Vi Va
pitasio

THE INDEPENDENCE OF MEXICO AND THE CREATION OF THE NEW NATION

UCLA Latin American Studies
Volume 69

Series Editor
Johannes Wilbert

Para
Linda
mi mejor y mas amada
amiga
Jaime

NON FECIT TALITER OMNI NATIONI

THE INDEPENDENCE *OF* MEXICO *AND THE* CREATION *OF THE* NEW NATION

Edited by

JAIME E. RODRIGUEZ O.

UCLA Latin American Center Publications
University of California, Los Angeles

Mexico/Chicano Program
University of California, Irvine

UCLA Latin American Center Publications
University of California, Los Angeles

Mexico/Chicano Program
University of California, Irvine

Library of Congress Cataloging-in-Publication Data

The Independence of Mexico and the creation of the
New Nation.

(UCLA Latin American studies ; v. 69)
Bibliography: p.
Includes index.
1. Mexico—History—19th century—Congresses.
2. Mexico—History—Wars of Independence, 1810-1821—Social aspects—Congresses. 3. Mexico—History—Wars of Independence, 1810-1821—Economic aspects—Congresses. 4. Mexico—Social conditions—19th century—Congresses. 5. Mexico—Economic conditions—19th century—Congresses. I. Rodríguez O., Jaime E., 1940- . II. Series.
F1231.5.I49 1989 972'.03 89-2665
ISBN 0-87903-070-4

Frontispiece: The Virgin of Guadalupe on the indictment of Father Miguel Hidalgo, 1811.

Jacket: Insurgent account book, 1818.

Endsheets: Battle between Insurgents and Royalists, 1812.

Photos: Courtesy of Archivo General de la Nación, Mexico City.

Jacket design: Linda M. Robertson.

Contents

PREFACE ix

CONTRIBUTORS xi

INTRODUCTION

Jaime E. Rodríguez O. 1

I. The Process of Independence

From Royal Subject to Republican Citizen: The Role of the Autonomists in the Independence of Mexico

Jaime E. Rodríguez O. 19

Las sociedades secretas durante el movimiento de independencia

Virginia Guedea 45

The Financial Disintegration of the Royal Government of Mexico during the Epoch of Independence

John Jay TePaske 63

"La Causa Buena": The Counterinsurgency Army of New Spain and the Ten Years' War

Christon I. Archer 85

Quetzalcóatl, King Ferdinand, and Ignacio Allende Go to the Seashore; or Messianism and Mystical Kingship in Mexico, 1800–1821

Eric Van Young 109

La minería durante la guerra de independencia y los primeros años del México independiente, 1810–1824

Hira de Gortari Rabiela 129

Caudillismo and Independence: A Symbiosis?

Hugh M. Hamill, Jr. 163

II. The Creation of the New Nation

The Iturbide Interregnum

Timothy E. Anna 185

Taxation and Tyranny: Public Finance during the Iturbide Regime, 1821–1823

Barbara A. Tenenbaum 201

Mexico's First Foreign Loans

Jaime E. Rodríguez O. 215

Modernidad, mito y religiosidad en el nacimiento de México

Jaime del Arenal Fenochio 237

Ilustrados, regalistas y liberales

María del Refugio González 247

El pensamiento económico moderno en el México independiente

Beatriz Urías Horcasitas 265

Territorial Integrity in Mexican Politics, 1821–1833

Nettie Lee Benson 275

III. Comparisons

Comparing Mexican Independence with the Revolution: Causes, Concepts, and Pitfalls

Paul J. Vanderwood 311

Independence and Revolution: Continuities and Discontinuities

Linda B. Hall 323

Mexican Independence in Comparative Perspective

Steven Topik 331

Random Thoughts Comparing the Role of the Army in the Independence Movement and the Fall of the Porfiriato

William F. Sater 339

BIBLIOGRAPHY 345

INDEX 363

Preface

THIS VOLUME OWES ITS ORIGINS to various discussions I shared in 1986 with two learned historians of Mexican independence: Virginia Guedea and Christon Archer. At that time, I was preparing the introductory chapters for a book on the early republic, and I wanted to clarify my views on the period. The conversations, however, convinced me that scholars lacked a genuine understanding of the causes, the process, and the consequences of the struggle for independence.

Although many historians have written about those crucial years, they tend to focus either on the great insurgent leaders, Fathers Miguel Hidalgo and José María Morelos; describe independence as a patriotic struggle; or concentrate on isolated provincial events. While a few scholars have attempted to provide a comprehensive interpretation of independence, none have equaled Lucas Alamán's classic nineteenth-century multivolume *Historia de Méjico desde los primeros movimientos que prepararon su independencia en el año 1808 hasta la época presente*, which still remains the best explanation.

Since various historians are presently reexamining the epoch, it seemed that we could benefit enormously from discussing our work. Because the process of independence profoundly affected the evolution of the new nation, I believed it necessary to extend our analysis to include not merely independence but also the early national period. Therefore, I proposed to my colleagues in the Mexico/Chicano Program that we devote our annual symposium to the topic "The Independence of Mexico and the Creation of the New Republic."

The Mexico/Chicano Program invited the leading specialists from Mexico, Canada, and the United States to a symposium held at the University of California, Irvine on February 20–21, 1987. The meeting proved extraordinarily successful. All the participants not only submitted excellent papers, but also engaged in stimulating and wideranging discussions. The symposium raised more questions than it resolved. But it proved extremely useful in opening new avenues of inquiry. All the participants, I believe, found the symposium rewarding. They have revised their papers for publications in light of the discussions held at Irvine.

The Mexico/Chicano Program and the School of Humanities of the University of California, Irvine, as well as the University of California

Consortium on Mexico and the United States, provided financial support both for the symposium and for the publication of this volume. The UCLA Latin American Center, which recognized the significance of these essays, agreed to publish a coedition. I am grateful to a number of individuals who assisted in these projects. My colleagues in the Mexico/Chicano Program, María Herrera-Sobek, Alejandro Morales, and Eloy Rodríguez, contributed to the success of the symposium. Linda Alexander Rodríguez, William F. Sater, Christon Archer, and Virginia Guedea read parts of the volume and provided suggestions for its improvement. In addition, Professor Guedea helped select and obtain the illustrations. I am also indebted to Lic. Leonor Ortiz Monasterio, Director of the Archivo General de la Nación in Mexico City, for permission to reproduce the illustrations. Geneva López-Iriani helped to coordinate the symposium and Karen Lowe assisted in preparing the papers for publication.

Jaime E. Rodríguez O.

Los Angeles
April 12, 1988

Contributors

Timothy E. Anna is Professor of History at the University of Manitoba. He has written extensively on the independence period. His works include *The Fall of the Royal Government in Mexico City* (Lincoln, 1978). He is currently working on a study of the early republic.

Jaime del Arenal Fenochio is Researcher at the Centro de Estudios sobre la Universidad at the Universidad Nacional Autónoma de México. He has published various studies of the early national period. He is currently working on an analysis of early constitutional thought.

Christon I. Archer is Professor and Head of the Department of History at the University of Calgary. He has written extensively on the army of New Spain. His works include *The Army of Bourbon Mexico* (Albuquerque, 1977) which received the Bolton Prize. He is currently working on the military during the war of independence.

Nettie Lee Benson is Professor Emeritus of History at the University of Texas, Austin and former Director of the Latin American Library which now bears her name. She has published extensively on the formation of the new Mexican nation. Her works include *La diputación provincial y el federalismo mexicano* (Mexico, 1955). She is currently working on political thought in early national Mexico.

María del Refugio González is Research Professor and Director of the Centro de Estudios sobre la Universidad at the Universidad Nacional Autónoma de México. She has published numerous studies on Mexico's legal history. Her works include *Estudios sobre la historia del derecho civil en México durante el siglo XIX* (Mexico, 1981). She is currently working on nineteenth-century conservative thought in Mexico.

Hira de Gortari Rabiela is Research Professor at the Instituto de Investigaciones Sociales of the Universidad Nacional Autónoma de México. He has published various articles on Mexico's social and economic problems. He is currently working on a study of social aspects of Mexican independence.

Virginia Guedea is Research Professor and Academic Secretary at the Instituto de Investigaciones Históricas of the Universidad Nacional Autónoma de México. She has published numerous studies of insurrections, particularly during the independence period. Her works include *José María Morelos y Pavón: cronología* (Mexico, 1981). She is currently working on secret societies during the independence.

Linda B. Hall is Professor of History at the University of New Mexico, Albuquerque. She has published extensively on the Revolution. Her works include *Alvaro Obregón: Power and Revolution in Mexico, 1911–1920* (College Station, 1981). She is currently working on the restoration of state power in the 1920s.

Hugh M. Hamill, Jr., is Professor of History at the University of Connecticut. He has published widely on the independence period. His works include *The Hidalgo Revolt: Prelude to Mexican Independence* (Gainesville, 1966). He is currently working on the royalists during independence.

Jaime E. Rodríguez O. is Professor of History and Director of the Mexico/Chicano Program at the University of California, Irvine. He has published widely on the early republic. His works include *Down from Colonialism: Mexico's Nineteenth-Century Crisis* (Los Angeles, 1983). He is currently working on the ideology of independence.

William F. Sater is Professor of History at California State University, Long Beach. He has published extensively on nineteenth-century Chile. His works include *Chile and the War of the Pacific* (Lincoln, 1986). He is currently working on a study of the Mexican military during the Porfiriato.

Barbara A. Tenenbaum is an independent historian living in Washington, D.C. She has published numerous studies of nineteenth-century Mexican finances. Her works include *The Politics of Penury: Debts and Taxes in Mexico, 1821–1856* (Albuquerque, 1986). She is currently working on a study of the impact of the Treaty of Guadalupe Hidalgo on Mexico.

John Jay TePaske is Professor of History at Duke University. He has published widely on Latin American colonial history, particularly finances. His works include *The Royal Treasuries of Spanish America* (with Herbert Klein), 3 vols. (Durham, 1983). He is currently working on taxation during the colonial period.

Steven Topik is Associate Professor of History at the University of California, Irvine. He has published extensively on the role of the state in economic development. His works include *The Political Economy of the Brazilian State, 1889–1930* (Austin, 1987). He is currently working on a comparative study of the role of the liberal state in Brazil and in Mexico during the late nineteenth century.

Beatriz Urías Horcasitas is Researcher at the Centro de Estudios sobre la Universidad of the Universidad Nacional Autónoma de México. She has several studies of nineteenth-century thought in press. She is currently working on early nineteenth-century education.

Paul Vanderwood is Professor of History at San Diego State University. He has published extensively on the problems of law and order in nineteenth- and early twentieth-century Mexico. His works include *Disorder and Progress: Bandits, Police, and Mexican Development* (Lincoln, 1981) which won the Herring Prize. He is currently working on social change in Chihuahua from colonial times to the present.

Eric Van Young is Associate Professor of History at the University of California, San Diego. He has published widely on rural Mexico. His works include *Hacienda and Market in Eighteenth-Centry Mexico: The Rural Economy of the Guadalajara Region, 1675–1820* (Berkeley, 1981). He is currently working on a social history of the struggle for independence.

Introduction

Jaime E. Rodríguez O.

One of the most vexing problems in the history of America is why one former colony, the United States, established a stable government and developed economically while the other former colonies, the Latin American countries, had to endure political chaos and economic decline during the nineteenth century. Most scholars link the post-independence political, economic, and social conflicts in Spanish America to a "negative" colonial heritage. In contrast, they assert that the colonial experience of the United States prepared it for self-government.[1] Thus, while the northern union rapidly developed after independence, most Latin American nations first had to struggle to overcome their "colonial heritage."[2]

Mexico is a special case in Latin America. Historically, it has been the largest, wealthiest, and most populous nation in the region. (Today, only Brazil is larger.) The pre-Columbian cultures of Mexico were not only more diverse and more numerous, but also more advanced than other Indian communities on the continent. During the colonial era, the Viceroyalty of New Spain developed a richer and more complex society than the rest of Iberian America. In many ways, the northern viceroyalty functioned as a metropolis of the Spanish empire in the New World. Indeed, by the eighteenth century, New Spain, with its prosperous economy and complex social structure, seemed to rival the mother country. In addition, Mexico has evolved in relative isolation from the rest of Latin America. For all these reasons, Mexico can be fruitfully compared and contrasted with the United States.

Elsewhere, Colin M. MacLachlan and I have argued that Mexico's colonial experience was not entirely negative. On the contrary, New Spain forged the strong base upon which the new nation could develop.[3] I have also

[1]Louis Hartz, *The Founding of New Societies* (New York, 1964). See also the essays in *Dos revoluciones: México y los Estados Unidos* (Mexico, 1976) and *Cardinales de dos independencias* (Mexico, 1978).

[2]See, for example, Romeo Flores Caballero, *La contrarrevolución en la independencia: los españoles en la vida política, social y económica de México, 1804–1838* (Mexico, 1969).

[3]Colin M. MacLachlan and Jaime E. Rodríguez O., *The Forging of the Cosmic Race: A Reinterpretation of Colonial Mexico* (Berkeley, 1980).

asserted that Mexico's "failure" to develop must be studied in light of what I have called "Mexico's Nineteenth-Century Crisis." The struggle for independence, according to this view, so severely damaged the structures of the viceroyalty that republican Mexico stumbled in the nineteenth-century race for national development.[4]

Any comparison between the United States and Mexico must consider the natural endowment of the two countries. The contrast is startling. The United States possesses vast, fertile agricultural lands while Mexico's agricultural regions constitute only about 15 percent of its territory, or an area about the size of Kansas. Thus, Mexico is impoverished in the most important resource known to man, agricultural land. The topographical contrast is also striking. Although mountains and deserts hampered national integration in the United States, they are relatively easy to overcome and located in regions peripheral to the core of the emerging nation. In contrast, Mexico's heartland is dominated by massive mountain ranges, great deserts, jagged cannons, and extensive rain forests which posed formidable barriers to national unity. While magnificent river systems in the eastern United States unified the young country and facilitated its development, Mexico lacked navigable waterways.[5] Mexico, therefore, is a relatively poor land—its mineral wealth not withstanding—characterized by a harsh environment. Thus, the destruction of the wars of independence was likely to affect Mexico more severely and to make recovery more difficult, even if all other factors had been comparable.

The nature and process of the struggles for independence were as different in the two countries as were their "material conditions." The war for United States independence became an international conflict in which the second and third most powerful nations in Europe—France and Spain—fought England both on land and on sea. At the height of the conflict, France fielded a force of more than 10,000 men in North America—an army comparable to the size of the Spanish army in New Spain—while Spain's soldiers harassed the English along its vast north American border with New Spain. At the same time, the combined French and Spanish navies neutralized the British fleet at sea. As a result of foreign involvement, the United States obtained its independence through an international settlement, the Treaty of Paris of 1783.[6]

[4]Jaime E. Rodríguez O., *Down from Colonialism: Mexico's Nineteenth-Century Crisis* (Los Angeles, 1983).

[5]On the geography of the United States see Gilly Glassborow and Gillian Freeman, eds., *The Atlas of the United States* (New York, 1986). The best work on Mexican geography is Jorge L. Tamayo, *Geografía general de México,* 4 vols., 2d ed. (Mexico, 1962). See also Claude Batallion, *Las regiones geográficas en México* (Mexico, 1969).

[6]The struggle for United States independence is discussed in John R Alden, *The American Revolution* (New York, 1954); Don Higgenbotham, *The War of American Independence: Military Attitudes, Policies, and Practice, 1763*–1789. (New York, 1971); Marshal

During the struggle for independence, the North American upper and middle classes shared moderate goals. The founders of the new nation, such as George Washington, Thomas Jefferson, James Madison, and John Adams, were members of the oligarchy. They represented wealth and power in the new nation. No social revolution threatened their interests. The United States' war of independence was characterized by traditional military engagements. Local insurgents with fundamentally different goals than the elite are noted for their absence. Certainly, no rural insurrection occurred. The black slaves did not revolt against their masters. And the Indians did not take the opportunity to recover the lands from which they had been dispossessed.[7]

Although regional tensions existed and although the first United States constitution, the Articles of Confederation, was rapidly discarded in favor of the stronger Constitution of 1787, the North American elite managed to direct the new nation without serious challenges from other social groups. To a great extent this was the result of the post-independence prosperity engendered by twenty years of war in Europe. The French Revolution of 1789 and the wars that followed created an insatiable demand for United States' products. Thus, the tensions that existed in the new nation were eased by the country's general prosperity.[8]

The Mexican wars of independence differed profoundly from the United States' experience. There, the struggle was characterized by a lack of consensus among the elite, mass rural insurrections, a race as well as a class conflict, and the rise of regionalism. The native upper and middle classes—the American Spaniards—were outmaneuvered by the small European Spanish minority. After nearly two decades of extortionate demands to support Spain's war efforts in Europe, the crown collapsed in May 1808 after Napolean invaded the peninsula. In New Spain, the European-born Spaniards, fearful of the American-born elite, overthrew the viceregal government on September 16, 1808. Thereafter, the tiny European-born

---

Smelser, *The Winning of Independence* (Chicago, 1972); and Willard M. Wallace, *Appeal to Arms: A Military History of the American Revolution* (Chicago, 1964).

[7]Historians of the United States have not tended to consider the struggle for independence as a social movement. James Franklin Jameson, *The American Revolution Considered as a Social Movement* (Princeton, 1926), is still useful. See also Merrill Jensen, *The American Revolution within America* (New York, 1975); and Jack P. Greene, "The Social Origins of the American Revolution: An Evaluation and an Interpretation," *Political Science Quarterly* 88 (1973), 1-22.

[8]The economic developments of the young republic are ably examined in Stuart Bruchey, *The Roots of American Economic Growth, 1607-1861* (New York, 1965). Also useful in understanding early United States development are: Merrill Jensen's *The Articles of Confederation*, 2d ed. (Madison, 1959), and his *The New Nation* (New York, 1950) as well as John C. Miller's *The Federalist Era, 1789-1800* (New York, 1960).

Spanish minority dominated New Spain. The American-born Spanish elite—the creoles—naturally chafed under a regime which they considered illegal and unconstitutional. Conspiracies for home rule abounded. One accidentally unleased a race and class war when on September 16, 1810, Father Miguel Hidalgo asked the masses to follow him.[9] Thus, two distinct movements—an urban drive for home rule and a rural struggle against exploitation—appeared to merge in the great Hidalgo insurrection. But, as the rural masses retaliated against their former oppressors, whether European Spaniards or American Spaniards, the elite of New Spain were forced to postpone their struggle for home rule while they sought to survive the new, unexpected, and dangerous rural insurgency.

In contrast to the experience of the United States, the elite of New Spain lost control of the movement for home rule to a mass-based rural insurrection. For months, tens of thousands of rural insurgents ravaged the Bajío and Jalisco, two of New Spain's most productive regions. When the royal army defeated the Hidalgo movement in March 1811, Father José María Morelos and his supporters continued the struggle. Although Spain sent crack troops in 1812 to quell the rebellion, the insurrection rapidly fragmented and spread to some of the viceroyalty's most prosperous regions. A massive, protracted, and extremely bitter struggle ensued.[10] When it ended in 1821, nearly a tenth of the country's population had died, the economy was wrecked, and the legitimacy of its institutions was destroyed.[11] The decade of insurgency, 1810–1821, had set the stage for the post-independence political instability, economic stagnation, and social conflicts.

[9]Virginia Guedea, "Criollos y peninsulares en 1808: dos puntos de vista sobre lo español," Licenciatura thesis, Universidad Iberoamericana, 1964; Luis Villoro, *El proceso ideológico de la revolución de la independencia*, 3rd ed. (Mexico, 1981), 41–63; Doris M. Ladd, *The Mexican Nobility at Independence, 1780—1826* (Austin, 1976), 89–94, 106–115; Hugh M. Hamill, Jr., "Un discurso formado con angustia: Francisco Primo de Verdad el 9 de agosto de 1808," *Historia Mexicana* 28:3 (January-March 1979), 439–474; and his *The Hidalgo Revolt: Prelude to Mexican Independence*, (Gainesville, 1966). Lucas Alamán, *Historia de Méjico*, 5 vols. (Mexico, 1849–1852), remains the best narrative of the period.

[10]The leading work on Hidalgo is Hamill, *The Hidalgo Revolt*. On the Morelos movement consult Virginia Guedea, *José María Morelos y Pavón: cronología* (Mexico, 1981), and Ernesto Lemoine, *La revolución de independencia, 1808–1821*, vol. 3 of *La república federal mexicana* (Mexico, n.d.). Alamán, *Historia de Méjico*, vols. 1, 2, and 3, remain the most detailed account of the period. Christon I. Archer has done the most extensive work on the Spanish military; see his "The Royalist Army in New Spain: Civil Military Relationships, 1810–1821, "*Journal of Latin American Studies* 13:1 (1981), 57–83; and his "Where Did All the Royalists Go? New Light on the Military Collapse of New Spain, 1810–1822," in Jaime E. Rodríguez O., ed., *The Mexican and the Mexican American Experience in the Nineteenth Century* (Tempe, 1989), 24–43.

[11]Hugh M. Hamill, Jr., "Was the Mexican Independence Movement a Revolution?" in Fomento Cultural Banamex, *Dos revoluciones: México y los Estados Unidos* (Mexico, 1976),

Because the Mexican insurgency consisted of various conflicting interests, New Spain's elite was divided. Some favored certain insurgents while others believed the liberal movement in Spain might provide them with a modicum of home rule. Still others, fearful of the race and class conflict unleashed by the insurgency, longed for the old order and the return of the monarch. Because of these divisions, the elite of New Spain failed to form a cohesive group which might have obtained support from foreign powers.[12] Unlike the United States, Mexican insurgents did not enjoy the aid of foreign armies and navies. Instead, adventurers entered New Spain seeking wealth and glory. Indeed, filibusters from the northern republic sought to dismember the country.[13]

The struggle for Mexican independence did not conclude in an international settlement. Spain and later the Holy Alliance continued to threaten the new nation after 1821. Thus, Mexico, unlike the United States, had to allocate a lion's share of its budget for defense during its first decade. When Iturbide took possession of the new Mexican government in September 1821, he found little sympathy abroad. True, the United States recognized the new nation in 1822 and, more importantly, Great Britain extended recognition in December 1824. Their actions, however, signified only partial international acceptance of Mexico. The United States was lukewarm in its support for the new American nation, despite the Monroe Doctrine. Although Great Britain opposed attempts by other European countries, particularly the Holy Alliance, to crush the Mexican republic, it did not object to Spanish attempts to reconquer its former colony. As a result, Spain did not recognize Mexican independence until 1836. France extended recognition only a few years earlier in 1832.[14]

Finally, Mexico achieved independence in 1821, *after* the European wars had ended. Not only did the new nation have to rebuild its shattered economy, but it also faced a lack of demand for its products. Instead, Europe and the United States were eager to flood Mexico with their own goods. Thus, Mexico did not enjoy prosperity during its formative years as the

---

43–61; John Tutino, *From Insurrection to Revolution in Mexico: Social Bases of Agrarian Violence, 1750–*1940 (Princeton, 1986), 41–212; Brian R. Hamnett, *Roots of Insurgency: Mexican Regions, 1750–1824* (Cambridge, 1986).

[12]Ladd, *The Mexican Nobility*, 112–131; Timothy E. Anna, *The Fall of the Royal Government in Mexico City* (Lincoln, 1978), 35–190.

[13]Harris G. Warren, *The Sword Was Their Passport* (Baton Rouge, 1943). See also Virginia Guedea, "The Beginning of Relations between Mexico and the United States," paper presented at the University of Calgary's "Mexico Week," March 21–26, 1988.

[14]Jaime E. Rodríguez O., *The Emergence of Spanish America: Vicente Rocafuerte and Spanish Americanism, 1808–1832* (Berkeley, 1975), 59–67, 85–178, 229–234; Carlos Bosch García, *Problemas diplomáticos del México independiente*, 2d ed. (Mexico, 1986).

United States had. Rather, the Mexican state had to face grave internal and external problems with increasingly diminishing resources.[15]

Although international conditions were adverse, it was the war of independence which profoundly affected the development of the new Mexican nation. The eleven-year struggle for Mexican independence was a critical period. The insurgency and the counterinsurgency not only undermined the old social, political, and economic structures, but in many instances destroyed them while creating new interests as well as new antagonisms. The conflicts became particularly virulent after the royal army defeated the mass insurrections of Hidalgo and Morelos and the insurgency fragmented into a series of violent guerrilla wars. The bitter struggle between the numerous insurgent bands and the recently arrived Spanish expeditionary forces ended forever the old colonial arrangement. And it made reconciliation with Spain impossible.

The protracted insurgency created new and formidable problems for the new nation. As Virginia Guedea and Christon Archer have argued, the Spanish counterinsurgency forces militarized New Spain. The European-born officers applied in New Spain the lessons which they had painfully learned from the French counterinsurgency in Spain. They disregarded civilian authority and imposed martial law in order to extract funds from local governments and obtain recruits for their forces. In their attempt to restore order and destroy the insurgency, the European-born Spanish officers not only disregarded traditional customs and practices, but they also acted with great brutality.[16] Only if one understands the novel and

[15]Barbara A. Tenenbaum, *The Politics of Penury: Debts and Taxes in Mexico, 1821–1856* (Albuquerque, 1986), 1–40.

[16]Virginia Guedea has worked extensively on the insurgency; see her *José María Morelos y Pavón*; "México en 1812: control político y bebidas prohibidas," *Estudios de Historia Moderna y Contemporánea* 8 (1980), 23–66; "José Nemesio Vázquez, un correo insurgente," in Antonio Pompa y Pompa et al., *De la historia: homenaje a Jorge Gurría Lacroix* (Mexico, 1985), 287–295; and "Los indios voluntarios de Fernando VII," *Estudios de Historia Moderna y Contemporánea* 10 (1986), 11–83. See also her essay "La organización militar," in Woodrow Borah, ed., *El gobierno provincial en la Nueva España, 1570–1787* (Mexico, 1985), 125–148. Christon I. Archer has studied the Spanish military in depth; among his works on the counterinsurgency consult "The Royalist Army in New Spain;" "Where Did All The Royalists Go?"; "The Officer Corps in New Spain: The Martial Career, 1759–1821," *Jahrbuch Für Geschichte von Staat, Wirtschaft und Gesellschaft Lateinamerikas* (1980), 137–158; "Banditry and Revolution in New Spain, 1759–1821," *Biblioteca Americana* 1 (November 1982), 59–89; "Los dineros de la insurgencia," in Carlos Herrejón Peredo, ed., *Repaso de la independencia* (Zamora, Michoacán, 1985), 39–55; and "Surviving the Chaos of Insurgency: Urban-Rural Relationships in Mexico, 1810–1821," in Roberto Moreno de los Arcos and Eric Van Young, *Proceedings of the VII Conference of Mexican and North American Historians* (Mexico, forthcoming).

Both Guedea and Archer maintain that the militarization of New Spain transformed the viceroyalty and had a profound effect on its population. (Personal communication, Mexico City, June 26, 1987.) My examination of the section "Operaciones de Guerra" of the Archivo

unusual, for New Spain, nature of their actions as well the brutality of the insurgency and counterinsurgency, can one comprehend the vehement hatred post-independence Mexicans later expressed for Spaniards. The expulsion of the Spaniards, which occurred in 1827 and 1829, did not represent "age old colonial grievances," as is often asserted.[17] It was the direct result of the ferocity of the counterinsurgency.

The militarization of New Spain also fostered the growth of regionalism. Although regionalist sentiments had existed in New Spain for centuries, they had not threatened the established order. The creation of the intendancies in the late eighteenth century, and the establishment of the provincial deputations by the Spanish Cortes in the early nineteenth century, further strengthened local feelings. Still, it was the realization that the civil government in Mexico City could not protect the provinces from either the depredations of the insurgents or from the excesses of the royal army that convinced local leaders to assume control of their areas. After independence regional elites imposed their notion of federalism on the nation with striking determination and rapidity.[18]

The violence and destruction of the insurgency seriously harmed the viceroyalty's economy. But, as John TePaske indicates, it was the incessant and increasing demands for money to sustain first the war in Europe and then the counterinsurgency in New Spain that destroyed the viceroyalty's finances and alienated the Mexican elite.[19] After independence they were unwilling to finance the government. Instead they put their hopes on foreign loans and on customs' revenues. But, as Barbara Tenenbaum has demonstrated, these resources were insufficient to sustain post-independence governments.[20] The independence struggle, thus, profoundly affected the way in which the new country was forced to cope in the first half of the nineteenth century.

General de la Nación has convinced me that they are correct. The documents are organized by military command and clearly demonstrate that army officers dominated regional governments.

[17]The most satisfactory explanation of the expulsion of the Spaniards is still Flores Caballero, *La contrarrevolución en la independencia*. Harold D. Sims' works, *La expulsión de los españoles de México, 1821–1828* (Mexico, 1974); *Descolonización en México: el conflicto entre mexicanos y españoles, 1821–1831* (Mexico, 1982); and *La reconquista de México: la historia de los atentados españoles, 1821–1830* (Mexico, 1984) provide the greatest detail on the question. Neither author, however, links the virulent anti-Spanish movement to the massive repression during the counterinsurgency, although Flores Caballero hints at it.

[18]Nettie Lee Benson, *La diputación provincial y el federalismo mexicano* (Mexico, 1955); Jaime E. Rodríguez O., "Intellectuals and the Constitution of 1824," in Roderic A. Camp, Charles A. Hale and Josefina Zoraida Vásquez, eds., *The State and Intellectual Life in Mexico* (Mexico and Los Angeles, forthcoming).

[19]See his "The Financial Disintegration of the Royal Government of Mexico during the Epoch of Independence" in this volume.

[20]Tenenbaum, *The Politics of Penury*, 17–175.

The new Mexican nation emerged almost by accident. The elite were deeply divided and unable to provide either a unified or strong direction. They, like the urban and rural masses and the army, were exhausted by eleven years of war. When an obscure officer, Colonel Agustín de Iturbide, pronounced the Plan of Iguala which called for independence, all sides joined the movement. The Spanish regime ended not because it was defeated militarily, but because Mexicans no longer supported it politically. The Plan of Iguala, however, provided no more than a temporary respite; it could not survive the political, economic, and social tensions that erupted after independence.[21]

Throughout the country, Mexicans received independence joyously. They widely acclaimed Iturbide as a great hero, a farsighted statesman, and the liberator of Mexico. However, his universal popularity proved as short-lived as the temporary concensus based on the Plan of Iguala; it evaporated after he crowned himself emperor and the new administration grappled with difficult economic and political questions. The Iturbide regime was the first of the post-independence governments to confront the new national reality—a loss of legitimacy and a loss of confidence. Unable to win either the political or the economic support of the elite, his empire failed.[22]

In an attempt to restore legitimacy, Mexicans established a federal republic in 1824. But the new regime faced the same problems as the previous one: economic stagnation, sectarian politics, regionalism, foreign threats, and, most important of all, lack of confidence. It collapsed in 1835 when a centralist republic was established. The new government, however, proved no more capable of restoring authority than the earlier ones. Between 1821 and 1848, only one president, Guadalupe Victoria (1824–1828), completed his term of office. And he owed his success primarily to the two large foreign loans negotiated in 1824 and 1825, which gave his administration financial stability. During the next twenty years, the republic endured three constitutions, twenty governments, and more than 100 cabinets.[23] As succeeding administrations proved unable to maintain order and protect lives and property, the country sank into anarchy. Fear and uncertainty became com-

[21]Alamán, *Historia de Méjico*, V, 50–130; William S. Robertson, *Iturbide of Mexico* (Durham, 1952), 51–104; Anna, *The Fall of Royal Government*, 191–209; Ladd, *The Mexican Nobility*, 126–128.

[22]Javier Ocampo, *Las ideas de un día: el pueblo mexicano ante la consumación de su independencia* (Mexico, 1969); Timothy E. Anna, "The Role of Agustín Iturbide: A Reappraisal," *Journal of Latin American Studies*, 17 (1985), 79–110.

[23]The political history of post-independence Mexico remains confused. Alamán's classic, *Historia de Méjico*, V, provides an excellent, but biased account. Among contemporary historians, the best are Carlos María Bustamante, *Continuación del cuadro histórico de la revolución mexicana*, 4 vols. (Mexico, 1953–1963); José María Bocanegra, *Memorias para*

monplace. Ex-soldiers turned bandits infested the highways obstructing commerce and threatening small towns. These and other manifestations of social dissolution contributed to Mexico's instability.[24]

The situation worsened when political conflict degenerated into civil war. Large sections of the country were ravaged as federalists and centralists, liberals and conservatives fought for political control. During 1835–1845, secessionists established the republics of Yucatán and Texas, although only the latter managed to consolidate its independence. The other regions, however, maintained autonomy, if not their independence from the national government, by force of arms.

The country's political instability made Mexico easy prey to foreign aggressors. The republic endured invasions by Spain in 1829, France in 1838, the United States in 1847, and England, France, and Spain in 1861. The nation's disintegration prompted many within and without to fear that Mexico would cease to exist. By 1848, the country had lost more than half its territory to the United States and national regeneration seemed unattainable.

Why did Mexico not recover soon after independence? Why did it sink into fifty years of economic depression and political turmoil? The answer appears to be both economic and psychological. The economy lay in ruins as a result of the post-independence political chaos. But in addition, Mexicans lost confidence in their country's institutions. Legitimacy, that elusive agreement about the nature of government and society, proved difficult to obtain. It required many conflicts, including the great civil war of 1857–1867, known as the Reforma, and the French intervention, before the country regained a sense of unity and purpose.[25]

Although the problems that resulted from Mexico's independence seem evident, we still lack definitive explanations for Mexico's nineteenth-century crisis. To examine these questions the Mexico/Chicano Program of the University of California, Irvine invited a group of distinguished scholars

---

la historia de México independiente, 1822–1846, 3 vols. (Mexico, 1986–1987); Lorenzo de Zavala, *Ensayo histórico de las revoluciones de México desde 1808 hasta 1830* (Mexico, 1985); and José María Luis Mora, *México y sus revoluciones*, 3 vols. (Mexico, 1986). The best modern works are Robertson, *Iturbide*; Flores Caballero, *La contrarrevolución*; Rodríguez, *The Emergence of Spanish America*; Michael P. Costeloe, *La primera república federal de México, 1824–1835* (Mexico, 1975); Charles Macune, *El Estado de México y la federación mexicana* (Mexico, 1978); Fernando Díaz Díaz, *Caudillos y caciques: Antonio López de Santa Anna y Juan Alvarez* (Mexico, 1972); Tenenbaum, *The Politics of Penury*; Stanley C. Green, *The Mexican Republic: The First Decade, 1823–1832* (Pittsburgh, 1987); Moisés González Navarro, *Anatomía del poder en México* (Mexico, 1977); and Carmen Vázquez Mantecón, *Santa Anna y la encrucijada del Estado: la dictadura (1853–1855)* (Mexico, 1986).

[24] Paul J. Vanderwood, *Disorder and Progress: Bandits, Police, and Mexican Development* (Lincoln, 1981), 25–89.

[25] Rodríguez, *Down from Colonialism,* 15–31.

to participate in a symposium titled "The Independence of Mexico and the Creation of the New Republic" held at the University of California, Irvine in February 1987. In addition to experts on the independence and the early national period, the Program also invited specialists on the Mexican Revolution asking them to compare that great upheaval with the independence. The authors of the papers presented at the symposium have revised them for publication. The essays in this volume examine many of the problems which emerged during independence and affected the new Mexican nation. The volume is divided into three parts: The Process of Independence, the Creation of the New Nation, and Comparisons.

The Process of Independence

The book begins with my essay "From Royal Subject to Republican Citizen: The Role of the Autonomists in the Independence of Mexico" which introduces some of the problems of the independence era. It argues that New Spain's elite desired *autonomy*, or home rule, rather than *independence*, that is, separation from Spain. They consistently maintained that position throughout eleven years of insurgency. Although New Spain's upper classes not only survived the vagaries of the insurgency and the royalists' counterinsurgency, but also gained power in 1821, they lost it two years later to an emergent regional elite. Instead of government by *hombres de bien*, early republican Mexico had to cope with mass politics at a time when representtive institutions were ill established.

Virginia Guedea examines the process of independence from the perspective of the cities in her essay "Las sociedades secretas durante el movimiento de independencia." She argues that, as a result of the insurgency, urban residents organized groups to press their interests. Although they often took the form of secret societies, they were not generally Masonic lodges. While these societies did not initiate or significantly affect the insurrection, as is sometimes alleged, they were important because they represented "la formación de distintos grupos que desde algunos de los principales centros urbanos buscaban alcanzar una participación cada vez mayor en la toma de decisiones." They were, in that respect, the embryonic groups which would form "las principales fuerzas políticas que controlarían la vida pública del nuevo país."

In his essay "The Financial Disintegration of the Royal Government of Mexico during the Epoch of Independence," John TePaske demonstrates that New Spain's fiscal crisis had its roots in the late eighteenth century. Although tax collection increased substantially during that period, expenditures, particularly for the military, expanded at an even faster rate. Deficits grew and the debt rose from 3 million in 1780 to 31 million by 1810. TePaske declares that the financial disintegration of the royal government in New Spain "was a gradual, inexorable process beginning in the early 1780s, and in fact, the financial collapse of the state was almost an accomplished fact by the time of the Grito de Dolores in 1810." But it was the long struggle for independence which led to the destruction of the fiscal system. Between 1809 and 1817, income declined by 70 percent because, as a result of the insurgency, regional treasuries stopped sending funds to Mexico City.

Christon Archer argues that New Spain underwent "one of the greatest guerrilla insurgencies in modern history," in his essay " 'La Causa Buena': The Counterinsurgency Army and the Ten Years' War." After the first large battles the struggle fragmented into regional insurgencies. General Félix María Calleja tried to deal with the insurrections by creating a tiered system of defenses, but it proved impossible to contain the rebels. The recently arrived European troops militarized the country. Army officers imposed taxes to support themselves and the militias. Contrary to the widely held view that New Spain was pacified by 1816, Archer argues against the "lull thesis," maintaining that the insurgency continued in an even more virulent form. The long protracted struggle not only weakened the Spanish army, but it also created discontent. As a result, when Agustín de Iturbide rebelled both Mexican and Spanish troops joined him. The royalists forces were not defeated; rather the military system imploded leaving no one to defend the Spanish regime.

Eric Van Young considers the problem of rural millenarianism in his "Quetzalcoatl, King Ferdinand, and Ignacio Allende Go to the Seashore: Or Messianism and Mystical Kingship in Mexico, 1810–1821." He demonstrates that Indian country people in central Mexico had messianic expectations in 1810. As a group these campesinos possessed very limited localist views which were backward looking. The messianistic strain in the Mexican independence struggle highlights the variegated nature of the process and the fundamentally different aspirations of urban and rural insurgents. In a sense, rural messianism calls into question whether such a diverse series of movements as occurred in New Spain during the period 1810–1821 can be considered a movement for independence.

Hira de Gortari Rabiela examines mining during the war for independence and the early years of independent Mexico in his essay "La minería durante la guerra de independencia y los primeros años del México independiente, 1810–1824." Mining constituted the principal motor force of New Spain's economy. Since agriculture and commerce depended upon a prosperous mining sector, damage to mining depressed the entire economy. De Gortari discusses the impact of the insurgency on the mining sector which was located in the regions of heaviest fighting. As a result of the destruction of the mining industry, the new nation faced grave difficulties in rebuilding its economy after independence.

In the final essay of Part I, "Caudillismo and Independence: A Symbiosis?," Hugh M. Hamill, Jr. considers the nature and origins of *caudillaje*. He argues that caudillos existed in colonial society but that they took special form during independence. Hamill examines the emergence of caudillaje by considering the careers of Hidalgo and Calleja. After a careful analysis, he concludes that Calleja represented true caudillaje and that the practice found its roots in colonial New Spain.

The Creation of the New Nation

Timothy Anna reassesses the brief administration of Agustín de Iturbide in his "The Iturbide Interregnum." He argues that the regime failed not because of his personality, but because of economic, political, and social forces that were beyond Iturbide's control. The growth of regionalism limited the ability of any national government to restore order. The country's financial crisis, moreover, prevented the formation of an effective national government. The internal political conflicts, which emerged during the struggle for independence, also severely hampered Iturbide's attempt to promote national unity. After examining the conflicting interpretations of Iturbide's role, Anna concludes that he was a well-meaning patriot who was overwhelmed by events.

Barbara A. Tenenbaum further expands this interpretation in her "Taxation and Tyranny: Public Finance during the Iturbide Regime, 1821–1823." She demonstrates that Iturbide inherited a hostility toward government because of earlier excessive taxation as well as a tendency toward atomization. To succeed the Iturbide regime had to win the loyalty of the population, establish fiscal as well as political control over the country, and create a new and workable tax system. But "the creole elites believed that independence meant liberation from the burdens of Spanish colonial taxation and its incessant demands for unsecured loans. They had no intention of giving any Mexican leader the funds required to run a stable government. They expected Iturbide (and his successors) to find those funds elsewhere." Unlike their North American counterparts, the Mexican elite refused to allow the formation of an effective tax system because they equated "taxation with tyranny." Without funds, the first empire failed.

My essay "Mexico's First Foreign Loans" examines the related issue of foreign loans as a way of solving the nation's fiscal crisis. From the outset Iturbide and his successors believed that Mexico was potentially quite wealthy and all it needed was time to restore its former prosperity. Therefore, they sought foreign loans as a way of solving their temporary fiscal crisis. Foreigners also believed in Mexico's legendary wealth and were eager to lend funds to the new nation. As a result, foreign loans helped Mexico consolidate its independence and contributed to the success of the Guadalupe Victoria administration. But the debt also became a serious burden which the nation overcame only with great difficulty.

Ideology and politics affected the new nation as profoundly as finances. Jaime del Arenal Fenochio studies the nature of independence ideology in his "Modernidad, mito y religiosidad en el nacimiento de México." He examines the principal documents that led to the creation of an independent nation. Although written at different times, and by different groups, these early political documents shared several major themes: they proposed that the Roman Catholic Church constitute Mexico's sole and official religion; they favored a constitutional monarchy; and they insisted on independence from Spain. While the theoretical basis of these documents was European naturalist law and rationalist thought, they were also influenced by the symbols of ancient Mexican culture.

In her essay "Ilustrados, regalistas y liberales" María del Refugio González examines the political thought in early national Mexico. She argues that neither liberalism nor conservatism existed in the republic's early years. Rather, the main currents of Mexican political thought were enlightenment ideas and regalism, ideological systems which possessed similarities to liberalism and which make it difficult to differentiate among them. The ideas of the Hispanic Enlightenment influenced Mexico during the late colonial era, the period of insurgency as well as the early republic. Regalism, with its rationalist and centralizing tendencies, was also present during those epochs. Liberalism, properly speaking, did not gain ascendancy until the Reforma. The issue, which in essence created both conservatism and liberalism, was the regalist stance toward the Church. After 1857, the constitution no longer protected the Catholic Church. Liberalism would triumph in Mexico only after a bloody struggle.

Beatriz Urías Horcasitas's "Pensamiento económico moderno en el México independiente" demonstrates how post-independence Mexicans used new liberal economic ideas to address the problems of poverty and massive unemployment brought about by the destruction of the economy during the wars of independence. Some argued for the government to create jobs because massive unemployment eventually affected adversely even those who were employed. Although ideally favoring a free market and individual entrepreneurship, the early national Mexicans agreed that without state intervention little could be achieved to restore the health of the economy.

In the final essay in Part II, the dean of historians of early national Mexico, Nettie Lee Benson, examines the problem of territorial integrity in her essay "Territorial Integrity in Mexican Politics, 1821–1833." Although all Mexicans, regardless of political persuasion, favored protecting the nation's territorial integrity, they were not above using the issue for their own ends. The extremely bitter partisan nature of early Mexican politics led opposing groups to use the issue of territorial integrity as a weapon against their opponents. As a result, the country was ultimately weakened and proved unable to defend its territory. While the southern border was settled to Mexico's satisfaction, the northern frontier dispute was not resolved, leaving the region prey to United States expansionism.

Comparisons

Paul Vanderwood maintains that comparisons between Independence and the Revolution are not possible at this time because historians of the two eras have not studied similar events and processes which might be compared. In "Comparing Mexican Independence with the Revolution: Causes, Concepts, and Pitfalls," he also criticizes the theories currently used to explain both events. Instead, he proposes that we "think of Indepenence and the Revolution not as singular events which occurred a century apart and somehow deserve comparison, but simply as two important conjunctures—two rather large bleeps—along the continuum of Mexican history." He suggests that one way of addressing the problem is to study the *mentalidad* or mindset of the groups involved.

Linda Hall, however, disagrees with Vanderwood. She asserts in her essay "Independence and Revolution: Continuities and Discontinuities" that "many similarities between the struggle for Independence and the Revolution a century later can be observed." She identifies a number of factors which were common to the two great upheavals: agrarian grievances; resistance to authority; the emergence of local leaders; periods of scarcity and financial crisis; and, most important of all, the political weakness of the national state. In her view, the principal difference rests in the outcome of the two movements. Post-Independence Mexicans failed to restore national order for nearly half a century, while post-Revolutionary leaders managed to establish national control within a decade and to put "in place a political system which has remained stable for more than sixty years."

In a related essay, "Mexican Independence in a Comparative Perspective," Steven Topik argues that Mexico's independence was the result of conjunctural events rather than the underlying causes usually used to explain the process. Comparing Mexico with Brazil, he demonstrates that both countries suffered from similar tensions. But while Mexico endured a violent upheaval, Brazil achieved its independence easily and peacefully. The difference, he argues, is that in 1807 the Portuguese crown fled to Brazil. What might have occurred in New Spain, he asks, if Fernando had fled there in 1808 or if a legitimate prince had gone there to initiate independence?

In the last essay, "Random Thoughts Comparing the Role of the Army in the Independence Movement and the Fall of the Porfiriato," William F. Sater argues that profound differences characterized the role of the army at independence and during the Mexican Revolution. Although both upheavals consisted of decade-long bloody conflicts and although violence and brutality marked both, the royal army and the Porfirian army acted quite differently. After fighting a bloody counterinsurgency campaign, the royal army betrayed the crown and joined Iturbide's rebels. In contrast the Mexican army remained loyal to the Díaz regime, fighting bravely and well.

Indeed, it did not suffer military defeat; rather, Díaz opted for a political solution, leaving the country.

The authors of these essays have brought a new understanding to a critical transitional era. It is clear that there are no convenient dividing lines between colonial New Spain and independent Mexico. Indeed, the evidence suggests that the period 1750–1854 might form a coherent century. The changes in the late colonial regime led naturally to the process of independence. And the protracted struggle for independence had profound and direct effects in the new nation.

I

The Process of Independence

From Royal Subject to Republican Citizen: The Role of the Autonomists in the Independence of Mexico

Jaime E. Rodríguez O.

THE HISTORIOGRAPHY OF MEXICAN INDEPENDENCE, although enormous, is both paradoxical and confusing.[1] Historians as different as Luis Villoro and M. S. Alperovich have commented on the diversity of interests involved in the process called the "movement for independence." As Villoro declared: " . . . many of the precursors of the movement became its most determined opponents the very moment that [the struggle for independence] erupted; . . . those who proclaimed independence did not achieve it, but their antagonists did; and finally, it is the revolutionary party which caused the failure of those who achieved independence."[2] Other interpretations abound: nationalists describe it as a patriotic struggle to break free from

AUTHOR'S NOTE: An earlier version of this essay was presented at the annual meeting of the American Historical Association held in Washington, D.C., on December 27–30, 1987. I am grateful to Virginia Guedea, María del Refugio Gonzáles, and Christon Archer for suggestions for improving this work. Research for this article was made possible by a grant from the University of California, Irvine Academic Senate Committee on Research.

[1]On this point consult Virginia Guedea, "The Historiography of Independence," paper presented at the University of Calgary's "Mexico Week," March 21-26, 1988. The best narrative remains Lucas Alamán, *Historia de Méjico*, 5 vols. (Mexico, 1849–1852). Among the contemporary works the best are Hugh M. Hamill, Jr., *The Hidalgo Revolt: Prelude to Mexican Independence* (Gainesville, 1966); Virginia Guedea, *José María Morelos y Pavón: cronología* (Mexico, 1981); Luis Villoro, *El proceso ideológico de la revolución de la independencia*, 3d ed. (Mexico, 1981); M. S. Alperovich, *Historia de la independencia de México, 1810–1824* (Mexico, 1976); Timothy Anna, *The Fall of the Royal Government in Mexico City* (Lincoln, 1978); Brian Hamnett, *Roots of Insurgency: Mexican Regions, 1750–1824* (Cambridge, 1986). See also the essays in *Cardinales de dos independencias* (Mexico, 1978) and *Dos revoluciones: México y los Estados Unidos (Mexico, 1976).*

[2]Villoro, *El proceso ideológico*, 14. See also Roberto Moreno, "Actitudes españolas ante la independencia de los Estados Unidos," *Cardinales de dos independencias* (Mexico, 1978), 37–53; Richard B. Morris, "The American Revolution and the Mexican War for Independence: Parallels and Divergences," *Dos revoluciones: México y los Estados Unidos* (Mexico, 1976), 11–30.

three hundred years of Spanish oppression; some call it a conservative reaction to Spanish liberalism; others argue that it was part of the "Age of Democractic Revolution"; finally a few assert that it was an aspect of the "bourgeois revolution" which formed the modern nation states.

Curiously, because these assertions contain a scintilla of truth, they do not explain the events that led to New Spain's emancipation. The process of Mexican independence may be best understood as a series of movements that erupted when the Spanish crown collapsed in 1808. Initially, two broad movements emerged: an urban upper class demand for home rule and a rural revolt against exploitation.[3] While these movements had their antecedents in the past, it was the Spanish imperial crisis which triggered them. Indeed, the ebb and flow of Spain's own bourgeois revolution and the counterinsurgency waged by the imperial government in New Spain further complicated these processes. Thus, exogenous forces transformed both the urban and the rural movements in the viceroyalty during the period 1808 to 1821. They fragmented the rural movement and created a ferocious guerrilla insurgency in the provinces of New Spain. The urban movement also splintered into two parts: the original elite, who sought home rule—that is, autonomy for the entire viceroyalty with the government in Mexico City—and a provincial element, who wanted to rule at home—that is, local autonomy from Mexico City.

This essay examines the elite quest for home rule. New Spain's upper class, a group which included the nobles, the great magnates, and intellectuals, among them clergymen, resided in Mexico City. Although many in the group possessed properties and interests in the provinces or had lived there, the elite was characterized by a proto-nationalist attitude. But they interpreted the well-being of the viceroyalty from the perspective of the

[3]Despite considerable research on rural conditions, we know little about the motives and aspirations of the rural masses. John Tutino attempts to understand the rural mindset through indirect means in his *From Insurrection to Revolution in Mexico: Social Bases of Agrarian Violence, 1750–1940* (Princeton, 1986). Although he develops a model to explain why peasants rebel, we really have no knowledge of the campesino's views. Eric Van Young has been more successful in examining the millenarian nature of rural thought in his "Millennium on the Northern Marches: The Mad Messiah of Durango and Popular Rebellion in Mexico, 1800–1815," *Comparative Studies in Society and History* 21 (1986), 385–413; and his "Quetzalcóatl, King Ferdinand, and Ignacio Allende Go to the Seashore: Or, Messianism and Mystical Kingship in Mexico, 1800–1821," in this volume. Virginia Guedea examines the reaction of Indian communities, particularly those of Mexico City, to the imperial crisis and to the insurgency in her "Los indios voluntarios de Fernando VII," *Estudios de Historia Moderna y Contemporánea* 10, (1986), 11–83. Other important works on rural conditions include Enrique Florescano, *Precios de maíz y crisis agrícolas en México, 1708–1810* (Mexico, 1969), 85–197; Enrique Florescano, ed., *Fuentes para la historia de la crisis agrícola, 1785–1786*, 2 vols. (Mexico, 1981); and Eric Van Young, *Hacienda and Market in Eighteenth-Century Mexico: The Rural Economy of the Guadalajara Region, 1675–1820* (Berkeley, 1981), 271–343.

capital. In that respect, they differed from the newly emerging provincial elites, who would play a significant role after independence.

New Spain's elite was not only wealthy, but also well educated. Because many members of the upper class were men of the Enlightenment, they were well versed in contemporary and classical thought as well as traditional Spanish ideology. Consequently, they were a progressive element who sought a moderate representative government for their country. Like the founding fathers of the United States, the autonomists of New Spain were not democrats. Rather, as *hombres de bien*, they favored an oligarchic regime. In that respect, they were no different than most other elites of the Western world in the latter part of the eighteenth and early nineteenth century.

Unlike their North American and European counterparts, however, the elite of New Spain lived in a predominantly nonwhite society. Thus, while they sought autonomy, they did not necessarily desire to sever their ties with the mother country because they, as well as the Indian and mestizo masses, held the monarchy in great respect. In addition, they feared that radical change might upset the hierarchical structure of New Spain's society. The elite, therefore, sought moderate changes. They wanted home rule, not independence. This distinction is crucial because when documents of the epoch refer to *independence*, they often mean *autonomy*. The actions of the upper class clearly prove this. As late as 1822, they proposed to the Spanish government that New Spain become part of a commonwealth and they specifically cited Canada as their model. Because they consistently sought home rule, the elite of New Spain are referred to as *autonomists* in this essay.[4]

The elite of New Spain favored home rule, in part, because of grievances arising from the Bourbon reforms which increased taxes while reducing their role in the government. The Law of Consolidation of 1804 constituted the greatest blow to the viceroyalty's interests. The law ordered the authorities to seize and auction the real estate belonging to the Church's *capellanías* and *obras pías*. Since the Church served as New Spain's principal banker and since nearly all entrepreneurs, large and small, owed money to the Church, enforcement of the measure would ruin New Spain. For the first time in nearly three hundred years, New Spaniards of all classes and castes, including European Spaniards residing in the viceroyalty, had a common cause to unite them. This was, surely, an instance of the *mal gobierno* which

[4]Nettie Lee Benson has indicated that the word *independence* was used in a number of ways during the period 1810–1821. For example, she points out that the Spaniards referred to their struggle against the French in the Peninsula as *la guerra de independencia*, and that in some instances when Mexican documents referred to "independence," they meant *independence from the French*. Nettie Lee Benson, "Comparison of the American Independence Movements," *Dos revoluciones*, 118.

traditional political theorists taught the people should oppose. Consequently, many among the elite concluded that autonomy would serve the best interests of New Spain. But they hesitated, fearing the dangers of ruling a hierarchical nonwhite society. As Alexander von Humboldt indicated in 1804: "They would no doubt prefer a national government and complete liberty of commerce . . . , but this desire does not sufficiently . . . impel them to long and painful sacrifices."[5] Thus, while relations between New Spaniards and the crown became strained, the tensions were not sufficient to precipitate a break with the mother country.

The reforms of the late eighteenth and early nineteenth century coincided with the emergence of new political ideas. In Spain nationalists reinterpreted history to create a new national myth. Enlightened Spaniards argued that the early Visigoths had enjoyed a form of tribal democracy. Supposedly, these Germanic ancestors forged the first Spanish constitution. Later, in the thirteenth century, Spain developed its own representative body, the cortes. According to this interpretation of history, medieval Spain had enjoyed democracy only to have it destroyed by the despotic Habsburg kings. Although earlier cortes had represented individual kingdoms, such as Aragon and Castile, not the entire nation, reformers had a unified national body in mind when they spoke of reconvening a cortes. Their ideas culminated in the work of Spain's foremost legal historian, Francisco Martínez Marina, whose massive work *Teoría de las cortes* implied that the restoration of a national representative body was necessary to revitalize the country.[6]

Like the Peninsulars, New Spaniards also looked to their past to forge a national myth which suited their needs. They advanced two concepts: the existence of a Mexican empire and of an American constitution.[7]

[5]There is an extensive literature on the eighteenth-century reforms. See, for example, Jean Sarraihl, *La España ilustrada de la segunda mitad del siglo XVII* (Mexico, 1957); Richard Herr, *The Eighteenth-Century Revolution in Spain* (Princeton, 1958). On Mexico see Ricard Rees Jones, *El despotismo ilustrado y los intendentes de la Nueva España* (Mexico, 1979); Horst Pietschmann, *Die Einfuhrung des Intendantensystem in Neu-Spanien* (Cologne, 1972); E. Arcila Farías, *El siglo ilustrado en América: reformas económicas del siglo XVIII en Nueva España* (Caracas, 1955); and David Brading, *Miners and Merchants in Bourbon Mexico, 1763–1810* (Cambridge, 1971). On the Law of Consolidation see Romeo Flores Caballero, *La contrarrevolución en la independencia: los españoles en la vida política, social y económica de Mexico, 1804–1838* (Mexico, 1969), 33–65; Asunción Lavrín, "The Execution of the Law of Consolidation in New Spain," *Hispanic American Historical Review* 52 (February, 1973), 27–49. Alexander von Humboldt, *Personal Narrative of Travels to the Equinoctial Regions of the New Continent During the Years 1799–1804*, 4 vols., 3d ed. (London, 1822), III, 329.

[6]Herr, *The Eighteenth-Century Revolution*, 337–347. Francisco Martínez Marina, *Teoría de las cortes*, 2 vols. Biblioteca de Autores Españoles, vols. 219–220 (Madrid, 1968). His critical introduction of the *Siete Partidas* has been reissued together with an excellent study of his thought as vol. 194 of Biblioteca de Autores Españoles (Madrid, 1966).

[7]Bernabé Navarro probed the dissemination of modern ideas in *La introducción de la filosofía moderna en México* (Mexico, 1948), and the character of the Mexican Enlighten-

As in the mother country, a new interpretation of history contributed to the formation of a new ideology. The study of the pre-Columbian past provided the basis for the notion of a Mexican empire and post-conquest history seemed to confirm the existence of an American constitution. This line of thought culminated in the writings of Father Servando Teresa de Mier. His *Idea de la Constitución dada a las Américas por los reyes de España antes de la invasión del antiguo despotismo* argued that New Spaniards were mestizos who possessed rights derived from two sources: their Indian progenitors, who originally possessed the land, and their Spanish ancestors, who in conquering Mexico obtained privileges from the crown, including the right to convene their own cortes. Mier declared: "Our kings, far from having considered establishing a colonial system in our Americas, not only made our [kingdoms] equal with Spain but also granted us the best [institutions] she possessed." He believed the early sixteenth century to have been "the age of the true constitution of America."[8]

Although the thesis of rights, based on a dual Indian and Spanish heritage, might have evolved into a rationale for independence, New Spaniards did not reach that conclusion. Instead, they considered themselves the true heirs of Spanish political tradition. They held that view not only because it served their own interests, but also because they believed that after 1808 the leaders of Spain had betrayed the nation to the French. The French Revolution and later Napoleon were anathema to the patriotic people of New Spain. Politically active New Spaniards refused to accept that their monarch, the embodiment of their sovereignty, could become a pawn of France. New Spaniards' hostility toward France and French practices became so pervasive that one cannot ignore it. For example, the premier issue of the first rebel paper, *El Despertador Americano*, was devoted to criticizing the failure of Spaniards to defend the nation from the French, accusing them of cowardice and treason. It concluded with an exhortation to the English to join the insurgents in their just struggle by declaring "We are now the true Spaniards, the sworn enemies of Napoleon and his lackeys,

ment in *Cultura mexicana moderna en el siglo XVIII* (Mexico, 1964). More recently Roberto Moreno has reinterpreted the Mexican Enlightenment in his *Joaquín Veláquez de León y sus trabajos científicos en el Valle de México* (Mexico, 1977). The nature of New Spain's political thought is examined in Villoro, *El proceso ideológico*, 41–63, 109–133; and with greater sophistication in José Miranda, *Las ideas y las instituciones políticas mexicana*, 2d ed. (Mexico, 1978), 211–355.

[8] *Idea de la constitución* is found in *La formación de un republicano*, vol. 4 of *Obras completas de Servando Teresa de Mier*, edited by Jaime E. Rodríguez O. (Mexico, 1988), 31–92. See also the "Introducción," 7–30; as well as Margarita Moreno Bonett, *Nacionalismo novohispano* (Mexico, 1983).

the legitimate successors of all the rights of the [Spaniards] who neither won [the war], nor died for Fernando [VII].[9]

As the quote indicates, the leaders of New Spain regarded themselves as more Spanish than the inhabitants of the Peninsula. Their desire to rule at home, of course, influenced their notion of correct Spanishness. In their minds, their right to self-rule was part and parcel of being true to Spanish traditions. The events of 1808 demonstrated that the American Spaniards, the creoles, remained true to Spanish legal traditions, which the European Spaniards, the gachupines, betrayed. It was the European Spaniards, after all, who carried out the first coup d'etat in Mexican history.

The issue came to a head in June and July 1808 when the people of New Spain learned that Carlos IV had abdicated; that his minister, Manuel Godoy, had been imprisoned; that the new king, Fernando VII, had renounced his crown; that French troops had occupied Madrid; and that Spanish officials had recognized French authority. The situation mystified the authorities in the viceroyalty. Who ruled Spain? Should anyone be obeyed? What ought to be done?

Two points of view emerged: one represented the position of the gachupines, the Spanish-born officals and entrepreneurs, the other the view of the American Spaniards. The European Spaniards wanted to maintain the established order. They declared: "In the present state of things, nothing has altered the nature of legitimately established authorities, and all should continue as they have until now. . . . "[10] The European Spaniards, of course, had powerful reasons for advocating such a stance. If they acknowledged that the Bourbon monarchy no longer existed, they would undermine their own position in New Spain. Consequently, they were trapped into arguing that whatever government existed in Spain was the authority that the viceroyalty had to obey.[11] Their policy, however, not only dismissed traditional Spanish political theory, but it also contradicted the actions of the Spanish provinces at that very moment.

The American Spaniards, conversely, enjoyed a superior legal and moral position, arguing that traditional Spanish political theory should guide the

[9]*El Despertador Americano*, no. 1 (December 20, 1810) in Juan E. Hernández y Dávalos, *Colección de documentos para la historia de la guerra de independencia de México de 1808 a 1821*, 6 vols. 2d ed. (Mexico, 1985), II, 312.

[10]"Voto consultivo del Real Acuerdo sobre la primera representación del Ayuntamiento de México," in Genaro García, *Documentos históricos mexicanos*, 7 vols., 2d ed. (Mexico, 1985), II, 38.

[11]Fray Melchor de Talamantes indicated the problem clearly when he declared: "No habiendo Rey legítimo en la nación, no puede haber vireyes; no hay apoderado sin poderdante; el obispo auxiliar cesa faltando el diocesano, y así de lo demás. Esta verdad la han conocido las provincias de España y por esto han nombrado juntas gubernamentales que las dirijieran." In "Proclama del Virrey Iturrigaray . . . anotada por Fr. Melchor de Talamantes," in Hernández y Dávalos, *Colección de documentos*, I, 518.

actions of the authorities in New Spain. The creoles based their actions on the principles: that New Spain was not a colony but a kingdom of the crown; that it was the coequal of the kingdoms in Spain; that in the absence of the monarch sovereignty reverted to the people; and that New Spain had the right to convene a cortes of cities in which Mexico City would be preeminent. The principle that New Spain was a kingdom, not a colony, constituted the basis upon which the rest of the American theory was founded. New Spaniards insisted on its recognition during the entire decade. Once that first principle was accepted all else followed.[12]

The creole-dominated ayuntamiento of Mexico City initiated the debate on July 19, 1808, with a proposal to Viceroy José Iturrigaray. The cabildo maintained that until the king returned and French troops evacuated Spain, the nation was not entirely free to act. Therefore the ayuntamiento proposed that the viceroy continue *provisionally* in charge of the government. The cabildo asserted that the viceroy no longer derived his authority from the crown, but governed provisionally only in the name of the Kingdom of New Spain as represented by its superior tribunals, the cities, Mexico City foremost among them, the clergy, and the nobility. As defined by the ayuntamiento, the representatives of the nation were virtually the same as those who had traditionally possessed the right to representation in the cortes of Spain.

The reasons the Mexico City ayuntamiento gave for its actions are significant. It held that the king could not alienate his kingdoms and that therefore his abdication was null. Such alienation was not only contrary

[12]These arguments were made in a number of documents, e.g., "Por su ausencia [la del rey] o impedimento reside la soberanía representado en todo el Reino, y las clases que lo forman, y con más particularidad en los Tribunales superiores que lo gobiernan, administran justicia, y en los cuerpos que llevan la voz pública." In "Testimonio de la sesión celebrada por el Ayuntamiento de México, el 19 de julio de 1808," in García, *Documentos*, II, 27. Similar views are expressed in "Representación del Ayuntamiento de Xalapa, 20 de julio de 1808." and "Representación del Ayuntamiento de Querétaro, 30 de julio de 1808," in García, *Documentos*, I, 35–37, 43–44. The marqués de Rayas provides an excellent account of these views in "La causa del Marqués de Rayas," Archivo General de la Nación (hereafter AGN): Infidencias, 91, f. 1–15. Various cities replied to requests of the Junta Suprema Central, among them Valladolid which insisted "que sea tenida esta América, no como colonia, sino como una parte muy esencial de la monarquía de España, y . . . que bajo este concepto fundamental e invariable en todas constituciones, providencias y deliberaciones, y aun variaciones de las leyes y gobierno nacional, sea considerada la Nueva España igualmente que la antigua sin variación alguna" AGN: Historia, 417, f. 300. Even the insurgents held such views as late as 1812. For example, the *Ilustrador Americano* published a *Plan de Paz* which included: "Principios naturales y legales en que se funda. 1. La soberanía reside en la masa de la nación. 2. España y América son partes integrantes de la monarquía, sujetas a la ley, pero iguales entre sí y sin dependencia o subordinación de la una respeto de la otra. 4. Ausente el soberano ningún derecho tienen los habitantes de la Península para apropiarse la suprema potestad y representarla en estos dominos." *Ilustrador Americano*, no. 3 (June 10, 1812).

to Spanish law, but also violated the oath which Carlos I gave to the city of Mexico in the sixteenth century that he would neither alienate it nor donate it. Thus, New Spaniards invoked not only Spanish legal traditions, but also the special historical rights, or constitution, of New Spain. The cabildo pointedly declared: "In the absence or during the impediment [of the king], sovereignty lies represented in all the kingdom and the classes that form it; and more particularly in those superior tribunals that govern it and administer justice and in those corporations that represent the public."[13]

It also proposed that a junta, composed of representatives from the cities, the nobility, the clergy, and the superior tribunals, be convened to govern New Spain. This proposal was consistent with Spanish and American traditions. In the sixteenth century, Carlos I had recognized Mexico City's preeminent position in any possible assembly of cities of New Spain. In the seventeenth century, during the debate over the Union of Arms, Mexico City and Puebla had petitioned the viceroy to convene a congress of municipal delegates. Although the viceroy had rejected their proposal, neither he nor the crown questioned the putative right of New Spain's municipalities to participate in the regional cortes.[14] Since many historians have interpreted the drive for autonomy as revolutionary, it is worth emphasizing that autonomy was a traditional concept. As Doris Ladd has indicated, it mirrored the historic struggle in Spain between the provinces and the core—between regional autonomy and Castilian centralism. Like the Catalans, the American Spaniards believed that their interests should take precedence over those of Spain. Following the classic formula, the autonomists of New Spain praised the king, but decried *bad government.*[15]

[13]"Acta celebrada por el Ayuntamiento de México, el 19 de julio de 1808," in García, *Documentos*, II, 15–34, quote on p. 27.

[14]Fray Melchor de Talamantes argued: "La Ley segunda, título octavo, Libro quarto de la Recopilación de Indias manda que, en atención a la grandeza y nobleza de la Ciudad de México, y a que en ellas reside el Virey, Gobierno, y Audiencia de la Nueva España, y fue la primera Ciudad poblada por Christianos, tenga el primer voto y lugar de las Ciudades y Villas de la Nueva-España. Esta Ley es una tácita declaración, o más bien verdadero reconocimiento del derecho que gozan para congregarse las Ciudades y Villas del Reyno, quando así lo exige la Causa pública, y bien del estado, pues de otra manera serían absolutamente inútiles e ilusorios el voto y el lugar que se les conceden." Melchor de Talamantes, "Congreso Nacional del Reyno de Nueva España," Luis González Obregón and Juan Pablo Baz, *Fray Melchor de Talamantes: biografía y escritos póstumos* (Mexico, 1909), 1–40, quote 3; John I. Israel, *Race, Class and Politics in Colonial Mexico* (Oxford, 1975), 178–180; Colin M. MacLachlan and Jaime E. Rodríguez O., *The Forging of the Cosmic Race: A Reinterpretation of Colonial Mexico* (Berkeley, 1980), 320–303.

[15]Among those who interpret the "autonomists' " actions as "revolutionary" are: Villoro, *El proceso ideológico*, 45–46 and passim; Hamill, *The Hidalgo Revolt*, 94–99; and Anna, *The Fall of the Royal Government*, 36–46. Doris M. Ladd, *The Mexican Nobility at Independence, 1780–1826* (Austin, 1976), 110. John H. Elliott, *The Revolt of the Catalans* (Cambridge, 1963), is a study of an imperial crisis similar to that of 1808–1821. See especially, 523–555.

The leading advocates of autonomy were the regidores Juan Francisco Azcárate, Francisco Primo de Verdad, and the Marqués de Uluapa; the alcalde de crimen in the audiencia, Jacobo Villaurrutia; and prominent citizens such as the Conde de Medina, the Conde de Regla, and the Marqués de Rayas. The principal ideologue of autonomy, Fray Melchor de Talamantes, composed a series of political tracts for the ayuntamiento. Talamantes proposed convoking a congress to govern New Spain and to reform the kingdom. The assembly would be empowered to appoint a viceroy, fill civil and ecclesiastical positions, manage the realm's finances, and name ambassadors. Talamantes also recommended that the congress abolish the Inquisition, as well as ecclesiastical *fueros*; introduce free trade; and promote mining, agricultural, and industrial reforms. The proposals resemble those subsequently enacted in Spain when a cortes met in Cádiz, indicating that these ideas were widely held throughout the Spanish world.[16] The main difference is that Talamantes proposed a regional congress for New Spain, something no European Spaniard tolerated.

Viceroy Iturrigaray appeared to accept the arguments of the American Spaniards. On September 1, 1808, he requested that the ayuntamientos of New Spain appoint representatives to a meeting in the capital. The following day he asked the Real Acuerdo if it considered "necessary the attendance of the deputies of all the ayuntamientos, or if it would be sufficient if these [ayuntamientos] delegated authority to the cabeceras of their respective provinces, and those . . . [deputies] represented them."[17]

The Real Acuerdo, composed of European Spaniards, objected to the convening of a congress.[18] Conservatives, especially peninsulares, considered any action as dangerous, given the uncertain circumstances in Spain. Some, like the wealthy entrepreneur Gabriel Yermo, *oidor* Ciriaco González Carvajal, and inquisitor Bernardo del Prado, maintained that the very idea of a congress was treasonable.[19] Bishop Manuel Abad y Queipo, long considered a progressive reformer, declared that "a national junta violated the

[16]Talamantes, "Congreso Nacional del Reyno de Nueva España."

[17]"Circular para que los ayuntamientos nombren apoderados para el congreso nacional, September 1, 1808"; and "El virey D. José de Iturrigaray al Real Acuerdo le consulta sobre el modo de concurrir los ayuntamientos al congreso general, September 2, 1808," in Hernández y Dávalos, *Colección de documentos*, I, 529–530.

[18]The only criollo on the court, Jacobo Villaurrutia, sided with the ayuntamiento. "Contestación y pedimento de los fiscales, September 3, 1808," in Hernández y Dávalos, *Colección de documentos*, I, 530–531.

[19]Ciriaco González Carvajal to Iturrigaray, August 7, 1808, in Hernández y Dávalos, *Colección de documentos*, 512–513; Bernardo del Prado to Iturrigaray, September 4, 1808, AGN: Historia, 417, ff. 375–380.

Constitution and was itself an act of rebellion."[20] The conservative criollo regidor Agustín del Rivero took the most extreme position: in his view, "to call the cities is to initiate civil war."[21]

When confronted by such opposition, Viceroy Iturrigaray decided not to convoke an assembly of cities. Instead, influenced by Primo de Verdad, on August 9, he invited the representatives of the principal corporations in Mexico City—the audiencia, the ayuntamiento, the consulado, the mining guild, the military, the fuero courts, the university, the monasteries of Guadalupe, Santo Domingo, and Carmen, the nobility, and three Indian governors of the metropolitan *barrios*—to advise him. In short, a body which resembled the one recommended by the ayuntamiento, but limited to Mexico City.[22]

The meeting was tempestuous. The *síndico del común*, Primo de Verdad, argued that in light of events in Spain, sovereignty now resided in the people. When the Spanish-born oidor Guillermo Aguirre inquired "Who are the people to whom sovereignty now devolved?"[23] Primo de Verdad replied that the constituted authorities represented the people. But Aguirre maintained that they were not *the people*, that the ayuntamiento's views were seditious, and that, in any case, the logic of Primo de Verdad's arguments would return sovereignty to the Indians who were "the original people." Despite these and other criticisms, the autonomists had advanced a powerful thesis that was consistent not only with Spanish political theory but also with the actions of Spaniards in the Iberian Peninsula.

In spite of the objections of the European Spaniards, Viceroy Iturrigaray convened four meetings, on August 9 and 31 and on September 1 and 9. Although the meetings resolved nothing, they convinced the gachupines that Iturrigaray constituted a threat to their position in the viceroyalty. News from Spain that mobs in Cádiz had removed Godoy's appointees, calling them French collaborators, only added to their apprehension. Most high officials in New Spain had been appointed during Godoy's long administration. In addition, European Spaniards were aware that they ruled a nonwhite society and that a mass uprising would be disastrous. Thus they were unwilling to permit the native elite, the American Spaniards,

[20]"Opinión del Obispo de Valladolid, D. Manuel Abad y Queipo, sobre la destitución del Sr. Iturrigaray," in Hernández y Dávalos, *Colección de documentos*, I, 756–758, quote on p. 757.

[21]Agustín del Rivero to Iturrigaray, September 6, 1808, AGN: Historia, 417, 292–305.

[22]Ladd, *The Mexican Nobility*, 207, and note 17, p. 256.

[23]"Relación de los pasajes más notables ocurridos en las Juntas Generales que el Exmo. Sr. D. José de Iturrigaray convocó en el Salón del Real Palacio en los días 9 y 31 de agosto, y 1 y 9 de septiembre de 1808," in García, *Documentos*, II, 137–138. See also Hugh M. Hamill, Jr.," Un discurso formado con angustia: Francisco Primo de Verdad el 9 de agosto de 1808," *Historia Mexicana* 28:3 (1979), 439–474.

to indulge in their penchant for home rule. Shortly after midnight on September 16, 1808, a small group of European Spaniards led by Yermo arrested Iturrigaray.[24]

Immediately after the coup, the archbishop and the audiencia gathered at two o'clock in the morning to approve the viceroy's removal from office and to appoint the 80-year-old field marshall Pedro Garibay acting viceroy. The conspirators subsequently arrested the leaders of the autonomy movement—Primo de Verdad, Talamantes, and Azcárate; Francisco Beye Cisneros, abbot of the Convent of Guadalupe; José Beristáin de Sousa, cannon of the Cathedral; and the auditor of war, José del Cristo y Conde. Primo de Verdad died in prison days later, probably the victim of his captors. In April 1809, Talamantes succumbed to yellow fever in jail, in Veracruz. Azcárate remained imprisoned for three years. The others were released shortly after their arrest.[25]

During the next two years, peninsulares dominated the government of Mexico. Garibay remained in office until July 19, 1809, when the "Spanish party" replaced him with Archbishop Francisco Javier Lizana y Beaumont. Lizana lasted only until May 1810 when the audiencia seized the reins of power. The government of the audiencia fell September 12, 1810, when a new viceroy appointed in Spain arrived in Mexico. During those two years, the authorities in Spain exercised little control over the viceroyalty. The European Spaniards ran New Spain to suit themselves, but they could not restore the earlier unity of the upper classes. Their coup d'etat ended legitimacy in New Spain.

Although the authorities in Spain did not reproach the European Spaniards, their actions acknowledged the correctness of the criollos' position. On January 22, 1809, the Junta Suprema Central recognized the equality between the American kingdoms and Spain, acknowledging the right of the New World to representation in the new peninsular government.[26] The actions of the authorities in Spain, however, did not redress the

[24]The principal work on the 1808 crisis is Virginia Guedea, "Criollos y peninsulares en 1808: dos puntos de vista sobre lo español," Licenciatura thesis, Universidad Iberoamericana, 1964. See also Miranda, *Las ideas*, 235–254; Villoro, *El proceso ideológico*, 41–69; Anna, *The Fall of the Royal Government*, 35–58: Ladd, *The Mexican Nobility*, 105–110; Hamill, *The Hidalgo Revolt*, 92–99. As usual, the most extensive account is Alamán, *Historia de Méjico*, I, 179–267.

[25]The standard studies of Iturrigaray and the coup are Enrique Lafuente Ferrari, *El Virrey Iturrigaray y los orígenes de la independencia de México* (Madrid, 1941), and Jack A. Haddick, "The Administration of Viceroy Iturrigaray," Ph.D. dissertation, University of Texas, Austin, 1954. See also Flores Caballero, *La contrarrevolución*, 58–65; Alamán, *Historia de Méjico*, I, 279–344.

[26]The wording of the decree is significant in light of events in New Spain. "Considerando que los vastos y preciosos dominios que España posee en las Indias no son propiamente colonias o factorías como las de otras naciones, sino una parte esencial e integrante de la

grievances caused by the 1808 coup. Criollos were particularly offended because the authorities in Spain failed to remove the European Spaniards who had broken the law and overthrown the king's viceroy. The deaths of Primo de Verdad and Talamantes fueled the discontent. The criollo autonomists never accepted the gachupines' usurpation of power. Some sought ways to recover their legal rights. Rumors of conspiracies and, more significantly, conspiracies abounded in New Spain.

In the fall of 1809, the authorities uncovered a serious criollo cabal. Lieutenant José María Michelena, of the royal infantry, and Captain José María Obeso, of the provincial militia, had organized a plot in the city of Valladolid. The conspirators obtained support in other important cities—Guanajuato, Querétaro, San Miguel el Grande, and Guadalajara. They had prepared an uprising for December 21, 1809, expecting backing from the army and the militia. In addition, they hoped to win the support of the Indians and castas by promising to abolish tribute. Once they gained control of New Spain, the rebels planned to convene a congress of cities to govern in the name of Fernando VII. The proposed plan differed from the earlier autonomy movement only in that the criollos relied on military force because the European Spaniards had seized the government. When the movement was exposed, the authorities brought the leaders to trial. But the prosecution could only prove that the conspirators planned to save New Spain from a possible French invasion. Noting that many important persons openly declared that the conspirators were guilty of using improper means to redress rightful grievances, Acting Viceroy Lizana ordered them released.[27]

The Valladolid conspiracy encouraged a similar movement in Querétaro, where militia captains Ignacio Allende and Juan Aldama and corregidor Miguel Domínguez began informal talks. By March 1810, the plotters had recruited Father Miguel Hidalgo and other disaffected criollos. They sought, as did Michelena, to depose the European Spaniards with the aid of the workers of the Bajío—the so-called Indians—and to establish a criollo junta to govern New Spain in the name of Fernando VII. The conspirators planned the uprising for October 1810, but they were discovered by the authorities on September 13, and the Querétaro group was arrested. The authorities were not initially frightened by the news of another intrigue. Quite the

---

monarquía española, . . . los referidos dominios deben tener representación nacional inmediata . . . y constituir parte de la junta central . . . por medio de sus correspondientes diputados." AGN: Reales Cédulas, 201, 13.

[27] José Mariano Michelena, "Verdadero origen de la revolución de 1809 en el Departamento de Michoacán," in García, *Documentos*, I, 467–471; Carlos María Bustamante, *Cuadro histórico de la revolución mexicana*, 3 vols., 3d ed. (Mexico, 1961), I, 22, 18–30; Alamán, *Historia de Méjico*, I, 314–320; Christon I. Archer, *The Army in Bourbon Mexico, 1760–1810* (Albuquerque, 1977), 290–295.

contrary, they were inclined to be lenient. Had events gone no further, most participants might have remained free like the Valladolid group.

Hidalgo, Allende, and Aldama, however, launched the revolt from the town of Dolores on the morning of September 16, 1810. According to Aldama, about eight o'clock in the morning:

> There were gathered more than six hundred men on foot and horseback for it was Sunday and they had come to mass from the nearby ranches, and the cura [Hidalgo] exhorted them to join him and help defend the Kingdom because they [the European Spaniards] wanted to turn it over to the French: that now oppression had reached an end; that there was no longer any tribute; that those who enlisted with horses and arms would be paid a peso daily, and those on foot four reales.[28]

Thus Hidalgo appealed to the traditional view that bad government should be removed, while the monarchy remained inviolate. As Hugh Hamill has declared: "What Hidalgo said in Dolores will probably never be known. It is reasonable to suppose, however, that the climax of his speech included one or all of the following: Long Live Ferdinand VII! Long Live America! Long Live Religion! and Death to Bad Government!"[29]

Father Hidalgo's exhortation resonated among the rural poor, not because he promised to abolish tribute or pay them a small sum, but because it offered them an opportunity to avenge the injustices they believed they had suffered. As recent research has indicated, from 1780 to 1810 the standard of living and the working conditions of rural people in central Mexico declined substantially. Hidalgo accidentally unleashed a rural uprising which did not discriminate between European Spaniards and American Spaniards. The insurgents attacked their oppressors regardless of their origins and political affiliations. Thus, a division between the European and the American Spaniards about who should rule turned into the first mass social revolt in the history of Mexico.[30]

The Hidalgo Revolt, which began as a criollo movement for autonomy, was initially favorably perceived by the elite of New Spain. The Marqués de Rayas, for example, described Hidalgo as a man of integrity and his followers as valiant. But any true alliance between the insurgents and the elite was unlikely. The great landowners feared the rural masses who had faced starvation during the drought of 1808–1809 while they profited; they

[28]Juan Aldama, Declaración rendida por . . . en la causa que se le instruyó por haber sido caudillo insurgente," in García, *Documentos*, VI, 529.

[29]Hamill, *The Hidalgo Revolt*, 123.

[30]On the social question, see Florescano, *Precios de maíz*, 85–197; Florescano, *Fuentes para la historia de la crisis*; Tutino, *From Insurrection to Revolution*, 41–98; Van Young, *Hacienda and Market*, 271–343.

knew that the agricultural crisis persisted and that the rural poor blamed their majordomos and them for the famine. Some magnates and other large property owners contributed food and supplies to the rebel cause hoping to save their properties from pillage. Whatever limited support the movement might have curried with the upper classes disappeared when it became apparent that the rebel leaders could not control their followers. Within a short time, the rebels began to plunder making no distinction between the property of good and bad peninsulares or even between that of European Spaniards and American Spaniards.[31]

The sack of Guanajuato constituted the turning point in the revolt; news of the massacre terrified not only the upper and middle classes, but also many in the lower classes. The looting, carnage, and destruction of the Bajian city clearly indicated that the insurrection promoted uncontrollable class conflict. The elite feared that a revolution would spark a race war. Indians and campesinos with communal lands also were afraid that they might be dispossed by the landless poor in Hidalgo's army. Royalists propaganda capitalized on these apprehensions. Bishop Abad y Queipo, for example, argued that the Haitian upper class had been the most prosperous in the world until race conflict destroyed them. The same fate, he claimed, would befall their counterparts in New Spain if the impious Hidalgo were not stopped. The horror of race conflict even frightened some of the rebel leaders. Allende considered poisoning Hidalgo in an effort to stop the violence.[32]

Despite the social dangers posed by the insurgency, the autonomists formed clandestine groups to advance their interests. In 1811, the authorities uncovered two conspiracies to form a governing junta in Mexico City. General Calleja identified the plotters as "counts and marqueses, judges, councilmen, and other individuals like doctors, lawyers and merchants,"[33] describing their network as "a kind of Freemansonry . . . that serves them as intelligence in all kinds of disloyal conspiracies. All are united; they seek a single goal; they work for the same principles: and they are never discovered."[34] Although the autonomists formed loose coalitions and used various names for their groups, some have become famous as the Guadalupes because correspondence with that name has been discovered.[35]

[31]Ladd, *The Mexican Nobility*, 111; Tutino, *From Insurrection to Revolution*, 142–147; Alamán, *Historia de Méjico*, I, 383.

[32]Alamán, *Historia de Méjico*, I, 211–226; José María Luis Mora, *Mexico y sus revoluciones*, 4 vols. [vol. II was never published.] (Paris, 1836), IV, 23; Hamill, *The Hidalgo Revolt*, 151–165, 200; Ladd, *The Mexican Nobility*, 112–114.

[33]Félix María Calleja to Melchor Alvarez, November 5, 1814, in Ernesto de la Torre Villar, ed., *Los "Guadalupes" y la independencia*, 2d ed. (Mexico, 1985), 120.

[34]Calleja to Ministro de Justicia, July 30, 1814, in ibid., 104.

[35]Virginia Guedea, "Los Guadalupes de México," *Relaciones. Estudios de Historia y Sociedad*, no. 23 (1985), 71–91. Guedea, who has been studying these so-called secret societies

The movement for home rule drew new impetus from events taking place in Spain. The Junta Suprema Central had been waging a losing battle against the French since 1808. Because it desperately needed the support of the American kingdoms, the Spanish national government invited the kingdoms of America, as well as the provinces of Spain, to elect representatives to the Junta. The decree of January 22, 1809, emphasized the equality of Spain and America, instructing local authorities to elect representatives to the Junta Central. The provisional government also decided to convoke a cortes to deal with the crisis, a Spanish tradition that antedated the monarchy's unification under Carlos I.

Initially the Junta had intended to call a traditional parliament consisting of representatives of the three estates: the clergy, the nobility, and the cities. New French victories, however, forced their hand. On January 1, 1810, the Junta Central decreed that elections be held. In Spain each provincial junta and each city entitled to representation in earlier cortes could elect a deputy. In addition, each province might select a representative for every 50,000 inhabitants. In America, each province, a vague and undefined term, could also elect a deputy. Since the Junta did not know the size of the population in Spanish America, it inadvertently provided the New World with great power by granting each American province individual representation. Apparently the Junta Central also intended to summon the clergy and the nobility—but this never occurred, because the Junta could not compile a membership roll for these two groups and because the supine attitude of the first two estates toward the invader gained them the antipathy of the people. The Spanish cortes, therefore, met as one body and became a national assembly.[36]

New Spain's autonomists enthusiastically responded to the invitation to elect representatives to the Spanish cortes. This was their opportunity to obtain the home rule, which Yermo and his clique had denied them in 1808. They worked avidly to ensure that their supporters won the elections. They were extremely successful. When elections were held throughout the viceroyalty from Yucatán to New Mexico during the months of June, July, and August 1810, autonomist candidates won everywhere. Despite the insur-

for some time, argues that they were neither secret societies nor formally organized groups. Instead, they were like-minded individuals who gathered in *tertulias* in various places where they discussed politics and sometimes planned actions. (Personal communication, December 17, 1986.)

[36]Jaime E. Rodríguez O., *The Emergence of Spanish America: Vicente Rocafuerte and Spanish Americanism*, 1808–1832 (Berkeley, 1975), 8–10. The decree specified that in America a deputy was to be elected "por cada capital cabeza de partido de estas diferentes Provincias." Ecuador, Archivo Nacional de Historia: Audiencia de Quito, vol. 460, 40–51.

gency at home and the war in Europe, fifteen of the twenty deputies elected in New Spain attended the 1810 cortes.[37]

Spain's first modern cortes, which convened in Cádiz, remained in session from September 24, 1810, until September 20, 1813. During those years it attempted to transform the Spanish world: it abolished archaic institutions, ended the Inquisition, and established firmer control over the Church. It extended freedom of the press, already a fact in Spain, to the commonwealth. The cortes also realized that the provinces of Spain and America resented the earlier Bourbon efforts toward centralization. Therefore, it recognized the diversity of the Spanish commonwealth by creating two new home rule institutions: the provincial deputation and the constitutional cabildo. The provincial deputation was an administrative body consisting of locally elected members and an executive appointed by the national government. Thus, Spanish provinces already ruled by local juntas and rebellious American provinces could retain local administration while retaining strong ties with the central government. With the creation of the provincial deputations, the cortes abolished the viceroyalty, transformed the audiencia from a quasi-administrative body into a high court, and divided the commonwealth into provinces that dealt directly with the central government in Spain. The second local body, the constitutional city council, substituted popularly elected officials for the hereditary elites, who had heretofore controlled city governments.[38]

The Constitution of the Spanish Monarchy, promulgated in March 1812, embodied these and other reforms. The new charter created a unitary state with equal laws for all parts of the commonwealth. A unicameral legislature, the cortes, would meet annually in the capital; the king was substantially restricted; and the cortes was entrusted with decisive power. Thus although the new government encouraged some decentralization, it still continued and, in some ways, strengthened the resented Bourbon policies of integration.

New Spain's deputies to the cortes were among the leading champions of American interests. José Miguel Ramos Arizpe, from Coahuila, was the chief architect of the provincial deputation. His compatriots, José Miguel Guridi y Alcocer and José María Couto, representing Tlaxcala and Mexico respectively, distinguished themselves as parliamentarians; Guridi served as president of the cortes in 1812, and Couto as vice-president in 1813.

[37]The best study of Mexican participation in the cortes is Nettie Lee Benson, ed., *Mexico and the Spanish Cortes* (Austin, 1966); Charles R. Berry, "The Election of Mexican Deputies to the Spanish Cortes," in Benson, *Mexico and the Spanish Cortes*, 12–13.

[38]On the provinical deputation see Nettie Lee Benson, *La diputación provincial y el federalismo mexicano* (Mexico, 1955). On the constitutional cabildo see Roger L. Cunniff, "Mexican Municipal Reform, 1810–1822," in Benson, *Mexico and the Spanish Cortes*, 59–86.

Two Mexican clergymen who subsequently became conservative bishops, Antonio Joaquín Pérez of Puebla and José Miguel Gordoa of Zacatecas, often sided with the liberals; as a member of the constitutional commission, Pérez supported the liberals against the *serviles*, the traditional faction. New Spain's deputies also joined other American representatives in arguing for autonomy for their areas. On August 1, 1811, all of the American deputies presented a statement in which they declared that, while only a tiny minority wanted independence, many overseas residents were dissatisfied with the government, particularly the illegitimate actions of the conservative European Spaniards. Dr. José Beye Cisneros, professor emeritus of law at the University of Mexico and a deputy for Mexico, argued forcefully in a separate representation that the New World required home rule. He declared that even "under the best of laws, the inhabitants of America suffer a weightier yoke than that of any other nation." He further stated that the Hidalgo insurrection had resulted from the Europeans' high-handed and illegal overthrow of Iturrigaray. He accused the new officials, including Viceroy Venegas, of anti-Americanism, urging the creation of provincial juntas to govern the American kingdoms.[39] This demand sought much more autonomy than even the Spanish liberals were willing to grant. Ultimately, the cortes reached a compromise through the skillful negotiations of Ramos Arizpe in introducing the provincial deputations, which partly satisfied the desire for home rule while maintaining strong ties with the mother country.

In New Spain, the royal authorities and the conservative European Spaniards viewed the actions of the Spanish cortes with alarm. Venegas, now reduced to political chief of the Province of Mexico—an area that included most of central Mexico—refused to implement all the reforms. He suspended freedom of the press in his area, fearing that it would not only serve the interests of the insurgents, but also of other malcontents in Mexico City. The political chiefs of other provinces, however, introduced the reforms. When the Constitution was promulgated, Venegas had no alternative but to institute it. The charter was formally proclaimed in Mexico City on September 30, 1812, and the week that followed was one of celebration. Thereafter the contending factions—European Spaniards and the autonomists—openly campaigned for the parish elections of November 29, 1812. A victory for the European-conservative faction would have vindicated Venegas and his supporters. But the autonomists were too well organized. The Guadalupes and others worked behind the scenes to ensure that the

[39]Cited in Anna, *The Fall of the Royal Government*, 101; Rodríguez, *The Emergence of Spanish America*, 10–13; Benson, *La diputación provincial*, 11–41; Gabriel Lovett, *Napoleon and the Birth of Modern Spain*, 2 vols. (New York, 1965), II, 449; Brian R. Hamnett, *La política española en la época revolucionaria* (Mexico, 1985), 11–152.

autonomists triumphed. The American Spaniards won an overwhelming victory throughout New Spain.

The Spanish cortes provided the autonomists with a peaceful alternative with which to obtain home rule. Fearful of continuing the race and class conflict which raged in the viceroyalty, they welcomed the new representative government which, while imposing constitutional limits on the monarchy, also possessed the appearance of legitimacy. The elite's attitude is understandable. The autonomists of New Spain, like the elites of other Western nations, wanted a limited representative government. They favored neither social revolution nor race war. But they were determined to rule at home. To this end they had formed loose political alliances to further their interests. In general, they engaged in political machinations to ensure that their candidates won the elections. But since they distrusted the authorities, even the cortes, they often cooperated with the insurgents. Because they courted both sides to assure that their interests remained secure, many autonomists were called *equilibristas*. As Virginia Guedea has argued, these groups which operated from "the principal urban centers sought to achieve a greater role in the decision-making process." They were, in that respect, the embryonic coalitions which would form "the principal political forces that would [later] control the public life of the new nation."[40]

In Mexico City all the successful electors were criollos associated with the autonomy movement. Fearful that the electors would select men of their own persuasion for office, Venegas suspended the election on the grounds of voting irregularities. He also moved against suspected insurgent sympathizers: he ordered Judge Villaurrutia to Spain; indicted the elector Juan Martínez on charges of corresponding with the rebels; jailed the writer José Joaquín Fernández de Lizardi; and put a price on the head of Carlos María Bustamante, who fled to join the insurgents. Thus, by the middle of December 1812, the authorities in Mexico City had again broken the law, frustrating the efforts of the autonomists. But this time, unlike 1808, other provinces of New Spain were being governed by the Constitution; the elections were carried out and the guarantees of the 1812 charter obeyed. Venegas' actions kept him in office only a few months. On March 4, 1813, he was replaced as *jefe político superior* by General Calleja, who ordered the suspended elections completed. Again, led by the Guadalupes, the autonomists dominated the elections. To the consternation of the gachupines,

[40]I am grateful to Virginia Guedea for the information on the term *equilibristas*; see her "Comments" in the session, "The Emergence of Independent Mexico," at the annual meeting of the American Historical Association held in Washington, D.C., on December 30, 1987. The quotes are found in Guedea, "Las sociedades secretas durante el movimiento de independencia," in this volume.

not a single European won a seat in the cabildo, the provincial deputation, or the cortes.

Calleja continued to pacify New Spain. He disobeyed the Constitution if it impeded his efforts to crush the insurgency in Mexico. The traditional formula, *obedezco pero no cumplo,* served the imperial bureaucracy. But Calleja no longer possessed viceregal authority. The cortes had divided the former Viceroyalty of New Spain into seven smaller districts, commanded for military purposes by captains-general: New Spain, Nueva Galicia, San Luis Potosí, the Eastern Interior Provinces, the Western Interior Provinces, Yucatán, and Guatemala. For administrative purposes, each of these districts was, in turn, divided into provinces with their own provincial deputations and political chiefs. For example, New Spain, the most populous region of the viceroyalty, consisted of nine provinces: Mexico, Puebla, Michoacán, Guanajuato, Oaxaca, Veracruz, San Luis Potosí, Tlaxcala, and Querétaro. The new constitutional cabildos and the provincial deputations asserted their rights to home rule, thus further weakening central authority. Dominated by New Spaniards, these bodies insisted that the imperial bureaucracy obey the constitution. In addition, New Spaniards possessed more than sixty seats in the cortes, not only giving them an important voice in commonwealth-wide affairs, but also the ability to restrict central authority and pursue home rule for New Spain. Thus, the once-powerful office of viceroy was reduced to captain-general of the Kingdom of New Spain and political chief of the Province of Mexico.

The political transformation wrought by the Spanish cortes substantially affected politics in New Spain. It encouraged the growth of regionalism. The provincial deputations and the constitutional city councils, moreover, gave provincial New Spaniards opportunities to assert their local interests. Building on the regionalism fomented earlier by the intenancies, the provincial deputations provided outlets for long repressed regionalist sentiments. That regionalism only increased when first Venegas, and later Calleja, attempted to annul or restrict their new provincial rights. These conflicts constituted the beginning of the political struggles between the center and the provinces which would plague post-independent Mexico. By restricting the ability of the royalist forces to deal with the insurgency, the reforms of the cortes indirectly aided the rebels. But they also forced the insurgents to take Spanish liberalism into account, if they were to win the support of most New Spaniards. As a result, the autonomists could play the royalists against the rebels in an effort to extract concessions from the Spanish government.[41]

[41] Berry, "The Election of Mexican Deputies,' 16–32; Anna, *The Fall of Royal Government*, 102–119; Brian R. Hamnett, *Revolución y contrarrevolución en México y el Perú* (Mexico, 1978), 37–54; W. Woodrow Anderson, "Reform as a Means to Quell Revolution," in Benson, *Mexico and the Spanish Cortes*, 185–196.

Events in Spain again radically altered the situation in the viceroyalty. In May 1814, when Fernado VII returned from captivity in France, he abolished the cortes nullifying all its acts. The constitutional structure fell like a house of cards. In Spain, the regular army pursued the liberals. Some escaped to France or Italy; countless others, including José Miguel Ramos Arizpe, were imprisoned. Fernando VII jailed or exiled thousands of liberals, among them the country's most important intellectuals, professionals, and scientists.[42] In New Spain, Calleja joyfully received the news of the king's return and acted energetically to reassert viceregal authority. Within a short time, he abolished all constitutional bodies and restored the older institutions. Subsequently, he imprisoned and tried the principal leaders of the movement for autonomy, among them many high-ranking criollos.

Restored to full viceregal power, and no longer hampered by the Constitution, Calleja was free to fight the insurgents. Nearly 15,000 Spanish soldiers had arrived in New Spain between 1811 and the end of 1815. No longer solely dependent upon local forces, Calleja relied increasingly on Spanish troops to garrison hostile regions, and on Spanish officers to administer unfriendly or uncooperative cities and towns. Consequently, large parts of New Spain fell under the heavy hand of military law. Again, New Spaniards found themselves subject to an arbitrary government which insisted that they place the interests of Spain before their own. But, as Christon Archer has indicated, despite Calleja's efforts, the insurgency did not end. Instead it fragmented into "one of the greatest guerrilla insurgencies in modern history."[43] Faced with a brutal guerrilla war in a nonwhite society, not knowing who was their enemy, many Spanish soldiers treated all New Spaniards as their foes.

The people of New Spain, particularly those who lived in areas of conflict, realized that an orderly government had almost ceased to function in the provinces. The viceroyalty's elite, those who had favored autonomy, continued to work clandestinely for home rule. The authorities considered them such a threat that in 1815 and 1816 Calleja arrested not only suspected rebels, but also four former regidores, an oidor, a *fiscal* of the audiencia, a marqués, and a canon who was a deputy-elect to the cortes. One former councilman, the Indian governor of San Juan, Francisco Galicia, died in prison, thus adding to the grievances against the government of Fernando VII. These high officials had been the leading partisans of the Constitution. Their imprisonment and harsh treatment demonstrated not only the

[42]Rodríguez, *The Emergence of Spanish America*, 15–16; Lovett, *Napoleon and the Birth of Modern Spain*, II, 828–829; Vicente Llorens, *Liberales y románticos: una emigración española en Inglaterra*, 2d ed. (Madrid, 1968), 10; Hamnett, *La política española*, 184–201.

[43]Christon Archer, " 'La Causa Buena': The Counterinsurgency Army of New Spain and the Ten Years' War," in this volume.

defeat of constitutional rule, but it also violated the traditional rights and privileges of their rank. Such actions reinforced the autonomists' desire for home rule.

Political unity had already been weakened by earlier shocks: the Bourbon centralization, the imperial crisis, the illegal actions of the European Spaniards, the rural uprisings triggered by the Hidalgo revolt, and the continuing upheaval in the provinces caused by the insurgency and the counterinsurgency. The actions of Viceroy Calleja, as well as those of Fernando VII, reinforced the fears of New Spaniards that they were living under *mal gobierno*. The consent of the governed that had sustained Spanish rule for nearly three hundred years had ceased to exist. New Spaniards obeyed the government principally because it possessed the monopoly of force. The situation seemed desperate. Yet most autonomists still refused to opt for independence. Although they had used the insurgency to gain their ends, particularly during the constitutional period (1810–1814), they were unwilling to join the rebels. It was one thing to participate in a moderate representative government and quite another to be at the mercy of a mass-based regime, especially when the masses had engaged for years in a race and class war.[44]

Again, events in Spain transformed the situation in the viceroyalty. Liberals rejected Fernando VII's policies by rebelling and restoring the Constitution in January 1820. As a result, the political structure of New Spain changed again. The constitutional cabildos and provincial deputations were restored, and elections held in May. The new situation presented autonomists with another opportunity to press their case legally. But they also realized that the situation had changed in the provinces. Local leaders refused to accept the status quo. Therefore, the autonomists had to act quickly if they expected to retain control of the politics of home rule. They followed two paths: conspiracy and parliamentary means. Manuel Gómez Pedraza and Lucas Alamán have left us accounts of their participation in conspiracies in Puebla, Jalapa, and Veracruz. Although much remains to be learned, it is clear the conspirators agreed on a program for autonomy. They pursued their plans in the cortes in Spain and clandestinely in the viceroyalty.[45]

New Spain's deputies, led by Ramos Arizpe, Michelena, and Alamán, proposed to the cortes that America be divided into three kingdoms: New Spain and Guatemala; New Granada and Tierra Firme; and Peru, Chile, and Buenos Aires. Each of the three kingdoms would have its own cortes and govern itself according to the Constitution of 1812. A Spanish prince,

[44]Alamán, *Historia de Méjico*, V, 166–174.

[45]Manuel Gómez Pedraza, *Manifiesto que . . . , ciudadano de la República de Méjico dedica a sus compatriotas, o sea una reseña de su vida pública*, 2d ed. (Guadalajara, 1831); Alamán, *Historia de Méjico*, V, 87–88.

or a person appointed by the king, would preside over each kingdom. Spain and the American kingdoms would enjoy special relationships in the areas of trade, diplomacy, and defense, and the new kingdoms would pay a portion of Spain's debt. The autonomists clearly wanted to retain ties with Spain, but they insisted on home rule. In presenting their arguments, the deputies named Canada as their model for a commonwealth. Their proposal would have granted New Spaniards the autonomy they had been seeking since 1808, if the Spanish majority in the cortes had not rejected it.[46]

The new Mexican nation emerged almost by accident. The country's elite, like the urban and rural masses and the army, were so exhausted by nearly eleven years of war that they all joined Colonel Agustín de Iturbide when he pronounced the Plan of Iguala, which provided an alternative method of achieving home rule. The Spanish regime ended not because it was defeated militarily, but because neither New Spaniards nor European Spaniards any longer supported it politically.[47] Throughout the country, people joyously received independence. They widely acclaimed Iturbide as a great hero, a farsighted statesman, and the liberator of Mexico.[48]

The Plan of Iguala resembled the proposal rejected by the cortes. It established an independent Mexican empire to be ruled by Fernando VII, or, if he did not accept, a Spanish prince; it proclaimed the Constitution of 1812 and the statutes passed by the cortes as the laws of the land; it guaranteed that the new country would remain Catholic; it preserved the fueros of the clergy and the military; it removed all ethnic distinctions, declaring all Mexicans, whether American- or European-born equal; and it proposed to convene a Mexican congress. Pending election, a Regency, a plural executive, and a Sovereign Junta composed of twelve members would govern the country. These bodies were modeled on the institutions which administered Spain between 1808 and 1810.[49]

The ideas of 1808 were accepted in 1821 as the bases for establishing the new nation. Through the Plan of Iguala, the autonomists, who had conspired since 1808 for home rule, gained power. The leaders of the movement signed the Declaration of Independence on September 28, 1821. They dominated first the Soberana Junta Provisional Gubernativa in 1821–1822

[46]"Exposición presentada a las Cortes por los diputados de ultramar en la sesión de 25 de junio de 1821," in Alamán, *Historia de Méjico*, V, Apéndice, 49–65; ibid., 477; Anna, *The Fall of the Royal Government*, 162–178.

[47]Archer, " 'La Causa Buena,' " and his "Where Did All the Royalists Go? New Light on the Military Collapse of New Spain, 1810–1821," in Jaime E. Rodríguez O., ed., *The Mexican and the Mexican American Experience in the Nineteenth Century* (Tempe, 1989), 24–43.

[48]Javier Ocampo, *Las ideas de un día: el pueblo mexicano ante la consumación de su independencia* (Mexico, 1969).

[49]"Plan de Independencia de la América Septentrional," in René Cárdenas Barrios, *1810–1821: Documentos básicos para la independencia* (Mexico, 1979), 274–286.

and then the first Congreso Constituyente Mexicano in 1822–1823. Once in office the Mexican elite failed to consolidate their power and establish an effective government. They engaged in petty conflicts with Iturbide, first as generalísimo and then as emperor, and among themselves. They seemed unable to translate the vigor and determination they had shown in opposition into governing the new nation. They appeared unwilling to accept the responsibilities of office.[50]

To succeed, the new regime had to win the loyalty of the population, end the tendency toward atomization by establishing fiscal, as well as political, control over the country, and create a new and workable tax system. But, as Barbara Tenenbaum indicates, "the creole elites believed that independence meant liberation from the burdens of Spanish colonial taxation. . . . They had no intention of giving any Mexican leader the funds required to run a stable government."[51] Unlike their North American counterparts, the Mexican elite refused to allow the implementation of an effective tax system because they equated "taxation with tyranny." Without funds, the first empire failed.

When Emperor Agustín I abdicated on March 19, 1823, the leaders of the First Constituent Congress attempted to establish a strong republic. To their shock and dismay provincial leaders emerged to challenge their authority. Ironically, one of the institutions created by the Spanish cortes, the provincial deputation, provided regionalists the means with which to challenge the power of the elite in Mexico City. Following Spanish tradition, the provincial deputations argued that sovereignty reverted to the people because Spain had repudiated the Plan of Iguala and because Iturbide's government had been illegal. They, naturally, argued that the provincial deputations were the rightful representatives of the people.[52] The Province of Guadalajara, or Jalisco, typified this view when it declared: "With the first and second allegiance destroyed, exempt from the obedience which we granted to the Spanish government, and later to the emperor which Mexico had, Guadalajara and its sister provinces entered naturally into liberty and independence."[53]

[50]See *Diario de las sesiones de la Soberana Junta Provisional Gubernativa del Imperio Mexicano* (Mexico, 1812) and *Actas del Congreso Constituyente Mexicano*, 2 vols. (Mexico, 1822–1823). See also Timothy E. Anna, "The Role of Agustín Iturbide: A Reappraisal," *Journal of Latin American Studies* 17 (1985), 79–110; and his "The Iturbide Interregnum," in this volume.

[51]Barbara A. Tenenbaum, "Taxation and Tyranny: Public Finance during the Iturbide Regime, 1821–1823," in this volume.

[52]These views are expressed in the following: Jalisco, Diputación Provincial, *Manifiesto . . . a los habitantes del Estado Libre de Xalisco* (Guadalajara, 1823); Puebla, Diputación Provincial, *Firmesa de los poblanos con la comisión de México* (Puebla, 1823); Querétaro, Diputación Provincial, *Ciudadanos* (n.p., 1823). See also the Mexico City paper *Aguila Mexicana* which printed many provincial manifestos during this period.

[53]Jalisco, Diputación Provincial, *Manifiesto*, 6.

During February and March 1823, when they had opposed Iturbide, the provincial deputations informed each other of their actions, and began to discuss the manner in which they should create a national government. On March 10, 1823, Puebla invited the provinces to send two delegates to a convention to form a provisional government. Three days later Michoacán proposed that representatives from Michoacán, Querétaro, San Luis Potosí, and the Eastern Interior Provinces meet in Querétaro to establish a national government, a suggestion it abandoned when it learned of Puebla's invitation. The majority of provincial representatives traveled to Puebla, but before most arrived, Iturbide reconvened the First Constituent Congress and then abdicated.[54] A rump session, calling itself the Junta of Puebla, recognized the reconvened congress but only for the purpose of convoking a new constituent congress.[55] The other provinces agreed. The provinces of Mexico insisted on electing a new constituent congress in order to ensure their own autonomy. Therefore, they declared that federalism was the only form of government possible for Mexico.

The provinces considered themselves the arbiters of the nation in mid-1823. Oaxaca, Yucatán, Jalisco, and Zacatecas installed provincial constituent legislatures while others, declaring themselves sovereign and independent states, created provincial governments. Most sent commissions to Mexico City to ensure that the First Constituent Congress obeyed their wishes. That body, however, refused to acknowledge provincial authority. Instead it attempted to impose its will upon the country by force. Rather than capitulating, the provinces raised militias to defend their territories, joining forces to oppose the national army. The national elite, which dominated congress, ultimately capitulated, declaring their support for the federal system and issuing instructions for convening a new constituent congress.[56]

The Second Constituent Congress, which met on November 7, 1823, faced very different circumstances than its predecessor. The provinces had not only asserted their sovereignty, but they had also restricted the authority of their delegates. Valladolid, for example, declared "This province in the federation does not want to give up much of its liberties and other rights, [it is willing to grant] only that which is necessary to assure the part which it retains."[57] Yucatán decreed that "The elected deputies are only granted the power . . . to constitute the nation in a government that is republican, representative, and federal," and that "The federal constitution which they, together with the other deputies in Congress, establish

[54]Benson, *La diputación provincial*, 85 and passim.

[55]Puebla, *Acta de la Junta de Puebla sobre la reinstalación del congreso mexicano* (Puebla, 1823).

[56]Benson, *La diputación provincial*, 167–198.

[57]*Aguila Mexicana* (October 23, 1823).

will not have force of law in the nation until the majority of federated states . . . ratify it."[58] Zacatecas was even more explicit, asserting that "The deputies in the future Congress cannot constitute the nation as they deem convenient; but [only] under a system of a federal republic."[59] Other provinces made similar declarations. The Second Constituent Congress represented the will of the provincial elites. As expected, it established a federal republic in 1824.[60]

The Mexico City–based national elite, which had been struggling for power since 1808, finally attained it in 1821 only to loose it two years later. The new Mexican republic, unlike the United States, began its life in the hands of a regional elite which resorted to mass politics. The Mexican upper class, the *hombres de bien*, as Lucas Alamán called them, were marginalized during the first decade of national life. Although they had struggled for a decade to achieve home rule, they were unable to establish the moderate representative government they desired. The federal republic had to cope with mass demonstrations, riots, and violence at a time when representative institutions were ill established. Instead of government by the hombres de bien, early republican Mexico fell into the hands of demagogues and military caudillos and was characterized by political instability. Little wonder that years later, Lucas Alamán would question the entire movement for independence.[61]

[58]Ibid. (October 17, 1823).

[59]Ibid. (August 22, 1823).

[60]Jaime E. Rodríguez O., "Intellectuals and the Mexican Constitution of 1824," in Roderic A. Camp, Charles A. Hale, and Josefina Zoraida Vásquez, eds., *The State and Intellectual Life in Mexico* (Mexico and Los Angeles, forthcoming).

[61]Alamán's *Historia de Méjico* is an attempt to understand the failure of the hombres de bien.

Las sociedades secretas durante el movimiento de independencia

Virginia Guedea

Es un hecho de todos conocido que la insurgencia novohispana se dio de manera primordial en el campo y que quienes en ella tomaron parte procedían en su gran mayoría de zonas rurales. La participación de grupos urbanos en la insurrección, ya fuera que abandonaran sus ciudades para unirse a la lucha armada, ya que desde ellas colaboraran con el movimiento, fue notoriamente menor. Sin embargo, no por minoritaria esta participación deja de tener gran interés para conocer cómo y en qué medida la insurrección afectó a quienes residían en los diversos centros urbanos de las regiones donde se dio y cómo y en qué medida, a su vez, se vio influida por ellos.

No pretendo explicar aquí el porqué del distinto tipo y grado de participación de los habitantes del campo y de la ciudad en el movimiento insurgente novohispano. Es éste un problema que rebasa, con mucho, los límites del presente trabajo. Lo que me interesa primordialmente es estudiar una determinada forma de respuesta, muy específica, que algunos grupos urbanos dieron a la insurrección. Esta forma de respuesta está constituida por las llamadas sociedades secretas, cuya existencia pone de manifiesto no sólo el interés de estos grupos urbanos de colaborar de manera activa con el movimiento insurgente, sino también una voluntad y una capacidad de organización que va más allá del simple impulso de actuar en su favor. Cabe aclarar que no todas las sociedades secretas que se dieron en la Nueva España durante este período estuvieron vinculadas directamente con la insurgencia. No obstante, las primeras de que tenemos noticia surgieron en estrecha relación con este movimiento; fue con posterioridad que aparecieron otras cuyos objetivos respondían a una problemática de dimensiones más amplias, como fue la lucha entre constitucionalistas y absolutistas que se dio por todo el imperio español.

El surgimiento de todas estas sociedades secretas revela la decisión de distintos grupos de la Nueva España de recurrir al empleo de un medio cada vez más utilizado durante esos años en otros países, sobre todo europeos, por algunos grupos que pretendían alcanzar una mayor participación política o incluso promover una revolución, pero de poca o ninguna tradición en la sociedad novohispana de entonces. Porque hasta donde sé o puedo inferir por los testimonios que conozco, la Nueva España de finales del siglo XVIII y principios del XIX no fue lo que pudiéramos llamar prolífica en cuanto a sociedades secretas se refiere. Ni siquiera se dieron fácilmente en ella asociaciones de otro tipo, como las filantrópicas, las económicas o las patrióticas, sino en forma muy aislada. En este aspecto, como en tantos otros y como no podía ser de otro modo dada su condición colonial, la Nueva España se vio influida de manera determinante por lo que ocurría en la península misma.

La masonería y las sociedades secretas

La posibilidad de formar ligas o juntas de cualquier clase se vio siempre limitada en todos los territorios del imperio español por la prohibición expresa, reiterada en varias ocasiones, que existía de hacerlo sin contar con el permiso del monarca.[1] La constante preocupación de la corona española de no permitir la existencia de agrupaciones que no fueran de su completo agrado o que pudieran significarle algún problema se vio exacerbada a mediados del siglo XVIII por la difusión cada vez mayor que por entonces alcanzaba en Europa la masonería. Este movimiento, más que por sus ideales de agrupar con un espíritu de fraternidad e igualdad a hombres de buena voluntad, sin tomar en cuenta diferencias religiosas o políticas, por las posibilidades que todas estas ideas venían a abrir, había sido visto con gran recelo por la Iglesia católica y prohibido por ella desde algunos años antes. Para "atajar" el problema, el rey Fernando VI, "informado de que la invención de los que se llaman Franc Massones es sospechosa a la Religión y al Estado", la prohibió en todos sus reinos mediante un decreto expedido en Aranjuez el 2 de julio de 1751.[2]

Ya fuera por las disposiciones de la Iglesia y del Estado español, ya por otros motivos, la masonería no encontró en la España de la segunda mitad del siglo XVIII un campo muy propicio para su florecimiento. Por la documentación que hasta ahora se conoce parece ser que durante esos años no existieron en la península sino unas cuantas logias masónicas y éstas no fueron propiamente españolas, sino fundadas e integradas en su gran mayoría por grupos de extranjeros. Extranjeros también lo fueron

[1]Véase la ley 1, tít. 12, lib. 12 de la *Novísima Recopilación*, entre otras disposicones en este sentido.

[2]Iris M. Zavala, *Masones, comuneros y carbonarios* (Madrid: Siglo Veintiuno de España Editores, 1971), 196.

los pocos individuos denunciados por entonces ante la Inquisición por masones. Por lo tanto, se puede decir que la masonería tuvo poca o casi ninguna importancia en España durante ese período.[3]

Esta situación prevaleció durante los primeros años del siglo XIX, hasta que se dio la invasión francesa que provocó la caída de la dinastía española en 1808. Bajo el dominio francés y con su franco beneplácito se comenzaron a fundar numerosas logias por toda la península, casi todas ellas integradas en forma mayoritaria por militares franceses, y se llegó a la formación de una Gran Logia Nacional en 1809.[4] Sin embargo, dado que la masonería era impulsada y controlada por el gobierno intruso, la inmensa mayoría del pueblo español no vio con buenos ojos a esta sociedad. Así la masonería, que se convertía ya para entonces en instrumento de lucha de numerosos grupos de disidentes europeos para la consecución de cambios políticos y sociales de importancia, no tuvo mayor éxito entre los patriotas españoles durante los años en que España estuvo sometida al dominio de Napoleón, ni siquiera entre los liberales que en Cádiz se enfrentaron a la difícil tarea de resistir a un régimen invasor al tiempo que intentaban renovar y modernizar el sistema político español. Tan fue así que en enero de 1812 el Consejo de Regencia confirmó por una real cédula el decreto de Fernando VI de julio de 1751 y se prohibió nuevamente la masonería en los territorios españoles y por los mismos motivos.[5] No sería sino a partir del regreso de Fernando VII en 1814, y el consecuente retorno al absolutismo, cuando la masonería y otras asociaciones secretas se desarrollarían en la lucha que los liberales españoles emprenderían contra el régimen absolutista.[6]

Igual o semejante proceso se daría en la Nueva España durante el siglo XVIII y primeros años del XIX, en donde ni siquiera encontramos, no ya digamos documentación, sino alguna referencia digna de tomarse en cuenta que nos permita suponer en ella la existencia de alguna logia masónica u otra sociedad secreta durante el siglo XVIII. Sí, en cambio, encontramos testimonios que prueban con toda claridad la presencia en ella de algunos masones, todos ellos extranjeros, los que fueron procesados por diversos motivos, entre ellos por sospechosos de pertenecer a la masonería.[7]

[3]José A. Ferrer Benimeli, *La masonería española en el siglo XVIII* (Madrid: Siglo Veintiuno de España Editores, 1974), 353 y ss.

[4]José A. Ferrer Benimeli, *Masonería española contemporánea, Vol. I, 1800–1868* (Madrid: Siglo Veintiuno de España Editores, 1980), 82–84.

[5]Ibid., 112-113.

[6]Zavala, *Masones*, 11. Marcelino Menéndez y Pelayo, *Historia de los heterodoxos españoles*, ed. dirigida y ordenada por Félix F. Corso (Buenos Aires: Librería Perlado, 1945), IV, 161.

[7]Véase, Nicolás Rangel, *Los precursores ideológicos de la guerra de Independencia: la masonería en México. Siglo XVIII*, t. II, Publicaciones del Archivo General de la Nación,

Por los primeros años del siglo XIX tenemos una referencia, registrada por varios autores que se han ocupado de la historia de la masonería en México, relativa a la introducción de esta sociedad en la Nueva España. Nos hablan de la fundación en 1806 de una logia masónica en la ciudad de México, que fuera establecida por un tal Enrique Muñí —al parecer español peninsular—, que se reunía en las casa del regidor Manuel Monroy Guerrero y Luyando, sita en la calle de las Ratas número 4. A esta logia pertenecieron el propio Monroy Guerrero y Luyando, el marqués de Uluapa, el licenciado Francisco Primo de Verdad y Ramos —lo que según José María Mateos explicaría en parte la actitud de los miembros del Ayuntamiento en 1808—, así como el corregidor Miguel Domínguez, el cura Miguel Hidalgo y el capitán Ignacio Allende, entre otros —lo que en parte explicaría también lo ocurrido en 1810—.[8] Tanto Mateos como Antonio Gibaja y Patrón, Richard Chism y demás autores que nos hablan de esta logia nos dicen que por desgracia no existe ninguna documentación que pueda darnos alguna luz sobre sus inicios, objetivos, duración, etc. "La historia del origen de esta logia se perdió hace muchos años en el mar de la revolución".[9] No nos aclaran tampoco si fue fundada espontáneamente por un grupo de personas o si estaba ligada a alguna de las Grandes Logias, ni cuál rito se practicaba en ella, aunque señalan que lo más probable es que haya sido el rito de York. Chism anota algo interesante al señalar que esta primera logia novohispana quizá no fuera "más que un club meramente político, el lobo revolucionario disfrazado con la piel del cordero masónico".[10] A partir de 1808, por las denuncias de que fueron objeto algunos de sus miembros, esta logia fue cambiando de sede, sin ubicarse ya en un lugar fijo. Despues de septiembre de 1810 muchos de sus integrantes pasaron a incorporarse a la insurrección, y desde entonces se desorganizó y "se perdió el hilo" de sus trabajos.[11] Dado que quienes registran esta noticia no ofrecen, ni hasta la fecha se ha encontrado, ninguna clase de prueba documental que avale la existencia de esta logia, cuesta trabajo pensar que la información que nos proporcionan sea algo más que un exceso de imaginación de algunos autores, casi todos masones, convencidos de la bondad e importancia de la masonería y de su decisiva influencia en la historia de México.

XXI, La vida colonial (México: Talleres Gráficos de la Nación, 1932); Richard E. Greenleaf, "The Mexican Inquisition and the Masonic Movement: 1751-1820," *New Mexico Historical Review* 44:2 (abril 1969), 92.117; Ferrer Benimeli, *La masonería española*, 293-301, 313-326.

[8]José María Mateos, *Historia de la masonería en México desde 1806 hasta 1884* (Mexico: "La Tolerancia", 1884) 8.

[9]Richard M. Chism, citado por Antonio Gibaja y Patrón, *Comentario crítico, histórico, auténtico a las revoluciones sociales de México*, la. ed. (México: Tipografía Universal, 1926), I, 398.

[10]Ibid., 399.

[11]Mateos, *Historia de la masonería*, 12.

Es a partir del inicio de la insurgencia cuando contamos ya con varios testimonios que demuestran positivamente la existencia de sociedades secretas en la Nueva España. Hasta donde todos sabemos fueron solamente dos las que funcionaron durante los años que estudiamos: la llamada de los Guadalupes y la masonería. Por supuesto que existieron además muchos otros grupos que desarrollaron distintas actividades, entre las que destacó la de prestar apoyo a la insurgencia; las numerosas conspiraciones que se dieron durante esos años son prueba indudable de su existencia. Pero su organización y funcionamiento no fueron los que corresponden a los de una sociedad secreta.

Son varias las características que hacen de una agrupación una sociedad secreta. Por una parte, la selección cuidadosa de sus integrantes, así como su jerarquización. Por otra, ciertos ritos que comprometen a sus miembros, como la iniciación, el juramento de velar por sus hermanos y por los fines de la sociedad y el de no revelar jamás su existencia. También ciertos gestos o símbolos para reconocerse entre los iniciados. Finalmente las más importantes: el contar con una organización que les permita actuar de la manera más eficiente posible para alcanzar sus objetivos y el funcionar dentro del más absoluto secreto.

Los Guadalupes

En el caso de la sociedad de los Guadalupes, sobre la que actualmente tengo una investigación en proceso, no he encontrado fuentes que permitan precisar si cumplía o no con todos los requisitos apuntados arriba. Sin embargo, lo que se sabe de los resultados de sus trabajos indica sin lugar a dudas que tuvo una muy eficiente organización. Asimismo se puede constatar que sus integrantes supieron guardar de manera casi absoluta el secreto más profundo sobre sus actividades. Casi todo lo que de ellos se conoce proviene de los insurgentes con los que estuvieron en contacto o de lo que las autoridades pudieron averiguar a costa de grandes trabajos.

De esta sociedad se tiene ya bastante información por los estudios que de ella han publicado Wilbert H. Timmons y Ernesto de la Torre.[12] Existen además numerosas referencias en los distintos autores contemporáneos de ella que se ocuparon de historiar el movimiento insurgente. También se cuenta con interesante documentación quitada por los realistas a varios jefes insurgentes, en especial la tomada a José María Morelos en Tlacotepec en febrero de 1814, así como las declaraciones de varios de estos jefes al ser tomados prisioneros. Lo que a continuación voy a exponer es un breve resumen de algunos aspectos, que de acuerdo con la investigación que he

[12]Wilbert H. Timmons, "Los Guadalupes: A Secret Society in the Mexican Revolution for Independence", *Hispanic American Historical Review* 30:4 (noviembre 1950), 453-479, y Ernesto de la Torre Villar, ed., *Los "Guadalupes" y la independencia, con una selección de documentos inéditos, 2a. ed. (México: Ed. Jus, 1985).*

llevado a cabo me parecen los más importantes, de su composición y actividades.

En primer lugar creo que es interesante hacer hincapié en que el lugar de sus operaciones fue la ciudad de México, capital del virreinato, sede de sus más altos poderes y el centro urbano de mayor importancia, con mucho, de toda la Nueva España. A pesar de que por todo esto la vigilancia y el control que sobre sus habitantes ejercían las autoridades fueron sin duda rigurosos, presentaba también ciertas condiciones muy propicias para el surgimiento y la organización de grupos de desafectos al régimen. La misma densidad de su población contribuyó a que se dieran numerosas oportunidades de comunicación entre ellos. Los sitios públicos de reunión —paseos, cafés, mercados—, así como las funciones tanto religiosas como civiles, permitieron un intercambio continuo de ideas y de opiniones. Pero fueron las diversas actividades sociales que en ella se daban, muy en especial las tertulias, las que facilitaron una comunicación mayor, más libre y más constante.

De quienes sabemos formaron parte de los Guadalupes o sostuvieron relaciones con esta sociedad sabemos también que en muchos casos tuvieron entre sí lazos de profesión, de amistad e, incluso, de familia. Además de abogados, el grupo mayoritario, entre los Guadalupes se contaron eclesiásticos, propietarios, comerciantes, alguno que otro noble y varias mujeres, familiares todas ellas de integrantes de la agrupación. Por lo que hasta ahora sabemos, muchos de ellos se conocían con anterioridad a la iniciación de la sociedad. También sabemos que los numerosos abogados que la integraban se visitaban mutuamente con cierta frecuencia, acudiendo a las tertulias o reuniones que se tenían en las distintas casas. Un ejemplo lo es la que se celebraba en casa del licenciado Juan Nazario Peimbert y Hernández; otro, las repetidas visitas que varios de ellos hacían a la hacienda de León, propiedad del doctor Manuel Díaz y su esposa Antonia Peña y que funcionó como centro de algunas de sus actividades. En cuanto a la posición económica de sus miembros, sólo mencionaré que entre los Guadalupes hubo varios individuos que contaban con amplios recursos y que estaban dispuestos a emplearlos en las distintas tareas que emprendió su asociación, como fue el caso del doctor Díaz o del licenciado Juan Bautista Raz y Guzmán. En buena medida el éxito de sus trabajos se debió a que pudieron disponer del dinero necesario en el momento preciso.

Una característica de esta sociedad que me parece vale la pena destacar es su vinculación con grupos de insurgentes que pretendieron consolidar el movimiento dándole una organización política y una coordinación militar. Aparentemente surgida esta asociación poco después de septiembre de 1810 con el nombre de El Águila e integrada por varios individuos de la ciudad de México que deseaban colaborar con el movimiento insurgente, sus actividades comenzaron a cobrar importancia y a llevarse a cabo de manera coordinada a partir del establecimiento en Zitácuaro de la Suprema Junta

Nacional Americana en agosto de 1811, con cuyos miembros, en especial con Ignacio López Rayón, entablaron al parecer una correspondencia regular. Aprovechando la información de interés para el movimiento que varios de ellos podían recabar dentro de la ciudad, así como la que podían conseguir relativa a otros puntos, enviaban noticias a los insurgentes, al igual que periódicos y otros impresos de dentro y de fuera de la Nueva España. También les remitieron hombres, dinero y armas. Y algo de gran importancia: una imprenta, la que hicieron llegar a Rayón en abril de 1812. Para todo esto les fueron de gran utilidad las relaciones que tenían establecidas con distintas partidas de insurgentes que rodeaban la ciudad en ese entonces, a las que ayudaban en sus esfuerzos y sobre las que ejercían cierto control. Otra actividad de interés en relación con la Junta Americana fue el que algunos Guadalupes, en especial el licenciado Raz y Guzmán, sirvieron de intermediarios a fines de ese año para preparar la celebración de una entrevista entre Rayón y el virrey Venegas. Y aunque dicha reunión no se llevó a cabo, lo ocurrido demuestra que varios de los Guadalupes ocupaban posiciones de relativa importancia dentro de la sociedad virreinal, que tenían establecidos contactos con personas y grupos de poder y que gozaban de prestigio.

Esto último se confirma en cierta medida por lo sucedido en las elecciones de noviembre de ese mismo año para nombrar a los electores que debían designar al nuevo ayuntamiento de la ciudad de México, en las que resultaron electos no sólo americanos simpatizantes del movimiento insurgente, o cuando menos desafectos al régimen, sino también varios miembros de la sociedad de los Guadalupes o relacionados con ella, como el canónigo José María Alcalá, Dionisio Cano y Moctezuma y Francisco Antonio Galicia, exgobernadores de la parcialidad de San Juan, y el oidor Jacobo Villaurrutia. También intervinieron exitosamente en las diversas elecciones celebradas en la capital en 1813. Estas actividades electorales, que implicaron, entre otras cosas, la movilización simultánea de grupos numerosos, demuestran una gran capacidad de organización y un conocimiento profundo de la sociedad capitalina. También son prueba de su habilidad para aprovechar al máximo la coyuntura —favorable en ciertos aspectos a la insurgencia, pero mucho más a los grupos urbanos descontentos con el régimen— que vino a ofrecer la promulgación en la Nueva España de la Constitución elaborada por las Cortes de Cádiz en 1812.

De todas estas actividades mantuvieron informados a los principales jefes insurgentes, en especial a José María Morelos, con quien los Guadalupes habían entablado una interesante correspondencia por lo menos desde septiembre de 1812, que es la que ha llegado hasta nosotros, y a quien remitieron auxilios semejantes a los enviados a la Suprema Junta. Fue entonces cuando se les comenzó a dar el nombre de los Guadalupes, que fue uno de los pseudónimos utilizados en su correspondencia. Por último, en relación con el grupo insurgente encabezado por Morelos y sus esfuerzos por establecer primero un congreso y elaborar más tarde una constitución, hay que recordar que algunos Guadalupes fueron consultados al respecto y sus opiniones tomadas en consideración.

Hasta donde sabemos, esta asociación poco a poco fue dejando de actuar en apoyo del movimiento insurgente a partir de las derrotas que sufriera Morelos a finales de 1813 y principios de 1814. A ello también contribuyó de manera decisiva el que ese mismo año fuera abolido el sistema constitucional, lo que dio mayor oportunidad a las autoridades de proceder en contra de los miembros de esta sociedad, varios de los cuales fueron puestos en prisión o enviados a la península para interrumpir sus trabajos en contra del régimen. Y creo que vale la pena anotar que aunque las autoridades, muy en especial el virrey Calleja, lograron a la larga poner freno a estas actividades, nunca llegaron a descubrir del todo quiénes eran los integrantes de la sociedad ni hasta dónde habían llegado sus trabajos en favor de la insurgencia.

Una última cosa en lo que se refiere a los Guadalupes. Quiero señalar que no he encontrado testimonios de que tuvieran relaciones establecidas con grupos semejantes de fuera de la Nueva España, aunque varios de ellos sí estaban en contacto con algunos individuos que residían en el exterior, muy en especial en la península. Parece ser, pues, que ésta fue una sociedad que surgió, se desarrolló y actuó sin influencias directas de fuera.

La sociedad de Jalapa

Mucho se ha hablado de la injerencia de la masonería en los movimientos de emancipación de las distintas colonias americanas. En cuanto a lo que se refiere a la Nueva España, se tiene conocimiento de la existencia de una logia de filiación masónica que de acuerdo con la documentación que he consultado funcionó en la ciudad de Jalapa en el año de 1812. Esta documentación se encuentra contenida principalmente en la causa iniciada en mayo de ese año contra el canónigo Ramón Cardeña por estar en relación con los insurgentes que actuaban en los alrededores de aquella ciudad.[13] También hay información de interés en la causa seguida a fray Servando Teresa de Mier en 1817 a resultas de su participación en la expedición de Javier Mina.[14]

Según nos dice Mier, a mediados de septiembre de 1811 fue iniciado en una sociedad que se reunía en el barrio de San Carlos, en Cádiz, fundada por el militar argentino Carlos Alvear y compuesta principalmente

[13]Archivo General de la Nación (en adelante AGN), *Infidencias*, v. 74, cuadernos 1 al 15.

[14]Juan E. Hernández y Dávalos, *Colección de documentos para la historia de la guerra de independencia de México de 1808 a 1821* (México: Biblioteca de "El Sistema Postal de la República Mexicana", José María Sandoval, 1881), VI, 638–950.

por americanos preocupados por la situación de España y la suerte que correrían sus dominios americanos si aquélla sucumbía ante Napoleón. La sociedad se llamaba de los Caballeros Racionales, "porque nada es más racional que mirar por su Patria y sus paisanos", según palabras del propio Alvear. Las obligaciones de sus miembros eran defender a la patria, socorrer a los demás socios y guardar el secreto de su existencia.[15] De esta sociedad, que según aclara Mier no era de masones, se fundaron también logias en Londres y algunos lugares de la América española, como en Buenos Aires. En la de Cádiz fueron iniciados varios novohispanos residentes por entonces en la península, entre ellos Vicente Acuña, conocido por el apodo de Tacones, quien en 1809 había sido remitido a España por escribir pasquines sediciosos. En septiembre de 1811, después de haber sido amnistiado, la sociedad de los Caballeros Racionales le encomendó que pasara a la Nueva España, según Mier para propagar en ella dicha sociedad.[16] El propio Acuña, en una declaración dada en Perote en junio de 1812, manifestó que sus miembros le dijeron en Cádiz que en América 'hallaría infinitos hermanos y juntas como las que había visto", y además precisó que "aquel congreso o logia" lo había habilitado de todo cuanto necesitó para su viaje.[17]

En los primeros meses de 1812 encontramos a Acuña ya en Jalapa, donde en unión de dos oficiales criollos del Regimiento de Lobera, Juan Bautista Ortiz y Evaristo Fiallo, llegados de la península en febrero de ese año, fundó una sociedad, cumpliendo así el encargo de los Caballeros Racionales de Cádiz. Según declararía más tarde el propio Ortiz, apenas llegado a Jalapa se encontró con Acuña, a quien conocía desde Cádiz, el que le dijo "que tenía conquistados varios sujetos para establecer en este reino la independencia y no reconocerse más gobierno que el americano", por lo que comenzaron a reunirse. Ortiz también precisó en su declaración que quienes entraban en la sociedad por ellos fundada debían ser decentes y honrados, además de jurar defender a la religión y no admitir gobierno extranjero alguno. En su opinión, el juramento se extendía a no aceptar tampoco el gobierno de España, porque tanto allá como acá se creía que éste era de franceses.[18]

Sin embargo, por las declaraciones de varios de los demás acusados de pertenecer a esta agrupación se puede ver que sus fines, por lo menos los que se manejaron de una manera más abierta —si es que esto se puede decir de los fines de una sociedad secreta—, no fueron exactamente los que señaló Ortiz sino los de sostener la religión católica, defender a la patria

[15]Declaración de Servando Teresa de Mier de 16 de nov. de 1817, en ibid., 817.

[16]Declaración de S. T. de Mier de 4 de dic. de 1817, en ibid., 821.

[17] Declaración de Vicente Acuña de 16 de jun. de 1812, en AGN, *Infidencias*, v. 74, cuad. 1.

[18]Declaración de Juan Bautista Ortiz de 6 de nov. de 1812, en ibid., cuad. 8.

y los derechos del rey y no admitir dominación extranjera alguna, en especial la francesa, "ni aun la de Morelos en caso de llegar a triunfar", así como evitar la efusión de sangre.[19] Los socios también debían socorrerse mutuamente en sus necesidades. En la ceremonia de iniciación, a la que concurrían muchos de los afiliados, los nuevos miembros debían prestar juramento de hacer cumplir todo lo anterior y de guardar el secreto de la sociedad bajo pena de la vida. De no respetar este juramento el puñal o el veneno pondrían fin a la existencia del traidor. Para reconocerse entre sí los integrantes tenían unas señas especiales: debían tocarse la frente y la barba con el dedo de en medio y luego deletrear la palabra *unión*, a veces seguida de las palabras *fortaleza y valor*. Cabe apuntar aquí que estas señas coinciden plenamente con las utilizadas por la logia de Caballeros Racionales establecida en Cádiz.

El canónigo de Guadalajara, Ramón Cardeña, había llegado a Jalapa, su ciudad natal, a principios del mes de febrero de 1812, aparentemente recién venido de España.[20] Según declararía más tarde, Cardeña no se enteró de la existencia de esta sociedad sino hasta mediados de marzo, cuando después de sostener una conversación con Acuña, Fiallo y Ortiz, en la que el canónigo dijo haberse expresado contra la insurgencia y contra Morelos, fue iniciado mediante la ceremonia de rigor en la sociedad fundada por aquéllos. Importante ha de haber sido su participación en ella porque para el 21 de ese mismo mes, a los pocos días de iniciado, se le nombró su presidente, cargo que debía ser rotativo y que duraba un mes, según él mismo precisó. Además del cargo de presidente, sabemos que la sociedad contó con un vicepresidente, un secretario y un tesorero. Este último encargado de recoger los dos pesos que debía dar todo miembro al ser iniciado y la cuota que debía pagar cada uno de ellos, que era de un peso al mes, aunque parece que esto no llegó a hacerse.

Además de Cardeña encontramos que fueron iniciados en ella numerosos individuos. Según se desprende de las declaraciones contenidas en el proceso seguido al canónigo, fueron alrededor de setenta. No se precisa la ocupación de todos ellos, pero entre los que se mencionan aparecen ocho militares, seis eclesiásticos, cuatro guardas, tres comerciantes, tres médicos, dos abogados, un escribiente, un carpintero, un relojero, un zapatero, un sastre, un notario de la curia, un platero, un literero y un boticario. Se menciona además a dos mujeres. De estas últimas no parece que hayan sido iniciadas en la sociedad, pero sí se registra su asistencia a alguna de sus reuniones.

[19]Declaración de Rafael Velad de 28 de jul. de 1812, en ibid., cuad. 2.

[20]Según Lucas Alamán, por su hermosa figura Cardeña fue conocido en Madrid como el Canónigo Bonito (Lucas Alamán, *Historia de Méjico*, 2a. ed. [México: Ed. Jus, 1942], IV, 293).

Por lo que se desprende de las distintas declaraciones del proceso, entre algunos de los miembros de la sociedad había relaciones previas de profesión, de amistad y hasta familiares, las que influyeron en cierta manera en su entrada a la sociedad. Sin embargo, no parecen haber sido tan decisivas en este sentido como lo fueron en el caso de los Guadalupes, y una prueba de esto es la diversidad de ocupaciones a que se dedicaban algunos de ellos. En cuanto a su posición económica, parece ser que fue tan variada como sus mismas ocupaciones.

La sociedad de Jalapa celebraba sus reuniones en distintos lugares. Se mencionan las casas de varios socios, como Manuel Cruz, que se dedicaba al negocio de las literas, Mariano Rincón, quien más tarde se uniría abiertamente a la insurgencia y sería uno de sus jefes más connotados en la región de Veracruz, y José Mariano Lucido, maestro carpintero. También se mencionan las casas del sastre Manuel Téllez, del patriota Velázquez, del licenciado Manuel Apolbón y de Teresa Medina como sitios donde se celebraron algunas reuniones.

Durante el corto tiempo que la sociedad estuvo en funciones, de febrero a mayo aproximadamente, parece ser que la mayor parte de sus energías fue empleada en organizarse y reclutar nuevos miembros. Sin embargo, sus integrantes sí alcanzaron a planear y llevar a cabo algunas actividades concretas, todas ellas en favor de los insurgentes que por aquel tiempo merodeaban por los alrededores de Jalapa, lo que pone en entredicho algunas declaraciones de muchos de los iniciados y que parece dar la razón a Juan Bautista Ortiz en cuanto a que el propósito fundamental de la sociedad era alcanzar la independencia y establecer un gobierno de americanos. Entre estas actividades se contaron el estrecho contacto con varios insurgentes, así como el enviarles pólvora, armas y caballos. Asimismo les enviaban noticias e información de interés. También se ocuparon de coordinar la salida de la ciudad de varios simpatizantes del movimiento, los que fueron a incorporarse a sus filas.

Pero su actividad de mayor interés en relación con la insurgencia fue la estrecha vinculación que tuvieron con el establecimiento de la Junta Gubernativa de Naolingo, ya que fueron varios los miembros de la sociedad que en distintos momentos pasaron a formar parte de aquélla. Entre ellos se contaron Mariano Rincón, su principal dirigente y organizador, el presbítero José María Tamariz, el licenciado Manuel Apolbón, el presbítero Joaquín Cardeña, así como Evaristo Fiallo y Juan Bautista Ortiz. Los dos últimos habían dejado Jalapa y pasado a Perote con su regimiento desde poco después de fundada la sociedad de Jalapa. Igual había hecho Vicente Acuña, quien pensaba pasar a la ciudad de México. Acuña, Fiallo y Ortiz, con varios otros militares, tramaron en Perote una conspiración para entregar el fuerte a los insurgentes, aparentemente apoyados por la Junta de Naolingo. Descubiertos los conspiradores el 8 de junio de ese año, fueron juzgados y los principales condenados a muerte, entre ellos el propio Acuña, quien murió fusilado.[21] Ortiz y Fiallo lograron escapar a poco de su prisión y pasaron a unirse a los insurgentes y a incorporarse a la Junta.

De hecho, la formación de esta Junta de Naolingo fue el resultado del proceso de desintegración que sufrió la sociedad de Jalapa desde poco tiempo después de haber sido establecida. Varios de sus miembros fueron acusados de actividades sospechosas, entre ellos el mismo Cardeña, por lo que suspendieron sus trabajos o se fugaron de la ciudad; otros consideraron que sus servicios a la causa serían más efectivos desde las filas insurgentes, por lo que se unieron a ellas, y otros, en fin, quizá los menos convencidos, simplemente dejaron de actuar. Por la documentación consultada parece ser que casi la mitad de los socios pasó, en distintas fechas, a unirse al movimiento, al que sirvieron de diversas maneras, aunque no todos los que lo hicieron permanecerían por mucho tiempo en el campo insurgente.

Un asunto de interés que aparece mencionado por Cardeña en su proceso, pero en especial por los testigos que presentó en su descargo y por algún otro de los llamados a declarar, fue la existencia en Jalapa de otra especie de sociedad secreta, compuesta exclusivamente de europeos, comerciantes los más, que se reunían al amparo de la noche a horas inusitadas y cuyos fines bien a bien no se conocían. Estas reuniones se efectuaban en las casas de Juan Lucas de Olabarrieta, de Francisco Rugama, de Francisco Cia y de un francés llamado Pemartin, y a ellas se presentaban armados todos los concurrentes. Éstos a menudo se expresaban contra los criollos, diciendo, entre otras cosas, que había que acabar con ellos, aun con los que no eran insurgentes.[22] Todo esto había alarmado enormemente a los nacidos en el país e incluso había provocado que algunos de ellos salieran de Jalapa y se unieran a los insurgentes. Por desgracia no tenemos mayor información de la existencia, organización, propósitos y funciones de esta sociedad más que las declaraciones mencionadas, las que parecen tener un fondo de verdad pero también ser un tanto parciales.

Dos últimos puntos relacionados con la sociedad de Jalapa. El primero se refiere a las menciones que se hicieron en el proceso de Cardeña que existían sociedades semejantes en La Habana, Veracruz y México, además de Cádiz y Jalapa. Cardeña declaró saber que había socios en Veracruz, pero que a él no le constaba nada. Acuña, por su parte, manifestó "que en La Habana había conocido a varios hermanos y su junta en Veracruz".[23] Desafortunadamente hasta ahora no he encontrado ninguna otra información que nos permita saber algo más de la existencia de logias

[21]Ibid., III, 149.

[22]Declaración de Mariano Montesinos de 10 de sep. de 1813, en AGN, *Infidencias*, v. 74, cuad. 13; declaración de Juan Bautista Ortiz de 8 de sep. de 1813, en ibid., y declaración de Ramón Cardeña de 26 de sep. de 1812, en ibid., cuad. 1.

[23]Declaración de Ramón Cardeña de 26 de sep. de 1812 y declaración de Vicente Acuña de 16 de jun. de 1812, en ibid.

en el puerto veracruzano o en la capital del virreinato. El segundo punto se refiere a si la sociedad de Jalapa era o no una verdadera logia masónica. Sus integrantes negaron en repetidas ocasiones su vinculación con la masonería, y es probable que en cierto sentido hayan dicho la verdad. En la causa de Cardeña no hay referencia alguna a que estuvieran en contacto directo con grupos de masones organizados. Pero independientemente de si fue o no masónica en un sentido estricto, lo que sí queda claro es que su establecimiento, composición y funcionamiento fueron de indudable inspiración masónica, aun cuando su principal objetivo, o por lo menos su principal actividad, haya sido ayudar a la insurgencia. Bien lo comprendieron las autoridades, las que se ocuparon primordialmente de descubrir sus relaciones con los insurgentes y dejaron un poco de lado el precisar si era o no masónica y si tenía o no relaciones con asociaciones de esta clase, tanto de dentro como de fuera de la Nueva España.

Entre la sociedad de los Guadalupes y la sociedad de Jalapa hay ciertas semejanzas y diferencias que conviene destacar. Una primera semejanza es que ambas funcionaron como apoyos del movimiento insurgente. Otra semejanza es que ambas se dieron en centros urbanos importantes: los Guadalupes en la capital del virreinato y la de Jalapa en una ciudad de importancia económica y estratégica dada su localización en el camino entre México y Veracruz. A su importancia se debió en gran medida el hecho de que ambas ciudades llegaran a encontrarse en un determinado período rodeadas de partidas de insurgentes, lo que facilitó el trato y las comunicaciones entre éstos y quienes dentro de ellas deseaban apoyar al movimiento. Otra semejanza de interés es la relación que estas sociedades establecieron con juntas insurgentes, a través de las que canalizaron principalmente este apoyo. Hay asimismo semejanzas en cierto tipo de auxilios brindados a la insurgencia, como en el envío de hombres, dinero y armas, aun cuando en lo que a auxilios se refiere los Guadalupes los proporcionaron en mayor cantidad y de maneras más variadas que la sociedad de Jalapa. Y esto se debió en parte a la diferencia que existió entre ambos grupos en cuanto a su duración. Por último, a pesar de esta diferencia en el lapso de tiempo en que funcionaron, más largo en un caso y muy breve en el otro, los dos grupos se dieron en un período que pudiéramos llamar de auge de la insurgencia. Fue, pues, esta coyuntura lo que en gran medida posibilitó su aparición.

Masones

En cuanto a otros grupos vinculados con la masonería que se dieron en la Nueva España con posterioridad a la sociedad de Jalapa, debo confesar que he dedicado mucho menos tiempo a su estudio, por lo que tengo mucho menos información y la que tengo pone de manifiesto que prácticamente ninguno de estos grupos tuvo una vinculación directa con el movimiento insurgente. Esto puede deberse en buena medida a que a partir de la prisión y muerte de Morelos la insurgencia contó cada vez menos con grupos armados bien organizados a través de los cuales pudiera ayudarse con efectividad al movimiento. Pero creo que se debió en primera instancia a que la lucha que se desató en la península a partir del año de 1814 entre los partidarios de un sistema constitucional y los del régimen absolutista se extendió también a sus dominios americanos y con ella se extendió la masonería. Por todo lo anterior, me ocuparé de ellos en forma muy breve.

Además de la sociedad de Jalapa, la única otra vinculación que he encontrado entre masones e insurgentes se refiere a la expedición de Javier Mina en 1817, algunos de cuyos integrantes fueron sin duda masones provenientes de distintos países. En la causa ya mencionada que se siguió al padre Mier se registra que entre los papeles que se le quitaron al ser hecho prisionero se encontraron "Varias cartillas que parece tratan de la secta de Francmasones. Apuntes para el tercer tomo de la revolución de América y muchos títulos de Francmasones, aunque quitados y arrancados los nombres".[24] Mier negó, como era natural, saber algo acerca de tales papeles, así como pertenecer a la masonería,[25] aunque sí confesó, como ya vimos, haber sido iniciado en la logia o sociedad de los Caballeros Racionales de Cádiz. En todo caso, nada concreto sabemos de cómo influyeron estos masones, en cuanto tales, en el movimiento insurgente.

En lo que se refiere a grupos de masones no relacionados directamente con la insurgencia, para el año de 1813 contamos con una noticia interesante. Según José María Luis Mora, a consecuencia de que se promulgara la Constitución de Cádiz nació en la ciudad de México "el partido *escocés*". Su programa lo constituían "el sistema representativo y las reformas del clero", que habían iniciado ya las Cortes españolas. Mora señala que la mayoría de sus iniciados se componía "de españoles por nacimiento y por sistema" y que de los partidarios de la independencia o "mexicanos" sólo lo fueron tres, entre los que se contaban José María Fagoaga y Tomás Murphy, ambos relacionados con los Guadalupes. Este partido escocés no desapareció al abolirse la Constitución en 1814, ya que a partir de entonces sus "notabilidades procedieron de un modo más circunspecto, por temor de la Inquisición, y su vulgo, que consistía en una multitud de oficiales de los regimientos expedicionarios españoles, se constituyó en *logias del antiguo rito escocés*". Por desgracia, Mora no precisa con exactitud cuándo se constituyeron estas logias, las que con gran sigilo se dedicaron a hacer prosélitos, a difundir libros prohibidos y a debilitar el prestigio del clero. Pero sí señala que para 1819 "era ya considerable el número de sus adeptos, pues los mexicanos, desesperando por entonces de la causa de la independen-

[24]La Inquisición al virrey Juan Ruiz de Apodaca, 9 de sep. de 1817, en la causa de Servando Teresa de Mier, en Hernández y Dávalos, *Colección de documentos*, VI, 682.

[25]Declaración de Servando Teresa de Mier de 4 de dic. de 1817, en ibid., 821.

cia, empezaban a tomar gusto a lo que después se llamó la *libertad*." El jefe de todas estas logias era el oidor peninsular Felipe Martínez de Aragón.[26]

Lucas Alamán coincide con varias de las afirmaciones de Mora. Para él, "hasta la venida de las tropas expedicionarias, esta sociedad contaba con pocos individuos que vivían aislados y ocultos por temor de la Inquisición, habiendo sido el primero en reunirlos y darles forma de cuerpo el oidor de México D. Felipe Martínez de Aragón". Entre los principales socios se encontraba Fausto de Elhuyar, director de Minería y suegro de Martínez, quien era el decano en el país, así como algunos religiosos franciscanos y otros individuos, todos ellos españoles, ya que los "mexicanos" no tomarían parte en ella sino hasta después. Según este autor, la llegada de las tropas expedicionarias le había dado nueva importancia a la masonería, porque casi todos sus jefes y oficiales pertenecían a ella, entre los que se hallaba el propio virrey Juan Ruiz de Apodaca. Alamán señala que "la primera logia que se estableció en México en 1817 o 18 [. . .] fue en la casa de los capellanes del convento antiguo de religiosas Teresas en la calle de este nombre, de donde pasó a la número 20 de la calle del Coliseo Viejo, y se titulaba la 'Arquitectura Moral' ", y que a partir de entonces aumentó el número de afiliados a la masonería.[27] Según José María Tornel, la regularización de la masonería en México no se daría sino hasta 1820, y quien la llevaría a cabo sería el oidor Felipe Martínez.[28] Para José María Roa Bárcena hasta 1820 la masonería, traída por las tropas expedicionarias, "apenas contó entre sus adictos a ningún mexicano, siendo españoles y del rito escocés todos sus miembros".[29]

1820 fue también el año en que se promulgó de nuevo la Constitución de Cádiz, y el que en la ciudad de México se haya hecho en forma precipitada se debió en gran parte, según Alamán, a la consideración del virrey Apodaca de que el movimiento que había restablecido el régimen constitucional en la península había sido promovido por la masonería, por lo que los muchos masones que sabía había entre las tropas expedicionarias podían haber recibido órdenes de llevar a cabo en la capital un movimiento semejante.[30] Apodaca tenía razón en temer algún movimiento por parte de las tropas

[26]José María Luis Mora, "Revista política de las diversas administraciones que la república mexicana ha tenido hasta 1837", en *Obras sueltas de . . . ciudadano mexicano*, 2a. ed. (México: Ed. Porrúa, 1963), 7-8.

[27]Alamán, *Historia de Méjico*, V, 48.

[28]José María Tornel y Mendívil, *Breve reseña histórica de los acontecimientos más notables de la nación mexicana, desde el año de 1821 hasta nuestros días* (México: Imprenta de Cumplido, 1852), 28.

[29]José María Roa Bárcena, citado por M. Menéndez y Pelayo, *Historia de los heterodoxos*, IV, 200.

[30]Alamán, *Historia de Méjico*, V, 48-49.

expedicionarias que se hallaban en la ciudad de México. Poco más de un año después, sus oficiales, descontentos con la actuación del virrey ante la rebelión que encabezaba Agustín de Iturbide, decidieron destituirlo después de discutir este asunto en la logia a la que asistían.[31]

Parece ser que grupos de masones organizados se dieron también por estos años en la península de Yucatán. Según Eligio Ancona, la masonería se introdujo en ella hacia 1818 y la primera logia se estableció en Campeche, fundada por varios partidarios de la Constitución de 1812 que habían sido desterrados de España y que a bordo de la fragata "Ifigenia" naufragaron en las playas de San Román, entre los que se contaban algunos masones. Las actividades masónicas en Yucatán se vieron reforzadas poco después por la llegada de España de varios oficiales jóvenes, ya iniciados en la masonería, que habían sido enviados a servir tanto en Campeche como en Mérida,[32] donde también se establecieron algunas logias. Los objetivos filantrópicos y humanitarios que aparentemente perseguía la masonería le atrajeron militares, ricos comerciantes, frailes, clérigos, empleados públicos, etc.[33] Entre ellos se contaron varios miembros de la antigua sociedad de San Juan, que había agrupado a numerosos yucatecos de tendencias liberales y partidarios del régimen constitucional y que había sido disuelta al reimplantarse en 1814 el régimen absolutista y ser puestos en prisión sus principales dirigentes.[34] Además de algunos sanjuanistas también se afiliaron a la masonería yucateca muchos de los llamados rutineros, grupo rival de los sanjuanistas, que habían sido los principales sostenedores del absolutismo en Yucatán.[35]

En 1820, al conocerse el levantamiento encabezado por Riego en España en favor de la Constitución, se reorganizó en Mérida la sociedad de los sanjuanistas, pero a ella se afiliaron además en esta ocasión numerosos masones, con lo que a poco "las diversas sociedades masónicas de la ciudad se refundieron públicamente en la Junta de San Juan". El promotor de todo esto lo fue Lorenzo de Zavala,[36] antiguo sanjuanista que había sido enviado preso a San Juan de Ulúa en 1814, donde había entrado en con-

[31]Ibid., 164.

[32]Eligio Ancona, *Historia de Yucatán desde la época más remota hasta nuestros días, Parte tercera, época moderna*, 2a. ed. (Barcelona: Imprenta de Jaime J. Roviralta, 1889), III, 117.

[33]Ibid., 119.

[34]Sobre esta sociedad véase J. Ignacio Rubio Mañé, "Los sanjuanistas de Yucatán I Manuel Jiménez Solís, el padre Justis", *Boletín del Archivo General de la Nación*, 2a. serie, VIII, n. 3-4, 1967, 1211-1234; IX, n. 1–2, 1968, 193-243; n. 3-4, 1968, 401-508; y X, n. 1-2, 1969, 127-252.

[35]Ancona, *Historia de Yucatán*, 118.

[36]Ibid., 121.

tacto con varios masones.[37] La antigua Junta de San Juan acabaría no sólo por cambiar de composición, sino también de nombre, y sería conocida como Confederación Patriótica.[38] Al saberse en Yucatán el triunfo del movimiento de Riego en España, como ocurriría también en la ciudad de México, los masones y los sanjuanistas promovieron que la Constitución fuera de nuevo jurada, tanto en Campeche como en Mérida, a pesar de la tenaz oposición del teniente del rey en la primera y del gobernador en la segunda.[39] Y poco después, a semejanza de lo que sus hermanos capitalinos harían con Apodaca, tomaron parte en la deposición del gobernador y capitán general de la península de Yucatán.[40]

A partir de entonces la masonería fue adquiriendo cada vez mayor fuerza en la colonia, y la llegada en 1821 de Juan O'Donojú, último jefe político con que contó la Nueva España, vino a darle un nuevo impulso.[41] Sin embargo, sería hasta después de consumada la independencia, y sobre todo a partir del establecimiento del sistema federal, cuando la masonería, a través de los distintos grupos a que daría origen, se convertiría en un factor de importancia realmente decisiva para la vida política del país.

Para terminar, quisiera hacer hincapié en que, por lo que hasta ahora sabemos, las sociedades secretas que funcionaron en la Nueva España en estrecha vinculación con la insurgencia no representaron una influencia determinante para su eventual éxito o fracaso. Aun en el caso de los Guadalupes, tan estrechamente ligados al movimiento insurgente y cuyas actividades le significaron contribuciones de importancia, no le representaron una influencia decisiva. Ésta se dio más bien en el otro sentido: fue la insurrección la que hizo posible en gran medida el surgimiento de esta sociedad, condicionó su desarrollo y provocó su extinción. Y mucho menor importancia para el movimiento tuvo la aparición de la sociedad de Jalapa. La expedición de Mina, integrada por numerosos masones, influyó en el movimiento insurgente, pero no por sus actividades masónicas, de las cuales, si es que las hubo, no sabemos prácticamente nada, sino por sus acciones militares. En cuanto a los grupos de masones que se dieron en la Nueva España sin vinculación directa con la insurgencia, sino como resultado de la lucha que se dio por todo el imperio español contra el régimen absolutista, tampoco en esta lucha desempeñaron un papel determinante, salvo, quizás, a un nivel muy local.

No obstante todo esto, y en parte precisamente por todo esto, creo que es indispensable el estudio de estas agrupaciones para comprender mejor este período y en particular las actitudes de ciertos grupos urbanos ante las circunstancias por las que atravesaba la colonia. Si bien estas sociedades

[37]Ibid., 117.
[38]Ibid., 145.
[39]Ibid., 136–142.
[40]Ibid., 153–154.
[41]Alamán, *Historia de Méjico,* V, 265.

en cuanto tales no desempeñaron un papel de primer orden en los acontecimientos ocurridos durante esos años en la Nueva España, sí son reflejo de un hecho que a mi parecer es de gran importancia: la formación de distintos grupos que desde algunos de los principales centros urbanos buscaban alcanzar una participación cada vez mayor en la toma de decisiones. Fue en cierta medida a través de los trabajos de organización de estas sociedades que estos grupos lograron consolidarse en muchos casos y llegar a constituirse en verdaderos grupos de poder, sobre todo después de consumada la independencia. Por esto también es necesario acercarnos a estas sociedades para entender lo ocurrido durante los primeros años del México independiente. No deja de ser interesante el hecho de que en unos cuantos años las llamadas sociedades secretas pasaran de ser prácticamente inexistentes y de poca importancia a convertirse en una de las principales fuerzas políticas que controlarían la vida pública del nuevo país.

The Financial Disintegration of the Royal Government of Mexico during the Epoch of Independence

John Jay TePaske

IN HIS THOUGHTFUL BOOK analyzing patterns of revolution, published almost half a century ago, Crane Brinton pointed out how difficult it is to establish a precise chronological starting point for any revolutionary movement.[1] Does the American Revolution, for example, begin at Lexington and Concord or can it be pushed back to the Boston Tea Party, Boston Massacre, Townshend Acts, Stamp Act, even to the very founding of the British colonies in the seventeenth century? The same is true for the wars of independence in Spanish America. The specific moment an independence ethos took hold in Mexico or any other part of the Spanish Indies is difficult to pinpoint. Some interpreters emphasize the advent of the Bourbons to the throne of Spain in 1700 and initiation of carefully orchestrated imperial reform; others feel that the penetration of Enlightenment thought and examples of the American and French Revolutions were crucial; still others believe that it was the moment that growing creole-Spanish tensions became so unbearable that independence became the only answer. Focusing as it does on the financial disintegration of the royal government in New Spain, this essay poses the same problem: there is no precise date for the onset of this fiscal collapse. Rather, it was a gradual, inexorable process beginning in the early 1780s, and, in fact, the financial collapse of the state was almost an accomplished fact by the time of the Grito de Dolores in 1810.[2]

AUTHOR'S NOTE: I wish to thank the Tinker Foundation, National Endowment for the Humanities, American Philosophical Society, and Duke University Research Council for providing the research funds that made this paper possible. This is part of a larger work (with Herbert S. Klein of Columbia University) analyzing the fiscal structure of Peru and Mexico.

[1]Crane Brinton, *The Anatomy of Revolution* (New York: Vintage Books, 1957), 73. The first edition was published in 1938 and revised in 1952.

[2]It should be made clear that this is a macro-overview of the financial state of the Mexican treasury system during this epoch based on quantitative data and a fairly extensive reading of the *expedientes de los reales oficiales* in the Archivo de Indias (AGI) in Sevilla, México,

The principal bases for this analysis are the royal accounts (*cartas cuentas*) of the various treasuries (*cajas*) of New Spain, financial records of income and expenditure for both the matrix treasury at Mexico City and the different regions of Mexico.[3] Unfortunately, despite the virtual completeness of the accounts for eighteenth-century New Spain, in the early nineteenth century the interruption of communications with the Peninsula and the outbreak of the wars of independence in 1810 meant that many accounts never got to the auditing bureau (Tribunal de Cuentas) in Mexico City or its counterpart (Real Contaduría) in Madrid and, thus, never found their niche in an archive. Accounts for the matrix treasury in Mexico City, for example run only through 1817, while those for the mining treasuries of Guanajuato and Sombrerete run only through 1816, but with gaps. For Durango extant accounts are available only through 1813, and for other regional treasuries, such as Veracruz, Acapulco, Guadalajara, and San Luis Potosí, there are either no cartas cuentas at all for the second decade of the nineteenth century or only a scattered one here and there. On the positive side, most of the cartas cuentas for the rich mining district of Zacatecas have survived for the epoch of independence; so too have mintage records, a series of annual treasury debt statements, and some published statistics on trade and Mexican customs house tax collections. Combined with the account data, these sources provide a fairly complete picture of the financial tribulations faced by the viceroyalty of New Spain during the turbulent independence period.[4]

Trends in Public Revenues and Expenditures at the End of the Colonial Period

During the latter decades of the colonial period in New Spain, tax collections were at an all-time high. In the matrix treasury of Mexico City, for example, revenues had risen from an average of about 2 million pesos annually in the first decade of the eighteenth century to over 14 million pesos or more per year in the first decade of the nineteeth century, a sevenfold increase (see Figure 1). If tax receipts deposited in the matrix treasury by the regional cajas between 1801 and 1810 are included (see Figure 2), total viceregal revenues averaged close to 20 million pesos annually in this

---

Legajos 2348–2386, also various documents found in AGI, Indiferente General, Legajos 41, 43, and 1707–1708.

[3]The first volume of accounts for the various treasuries of Mexico has finally been published. John J. TePaske and Herbet S. Klein, *Ingresos y egresos de la Real Hacienda de Nueva España*, I (Mexico: Instituto Nacional de Antropología e Historia, 1986). This first volume includes the accounts for the *cajas* of Acapulco, Arispe, Bolaños, Campeche, Chihuahua, Durango, Guadalajara, Guanajuato, and Mérida.

[4]The specific sources for this analysis may be found in the accompanying figures.

decade, and in 1809, the year before the Hidalgo revolt, amounted to over 28 million, although this spectacular rise in viceregal income was vitiated by inflation.[5]

Generally, regional treasuries in Mexico reflected the same pattern as the Mexico City matrix caja. In the Guadalajara district, for example, income averaged 163,000 pesos annually in the first decade of the eighteenth century and almost 740,000 pesos in the first decade of the nineteenth century, over a fourfold increase.[6] For the same decade (1801–1810) in Guanajuato, Zacatecas, and Sombrerete, collections were at their peak, at least nominally, and demonstrated, in general, rates of increase exhibited in Mexico City and Guadalajara. With occasional annual or cyclical deviations then, both the matrix treasury in Mexico City and the provincial cajas all gathered in greatly increased revenues as the eighteenth century wore on, and by the time of the Hidalgo revolt in 1810, viceregal tax receipts had reached their highest point ever. In broad terms, this increase in viceregal income over the century occurred because of the fourfold increase in silver production and resulting increases in silver tax collections; the more efficient, more rational collection of existing taxes; imposition of a series of new taxes by the Bourbons and their ministers, particularly in the last quarter of the eighteenth century; and the rise in the population of New Spain.[7]

But this roseate picture of increased revenues on the income side of the account ledgers had a bleaker visage on the expenditure side. Beginning in the 1770s and 1780s, at the same time inflation was beginning to take its toll on royal treasury income, expenditures for war and defense jumped sharply. These included treasury funds for *situados* and extraordinary allocations for the *presidios* dotting the Greater Caribbean, the outfitting of privateers and naval vessels guarding the treasure fleets, and support for the military and naval establishment in the Philippines. Also, in the 1770s remissions to Castile increased precipitously, jumping from an annual average of less than 1 million pesos in most of the previous decades

[5]See John J. TePaske, "Economic Cycles in New Spain in the Eighteenth Century: The View from the Public Sector," in R. L. Garner and W. B. Taylor, *Iberian Colonies, New World Societies: Essays in Memory of Charles Gibson* (University, Pa.: privately printed, 1985), 119–142, and John Coatsworth, "The Limits of Colonial Absolutism: The State in Eighteenth-Century Mexico," in K. Spalding, ed., *Essays in the Political, Economic and Social History of Colonial Latin America* (Newark, Del.: University of Delaware Latin American Studies Program, 1982), 25–52.

[6]The average annual income for Guadalajara is based on the quinquennium 1801–1805; full data are not available for the five years 1806–1810.

[7]In the first decade of the eighteenth century, there were about thirty entries on the income side of the Mexico City ledgers; by the end of the century there were over a hundred.

of the century to almost 5 million pesos yearly in the 1790s.[8] In addition, some of the new taxes the crown had imposed to support innovative social or economic programs locally such as road building, the support of hospitals and legal protectors for Indians, and pensions for military and government retirees were not paying their way and had to be supported by other treasury sources. At the same time some new imposts, such as the royal assessments made on each Mexican bishopric for the Royal Order of Carlos III, simply drained monies needed locally out of Mexico to Spain.

Deficits thus began to grow. In the early 1770s debts owed by the *real hacienda* in Mexico amounted to a bit over 3 million pesos. By 1810 this debt had risen to over 31 million pesos (see Figure 7), a tenfold increase, and this did not include the burgeoning debts for situados never delivered to garrisons in Florida, Cuba, Puerto Rico, Santo Domingo, or the Philippines.[9] Royal officials used various methods to make up for these deficits. As noted, one device was simply not to pay its annual or extraordinary obligations to the presidios of the Greater Caribbean or to the Philippines, to throw these garrisons on their own resources. Another was to force religious and lay institutions to provide monies out of their capital funds in return for government bonds issued at 4 or 5 percent interest guaranteed by receipts from the tobacco monopoly or the Mexico City customs house. Still another was simply to request or demand loans periodically from institutions such as the *consulado* or *tribunal de minería*, again at interest, although sometimes with none at all. By 1810, for example, debt accumulated by dipping into the capital reserves of clerical and lay institutions was about 18.5 million pesos; debt accrued from loans amounted to over 8.5 million pesos.[10] Outright donations, a method used virtually from the founding of New Spain, remained a ploy also for raising money in extraordinary circumstances.

To 1810 royal officials also met the heavy demands on the treasury by tapping reserves of the *ramos agenos* or *ramos particulares*[11] of the treasury in which large sums had accumulated and allocating these funds to the real hacienda. In Mexico the ramos most susceptible were indulgences

[8]See John J. TePaske, "La política española en el Caribe durante los siglos XVII y XVIII," in Antonio Acosta and Juan Marchena, eds., *La influencia de España en el Caribe, la Florida y la Luisiana, 1500–1800* (Madrid: Instituto de Cooperación Iberoamericana, 1983), 76–82.

[9]The viceroy generally included amounts owing for back *situados* when he wrote to the king concerning his financial tribulations and the debts piling up for the treasury. These delinquent payments were not included in the debt statements submitted annually to Spain by the royal treasury officials.

[10]AGI, México, Legajo 2023. Estado que manifiesta los débitos en que quedó la Tesorería General de Ejército y Real Hacienda de esta capital en 31 de diciembre de 1810 . . . , México, 29 enero 1811,

[11]These were revenues specifically reserved or allocated for the crown, charitable work, defense, road building, or the like. They were distinguished from the *ramos de real hacienda*.

(*bulas de santa cruzada*) and tithes (*novenos*). By 1798, in fact, royal treasury officials had borrowed over 16 million pesos from these reserves, exhausting them in the process. As a way of writing off the debt, officials in Spain ultimately declared both *bulas* and tithes *ramos* of the real hacienda and in so doing reduced treasury debt in one fell swoop by 16 million pesos, but this was only a temporary reprieve as debt began to rise once again in 1805 (see Figure 7). *Depósitos*, bonds and guarantees placed in the treasury by public officials and institutions, were also a favorite target of desperate treasury officials as were the reserves of seized Jesuit estates (*temporalidades*), both of which were also completely stripped by 1810. By the time of the Hidalgo revolt, in fact, there were virtually no reserves left in any of the special ramos; all the surplus had been used up meeting military and naval needs in the Indies and Peninsular demands for supporting the war effort at home. Clerical and lay institutions and wealthy Mexicans had already been squeezed very hard, almost to the point where they had little more to provide a needy but demanding viceregal government.

Treasury Receipts and Expenditures in the Decade of Independence

The outbreak of the wars of independence dealt still another catastrophic blow to the reeling Mexican treasury system. As pointed out above, in 1809, including those revenues being remitted to Mexico City from the other cajas in New Spain, total income flowing into the matrix treasury amounted to over 28 million pesos, the greatest amount ever collected by royal treasury officials in the capital. In 1810, however, total income dropped by 10 million pesos to a bit less than 18 million. Then in 1811 it fell even further to 13.5 million, the last year income into the Mexican caja amounted to more than 10 million pesos. In 1812, the nadir year in the epoch of independence, total revenues reached only 8.7 million pesos and never approached the 10-million-peso level again, at least not through 1817. Put another way, income declined 36 percent between 1809 and 1810, another 31 percent between 1810 and 1811, and still another 36 percent between 1811 and 1812. Overall, the drop between 1809 and 1817, the last year for which there are extant matrix treasury accounts, was almost 70 percent. In fact, in 1817 nominal tax revenues were no greater than those being collected in the late 1770s.

The major cause of this sharp drop in revenues was the sudden end of remissions to Mexico City by subsidiary regional treasuries throughout the viceroyalty. Prior to 1810, provincial cajas had consistently sent large sums to royal treasury officials in the capital, funds to be dispensed for viceregal and imperial needs. In fact, from 1795 through 1810, these remissions to Mexico City amounted to over 98.4 million pesos (see Figure 2), an average of 5.8 million pesos per year, one-third of all revenue reported in the Mexico City tax ledgers. From 1811 through 1817, monies from subsidiary treasuries reaching Mexico City amounted to only 1.9 million pesos, an average of only about 318,000 pesos a year or one twenty-fifth of total receipts into the Mexican treasury—dramatic testimony to loss of income from the provinces both in real and percentage terms.

The magnitude of these losses for the matrix treasury can also be seen in an analysis of the figures for three subsidiary cajas—Zacatecas, Durango, and Guanajuato. From 1791 through 1810, for example, royal officials of Zacatecas remitted approximately 85 percent of all tax receipts to Mexico City; between 1811 and 1821 they sent less than 25 percent. In Guanajuato approximately 80 percent of all taxes collected in the district went to Mexico City between 1791 and 1807, remissions which averaged almost 1.5 million pesos a year. During the wars of independence (1812–1816), these transfers dropped to only 28 percent of total treasury income, but more importantly, annual treasury receipts in Guanajuato now averaged only 800,000 pesos a year, half of what they were prior to the Hidalgo uprising. For the treasury of Durango, to 1813 remissions to Mexico City in the period 1791–1810 amounted to approximately 75 percent of total revenues, an average of about 375,000 pesos annually; from 1811 through 1813 these remissions dropped to only 31 percent of total income into the Durango caja.

The sudden drop in remissions from the regional cajas to Mexico City did not always reflect woeful financial conditions in the provincial treasury districts. Although income generally declined in most cajas from 1810 to 1812, after the initial impact of the revolt had passed, particularly after the defeat of José María Morelos and the end of the Peninsular War, income rose once again, although never to pre-1810 levels. In the Zacatecas district, for example, the years 1813–1814 saw some recovery as did 1816–1817 although after 1812 the general trend was downward (see Figure 4). Also, despite the shortage of mercury, silver production recovered somewhat in Zacatecas, not to the pre-independence level, but significantly enough to generate some income into the treasury (see Figure 5). Sales tax collections also remained high, most probably because of the increase in the *alcabala* rates.

The significance of the sudden end to remissions from the provincial treasuries to Mexico City after 1810 cannot be overstated. Whatever their reasons, royal officials in Zacatecas and elsewhere retained tax monies generated in their districts, rather than see them heaped upon the backs of mules for the arduous and now perhaps dangerous trek to Mexico City. Most of these funds, formerly shipped to Mexico, now went to pay military salaries locally, which had grown enormously during the independence epoch. In Zacatecas, for example, military expenditures were less than 1 percent of total revenue annually prior to 1810; to 1817 they were almost 30 percent. For Guadalajara, where military costs were 37 percent of total revenue in the early 1800s, the percentage doubled by 1816 to 73 percent. The Guanajuato district spent roughly 2 percent of its income on defense prior to 1810; after that it amounted to 43 percent. Other local expenses also grew. In Zacatecas, as an example, operation of the ad hoc mint set up in Zacatecas to stamp *pesos fuertes* was one of these. Clearly, though, the outbreak of the wars of independence gave local treasury officials the opportunity or excuse to stop sending tax receipts to Mexico City to pay the costs of empire. Officials in those regional treasuries made the decision to use tax revenues to preserve their financial and military security and autonomy locally rather than to feed the seemingly insatiable needs of viceregal authorities in Mexico City. The financial network which had bound the treasuries of New Spain together during the entire colonial epoch almost symbiotically was suddenly shattered.

The collapse of silver production—and the loss of revenues from taxes on silver—was still another cause of the financial woes of the viceroyalty. Despite a bit of recovery at Zacatecas, analysis of mintage records indicates, not surprisingly, that bullion production generally declined in Mexico during the second decade of the nineteenth century (see Figure 6). From 1791 to 1810, the Casa de Moneda minted an average of 23 million pesos annually. From 1811 to 1821 it amounted to only 8.5 million pesos annually, almost a two-thirds drop. During this time, the worst year was 1812 when the mint only coined 4.4 million pesos (compared with the peak 27.1 million pesos in 1805). After that, mintage activity rose modestly until 1817, then dropped a bit, rising once again to a peak of 12 million pesos in 1819. By 1821, however, Mexican mints stamped only 5.9 million pesos, testimony that the Army of Three Guarantees had made its mark on Nueva España.[12]

Response to the Financial Crisis of the Wars of Independence

Financially, the Hidalgo revolt could not have come at a worse time. Over the previous thirty years prior to the outbreak of hostilities, Mexican treasuries had been stripped of their tax surpluses and tax reserves. Tapped for loan after loan and donation after donation, clerical and lay institutions had little left to provide for the defense of the kingdom; debts for nonpayment of situados to presidios in the Greater Caribbean were growing exponentially; and financial experts in both Spain and Mexico had seemingly taxed everything and everybody who had any disposible wealth, except

[12]Mint figures are an excellent index to bullion production. For 1691–1810 the correlation between mintage and bullion production is .98828 and for the years 1731–1810 it is .98138.

for the Indians whose tribute payments had been eliminated. In 1810 with a serious civil insurrection to put down, the viceroy and his treasury officials were now severely pressed to find monies to pay for the regular troops, militia, and equipment needed for carrying on war effectively against the rebels. Despite the obstacles they tried valiantly, using some time-tested methods and some new expedients, which were absolutely imperative in view of the sudden loss of revenue from the provincial treasury districts.[13]

Some old ploys were at least partially successful in raising new funds. These included forced lotteries and raising existing rates on well-established taxes such as the alcabalas and *almojarifazgos*. By 1815 and 1816, for example, the tax rate for the alcabala had risen to 8 percent from the 3 to 5 percent levels of the pre-independence period. The viceroy laid new imposts on items such as pulque and tobacco to provide for military needs, called for new donations and loans, and discounted salaries of all public officials. In 1812 Viceroy Francisco Xavier Venegas also imposed higher rates on virtually all commodities consumed in the cities (new *propios e arbitrios*) for the exigencies of war. About the only method royal officials could *not* use was diversion of treasury funds from one ramo to another: the ramos agenos and ramos particulares stood empty, already stripped bare by desperate treasury officials. At the same time these same officials continued to ignore payment of normal treasury obligations—administrative or military salaries, the situados of the garrisons and naval forces in the Greater Caribbean, pensions, support of educational and pious foundations and institutions, and remissions to Spain. But none of this was new. Since the 1780s special propios e arbitrios, temporary wartime exactions, and increased rates on established taxes were all too familiar to Mexicans as methods for raising revenues in time of crisis. So too were the forced and voluntary loans, requests for patriotic donations, and discounted salaries for public officials. Only the tapping of reserves in the ramos particulares and ramos agenos was no longer available.

Badly in need of money, however, colonial leaders in Mexico City showed surprising ingenuity in devising new taxes. In Mexico City they imposed both a real estate tax and—shades of the twentieth century—a graduated income tax. A 10 percent tax on all urban real estate went into effect on February 24, 1812, with renters contributing a portion of the impost along with the property owners. Over the next four years, to March 1816, the tax produced a net revenue of over 277,000 pesos, an average of almost 70,000 pesos a year[14]. Established by viceregal decree in mid-

[13]The burden of new or raised taxes fell primarily upon the urban population. For an excellent description of these policies as they affected Mexico City, see Timothy E. Anna, *The Fall of the Royal Government in Mexico City* (Lincoln: University of Nebraska Press, 1978), 140–161.

[14]AGI, México, Legajo 1489. Informe del virrey, México, 4 marzo 1816.

December 1813, the graduated income tax set a 3 percent rate on salaries of 300 pesos to 12.5 percent on income of 12,000 pesos or more, although just how much this new levy produced is not clear.

Aduana officials somehow managed to keep tax receipts at the Mexico City customs house remarkably stable (see Figure 8). Although sales taxes declined somewhat—despite the increase of the tax rate to 8 percent—income from other taxes such as those on *aguardiente* actually rose, particularly after 1815. Authorities also levied a special convoy tax to pay for a force of 1500 cavalrymen to keep the road to Veracruz open, which maintained the flow of at least a modicum of goods into Mexico City.[15] Interestingly, aduana revenues in Mexico City were some 600,000 pesos greater in 1820 than in 1810, reflecting the ability of the customs house to keep its revenues up by increasing its rates on established taxes and by imposing new levies. If income from provincial cajas had dried up, the aduana was at least doing its part to keep a steady flow of funds into the real hacienda. Unfortunately, these revenues were not enough to compensate for the loss of income from the provinces.

And the money was so sorely needed. In 1795, for example, total local military and defense expenditures in the matrix treasury of Mexico amounted to about 600,000 pesos, which included monies spent for support of both regular troops and militia in Mexico (see Figure 3). By 1810 these costs had almost tripled to 1.6 million pesos, and by 1812 had quintupled to 3 million pesos. After 1812, however, because of the lack of funds or because the war effort against the rebels was going better, military expenditures began to decline, and by 1817 were only a bit more than 900,000 pesos. Lack of funds seems to be the principal reason; the viceregal government simply had no funds to dispense. The desperate efforts made in Mexican provincial villages and towns to raise funds for military endeavors during this period also gives testimony to the financial failures at the viceregal level, which traditionally had financed such enterprises.[16]

On the fringes of New Spain, military establishments suffered even more severely from the disruption of the wars of independence—the garrisons and outposts in the Greater Caribbean such as Florida, Cuba, Puerto Rico, the Presidio del Carmen and other Spanish fortresses (see Figure 3), and also the Philippines. From 1795 to 1810, for example, situados sent from Mexico to these outposts averaged about 1.7 million pesos annually.

[15]AGI, México, Legajo 1494. Carta del Virrey Juan Ruiz de Apodaca al Ministro de Real Hacienda, México, 11 noviembre 1817.

[16]Failure of the viceregal government to provide troops and equipment for fighting the rebels is clearly the reason for the extreme measures taken at the town and village level to get funds for defense. See particularly the article in this volume by Christon Archer, " 'La Causa Buena': The Counterinsurgency Army and the Ten Years' War."

From 1811 to 1817 these same military and naval subsidies amounted to an annual average of only 80,000 pesos, and in the years 1815 and 1817 were virtually nothing. Thus, those hurt most in the wars of independence were Spanish outposts in other parts of the Indies or in the Philippines which depended upon yearly subsidies from Mexico. That many of them survived without support from New Spain is indeed remarkable.

As might be expected, royal treasury debt continued to grow during the epoch of independence (see Figure 7). During the twenty years from 1791 to 1810, the strains put on the royal treasuries of Mexico by the exigencies of war in Europe and the Indies had left the Mexican treasury in a miserable state. During the early 1790s its debt had grown from 13.9 million in 1791 to over 34 million in 1798, a debt reduced the next year to 22.7 million after indulgence and tithe income were made ramos of the royal treasury. Over the next seven years to the end of 1805, good years for the real hacienda of New Spain, the debt was reduced significantly to 17.4 million pesos, but during the following quinquennium, income simply could not keep pace with expenditures as deficits increased and debts almost doubled to 31.1 million pesos by the end of 1810.

Interestingly, although the debt continued to grow after 1810—to 37.5 million pesos by the end of 1815—the *rate* of increase slowed considerably—and for good reason. Royal treasury officials simply could not pry more revenues out of an economically exhausted populace, which had little wealth or property left to lend or be sequestered. Even church and household silver had been used to finance the war effort, and many of the rich had sent their remaining capital elsewhere. With inflation rampant, supplies of goods difficult to obtain, and high tax rates driving commodity prices upward, the consulado had not prospered enough to provide additional loans, silver production had declined, and special ramos of the royal treasury had no more reserves. By the end of 1816, in fact, one estimate indicated that the treasury of Mexico owed almost 81 million pesos, including over 24 million pesos in delinquent situado payments. The official drawing up the estimate believed that over 41 million could be defaulted—monies owed to the mint, tobacco monopoly, ramos particulares e agenos, and the situados which remained unpaid—among others. An additional 7.7 million, he felt, might also be written off, unless those to whom the money was owed could establish the legitimacy of the debt—institutions such as consulado, juzgado de intestados, and royal *audiencias* in Mexico City and Guadalajara; the Indian communities of Mexico, Valladolid, and Oaxaca; the ecclesiastical *cabildos* of Nuevo León, Valladolid, and Guadalajara; the tribunal de minería; and the royal lottery. The remaining 32 million, however, had to be repaid in order to preserve the good faith and credit of the government and to insure the survival of religious institutions in Mexico which had lent so much to ensure the success of the war effort over the previous thirty years.[17] A small beginning came in 1817 when almost 2 million pesos were repaid to various creditors of the treasury, and a bit more may have been paid back over the next three years, but in 1821 the success of the Army of Three Guarantees meant the end of Spanish rule in Nueva España, making most debt questions irrelevant.

In summary, this analysis of the breakdown of the Mexican treasury system in the epoch of independence clearly shows that disintegration came in stages. The first began in the 1780s when heavy, new demands were made on the real hacienda in Mexico to finance war in Europe and the Indies. This meant first borrowing from and then completely stripping the reserves of certain ramos of the treasury—*bulas de santa cruzada, temporalidades, novenos, depósitos*, and others. It also meant borrowing from wealthy lay and clerical institutions at interest rates of 4 and 5 percent, guaranteed by the income from the tobacco monopoly or customs house receipts. Then in the first decade of the nineteenth century, the viceregal government appropriated and sold landed properties belonging to pious foundations and chantries in still another move to meet fast-rising Peninsular and local expenditures.[18] By 1810, in fact, viceregal treasury officials had tapped seemingly all the financial resources available in Mexico and had begun ignoring normal treasury obligations, particularly those to the military outposts on the fringes of New Spain.

In essence, the Hidalgo revolt in 1810 was just another in a series of bitter blows to the treasury, heaping still another new obligation on an already overburdened system. Most significantly, though, the independence movement marked the end of remissions of tax receipts to Mexico City from the wealthy mining districts and other treasuries of the viceroyalty, traditionally a vitally important source of income for paying the larger costs of empire in Nueva España and Spain. Temporary expedients enabled viceregal officials to meet the costs of quelling the initial revolt (1810–1815) but at the expense of the presidios of the Greater Caribbean and the Philippines and of the tax-burdened urban residents of New Spain. Although there was some recovery in a few treasury districts after the defeat of Morelos in 1815, this was not substantial enough to help revive the old structure. The events of 1810 had destroyed the network which had joined Mexico City to the rest of New Spain, fiscal ties with the periphery that had made the system work for almost three centuries. The monumental task of reconstructing these links is still another tortuous story of Mexican state building in the nineteenth and early twentieth centuries, almost as tortuous as their destruction.

[17]Sala de Manuscritos, Biblioteca Nacional, Madrid, doc. 19710, f. 23. Sobre la deuda de la R. Hazienda y medio de restablecer su crédito. Año de 1817.

[18]Brian R. Hamnett, "The Appropriation of Mexican Church Wealth by the Spanish Bourbon Government," *Journal of Latin American Studies*, 1 (1969), 85–113.

Appendix

Figure 1

Net Revenues, Treasury of Mexico, 1795–1817

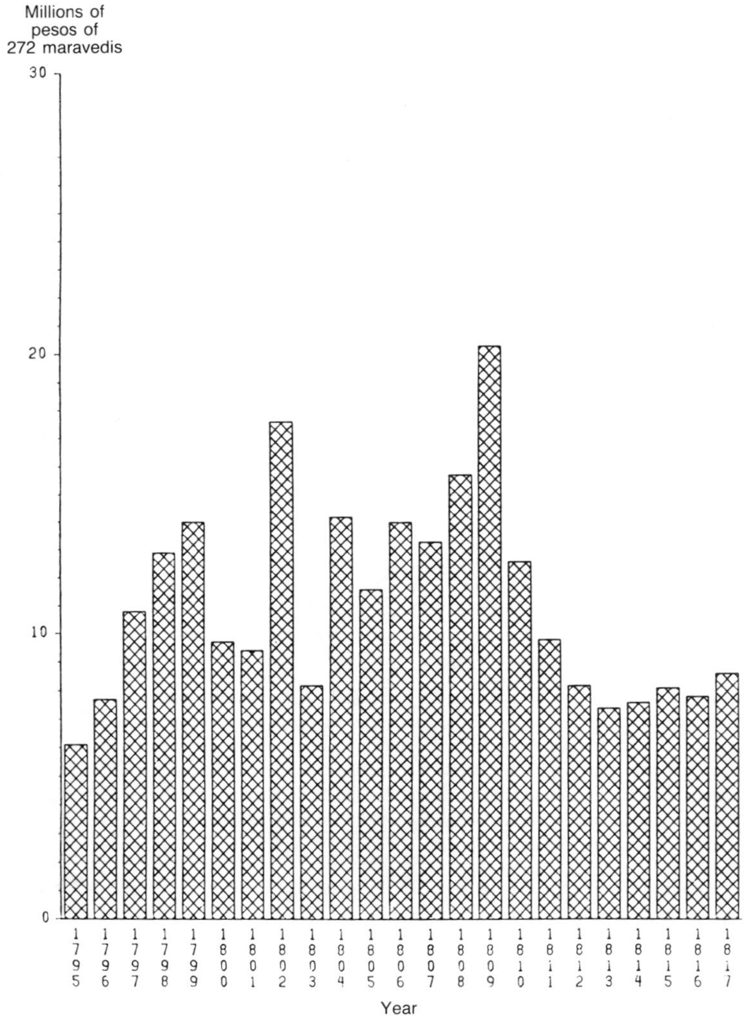

Source: From the *cartas cuentas* found in Archivo General de las Indias (AGI), México, Legajos 2029 and 2061–2072, and in the Archivo General de la Nación, México, Libros de Hacienda, 68 and 81. The account for 1817 comes from this same archive and was graciously provided me by my friend and colleague Dr. Juan Carlos Garavaglia.

Figure 2
Remissions of the Treasury of Mexico, 1795–1817

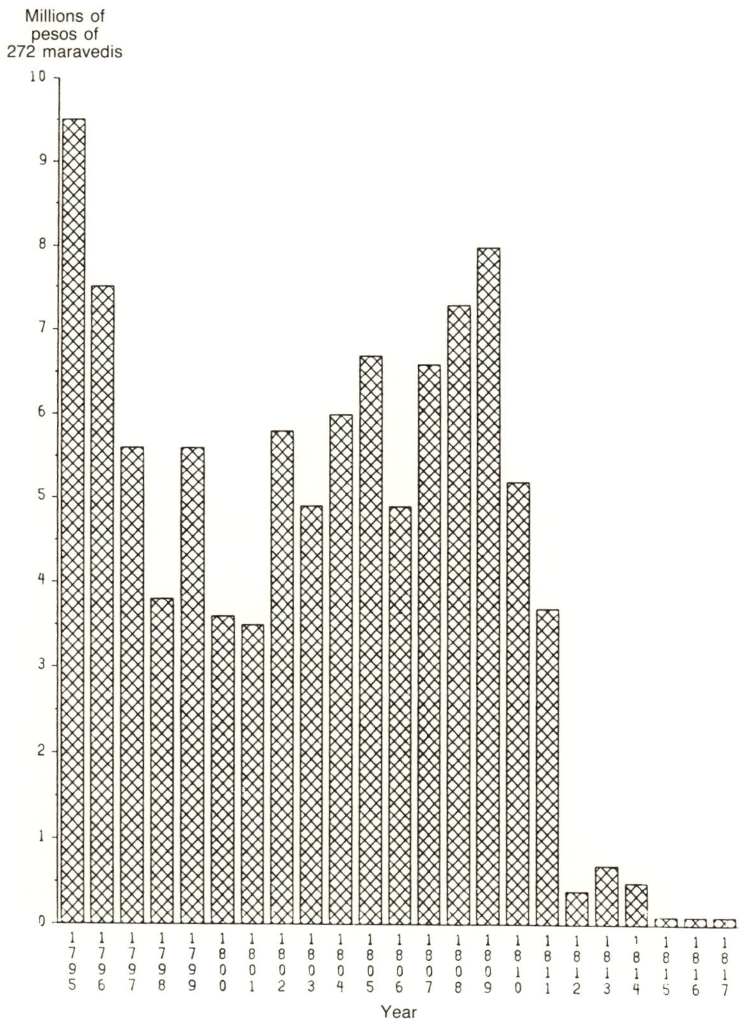

Source: From the *cartas cuentas* found in Archivo General de las Indias (AGI), México, Legajos 2029 and 2061–2072, and in the Archivo General de la Nación, México, Libros de Hacienda, 68 and 81. The account for 1817 comes from this same archive and was graciously provided me by my friend and colleague Dr. Juan Carlos Garavaglia.

Figure 3
War and Situado Expenditures, Mexico, 1795–1817

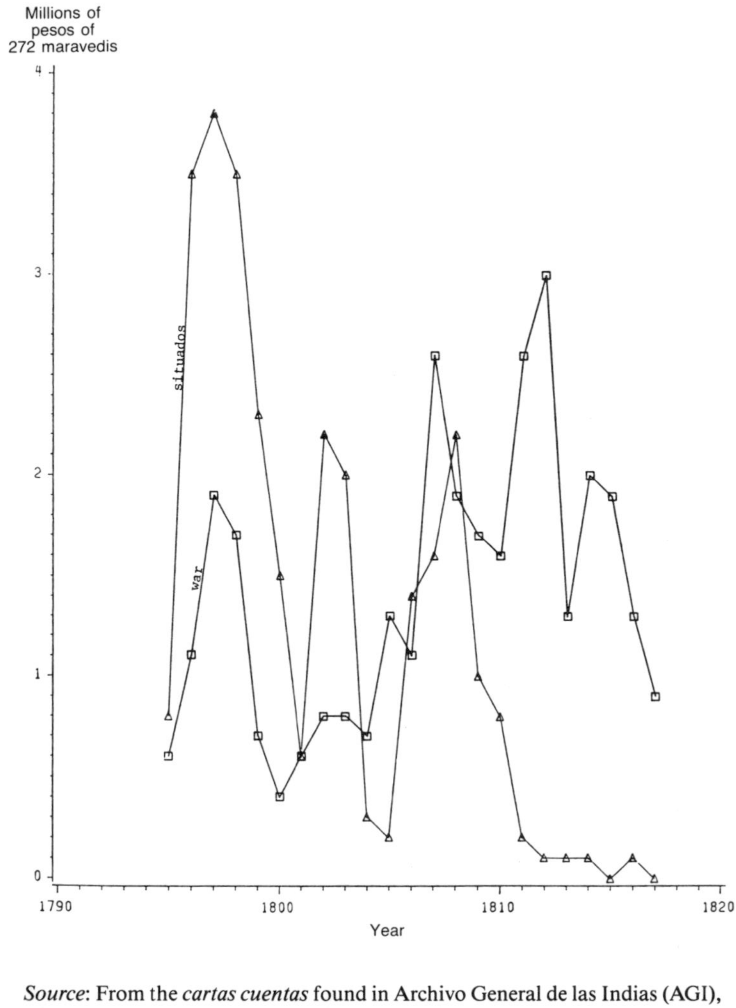

Source: From the *cartas cuentas* found in Archivo General de las Indias (AGI), México, Legajos 2029 and 2061–2072, and in the Archivo General de la Nación, México, Libros de Hacienda, 68 and 81. The account for 1817 comes from this same archive and was graciously provided me by my friend and colleague Dr. Juan Carlos Garavaglia.

Figure 4
Total Revenue, Treasury of Zacatecas, 1791–1821

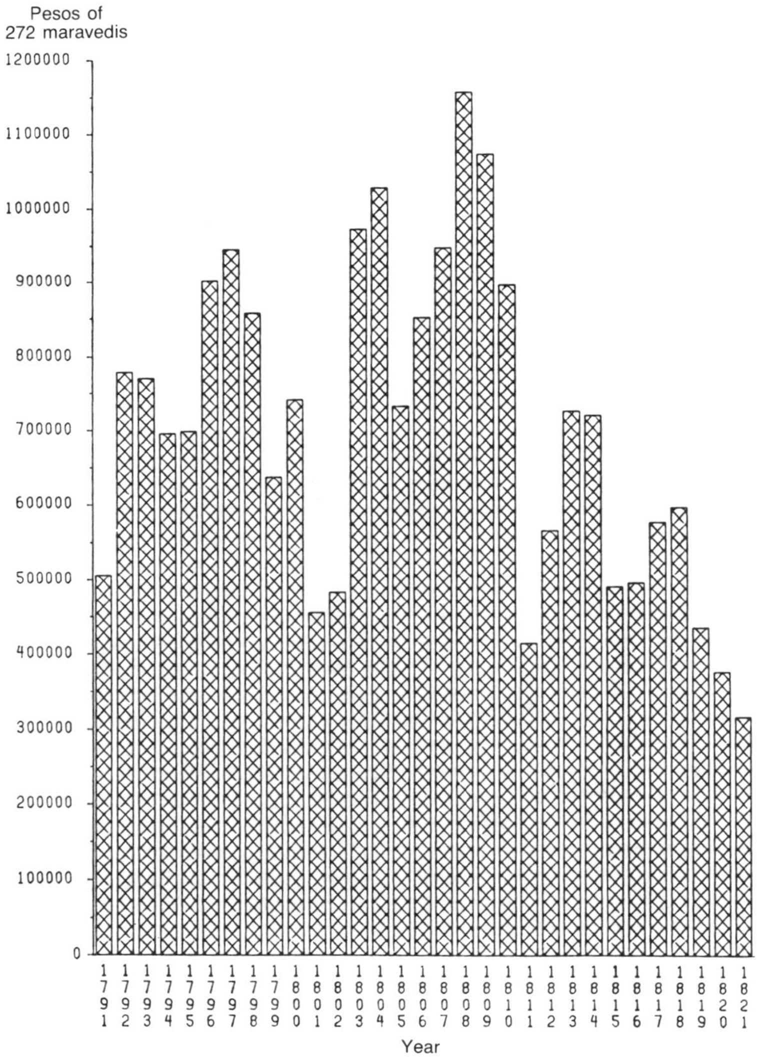

Source: The accounts for Zacatecas may be found in AGI, Guadalajara, Legajos 481–482, and AGI, México, Legajos 2032, 2034, and 2376. The William Clements Library in Ann Arbor, Michigan, houses the accounts for 1807–1812, 1814–1815, 1817–1819, and 1821 in its Zacatecas Collection.

Figure 5
Silver Taxes, Zacatecas, 1791–1821

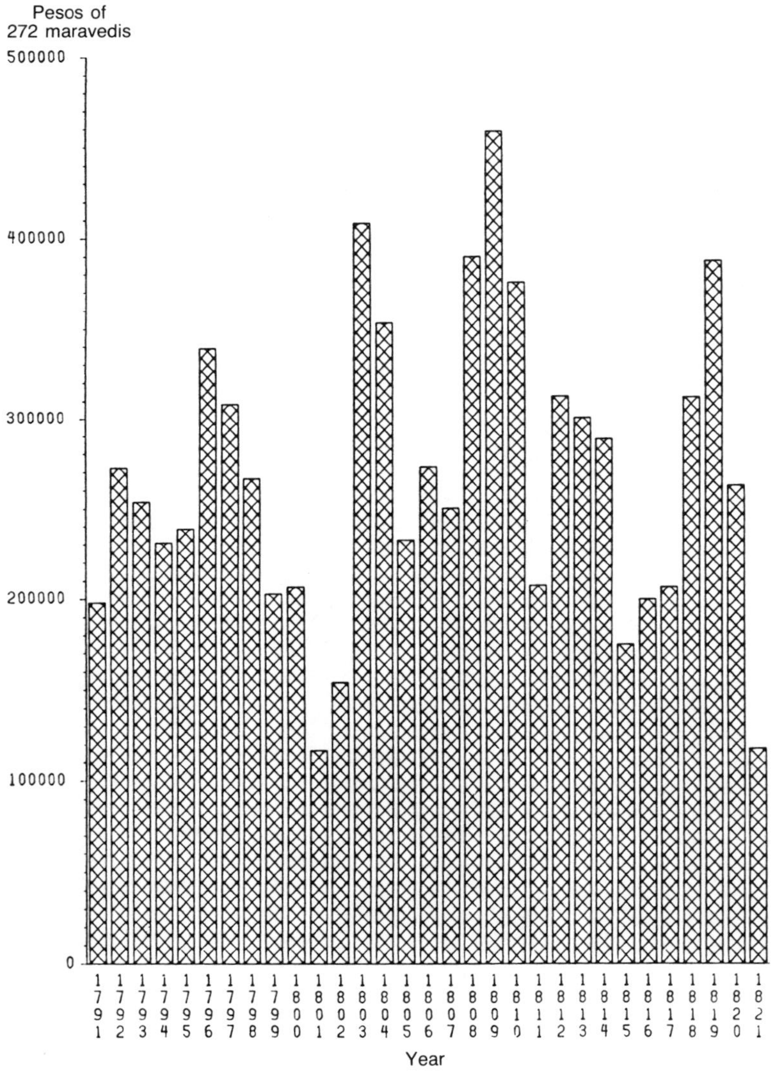

Source: The accounts for Zacatecas may be found in AGI, Guadalajara, Legajos 481–482, and AGI, México, Legajos 2032, 2034, and 2376. The William Clements Library in Ann Arbor, Michigan, houses the accounts for 1807–1812, 1814–1815, 1817–1819, and 1821 in its Zacatecas Collection.

Figure 6
Mintage of Bullion in Mexico, 1791-1821

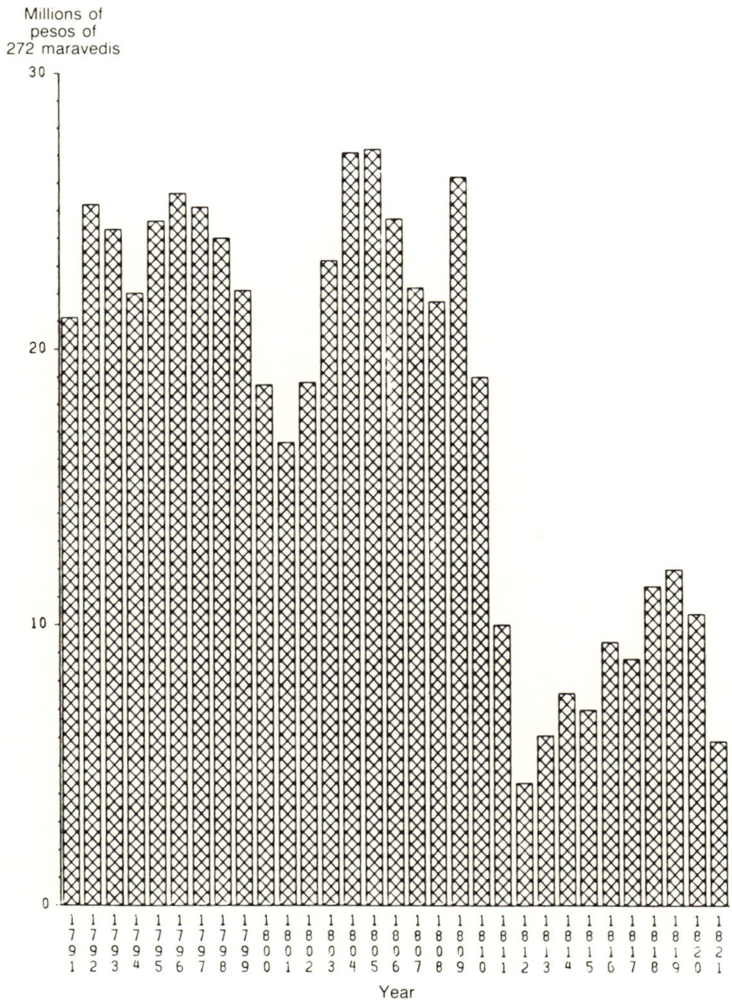

Source: Mintage figures are listed in Walter Howe. *The Mining Guild of New Spain and Its Tribunal General, 1770–1821* (Cambridge, Mass.: Harvard University Press, 1949), 453–459. These have been checked against those listed in AGI, México, 1489, 2800, 2802–2803, 2806, 2819–2820, 2827–2829, and 2831, also in AGI, Indiferente General, Legajo 1714. Mintage figures can also be found in the Sala de Manuscritos, Biblioteca Nacional, Madrid, Ms. 1399.

Figure 7
Debt Owed by the Treasury of Mexico, 1791–1817

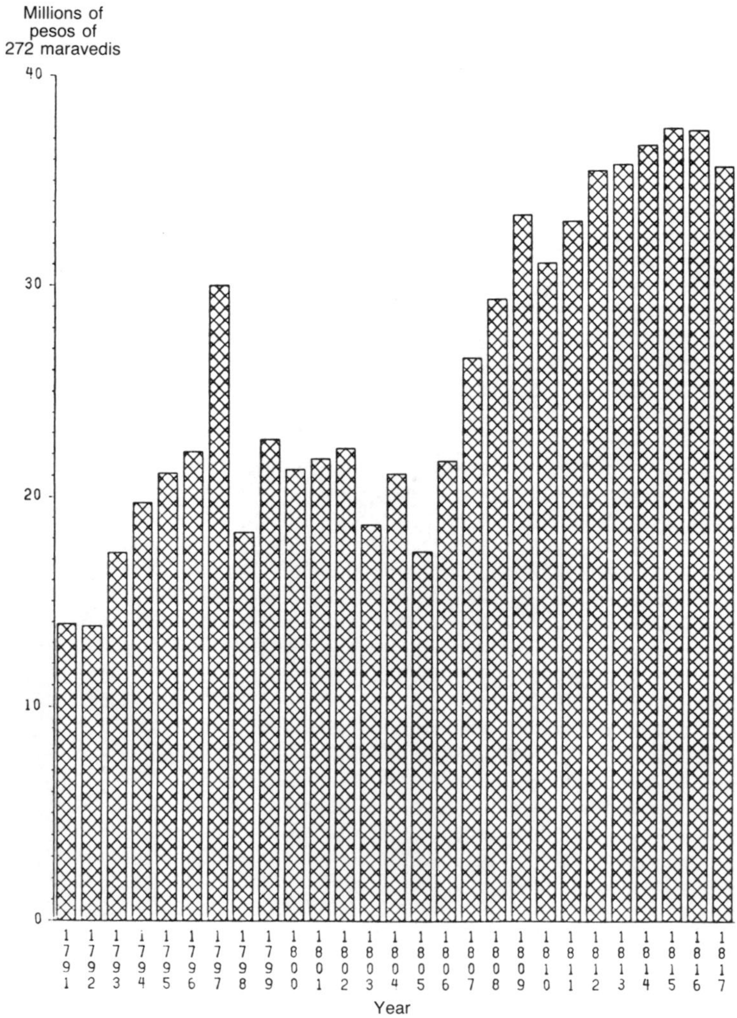

Source: Annual statements of the debt of the *real hacienda* in Mexico may be found in AGI, México, 2020, 2022–2023, 2026, 2355–2358, 2360, 2366, 2373, 2375, and 2387.

Figure 8
Net Income, Aduana of Mexico City, 1810–1821

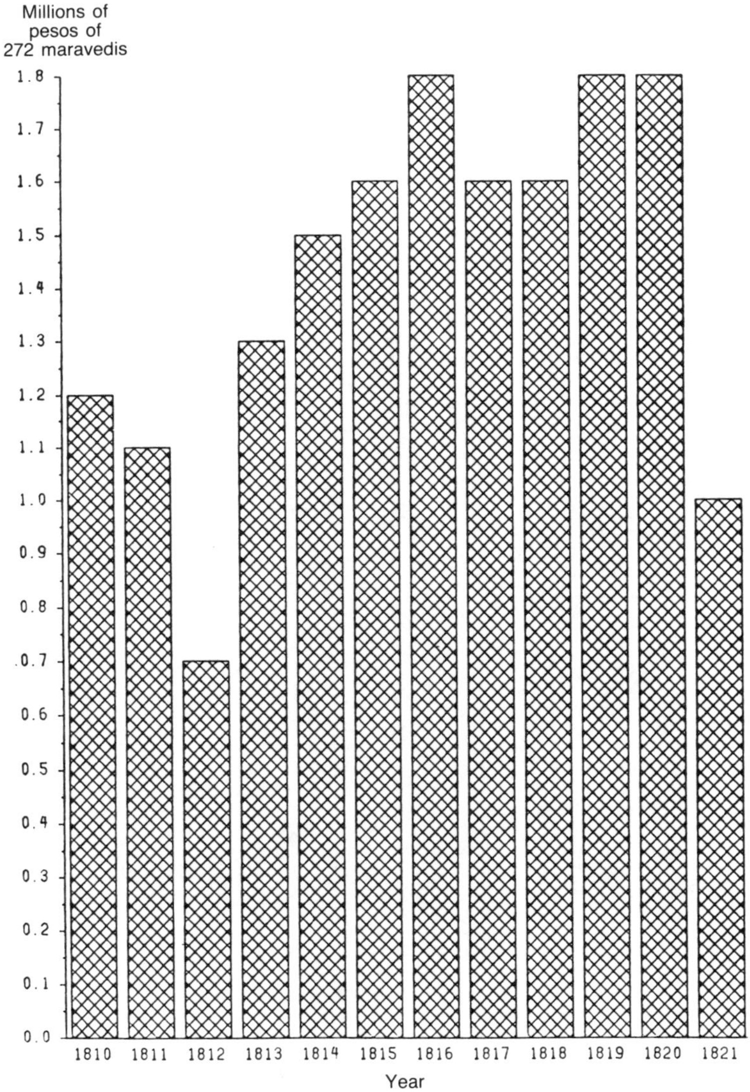

Source: Lucas Alamán's magesterial five-volume work, *Historia de Méjico* . . . (México: Colección de Grandes Autores Mexicanos, 1942), a republication of the original published between 1849 and 1852, includes a host of statistics on the independence and early national periods from which these customs house figures are taken. See also Tadeo Ortiz de Ayala, *Resumen de la estadística del imperio mexicano* (Mexico: Imprenta de doña Herculena del Vilar y Socios, 1822).

Figure 9
Total Gross Revenues, Treasury of Mexico, 1795–1817

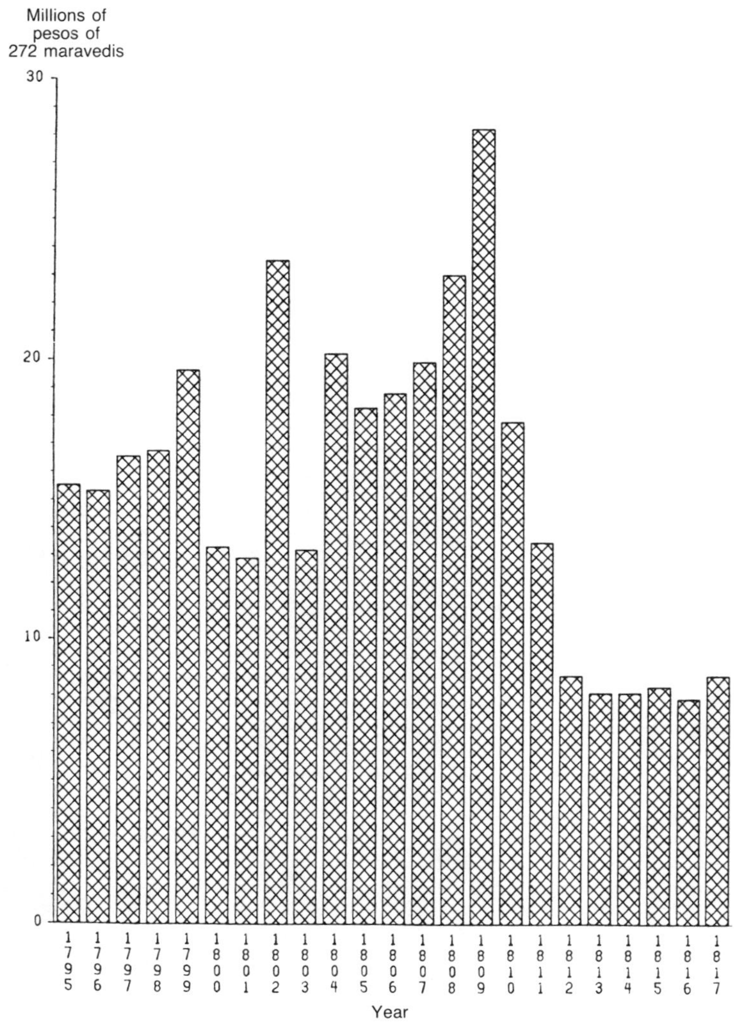

Figure 10
Total War Expenses, Treasury of Mexico, 1795–1817[a]

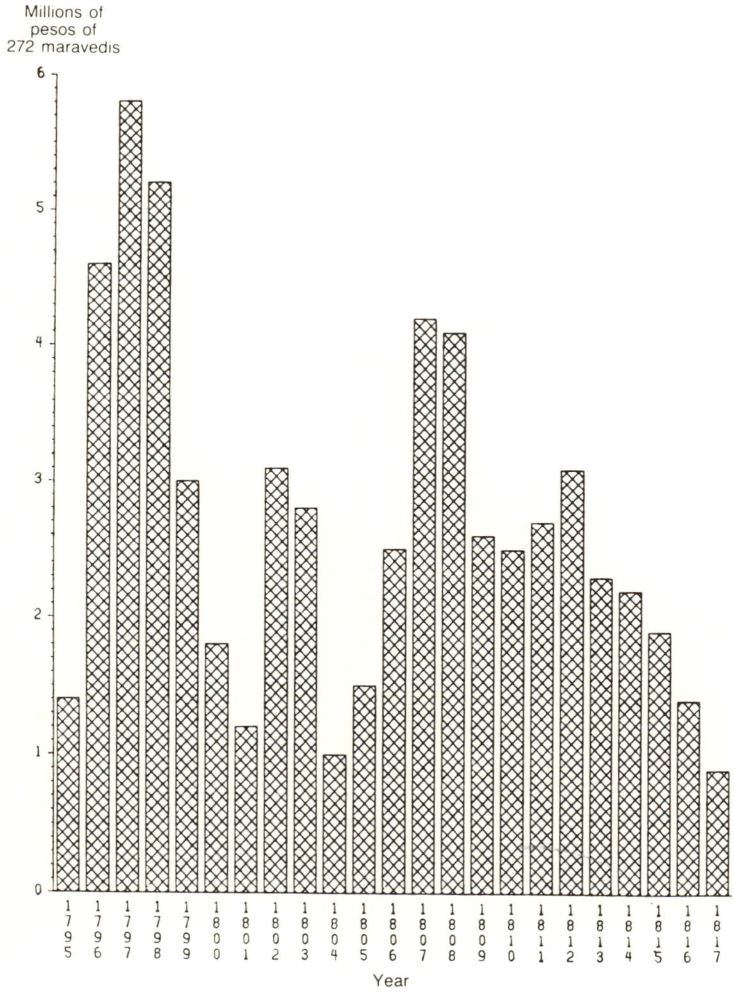

a. Includes situados remitted elsewhere.

"La Causa Buena": The Counterinsurgency Army of New Spain and the Ten Years' War

Christon I. Archer

> Comandante: "¿Juráis a Díos, y prometéis a la Patria, y a la Religión de defenderla hasta perder la última gota de vuestra sangre, de mantener estas ricas posesiones a Vuestro Augusto Soberano y de obedecer a los Cabos, Sargentos, y demas Jefes que compongan el Exército?"
> Soldados Realistas: "Sí Juramos."[1]

WRITING IN JUNE 1815, after almost five years of revolution, Bishop Manuel Abad y Queipo had good reason to believe that he possessed considerable expertise on the "mortífero contagio" of insurgency that devoured New Spain. During his journey from Valladolid (Morelia) to Mexico City, where he reported to the king on the origins and state of the revolution, Abad y Queipo's convoy suffered two violent attacks in which the 400 escort troops managed to repulse the insurgents. In the bishop's view, the royalist struggle against a powerful coalition of rebel forces was all that stood in the way of a descent into "a frightful anarchy."[2] The revolution of Santo Domingo provided graphic evidence of the absolute ruin that could destroy Mexico. Abad y Queipo identified a criollo faction that employed "the most refined Machiavellianism" to convert submissive and pacific Mexicans into "monstruos feroces." In fifteen horrendous days during September, 1810, more than a million Indians, Negroes, and mulattoes had been seduced into joining the rebellion.[3]

[1]Sobre la formación del Batallón de Voluntarios de Fernando VII de Puebla, 1810, Archivo General de la Nación, México, Ramo de Indiferente de Guerra (cited hereinafter as AGN:IG), vol. 200-A.

[2]D. Manuel Abad y Queipo, obispo electo de Mechoacán representa a S.M. sobre el estado de Nueva España y origen de la Revolución, México, 20 June 1815, Archivo Histórico Nacional, Madrid, Spain, Ramo de Hacienda, leg. 229-A. Abad y Queipo was in Madrid in January 1816.

[3]Ibid.

By identifying a conspiratorial leadership, Abad y Queipo drifted away from any true understanding of the Mexican insurgency. Like so many contemporary participants, nineteenth-century observers, and recent historians who have written on the Mexican independence period, the bishop could not acknowledge the fact that what gripped New Spain was nothing less than one of the greatest guerrilla insurgencies in modern history. In response, the royalist army introduced a counterinsurgency program that was a classic of its type comparable with similar twentieth-century campaigns waged by the French in Algeria, the French and Americans in Vietnam, and the Russians in Afghanistan. The fact that the Mexican counterinsurgents failed to subdue guerrilla insurgents involved in a totally fragmented people's war of ten years evokes further comparisons with modern wars of national liberation. For Abad y Queipo and Mexico's first generations of historians, proximity to the events and the need to create a Mexican national identity blurred the major themes, creating a generation of national heroes and evil scapegoats. In Mexico, long-term insurgency and counterinsurgency led to decentralization and regionalism and to the enthronement of reactionism over progressive or modern tendencies. After independence, Mexican nation builders, struggling with the heritage of such debilitating factors, had no reason to glorify a deep guerrilla tradition or the continuation of regional centrifugal forces that threatened the existence of the nation.

For Abad y Queipo, the royalist failure to end insurgency quickly appeared to be the direct result of poor leadership by the army commander, Brigadier Félix Calleja, rather than of a confrontation of monumental proportions between parties that would fight to their death or total exhaustion. No royalist supporter wanted to admit that the army of New Spain had engaged what Calleja described as a "hydra reborn as fast as one cuts off its heads."[4] Abad y Queipo focused criticism on Calleja whom he described as " . . . a man sold on himself, and very sensitive to flattery."[5] The bishop agreed that initially Calleja had done well enough, leading his Army of the Center to brilliant victories over Padre Miguel Hidalgo's rebel masses at Aculco, Guanajuato, and Calderón. Yet he failed to pursue the rebels with sufficient dedication and energy to liquidate them totally. Calleja's difficulties at Zitácuaro, and in the protracted siege of José María Morelos's army at Cuautla Amilpas, caused many nonmilitary observers to criticize the royalist general and his army. To Abad y Queipo, the fault lay with army commanders who lacked the talent and knowledge needed to prosecute an effective campaign. What was worse, Calleja had convinced

[4]Calleja to Viceroy Francisco Javier de Venegas, 20 August 1811, Archivo General de la Nación, México, Ramo de Operaciones de Guerra (cited hereinafter as AGN:OG), vol. 190.

[5]D. Manuel Abad y Queipo . . . representa a S.M. sobre el estado de Nueva España, 1815.

Viceroy Venegas that the insurrection was all but over in 1811 when in fact it was about to enter a powerful new stage. Then as viceroy, beginning in 1813, Calleja failed to end the revolution. In the mind of the unmilitary bishop, the army appeared to increase its oppression without results. Military discipline declined, many commanders seemed indolent, and the royalist forces controlled only the garrisoned towns and cities. A bloated army of some 80,000 troops could not handle 25,000 to 30,000 poorly armed and undisciplined insurgents who were "the true sovereigns of the country."[6] The rebels controlled agriculture, industry, and commerce; they robbed, destroyed, or taxed everything outside of the royalist fortifications.

Although there was an element of truth to each of Abad y Queipo's charges against the royalist army, the bishop was guilty of gross oversimplifications and misunderstandings that made him a poor observer of a guerrilla war. It would take time for a conventional army to learn the art of irregular war and to apply a program designed to control, if not to obliterate, insurgency.

Many of the complaints lodged against the royalist army demonstrated little more than the advanced level of petty backbiting, fears, and jealousies prevalent in Mexican society. Calleja although a brillant soldier in many respects, lacked training or experience in the area of counterinsurgency. Like most senior officers stationed in Mexico prior to 1810, his major mission had been to prevent a European enemy from landing on the Veracruz coast and, to a lesser degree, to control the northern frontier, where Indian tribes posed regional threats, but never the prospect of total annihilation. The mass appeal of Hidalgo's uprising surprised army officers, like everyone else. In anticipation of a French invasion, many of the provincial militia units, and the few regular infantry battalions, had been mobilized and cantoned in Puebla and near the mountain towns overlooking Veracruz. Administrators and army commanders looked on dumbfounded as the insurgency expanded.

Calleja, commander of the Tenth Militia Brigade at San Luis Potosí, possessed no mobilized units even at the company level that could be committed to battle against the insurgents. When he received word of the uprising, at 10:30 A.M. on September 19, Calleja had to create an army from scratch, one not based on an existing force.[7] He met with the commanders of his brigade, assembled green ranch hands from the rural haciendas, and ordered the construction of weapons. The only firearms available in his brigade were ancient worn out muskets used by the Provincial Dragoon

[6]Ibid.

[7]Félix Calleja to Viceroy Venegas, San Luis Potosí, no. 2196, 21 September 1810, AGN:OG, vol. 169.

Regiments of San Luis and San Carlos.[8] Ordered by Viceroy Venegas to concentrate his brigade at Querétaro with other royalist units marching there from Puebla, Calleja saw no alternative but to defer. Even the recruitment of Indian bowmen and the mobilization of artisans to construct lances, the most basic weapon used by mounted forces, would take weeks. If there had been a theoretical opportunity for the army to crush Hidalgo's insurgency in its formative stages, neither the provincial units of the cantonments nor Calleja's hastily recruited countrymen were able to act decisively. By 9 October 1810, the Marqués del Xaral del Berrio, commander of Calleja's advance guard, sighted an insurgent force of 40,000 to 50,000 against San Luis Potosí. They came by roads and through the barrancas loaded down with booty from robberies like "a swarm of ants" determined to incite the countryside to rebellion.[9]

Calleja might have viewed many aspects of his situation as humorous if he and his province had not been in mortal peril. He lacked infantry and artillery needed to force the insurgent-occupied passes at Carrasa and Nieto on the road to Querétaro. A junta of artisans knowledgeable about casting iron and bronze promised to make artillery pieces, but produced poor quality cannon. The first casting failed completely and the second effort produced one flawed barrel and two others that were so small that they would not do much damage in battle. It was quite obvious, during the experiments, that no one possessed sufficient technical knowledge about casting cannon and that improvements would come only after a period of trial and error. Even after mid-October, only one barrel was ready to be mounted on a carriage.[10]

For all of his efforts to recruit troops, by mid-October Calleja had only 1,500 foot soldiers "of the very worst sort," and 2,600 horsemen composed primarily of rural vaqueros armed only with lances. Not only did the precipitous nature of the recruitment and training of his soldiers bother Calleja, but also he could not forget the expanding contagion of insurgency and the frequent desertions from his cantonment.[11] Such were the origins of the Army of the Center.

Uncertain about the loyalty of his own troops and civilian populace, Calleja was helpless to prevent disasters befalling the city and province of

[8]Calleja to Venegas, no. 2197, 28 September 1810, AGN:OG, vol. 169.

[9]Calleja to Venegas, no. 33, Campo de la Pila, 9 October 1810, AGN:OG, vol. 169.

[10]Intendente de San Luis Potosí, Manuel de Acevedo, to Calleja, 13 October 1810; and 17 October 1810, AGN:OG, vol. 91.

[11]Calleja to Venegas, Campo de Pila, 15 October 1810, AGN:OG, vol. 169; and Calleja to Conde de la Cadena (Manuel de Flon, Intendente de Puebla), San Luis Potosí, 2 October 1810, AGN:OG, vol. 94-A. Cadena, second in command to Calleja, marched from Puebla to Querétaro where confusion, disorder, and fear in the city prevented him from any decisive activities.

Guanajuato. On September 23, 1810, Intendente Juan Antonio Riaño of Guanajuato reported that he was in dire straits surrounded and cut off from provisions. Irapuato had fallen the day before and Riaño knew that his own large urban populations had begun to waver. The intendente begged assistance and information on Calleja's operations and the size of his forces.[12] In reply, Calleja prevaricated with a promise he knew was untrue; he told Riaño to sustain his position with vigor and to expect relief from San Luis Potosí in a week.[13]

Poor Riaño, his lifeline had almost run its course. Far from being able to defend himself, on September 26 he informed Calleja that with 500 men he had fortified himself in the city *alhóndiga*. He informed Calleja that Dolores, San Miguel, Celaya, Salamanca, and Irapuato had fallen and that Silao was on the point of declaring for insurgency. Guanajuato seethed with discontent, his few cavalrymen were poorly mounted and armed with "glass swords," and his untrustworthy infanty possessed only patched and mended muskets. Riaño told Calleja that ever since September 17, he had not taken off his clothing or been able to obtain minimum rest. For the past three days, he had not managed to sleep for even an hour.[14] By September 27, rebel forces surrounded and besieged the granary. Cut off from news and short of gunpowder, Riaño did manage to send a dispatch to Calleja and another to the presidente of Guadalajara requesting relief forces. Despite the hopelessness of the situation, Riaño was certain that the royalist columns, in combination with his garrison, would inflict exemplary punishment upon the rebels.[15] The idea was a good one, but others would have to take up the cause of counterinsurgency. At 11:00 A.M. on September 28, Riaño managed to smuggle out one last runner with a terse note for Calleja:[16] "I am going to fight because I am going to be attacked this instant: I will resist as long as I can because I am honorable: Your Excellency, come to my aid." Riaño was dead within hours, insurgents had sacked the granary killing its European and criollo defenders, and Guanajuato was in rebel hands.[17]

Far from acting decisively to introduce a counterinsurgency program, the royalist commanders staggered before a frightening new power that threatened to sweep aside all military resistance. European Spaniards and other members of the governing elite fled from the provincial cities in "terror

[12]Juan Antonio Riaño to Calleja, Guanajuato, 23 September 1810, AGN:OG, vol. 809.
[13]Calleja to Riaño, San Luis Potosí, 24 September 1810, AGN:OG, vol. 809.
[14]Riaño to Calleja, 26 September 1810, AGN:OG, vol. 809.
[15]Riaño to Calleja, 27 September 1810, AGN:OG, vol. 809.
[16]Riaño to Calleja, 28 September 1810, AGN:OG, vol. 809.
[17]For additional detail, see Hugh M. Hamill, Jr., *The Hidalgo Revolt: Prelude to Mexican Independence* (Gainesville, 1966), 139-140; and José María Luis Mora, *México y sus revoluciones* (Mexico, 1965), III, 37-45.

pánico" to seek refuge in Querétaro, Mexico City, and in regions distant from the insurgency.[18] At Querétaro, the Conde de la Cadena and the urban government feared dispatching any forces from the city that would allow the 60,000 inhabitants to launch their own uprising. Cadena placed little confidence in his troops and found that his senior officers exhibited no desire to lead relief expeditions against the insurgent-occupied cities.[19] Large segments of militia units from the Bajío towns joined the rebellion and Querétaro soldiers who had their wives with them appeared especially untrustworthy. In only two days, 74 soldiers of the Provincial Regiment of Celaya garrisoned at Querétaro deserted into rebel territory two leagues outside of the city.[20] Cadena asked Viceroy Venegas to transfer loyal troops from Puebla, Veracruz, Tlaxcala, and Toluca. In cities and provinces not yet affected by insurgency, however, recruitment of patriotic militias lagged as men debated terms of service and resisted any suggestion that they might be required to march beyond their city walls. At Veracruz, soon a major center of revolution, residents foiled all efforts to raise a Cuerpo Urbano of 1,000 men.[21]

Depression and defeatist attitudes turned to euphoria as the royalists concentrated scattered units and Calleja marched southward from San Luis Potosí. The invulnerability of the Indian and mestizo masses had much more to do with appearance and psychology than with real military might. The massed musketry, grapeshot, and fairly well disciplined soldiers of the Army of the Center crushed the insurgents at Aculco, Guanajuato, and Calderón. Even describing these affairs as battles is misleading since they were so one-sided. The insurgent commanders committed the tragic error of believing that they could engage in conventional battle with the royalist army. They lacked the arms, leaders, and discipline. Once the royalists banished their own fears of rebel omnipotence, they found that they had been combatting an illusion of military power rather than a real army. Cadena informed Venegas that after the pacification of the Bajío cities and towns that had supported the insurgency, "I will return to Mexico City without having fired a shot."[22] Upon further reflection and with time to evaluate the true nature of the insurgency, Cadena was less optimistic about a rapid conclusion. In his view, two months more of inaction and paralysis by the military might have been enough to lose New Spain. On

[18]Jacobo María Jantos to Calleja, Venado, 26 October 1810, AGN:OG, vol. 169.

[19]Cadena to Ignacio García Revollo, 30 September 1810, AGN:OG, vol. 94-A; and Cadena to Venegas, 5 October 1810, AGN:OG, vol. 94-A. Cadena was shocked by the fall of Guanajuato and the death of his brother-in-law, Juan Antonio Riaño.

[20]José Alonso to Cadena, 12 October 1810; and Cadena to Venegas, 12 October 1810, AGN:OG, vol. 94-A.

[21]Carlos de Urrutía to Venegas, Veracruz, 13 October 1810, AGN:OG, vol. 882.

[22]Cadena to Venegas, Hacienda de la Erre, 27 October 1810, AGN:OG, vol. 882.

the eve of the battle of Calderón, which was to take his own life, Cadena realized that the Hidalgo movement was a general insurrection including all inhabitants and not merely a peasant uprising. Fear and even terror of military retribution might restore order, but in their hearts the Mexicans had come to abhor Spaniards and Spanish rule.[23]

The problem for any counterinsurgent is to balance naked force with a desire to introduce pacific reform policies designed to extirpate the root of insurgency. Calleja could not forget for an instant that his Army of the Center was a force composed principally of Mexicans. He knew that a revolt based simply upon separation from Spain, unencumbered by the racial overtones of the Hidalgo uprising, would appeal to the great majority of Mexicans.[24] From the military point of view, Calleja knew that his victories were flawed to the extent that his green troops wavered when rebel units stood to fight. There was, for example, considerable vacillation in the royalist lines at Calderón before the insurgents broke and turned the battle into a massacre.[25] Worse, the rebels learned very quickly from their disasters, and adopted guerrilla warfare and constructed fortifications that would require lengthy conventional sieges. A general proliferation of insurgent bands presented the royalist army with insuperable challenges that would require the introduction of a full-blown counterinsurgency system. Even in 1811, the insurgents had the royalist army running from point to point to meet a multiplicity of minor irritations. In Guanajuato province, the rebel chief Albino García operated with a guerrilla force of about 1,000 men out of the steep mountains and canyons of Valle de Santiago. An army division under Major Agustín Viña chased García, but could not engage the guerrillas because of the rough country. When the royalists moved out, the insurgents followed, destroying water tanks, digging pits in roads to prevent the passage of artillery and cavalry, and diverting streams to flood roads. Viña became so frustrated by his inability to engage Albino García's guerrillas that he returned to the town of Salamanca to apprehend and jail some rebel women and children. In Viña's view, they had to be made " . . . to feel the evils of war in every way."[26]

News in 1811 of Morelos's threats to Puebla forced Calleja to move the Army of the Center out of the unpacified Bajío region. Insurgent forces

[23]Cadena to Venegas, Villa de Lagos, 7 January 1811, AGN:OG, vol. 94-A; and Calleja to Venegas, Guanajuato, 12 August 1811, AGN:OG, vol. 190.

[24]Calleja to Venegas, reservado, 29 January 1811, AGN:OG, vol. 171.

[25]Calleja to Venegas, Campo de Zapotlanejo, 18 January 1811, AGN:OG, vol. 171. The estimates of royalist dead and wounded were about 150 while the insurgents were thought to have lost 6,000 to 7,000.

[26]Calleja to Venegas, Guanajuato, 30 October 1811, AGN:OG, vol. 192. Also see Brian R. Hamnett, *Roots of Insurgency: Mexican Regions, 1750–1824* (Cambridge, 1986), 180–183.

concentrated first at Zitácuaro, fortifying the town and challenging the army to exhaust itself in a debilitating siege. Calleja's critics had no idea about the difficulties entailed in moving approximately 5,000 troops. Cold weather caused sickness and many soldiers suffered from venereal disease " . . . that is endemic in this country and which devours the army."[27] As the provincial soldiers left their home districts, desertion eroded the army's vitality. Supplies of biscuit became precarious and many units ran short on tobacco "so essential for soldiers on campaign."[28] As the royalists approached Zitácuaro, the rebels dug great pits in the road which delayed progress and required considerable energy to fill before artillery and baggage carts could be moved. There was no possibility of living off the land since the enemy implemented an effective scorched earth policy.[29]

Calleja was not a sanguinary general compared with some other counterinsurgent commanders who served in New Spain. Nevertheless, debilitating dysentery combined with Venegas's impatient demands for rapid movement made Calleja anxious to avoid a lengthy siege at Zitácuaro. He followed his victory with a draconian punishment designed to provoke terror in other insurgent districts. Zitácuaro and eleven Indian villages were razed to ashes.[30] Following the lengthy and debilitating siege of Cuautla Amilpas, on May 6, 1812, Calleja ordered the demolition of the defenses and the burning of the town. At this point, Viceroy Venegas intervened to suspend the order which in his view applied counterinsurgency terror indiscriminately against both guilty and innocent.[31] Unfortunately, either by design or error, Calleja's order halting the sacrifice of Cuautla did not reach Brigadier Ciriaco de Llano who had been left in charge. Llano informed Calleja that the order containing the "pious resolution" to suspend the destruction had reached him a day late—only the churches and a few other buildings had been spared a fiery end.[32]

It is interesting that when he became viceroy, Calleja renounced this form of counterinsurgency terror. In 1813 near Veracruz, when his forces encountered resistance, Colonel Ramón Monduí torched the towns of Medellín and Rancho de Tejar. Monduí expressed satisfaction at having captured rebel standards, a cannon, arms, and horses, and at leaving the insurgents and "their wretched families" without houses. While he agreed

[27]Calleja to Venegas, 14 December 1811, AGN:OG, vol. 195.

[28]Ibid.

[29]Calleja to Venegas, Cañada de San Mateo, 31 December 1811, AGN:OG, vol. 195.

[30]Calleja to Venegas, 20 January 1812, AGN:OG, vol. 197; and Bando de Félix Calleja, Zitácuaro, 5 January 1812, AGN:OG, vol. 165.

[31]Calleja to Venegas, 6 May 1812; and Venegas to Calleja, 8 May 1812, AGN:OG, vol. 201.

[32]Calleja to Ciriaco de Llano, 9 May 1812; and Llano to Calleja, Sacatepec, 10 May 1812, AGN:OG, vol. 288,

that Medellín deserved having been reduced to ashes, Calleja informed his commander: " . . . the politics of our living together requires that you have certain consideration for the towns that obliges one to keep the buildings in provinces of small population. We do not wish to convert the country into a frightful desert and increase the evils that exist and the hatred with which measures of this nature are viewed."[33]

The implementation of counterinsurgency policies in New Spain depended upon the nature and extent of insurgent activities. Viceroy Venegas ordered army commanders to offer amnesty and pardon to those who truly eschewed violence. However, when soft persuasion and reason did not work, "extraordinary rigor," exemplary punishment, and terror became the operative policies. Summary executions of rebel officers and soldiers were common in the first few years. Given the widespread popularity of the rebellion, many royalist commanders adopted arbitrary and even cruel responses designed to bludgeon would-be insurgents into acquiescence if not support for the royalist cause. At Guanajuato during November, 1810, Calleja imposed the draconian punishment of decimation upon a group of men accused of tearing down during the night his proclamations pardoning rebels. Failing to identify the real culprits, soldiers arrested forty men of the lower classes who happened to be in the general area where the incidents had taken place. When the prisoners could not or would not denounce those responsible for the offenses, the names of four men were drawn by lot and they were executed by firing squad.[34]

In their application of counterinsurgency programs and policies, royalists officers arriving in Mexico from the Spanish army knew a great deal about the subject firsthand from their unfortunate experiences against the French invasion and occupation armies. It is interesting that soldiers who had supported the resistance and insurgency in Spain switched roles in Mexico to introduce many of the counterinsurgency techniques they had seen used by the French. They recognized that effective counterinsurgency demanded mobility, speed, and the flexibility to pacify rebellious districts effectively. Their methods included the use of exemplary terror and of *destacamentos volantes* (flying detachments) designed to chase down and to punish guerrilla bands and the civilian populace that supported insurgency.

The destacamento volante set units of counterinsurgent hunters against the mobile guerrilla bands. While some isolated and mountainous provinces, such as Veracruz, became permanent *foci* of insurgent activity that required major military incursions to achieve any real results, flying

[33]Intendente de Veracruz José Quevedo to Calleja, 4 April 1813; and Calleja to Quevedo, 2 May 1813, AGN:OG, vol. 692.

34Calleja to Venegas, 23 November 1810, AGN:OG, vol. 170.

detachments served to patrol the margins of major roads, to prevent the coalescence of insurgent bands, and to keep the guerrillas out of towns from which they drew sustenance and support. Counterinsurgency of this sort demanded enthusiasm, dedication, and constant energy from officers who had to endure difficult conditions for lengthy periods. In Mexico, the steady flow of Spanish expeditionary officers and soldiers between 1811 and 1816 stiffened locally recruited units and brought renewed vigor at times when existing counterinsurgent commanders approached a state of exhaustion. Although many historians have tended to dismiss the expeditionaries, they played a major role in keeping New Spain within the empire. Without them, independence might have come years earlier.

The first to organize flying detachments or columns was Brigadier José de la Cruz who arrived from Spain in early November, 1810. His first mission as commander of the army of the Right was to open the strategically important road between Mexico City and Querétaro that had been cut by guerrilla bands operating out of Tula, Huichapan, and other towns. Cruz advocated the use of terror against entrenched village and district rural clans led by families such as the Villagráns and Anayas. In this region, as well as in other provinces, members of these clans acted as linking agents who articulated existing grievances and recruited support from more isolated Indian communities. With backgrounds in contraband trading and banditry, and legitimization through recognition by the major rebel leaders, these insurgents were extemely difficult to check. Despite his recent arrival in Mexico, the volatile Cruz wasted little time before he vowed to use terror and mobile counterinsurgency to obliterate opposition.[35] Rebels captured with arms in their hands were taken to towns such as Nopala and Huichapan where they were executed before the assembled populace. Cruz informed Venegas: "Your Excellency, it is no longer possible to suffer more from this vile scum; only examples of exemplary terror will make them understand their duty."[36] Flying detachments received orders to apply a policy of "fire and blood" against any rebel village. Anyone caught with arms, unable to produce a passport, or who acted suspiciously was to be shot and the bodies were to be displayed at the places of execution.[37]

By December, 1810, Cruz had formed three destacamentos volantes financed by a combination of donations, forced contributions, and outright confiscations. These mounted forces employed lightning speed, deception, and the cover of night to confuse the insurgents and to appear in areas where they could strike quickly and withdraw. Villages, haciendas, and ranchos located in rebel zones were stripped of all horses, arms, and weapons,

[35]José de la Cruz to Venegas, 17 November 1810, AGN:OG, vol. 141.
[36]Cruz to Venegas, 27 November 1810, AGN:OG, vol. 141.
[37]Cruz to Venegas, 30 November 1810, AGN:OG, vol. 141.

even small kitchen knives. They rounded up all blacksmiths and destroyed forges which could be employed in the construction of lance points and other weapons.[38] Although the destacamentos volantes of 1810 were a stopgap measure to match the mobility of guerrilla warfare north of Mexico City, the concept took hold as the royalists introduced a thoroughgoing system of counterinsurgency. For most of the decade of war, regular and militia garrisons throughout New Spain operated flying detachments in cooperation with regular army formations. The major weakness of the mobile forces was that the detachment commanders often lacked intelligence data on insurgent activities. Arbitrary punishments, confiscations, and brutalities committed by counterinsurgent troops deepened bitter enmities and created many more enemies than friends. In 1811 veteran criollo officer Colonel José Antonio de Andrade reported that the enemy simply fled from any action and reformed elsewhere. The royalist troops had no idea how to identify insurgents since the campesinos dressed alike and no one gave information for fear of later reprisals.[39]

Despite these weaknesses, the flying detachments or variations on the system worked well in guerrilla insurgent zones where the population was known to be committed and excessive violence by the army posed little danger to royalist interests. In 1816, José de la Cruz operated a series of *cuerpos volantes* south of Guadalajara around the margins of Laguna de Chapala to create a tight cordon designed to prevent the Indians from supplying the rebel island fortress of Mezcala. Amnestied on numerous occasions and never repentant, Cruz described the population as "perfidious, and treacherous—using hypocrisy as their emblem."[40] Elsewhere, the creation of commandancies general in provinces of major guerrilla activity employed many characteristics of the mobile flying companies. In 1814, for example, Viceroy Calleja created a special military province under Colonel José Joaquín Márquez y Donallo, commander of the Regiment of Lobera which embraced portions of the Intendancy of Mexico including the Llanos de Apan, Tulancingo, Pachuca, Otumba, Zempoala, Texcoco, and San Juan Teotihuacán. Small garrisons of regular infantry and dragoons were stationed in each of the towns and the second in command, Major José Barradas, headed a mobile division based at Apan composed of the Light Infantry Regiment of San Luis, a company of Lobera, 75 dragoons of the Regiment of Mexico, 55 dragoons of the Regiment of Querétaro,

[38] Cruz to the Subdelegado of Huichapan, 6 December 1810, AGN:OG, vol. 142; and Instrucción a que deben arreglarse los Comandantes de los destacamentos volantes, December, 1810, AGN:OG, vol. 142.

[39] José Antonio de Andrade to Venegas, Jilotepec, 17 July 1811, AGN:OG, vol. 95.

[40] Instrucciones para los comandantes de los cuerpos volantes que deben establecerse . . . para cubrir toda la orilla de la Laguna de Chapala, 1816, AGN:OG, vol. 151.

and 60 mounted artillerymen with two mobile artillery pieces and a howitzer. The first mission of the mobile force was to crush insurgent congregations and to reorganize the towns. Since the residents had opted for the rebels and withheld taxes for years, they were to be heavily taxed and to provide meat, grain, and other provisions consumed by the royalist troops.[41]

As early as 1811, Félix Calleja realized that a general fragmented insurgency employing guerrilla warfare would rapidly exhaust the available regular and militia units of the royalist army. Certainly as Abad y Queipo charged, it was premature for Calleja to declare a unilateral end to the insurgency. However, by reducing the opposition to bandits, thieves, and delinquents, he sought to gain a propaganda victory. Calleja endeavored to construct a tiered system of counterinsurgent defense that would be based upon patriot militias organized in cities, towns, and rural districts. His Reglamento Político Militar of June 8, 1811, became one of the most important and controversial documents of the counterinsurgency. With his tiered system, Calleja hoped to regain control over the countryside, isolate and marginalize the insurgents, and to harden town defenses so that the lightly armed rebels would not dare attack without artillery. As he explained to the district subdelegados, the army could not dispatch small forces every time a village or hacienda received a threat. The army divisions and flying detachments could not be present everywhere and the people had to take up arms in their own defense.[42] Once this took place, the royalist army would be able to unite scattered garrisons and to concentrate forces against the major foci of insurgency.

Depending upon the districts or towns involved, Calleja's Reglamento Político Militar could be either quite successful or an abject failure. At insurgent-wracked San Miguel, Colonel Diego García Conde organized three companies of 50 men each—one of infantry and two of cavalry. During August, 1811, the militiamen received daily training and appeared to exhibit a positive attitude toward "la justa causa." One of the cavalry companies had some pistols and sabers and the other two companies received lances which were the normal weapons assigned to such units. García Conde embarked upon an ambitious project to manufacture firearms for these militias.

[41]Calleja to José Joaquín Márquez y Donallo, 18 June 1814; and Instrucciones para el Comandante General de Llanos de Apan, 1814, AGN:OG, vol. 530. For other examples see Brian R. Hamnett, "Royalist Counterinsurgency and the Continuity of Rebellion: Guanajuato and Michoacán, 1813–1820," *Hispanic American Historical Review* 62:1 (February 1982), 19–48.

[42]Reglamento político militar que deberán observar bajo las penas que señala los pueblos, haciendas, y ranchos a quienes se comunique por las autoridades legítimas y respectivas . . . , Aguascalientes, 8 June 1811, AGN:OG, vol. 278; and Calleja to the Alcalde of León, Ildefonso Seprién, Guanajuato, 13 August 1811, AGN:OG, vol. 177.

Outside the town, the Indian communities formed two companies and contributed 30 men daily to active duty and more in emergencies.[43]

In contrast with this apparent success, at San Luis de la Paz dependent upon San Miguel, the subdelegado, Antonio de Flon, convened a meeting of 60 men who were to form the town militia. From their looks, all appeared to Flon as frightened and cowardly. None had arms or horses to form cavalry and there was no money available. Later, Flon convoked a junta of the rural hacienda mayordomos and workers. The mayordomos showed up, but explained that the hacienda workers fled " . . . for fear of the army and the insurgents." They said that if they declared for the royalists, they would be killed by the rebels. Since they had to travel alone in the mountains, it seemed likely that they would fall into the clutches of the bands that constantly sacked the haciendas. Flon described the few rancheros who appeared as " . . . absolutely wild men, who in general are malicious, cowardly, and rotten to the heart."[44] His general impressions notwithstanding, Flon explained the benefits of joining "la causa buena" and the evils of not doing so. All listened " . . . with arms crossed and their eyes on the ground." As soon as he released them, one rode out immediately to report the contents of the junta to the rebels at Sichú. Given this state of affairs, Flon recommended against arming such elements until the army dislodged the insurgent bands in the mountains.[45]

One major criticism of Calleja's counterinsurgency plan was that he conceived a design specifically for a region of towns and large rural haciendas where there was sufficient population and financial resources to raise infantry and mounted patriot companies. Calleja called for haciendas of the first class to offer 50 militiamen, second class 35 militiamen, and third class 25 militiamen. In Querétaro province, for example, the haciendas were small and none reached the status of first class. In San Luis Potosí, Calleja's model and home province, the hacienda of Jaral and other estates were vast in magnitude and contained settled populations of up to 11,000 inhabitants. To fund 50 militiamen cost 13,000 pesos annually, 25 men cost 6,500 pesos, and 10 men cost 2,600 pesos. Of the 64 haciendas of Querétaro jurisdiction, not including San Juan del Río, there were only four estates valued at 200,000 pesos that would produce approximately 10,000 pesos annually. Even the largest estates could not afford royalist companies of 50 militiamen. In his 1818 report on Querétaro province, José Miguel Barreiro concluded that recent annual sales from haciendas totaled 3,687,000 pesos, contributing a profit after expenses and taxes of only 184,350 pesos.

[43]Diego García Conde to Calleja, San Miguel, 14 August 1811, AGN:OG, vol. 899.

[44]Antonio de Flon to García Conde, San Luis de la Paz, 13 August 1811, AGN:OG, vol. 899.

[45]Ibid.

Naturally, only part of this sum could be used for militias since a large portion went to the owners for subsistence, payments on debts, and for other obligations.[46] Barreiro pointed out that hacienda owners had also been paying the insurgents special taxes for safety and protection. However, success in the plan to establish royalist companies would allow the hacendados to terminate paying rebel taxes which drained the royalist cause.[47]

The weaknesses of Calleja's Plan Político Militar were even more evident in Veracruz province which became a primary zone of insurgent dominance and of royalist concern. The tropical lowlands and mountainous highlands offered guerrillas every possible advantage. Yellow fever consumed European expeditionary battalions and Mexican highland regiments equally while sparing the indigenous insurgents who enjoyed inborn immunity. As viceroy, Calleja knew that Spanish expeditionaries arriving at the port suffered severe losses to tropical disease and as an experienced commander of Mexican forces, he was fully aware of the terror generated in highlanders by mere mention of *vómito negro.* In 1813, Calleja ordered the governor of Veracruz, José Quevedo, to implement his general counterinsurgency plan and to recruit the coastal inhabitants into patriot companies. Quevedo, like many Veracruz governors before him, resisted a defense program based upon the local population and designed to keep Europeans away from the zones of tropical disease. He wanted the commander of the Army of the South, the Conde de Castro Terreño, to station a flying division in the lowlands to keep the roads inland open and to garrison Puente del Rey.[48]

Almost all of the available arable land in Veracruz province was held by absentee owners. The insurgency, fragmented as in other provinces, took on many aspects of agrarian revolution with the landless peasants attracted to guerrilla warfare as a means to possess land. Since the inhabitants were acclimatized to yellow fever and knew the thick forests, swamps, ravines, and trackless mountains, they evaded counterinsurgency flying divisions. Calleja's Plan Político Militar demanded the proximity of garrisons and of flying divisions in order to strengthen the ability of the organized royalist companies to resist. While the walled city of Veracruz contained a fairly large population, after 1812–1813, the insurgents dominated the villages and countryside beyond its crumbling parapets. Even more significant, the rural and village populations of Veracruz possessed traditions of antigovernment activities and dedication to contraband trading. Unlike many other Mexican insurgents, they enjoyed strong maritime links to New Orleans

[46]A la ciudad de Querétaro le es conducente para el buen orden, José Miguel Barriero, México, 8 August 1818, AGN:OG, vol. 511.

[47]Ibid.

[48]José de Quevedo to Calleja, Veracruz, 5 April 1813; and Calleja to Quevedo, 13 May 1813, AGN:OG, vol. 692.

and access to fairly high quality arms and munitions. After the War of 1812 between Britain and the United States, this traffic brought significant numbers of weapons into the hands of the Mexican rebels.

Urban defense presented innumerable challenges and problems for counterinsurgency planners. Even the best protected cities such as Querétaro were quite porous and exposed to insurgent infiltration. Sometimes this could become extremely embarrassing and dangerous. On the night of February 6, 1818, over 100 insurgent horsemen rode into Querétaro and dashed through the streets to the central palace and square before they departed—hastened along by 20 random cannon shots from the parapets.[49] The placement of guardhouses and barracks had much to do with the lack of security, but fully a third of Querétaro's population resided outside the lines of fortification where they were exposed to rebel incursionists and robbers. At Jalapa, the majority of the plebeian inhabitants lived outside of the precinct guarded by the city parapets. To make matters worse, the gates closed at 9:00 P.M. during summer and at 8:00 P.M. in winter. For a significant portion of the day, the common people locked out of the town were cut off from doctors, medicines, their confessors, and other necessities. There were small entry ports in the gates, but nervous sentinels kept them locked; even if they were open, the entry points were located half way around the town from the main residential district.[50] As in the case of Querétaro, the poor of Jalapa suffered many robberies and assaults. Army patrols lacked the frequency and flexibility to assist civilian victims who were often thought of as insurgent sympathizers. Even at heavily fortified and well defended Puebla, rebel horsemen enjoyed the challenge of mocking urban guards by wreckless rides through the city. On February 15, 1815, at 2:30 A.M., six insurgent horsemen caused a general alarm when they managed to bypass the guardposts, night patrols, and other precautions to appear in the plaza de armas. Finally, sentinels opened fire and the audacious visitors withdrew to a point just outside the city where they were met by about 50 cavalry.[51]

The protection of populous Mexico City from insurgent incursions, spies, and plotters was a counterinsurgent's nightmare. By 1811, the city had been divided into districts with *tenientes de policía* in charge of each. Despite severe difficulties with administration, the police authorities introduced a system of passports. There were few problems with merchants,

[49]Brigadier Domingo Luaces to Viceroy Apodaca, Querétaro, 4 February 1818, AGN:OG, vol. 514.

[50]García Dávila to Viceroy Conde de Venadito (Apodaca), 6 July 1820, no. 72, AGN:OG, vol. 266.

[51]Francisco Palacio to Brigadier José Moreno y Daoiz, Puebla, 15 February 1815; and Calleja to Moreno y Daoiz, 28 February 1815, AGN:OG, vol. 536.

muleteers, and transporters who obtained perpetual passports to allow them to conduct their businesses, but the regime was hard pressed to control the innumerable Indians who came to the city irregularly with vegetables, fruit, and other produce.[52] Soldiers at the sentry posts into Mexico City often required these people to pay bribes for entry whether or not they possessed documents.[53] Within the city, crime increased dramatically during the years of war—murders, assaults, woundings in pulquerías, sexual crimes, thefts, robberies, drunkenness, and many other offenses. Certain that there were spies everywhere, police authorities even worried about suspicious behavior of actors who put on marionette shows and comedies. To advertise their performances, they sent drummers through the city at all hours of the day and night. Antonio Columna of the Tribunal de la Acordada worried that night comedies were a constant source of abuses and were bound to produce "evil consequences."[54]

As might be expected, the presence of a large garrison of soldiers compounded the potential for disorder. Because the regime feared illegal meetings and other gatherings that might signify insurgent plotting, all inhabitants of the capital were encouraged to report anything unusual. In April, 1818, an anonymous complainant named "El Deseoso del Sosiego" reported all-night parties in a building adjoining a wine shop called La Fruta in Calle del Refugio. These events were so wild that the writer described them as a "whores and knaves market." A police raid resulted in the arrest of 40 revelers—a colonel, several subaltern officers, a curate, a friar, and an assortment of civilian women and men.[55] Ordinary soldiers could not afford to spend their time in wine shops. When the pulquerías closed, they congregated in cemeteries or wherever they thought that they might evade the roving patrols. In May, 1820, for example, at 1:00 A.M. vigilance patrol discovered three women, a civilian male, and two drummers from the Regiment of Ordenes Militares "committing lewd acts" in the cemetery of the Bethlemite friars.[56] Although the authorities wished to uphold morals and to prevent soldiers from meeting the large numbers of prostitutes in the city, there were fears of security lapses and of threats posed by insurgent agents. Viceroy Calleja ordered the operators of inns and hostelries to submit daily lists of their guests to the *sargento mayor* of Mexico City.[57]

[52]Agustín Pomposo Fernández to Pedro de la Puente, 28 August 1811, AGN:OG, vol. 671.

[53]Bando del Virrey Venegas, 5 December 1811, AGN:OG, vol. 979.

[54]Antonio Columna, Tribunal de la Acordada, to Venegas, 17 August 1811, AGN:OG, vol. 673.

[55]Anónimo, El deseoso del sosiego to Apodaca, 18 April 1818; and Capitán de Comisarios Antonio Acuña to Apodaca, 19 April 1818, AGN:OG, vol. 599.

[56]Report of José Salazar, Compañía de Policía, 26 May 1820, AGN:OG, vol. 597.

[57]José Juan Fagoaga to Calleja, 1 October 1815, AGN:OG, vol. 596.

From the beginning of the counterinsurgency war, there was danger that in a futile struggle to combat the fragmented revolution, the royalist army would subdivide itself into impotence. Calleja's Plan Político Militar was to have given the tiered defensive system a broad rural and urban base. Unfortunately for royalist interests, however, the insurgency endured to erode the best guarded provincial defenses. In Veracruz province and the vast region to the south and west of Guadalajara, Valladolid, and Mexico City, just to mention two of the permanent guerrilla foci, the insurgents exercised complete control except during periodic sweeps by large regular army divisions. As early as 1812, Calleja wanted to concentrate many of the dispersed garrisons into two armies of the North and South. He worried about loss of discipline, laxity, and the development of vices among soldiers separated from their regimental or battalion commanders.[58] The units of the Army of the Center which had crushed the first phase of the rebellion were broken up and parceled out in companies to garrison provinces, to provide convoy service, or to organize the various flying detachments. Away from their regimental headquarters and command structure, companies deteriorated quickly and soldiers forgot their discipline. Counterinsurgency was difficult when some of the best cavalry units lost their horses and equipment.[59] Even the Spanish expeditionary regiments and battalions ended up divided and dispersed in many different locations.

Although senior officers complained bitterly about the difficulties with military administration, recruitment, and deterioration of discipline, Viceroy Apodaca saw no alternatives in a war against fragmented guerrilla bands spread over the surface of an enormous country.[60] In 1818, Colonel Matías de Aguirre of the Regiment of Dragones Fieles de Potosí informed Apodaca that he had lost touch with many detachments from his regiment and could not report on the state of some squadrons and companies. Men of the regiment had been mobilized in 1810 and marched off into action where they had remained for eight years. Their officers were unschooled in preparing status reports and accustomed only to chasing guerrilla bands.[61] Sub-Inspector General Fernando Miyares Mancebo noted that it was common in Mexico to have a division of 1,000 troops formed of as many as eleven different units. The results for training and discipline were "monstrous." Separated officers charged enormous debts to units that were

[58] Calleja to Venegas, 11 February 1812, AGN:OG, vol. 165.

[59] Calleja to the Minister of War, no. 14, 5 September 1813, Archivo General Militar de Segovia (cited hereinafter as AGMS), Ramo de Ultramar, leg. 232.

[60] Apodaca to Brigadier Pascual de Liñan, 1 September 1818, AGN:OG, vol. 488; and Liñan to Venadito, 3 January 1820, AGN:OG, vol. 493.

[61] Liñan to Apodaca, no. 1561, 27 October 1818, AGN:OG, vol. 501.

not inspected or audited. By 1820, José de la Cruz warned that subdivision of army units had created dangerous vulnerability that could lead to disaster.[62]

As so often occurs in counterinsurgency conflicts, the royalist army of New Spain sacrificed its strength in efforts to hold down the country and to chase guerrilla bands. After 1816 Spain no longer dispatched new expeditionary battalions, leaving the Mexican royalist army without sufficient operational forces to crush the major guerrilla strongholds. Lacking continued infusions of dynamic fresh battalions to stiffen morale and to lead offensive operations exhaustion became a factor of increasing significance.[63] Aware of the developing stalemate, between 1816 and 1821 Viceroy Apodaca initiated a new program to amnesty insurgents and to convince the world that the revolt was ending. While he convinced many contemporary observers and later historians that he had discovered a better means to pacify insurgency, the reality of the situation proved quite different.

Beginning in 1816, many historians have identified a lull in the independence war. Lucas Alamán described a situation in which the royalist army backed by the hammer of effective counterinsurgency repression restored communications and set Apodaca's amnesty machinery on the right track. With the liquidation of Javier Mina, and the destruction of a number of important rebel fortifications, Alamán declared the insurgency ended except for minor mopping up operations against small bands in the mountainous zones of Veracruz and the region south and west of Jalisco and Michoacán.[64] More recently, Timothy Anna declared that " . . . the restoration of royal power over New Spain was a remarkable achievement, one of the Spanish Empire's greatest victories."[65] Brian Hamnett noted that " . . . by the end of 1819 the insurgency consisted of little more than raiding parties dedicated to the theft of cattle and horses."[66] These historians, and many others, may be described as supporting "the lull theory" of the latter stages of Mexico's independence period. Backing their interpretation were Apodaca's confident dispatches of victories, impressive lists of insurgents applying for amnesties, and effective royalist army counterinsurgency in some regions. There is no doubt that many contemporary administrators and army officers believed these indicators of victory. In fact, the apparent royalist victory was a will-o'-the-

[62]Cruz to Venadito, 4 October 1820, AGN:OG, vol. 157.

[63]For one interesting comparison, see Alister Horne, *A Savage War of Peace: Algeria, 1954–1962* (London, 1977).

[64]Lucas Alamán, *Historia de Méjico* (Mexico, 1969), IV, 287, 409.

[65]Timothy E. Anna, *The Fall of the Royal Government in Mexico City* (Lincoln, 1978), 179. See pp. 179–187.

[66]Hamnett, "Royalist Counterinsurgency and the Continuity of Rebellion," 46.

wisp illusion that was not substantiated by reality. Exhaustion after six, seven, or eight years of debilitating guerrilla war made some royalists and some rebels willing to recognize a status quo.

After 1816, there were fewer large insurgent forces remaining in the field. While Apodaca celebrated this fact, he misunderstood the real nature of the fragmented revolution. Throughout New Spain, the insurgents had broken up into smaller units that continued autonomous existence in their regions and, in some cases, maintained loose ties with the isolated guerrilla foci. While the army sought to chase down "escaped" communities and to concentrate populations, there was simply too much territory to cover and too few soldiers. Where the royalist army managed to exert superior force, the rebels accepted amnesties, entered the provincial defense structure in their units, and waited for new opportunities. In some respects, Apodaca disregarded negative information that should have caused him to be less sanguine about the future. In 1815, the Veracruz insurgents became so strong that they were able to blockade the road between Jalapa and the port for months. One convoy languished in Jalapa for almost half a year.[67] The Consulado of Veracruz referred to "a mortal paralysis" of internal and external trade, attacking the royalist army for its military failures and repressive policies.[68] Travelers and merchants paid insurgent taxes for the right to move while the army responded with an inefficient and ineffective program of escorted convoys.[69]

Matters reached such a low state that the imperial government became extremely worried about New Spain. Severed communications and pleas from Veracruz merchants caused major changes in military planning. An expedition of almost 2,000 troops, consisting of the Infantry Regiments of Ordenes Militares and Voluntarios de Navarra, under Field Marshal Pascual de Liñan and Brigadier Fernando Miyares y Mancebo, ready to sail from Cádiz for Peru was redirected by the minister of war to Veracruz. The imperial government ordered General Pablo Morillo to dispatch 4,000 troops from his expeditionary army in Venezuela and the transfer of some acclimatized Mexican soldiers from Havana back to New Spain. While not all of these units reached Veracruz, the imperial war ministry placed major emphasis upon opening communications between Veracruz and Mexico City and in garrisoning a defended "camino militar" that could repel the Veracruz insurgents.[70] Even with this massive pressure, the army could only temporarily contain these guerrillas. By 1818, the rebels of the fragmented

[67]Consulado of Veracruz to Calleja, 13 April 1815, AGN:OG, vol. 216.

[68]Consulado of Veracruz to the Secretary of State, 23 June 1815, AGN:OG, vol. 216.

[69]Brigadier José Quevedo to Calleja, 27 March 1815, AGN:OG, vol. 699.

[70]Xavier Abadía to the Governor of Veracruz, Cádiz, 7 April 1815, AGN:OG, vol. 699; and Miyares y Mancebo to Abadía, Veracruz, 2 August 1815, AGMS, Ultramar, leg. 226.

bands coalesced once again to interdict commerce and to apply their system of tolls. Viceroy Venadito had to dispatch Field Marshal Pascual de Liñan to assume the interim governorship of Veracruz with orders to introduce a new program to establish fortified villages, to amnesty rebels, and to search out and destroy recalcitrant insurgent bands.[71]

If Veracruz province suffered a constant and bitter confrontation rather than a lengthy period of lull, the same was true in some other significant regions. In July, 1818, José de la Cruz reported frequent insurgent incursions from the mountains of Guanajuato, "the seedbed of rebellion," into the districts surrounding Valladolid and Guadalajara. Similarly, the region south of Valladolid and Uruapan became the base for small bands that coalesced to raid Nueva Galicia. While they numbered only approximately 1,430 men, Cruz noted that they were "old and resolved insurgents."[72] He underscored the need for total dedication by counterinsurgent forces that had to emulate guerrilla tactics and to be ready to live in the sierras for lengthy periods. Cruz saw little use for fruitless chases that went on for 15 or 20 days, only to end with the insurgents still on the loose. He criticized royalist commanders who believed that the countryside was pacified because they occupied a fortified town. Always quite perceptive about counterinsurgency, Cruz understood that there was not sufficient force both to pacify the regions and to contain and repress the inhabitants.[73] He was particularly upset by the fact that after years of conflict both royalists and rebels accepted a status quo and spheres of influence to permit active commercial exchanges. Army patrols in mountainous districts often encountered merchants, muleteers, and travelers from royalist zones who engaged in trade with insurgent-occupied areas.[74]

Although the royalists did manage to pacify some provinces, insurgent activities were by no means confined to isolated mountainous regions far from settled populations. In February, 1816, Pedro el Negro with about 55 insurgents attacked the village of Nononalco near Tacuba just outside Mexico City. He went to the house of his cousin, a loyal realista of the Tacubaya companies, whom he robbed and hacked to death before the rebels fled.[75] On the night of May 27, 1816, mounted insurgents appeared near the royalist powder magazines at Chapultepec. The royalist garrison fired 484 cartridges before the guerrillas withdrew. This audacious attack followed a series of raids against flour mills and against the first houses at Tacubaya

[71]Liñan to Venadito, 22 April 1819, AGN:OG, vol. 490.

[72]Cruz to Apodaca, 18 December 1818, AGN:OG, vol. 155. For a useful regional study, see Jaime Olveda, *Gordiano Guzmán: un cacique del siglo XIX* (Mexico, 1980), 81–82.

[73]Cruz to Apodaca, 10 July 1818, AGN:OG, vol. 154.

[74]Cruz to Apodaca, 26 December 1818, AGN:OG, vol. 155.

[75]Sargento Mayor José Mendivil to Calleja, 22 February 1816, AGN:OG, vol. 596.

on the outskirts of the capital. One of these was directed against the main buildings of the Hacienda de los Morales, today a famous Mexico City restaurant in Polanco district.[76]

The fact of the matter was that there was no general lull in the ten years' war of New Spain. In 1818 at Querétaro, Brigadier Luaces reported that bands of 200 to 300 insurgents almost daily assaulted various targets, mostly against the haciendas of the district. The constant pressure exhausted and frightened the local militia companies. Luaces described a state of exhaustion that infected his command. Despite constant patrols and pursuits, he reported that the haciendas were " . . . isolated, destroyed, sacked and ruined." The troops of Querétaro garrison had too many missions. Luaces asked for a regiment of dragoons to form flying detachments that might recover the outlying haciendas from rebel control.[77] However, efforts to recruit replacements for the Querétaro units accomplished little more than to provoke a flight of young men out of the city.[78]

Given this situation, the morale and psychological mood of the counterinsurgent army faltered. Even in the European expeditionary battalions and regiments, feelings of hopelessness and anger made the soldiers listless and amenable to desertion. Financial crisis in the general treasury and in army taxation further exacerbated the demoralization. During the so-called lull period, the viceregal government failed to make regular salary and maintenance payments to army units, leaving some in desperate financial need. In August 1818, for example, the treasury owed the Infantry Regiment of Zaragoza 14,000 pesos in back payments. The situation became so bad that officers borrowed money to help pay their men for daily provisions. Although uniforms, shoes, and equipment had deteriorated over years of hard usage, there was no money available for repairs and replacements. Some units reported that, due to their indecent nakedness, the soldiers were embarrassed to appear in public.[79] Disgruntled soldiers circulated anonymous papers and petitions criticizing their officers and demanding better treatment. On some occasions, ridiculous rumors spread through units that would have been dismissed during normal times. Desertion depleted a flying detachment north of Zacatecas when the soldiers suspected that they were being marched to Perote where they would be traded into slavery for cloth! Although the commander exhorted them to remember their oaths of loyalty and told them that they were destined only for Aguascalientes, 70 men including some noncommissioned officers deserted in two nights.[80]

[76]Mendivil to Calleja, 13 March 1816; and 22 July 1816, AGN:OG, vol. 596.
[77]Luaces to Apodaca, Querétaro, 4 February 1818, AGN:OG, vol. 514.
[78]Liñan to Apodaca, no. 1833, n.d., 1818, AGN:OG, vol. 486.
[79]Liñan to Apodaca, no. 1032, 6 August 1818, AGN:OG, vol. 499.
[80]Brigadier José Gayangos to Apodaca, 23 May 1818, AGN:OG, vol. 584.

Given these developments, the collapse of the counterinsurgency army may have appeared predictable. However, there were many other factors that accelerated the process even further. Venadito's urgent requests in 1818 for 3,000 replacements from Spain to fill the depleted expeditionary battalions came to nothing. Mired in its own developing crisis, the imperial cabinet continued to delay the matter until 1821 when it was much too late to send reinforcements.[81] Insubordination and rebellion within the Spanish metropolitan army prevented the dispatch of any new units to save the disintegrating colony. Summing up the situation, the Consejo de Guerra in Madrid felt that it was impotent to act; there was no sense sending new units to America. Without good morale, discipline, and obedience, the soldiers would desert or surrender without a fight.[82]

Spain's crisis had an even greater immediate impact upon the ability of the Mexican royalist army to maintain its tiered counterinsurgency system. While historians have recognized the significance for Mexico of the liberal revolt of Rafael Riego in January, 1820, which led to the restoration of the Spanish Constitution of 1812, it was not the radicalism of the new Spanish regime that caused a backlash in conservative Mexico. The Constitution permitted towns and cities throughout Mexico to cast off the crushing burden of local taxation required to support the royalist military system. After ten years of counterinsurgency, the taxes to support the army weighed unbearably upon all segments of the population. Taxes, called *arbitrios de milicias*, increased the costs of food, commercial transactions, manufactured goods, and mine output, and inflated the costs of whatever economic activities took place in a specific district or province. At the local level, juntas appointed by town *ayuntamientos* searched for new ways to tax regional and urban populations for military support. These needs included the construction of fortifications, purchases of arms, uniforms, mounts, and utensils, and the debilitating expenditures required to pay garrison troops in case the guerrillas attacked.

Throughout royalist zones, the juntas and the regional commanders surveyed the population to levy *contribuciones militares* or wealth taxes upon all inhabitants depending upon their total assets.[83] Over the war

[81]José de Ymar to the Secretrio de Hacienda de Indias, Palacio, 5 October 1819, Archivo General de Indias, Ramo de México, leg. 2420; and Report of the Consejo de Guerra, 1 September 1821, Madrid, AGMS, Ultramar, leg. 227.

[82]Report of the Consejo de Guerra, 1 September 1821, Madrid, AGMS, Ultramar, leg. 227.

[83]For the origins of the military support system, see José Moreno y Daoíz to Valleja, no. 300, Puebla, 10 March 1815, AGN:OG, vol. 536; and Christon I. Archer, "Not with a Bang but a Whimper: The Decline and Defeat of the Royalist Army of New Spain," paper presented at the Midwest Association of Latin American Studies, St. Louis, Missouri, October 1986; and "Where Did All of the Royalists Go? New Light on the Military Collapse

years, sources of funds dried up and many formerly prosperous landowners, miners, merchants, and artisians were left destitute. Some individuals who possessed estates occupied by insurgents or abandoned in war zones initiated legal proceedings to stop juntas that appraised their assets at high values and then levied taxes that had to be paid in specie. As was always the case, the poor suffered the brunt of arbitrary and violent acts by the tax collectors. In many instances, those Indians, even women, who lacked a half *real* or *real* were stripped of their "miserable rags" and left naked in the streets. The ayuntamiento of Miacatlán reported that some men committed suicide rather than endure cruel treatment and threats of the tax collectors.[84] Needless to say, many more men chose life with the rebels rather than meet continuous exactions by the royalist tax collectors.

Almost spontaneously, the base level of Calleja's tiered defense structure collapsed. Through 1820, horrified regional commanders passively witnessed a process that they could not arrest. All over royalist Mexico, viceregal orders and insistence that the Constitution had not altered military support taxes fell upon deaf ears.[85] Everyone argued that the Constitution abolished the existing militia structure and decreed the establishment of a new national militia system. Urban and rural companies evaporated, leaving a vacuum that the royalist army simply could not fill. With the appearance of Agustín de Iturbide, a large part of the army joined his Plan de Iguala, while the remainder abandoned its garrisons and literally imploded upon Mexico City. Much of Mexico was stripped of any royalist forces based in the towns and districts to resist the many new insurgencies or regenerated insurgencies that now operated in the name of Iturbide. From Puebla, Brigadier Ciricao de Llano felt a little ironic satisfaction when towns that had disbanded their defense forces complained to him that they had been robbed and raided by Iturbide's guerrillas.[86]

After over ten years of insurgency and counterinsurgency, independence came with shocking speed and finality. As is so often the case, the defeat of the counterinsurgent army was definitive. Iturbide's rebellion permitted a rapid shift from the stage of insurgent guerrilla bands to a conventional confrontation that ended the war. Concentration of village populations of amnestied insurgents formed excellent pools of recruits for Iturbide and new insurgent leaders. Efforts by royalist commanders, such as Pascual

---

of New Spain, 1810–1822," in Jaime E. Rodríguez O., ed., *The Mexican and the Mexican American Experience in the Nineteenth Century* (Tempe, 1989), 23–43.

[84]Ayuntamiento of Miacatlán to Presidente y vocales de la Exma. Diputacíon Provincial de México, 4 November 1820, AGN:OG, vol. 455. Many similar complaints could be listed of mistreatment directed against the poor.

[85]Ayuntamiento of Jilotepec to the Intendente de México, Ramón Gutiérrez de Mazo, 8 February 1821, AGN:OG, vol. 455.

[86]Llano to Venadito, no. 1292, AGN:OG, vol. 326.

de Liñan, to introduce land reform programs in Veracruz province came too late to have any impact on the outcome of the war. Corruption and loss of mission left most of the royalist army incapable of further sustained resistance. Moreover, Iturbide absorbed so much of the royalist army that the final struggle was anticlimactic. However, Iturbide's victory and the arrival of Mexican independence obscured the fact that few if any of the insurgents involved in the fragmented revolution achieved their goals. With changed names and slightly altered institutions, Mexico began its independent life without having solved any of the basic questions behind the struggle. These remained for the future.

Quetzalcóatl, King Ferdinand, and Ignacio Allende Go to the Seashore; or Messianism and Mystical Kingship in Mexico, 1800–1821

Eric Van Young

In the years around 1810 Indian country people all over central Mexico seem to have been awaiting some sort of a messiah to lead them to a more perfect time and place, ill-defined or unconscious as these hopes may have been. Popular messianic hopes had not arisen, of course, just with the eruption of Miguel Hidalgo's revolt. The year 1801 may even have marked the advent of an Indian millennium in Mexico, or so it seemed to substantial numbers of village-dwelling peasants in the western central area of the country and in parts of the near north. In the very first years of the new century rumors of conspiracy, foreign invasion, Indian saviors and kings, and massive rural uprising ricocheted about the countryside. At least two Indian pseudo-messiahs were reported to have appeared, one in the area of Durango and another near Tepic, evoking near-hysterical responses from the central authorities in Mexico City and weary embarrassment on the part of these same authorities when no massive insurrections materialized.[1] The Tepic episode, occurring in the twilight years of Spanish

[1]For a detailed discussion of the Durango messiah, see Eric Van Young, "Millennium on the Northern Marches: The Mad Messiah of Durango and Popular Rebellion in Mexico, 1800–1815," *Comparative Studies in Society and History*, 28 (1986), 385–413. The Indian "uprisings" of the Tepic area are dealt with by Christon I. Archer, *El ejército en el México borbónico, 1760–1810* (Mexico, 1983), 132–135. Important documentation on the Tepic episode is to be found in Biblioteca Pública del Estado, Fondos Especiales, Guadalajara (hereafter BPE), Criminal, paquete 34, exp. 9, ser. 763, 1801–1806. Other documentary references include Archivo General de la Nación, México, Mexico City (hereafter AGN), Historia, vol. 428, fols. 37r–76r, 1801; AGN, Historia, vol. 413, exp. 5, fols. 248r–339r, 1801; AGN, Infidencias, vol. 13, exp. 6, fols. 125r–155r, 1816–1817; and AGN, Indiferente de Guerra, vol. 46A, no pagination, 1801. I am grateful to Christon Archer for bringing some of these sources to my attention. Lic. Juan López, official city historian (*cronista*) of Guadalajara, has done the community of historical scholars an invaluable service by publishing the massive documentation on the Mariano rebellion still to be found in the Archivo General de Indias, Seville, along with a useful

colonial rule in Mexico, had a number of predecessors in the form of messianic/millenarian movements among the rural Indians of the country. One may thus legitimately speak of a long tradition of such collective manifestations beginning immediately after the conquest and stretching through the eighteenth century, with something of a hiatus after about the early 1760s.[2]

In a doubly sharp irony, in many instances around 1810 these messianic hopes were focused on the ferociously reactionary figure of the Spanish King Ferdinand VII ("El Deseado" – "The Longed-for One"), who would have found himself perfectly in sympathy with the ruthless military repression carried out in his own name by some royalist commanders in New Spain. One group of captured young Indian rebels from Celaya, for instance, believed that the King had appeared in the countryside near their village in a mysterious dark coach and had enjoined them, through the headman (*gobernador*) of their village, to kill the viceroy and all other European-born Spaniards and divide their property among the poor. A woman from a village near Cuautla told her neighbors that the King was traveling in the company of Father Hidalgo and was wearing a silver mask. In the late winter of 1810 and spring of 1811 King Ferdinand VII was variously reported to be approaching Cuauhtitlán, or with Ignacio Allende's insurgent forces at Querétaro.[3] The King was masked; he was invisible; he was traveling alone in a closed coach; he was with Hidalgo or Allende; he was working in concert with the Virgin of Guadalupe to defeat the Spanish armies. And yet while much of the Mexican countryside was awash with this amalgam of rumor, hope, and messianic expectation centering on the King of Spain or (as we shall see) surrogate figures, Indian peasants were brutally assassinating European-born Spaniards in village jacqueries and on back-country roads. Thus we are faced with an apparent sharp contradiction between two elements of collective belief and their associated forms of social action: the monarch, the archetypal figure of instrusive

---

in Juan López, ed. *La rebelión del Indio Mariano – un movimiento insurgente en la Nueva Galicia, en 1801; y, documentos procesales*, 3 vols. (Guadalajara, 1985).

[2]For an interesting and exceedingly suggestive treatment of four such figures and their followers, see Serge Gruzinski, *Les Hommes-dieux du Mexique. Pouvoir indien et société, XVIe-XVIIIe siècles* (Paris, 1985); and for a discussion of messianic/millenarian elements in the Tzeltal revolt in early eighteenth-century Chiapas, Robert Wasserstrom, *Class and Society in Central Chiapas* (Berkeley, 1983), 76–86 and passim.

[3]AGN, Criminal, vol. 134, exp. 3, no pagination, 1810; vol. 175, no exp. no., fols. 369r–392v, 1811; vol. 204, exp. 10, fols. 191r–205v, 1811; vol. 194, exp. 1, fols. 1r–13r, 1811. The figure of the messianic, disguised king ("*el encubierto*") is familiar from Spanish history, as Angus MacKay points out in his interesting paper "Ritual, Violence, and Authority in Castile," delivered at the Bronowski Renaissance Symposium: The Art of Empire – Culture and Authority in the Spanish Empire, 1500–1650, University of California, San Diego, April 1986.

and oppressive colonial authority, was being venerated with messianic fervor while European-born colonists were being slaughtered with an almost ritualistic enthusiasm.[4]

The central question examined in this paper is: how did Indian messianism function as an element of popular ideology in the Mexican struggles for independence from Spain? More concretely, an approach to this issue can help us begin to resolve the interesting contradiction embodied in the messiah-king/victim-Spaniard opposition. In answer to the question I will develop the following hypothesis: that messianic belief within the context of large-scale political upheaval functioned to focus popular—that is to say, largely Indian and peasant—energies on the struggle for a political break with Spain, but for reasons very different from those of the elite creole ideologues of the movement, and even in substantial degree opposed to them. It is my contention, in fact, that Indian messianic hopes represented a primitive political irredentism: a basically conservative, even reactionary, ideology combining elements of naive monarchical legitimism with those of a rigidly localocentric world view, a kind of spontaneous peasant Fourierism. I shall be concerned in this paper with accounting somehow for the centrality of notions of mystical kingship in linking ideas about social structure, political constitution and legitimacy, and religion. It is this concept largely that provided the interface between elite and popular idealogy, and which allowed apparently concerted action at certain points. Behind it, however, lay very different goals and ideas about the structure of social and political relationships. Furthermore, the different forms messianism took in different regions of colonial Mexico indicate a good deal about the spatially and temporally uneven process of acculturation which took place during the colonial period. Finally, the fact that one sees messianism linked to mystical kingship in popular ideology, and in *no instance* to a full-blown millenarian formulation, but only to the vaguest of programs provides some hints as to the overall shape of colonial popular culture

[4]Numerous instances of what I have elsewhere described as almost ritualistic, preternaturally violent assassinations occurred; some of the more spectacular examples are to be found in AGN, Criminal, vol. 299, no exp. no., fols. 263r–413v, 1811, and vol. 231, exp. 1, fols. 1r–59r, 1811, both on the same case; AGN, Criminal, vol. 156, no exp. no., fols. 20r–167v, 175r–416v, 432r–450v, 521r–530v, 1810; vol. 147, exp. 15, fols. 443r–574v, 1810; and vol. 26, exp. 9, no pagination, 1818. These and other examples are discussed and analyzed in Eric Van Young, "Who Was That Masked Man, Anyway?: Popular Symbols and Ideology in the Mexican Wars of Independence," Rocky Mountain Council on Latin American Studies, Annual Meeting, *Proceedings* (Las Cruces, New Mexico, 1984), I, 18–35, and "Millennium on the Northern Marches." Jan Szeminski, in his analysis of the Túpac Amaru rebellion in Peru (1780–1782), "Why Kill The Spaniard? New Perspectives on Andean Insurrectionary Ideology in the Eighteenth Century" (unpublished ms., 1986), cites evidence of similar savagery, including dismemberment, sexual mutilation, the eating of hearts and blood, and so forth, linking such behavior to religious ideas.

and the world view of major segments of the Mexican population. In examining my hypothesis I shall look first at the evidence concerning the cultural antecedents of popular messianic beliefs—at the necessary but not sufficient preconditions, as it were, for the development and activation of such ideas at the end of the colonial period, and then at the concrete manifestations of these ideological elements and their meanings within the political context of the revolt for independence from Spain.[5]

The connection in Western religious/eschatological thought of the millennium with a cyclical closure or recurrence in time is too well known to require extended comment. Indeed, the idea of the Second Coming itself partakes of such a circularity, even though the outcome of this central event of Christian eschatology, in which messiah and millennium are inextricably associated, is traditionally thought to be an end of history, a kind of perfect stasis, and not the initiation of a new cycle.[6] This is a particularly notable characteristic of the nativistic or revitalization movements which have frequently sprung up in the ex-colonial world, and which often assume the form of messianic/millenarian cults or uprisings. In such collective fantasies the perfect age to come may appear as a regeneration, the recovery by oppressed social groups of what has previously been lost—political autonomy, economic resources, cultural integrity, cosmological coherence, and so forth—so that, in Sylvia Thrupp's words, "time [is] being bent back . . . to recapture some state of harmony in which the world began."[7]

[5]It should be stressed that the conjunctural circumstances which gave rise to popular protest and rebellion in this relatively short period—long-term changes in demographic and agrarian structures, market conditions, short-term conditions of dearth in the countryside, the political crisis in Napoleonic Europe and the attendant loss of legitimacy by the Spanish colonial regime, and so forth—are not dealt with here, but only the associated messianic expressions and the reasons for messianic object-choice.

[6]The basic New Testament source on the advent of the Millennium is Revelations 20. Stimulating discussions of millenarian doctrines upon which I have leaned heavily, though not exclusively, in the present treatment are to be found in Norman Cohn, *The Pursuit of the Millennium: Revolutionary Messianism in Medieval and Reformation Europe and its Bearing on Modern Totalitarian Movements*, 2d ed. (New York, 1961), esp. 1–32; Sylvia L. Thrupp, "Introduction," in Sylvia L. Thrupp, ed., *Millennial Dreams in Action: Studies in Revolutionary Religious Movements* (New York, 1970), 11–27; Norman Cohn, "Medieval Millenarism: Its Bearing on the Comparative Study of Millenarian Movements," in ibid., 31–43; George Shepperson, "The Comparative Study of Millenarian Movements," in ibid., 44–52; Janos Bak and Gerhard Benecke, "Introduction," in Bak and Benecke, eds., *Religion and Rural Revolt* (Manchester, 1984), 2–13 (and the other essays in that volume); J.F.C. Harrison, *The Second Coming: Popular Millenarianism, 1780–1850* (London, 1979), esp. 1–54; Jacques Lafaye, *Mesías, cruzadas, utopías: el judeo-cristianismo en las sociedades ibéricas* (Mexico, 1984), 7–26 and passim; Michael Adas, *Prophets of Rebellion: Millenarian Protest Movements against the European Colonial Order* (Chapel Hill, 1979); and Eric J. Hobsbawm, *Primitive Rebels: Studies in Archaic Forms of Social Movement in the 19th and 20th Centuries* (New York, 1959).

[7]Thrupp, "Introduction," 12; and on revitalization movements in general, see the remarks of Adas, *Prophets of Rebellion*, xvii–xxi.

How much more powerful must the appeal of such doctrines be, therefore, if they resonate strongly with an indigenous intellectual and religious tradition of cyclical cosmology, even if the latter has been systematically suppressed in the name of a hegemonic evangelical Christianity?

Such a resonance was, in fact, one of the major antecedents of popular messianic belief in late colonial Mexico, and played an important role in the link between messianic expectation and collective violence. As with the cyclical aspect of millennial belief, the cyclical (or perhaps helical, Aztec thought allowing for some evolution) nature of Mesoamerican cosmological thought is familiar enough to require only brief comment here.[8] Intertwined with this cyclical view of time there existed a strong mythico-historical tradition of man-gods and messianic prophecy, stretching back through the Mesoamerican Classic era and embodied most strikingly in the figure of Quetzalcóatl, a pan-Mesoamerican deity who was also regarded as having been a real historical figure. Exactly how explicitly or widely preserved by the eighteenth century were the Aztec traditions of cyclical cosmology and messianic expectation is impossible to determine given the conditions prevailing in the colony and the surviving documentation, but it seems likely that they existed side by side with other beliefs (shamanism, for example) as part of the substrate of Indian popular culture.[9] At the very least such beliefs would have predisposed large segments of the colony's rural masses, in times of stress, to form the highly cathected relationship with a single charismatic figure typical of messianism.[10]

The enduring matrix of popular messianic expectation, however, was only one of the ingredients in the singular alchemy of collective action. Another was the existence and wide recognition among the colonial rural masses of a protective, patriarchal tradition of monarchical government at whose center stood the quasi-thaumaturgical figure of the Spanish King

[8]See, for example, Miguel León-Portilla, *Aztec Thought and Culture: A Study of the Ancient Nahuatl Mind* (Norman, 1963); Laurette Sejourné, *Burning Water: Thought and Religion in Ancient Mexico* (London, 1957); Jacques Soustelle, *La Pensée cosmologique des anciens mexicains* (Paris, 1940); and Burr Cartwright Brundage, *The Fifth Sun: Aztec Gods, Aztec World* (Austin, 1979).

[9]For the notion of such a cultural substrate among an Indian group both in colonial and modern times, see Victoria Reifler Bricker, *The Indian Christ, the Indian King: The Historical Substrate of Maya Myth and Ritual* (Austin, 1981).

[10]Gruzinski suggests that the mythico-historical lineage of the "hommes-dieux" in fact ended among the Nahuas about 1403 (a century before the Spanish conquest) because of the need for political stabilization in central Mexico, thus divorcing political power and divinity to a certain degree. Of the Aztec imperial leadership (*tlatoani*) of the fifteenth and sixteenth centuries he writes: "Tournant les dos aux héroes culturels, aux Quetzalcóatl, ils esquissent la figure de despote et evoluent vers des formes que l'on pourrait qualifier d'absolutistes" (*Les Hommes-dieux du Mexique*, 18–19). I shall return to this argument below.

himself. The great rambling edifice of royal Indian protectionism constructed piecemeal during the three centuries of colonial rule leaked like a sieve, to be sure, and laws for the protection of the Indian populations were frequently honored more in the breach than in the observance. Nonetheless, the Indians of New Spain (and elsewhere) enjoyed protections which significantly interfered with their complete integration into colonial society, and kept them in a legal bubble of tutelage ruptured only with the advent of independent Mexican nationhood in the third decade of the nineteenth century.[11]

On the negative side this protected status meant demeaning tribute payments, a serious abridgment of civil rights, and perennial interference in Indian affairs from secular and ecclesiastical authorities. But on the positive side it meant exemption from certain kinds of taxes, generally more lenient criminal penalties than meted out to non-Indians, a high degree of municipal political autonomy (the interference mentioned above notwithstanding), access to a special court system, and so forth.[12] Where legal remedies were applied in favor of the Indians of colonial New Spain, they were applied in the King's name. Furthermore, religious and civic ritual of all kinds constantly stressed the centrality of the Spanish King to the colonial commonweal, and his benevolence and fatherly concern with the welfare of his weakest subjects.[13] Such associations surely contributed powerfully to popular veneration of the Spanish King, especially among the Indians who often sheltered under his protective, patriarchal mantle, and made of his figure a preeminent candidate for messianic expectation.

In addition to considerations of politics, culture, and cosmology, we must take into account the particular social and intellectual circumstances under which the mass of rural Indians lived in Mexico at the close of the colonial period. While it is true that messianic and millenarian movements have been common enough in the West and in Western-dominated areas of the world since the medieval period, it is also true that in terms of mainstream religious belief these cults and movements must be regarded

[11]On the legal status of Indians, see, among others, Paulino Castañeda Delgado, "La condición miserable del indio y sus privilegios," *Anuario de Estudios Americanos*, 28 (1971), 245–335.

[12]For an exhaustive and fascinating treatment of the General Indian Court, an institution unique to New Spain, see Woodrow W. Borah, *Justice by Insurance: The General Indian Court of Colonial Mexico and the Legal Aides of the Half-Real* (Berkeley, 1983).

[13]Indeed, the King occupied an almost suprapolitical position in the Spanish political tradition, and often remained inviolate in the midst of popular rebellion, his authority being split off from the legitimacy of government, as in the traditional cry of rebels and rioters, "Long live the King! Death to bad government!" For a thoughtful treatment of this political habit of mind in the New World, see John L. Phelan, *The People and the King: The Comunero Revolution in Colombia, 1781* (Madison, 1978); and see also MacKay, "Ritual, Violence, and Authority."

as heterodox, even (or most especially) if they adapt, distort, or invert ideological elements from orthodox religious thought. Many observers of such collective phenomena have noted that they tend to flourish in culturally "backward" or isolated areas or among marginal or transitional populations, where heterodox beliefs or older cultural elements are likely to persist.[14] Heterodox belief, a longstanding tradition of religious syncretism, lack of education, and geographical and cultural isolation were certainly typical of large parts of New Spain even at the end of the colonial period. The characterization of the rural Indians constantly repeated by many parish priests and local officials at the end of the colonial period—that they were ignorant, lazy, drunken, vicious sodomites, naturally prone to violence, barbarism, and rebellion—must certainly be taken with a large grain of salt.[15] Nonetheless, there is plentiful evidence that ignorance and heterodoxy, or at the very least an exceedingly imperfect understanding of approved religious teachings, was widespread, and it seems reasonable to assume that these conditions provided an environment nourishing to messianic beliefs.

Institutions of secular education—village schools— for Indians and other country-dwellers were common in New Spain at the close of the colonial period, but they seem to have achieved indifferent results at best. Aside from village financial constraints, Indian attitudes about non-Indians (schoolmasters were often drawn from this group) living in their villages, resistance to acculturation, and the oft-mentioned need to have children working in the fields and other productive activities rather than attending school made school attendance very low and progress in educating Indian children slow or nonexistent.[16]

[14]For example, in analyzing millenarian movements in modern Brazil René Ribeiro stresses the necessary background conditions of "social isolation . . . and lack of real religious help" in addition to extreme poverty in making apocalyptic preaching appealing; Ribeiro, "Brazilian Messianic Movements," in Thrupp, *Millennial Dreams in Action*, 59. Similarly, Roger Bastide, *Les Religions africaines de Brésil* (Paris, 1960), 495 ff, emphasizes that modern millennial movements have found their origins in " . . . frustration and backwardness through participation in a kind of 'archaic culture' which persists because of geographical and cultural isolation."

[15]For more on this point of view, reflecting as it does a subtle mixture of aggression, fear, and racist ideas, see Van Young, "Millennium on the Northern Marches," 400–401.

[16]A survey of Indian schools in various provinces, indicating almost uniformly negative findings particularly with regard to Spanish language acquisition, is to be found in AGN, Historia, vol. 494, exp. 4, fols. 18r–105v, 1774, and another of a decade later in AGN, Historia, vol. 495, exps. 6, 7, 8, 10, 14, 15, and 19, 1784. All of these reports discuss similar problems of finance and Indian resistance to the schooling of children, though in some districts the outcome was better. To be fair, it should be noted that local priests sometimes opposed the establishment or continuance of secular schools, presumably for fear that their control over their parishioners would be diluted. The parish priest of Tecali (to the southeast of Puebla), for example, had always opposed the teaching of Spanish to the Indians in his parish, and likewise openly preached from the pulpit against the establishment of a village school, though

Even more important than the lack of secular education among the Indian population in nourishing a tradition of messianic expectation, however, was religious heterodoxy of various sorts. Both the active practice of heterodox religious rites and the more passive resistance to traditional religious indoctrination at the parish level were explicitly acknowledged by colonial authorities as often being linked to an overall rejection of the Spanish colonizers and their culture. To cite but one example, the Franciscan curate of the Indian town of Poncitlán, on the northern shore of Lake Chapala, reported in 1731 concerning the hostility of the local Indian villagers, particularly in the nearby pueblo of Mezcala. The problem of inducing the local villagers to attend mass and observe the other Christian sacraments had for decades past been a difficult puzzle (*quebradero de cabeza*) for all the priests who had dwelt there. The Franciscan stressed, however, as did other local Spanish witnesses, that the Indians also held an "enmity . . . to the Spaniards" and a "repugnance" to have any non-Indian living in their villages. Riots against their curates and the occasional attack upon local secular authorities (on one occasion resulting in the murder of a royal deputy magistrate) were fairly regular occurrences. In one pueblo of the district in the 1720s the Indians had attacked the priest in his church. One man among the rioters had broken into the sacristy, eaten all the sacramental wafers, and to the horror of several onlookers, while running through the cemetery to his home he burst open and died on the spot.[17]

The complaints of parish clergy regarding the irreligion and ignorance of their Indian flocks were so generalized over New Spain right up to the end of the colonial era (and beyond) as to indicate that evangelization had indeed been shallow, at least insofar as formal religious observance was concerned. The priest of Calimaya, for example, just a few miles west of Mexico City, asserted in 1792 that of his 5,000 backsliding parishioners,

he encouraged attendance at the doctrinal lessons in the Church, which were given in Náhuatl; AGN, Historia, vol. 494, exp. 1, fols. 3r–6v, 1770. See also the case of Miaguatlán (in the south of Oaxaca), where schools became a political football between the local priest and royal officials in the 1780s; AGN, Historia, vol. 495, exp. 7, fols. 80r–130r, 1787. Particularly gloomy overall assessments of Indian rural schooling by high viceregal officials, separated by 25 years, are to be found in AGN, Historia, vol. 495, exp. 20, fols. 293r–303r, 1784, and AGN, Historia, vol. 493, exp. 12, fols. 114r–136r, 1811. The last royal decree of the colonial period commanding the establishment of Indian schools noted the frequent lack of compliance and generally indifferent results of earlier decrees; AGN, Historia, vol. 493, exp. 15, fols. 212r–218r, 1816.

[17]BPE, Civil, caja 49, exp. 4, ser. 637, 1731. It is interesting to note that the pueblo of Mezcala, with other surrounding Indian villages, became a center of prolonged armed rebellion after 1810, and the center of a famous episode of siege by the royalist forces of an insurgent garrison on the island of the same name in Lake Chapala; see Alvaro Ochoa, *Los insurgentes de Mezcala* (Morelia, 1985).

mostly Indians, not a hundred knew the simplest prayers.[18] Indian parishioners in many villages regularly went for years without hearing mass, taking communion, or confessing, and they lived together out of wedlock, refused to baptize their newborn, and buried their dead outside church cemeteries.

If ignorance of formal religious elements, resistance to indoctrination, and conflict with ecclesiastical authorities were endemic in the late colony, more active forms of heterodox behavior seem to have been common enough, although by their very nature less well documented. The most extreme form of this, of course, was the advent of Indian messiahs. One such figure was Antonio Pérez, active in the area of Yautepec, in the Morelos sugar zone, about 1760. He preached nothing less than a total inversion of the social order then prevailing in the colony, clothing his prophetic visions in a language compounded of traditional apocalyptic and pre-Columbian imagery (the soul of Christ was composed of kernels of maize, etc.).[19] Similar though less well studied cases of Indian messianism were those of Mariano, in the Tepic area in 1800–1801, and the mad messiah of Durango, about the same time, both cited above.

But these spectacular manifestations of Indian heterodoxy were certainly outnumbered by the day-to-day practices of shamanism, witchcraft, fertility cults, and so forth. In 1817, for instance, the vicar of the village of San Lorenzo Huichichilapan, near Toluca, just a few miles west of Mexico City, reported the arrest of a number of men of the pueblo for participating in what were apparently propitiatory rites dedicated to a traditional Indian god of the hills. The celebration of the cult included icons of Christ and the Virgin, but also certain "dolls" (*muñecos*) presumably representing pagan deities; dancing and singing by both sexes, offerings of food (tamales,

[18]AGN, Clero Regular y Secular, vol. 131, exp. 1, fols. 1r–110r, 1792. For a number of cases of a similar nature, see: Apaxtla—AGN, Clero Regular y Secular, vol. 126, exp. 2, fols. 286r–294r, 1809; Zacualpan—ibid., vol. 5, exp. 8, fols. 418r–453v, 1801; Celaya—AGN, Historia, vol. 500, exp. 3, fols. 168r–187r, 1797; Actopan—AGN, Clero Regular y Secular, vol. 179, exp. 13, fols. 398r–428v, 1763; Tlacotalpan—ibid., vol. 188, exp. 7, fols. 115r–137r, 1790; ibid., vol. 213, exp. 15, fols. 243r–256r, 1794 (a report on all the secularized missions of New Spain); Huasteca and Sierra Gorda in general—ibid., vol. 126, exp. 11, fols. 281r–285v, 1809; Metztitlan—AGN, Bienes Nacionales, leg. 472, no. exp. no., no pagination, 1819; and the extensive report on a pastoral inspection of the sierra of Metztitlan and the Huasteca—ibid., leg. 716, 1819.

[19]On Pérez, see Gruzinski, *Les Hommes-dieux du Mexique*, 114 ff. Some years later memories of Pérez, his cult, and his followers were still fresh in the area, and by the late 1770s there was even some suggestion that traces of the cult survived in and around Tepoztlan; AGN, Criminal, vol. 203, exp. 4, fols. 109r–268r, 1778. See also the interesting remarks on the Indian prophetic tradition in David A. Brading, "Images and Prophets: Indian Religion and the Spanish Conquest," unpublished ms. (1985).

most prominently), and other ritual elements.[20] Furthermore, parallel with resistance to religious indoctrination, messianism, and active heterodoxy ran a strong tradition of what can most appropriately be called popular piety—religious celebrations, processions of various kinds associated with liturgical events or the veneration of local icons, spontaneous cults and chapels, and so forth. In the late eighteenth century, these forms of popular piety were increasingly sanitized, restricted, or suppressed outright by the enlightened Mexican Church, provoking considerable resistance, even violent resistance, on the part of Indian villagers in particular.[21] Thus identified as noxious by the Church, these practices entered, ipso facto, the substratum of Indian ideology which nourished heterodoxy and an oppositional political stance readily associated with it.[22]

[20]AGN, Bienes Nacionales, leg. 663, no exp. no., no pagination, 1817. Roughly similar cases were uncovered in Xochimilco and Tecualoya around the same time, for which see AGN, Bienes Nacionales, leg. 976, exp. 39, no pagination, 1813, and ibid., leg. 663, no exp. no., no pagination, 1818, respectively.

[21]David A. Brading, "Tridentine Catholicism and Enlightened Despotism in Bourbon Mexico," *Journal of Latin American Studies* 15 (1983), 1–22; Brading, "Images and Prophets;" Gruzinski, *Les Hommes-dieux du Mexique*, 161–167. See the series of reports and viceregal decrees regarding "abuses" (excess spending by Indians and others, gambling, drinking, commercial activity, etc.) during Holy Week in Mexico City, Pátzcuaro, and Silao in the 1790s, in AGN, Historia, vol. 437, exps. 3, 5–11, 1791–1798; and the refusal of viceregal authorities to grant licenses (to Indians) for the establishment of popular chapels in the villages of Huayacocotla and Atotonilco el Alto, in AGN, Clero Regular y Secular, vol. 22, exp. 14, fols. 240r–246v, 1791, and vol. 22, exp. 13, fols. 225r–238v, 1794, respectively. It seems possible that several of the village jacqueries that erupted in connection with the Hidalgo rebellion in late 1810 may have been linked to frustrations with clerical attempts to suppress popular religious celebrations, especially those of All Saints. See, for example, the case of the riot and murders of several European-born Spaniards by the Indian villagers of Atlacomulco in November 1810, in AGN, Criminal, vol. 229, no exp. no., fols. 263r–413v, 1810, and vol. 231, exp. 1, fols. 1r–59r, 1811; and also the riot during *carnaval*, 1806, by the villagers of Amecameca, in AGN, Criminal, vol. 71, exp. 6, fols. 167r–241v, 1806–1810.

[22]Brading, "Images and Prophets," 16, makes much the same point. It should be noted in passing that a possible relationship exists between the occurrence of messianic/millenarian beliefs or movements among Indian populations and earlier missionary activity by the Franciscans, who in the New World harbored in their thought and teachings a definite strain of millennial expectation harking back to Joachim of Floris in the twelfth century. Certainly the two Indian pseudo-messiahs of Tepic and Durango originated in regions strongly influenced by Franciscan evangelization. Such beliefs among the Indians also occurred elsewhere in New Spain, in areas missionized by the Dominicans and Augustinians, as Gruzinski demonstrates in *Les Hommes-dieux du Mexique*. Brading suggests that the Franciscan influence may have been important in encouraging millenarian belief among the Yucatec Maya, but leaves the question open for lack of data ("Images and Prophets," 15). On early evangelization activity in New Spain, see Robert Ricard, *The Spiritual Conquest of Mexico; An Essay on the Apostolate and the Evangelizing Methods of the Mendicant Orders in New Spain: 1523–1572*, translated by Lesley B. Simpson (Berkeley, 1966), especially the map on pp. 62–63. For millenarian thought among the Franciscans, see Jacques Lafaye, *Quetzalcóatl and Guadalupe: The Formation of the Mexican National Consciousness, 1531–1813*, translated by Benjamin Keen (Chicago,

In the heated political atmosphere of the years around 1810, it should come as no surprise that political imagery and religious imagery were widely blended in both rhetoric and action. The communal identity of villages under attack by internal and external pressures – a long-term process with significant political dimensions – had traditionally been linked to religious expression, a relationship most economically described by the concept of "campanillismo" – the tendency of villagers to see the social (and political) horizon as extending only as far as the view from the church tower. Indian villagers were forever ringing their church bells as a symbol of community identity, even (or perhaps especially) over the strong objections of parish clergy. In one case, in the pueblo of Atlautla in the Chalco district near Mexico City, for example, villagers in an argument with the local curate, when enjoined by another local priest to stop ringing the church bells to gather people in the plaza, replied to him " . . . that they would ring them as much as they wanted, since they had paid for the bells and not I."[23] And of course once the rebellion itself had broken out, formal and informal rhetoric and collective action were suffused with religious imagery on both sides of the conflict, though this was perhaps most notable among the insurgents because of the popular nature of the revolt.

It is in such an atmosphere, then, that one sees the invocation of the Spanish King Ferdinand VII up and down a continuum ranging from revilement to veneration. References to regicide (especially worrisome to the authorities because of the Paris events of 1791) were reported, as well as punishments less terminal but more earthy, such as sodomizing the King and defecating upon him.[24] In the rural setting, denials of the King's authority or even in his person occasionally are recorded, as when the Indian insurgent chieftain (*cabecilla*) Luis Vite, in the remote mountainous area of Molango in the sierra of Metztitlán to the north of the capital, insisted that his followers " . . . not believe [or] obey the king."[25]

1976), 28–34 and passim; and John L. Phelan, *The Millennial Kingdom of the Franciscans in the New World*, 2d rev. ed. (Berkeley, 1970).

[23]AGN, Criminal, vol. 157, exp. 3, fols. 93r–155v, 1799. Also on the relationship of church bell ringing to communal identity and solidarity, see the case of the village of Zapotlan el Grande, in the Lake Chapala area, in BPE, Civil, caja 143, exp. 5, ser. 1564, 1797.

[24]For an early reference to the question of regicide, suggested obliquely but unmistakably in connection with King Carlos IV, Ferdinand's father, see the inquiry into the statements of the creole militia officer don Francisco de Solano Gil, in Toluca, in AGN, Criminal, vol. 454, no exp. no., no pagination, 1794; and for the statements of a priest, AGN, Inquisición, vol. 1416, exp. 21, fols. 269r–270v, 1817. For "screwing the King," see AGN, Infidencias, vol. 2, exp. 6, fols. 134r–144r, Oaxaca, 1811, and vol. 2, exp. 2, fols. 40r–57v, also Oaxaca, 1811; and for "shitting on the King," ibid. This same scatologically imaginative seditionary, referring to King Ferdinand's house arrest by Napoleon, suggested he should be known as "Fernando Suéltame" instead of "Fernando Séptimo."

[25]AGN, Criminal, vol. 251, exp. 10, fols. 309r–319v, 1812. Interestingly enough, the only seditious statement of this sort from Indians in an urban setting that I have been able to

A more normal or expectable range of expression from Indians regarding the figure of the Spanish King fell in the category of what we may call naive monarchism. This was ideologically associated, certainly, with the patriarchal stance of the monarchy toward the Indians and their veneration of the King, but was pre-messianic and found its own spontaneous forms of expression. The Indian commune of Juchipila, for example, in western central Mexico (in an area which, like parts of the Huasteca and the eastern sierra madre on the other side of the country, was to be an endemic focus of rebellion for several years after 1810), annually celebrated a fiesta dedicated to the King of Spain, even when the local curate tried to discourage it.[26] Within the context of the insurrection, it is in this naive monarchical legitimism that one begins to see the "splitting" of Spaniards into "good King" and "bad gachupines" alluded to above.[27]

In its most sophisticated and secularized aspect this might appear as a discussion of French "usurpation" of the Spanish throne, a form of sedition apparently more likely to appear among Indian villagers in the center of the country, near the capital or other large cities. One particularly droll manifestation of this was the story circulating in 1808 among the Indians of the market town of Zempoala, to the northeast of the capital, that the Spanish royal family had been sent back to Spain by Napoleon, but all embalmed, in wooden boxes (a metaphor of legitimacy without authority?).[28] More crudely, Indian villagers occasionally made emphatic pronouncements against the gachupines in general, while exempting the King as the object of special veneration. An example of such behavior occurred in a public procession in the village of Epazoyuca, just a few miles to the northeast of Mexico City, during a public procession in the fall of 1808. The Indian official Pablo Hilario, bearing a standard with the image of the Virgin of Guadalupe on it, was standing next to the Indian governor

document comes from mid-1809, before the outbreak of the insurrection, and was made in a tavern in the heat of a drunken argument by an Indian pulque-seller from one of the Indian districts of Mexico City, apparently in response to what he considered a racial insult from a non-Indian. This was a veiled reference to regicide, cast in the quite sophisticated form that the French [regicides] had had the right idea, " . . . and that the time will come when the Indians will do the same;" AGN, Infidencias, vol. 6, exp. 8, no pagination, 1809.

[26]BPE, Civil, caja 140, exp. 5, ser. 1518, 1791. For an interesting recent work on this under-studied area, called the region of *los cañones*, see Agueda Jiménez Pelayo, "Historia rural en México colonial: el sur de Zacatecas, 1600–1820" (Ph.D. dissertation, University of New Mexico, 1985). The idea of "naive monarchism" is borrowed from MacKay, "Ritual, Violence, and Authority."

[27]On the psycho-social origins of this "splitting," a concept drawn from the object-relations school of psychoanalytic theory, see Van Young, "Who Was That Masked Man, Anyway?" and "Millennium on the Northern Marches."

[28]AGN, Criminal, vol. 226, exp. 5, fols. 267r–361r, 1808. Also on the usurpation theme, see AGN, Criminal, vol. 207, exp. 22, fols. 306r–327v, Ocoyoacac (near Toluca), 1810.

of the village, bearing upon another standard the likeness of King Ferdinand VII. When the large ethnically mixed crowd began yelling "Viva Fernando Séptimo!," Pablo Hilario chimed in with "Viva Fernando Séptimo y mueran todos los gachupines!" ("Long live King Ferdinand VII and death to all Spaniards!"). One Spanish witness to the incident observed that Hilario's statements were " . . . very like those indecorously repeated even in the public plazas."[29] Translated into action, such naive monarchism very often took the form of Indians being recruited to the insurgent cause by rebel leaders astute enough to invoke the name of the King in calling for adherence to the cause of Hidalgo and Allende. The statements of captured Indian rebels show no trace of any cognitive dissonance in this regard: apparently the yawning contradiction in terms was for them no contradiction at all.[30]

The most extreme form of this veneration, noted already, was the tone of messianic expectation attached to the person of the Spanish King in a number of instances. Although the documented cases of this are comparatively few, it is safe to assume that the recorded pronouncements represented a more generalized belief among the Indian rebels of the colony,

[29]AGN, Criminal, vol. 226, exp. 5, fols. 267r–361r, 1808. It is worth noting that Pablo Hilario, after spending a year in jail while his case was investigated and tried, was released and deprived of his civil rights for ten years; after 1810 the sentence would certainly have been much more severe. For another similar incident, see AGN, Operaciones de Guerra, vol. 9, no exp. no., fols. 91r–v, 1817, relating to an occurrence in Tula in 1810. Virginia Guedea (personal communication) has pointed out that the expression "gachupín" may have been applied only to European-born Spaniards living in Mexico, and not to the same people living in Spain, so that statements like Pablo Hilario's would embody a perfectly consistent contrast rather than an irony or self-contradiction. While this may be correct from a strictly semantic point of view, the "splitting" hypothesis, if true, suggests a level of meaning beyond the semantic, in which all whites were in fact the object of hostility, whether creole or European-born, and that application of the "gachupín" epithet was a way of creating an artificial distinction among them, the reasons for which I have explored elsewhere (Van Young, "Millennium on the Northern Marches"). What is fundamentally at issue is why the Spanish King should have been the object not only of veneration, but also messianic expectation. After all, he *was* thought to be physically present in New Spain, much as were the gachupines who were attacked and killed with such ferocity by popular rebels, and also the creoles who were for the most part exempted from such treatment. On this same point, Szeminski ("Why Kill the Spaniard?") shows that Indian rebels understood the term "Spaniard" (*español*) to include *all* whites, whether of New or Old World origin, as well as Indian notables and others associated with them – in other words, members of the upper class – and that all such people were to be killed. He also draws attention to edicts to this effect putatively authored by the King of Spain and published by rebel leaders, as occurred in New Spain. Szeminski notes, however, that the Spanish King's legitimacy and authority may not, strictly speaking, have extended to Peru, where Túpac Amaru, as heir to Inca dynasty and Andean gods, was to reign supreme – something of a contradiction he does not attempt to resolve.

[30]For some instances of this, see AGN, Infidencias, vol. 5, exp. 8, no pagination, Yurirapúndaro, 1810; ibid., exp. 10, no pagination, Huichapan, 1810; AGN, Infidencias, vol. 14, exp. 1, fols. 1r–92v, Sichu, 1811; AGN, Criminal, vol. 241, exp. 4, fols. 106r–115r, Tula, 1811.

and probably even among many thousands or tens of thousands of Indian villagers who did not take up arms actively. Of the group of young Indian insurgents of both sexes from Celaya captured in November of 1810, for example, all but two clearly believed that they were following the orders of the King of Spain, who was physically present in Mexico, riding about the countryside in a black coach, and who had himself commanded Father Hidalgo to take up arms against the Spanish colonial authorities. Another captured rebel stated emphatically that King Ferdinand had appeared in New Spain by a particular and miraculous intercession of the Virgin of Guadalupe.[31] One of the most interesting of these "sightings" of the King in Mexico was that by two Indians in the area of Cuernavaca in early 1811, who sought to defraud a number of local village officials of a small quantity of cash by concocting a letter supposedly authored by the Indian governor of Tlaxcala (a significant echo of the Mariano and mad messiah episodes mentioned above, in which both men claimed to be the son of the governor of Tlaxcala). The letter stated that the King was about to enter the village of Cuauhtitlán, to the north of Mexico City, and that he commanded complete secrecy from the gachupines as well as financial support from Indian village officials, on pain of death.[32] What is interesting about this incident, of course, is not the fraud itself, but the fact that its perpetrators thought it credible.[33]

There were, however, candidates alternative to "El Deseado" to whom messianic expectation was attached. Although the reasons for this are rather vague, a brief discussion of the evidence and some speculation about its significance add interesting subtleties to the argument about messianism among the Indians of New Spain. It is often stated and widely believed that the objects of messianic veneration by the Indian masses of the country were the priest who led the rebellion in its early phases, most especially

[31]On the rebels from Celaya, see AGN, Criminal, vol. 134, exp. 3, fols. 36r–50r, 1810. Another captured rebel was reported to have said that " . . . a person is coming in a veiled coach, and when people come to see him, they kneel down and go away very happy;" AGN, Criminal, vol. 454, no exp. no., no pagination, 1811. On the association of the King and the Virgin, see AGN, Infidencias, vol. 22, exp. 10, fols. 179r–183v, 1810. The miraculous intercession of the Virgin, by the way, goes some way toward meeting the criterion of supernatural intervention seen to be essential in the definition of messianic/millenarian expectation developed by Cohn, "Medieval Millenarism," 31 ff.

[32]AGN, Criminal, vol. 204, exp. 10, fols. 191r–205v, 1811.

[33]Some rebel leaders even feared that news of King Ferdinand's restoration to the throne in 1814 might undermine the loyalty of their Indian followers. This thinking apparently lay behind the effort of Father Marcos Castellanos, the insurgent commander of the besieged island of Mezcala in Lake Chapala, to suppress the information from his entirely Indian force as late as 1815; University of Texas at Austin, Benson Latin American Collection, Hernández y Dávalos Collection (hereafter UT-HD), 1.212, 1815.

Miguel Hidalgo and José María Morelos.[34] While this is not an unreasonable assumption, it is probably due more to the retrospective mythification of the progenitors of Mexican national identity than to any marked popular sentiment at the time of the independence struggle itself. If this were not the case, one would expect to see more statements on the part of captured rebels from the Mexican popular classes who acclaimed the priests as messiahs or at least, in Lafaye's words, as "providential" men, but such pronouncements are in fact conspicuous by their absence. Apart from a very few scattered references to the imminent return of Hidalgo and Morelos at the head of avenging armies after their widely publicized deaths, there is very little evidence of the kind of apotheosis ("spontaneous canonization" in Lafaye's expression) of these popular leaders undergone in more recent times by such men as Emiliano Zapata, Pancho Villa, or Che Guevara. There may have been some popular belief in Hidalgo's thaumaturgical or miraculous powers, but again almost no written evidence remains of it apart from a reference (revealing in itself) to his " . . . very miraculous soul," not by an Indian peasant but by a Franciscan friar in Sonora.[35] Father Morelos could not even perform his own miracles, according to the testimony of one Indian rebel captured outside the besieged town of Cuautla in March 1812. This man, locally born and 25 years old, upon being sentenced to death by a royalist court martial and asked what disposition he wanted made of his body after his execution, asked his captors to send his corpse back across the siege lines into the town. There he expected Father Morelos to bring him back to life through the agency of a miraculous child the rebel *generalísimo* had brought with him from the hot country of the Pacific coast, and who was believed to have the ability to resuscitate dead people after three days. The tough and talented royalist commander of western Mexico, José de la Cruz, in a typically snarling irony in a letter of 1811 to his military colleague (and the future Viceroy) Calleja, made a passing reference to the commonly held belief among the rebels that Hidalgo could revive them from the dead.[36]

[34]Lafaye, *Mesías, cruzadas, utopías*, 87–88 and passim; and Lafaye, *Quetzalcóatl and Guadalupe*, 28. Lafaye, it seems to me, fails to make a sufficiently sharp distinction between messianic and charismatic leadership, which are not necessarily the same thing. Michael Adas has some peerceptive comments to make on this confusion, even in the original formulation of charismatic leadership by Max Weber; Adas, *Prophets of Rebellion*, xx–xxi. For an interesting but not entirely convincing, broadly psychohistorical interpretation of Hidalgo and the rebellion he led, which casts the struggle in oedipal terms, see Victor Turner, "Hidalgo: History as Social Drama," in turner's *Dramas, Fields, and Metaphors: Symbolic Action in Human Society* (New York, 1974), 98–155.

[35]BPE, Criminal, leg. 6, exp. 28, no pagination, 1815.

[36]On Morelos and the miraculous child, see UT-HD, 4.71.371–383, 1812; and for Cruz's letter, AGN, Operaciones de Guerra, vol. 145, no exp. no., fols. 229r–232r, Cruz to Calleja, Guadalajara, 2 September 1811.

A more widely venerated, or at least more widely spoken of, figure in the messianic mold, oddly enough, was Ignacio Allende, the wealthy creole militia officer from the Bajío town of San Miguel el Grande and co-conspirator of Hidalgo's who became the priest's second in command during the short-lived 1810–1811 rebellion. A less likely candidate for popular veneration would be hard to imagine, but Allende was apparently nonetheless more closely associated with messianic expectation himself, and also with the figure of King Ferdinand, than the priests. In a number of documents Allende was linked closely with 'El Deseado," or even conflated with him and the Virgin of Guadalupe, as very notably in the case of an Indian uprising and rebel invasion in the Cuernavaca area in late 1810.[37] Allende was quite widely perceived among Indian villagers and many other insurgents as the paramount leader of the rebel forces even during the apogee of Hidalgo's power, until he engineered a kind of coup against the older man in early 1811. A seditious Indian magistrate from a small pueblo in the Chalco district said in the early summer of 1811 that " . . . would to God Allende would come, and he would go with him though it cost him his home." In the Texcoco district, near the viceregal capital, many Indian officials sympathetic to the rebellion were awaiting an emissary from Allende (not Hidalgo) in November of 1810, and the insurgent army was on more than one occasion referred to as Allende's army (rather than Hidalgo's).[38] His name appeared in seditious verses espousing national liberation (in one case substituted for that of Archduke John of Austria, with America replacing Italy) and his image in an allegorical sketch purchased by an Indian peasant from the country in one of the capital's major plazas; he was mentioned in people's prayers and seen by some to have been sent by God as a scourge for the gachupines; and one ingenuous captured rebel even referred to him in his judicial confession to the royalist authorities as "His Serene Highness."[39] Among the ranks of the creole insurgent leadership Ignacio Allende was more socially conservative than many, yet he was seen by many Indians as a great avenger and killer of gachupines, social equalizer,

[37] Allende was supposed to be with King Ferdinand in Querétaro in the spring of 1811; AGN, Criminal, vol. 194, exp. 1, fols. 1r–13r, 1811; for the Cuernavaca incidents, see AGN, Criminal, vol. 47, exp. 15, fols. 443r–574v, 1810.

[38] AGN, Criminal, vol. 2, exp. 21, no pagination, 1811; ibid., vol. 143, exps. 13–15, fols. 215r–333r, 1810; ibid., vol. 500, no exp. no., no pagination, 1810; ibid., vol. 241, no exp. no., fols. 173r–182r, 1810.

[39] AGN, Operaciones de Guerra, vol. 9, no exp. no., fols. 133r–134r, 1817; AGN, Infidencias, vol. 2, exp. 8, fols. 154r–162v, 1810; AGN, Inquisición, vol. 1416, exp. 11, fols. 173r–178v, 1811; AGN, Operaciones de Guerra, vol 9, no exp. no., fols. 41r–v, 1817; and AGN, Infidencias, vol. 2, exp. 4, fols. 100r–116v, 1811. Allende's fate (arrest, trial, and execution in 1811) was, like that of Hidalgo, the subject of popular speculation, and his expected return believed imminent; see AGN, Criminal, vol. 262, exp. 19, fols. 235r–256v, 1811.

abolisher of tributes and fixer of prices, and even as an agrarian reformer.[40] In at least one instance—significantly, in the rough and isolated further reaches of the sierra of Metztitlán—while his capture was being denied as a lie (at almost exactly the same time that he was being executed in the north of the colony, in Chihuahua), Allende was being proposed as a popular candidate for King: " . . . and he is going to obtain the crown of Mexico and in a few days we will fall at his feet, and kiss his feet and hands, because he is going to be our Catholic King [*nuestro católico*]."[41]

Let is now take up some of the evidence from an interpretive point of view. To begin with, how are we to account for the central importance of Ignacio Allende, himself an improbable candidate for messiah-hood, in popular ideology in this period? A possible explanation—a working hypothesis—lies in the nature of the mediating role played by the lower clergy in village cosmology. Rural priests like Hidalgo and Morelos, along with hundreds of other country clerics who fought under the banner of the Virgin and many more who did not, were mediators between their parishioners and the supernatural powers represented by God, Jesus, the Virgin, and the Saints.[42] As such, their brokerage function may have been such an inherent aspect of their personae, and their personalities so familiar, that they were able to attract little if any of the powerful emotional cathexis whose formation was necessary to the development of a popular messianic figure. Perhaps priests, therefore, were simply not expendable in the moral economy of the peasant village universe. Then, too, Allende ostensibly shared a number of characteristics with the king against whom he rebelled: relative youth, whiteness, social distance, a politico-military vocation, and so forth.

Furthermore, if it is true, as has been suggested, that the priestly and political functions earlier fused in the Mesoamerican tradition were split apart in the post-Classic period, before the advent of the Europeans, then it would appear that by the late colonial era, despite the tendency of the Spanish state to conflate divine and secular authority, the split had become

[40]AGN, Criminal, vol. 240, no exp. no., fols. 355r–364r, 1810; ibid., vol. 241, exp. 7, fols. 233r–243v, 1811; ibid., vol. 57, exp. 6, fols. 101r–116r, 1810; ibid., vol. 204, exps. 11–12, fols. 206r–262r, 1810; ibid., vol. 13, exp. 6, no pagination, 1810; ibid., vol. 53, exps. 16–17, fols. 196r–224r, 1810.

[41]AGN, Criminal, vol. 163, exp. 18, fols. 307r–320r, 1811.

[42]Gruzinski, *Les Hommes-dieux du Mexique*, 139, 163–167, makes an approach to this question, but from the angle of the widespread popular anticlericalism he sees as a result of the enlightened policies of the Bourbon Church, and from the preachings of the Indian messiah Antonio Pérez on the inefficacy of such priestly mediation in the salvation of souls. In passing it should be mentioned that many more priests in New Spain remained loyal to the Spanish crown than took up arms.

a permanent one.[43] This would explain why the specialized priestly class of the colony—parish curates such as those who led the insurgency in many areas—failed to emerge as political/religious messiahs. From this point of view, Father Hidalgo may have been just another Nahua priest reciting auguries. Following this same interpretation, the hints of fusion—expressed as chiliastic grandiosity—one sees in Mariano and the mad messiah of Durango would be characteristic of the colonial periphery because of the less thorough process of acculturation (or deculturation) there. Furthermore, the lack of specific programmatic elements, for the most part, in the ideology of Indian rebels in the more central regions of the colony would correspond precisely to the same considerations, since one does see such programmatic elements in the earlier, more peripheral movements, as also in earlier messianic episodes in central New Spain.[44] Even if the peripheral Indian prophet-kings elaborated only primitive millenarian programs, this was still more than one saw a decade later in the center of the country. Here Indians of a messianic persuasion seem to have been operating with an amputated cosmology in which, if a New Jerusalem existed, it was coterminous with the edge of each embattled peasant village which looked to the King or his surrogate as messianic figures.

Finally, messianic expectation among the Indian villagers of New Spain may have served them as a kind of ideological lever against the local political structure—against local officials, merchants, landowners, and sometimes against their own priests. It represented in a time of social crisis the invocation of a reciprocal relationship in which the distant royal government (and by extension its viceregal surrogates) had done much the same thing in reverse—built the large, rambling, leaky edifice of royal Indian protectionism as a counterweight to the centrifugal tendencies present in the New World in general and New Spain in particular. This political symbiosis, of course, had its limits, and there were strains within it which neither party, on its side, openly admitted. The village-dwelling Indians almost certainly looked no further than the boundaries of their communes, and admitted as legitimate only certain claims on the part of the monarch, while the monarchy (or Spanish state) on its side saw the Indians not as potentially free and equal citizens, but as perennial minors living under royal tutelage, paying

[43]Gruzinski, *Les Hommes-dieux du Mexique*, 18 ff. For an equally stimulating but somewhat different point of view, positing a multilevel model of religious understanding of which the Maya Indians lost the uppermost, corresponding to universal religion, see Nancy M. Farriss, *Maya Society Under Spanish Colonial Rule: The Collective Enterprise of Survival* (Princeton, 1984), 286–351.

[44]See Gruzinski's discussion of Antonio Pérez, for example, in *Les Hommes-dieux du Mexique*. Pérez's uprising seems to have been the last genuinely millenarian episode in the center of the country during the colonial period, leading one to suspect a situation of rapidly changing social conditions and accelerated acculturation there for the next half-century.

taxes and supplying labor.[45] The system represented, therefore, a kind of disingenuous alliance. There was about this situation a certain structural symmetry if one places the creole elite with its allied social groups in the middle, its aims radically opposed to both Indian villagers and monarchy since it sought to seize and, to a degree, spread political power on the one hand and pulverize Indian communitarian values on the other. The focus of Indian messianic expectation on the Spanish King (or on Ignacio Allende) embodies the kind of contradiction between popular and elite ideology often found in mass insurrectionary movements, therefore, and undermines the traditional wisdom that all the rebels in New Spain had the same thing in mind when they took up arms against the Spanish regime.

[45]For the most highly developed discussion of Indian peasant worldview and the relationship of Indian villages to structures of authority, see William B. Taylor, *Drinking, Homicide, and Rebellion in Colonial Mexican Villages* (Stanford, 1979).

La minería durante la guerra de independencia y los primeros años del México independiente, 1810-1824

Hira de Gortari Rabiela

El propósito fundamental de este ensayo es revisar los efectos que la guerra de independencia trajo a la economía y particularmente a la minería, un sector económico fundamental de la Nueva España.

Para analizar dicho problema revisaré cómo el dislocamiento y destrucción de la minería contribuyó a trastornar el orden colonial y se convirtió en una pesada carga para los primeros gobiernos independientes, los cuales, como parte de sus primeras medidas, se dieron a la tarea de intentar rehabilitarla como una de las prioridades para afianzar al nuevo régimen.

Para comprender cabalmente el asunto no podemos circunscribirnos a una crónica detallada sobre el estado de los yacimientos e instalaciones mineras durante y después de concluida la guerra, sino también es indispensable adentrarnos en sus características para escudriñar de qué manera los fragores de los combates trajeron la destrucción, paralización y reducción de la producción minera; aquéllos también contribuyeron a construir realidades inéditas con nuevos actores que se fortalecieron en la escena gracias a su enriquecimiento durante la contienda, aprovechándose del trastorno en las actividades y circuitos económicos.

La guerra heredó al país recién independizado una economía seriamente afectada y trastornada y que para ponerla nuevamente en marcha supuso varias décadas de esfuerzo y el enfrentamiento de proyectos distintos de cómo avanzar y reencontrar el camino.

En lo inmediato, el dislocamiento económico de algunas de las regiones más prósperas de la Nueva España contribuyó al debilitamiento paulatino del orden colonial y a la pérdida de la legitimidad y de autoridad del gobierno español, abriendo con esto el camino a la independencia.

Nota del Autor: Una versión preliminar se presentó en el XII simposio de Historia Económica, CLACSO, 1986.

Cuando analizamos un problema como el que nos ocupa, es cada vez más clara la necesidad de abordarlo desde una perspectiva temporal que vaya más allá de la guerra y nos interne en la vida nacional para captar con mayor profundidad la magnitud y significado de los cambios ocurridos a finales del siglo XVIII y principios XIX.[1]

La economía y los escenarios de la guerra

Prácticamente imposible sería reproducir los escenarios de la guerra y analizar los efectos que trajeron a la economía novohispana. Más aún, no se puede contemplar el movimiento de independencia como unitario y homogéneo, sino que es indispensable considerar que fue una contienda en donde lo regional tuvo un peso decisivo y por tanto la existencia de participantes con ideas y propósitos distintos que formaron un mosaico compuesto por reivindicaciones, acciones y motivaciones que respondían a imperativos locales o regionales. Esta mirada recién iniciada apunta a estudiar movimientos a otra escala y cuyos resultados seguramente nos proporcionarán un panorama más complejo y apasionante de la guerra de independencia.[2]

En este ensayo no pretendo analizar todos y cada uno de los movimientos y sus características pero sí contribuir a mostrar cómo, en las distintas fases de la guerra, la economía y en particular la minería fueron afectadas severamente.

El inicio de la guerra: el Bajío escenario principal

El Bajío, una de las regiones más prósperas de la Nueva España donde se desarrolló "un complejo único de minería, agricultura e industria" , de donde se extraía una cuarta parte de la plata mexicana y una sexta de la producción mundial, fue la cuna principal de la guerra.[3] Su papel estratégico se debió tanto a su importancia agrícola y minera como a su

[1]Christon I. Archer, "Los dineros de la insurgencia" , en Carlos Herrejón Peredo, ed., *Repaso de la independencia*, Memoria del Congreso sobre la Insurgencia Mexicana, octubre de 1984 (Morelia, Michoacán: El Colegio de Michoacán, 1985), 39–70.

[2]Lucas Alamán, *Historia de Méjico, desde los primeros movimientos que prepararon su independencia en al año de 1808 hasta la época presente* (México: Instituto Cultural Helénico y F.C.E., 1985; edicion facsimilar de la editada por la Imprenta de J. Mariano Lara, 1849–1852), 5 vols., II, 212.

[3]Eric R. Wolf, "El Bajío en el siglo XVIII (Un análisis de integración cultural)", en David Barkin, *Los beneficiarios del desarrollo regional* (México: Secretaría de Educación Pública, 1972 [Sepsetentas 52]), 63–94, David A. Brading, "El Bajío", en *Mineros y comerciantes en el México borbónico (1763–1810)* (México: Fondo de Cultura, Económica, 1975), 301–330.

localización geográfica, como paso obligado entre la ciudad de México y las provincias internas.[4]

Esto se hizo patente desde septiembre de 1810 con la toma de Guanajuato, la cual marcó el inicio de la desarticulación económica e interrupciones del tráfico y los primeros saqueos. Tan estratégica era la zona que una de las primeras estrategias realistas fue su recuperación.

La ciudad fue tomada, como sabemos, a sangre y fuego y cuyas estrujantes escenas de pillaje y destrucción nos fueron relatadas por Lucas Alamán; éste escribe "La destrucción y el saqueo . . . no se limitó a las casas y tiendas de los europeos en la ciudad . . . lo mismo se verificó en las de las minas, y el saqueo se hizo extensivo a las haciendas de beneficiar metales."[5]

Desde los primeros enfrentamientos la economía del Bajío sufrió principalmente las consecuencias, ya que la:

> riqueza fue desapareciendo rápidamente, a medida que la revolucion se generalizó. Arruinadas u ocupadas las fincas rústicas; interceptados los caminos y cortadas las comunicaciones, todos los giros cesaron, las fortunas particulares fueron decayendo. . . . Y en particular la . . . minería fue la primera que resintió los efectos de la revolución, pues ocupadas por los insurgentes los principales y más productivos minerales, como Guanajuato y Zacatecas; muertos o privados de sus bienes los que principalmente ejercían aquella industria; escaseando el dinero en los distritos de minas aunque hubiese plata en pasta, por no poderla mandar a México donde estaba la única casa de moneda que en el país había; hubieron de suspenderse las labores, por la primera vez después de la conquista y abandonados los desagües de las minas, éstas se inundaron y las haciendas o ingenios de beneficio se redujeron a ruinas, las unas por sólo el efecto del tiempo y el abandono; otras quemadas o destruidas por los independientes.[6]

Los efectos de la guerra se pueden apreciar en la reducción drástica de la acuñación de moneda, tanto por las dificultades para la circulación de los metales, el apoderamiento de minerales, como la destrucción de las instalaciones. Las cifras de amonedación que se incluyen a continuación son más que elocuentes.

[4]Brian R. Hamnett, "The Economic and Social Dimension of the Revolution of Independence in Mexico, 1800–1824", *Ibero-Amerikanisches Archiv* 6:1 (1980), 1–27.

[5]Alamán, *Historia de Méjico*, I, 435–438.

[6]Ibid., 241–242.

Ano	Plata (pesos)	Oro (pesos)
1809	24,708,164.2 6	1,468,818
1810	17,950,684.3 6	1,095,818
1811	8,956,432.2 9	1,085,364
1812	4,027,620.0 9	381,646

La acuñación no alcanzó más los niveles anteriores al desencadenamiento de las hostilidades y debe notarse que que 1812 fue el año de menor cuantía durante la guerra, el cual coincide con la campaña de Morelos.

La toma y destrucción de los reales de minas

Los reales de minas fueron lugares codiciados por los insurgentes y su defensa o recuperación ocupó muchos de los esfuerzos de las tropas realistas por su papel vital en la economía novohispana. Para los insurgentes durane la guerra los yacimientos mineros fueron lugares estratégicos para proveerse de fondos, aunque muchos fueron destruidos y paralizados, trayendo consigo mermas cuantiosas en los ingresos públicos, esenciales, para sostener la contrainsurgencia, así como serios problemas en la agricultura y el empleo.

Las incursiones a las minas fueron frecuentes y una de las tácticas más socorridas. Guanajuato no sólo fue ocupada por Hidalgo, sino en noviembre de 1811 la ocupó Albino García al quedar abandonada por las tropas realistas que habían salido a persequir a Hermenegildo Galeana y también fue el caso Pachuca ocupada por gente de Osorno; en ambas ciudades la ocupación fue pasajera y no significó su paralización.[7]

Los asaltos no siempre fueron exitosos, pero mantenían a la población en zozobra y contribuían a desanimar cualquier intento por poner en marcha las actividades mineras, sobre todo en las zonas más afectadas por ejemplo Guanajuato, Zacatecas, Temascaltepec, Sultepec. Muchas de las incursiones no sólo fueron para proveer de fondos a los grupos insurgentes, sino también de bandas cuya única finalidad era el robo.[8]

Los ejemplos que pueden encontrarse de los insurgentes tratando de poner en marcha las minas abandonadas como de los realistas protegiendo aquellas que seguían en funcionamiento son numerosos. Rayón —nos cuenta Alamán— en Zacatecas al encontrar la mina de Quebradillo abandonada, para hacerse de fondos, la mandó abrir:

> que estaban entonces en abundantes frutos y cuyos dueños eran españoles, siendo el principal D. Fermín de Apezochea, emigrado entonces en Méjico, para que bajasen a trabajar todos los que quisiesen, donde y cómo les pareciese,

[7]Hamnett, "Economic and Social Dimension", 10-11.
[8]Alamán, *Historia de Méjico*, II, 353, 395, 418, 435-436 y 578-580.

> dando la tercera parte de lo que extrajesen para el ejército, la que se beneficiaba en la hacienda de Bernárdez y la Sauceda, con lo que en poco tiempo se sacó una gran cantidad de ricos minerales, quedando la mina despilarada y arruinada, y para que no faltase la moneda circulante, dispuso se continuase la fabricación de la provisional ya establecida.[9]

La puesta en marcha de minas abandonadas o tomadas por los insurgentes fue una práctica utilizada, pues además de proveerse de fondos les permitió garantizar la acuñación de moneda, la cual podía circular en las zonas que controlaban. Morelos en 1811 hace referencia al asunto mencionado que si ahora utilizan cobre para dicho propósito: "concluida la conquista, o antes, luego que tenga reales suficientes en plata o en oro, lo que no es difícil, porque los minerales comenzarán a trabajarse".[10]

Todavía en la campaña de Javier Mina en octubre de 1817, uno de sus hombres, Francisco Ortiz: "al paso por la Valenciana . . . que poco tiempo antes asaltó aquella mina, pego fuego al tiro general de ella, en el cual siendo los techos de todas las oficinas de madera, se levantó en momentos una gran llamarada".[11]

El control o destrucción de las haciendas

Para los ejércitos insurgentes como el realista, el control sobre la producción agrícola fue un asunto vital, pues de ello dependía la supervivencia de sus tropas; también para los realistas era indispensable para mantener el sistema de abastecimiento de las ciudades y poblaciones novohispanas.

Los ejércitos insurgentes muchas veces no buscaron el control sino el destruir sistemáticamente las haciendas y en esta forma trastornar la economía del enemigo. Gabino García por ejemplo en 1811:

> inundó todo el Valle de Santiago y las inmediaciones de Salvatierra, soltando las compuertas de los vallados en que se recoge el agua para la siembra de los trigos, inutilizando así los caminos y, además hizo abrir en muchas partes zanjas profundas cubiertas con ramas para impedir el paso de la artillería.[12]

Esta práctica se mantuvo y cuando los insurgentes no podían tomar las poblaciones por falta de contingentes suficientes se dedicaron a hostilizar

[9]Ibid., 263.

[10]José María Morelos y Pavón, "Proclama de Morelos emitida en Cuautla donde reafirma la causa de la independencia. 8 de febrero de 1812", en Lillian Briseño Senosian et al., eds., *La independencia de México: textos de su historia* (México: Instituto de Investigaciones Dr. José María Luis Mora, 1985), I, 291–296.

[11]Ibid., IV, 399.

[12]Ibid., II, 295.

a las haciendas y a los pueblos; en referencias posteriores se menciona cómo la junta de Zitácuaro instigaba a sus seguidores a destruir haciendas y las semillas almacenadas y en esta forma lograr la rendición de los pueblos fortificados merced a la falta de medios de subsistencia, táctica que se puso en práctica en Valladolid, Guanajuato y en el valle de Toluca.[13]

En la guerra se cometieron muchos excesos a tal punto que José María Morelos tuvo que hacer llamados y condenas en contra del saqueo y la rapiña. Por ejemplo en 1814 expresaba:

> La peste destructora de hombres viciosos que entregados a la rapiña talan y asolan las propiedades de sus conciudadanos con notable descrédito de la santa y justa causa que sostenemos, abusando del honroso nombre de americanos, ha llegado a tal punto, que nada ha estado exento de la depravación de estos malvados; y para que en lo sucesivo no sufra iguales extorsiones en su persona y bienes de la nación . . . mando que ninguno de los jefes militares y subalternos que por ahí transitaren, puedan exigir cabalgaduras, reales o alguna otra cosa que pertenezca a dichas estancias, sin expresa autoridad mía, que deberán presentar cuando les sea librada . . . .[14]

Esto no supuso el evitar la destrucción de los medios de abastecimiento del enemigo, pero sí trató de evitar la anarquía y el desorden entre las tropas insurgentes. En una proclama de Morelos en el mismo año de 1814 señalaba:

> Cuando queden por nuestra parte los ataques que dé Ud. a las Plazas enemigas, deben éstas arrasarse, destruirse e incendiarse, de modo que ni aun para habitaciones queden servibles, pasando por las armas a todo militar que se haga prisionero, y entrando a degüello en los expresados pueblos: teniendo presente que ningún Comandante es ádvitro [sic] a perdonar la vida a ningún delincuente. Cuya orden hará Ud. circular a sus Subalternos para su puntual cumplimiento.[15]

En cuanto al trato de la población con el enemigo estipulaba:

> Prohibo que al enemigo o población que por él esté ocupada pueda vendérsele carne, semillas ni otra cosa de primera o segunda necesidad; todos sus comercios deben tenerlos en los países conquistados, bajo la pena por

[13]Ibid., III, 385-386.

[14]"Morelos condena la rapiña: de modo especial en el caso de Sinagua, 30 de junio de 1814", en Carlos Herrejón Peredo, *Morelos: antología documental*, Colección Cien de México (México: Secretaría de Educación Pública, 1985), 141-142.

[15]"Circular sobre el tratamiento a las plazas enemigas, 22 de noviembre de 1814", en Xavier Tavera Alfaro, *Dos etapas de la independencia: documentos* (Morelia, Michoacán: Universidad Michoacana de San Nicolás de Hidalgo, 1966), 84.

> primera vez de decomisar las semillas y mulas y un mes de carcel a los arrieros, y por la segunda, destierro a cien leguas.[16]

La destrucción en los años siguientes de haciendas y pueblos continuó siendo una práctica sistemática; José Francisco Osorno en 1816 dispuso que: "los pueblos de Singuilucan, Zempoala y Otumba y las ricas haciendas de Tepetates, Jala y Ometusco, antes de que en ellas se estableciesen destacamentos (realistas) fueran incendiadas. . . .[17]

Hasta ahora es difícil calcular los costos que la guerra trajo a la agricultura novohispana; sin embargo, en investigaciones recientes como las de Brian Hamnett se aborda el problema y se intenta hacer un balance.

Como ya se ha señalado, nos dice Hamnett que la insurrección trajo inicialmente serios daños en las propiedades del Bajío; así desde octubre de 1810 muchas haciendas fueron abandonadas por sus propietarios, arrendatarios o superintendentes. Para enero y febrero de 1811 las ciudades situadas en la principal región cerealera, como Salamanca, Irapuato y Celaya, estaban en completo estado de anarquía. Así las familias más ricas y las autoridades de Celaya huyeron a Querétaro— ciudad refugio— dejando sus propiedades abandonadas.

Posteriormente durante la etapa de la guerra encabezada por Morelos (1811-1815) las bandas insurgentes en los años de 1811 a 1812 rondaron las haciendas de la intendencia de Puebla, quemando algunas productoras de azúcar y causando daños duraderos en muchas de ellas.

En la intendencia de Oaxaca, en la Mixteca alta y baja, en los años de 1811 a 1814 la insurrección causó destrozos permanentes en las zonas productoras de azúcar, trigo, algodón y colorantes (añil y grana cochinilla). Un comandante realista en 1814 calculaba que entre 1811 y 1813 se habían perdido más de dos millones de pesos.

A juicio de Hamnett, no fueron los cereales los cultivos más afectados por la guerra sino productos como el pulque; sin embargo la presencia de los insurgentes en el valle de México y los valles de Puebla afectaron las propiedades productoras de cereales, bajando el valor de sus rentas e ingresos.[18]

En 1819 se hacía un análisis razonando acerca del estado del crédito agrícola después de la guerra. Su autor expresaba preocupación acerca de la suerte de los deudores, incapaces de pagar los préstamos contraídos, y las exigencias de los acreedores por intentar recuperarlos. La situación era delicada y justificando a los deudores señalaba:

[16]"Plan de Morelos por el que se reorganiza la población y la guerra insurgentes, 7 de julio de 1813", en Herrejón, *Morelos*, 119-124.

[17]Alamán, *Historia de Méjico*, IV, 621.

[18]Hamnett, "Economic and Social Dimension", 15-17.

Todos y cada uno de los deudores de capitales tomados a réditos antes de la insurrección, que hemos sido perjudicados en nuestros respectivos haberes, tenemos un interés inmediato para exponer los robustos derechos que favorecen nuestra causa . . .[Ya] que los que somos responsables a los réditos de capitales impuestos antes de la revolución, por la que se ha menoscabado nuestra fortuna, y ha dejado de producir nuestra industria, tenemos de nuestra parte para no pagar los réditos, o para que se nos minoren a proporción del estado productivo de nuestros giros, no solamente la autoridad del derecho, la voz imperiosa de la justicia, y la protección de las leyes, sino también la conveniencia política del estado, y el interés bien entendido de nuestros propios acreedores.[19]

Ante la situación causada por un acontecimiento de la magnitud de la guerra por nadie prevista, solicita una reducción de los intereses o el no pago de los préstamos, dado que:

los acreedores [se] encuentran bajo los escombros . . . los miserables restos de [su] fortuna . . . pudieron haber perecido . . . en la agricultura, en el comercio, y en las fábricas, por los robos, saqueos, incendios y destrozos ejecutados: [y] que en moneda [han] estado expuestos a la rapacidad de la muchedumbre ocupada en disipar y devorar los caudales . . . [y] . . . que los capitales impuestos antes de la insurrección, unos se han perdido con motivo de ella, y otros en mayor número existen, a pesar de los desastres de la guerra revolucionaria. . . . [20]

Advertía que no debían tomarse en cuenta las pérdidas originadas directamente por la guerra:

aún no para aquí el daño, porque todavía hay que atender otro género de pérdidas sumamente considerable. Tal es, entre otros, la del valor estimativo de las fincas, regulada en las dos terceras partes, así como lo que han padecido en su valor intrínseco se computa en más de la mitad: tal es también lo que se ha seguido de haberse paralizado la circulación del dinero, pues a proporción que es mayor y más rápida, se necesita menos numerario, que puede emplearse útilmente en la producción: tal es igualmente la del crédito. . . .

La escasez de crédito ha intensificado el del agio, ya que éste:

se introduce en los casos de desorden es otro perjuicio que deja un vacío inmenso . . . en sí evento de trastorno y calamidad, tratan los agiotistas y

[19]José María de Jauregui, "Discurso en que se manifiesta que deben bajarse los réditos a proporción del quebranto que hayan sufrido en la insurreción los bienes y giros de los deudores" (México, 1820), en Luis Chávez Orozco, ed., *La guerra de independencia y el crédito agrícola*, Documentos de la Historia del Crédito Agrícola en México (México: Banco de Crédito Agrícola y Ganadero, 1953), I, 2, 6–7.

[20]Ibid., 9 y 11.

bribones, no sólo de cargar trabajo, sino de sacrificar al hombre industrioso, haciendole su víctima. Hay ganancias pero sin producción, y hay pérdidas sin consumo. . . . [21]

Una secuela más, heredada de la guerra, que no podía pasarse por alto era la:

otra pérdida que no se sujeta a cálculo, resultante de la falta de brazos y de personas industriosas, bien se atienda a la muchedumbre que se reunió en masa para sostener la causa de los rebeldes, bien se considere la que tomó las armas para defender la del legítimo gobierno, bien la que ha perecido de una y otra parte, bien la que ha emigrado hasta con sus caudales, pues se situaron varias sumas en los países extranjeros, y se negociaron otros sobre Cádiz, fuera de los que salieron con registro.[22]

En 1817 José María Quirós, aunque convencido de que los minerales no eran la riqueza fundamental de la Nueva España, llegó a calcular que aquellos:

ofrecían anualmente en tiempos tranquilos a la circulación interna y externa la gruesa suma de doscientos veinte y siete millones y medio de pesos; que esta gran masa casi ha desaparecido, quedando reducida a una tercera parte. . . . [23]

El estado de la finanzas públicas e insurgentes

En la medida que la guerra se extendía más allá del Bajío, sus efectos se prolongaban sobre las finanzas virreinales, haciendo cada vez más apremiante la necesidad de obtener ingresos extras para sostener la causa realista que exigía mayores gastos. Obtenerlos era cada vez más difícil en la medida que los ingresos originados en la producción minera y agrícola habían mermado, por lo que se tuvo que recurrir con mayor frecuencia a impuestos extraordinarios para aliviar la carga del erario.

[21] Ibid., 45–46.

[22] Ibid., 45.

[23] José María Quirós, "Memoria de estatuto. Idea de la riqueza que deban a la masa circulante de Nueva España sus naturales producciones en los años de tranguilidad, y su abatimiento en las presentes conmociones, 1817", en Enrique Florescano e Isabel Gil, eds., *Descripciones económicas generales de la Nueva España, 1784–1817*, Fuentes para la Historia Económica de México (México: Secretaria de Educación Pública e Instituto Nacional de Antropología e Historia, 1973), I, 259.

Cuando Félix María Calleja ocupó en 1813 el cargo de virrey, constató que:

> El erario público . . . se halla en agonía, y muy próximo a disminuir o acaso a no pagar los sueldos de empleados, con una deuda de más de treinta millones de pesos, y con un deficiente mensual de más de seiscientos sesenta mil, consumidos todos los fondos públicos . . . y algunos de los extraordinarios, recargados de deudas las más privilegiadas, como alcances de las tropas que nos defienden. . . .[24]

Los esfuerzos del gobierno virreinal para costear la guerra no fueron siempre efectivos pues:

> En todos los pueblos se cobraban las que se habían establecido . . . y para el pago de la tropa se echaba mano de todos los fondos que existían y de que disponían los comandantes: las rentas eclesiásticas habían sufrido más que ningunas otras, pues ocupadas por los insurgentes o destruidas las fincas rústicas, los propietarios no pagaban réditos de los capitales que sobre ellas reconocían, y los diezmatarios estaban los más en poder de los insurgentes y, de los que estaban libres, los comandantes de las tropas reales tomaban casi todo lo que rendían.[25]

Las cargas impositivas extraordinarias fueron agobiando más a la población, pues nunca alcanzaban los ingresos ordinarios para atender los gastos y su efecto inmediato fue la irritación. Lentamente erosionaron la confianza y legitimidad de la autoridad colonial porque: "la recaudación . . . se había hecho con desigualdad, imponiéndose además de las establecidas por el gobierno, otras muchas por los comandantes locales, los cuales también exigían a su arbitrio préstamos forzosos que a veces eran exorbitantes."[26]

La distribución de los ingresos entre las provincias fue causa de disputa con los poderes del interior, los cuales mostraron su inconformidad acerca de la forma en que se hacía, dando a la luz fenómenos que eran señales de posteriores barruntos de autonomía en algunas intendencias y que, a juicio de Alamán, habían llevado a " . . . un estado casi de independencia del virreinato . . . " y que traerían en los años futuros graves consecuencias una vez declarada la independencia.[27]

En la estrategia diseñada por Calleja para ganar la guerra a los insurgentes fue indispensable reanimar las actividades económicas, tanto para

[24]Alamán, *Historia de Méjico,* III, 391.
[25]Ibid., 262.
[26]Ibid., IV, 470.
[27]Ibid., 472.

obtener los ingresos necesarios, como para normalizar la vida de la Nueva España. La palanca estratégica fue el activar la minería y el comercio, para lo cual fue necesario asegurar el tráfico por las principales rutas comerciales.[28]

Las dificultades para mantener un tráfico normal fueron innumerables, como veremos; así fue indispensable que el ejército virreinal dedicara constantemente una parte importante de sus tropas a custodiar y vigilar los convoyes que transportaban numerario y mercancías principalmente y pudieran circular sin peligro de caer en manos de los insurgentes o bandidos que habían proliferado.

La estrategia de Calleja de normalizar las actividades no dió frutos de inmediato. En el caso de la minería no se resolvieron los principales problemas que la afectaban, pero a pesar de esto la amonedación creció si la comparamos con el año de 1812 como se observa en las cifras siguientes:

Año	Plata (pesos)	Oro (pesos)
1812	4,027,620.09	381,646
1813	6,133,983.60	–
1814	6,902,481.40	618,069
1815	6,454,799.50	486,464

Las finanzas del campo insurgente

No es posible por ahora adentrarnos en las finanzas de la insurgencia, pues aún carecemos de estudios sobre el asunto. Nos hemos referido a algunas formas de allegarse fondos, siendo una de las más socorridas el exigir cuotas en el tráfico comercial y el apoderarse de pastas y minerales provenientes de los reales de minas.

Morelos desde sus primeras proclamas se ocupó de la cuestión impositiva, comprendiendo la importancia que la recaudación tenía como uno de los medios para sostener la guerra contra los realistas. Para este fin aprovechó el sistema de recaudación imperante, pero para beneficio de la insurgencia.

En 1811 ordenaba:

> Por el presente comisiono en toda forma . . . para que [algunas personas autorizadas expresamente] pasen a los pueblos y lugares conquistados en las tierras calientes y costas del sur, a reconocer las existencias de los estancos, alcabalas, como también las de bulas y nuevo indulto de carne, tomando cuenta de ellos a las personas que las manejan, sus fiadores etc., y demás que llaman rentas reales, y que por lo mismo entraban en cajas reales, comprendiendo los de comunidad producidos de renta de los pueblos, recogidas

[28]Ibid., III, 400–401.

hasta esta fecha en algún juzgado, caja o particular: todas las que recogerán dichos comisionados para socorro de las tropas de mi mando. . . . [29]

También se hizo uso del recurso de contribuciones forzosas en las zonas bajo su control, principalmente de las haciendas y ranchos a los cuales se les había fijado una cuota, dado que:

Para sostener . . . [sus] fuerzas, los recursos con los [que] . . . contaban consistían, en lo que producían las haciendas de los europeos y de los americanos adictos al partido real de que se habían apoderado; más estos productos eran escasos tanto por la dificultad de realizar los frutos, como por la infidelidad de las manos que administraban las fincas.

A juicio de Alamán,

Morelos regulaba su importe en un millón anual de pesos; Osorno subsistía a expensas de las haciendas de pulque de los llanos de Apam; Terán con lo que producían las contribuciones que impuso a los maíces del rico valle de San Andrés y el P. Torres con las que pagaban todas las del Bajío. Además . . . cobraban alcabalas de 4 a 6 por 100, sobre los artículos del giro interior; derechos sobre las carnicerías, y se apoderaban de los productos de los diezmos en los lugares que ocupaban.[30]

El propio Morelos comprendía lo gravoso que resultaba para gran parte de la población el pago de impuestos forzosos, como también la posible irritación que provocaba; al respecto es elocuente un comunicado en el cual se lamenta de la imposibilidad de dejar de cobrar ciertas cantidades a los vecinos e indios:

impuestos a los que no asisten en los ejércitos para socorro de las tropas . . . porque siendo auxilio de los más principales para el socorro de mis ejércitos, seguramente [si se suspendieran] resentiría grave perjuicio, y acaso me expondría a la deserción de mis tropas no teniendo socorros para subsistir; pues aunque por aquí hay muchos caudales secuestrados, pero estos consisten en haciendas, que los más de ellos están paradas por falta de fomento.[31]

[29] José María Morelos, "Nombramiento de comisionados para el reconocimiento de las existencias de las rentas reales y administración de estas, 18 de abril de 1811", en Manuel Dublán y José María Lozano, *Legislación mexicana o colección completa de las disposiciones legislativas expedidas desde la independencia de la república ordenada por los licenciados . . .* (México: Imprenta del Comercio, a cargo de Dublán y Lozano, Hijos, 1876), I, 344–345.

[30] Alamán, *Historia de Méjico*, IV, 391–392.

[31] J. E. Hernández y Dávalos, *Colección de documentos para la historia de la guerra de independencia de México de 1808 a 1821. Coleccionados por . . .* (México: José María Sandoval, Impresor, 1877), IV, 37.

La guerra llegó a tal grado de indefinición en regiones, como los llanos de Apam, que permitió a los insurgentes encontrar una entrada cuantiosa de ingresos, al igual que a los agentes del gobierno virreinal, donde ambos cobraban impuestos por la extracción del pulque.[32]

Dificultades en el tráfico comercial: arreglos y realidades nuevas

A medida que la contienda se extendió, sus efectos se hicieron más palpables en la economía y el costo para mantener al ejército en pie de guerra se incrementó. Como hemos señalado, los trastornos en la minería hicieron de 1812 el año de menor amonedación registrada y sus consecuencias fueron más que severas, tanto por que eran una prueba palpable de los trastornos que la guerra había traído en el sector más importante de la economía novohispana después de la agricultura, pero también porque agravó la ya conocida escasez crónica de numerario, lo cual contribuyó a minar la economía interna al dificultar aún más el tráfico y las transacciones comerciales.

El problema tomó tal gravedad que no solo el gobierno español tuvo que ordenar la acuñacion de moneda de cobre, sino que algunos grupos insurgentes buscaron la forma de amonedar cobre, plata y oro para no interrumpir el comercio y proveerse de los alimentos y pertrechos indispensables para sostener la guerra.

El ejército virreinal tuvo, como ya lo hemos mencionado, la tarea de salvaguardar los enormes convoyes que transportaban el numerario junto con las mercancías y artículos indispensables para la producción minera en particular.

Hamnett señala como la insurgencia afectó las principales líneas de comunicación de la Nueva España:

1. El nexo entre la ciudad de México y el Bajío
2. La ruta del Bajío con su hinterland del norte, las provincias internas
3. El camino a Acapulco
4. El del principal puerto, Veracruz, pasando por Puebla, estuvo permanentemente asediado por grupos de insurgentes y gavillas[33]

Los convoyes necesitaron cada vez más tropas para custodiarlos; por ejemplo, uno que salió de la ciudad de México en abril de 1812 rumbo a Guanajuato llevando un cargamento del rey y de particulares

[32]Alamán, *Historia de Méjico,* IV, 216.
[33]Hamnett, "Economic and Social Dimension, 18-19.

con los reales destinados a aquel mineral y gran cantidad de efectos mercantiles que habían de distribuirse en todas las provincias del interior [fue atacado en Salamanca por la gente de Albino García] . . . el destacamento militar logró salir tan bien librado del ataque a pesar de que era . . . un cargamento tan considerable, que era tan difícil defender en la larga extensión de una legua larga que ocupaba más de mil mulas. . . [34]

La magnitud de algunos convoyes fue impresionante; Lucas Alamán nos describe en el que se dirigía a Veracruz en enero de 1814. Escribe:

se pusieron en camino para aquella plaza y Puebla ochenta y siete coches con pasajeros, multitud de estos a caballo, más de siete mil mulas cargadas con cinco millones de pesos y cantidades grandes de efectos del país. Los exorbitantes fletes que se pagaron, prueban las dificultades que había para caminar en aquel tiempo . . . las cuales no dejaron de aparecer en el camino, ya que en el tránsito a Puebla ocurrió una desgracia lamentable: varios pasajeros a caballo impacientes de las molestias de tan lenta caminata, creyendo que no había riesgo en lo que restaba que andar hasta aquella ciudad, se adelantaron desde Rio Frío, y fueron muertos por los insurgentes, quedando los cadáveres colgados en los árboles del camino por donde había de pasar el convoy.[35]

El tráfico de mercancías y el resguardo de los convoyes se convirtieron en un pingüe negocio para algunos de los propios encargados de custodiarlos. La protección del ejército realista a los convoyes en ocasiones no se hizo como servicio, sino que supuso un pago a los propios militares por los particulares interesados en garantizar la seguridad de sus envíos. En estos años se mencionó con insistencia a Agustín de Iturbide como uno de los oficiales realistas que se beneficiaron con tales operaciones, y que fue el inicio —según lo señalan sus acusadores— de una fortuna gracias a que prestó sus servicios en el resguardo del tráfico y participando directamente en la compra de productos, en los lugares donde la inseguridad y el peligro contribuían a despreciarlos y, posteriormente los vendía a precios más altos en las zonas en donde se carecía de ellos.

Iturbide también fue acusado de que en 1814 en la campaña de pacificación de Guanajuato se aprovechó de su cargo y

llevó consigo un cargamento de azogue y otros artículos de consumo de las minas, dejando establecidas sus relaciones en la capital, para continuar el giro lucrosísimo de llevar estos y otros efectos que vendía muy caros, recibiendo su importe en plata al precio ínfimo de cuatro y medio pesos el marco, a que los mineros se veían obligados a realizarla por escasear mucho el numerario, pudiendo . . . , como comandante, retardar la llegada de los

[34]Alamán, *Historia de Méjico*, III, 178–181.
[35]Ibid., IV, 37, 39 y 473–474.

convoyes según le convenía, de donde resultó la ruina de aquella minería y gravísimos perjuicios al comercio. . . . [36]

Los negocios de Iturbide no quedaron impunes, pues un grupo de notables de Guanajuato envió una representación al virrey solicitando su remoción; éste se vio obligado a suspenderle en el mando, pero considerando que era un hombre indispensable a su estrategia para sofocar la rebelión, decidió dejarle el mando de tropas, justificándose en que otros informes le eran favorables a Agustín de Iturbide.

El asunto no dejó de ser un contencioso en la carrera del antiguo comandante realista, pues en 1822 se publicaron unos comentarios de un antiguo conocido suyo el cual hacía aseveraciones que empañaban su prestigio; éste lo acusaba de que otro de los medios de que se había valido para hacerse de dinero consistía en mandar: "vender a vil precio los acopios de granos de algunas haciendas, a pretexto de evitar que se hiciesen dueños de ellos los insurgentes comprándolos él mismo por tercera mano, para venderlos por cuadriplicada cantidad. . . . "[37]

Los abusos de los militares no se limitaron a Iturbide pues:

habían ido creciendo a medida que la seguridad del tráfico con las provincias había abierto campo más amplio a las especulaciones mercantiles. Por ejemplo se menciona el caso de dos comandantes La Madrid y Samaniego . . . de quienes dependía la conducción de los convoyes de Puebla a Oaxaca, disponían la salida y tránsito de éstos, según el estado de los precios del azúcar y otros artículos . . . dejando que escaseasen en aquel mercado, para sacar mayor ventaja en las remesas que por su cuenta hacían.

Se menciona el caso de otro comandante realista que:

había venido a ser monopolista en todas las poblaciones que comprendía su comandancia del Sur, y aplicando a su provecho las presas que sobre los insurgentes solían hacerse, especialmente en las cosechas de algodón, reunió en poco tiempo un capital tan considerable, que pudo adquirir fincas muy valiosas en el mismo departmento. . . . "[38]

También en el campo insurgente, como hemos mencionado, gracias al control de caminos o regiones claves se exigían pagos forzosos para permitir la circulación de mercancías en la ruta de Veracruz, lo que a ojos de los comandantes realistas eran arreglos a los que habían llegado los miembros del consulado del puerto con los insurgentes; los militares se

[36]Ibid., IV, 42.
[37]Ibid., IV, 446–447.
[38]Ibid., IV, 445.

quejaban de que a pesar de las prohibiciones de circular, salvo con los permisos concedidos por el virrey, veían como entraban al puerto mercancías en hatos de mulas, por lo que no dudaban en acusar:

> al comercio de Veracruz, de ser la causa del grande aumento que había tenido la revolución en aquella provincia, por el fomento que recibían los insurgentes con los derechos de tránsito que les pagaban los comerciantes, sobre los efectos que aquellos dejaban libremente pasar.[39]

A las dificultades e interrupción del tráfico por las principales rutas habría que añadir los daños causados en los caminos, ya fueran provocados intencionalmente, o por el uso que para fines militares se les dio. Años después, recién independizado el país, se nos describe cómo sus efectos aún eran visibles:

> en que los más de ellos fueron estropeados para impedir el paso de las tropas o echados a perder por el acarreo de la artillería, han quedado abandonados a merced de los viajeros y de las inclemencias del tiempo, de manera que, en realidad de verdad (salvo tan solo el camino a Veracruz, recién restaurado) apenas si hay carretera en la República que no parezca antiguo lecho de arroyo de montaña más bien que obra llevada a cabo con el propósito de facilitar las comunicaciones.[40]

Intentos por restablecer la normalidad

El panorama empezó a cambiar con la derrota y fusilamiento de Morelos. En 1815 Calleja podía anunciar:

> Destruido Morelos que tuvo el designio y los medios de formarla, no es fácil a lo menos en algún tiempo que ningún otro lo consiga, por los odios y rivalidades que los desune y que procuro fomentar. Las comunicaciones se hacen cada día más fáciles y expeditas de unas provincias a otras; muchos territorios van volviendo al orden y algunos están tan pacíficos que casi no conocen la insurreción, como la mayor parte de las provincias de San Luis Potosí y Guadalajara y las siete internas de Oriente y Poniente. La capital del reino es provista y abastecida desde las partes más remotas de él, con toda clase de comestibles y efectos y con una abundancia y baratura tal que a juicio de las personas más imparciales hace muchos años que no se veía en un estado tan ventajoso, ni gozaba de tanta tranquilidad.[41]

[39]Ibid., 97–98 y 242–243.

[40]Brantz Mayer, *México lo que fue y lo que es* (México: Fondo de Cultura Económica, 1953), 368.

[41]"Carta de Calleja al ministro de Indias sobre la aprehensión de Morelos y estado de la revolución, 30 de noviembre de 1815", en Herrejón, *Morelos*, 155–161.

Para principios de 1816 las aguas parecieron volver a la tranquilidad en la mayoría de los frentes de la guerra pues después de la muerte de Morelos el reflujo de las fuerzas insurgentes era patente y recordaba en cierta manera a la situación que había prevalecido después de la aprehensión y fusilamiento de Miguel Hidalgo, con la diferencia de que ahora no había ningún dirigente entre los sobrevivientes que lograra agrupar y reorganizar las diezmadas fuerzas que restaban de la revolución, por lo que empezaron a prevalecer grupos y bandas carentes de organización y que muchas veces se confundían con bandidos.

El triunfo de las armas realistas no significó en forma alguna un regreso a la situación imperante anteriormente, pues la guerra había en parte destruido y desorganizado la economía novohispana y en él ánimo de muchos de los sectores más influyentes de la población cundía el desaliento y pesimismo sobre el futuro.

Este clima se tradujo en la salida sin control de importantes volúmenes de moneda que drenaban la riqueza de la Nueva España aprovechando el descontrol reinante, particularmente "por los puertos del mar del sur". Calleja se vio obligado a promulgar una serie de medidas con el fin de detener tal práctica. Las más importantes eran las siguientes:

> Se declaran incursos en la pena de comiso todos los metales que se encontraren sin las correspondientes marcas de la Tesorería . . . de cuyo importe se aplicará la parte respectiva al denunciante y aprehensores.
>
> Todas las aduanas marítimas de esta Nueva España remitirán mensualmente a este Virreinato una razón o estado circunstanciado, del número de barras que se hayan embarcado en sus respectivos territorios, con expresión de su peso y ley, y la de los asientos de minas de su procedencia, explicando los nombres de los sujetos que los extraigan, los fiadores de la presentación de la tornaguía, y finalmente, las de los puertos de la Peninsula, o de este Reino, a que se dirijan.[42]

Los esfuerzos por rehabilitar la minería continuaron, pero tropezaron con serios escollos, pues si bien la amonedación había tomado un paso más firme, como se aprecia en las cifras siguientes:

Año	Plata (pesos)	Oro (pesos)[43]
1815	6,454,799.50	486,454
1816	8,325,616.03	960,393
1817	7,994,951.00	854,942
1818	10,852,367.76	533,921
1819	11,491,138.50	539,377
1820	9,897,078.10	509,076

[42]*Ordenanzas de minería y colección de las órdenes de esta materia posteriores a su publicación a las que van agregadas las reformas de que son susceptibles algunos de los artículos vigentes de las mismas ordenanzas y dos láminas para explicar los metodos más económicos de despuntar las vetas*, Nueva edición (Paris: Librería de Rosa, Bouret y Cia., 1851), 170–171.

[43]Alamán, *Historia de Méjico*, I, 4, 17.

La situación real de la minería no se reflejaba en los resultados de la amonedación, ya que faltaba evaluar el estado de los yacimientos y las pérdidas ocurridas durante la guera. Al respecto la memoria presentada por José María Quirós al consulado de Veracruz en 1817 nos proporciona una idea más exacta de la situación; éste señalaba:

> basta para conocer . . . la decadencia! de la minería la que han sufrido los preciosos metales de oro y plata, que son en los que consiste principalmente la entidad de sus productos, y lo acredita haberse reducido de seis a siete millones de pesos la amonedación anual de la Real Casa de México, en lugar de los veinte y siete que se acuñaban en los últimos años en que no se había alterado el sosiego y el orden público . . . [y explicaba] como habiéndose hecho las minas el primario objeto de los jefes de la rebelión para rehacerse en ellas de caudales con que concitar a la incauta plebe y sostener sus proyectos, experimentaron los mayores estragos, perdiendo los metales existentes, sus operarios, tiros y menesteres e interrumpiéndose sus labores; con lo que las unas se anegaron, las otras se emborrascaron y todas han contraído lamentables atrasos, incapaces de restaurarse en un siglo, aun impendiendo en ello sumas considerables.

Para Quirós las pérdidas calculadas en el monto de la masa circulante:

> en cada año de revolución un quebranto de más de treinta y un millones de pesos, elevándose en los seis corridos hasta fin de diciembre del próximo pasado [1816] por cima de setecientos ochenta y seis millones. . . . [44]

A las pérdidas contabilizadas por Quirós habría que añadir la situación del crédito minero, mecanismo vital en el refaccionamiento de los mineros. A propósito, José Joaquín de Eguía, autor de una Memoria elaborada en 1817 sobre la utilidad e influjo de la minería en el reino, explicaba:

> Antes de las conmociones populares tenían los mineros el recurso de recoger a cambio de libranzas cuanta moneda acopiaban los mercaderes y los administradores de las rentas Reales y eclesiásticas. Otras veces giraban libranzas pagaderas cuando enviasen sus platas, y recibían de contado el valor de aquellas, con el cual continuaban las operaciones de sus minas y haciendas, o tal vez compraban con utilidad las platas con que habían de hacer el pago. Tenían además algunos mercaderes y hacendados que los habilitaban. Finalmente en las Reales Cajas había un banco de rescate donde sin más demora que la necesaria para el camino se les compraban sus platas por todo su valor. Sin embargo se veía con frecuencia que apenas llegaba la cantidad correspondiente al envío que de platas pastas se había hecho por cuenta del fondo de este banco, cuando ya se hallaba convertida en nuevas pastas, porque

[44] Quirós, "Memoria de estatuto", 231-264.

los mineros . . . carecían de moneda; por lo cual empleaban los ruegos y empeños solicitando cada uno ser preferido en la compra, porque regularmente no alcanzaba el fondo para la de todas las pastas que se habían acopiado. ¿Que sucederá en el día que han desaparecido todos estos recursos?

Se respondía:

> Lo que debe suceder es que cada uno gire con su fondo propio. Pero, ¿no sabemos que la emigración, la paralización de los giros y las invasiones de los insurgentes han disminuido las fortunas de unos y arruinado las de otros, dejando a muchos con sólo un corto rezago que pudieron consigo cuando emigran? ¿Será suficiente este para emprender el desagüe de las grandes inundaciones que la suspensión de la maniobra ha causado; el reparto de las ruinas que el tiempo y los rebeldes han hecho en las obras interiores de las minas; los nuevos tiros que algunas necesitan; el reedificio de las haciendas y reposición de máquinas y herramientas . . . y de las minas que han sido quemadas o robadas; y el acopio de cal, sal, magistral, sebo, jarcia, madera, acero, hierro, azogue, etc.?[45]

Para aliviar la situación en 1820 se llevaron a cabo nuevos intentos por sacar adelante a la minería, y como el gobierno carecía de los fondos suficientes para una tarea de tal magnitud, se invitó incluso al consulado de México a patrocinar la empresa y aunque dicho cuerpo presentó un proyecto conducente a rehabilitar la minería, éste no se llevó a la práctica. Se hicieron también esfuerzos por parte de las autoridades, que resultaron infructuosos, mediante la política de conceder indulto " . . . a todos los dueños y trabajadores de minas, mandando se pusiesen en libertad los que estuviesen presos y procesados por infidentes . . . ".[46]

En resumen, la grave situación por la que atravesaba la minería y que heredó el nuevo régimen independiente —como señala Hamnett— se debió a que en este sector ocurrieron los cambios más drásticos como resultado de la guerra, particularmente por el desplazamiento de los inversionistas —comerciantes de origen peninsular, intermediarios indispensables en la capitalización de la producción minera, debido a que la guerra socavó la cadena de comunicación de aquéllos con los operadores de minas.

De esta manera se desorganizó el funcionamiento de la amalgamación que supervisaban los rescatadores, los cuales habitualmente compraban el mineral a los mineros y se lo suministraban a los comerciantes, los cuales a cambio financiaban sus operaciones.

[45]*Memoria sobre la utilidad e influjo de la minería en el reino: necesidad de su fomento, y arbitrios de verificarlo* (México: Impresa en la Oficina de don Juan Bautista de Arizpe, 1819).

[46]Alamán, *Historia de Méjico,* IV, 706-707.

Aunque también la presión financiera ejercida sobre los comerciantes por las autoridades virreinales y metropolitanas, urgidas de fondos para sostener los gastos bélicos en Nueva España y ultramar, hicieron recaer sobre aquéllos cargas fiscales extraordinarias, que paulatinamente debilitaron su lealtad a medida que disminuían sus recursos. Se debe añadir a lo anterior las inversiones perdidas, la emigración de personal preparado y sobre todo la fuga de capitales, la cual, según diferentes cálculos, anduvo por los 80 a 140 millones de pesos.[47]

La paralización de una parte importante de la producción minera

El panorama que presentaba la minería mexicana a principios del México independiente era desolador pues: "Exceptuando algunas minas en Zacatecas y en Taxco, no se trabaja formalmente ninguna: que el laborío actual está reducido a arrancar sobre el nivel de la inundación los restos de la antigua riqueza. . . . Por lo cual la extracción se ha reducido a poco más de la cuarta parte de antes de la revolución. . . . "[48]

La inundación y el azolvamiento de los tiros de las minas por abandono o destrucción intencional eran los problemas más frecuentes a los que se enfrentaron las mineros. Para reanudar la extracción era indispensable primero limpiar las minas, para lo cual era necesario invertir en la compra de maquinaria adecuada, pero en la medida que la mayoría de los mineros se encontraba sin fondos poco podía hacerse, ya que " . . . nuestras minas no pueden explotarse porque se hallan insolvadas, y nosotros sin fondos para desaguarlas y ponerlas al corriente".

La escasez de fondos estaba estrechamente relacionada con la guerra pues las minas habían sido uno de los recursos más socorridos por los ejércitos en armas, gravando " . . . a todas las minas con pensiones exorbitantes que aniquilaron sus poblaciones; y arruinaron las manos benéficas que las fomentaban".[49] La disminución o paralización de la producción minera provocó desocupación, la cual, junto con el enlistamiento de muchos mineros en los ejércitos, contribuyó a la dispersión de la mano de obra.

Los trabajadores mineros después de la guerra tuvieron que buscar empleo o dedicarse a otro oficio, así por ejemplo:

[47]Henry George Ward, *México en 1827* (México: Fondo de Cultura Económica, 1981), 314-337; Hamnett, "Economic and Social Dimension", 20-21.

[48]Lucas Alamán et al., *Dictamen de la comisión especial nombrada para informar sobre el importante ramo de minería*. Impreso de orden de las Cortes (México: Reimpreso en la Oficina de D. Celestino de la Torre, 1821), 3-4.

[49]*Gaceta Imperial de México*, n. 22, I, 10 de noviembre de 1821, 189-192.

> la decadencia [de] las minas [en San Luis Potosí] . . . hizo que la mayor parte de las mineros de este estado se dedicasen a la agricultura en los mismos terrenos que antes sirvieron para los usos de la minería. De ahí que resultaron en los contornos de esta ciudad y en el distrito de su Alcaldía mayor varios terrenos de laboría pequeños . . . de los que juntándose algunos se formaron posesiones rurales de mucha cuantía. Resultó de ahí que tantos brazos que la indicada decadencia de las minas dejó sin ejercicio, se aplicaron a los trabajos de campo con los indígenas que naturalmente propenden a ellos.[50]

Formación de comisiones oficiales para rehabilitar la minería (1821–1822)

La preocupación por resolver la crisis de la minería ocasionada por la guerra se puso oficialmente de manifiesto nuevamente en 1821 por el régimen español, específicamente por las Cortes, para lo cual formó una comisión integrada por diputados entre los que se encontraba Lucas Alamán, la cual se encargo de estudiar el caso y proponer soluciones. En junio de 1821 se aprobó el dictamen siguiente con excepción del articulo 11:

> Art. 1. Abolición derechos: quintos, uno por ciento y señoriaje. / Art. 2. Contribución única del 3 por ciento sobre oro y plata. / Art. 3. Los mineros no pagarán ningún otro impuesto. / Art. 4. El cobro de la amonedación importará sólo su costo haciendo promedio. / Art. 5. Se dejará de cobrar por la afinación y las mermas. / Art. 6. La diferencia de ley entre monedas duras y flebes será para el cuerpo de minería. / Art. 7. Se tratará de reducir los costos de apartado (en oro y plata). / Art. 8. Suspensión del derecho de bocado. / Art. 9. Una vez que se fijen los impuestos y sellos el precio de venta será fijado por los dueños. / Art. 10. Franquicias de alcabalas. Ratificando las de 1783, 1791 y 1796. / Art. 11. Libre circulación a ultramar y se instale una fábrica de pólvora. / Art. 12. Quedan abolidos derechos fijados por la revolución al consumo, como a la producción. / Art. 13. Que se mande azogue a las diputaciones de minería y se tenga una reserva. / Art. 14. Que se contraten personas con conocimientos sobre minería y nociones fiscales para las casas de moneda.[51]

Para la comisión de las Cortes sólo había una política que pudiera poner en marcha nuevamente al sector minero y consistía básicamente en brindar estímulos y apoyos consistentes en la reducción o suspensión de cargas fiscales; además solicitaban se les suministrara regularmente azogue,

[50] *Aguila Mexicana*, n. 134, 24 de agosto de 1824, 2–4.
[51] Alamán, *Dictamen de la comisión*, 6–10.

pólvora y maquinaria sin trabas fiscales. Tenían confianza que con los recursos ahorrados pudieran ser destinados a gastos de recuperación de que tanto necesitaba la minería.

La inquietud de las Cortes fue compartida por el nuevo régimen independiente. La soberana junta provisional gubernativa del imperio formuló una serie de medidas en noviembre de 1821 cuyo contenido seguía en lo esencial las promulgadas por las Cortes y con las cuales se buscaba contribuir a resolver

> el deplorable y decadente estado de la minería, y la urgencia que hay de proporcionarle a este importante ramo cuantos medios se hallen en su alcance que contríbuyan a su mayor prosperidad, ha tenido a bien decretar y decreta:
>
> 1. Quedan suprimidos los derechos de uno por ciento, diezmo, y real de señoriaje. / 2. Queda también suprimido el derecho . . . por la afinacion de las pastas . . / 3. . . . queda suprimido el derecho . . . de las pastas mixtas que se cobra por razón de mermas de la plata en el Apartado. / 4. . . . queda suprimido el derecho . . . que se cobra a título de bocado. / 5. . . . quedan suprimidos todos los derechos que se impusieron a las pasta . . . y la moneda durante la revolución. / 6. Por única contribución se cobrará sólo el tres por ciento sobre el verdadero valor de la plata, y lo mismo sobre el del oro. . . . / 7. En la casa de moneda de la capital, sólo se cobrarán dos reales a cada marca de plata y lo mismo en cada marco de oro por total costo de amonedación. . . . / 8. (Se reducen costos de apartado.) / 9. (Se cobrará sólo el costo real de los ensayes, quedando suprimido el derecho de bocado.) / 10. (Una vez pagados los derechos que estipula el artículo 6 y con los sellos que lo acrediten, sus dueños quedan en la más absoluta libertad de venderlos o utilizarlos como más les convenga y al precio que ellos mismos fijen.) / 11. (Se reducen los granos de feble en la moneda. / 12. (Sólo se emplearán en las casa de moneda y en la del Apartado personas con los conocimientos necesarios en física, química y mineralogía.) / 13. Queda absolutamente libre de derechos el azogue en caldo, ora proceda de Europa o Asia, ora se saque de los criaderos del imperio. / 14. La pólvora que necesiten los mineros para el laborío de las minas, se las franqueará el gobierno al costo y costas.[52]

Le preocupación sobre la materia fue constante y con tal propósito se formó una comisión para estudiar la situación de la minería. De la comisión formaron parte mineros destacados como José María Fagoaga; ésta trató de solucionar los trastornos que ocasionaba al gobierno la falta de impuestos por la reducción de la producción, así como trató de impedir la evasión fiscal y naturalmente coadyuvar a que los mineros volvieran a obtener ganancias. La comisión ratificó las 14 medidas tomadas en noviembre de 1821.

[52]Dublán y Lozano, *Legislación Méxicana*, I, 563–564.

En su informe presentado en 1822 señalaba:

> La Comisión examinó el lánguido y moribundo estado a que diez años continuos de la más ominosa y desastrosa guerra, habían reducido todas las ramas, todas las fuentes de su riqueza y prosperidad. Inmensos capitales han sido presa de la más escandalosa rapiña, y los que se salvaron del naufragio general, buscaron los unos su seguridad refugiándose a países extraños y los que permanecieron, condenados a la ociosidad más absoluta por falta de empleo, se extinguieron sucesivamente, como debió suceder.[53]

En ambas comisiones, la de Cortes y la de la junta gubernativa, había el convencimiento de que la minería había sido y debería seguir siendo un sector clave en la economía, por lo que de su recuperación dependía la suerte del resto de las actividades económicas, y así lo señalaban: "En esta relación íntima entre la minería y la industria agricultora y el comercio, proviene el que la decadencia o prosperidad de estos haya seguido exactamente los pasos de aquélla, de donde se deduce que el restablecimiento de las unas es también dependiente de la otra".[54]

Los miembros de la comisión formada por la Junta estaban plenamente convencidos que a partir de la reanudación de:

> Las actividades mineras pueden y deben ocupar y dar empleo a muchos cientos de miles de habitantes, proporcionándoles subsistencia cómoda para sí y sus familias [y ademas] . . . la producción y preparación de los artículos que componen esta subsistencia (consumo de los mineros) ocupará y dará . . . ventajas a otro número igual o mayor de familias.

Estaban convencidos que una de las secuelas de la guerra era la existencia de una gran masa de desocupados que "Con la guerra y la destrucción consiguiente faltó ocupación a gran número de brazos y con ella los medios de conseguir su subsistencia y la de sus familias: de aquí la miseria y el empobrecimiento universal".[55]

Ambas comisiones coincidían en cuanto a la magnitud de los daños que impedían reanudar la extracción. Las reparaciones implicaban —a su juicio— una cantidad enorme de recursos y cuya suma era imposible de alcanzar con los fondos de que disponían los concesionarios de minas.

[53]José María Fagoaga et al., *Exposición hecha por la comisión especial a la soberana junta gubernativa, sobre la necesidad de fomentar este ramo principal de industria con la baja de derechos que propuso su dictamen de 24 de octubre próximo pasado* (México: Imprenta de D. Mariano de Zúñiga y Ontiveros, 1822), 4-5.

[54]Alamán, *Dictamen de la comisión*, 4-5.

[55]Fagoaga, *Exposición*, 4-5 y 7-8.

A los problemas acarreados por la guerra, se añadían aquellos inherentes a la naturaleza de los yacimientos, siendo el principal la baja proporción de plata contenida en los materiales extraídos, por lo que era indispensable extraer grandes cantidades para conseguir la ley requerida, lo que a su vez hacía necesario emplear un mayor número de trabajadores, elevando los costos de producción. A esto se añadían las tradicionales dificultades para conseguir el azogue y la pólvora vitales para la producción y que en los últimos tiempos sólo se conseguían por medios fraudulentos.[56]

Los miembros de la comisión formada por la Junta estaban convencidos que el gobierno, al acceder a las demandas de los particulares, obraba en detrimento de sus ingresos, pero también que era la única política que podría salvar a la minería.

La argumentación no convenció a todos y no faltaron los que la criticaron argumentando el predominio de los intereses particulares en las decisiones del gobierno. Los defensores de la política gubernamental que —como hemos visto— seguía en los fundamental las medidas recomendadas y puestas en vigor por el régimen anterior respondieron:

> La comisón . . . cuando propuso la rebaja de derechos a las platas no lo hizo por favorecer a los individuos que se ocupan en el giro de las minas: semejante idea era muy indigna de la alta penetración e ilustrado celo de V.M. que no puede ver a todos los habitantes del Imperio, sino como miembros de una misma y única familia, cuya felicidad es el resultado de la que disfruta cada uno de los que la componen.[57]

Reformas a las condiciones de usufructo de las minas (1821-1824)

La separación de la metrópoli abrió al nuevo régimen la posibilidad de legislar sobre el sistema de propiedad y al establecerse los acuerdos de Iguala se sancionó comó principio fundamental el respeto a la propiedad privada, salvaguardando los intereses privados de los diversos sectores de la economía.

Augustín de Iturbide prometió respetar la propiedad privada disipando cualquier duda sobre la actitud de su gobierno: "La conservación de las propiedades que los hombres adquieren con penosos afanes, son, han sido y serán siempre respetados por todos los pueblos y legislaciones".[58]

[56]Juan A. Mateos, *Historia parlamentaria de los congresos mexicanos de 1821 a 1857* (México: Vicente S. Reyes, 1877), I, 75; *Gaceta Imperial de México*, n. 25, I, 181-183.

[57]Alamán, *Dictamen de la comisión*, 19; Fagoaga, *Exposición*, 3-4; Dublán y Lozano, *Legislación mexicana*, I, 563-564.

[58]Juan O'Donojú, *Manifiesto que por conducto del señor gobernador intendente y jefe político de esta provincia hace a sus moradores el Excmo. Señor Capitán General y Jefe Superior político D . . .* (Veracruz y después Puebla: Imprenta Imperial, 1821).

En principio se mantuvo el régimen de propiedad colonial de los yacimientos mineros que, como parte del subsuelo, eran considerados propiedad del Estado y que para su explotación privada requerían de una concesión del monarca con el requisito indispensable de que el concesionario fuera nacido en un territorio perteneciente a la Corona o tuviera permiso expreso. Dicho permiso era temporal y estaba especificado que la concesión caducaba si en un plazo de cuatro meses no se trabajaba el mineral, medida con la que se pretendía garantizar el trabajo permanente en las minas.[59]

En la práctica el régimen de propiedad estuvo amenazado durante la contienda, dado que muchas minas fueron ocupadas por pequeños mineros sin autorización expresa, amparados en la legislación vigente que permitía la denuncia de las minas no trabajadas durante más de cuatro meses, debido a que habían sido abandonadas por sus concesionarios en espera de tiempos mejores o del financiamiento indispensable para ponerlas nuevamente en condiciones de producir.

Henry George Ward nos describe la situación:

> Bajo la denominación de buscones, nunca han cesado de trabajar; y aunque, por falta de método en sus operaciones, ellos mismos han causado a las minas los más graves daños, en general han logrado extraer, de los niveles superiores o de operaciones abandonadas en tiempos mejores por otras de mayor promesa, una muy considerable cantidad de plata. Este irregular sistema todavía se sigue en muchas partes del país; y en Zimapán, Zacualpan, El Doctor y muchos de los distritos del norte, gran cantidad de la población se mantiene así aun hoy. La plata así obtenida se vendía en cada real de minas en un precio de cuatro o seis, ocho y hasta doce reales por marcos más abajo del precio de la casa de moneda, a aquellos habitantes que en tales términos se podían permitir esperar una oportunidad de llevarla, en convoy, hasta la casa de moneda más cercana, en donde era cambiada. . . . [60]

El uso por buscones de las minas, amparados en la legislación vigente, encontró un eco favorable en la prensa y así aparecieron notas apoyándolos:

> El dominio eminente o directo de las minas, reside en la nación: ésta concede el útil al ciudadano que las denuncia, con la condición precisa de

[59]"1°. Todo yacimiento minero, cualquiera que, fuese su calidad, y lo mismo si se encontrase en lugares públicos que en tierras y posesiones de personas particulares, debía ser considerado como regalía de la Corona. 2°. El dominio del suelo no daba derecho ninguno al dominio del subsuelo", en. J. M. Ots Capdequi, *España en América: el régimen de tierras en la época colonial* (México: Fondo de Cultura Económica, 1959), 65. La ley de la recopilación de Indias era: Ley 12, tit. 10, lib. 5 y 5a, t. 18, lib. 6; de la recopilación de Indias: Ley 1, tit. 10, lib. 8 y t. 27, lib. 9; de las ordenanzas de minería: art. 1 del tit. 7. En las cuales se exigía a los extranjeros para trabajar y adquirir minas estar naturalizados o tener licencia expresa. *El Sol*, n. 89, 11 de septiembre de 1823, 354.

[60]Ward, *México en 1827*, 323.

trabajarlas incesantemente: dejarlo de hacer por cuatro meses continuos con menos de quatro operarios, basta para que otro pueda denunciarlas.[61]

Los nuevos denunciantes, para legitimar el usufructo de estas minas, presentaron solicitudes al Congreso, órgano encargado ahora de atender y dar validez a dichas peticiones. La respuesta de un diputado – minero también – fue: "la malicia de algunos individuos se vale por medio de denunciarlas conforme a sus ordenanzas . . . dejando perdidos a los desgraciados que consumieron sus caudales y tal vez quedaron adeudados".[62]

La práctica tendió a generalizarse por lo que aumentó la preocupación de los mineros reconocidos por el antiguo régimen, pues *stricto sensu* las denuncias eran legalmente válidas.

Esta situación trajo cada vez mayor inquietud entre los grandes mineros precupados por la práctica que iba ganando adeptos incluso en el congreso y en medios interesados. Los diputados favorables a la posición de los antiguos mineros argüían que la legalidad de las ocupaciones era relativa, apoyandose en que los sucesos que había vivido el país no podían haber sido previstos por nadie, rompiendo abruptamente la normalidad y por lo tanto solicitaban al Congreso que suspendiera la aplicación de las disposiciones a las que se acogían los pequeños mineros, pues ponía en aprietos sus intereses y propiedades en tanto las condiciones para las actividades económicas no fueran las normales.

En la sesión del 2 de julio de 1824, el diputado M. M. Bustamante hizo una proposición acerca de la situación reinante en la minería diciendo:

> llamo la atención del Congreso hacia la facilidad con que por medio de denuncias, se está privando de las minas a sus poseedores . . . [por lo que]. Pido a V. Soberano que se suspenda por tiempo limitado la ley de la denuncia de minas que tienen poseedores, para evitar los grandes perjuicios que está causando en el día su cumplimiento.[63]

Su postura fue suscrita también por los diputados Zavala, Paz, Farías, Mier y Covarrubias y fue enviada a la comisión de minería.

La proposición de Bustamante fue aprobada por el Congreso, no sin dejar de suscitar las protestas de los nuevos denunciantes, las cuales se dejaron oír en la prensa; una carta dirigida a la redacción del *Aguila Mexicana* y escrita por alguien que se firmaba "un minero pobre de Real de Catorce" escribía:

[61]*Aguila Mexicana,* n. 78, año 2, 1 de julio de 1824, 3-4.
[62]Ibid., n. 81, año 2, 4 de julio de 1824, 3-4.
[63]Mateos, *Historia parlamentaria,* II, 826.

> En este mineral hay cinco o seis, que con sus escasos y pobres frutos, mantienen el vecindario, tienen en movimiento las haciendas de sacar plata; los entrantes con efectos, granos y víveres, se llevan bastantes reales, y con treinta barras de plata poco más o menos, que cada mes producen sus metales, se sostiene el comercio, la nación cobra sus respectivos derechos hasta que en fin se la lleva el extranjero. [Y concluía escribiendo] si el congreso suspende la aplicación de la legislación vigente, provocará que muchos mineros que se han acogido a ella se quedarán sin trabajo y se convertirán en salteadores.[64]

El Congreso, como señalábamos, aprobó suspender la aplicación de la legislación en lo que toca a la posibilidad de denuncia de minas abandonadas y de esta manera decidió proteger los intereses de los antiguos concesionarios. Con esta decisión se ponía un freno a una de las secuelas que la guerra había provocado e impedía drásticamente que aquellos que se habían acogido a la legislación española aprovechando la situación reinante pudieran legitimar sus actos.

El Congreso, al decidir suspender la legislación en este aspecto, posibilitaba un cambio en cuanto al derecho de que disponía el Estado como propietario del subsuelo y por tanto el único que podía autorizar concesiones sobre su explotación. Al refrendar su uso a los antiguos concesionarios, supuso el reconocer que éstos tenían derechos sobre las minas y en la práctica darles trato de propietarios, ganándose de esta forma el apoyo de un grupo aún influyente en la economía y la política nacional.

Acogida al capital extranjero: la necesidad de crédito, 1823–1824

Los progresos en la reanudación de la producción fueron demasiado lentos, a pesar de la reducción y suspensión de la mayoría de las cargas fiscales, las cuales contribuyeron a posibilitar la disposición de fondos indispensables para rehabilitar la minería y, en particular la adquisición de maquinaria importada adecuada para desaguar los tiros de las minas, así como el pago de materiales indispensables para reanudar la producción y el pago de mano de obra.

Para 1823 tuvo que reconocerse que la política puesta en marcha era insuficiente para resolver los problemas que aquejaban a la minería y, que solo con la obtención de créditos y nuevas inversiones se podría poner en marcha la mayoría de las minas.

Ante la insuficiencia de los recursos internos, dados los daños, la salida de fondos y el descalabro de los medios tradicionales de financiamiento,

[64] *Aguila Mexicana*, n. 116, año 2, 8 de agosto de 1824, 3.

el único camino posible —a ojos de los de los interesados— era recurrir a la inversión externa; ésta se justificaba dada la:

> situación actual de los mineros les obligará sin duda a admitir habilitación extranjera, que no tendrán dificultad de conseguir por la abundancia de capitales ociosos que existen en Europa, y de que seguramente tendríamos una parte en nuestro país, si el libertador del Anahuac no hubiese destruido la confianza pública con sus latrocinios. Conviene, pues, tener presente que los extranjeros han concebido mejor idea de nuestras minas, que la que nosotros nos hemos formado, a fin de no proponerles partidas excesivamente ventajosas y adquirir capitales al menor costo posible.[65]

Esta posibilidad pudo concretarse debido a que desde el fin de las guerras napoleónicas la inversión externa —principalmente inglesa— cobró gran ímpetu; por lo que hubo una coincidencia entre la necesidad interna de capital para financiar actividades como la minería y la disponibilidad de éste en el exterior. Dicho flujo se canalizó por instituciones financieras, tales como bancos comerciales, así como con el desarrollo de casas de inversión y mediante instrumentos como las letras de cambio. Es así como a partir de 1815 se inició una corriente de inversiones a distintos sectores y regiones, entre los cuales se encontró la minería mexicana a partir de los años veinte del siglo pasado.[66]

Sin embargo, para la participación de inversionistas extrajeros había un impedimento fundamental en la legislación colonial —aún vigente— dado que estaba explícitamente prohibida su calidad de concesionarios de los yacimientos mineros, salvo excepciones autorizadas directamente por el monarca.

El único camino posible era ahora pedir opinión al Congreso como el órgano autorizado para modificar la legislación. Para esto fue necesario su discusión en la cámara. El diputado Lucas Alamán se convirtió en el principal vocero de este nuevo proyecto.

Alamán elaboró una iniciativa que fue aprobada casi en su totalidad por el pleno del Congreso y en ella imperaba una gran identificación entre los intereses particulares y los gubernamentales. En su intervención se pronunció en favor del dictamen, señalando la urgencia de habilitar la minería que carecía de capitales, perdidos durante la guerra o porque hubieran salido del país, convencido que: "parece tanto la necesidad, como la utilidad y conveniencia de la nación, exigen que nos aprovechemos de

[65] *El Sol*, n. 16, 30 de junio de 1823, 309.

[66] A. G. Kenwood y A. L. Lougheed, *Historia del desarrollo económico internacional desde 1820 hasta la primera guerra mundial* (Madrid: Ediciones Istmo, 1973), 50–51; Eric J. Hobsbawm, *Industria e imperio: una historia económica de Gran Bretaña desde 1750* (Barcelona: Editorial Ariel, 1977), figuras 32 y 33.

esta propensión natural que manifiestan los extranjeros, de habilitar nuestras minas, mediante contratos que a unos y a otros nos ofrezcan".[67]

La discusión fue ardua en ciertos momentos debido a que hubo opositores al dictamen y que expresaron su preocupación por la posibilidad de que la participación extranjera terminara por apoderarse de los principales yacimientos de minerales del país. Un diputado mencionó tal posibilidad: "no puedo convenir con (el dictamen) en términos tan generales como propone, porque ya veo a las más ricas negociaciones del reino en poder de los extranjeros . . . y quedar los nacionales de simples espectadores".[68]

La participación de los créditos foráneos no estuvo extenta entonces de suspicacias y recelos, por lo que incluso se llegó a proponer que como medio para evitarlo se debría obligar a los extranjeros a naturalizarse y en esta forma no caer en la formación de un "imperio dentro de otro imperio" por la condición privilegiada que les garantizaban las leyes a los extranjeros.

Los más radicales llegaron a opinar que el gobierno debería prohibir la presencia de créditos externos por las desigualdades que se creaban entre los mineros nacionales, dado que sólo se financiaba a unos cuantos, lo cual iba en contra de la política que el nuevo régimen debería llevar a cabo de favorecer las actividades económicas de todos los nacionales.[69]

Lucas Alamán defendió el dictamen y respondió a los que lo impugnaban que si tales medidas no se ponían en práctica, los capitalistas extranjeros buscarían la forma de invertir subrepticiamente por medio de prestanombres.

Finalmente el Congreso aprobó la proposición suscrita por Lucas Alamán, referente a la suspensión temporal de los artículos de la Recopilación de Castilla y de las Ordenanzas de minería que impedían la intervención de extranjeros en el usufructo de las minas. La parte medular consistió en la suspensión de aquellos artículos como los que "exigían a los extranjeros, para poder adquirir y trabajar minas propias, el de estar naturalizados o tolerados con expresa licencia del gobierno."

Hubo sin embargo, una precisión que limitaba estrictamente la inversión de los extranjeros y que salvaguardaba para los nacionales el usufructo de minerales sin explotar anteriormente, para lo cual se aprobaron dos artículos en los cuales se especificaba:

> Esta suspensión unicamente habilita a los extranjeros para pactar con los dueños de minas que necesiten habilitación de toda clase de avíos en los términos que ambas partes tengan mas conveniente, hasta poder adquirir

[67] *El Sol*, n. 85, 7 de septiembre de 1823, 339.
[68] Ibid., n. 84, 6 de septiembre de 1823, 333–335.
[69] Ibid., n. 85, 7 de septiembre de 1823, 339–340.

en propiedad acciones en las negociaciones que habiliten advertidos de quedar sujetos en todo a nuestras ordenanzas para el laborío de las minas y beneficio de los minerales, y a las demás obligaciones y cargos que la nacion concede la propiedad en tales fundos a todo ciudadano.

El otro señalaba:

> En consecuencia, se les prohibe el registrar minas nuevas, denunciar las desamparadas ni adquirir parte en otras minas que las que habiliten, sea cual fuere el título con que pudieran cohonestar su adquisición.

El pago de alcabala se mantenía tal como se había acordado anteriormente y en el caso del azogue libre de cargas fiscales con excepción del resto de los materiales indispensables, que pagarían los impuestos que les correspondieran.[70]

Una vez que quedaron suspendidas las disposiciones que imposibilitaban la participación extranjera y delimitaban sus alcances, se dió un paso más con la formación de compañias por acciones para canalizar la inversión inglesa.

Con la llegada de los primeros capitales, Aristides Franklin Mornay fungió como uno de los primeros representantes de los intereses británicos en México. Éste, como parte de sus funciones se dirigió al público interesado por medio de la prensa; en una carta al periódico *El Aguila Mexicana* justificaba la presencia de sus compatriotas debido a la situación imperante. Precisó, asimismo, la posición de los inversionistas ingleses respetuosos de la suspensión de la denuncia de minas que anteriormente la legislación permitía, por lo que advertía a posibles solicitantes de fondos que no hubieran acatado las disposiciones del Congreso, no contaran con la ayuda de sus compatriotas. En la carta explicaba cómo:

> una consecuencia inevitable de la guerra intestina que ha padecido este país en sus esfuerzos para conseguir su independencia y libertad, ha sido la destrucción de su minería, el ramo más importante de la industria de sus habitantes, y la ruina casi total de los propietarios de las minas. Se hallan, pues, estos incapaces de continuar sus laboríos, y entiendo que ciertas personas de duras entrañas procuran aprovecharse de esta circunstancia para arrancar de manos de los legítimos dueños, por medio de denuncias, estas minas, la última y sola esperanza que queda a estos hombres estimables para resarcirse de sus enormes pérdidas y reponer sus fortunas en el estado que corresponde al rango que merecen ocupar en la sociedad.
>
> Los tales denunciantes proceden en el concepto errado que los capitalistas ingleses les ministraran los fondos necesarios para trabajar sus mal adquiridas

[70]Dublán y Lozano, *Legislación Mexicana*, I, 681; Mateos, *Historia parlamentaria*, II, 531.

> minas, y así creo que es mi deber declarar que en mi opinión, no se hallará un inglés capaz de fomentar sistema tan injusto y cruel, y que ninguno de mis paisanos amortizará sus capitales en semejantes negociaciones por grandes que sean las ventajas ofrecidas. Por mí individualmente y en nombre de mis amigos y conocidos en el proyecto de habilitar minas mexicanas (Herring, Graham y Powels) . . . protesto formalmente que no habilitaremos con nuestros caudales mina alguna que se halle en este caso, y que usaré de mi influjo con la nueva compañía formada en Londres para que resuelva obrar en conformidad con nuestros principios en este respecto.

La posición anunciada por Mornay canceló cualquier oportunidad de que los nuevos denunciantes se beneficiaran de los capitales británicos. Los nuevos inversionistas acataban las disposiciones del Congreso y respetaban a los antiguos concesionarios de minas, los únicos ante los cuales podía en caso necesario hacerse alguna reclamación en tanto que podían garantizar con su concesión cualquier contratiempo, asegurando de esta manera la suerte de sus fondos.[71]

Una de las primeras compañías, la Unión, se formó en Londres y tuvo como miembro prominente y representante en México a Lucas Alamán. Este describe a la compañía, la cual contaba con un capital de 1,200,000 pesos y el cual podía crecer en caso necesario para el avío de las minas. La Unión exigía como requisitos indispensables para la concesión de un crédito contar con:

1. título de propiedad
2. que no proceda de una denuncia reciente
3. un cálculo sobre el rendimiento de la mina anterior a 1810
4. un informe acerca del estado actual interno y externo de la mina
5. detallar en cuanto a los túneles la altura de las aguas, fuerza de sus viveros, número y tamaño de los volúmenes de agua antes de la guerra
6. mencionar la capacidad de las máquinas necesarias para desaguar los túneles
7. detallar el capital necesario para rehabilitar la mina
8. precio y distancia de los combustibles indispensables para la producción.[72]

La compañía Unión buscó proteger sus inversiones con condiciones que difícilmente podían ser cubiertas por muchos mineros y así privilegió el trato con los grandes concesionarios, los únicos que podían cubrir la totalidad de los requisitos impuestos por la compañía.

[71] *Aguila Mexicana*, n. 14, año 2, 28 de abril de 1824, 3 y n. 78, año 2, 1 de julio de 1824, 3-4.

[72] *El Sol*, n. 33, 10 de mayo de 1824, 132; *Aguila Mexicana*, n. 28, año 2, 12 de mayo de 1824, 3.

Era imposible prácticamente garantizar el cien por ciento del crédito y en caso dado de que la deuda no pudiera ser pagada, el acreedor adquiría derechos según el monto del crédito e inclusive, si lo ameritaba el caso, la concesión pasaba a ser dominio del acreedor. Así, el posible fracaso de las operaciones de rehabilitación hizo posible la transfencia del usufructo a inversionistas externos. Este tipo de acuerdo protegía al capital foráneo y constituía un reconocimiento del usufructo privado que de las minas podían hacer sus concesionarios e incluso la posibilidad de ser traspasadas para el pago de una deuda, e implicaba un acuerdo entre particulares donde la presencia del gobierno se iba diluyendo.

En este ambiente favorable, los mineros, como cuerpo organizado en el Tribunal de Minería, elaboraron un informe a solicitud del gobierno, dándolo a conocer en mayo de 1824. En él reconocían los esfuerzos de las autoridades en cuanto a continuar con la política fiscal de reducción impositiva elaborada tanto por la Corona como por las Cortes, así como las facilidades que se le daban a la inversión externa, pero consideraban que no eran las medidas suficientes para recuperar los niveles de producción anterior.

Ahora solicitaban que, además de lo ya establecido, se redujeran aún más las alcabalas, así como el pago del sello de la moneda, precios más reducidos y mayores facilidades en el suministro del azogue, pólvora y sal. Abordaban también el asunto del crédito, señalando que el uso de las libranzas no funcionaba, por lo que los mineros debían vender su plata a aquellos que disponían de capital y podían esperar el pago de la casa de moneda, operación en la que los mineros perdían entre un 10 a 13 por ciento del valor del metal.

Para remediar el problema de romper el monopolio del control sobre la plata que se llevaba a amonedar, establecido por los comerciantes y los militares, estaban convencidos de que la única forma era abriendo nuevas casas de moneda, ahí donde las necesidades y condiciones lo permitieran. Su proposición no excluía a las ya existentes, es decir, la de México y las que se habían establecido en Guanajuato, Guadalajara, Durango y Zacatecas durante la década anterior.[73]

La solucion no era sencilla así lo hacía notar Alamán en la memoria que presentó en 1825 como ministro de relaciones exteriores e interiores.

[73]*Memoria acerca de los medios que se estiman justos para el fomento y pronto restablecimiento de la minería, presentada por el Tribunal del mismo cuerpo al Supremo Poder Ejecutivo. Precede el discurso con que el tribunal dio cuenta a la junta general del cuerpo de las pretensiones y negocios que tenía pendientes, en el que se recapitula cuanto se expuso al gobierno supremo en la Memoria,* (México: Imprenta a cargo de Martín Rivera, 1824).

En tono prudente, señalaba que la recuperación de la minería no era un asunto a resolver en un plazo corto, pues afirmaba:

> Si restablecer fuese tan fácil como destruir, tendríamos motivo para extrañar que después de cuatro años que sacudimos el yugo extranjero aún no se halle la nación en aquel estado de abundancia y prosperidad que presentaba antes de la guerra, pero si se considera que en este período las conmociones y trastornos políticos han sido continuos, y si se reflexiona que el sanar las heridas profundas que aquella abrió, y reparar los inmensos males que en ella se causaron, es obra no sólo de una prudente política, y de una administración ilustrada, sino también del tiempo, de la tranquilidad y de la confianza pública. . . .[74]

Epílogo

El entusiasmo y esperanza que suscitó la presencia del capital inglés como el principal punto de partida para la rehabilitación de la minería perdió fuerza, debido a los fracasos ocurridos en distintas minas. En la voz del propio Alamán años después se hacía patente su desilusión sobre los resultados obtenidos.

> Hablo de este modo, con tanto más calor cuanto que es un error en que yo mismo he caído; pero del que me he desengañado enteramente. A mí me parece habrá pocas cosas en que las bombas de vapor puedan ser útiles en este país.

Hacía también ver su experiencia en la Compañía Union:

> Nada es tan incierto en materia de minas, como hacer elección de las que se deben trabajar. Con un capital de seis millones de pesos a mi disposición para invertirlo en las minas que me pareciese, y con el mayor deseo de acertar, se me propusieron entre otras las que después han dado tantas ríquezas, con la que la Compañía . . . habría tenido el resultado más brillante y por diversos motivos no quise entrar en ellas . . tuve, pues, en mi mano las negociaciones que han sido más ricas, y anduve tan desacertado que no me aproveché de ninguna de ellas. Todavía sin embargo, la Compañía unida no fue de las que tuvieron peores resultados . . . sin embargo . . . sufrió la pérdida de una gran parte de su capital.[75]

[74]*Memoria presentada a las dos cámaras del Congreso General de la Federación, por el Secretario de estado y del despacho de Relaciones Exteriores e Interiores al abrirse las sesiones del año de 1825. Sobre el estado de los negocios de su ramo* (México: Imprenta del Supremo Gobierno de los Estados Unidos Mexicanos, en Palacio, 1825), 2.

[75]*Memoria que el Secretario de estado y del Despacho de relaciones exteriores e interiores presenta al soberano congreso constituyente, sobre los negocios de la Secretaría a su cargo. Leida en la sesión del 8 de noviembre de 1823. Impresa de orden del soberano Congreso* (México: Imprenta del Supremo Gobierno, en Palacio, 1832); Alamán, *Historia de Méjico*, V, doc. 25, 82–83; R. W. Randall, *Real del Monte: una empresa minera británica en México* (México: Fondo de Cultura Económica, 1977), 45–78.

Caudillismo and Independence: A Symbiosis?

Hugh M. Hamill, Jr.

MORE THAN HALF A CENTURY AGO, W. H. Callcott concocted a subtitle for his biography of Santa Anna which reads: *The Story of an Enigma Who Once Was Mexico.*[1] Perhaps this was a biographer's unwitting confession that he had failed in his attempt to recreate a life. And maybe he did fail, for few argue that Callcott's study of Antonio López de Santa Anna is definitive. I find wisdom and a valuable caveat, however, in Callcott's use of the word "enigma," which means something that is hard to understand. The essay which follows is by a Gringo Anglo-Saxon Protestant—a GASP—and it probes some historical problems which deal in values which are not my own and are hence obscured. Callcott and all of us historians who are aliens in the world of Hispanic—and particularly Mexican—culture possess a certain degree of either hubris or foolhardiness. Certainly any GASP who explores caudillismo, as I intend to do, is demented. For example, given the destruction of royal legitimacy at independence, it could be argued that caudillos were not necessarily bad or inappropriate for Mexico for the first generation. GASPs, however, are notoriously apt to deplore the presence of caudillos and to bemoan the abscence of "Democracy." GASPs, then, must beware of themselves and their own value-laden instincts.[2]

Callcott also indirectly admitted that Santa Anna's Mexico during the first three decades of the Republic likewise puzzled him. The last fifty-odd years of scholarship have surely fitted all the straight-edged pieces of the jigsaw together. I suspect, however, that everyone would agree that the Early

[1]Wilfred Hardy Callcott, *Santa Anna: The Story of an Enigma Who Once Was Mexico* (Norman: University of Oklahoma Press, 1936).

[2]GASPs, in particular, and all those, in general, who are interested in fresh approaches to caudillismo should read Alain Rouquié, 'Dictadores, militares y legitimidad en América Latina," in Julio Labastida Martín del Campo, comp., *Dictaduras y dictadores* (Mexico: Siglo Veintiuno, 1986), 10–26; and Frank Safford, "Politics, Ideology and Society in Post-Independence Spanish America," in Leslie Bethell, ed., *The Cambridge History of Latin America, Vol. III: From Independence to c. 1870* (Cambridge, 1985), 347–421. Also useful is Glen C. Dealy, "Prolegomena on the Spanish American Political Tradition," *Hispanic American Historical Review* 48:1 (February 1968), 37–58.

Republic has been much less extensively researched than Independence, the Reforma, the Porfiriato, and the Revolution of 1910.[3]

The early republican era has received relatively less attention because it was a period of ambiguity and of what Stanley Stein would call "disappointing fulfillment."[4] Instability associated with great events like revolutions attracts scholars (and the readers and students who support scholars), but enervating violence spread over thirty years, ill-formed institutional patterns, inchoate politics, and unprincipled leaders beckon the researcher less strongly.

Now, however, the Early Republic – Santa Anna's Enigmatic Mexico – is being discovered. Colonial and Independence scholars, saturated in the Bourbon reforms and Insurgent heroics, along with a new generation of talented historians have begun to move forward into the 1820s and 1830s.[5] As they do, the most compelling problem they face is to explain why newly independent Mexico became mired in a slough of despond. To promote debate on this matter let me propose two conflicting explanations for the phenomenon each of which is ably defended by a distinguished contemporary historian. One school of thought blames the colonial experience for its failure to prepare New Spain for nationhood and finds systemic weaknesses in the conduct of affairs which became obstacles to economic development after independence. This view is held by John Coatsworth. The other school argues that late colonial New Spain was a stable and essentially progressive viceroyalty. The decade of sanguinary civil war leading to independence, however, so badly disrupted that prosperous polity that it could not recover. Jaime Rodríguez defends this position.[6]

The essence of Coatsworth's argument is that the late colonial era was "a seriously deficient institutional environment for entrepreneurial activity." The "system of government made 'free' enterprise impossible. It was not merely a matter of specific policies, laws, and institutions or their collective impact at a particular point in time that discouraged enterprise.

[3]There are, of course, some outstanding modern works from this period by well-known scholars like Jan Bazant, Michael Costeloe, Fernando Díaz Díaz, Charles Hale and Robert Potash, but the statement stands.

[4]Stanley J. Stein and Barbara H. Stein, *The Colonial Heritage of Latin America* (New York: Oxford University Press, 1970), viii.

[5]Among the works that have appeared most recently are Silvia M. Arrom, *The Women of Mexico City, 1790–1857* (Stanford: Stanford University press, 1985); Donald F. Stevens, "Instability in Mexico from Independence to the War of the Reform," (Ph.D. dissertation, University of Chicago, 1984); and Barbara A. Tenenbaum, *The Politics of Penury: Debts and Taxes in Mexico, 1821–1856* (Albuquerque: University of New Mexico Press, 1986).

[6]John H. Coatsworth, "Obstacles to Economic Growth in Nineteenth-Century Mexico," *American Historical Review* 83:1 (February 1978), 80–100; Jaime E. Rodríguez O., "Down from Colonialism: Mexico's Nineteenth-Century Crisis," University of California, Irvine, May 28, 1980.

The chief obstacle was the nature of the state itself, its operating principles, the basis for all of its acts." He further argues that

> the interventionist and pervasively arbitary nature of the institutional environment [in New Spain] forced every enterprise, urban and rural, to operate in a highly politicized manner, using kinship networks, political influence, and family prestige to gain privileged access to subsidized credit, to aid various stratagems for recruiting labor, to collect debts or enforce contracts, to evade taxes or circumvent the courts, and to defend or assert titles to land. Success or failure in the economic arena always depended on the relations of the producer with political authorities—local officials for arranging matters close at hand, the central government of the colony for sympathetic interpretations of the law and intervention at the local level when conditions required it. Small enterprise, excluded from the system of corporate privilege and political favors, was forced to operate in a permanent state of semiclandestinity, always at the margin of the law, at the mercy of petty officials, never secure from arbitrary acts and never protected against the rights of those more powerful.[7]

Post-independence problems were in part the result of the desire by many elite Mexicans—especially in Mexico City—to recreate the arbitrary centralized state which had disappeared with the disruption of the independence wars. The bitter struggles which led to the final triumph of the Liberals in 1867 negated any positive result of independence, further delayed Mexican development, and left the country with a "long-term dependence on foreign technology, resources, and markets."[8]

Although Coatsworth addresses other fundamental problems of the colonial era—most notably geographically conditioned high freight costs—it is structural dysfunction in what might be called "the Mordida Society" which did most to inhibit Mexico's growth in the nineteenth century.

The title of Jaime Rodríguez's Distinguished Faculty Lecture at the University of California, Irvine in 1980, "Down from Colonialism: Mexico's Nineteenth-Century Crisis," suggests a quite opposite view. In that published lecture he holds that "colonial Mexico (New Spain) was a vast territory characterized by a stable and responsive government, a wealthy and balanced economy, and a multi-racial society which enjoyed considerable social mobility. . . . The wars of independence and the chaos that followed ruined the nation's economy and destroyed the legitimacy of its institutions." In short, Mexico experienced "a decline from colonial well-being to republican disaster." For Rodríguez "the Viceroyalty of New Spain was the Western Hemisphere's most imposing political structure at the end of the eighteenth century." The government was held in confidence and

[7]Coatsworth, "Obstacles to Economic Growth," 92, 94.
[8]Ibid., 100.

seen as legitimate by its citizens. "There was general agreement in New Spain that royal government, both at the local and at the imperial level, served the public interest." When social violence occurred, it was ad hoc and localized. The Kingdom's enormous wealth, its engine of prosperity, was not merely based in silver exports but in the viable diversity of agricultural and early industrial development. In short,

> eighteenth century Mexico can be described as a wealthy, capitalist society whose economy was characterized by private ownership of the means of production, by profit-oriented entrepreneurs, by a free wage labor force, and by the exchange of capital, labor, goods and services in a free market. While there were some limits on the mobility of these economic factors, present research indicates that these restrictions posed no greater obstacles than those existing in eighteenth century England and the United States.[9]

"Ironically," says Rodríguez, "Mexico in 1850 possessed the sort of society and economy which many today mistakenly believe to have characterized colonial Mexico." Rodríguez hints at some agreement with Coatsworth when he acknowledges that "New Spain developed a costly and complex, but extremely fragile, infrastructure in a land that is both poor and harsh."[10] The fragility of that infrastructure was revealed by the cataclysmic destruction of the wars of independence. Rodríguez devotes much space to estimates of damages to all economic sectors and emphasizes that drastic losses of capital and of public confidence prohibited post-war recovery.

In sum, to overdraw the question, Coatsworth blames the mechanisms of the colonial state and Rodríguez blames the more immediate horrors of independence for the disastrous early republican experience in Mexico. This controversy is akin to the insoluable debate over heredity versus environment in human development: insoluable, perhaps, but exciting to pursue.

The approaches of these two scholars are both provocative and selective. As with all grand interpretive theses, they stir the imaginations of their readers and may well be responsible for stimulating much current historical research. Their common concern, though, is primarily economic. Very little is said on either side about political leadership. It occurs to me, then, that there is a need to comprehend the consequences of the breakdown of authority and the efforts to fill that vacuum of legitimacy at all levels by caudillos and caciques.

[9]Rodríguez, "Down from Colonialism," 1, 2, 9.
[10]Ibid., 15–16.

This cursory exploration of the roots of the highly visible phenomenon of caudillismo — or Santanismo — fits well within the context suggested by the Coatsworth-Rodríguez controversy. Was there a caudillaje spirit at work within the colonial scheme of things which responded to and perhaps contributed to the structural dysfunction Coatsworth identifies? Or were caudillos one of the new destructive elements struck off in the violence of independence which Rodríguez finds so fundamental?[11]

This tentative inquiry also responds to the criticism made by Brian Hamnett that "we still tend to identify the emergence of caudillaje (the political dominance of regional bosses) and caciquismo (the power-broking of local notables) as a phenomenon of the post-independence period, rather than seek their origins in colonial Latin America."[12] It is in fact very tempting to devote most of the remainder of this essay to a treatment of the droves of insurgent and royalist leaders who became caudillos during the independence struggle and to those survivors among them who dominated early republican politics.[13] It would not be difficult to sustain the view that Rodríguez's wartime economic destruction was matched by political attrition in the form of atomistic insurgent chieftains like Villagrán in the Huasteca and venal royalist commanders like Iturbide in Michoacán and the Bajío. There is also more subtle evidence that the independence years brought about an erosion of civil rights which helped create favorable conditions for caudillaje. As Nancy Farriss has made plain, cutthroat warfare and widespread civil war "resulted not only in elimination of ecclestiastical immunity but also of the basic legal rights traditionally enjoyed by both laity and clergy."[14] The question that perplexes me the most, however, is what evidence is there that caudillismo was present in colonial society before the patterns of insurgency and counterinsurgency were set in 1811?[15]

[11]For a stimulating exploration of the meaning of "caudillaje spirit," see Glen C. Dealy, *The Public Man: An Interpretation of Latin American and Other Catholic Countries* (Amherst: University of Massachusetts Press, 1977).

[12]Brian R. Hamnett, *Roots of Insurgency: Mexican Regions, 1750–1824* (Cambridge: Cambridge University Press, 1986), 214, n. 4.

[13]See Fernando Díaz Díaz, *Caudillos y caciques: Antonio López de Santa Anna y Juan Alvarez* (Mexico: El Colegio de México, 1972). Donald Stevens) ("Instability," 117–118) argues that "few insurgent leaders survived the wars" and that Mexico's "post-independence army relied heavily on former royalists who had defended the crown in the creole militias and Spanish army."

[14]Nancy M. Farriss, *Crown and Clergy in Colonial Mexico: 1759–1821* (London: Athlone Press, 1968), 203.

[15]H. M. Hamill, Jr., "Royalist Counterinsurgency in the Mexican War for Independence: The Lessons of 1811," *Hispanic American Historical Review* 53:3 (August 1973), 470–489. For an especially durable essay which explores the roots of both Thomistic and Machiavellian authority during the empire and after, see Richard M. Morse, "Toward a Theory of Spanish American Government," *Journal of the History of Ideas*, 15 (1954), 71–93.

One way to test the degree to which caudillaje may have been engrained in the colonial society is to examine the nature of the very earliest responses to leadership in the crisis years leading up to the insurgency of late 1810. That is, leadership before the post-Calderón atomization of the conflict set its particular stamp on the enervating conflict. Who became the immediate caudillos? What purposes did they propose? What postures did they assume? What pasts did they reflect? What values did they exhibit? And whom were they able to attract? Coming as they did at the very outset of the disruption of independence the individual exponents of caudillaje were not the products of Independence or the Early Republic. At the same time, however, their prominence and fame made them the prototypes of many future caudillos.

The two paramount caudillos who were products of their societies and who made their marks indelibly on Mexico's future were, of course, Félix María Calleja del Rey and Miguel Hidalgo y Costilla. These famous adversaries deserve to be compared with other pairs in Mexican history like Cortés and Montezuma, Juárez and Maximilian, and Díaz and Madero. At first glance Calleja and Hidalgo were completely different men. Calleja was a gachupín, Hidalgo was a criollo; Calleja was supremely self-disciplined, Hidalgo was impetuous and erratic; Calleja was a methodical calculating military strategist, Hidalgo was a mercurial and tempermental priest without military training. To look behind these obvious differences, however, is to find that both men fit into the colonial ambience of social networks and influence which Coatsworth finds a weakness and Rodríguez finds a strength in pre-independence New Spain.

Calleja and Hidalgo complemented each other and shared the attributes of caudillo leadership which would become so visible later in the century. Let us accept that the power and authority which undergirded caudillismo were composed of an intricate combination of personal forcefulness of character, perhaps although not necessarily charismatic; something of that peculiarly Mexican masculinity we call machismo; a shrewd capacity to aggregate followers through kinship, compadrazgo, and professional and social ties; appeals to tradition if possible to solidify legitimacy; prior status through class, wealth, or profession; and technical and administrative expertise.[16]

Both Hidalgo and Calleja had already intuitively built into their respective clerical and military careers solid bases upon which to operate as

[16]For appraisals of Weber and post-Weber contributions to theories of authoritarian leadership, see Díaz Díaz, *Caudillos y caciques*, 1–7; Dealy, *The Public Man*; and Peter H. Smith, "Political Legitimacy in Spanish America," in Richard Graham and Peter H. Smith, eds., *New Approaches to Latin American History* (Austin: University of Texas Press, 1974), 225–255.

caudillos when they were suddenly catapulted to positions of power. Their caudillaje qualities were, of course, uneven. Hidalgo's charisma was greater than that of Calleja. For his part Calleja could far more readily claim legitimacy as a defender of the status quo than the renegade priest. Nevertheless, the society and its mores provided those conditions which could nurture a caudillo when circumstances favored their appearance. Just because the evidence of caudillaje is much less abundant before 1810 than afterward is no reason to assume that it did not exist. To demonstrate this fully requires examination of the subtle patterns of leadership in business affairs, government, extended families, corporate especially church hierarchies, provincial village structures, and social banditry as all these developed over much of the colonial past. Such an agenda is beyond this essay. So too is a thorough exploration of the effects which the more immediate years prior to the Grito de Dolores had on caudillaje culture. The mystique of Napoleon filtered into the novo hispano world and stirred subliminal admiration for the French emperor on the one hand, and, then, after 1808 drew outraged but highly revealing patriotic attacks on the other. When Agustín Pomposo Fernández de San Salvador, the Rector of the University of Mexico, struck out at Napoleon in a pamphlet, he warned the Scourge of Europe that

> ya el Caudillo de Israel, es el Caudillo
> de la Española gente.[17]

The spectacle of telluric Spanish military heroes suddenly appearing to defend the Iberian patria against the French invaders in 1808 is another source of inspiration for a coming generation of Mexican warriors who would soon have their own chances for glory on either side of the military equation: insurgent or royalist.

On balance Calleja was more important as a model for future caudillos than Hidalgo. Hidalgo may have opened the path to insurgency for other criollo priests like Matamoros and demonstrated to later prelates like Bishop Munguía the power of the cloth for attacks on established governments, but he was clearly unique as a charismatic curate generalísimo. Hidalgo was also ephemeral because he was quickly destroyed. Only the process of early republican nation building resurrected him in mythic proportions. Calleja, by contrast, was far closer to the stereotype of the military caudillo, and dozens of leaders great and small were cast in his mold. Calleja was also victorious, a peculiarly desirable attribute for any practitioner of caudillismo.

[17]Agustín Pomposo Fernández de San Salvador, *Selva Libre* (Mexico, July 30, 1808), 3. Sutro Library.

Ephemeral as he may have been, Miguel Hidalgo is among the most studied of Mexican heroes. For all the biographical detail, however, there is much more that we would like to know about the itinerant priest. He surely had a vast network of friends and relatives throughout the Bajío, Michoacán, Querétaro, and into San Luis Potosí and Nueva Galicia. He naturally exploited these linkages as the conspiracy of Querétaro matured. For example, in September 1800 Hidalgo was invited to celebrate the mass of dedication of the new temple of Nuestra Señora de Guadalupe in San Luis Potosí, where he also chanced to attend a *corrida de toros* with Félix Calleja. Was it at that time or another that he made the ties with local clergy who would promote his cause in that city a decade later?[18] Any future biographer of the Cura of Dolores must explore this network systematically, for therein lies a partial explanation of Hidalgo's initial success.

Hidalgo exploited his priestly status in multiple ways and yet did not let it interfere with his machismo. He was Padre de la Patria in not only symbolic ways. Even the mystery of the transvestite girl "La Fernandita" in his entourage may have added sexual spice to his appeal among his supporters.[19]

His insurgency had many of the trappings of a religious crusade. This helped Hidalgo to justify his leadership and served as a necessary legitimizing force for the "curadillo". Hidalgo perhaps emphasized his appeals to the True Faith and sought the protection of the Virgin of Guadalupe precisely because he knew he would be attacked for usurping authority. Indeed a royalist pamphleteer reproached him thus:

> No tiene autoridad ese caudillo de los insurgentes para hacernos la guerra . . . ; pues esta autoridad es un derecho inseparable, un derecho inmanente de la Soberanía, y esta reside en . . . Rey Fernando.[20]

(Note that Hidalgo was dubbed a caudillo, which is evidence—along with the rector's use of the term in 1808—that "caudillo" was in common parlance by the earliest stages of the struggle over independence.)

Of course, Hidalgo was well aware of the traditional power of the Spanish King, who was excused for being a gachupín by his admiring

[18] José de J. Núñez y Domínguez, *La Virreina mexicana: Doña María Francisca de la Gándara de Calleja* (Mexico: Imprenta Universitaria, 1950), 47–53.

[19] H. M. Hamill, Jr., *The Hidalgo Revolt* (Gainesville: University of Florida Press, 1966; 2d ed. Westport, Conn.: Greenwood Press, 1981), 204, 248, n. 61.

[20] Francisco Estrada, *El centinela de Santiago: diálogo entre la ronda de la Tecpan y un clérigo* (Mexico 1810), 2. Sutro Library.

Mexican subjects, as Eric Van Young has explained.[21] The curate skillfully employed the exhortation "Viva el Rey!" as yet another source of his charismatic legitimacy. Hidalgo also called upon his knowledge of the dynamics of Bajío villages and rural estates and his awareness of economic tensions to evoke King and Virgin and to tap a strain of intense xenophobia which focused upon the gachupines but also included those exotic monsters the French *and* the English.[22] But Hidalgo's brand of caudillismo had its limits. As Hamnett has suggested, Hidalgo only briefly bound together the region's disparate social groups.

> Since the ultimate objective was the furtherance of the political ambitions of the frustrated 'provincial bourgeoisie' this revolutionary coalition of rural workers, villagers, dispossessed tenants, unemployed urban or mine workers, *rancho*-owners, muleteers, estate administrators, small town lawyers, lower clerics, provincial intellectuals, local *caciques*, men on the make, bandits and criminals suffered internal contradictions from the start.[23]

Félix Calleja came to New Spain in 1789 in the entourage of Viceroy Revillagigedo. That the wisest of Bourbon administrators should have favored the young officer from Medina del Campo in Old Castile is itself significant. Through a series of military assignments, chiefly in the north of the viceroyalty, Calleja became an expert in the geography of the realm. He was also an avid reader of history and could see himself in perspective. In 1797 Lieutenant Colonel Calleja was posted to the city of San Luis Potosí, where he became in due course the commander of the 10th Brigade headquartered there. Almost at once he began the process of rooting himself in the Potosino earth and society. Within two years he had acquired land, an orchard, and a house and had the base for a future patrimony.[24]

It was Calleja's capacity to draw about himself a powerful coterie of local members of the elite which showed his emergent caudillaje. In one lawsuit against the local intendente, which Calleja brought in 1800, he managed to gather twenty-two supporters including a conde, a caballero of the Order of Charles III, an alférez real, 5 regidores, 2 alcaldes, the local tobacco monopoly administrator, 17 hacendados, and 10 merchants.[25]Calleja spun Potosino society more tightly into his web when he

[21]Eric Van Young, "Millennium on the Northern Marches: The Mad Messiah of Durango and Popular Rebellion in Mexico, 1800–1815," *Comparative Studies in Society and History* 28:3 (July 1986), 404–407.

[22]Hamill, *The Hidalgo Revolt*, 133.

[23]Hamnett, *Roots of Insurgency*, 205. See also John Tutino's fundamental study of the crisis of rural conditions in the Bajío in his *From Insurrection to Revolution in Mexico: Social Bases of Agrarian Violence, 1750–1940* (Princeton: Princeton University Press, 1986), esp. 41–137.

[24]Núñez y Domínguez, *La Virreina mexicana*, 29–44.

[25]Ibid., 54–55.

married the niece of don Manuel de la Gándara, the city's alférez real and proprietor of the great hacienda complex of Bledos.[26] The wedding in 1807 of the forty-eight-year-old Castilian and his twenty-year-old bride was a spectacular social event. In spite of his late marriage, Calleja's machismo had never been in doubt. It was said that he had a son by a Spanish ballerina.[27] Later when he was Viceroy his wife, María Francisca, bore him two children and three more after his term expired.[28]

His marriage to a member of the elite de la Gándara family was the capstone of Calleja's Mexicanization. It brought him closer contact with the criollo aristocracy including the Marqués de Jaral de Berrios, who later offered his sumptuous town house on Calle San Francisco (today Madero) in Mexico City to Calleja in 1812.[29] More to the point, Calleja soon became a frequent visitor to the Bledos hacienda and seems to have played a significant role in the management of the estate. It was at Bledos that tradition has it that Calleja heard the bad news from Dolores. Well before 1810, however, Calleja had enlarged his network in other ways. Austere as he may have been, the gachupín brigadier had a common touch, and was known among the campesinos as well as among his soldiers of the rank and file as "el amo don Félix."[30] Whether this note of respectful affection was enhanced by his apparent taste for pulque is impossible to say.[31]

The military was the obvious other network which Calleja's native instincts led him to cultivate. Not only did the chain of command and his own prominence in it establish formal ties of value, but he also assiduously cultivated particular soldiers of talent who were destined to aid him in what Christon Archer calls "La Causa Buena."[32] It has also been argued that a surprising number of early republican caudillos served their military apprenticeships not as insurgents but as royalists after the fashion of the enigmatic Santa Anna. To a certain degree this may have been because of Calleja's capacity to recruit able criollos and to give them opportunities which they effectively transformed into post-independence patriot careers. Thus Calleja, the proto-caudillo, nurtured as he was in the late viceregal

[26]For a history of Bledos, see Jan Bazant, *Cinco haciendas mexicanas* (Mexico: El Colegio de México, 1975), 73–94.

[27]Ibid., 84.

[28]Núñez y Domínguez, *La Virreina mexicana*, passim.

[29]Doris M. Ladd, *The Mexican Nobility at Independence, 1780–1826* (Austin: University of Texas Press, 1976), 64–65.

[30]Núñez y Domínguez, *La Virreina mexicana*, 43.

[31]Ernesto Lemoine Villicana, *Morelos: su vida revolucionaria . . .* (Mexico: Universidad Nacional Autónoma de México, 1965), 57.

[32]Christon I. Archer, " 'La Causa Buena': The Counterinsurgency Army and the Ten Years' War," in this volume.

time frame, left a legacy of caudillismo for the new Republic. Among those to whom Calleja was able to turn when the crisis came in September 1810 were two young landed aristocrats, Miguel Barragán and Manuel Gómez Pedraza, from Valle del Maíz and Río Verde respectively, and a young military physician named Anastasio Bustamante, who came to San Luis Potosí in 1808 and helped cure doña Francisca's infected eye. All three would eventually pass through the revolving door of the Mexican presidency.[33] Another key officer was Bernardo Fernández de Villamil, a peninsular whom Calleja brought into his intimate circle by marriage in January 1810 to his wife's cousin, María Josefa de la Gándara. Fernández de Villamil later became Calleja's trusted adjutant and secretary during the Hidalgo insurgency.[34] Further linkages combined Calleja's family, the noble elite, and the military. For example, Manuel José Rincón Gallardo was the first Marqués de Guadalupe Gallardo and several ways related to the de la Gándara clan. The Marqués was also commander of the Regiment of Dragoons of San Luis and thus Calleja's subordinate. In 1815 he became godfather to Calleja's son.[35]

When the news of the Hidalgo revolt reached him on September 19, 1810, Calleja moved at once to prepare a defense of his region. He did so, however, with a deliberation which would be characteristic of all his future military planning. One of his attributes as a caudillo was his technical proficiency and attention to detail. His first act was instructive. He chose that very day not to raise troops but to round up funds and to interdict convoys with money and supplies he feared might fall into insurgent hands. He saw funding as a fundamental step to mobilization of what would eventually be called the Army of the Center.[36]

It was only then that Calleja cashed in on his elaborate networks. "El amo don Félix" took full advantage of his extended family, his elite coterie, and his military command. Within ten days he was able to report to the

[33]Núñez y Domínguez, *La Virreina mexicana*, 120–121; Brian R. Hamnett, "Anastasio Bustamante y la guerra de independencia, 1810–1821," *Historia Mexicana* 28:112 (April–June 1979), 518.

[34]Núñez y Domínguez, *La Virreina mexicana*, 115. See also Fernández de Villamil's service record, ibid., 291–294.

[35]Ladd, *Mexican Nobility*, 261, n. 80; Núñez y Domínguez, *La Virreina mexicana*, 37, n. 28.

[36]Calleja to Venegas, San Luis Potosí, September 21, 1810, in Núñez y Domínguez, *La Virreina mexicana*, 121, n. 5. Calleja's methodical behavior fits into Timothy Anna's later assessment of Calleja and the other Spanish wartime viceroys. It is Anna's thesis "that the viceroys were not incompetent, but on the contrary, extraordinarily competent politicians and military leaders" and, as a consequence, it was they who "proved Spanish imperialism unsuited to America. Actual circumstances and events forced them to contradict their stated principles and the principles on which imperial political institutions were grounded." Timothy E. Anna, "The Last Viceroys of New Spain and Peru: An Appraisal," *American Historical Review* 81:1 (February 1976), 39–40.

new Viceroy Venegas that the Marqués del Jaral de Berrios had agreed to make 500 armed men available from his haciendas and that he had already put a hundred mounted men armed with *cuchillos* at Calleja's disposal. This was indicative of the instant support Calleja enjoyed and is especially significant in that the Marqués might have contented himself with his role as commander of the Regiment of San Carlos which he commanded in Calleja's brigade. (Jaral de Berrios was then the second criollo Marqués to serve under the Spanish Brigadier.) By the time he left San Luis Potosí on October 24 the Mexicanization of Calleja had paid off. The army which marched out that day to join a troop from Puebla had 3,000 cavalry, 600 infantry, and 4 cannon founded during the weeks after the Grito. The caudillo's primary task of basic mobilization was accomplished.[37]

The two caudillos, one a priest and the other a soldier, were both authentic products of their societies and of the value systems which rewarded public men. They each fully expected their respective righteous causes to triumph in the collision which ensued. Yet it was Calleja and not Hidalgo who brought home to Mexico City the first triumphant military parade. This occurred on February 5, 1812, just after Calleja had left the insurgent headquarters at Zitácuaro "arrazada, incendiada y destruida."[38] The dramatic spectacle of a victorious army on parade with a caudillo at its head inaugurated a new era in Mexican history. The Age of Caudillismo had arrived. It would mature rapidly during the balance of the independence wars as personalist leaders increased their roles in politics at all levels. Nevertheless, Caudillismo was firmly rooted in colonial New Spain.

[37]Calleja's successful mobilization of the San Luis Potosí region was not due only to the Brigadier's caudillismo. John Tutino has demonstrated that conditions for estate residents in San Luis Potosí were significantly better than those in the Bajío (*From Insurrection to Revolution*, 151–164). Christon Archer suggests, however, that Calleja had serious difficulties with recruitment and with founding cannon at least until mid-October (" 'La Causa Buena,' " in this volume). For the specifics of Calleja's military by October 24, see Carlos María de Bustamente, *Cuadro histórico de la revolución mexicana* (Mexico, 1961), I, 49.

[38]Proclamation of Calleja, San Juan Zitácuaro, January 5, 1812, in Carlos María de Bustamante, *Campañas del General D. Félix María Calleja* (Mexico, 1828), 144. For the parade, see ibid., 167, and Alamán, *Historia de Méjico*, II, 475–478.

N.A. M. S. D. FERNANDO VII

Fernando VII, King of Spain, 1810

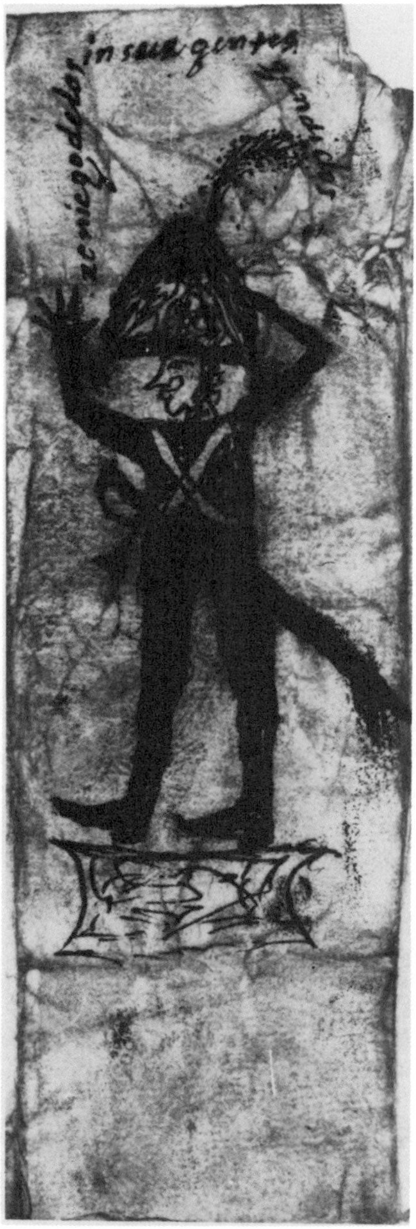

Insurgent

Father Miguel Hidalgo celebrating Mass for his troops before battle

Proposed monument to Hidalgo

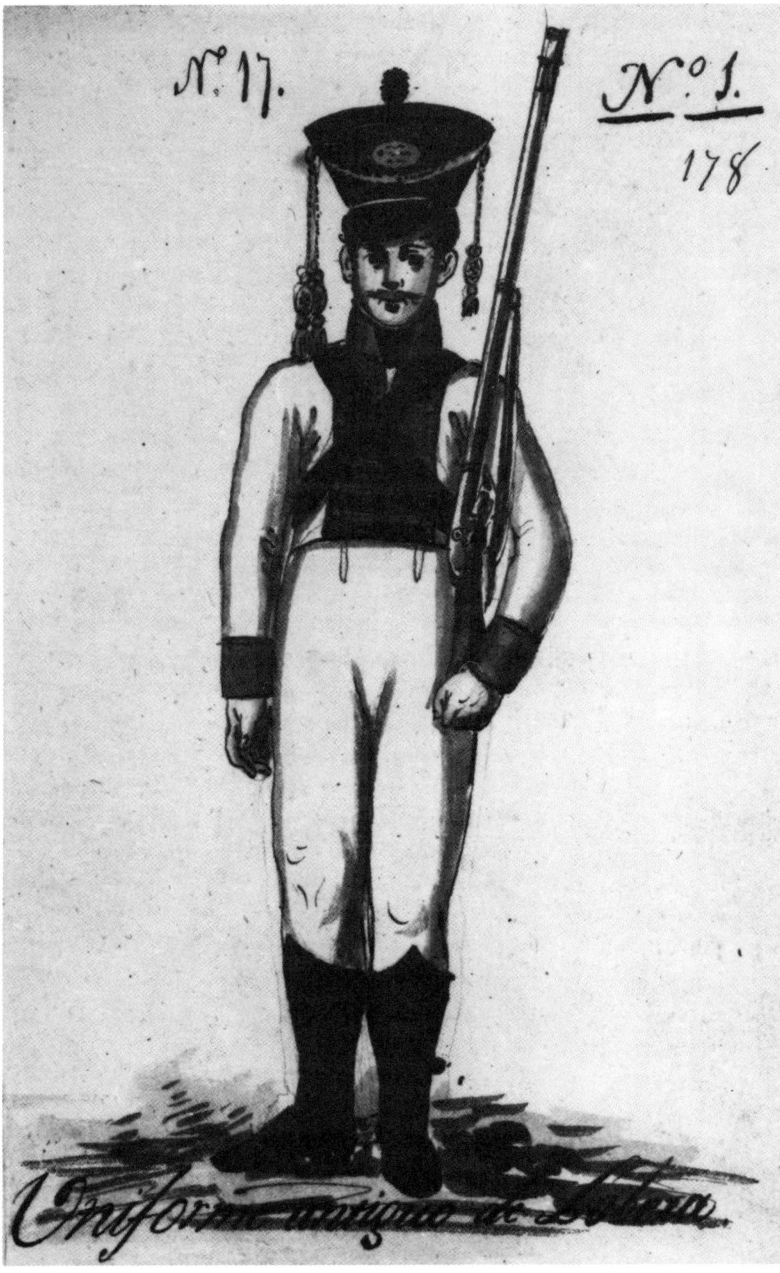

Soldier of the Lobera Regiment

Royalist standard celebrating the victory over Mina 1817

Iturbide defeating the Royalists while Guadalupe Victoria prays for victory in the background

Coat of arms of the Mexican Empire

Uniform of the Mexico City Council, 1828

Civic militia of Puebla, Oaxaca, and Mexico

II

The Creation of the New Nation

The Iturbide Interregnum

Timothy E. Anna

THE PERIOD OF DOMINANCE of Agustín de Iturbide over the government of Mexico—from his triumph as Liberator in September 1821 to his abdication as emperor in March 1823—continues to be a source of controversy in the historiography of Mexico. The prevailing view of history is that Iturbide was a crass opportunist, a false hero, and a man whose political solutions were rejected by his nation. Modern antipathy to the person and personality of Iturbide—whether well-founded or not—leads historians to overlook the fact that the eighteen-month period of his dominance was the critical period of transition during which Mexico went from political autonomy to full independence. This is the period when Mexicans began to come to grips with and define independence, a time of the greatest signficance. It was, in the words of Carlos Navarro y Rodrigo, "a prolonged and turbulent interregnum."[1]

The Iturbide interregnum could not have been anything but turbulent, as a result of the political and military developments that preceded it. From 1810 to 1821 the nation had been swept up in a truly destructive war which cost the lives, according to the most conservative estimates, of 200,000 persons, and according to the most extreme estimates, of one in ten Mexicans, or 600,000 persons. The Mexican War for Independence was actually a civil war among factions of Mexicans, some loyal to Spain and some in rebellion. To follow Hamnett's recent distinction, it began under Hidalgo as an insurrection but then deteriorated into a series of regionally based insurgencies.[2] A decisive military outcome proved impossible until the stalemate was finally broken by the brilliant political compromise of Iturbide's Plan of Iguala. Everyone, from servile royalist to long-time rebel,

[1]Carlos Navarro y Rodrigo, *Vida de Agustín de Iturbide* (Madrid, 1919), 136.

[2]Brian R. Hamnett, *Roots of Insurgency: Mexican Regions, 1750–1824* (Cambridge, 1986).

recognized the value of the Plan in permitting consensus in favor of separation from Spain. Even Father Servando Teresa de Mier, a source as hostile to Iturbide as any that existed, in a private report written in the summer of 1821 in Philadelphia, said of the Plan of Iguala: "The object is independence, the rest is calculated to avoid the scoffing of rebels and to make all parties enter in it, conciliating their interests."[3] The Plan of Iguala forged an alliance of many and varied interests—liberal and conservative, rebel and royalist, creole and Spaniard—which, although unstable, accomplished the desired end of political separation from Spain. Although Vicente Rocafuerte—another original source hostile to Iturbide—argued that Juan O'Donojú would have capitulated without the Plan of Iguala because he knew the Spanish were effectively defeated,[4] the simple fact is that the political consensus that O'Donojú found waiting him when he arrived in Mexico could not have been achieved without Iguala.

Although one might argue that the Treaty of Córdoba was not strictly necessary, since O'Donojú himself told Spain he had no choice but to acquiesce in the will of Mexicans,[5] it is clear that Iturbide chose to complete the enterprise by signing a treaty with the Spanish Superior Political Chief because he preferred to view independence as a diplomatic triumph rather than as the result of a civil war.[6] Whether Iturbide honestly expected the Treaty of Córdoba to be accepted by Spain can never be known for certain. It does, however, seem a mark of their bias that Mier and Rocafuerte—and many authors who have followed them since—argue that the Plan of Iguala and Treaty of Córdoba were nothing but tricks by Iturbide to engineer himself onto the throne. Monarchy was still the preferred form of government in 1821; republicanism as yet had few advocates. It is clear that the support of the peninsulars in Mexico and their clients was essential to political separation from Spain, that the interests of those peninsulars had to be protected or else they and their many Mexican allies would have continued to resist political separation, and that Iturbide would probably have continued to lead the government, whether as monarch or in some other capacity, in the first phase after September 1821.

Lorenzo de Zavala himself admitted he did not know, at that time, what form of government was best suited to a new country.[7] As opin-

[3]Report in Mier's handwriting, Philadelphia, no date, Benson Latin American Collection, University of Texas at Austin (hereafter cited as BLAC), García collection.

[4]Vicente Rocafuerte, *Bosquejo ligerísimo de la revolución de Méjico* (Philadelphia, 1822), 68.

[5]O'Donojú to Minister of Ultramar, Córdoba, 31 August 1821, Archivo General de Indias, Seville, Mexico, 1680.

[6]Harold Sims, *Descolonización en México: el conflicto entre mexicanos y españoles, 1821-1831* (Mexico, 1982), 13.

[7]Lorenzo de Zavala, *Ensayo crítico de las revoluciones de México desde 1808 hasta 1830*, 2 vols. in *Orbras* (Mexico, 1969), I, 172-173.

ionated a source as Francisco Bulnes admits that Iturbide was the unanimous choice of the people, arguing that if democracy consists of the vast majority choosing their leader, then Iturbide and his empire represented democracy.[8] Tadeo Ortiz de Ayala argues that Iturbide's empire adhered to the customs and tradition of Mexico.[9] In September 1821 and even, indeed, in May 1822 when Iturbide was elected emperor, there were few republicans active in the country. Though Joel Poinsett and others naturally gave the impression that republicans constituted a majority, Bulnes put it best when he said the few republicans then active were building castles in the air.[10] Bulnes summarizes the existing bias of the early authors whose writings have so prejudiced the historiógraphy when he points out that:

> Alamán sincerely believes that if Iturbide had proposed to comply with the Plan of Iguala he would have established in Mexico a monarchy as solid as that of England. José María Tornel is not of his opinion, and assures us that if Iturbide had established the centralist republic the peace would never have been disturbed. Zavala opines that Iturbide would have triumphed over his enemies and established his empire always if he had been democractic. Cuevas assures us that Iturbide would have submerged his nation in happiness if he had established an aristocratic conservative republic. Servando Teresa de Mier bitterly censures Iturbide and denigrates him for not having proclaimed a decentralized parliamentary republic. . . . Valentín Gómez Farías declares Iturbide a criminal for not having established a demagogic federal republic; and ultimately, the jacobins of 1861 make Iturbide responsible for all the misfortunes of the country for not having proclaimed Federalism and the Laws of the Reform.[11]

It is clear that the historiography about Iturbide consists largely of judgments about what he should or should not have done. None of this helps very much in determining why the Iturbide interregnum was so passionately debated, or how Iturbide failed. A more useful approach would be to look at a number of specific weaknesses or defects that prevailed during the Iturbide interregnum and that helped to guarantee the fundamental power struggle that lies at the heart of Iturbide's failure.

It is important, to begin with, to remember that the Plan of Iguala was conceived of as a compromise document, which together with the Treaty

[8]Francisco Bulnes, *La guerra de independencia: Hidalgo-Iturbide* (Mexico, 1910), 347, 378. See also Timothy E. Anna, "The Rule of Agustín de Iturbide: A Reappraisal," *Journal of Latin American Studies* 17: 1 (May 1985), 79–110.

[9]Tadeo Ortiz de Ayala, *México considerado como nación independiente y libre*, 2 vols. (Burdeos, 1832; reprint Guadalajara, 1952), I, 17.

[10]Bulnes, *La guerra de independencia*, 384.

[11]Ibid., 393–394.

of Córdoba brought about a status that was not quite full independence. This fact is only now being emphasized by such historians as Brian Hamnett, who doubts if there ever was a "war of independence," and by Linda Arnold, who consistently refers to 1821 as the date of the achievement of autonomy rather than independence.[12] What the Mexican elite aspired to was some degree of political autonomy from Spain, and guarantees of social stability, protection of property, and advancement to office. In calling for a monarchy, presided over by Ferdinand VII or a member of his family, and governed by the Spanish Constitution of 1812, the two fundamental treatises of Iguala and Córdoba created autonomy. As Iturbide himself put it in his *Memoria de Livorno,* "The Plan of Iguala guaranteed the religion of our forefathers; it offered to the reigning house of Spain the only means left to keep those extensive and rich provinces; it allowed the Mexicans to give laws to themselves and to have the government residing on their own territory."[13] That, of course, is the definition of autonomy, not of independence. In choosing to call the country the Empire of Mexico or Anáhuac, Iturbide harkened back to the roots of the nation, while continuing to govern through the moderate constitutional monarchical system of Spain. As Luis Villoro has argued, this was an organic transformation, or evolution, not a revolution, based on the native and European historical foundations of the country. Iguala and Córdoba were examples of "loosening but not breaking the link with the past." Villoro continues: "The abdication of Iturbide and the reinstallation of Congress, in March 1823, may be considered the end of the Revolution for Independence because they mark the accession to power of the creole middle class which had initiated the movement."[14]

The constitutional monarchical regime was conceived as an intermediate condition of indeterminate duration, and the leading periodicals in the months ahead were filled with discussion of whether Mexicans were mature enough for a more complete fulfillment of independence, normally concluding that, unlike their North American neighbors, they had not yet reached that state of civic order and enlightenment necessary for total abandonment of the institutions of the past. Iturbide, like most Mexicans of the time, believed that a republic was not suitable to the Mexican tradition and history. Historians must somehow overcome their tendency to

[12]Hamnett, *Roots of Insurgency*; Linda J. Arnold, "Bureaucracy and Bureaucrats in Mexico City, 1742–1835," ms.

[13]Augstín de Iturbide, *Memoria de Livorno*, 27 September 1823, BLAC, Hernández y Dávalos collection. I used the handwritten first draft English translation of Michael Joseph Quin.

[14]Luis Villoro, "The Ideological Currents of the Epoch of Independence," in Mario de la Cueva et al., *Major Trends in Mexican Philosophy* (Notre Dame, 1966), 215, 217–218.

assume that creation of a republic was an inevitable and immediate consequence of separation from Spain (in Mexico or anywhere else in Latin America).

The simple attainment of home rule, however, did not solve the problem of who was to rule at home. Since the Plan of Iguala loosened but did not break the link with the past, it naturally followed that Iturbide had to staff his new government with representatives primarily drawn from the old elite—the Spanish, the aristocrats, the holders of high office in the viceroyalty, the upper clergy, and high military. Thus Iturbide attempted to minimize the influence of the "old rebels," such as Vicente Guerrero, Nicolás Bravo, and Guadalupe Victoria.[15] Enemies of Iturbide, such as Rocafuerte, would claim that the Supreme Provisional Governing Junta was made up of the most disliked lowlifes in the empire and Iturbide's adulators—a patently false charge but understandable from an author who could not help but notice that the thirty-one Junta members who first took office consisted of seven officers, six audiencia lawyers, five high clergy, two audiencia judges, four titled nobles, two city councilors, one intendant, one magistrate, and three landowners and merchants.[16] Iturbide had to incorporate such people; to have done otherwise would have been to break the promise of Iguala while disrupting the fragile alliance that the consensus of Iguala depended upon. There was a very real danger, however, in Iturbide's dependence on the old elite, and one he perhaps did not recognize (since his own preferences corresponded to the class interests of the elite). For one thing, the hatred of gachupines and their privileges was fundamental and would continue to grow until it reached uncontrollable bounds. At a more fundamental level, however, the higher clergy and upper military whom Iturbide depended on were appointees of a previous regime, only some of whom had deep roots in the Mexican polity; most of them had converted to the cause of Iguala very late; they were royal appointees and functionaries. Mexico thus lacked, as Bulnes pointed out, a domestic "agrarian-military aristocracy" of its own upon which to base a monarchy.[17] Iturbide was attempting to construct a remodeled edifice on old foundations. Behind the scenes of this autonomy that called itself independence, there would obviously prevail the most profound power struggle.

The old insurgents and the Iturbidists also had profound differences of philosophy. One can, I think, reject the arguments of Iturbide's enemies that he was a servile adulator of Spain and the Bourbon dynasty. However, there can be no doubt that he believed the third guarantee—promising a

[15]Javier Rondero, "Diseño crítico de la consumación de la independencia," *Cuadernos Americanos*, 180 (January–February 1972), 128–142.

[16]Rocafuerte, *Bosquejo*, 74; Javier Ocampo, *Las ideas de un día: el pueblo mexicano ante la consumación de su independencia* (Mexico, 1969), 351, n. 2.

[17]Bulnes, *La guerra de independencia*, 347.

place in the new order for the Spaniards living in Mexico and protections for their jobs and properties—was fundamental to future stability. In the beginning Iturbide was motivated by the desire to win the support of the old Spaniards for his enterprise of autonomy. Subsequently he was motivated by a desire to see the Treaty of Córdoba accepted by Spain. In the end, he was motivated by a belief that protection for the Spaniards was fundamental to good order and justice.

Iturbide's elite followers could not have felt any sense of Mexican nationalism. The process of Iguala failed to produce nationalism, and in this it does not differ from the independence movements in Spanish America in general. Nonetheless, the failure of the autonomy process to produce a nationalist sentiment is surely related to Iturbide's failure to obtain agreement on the creation of a centralized state system.

The Iturbidists believed that basic reforms in society were evolutionary, not revolutionary. They despised the image of the French revolution. They were conservative reformers, but not counterrevolutionaries. In reflecting on the errors of the earlier revolutionaries, particularly Miguel Hidalgo, Iturbide wrote: "Hidalgo, and those who came after him, and who followed his example, desolated the country, . . . sacrificed millions of citizens, obstructed the sources of riches, . . . destroyed all kinds of industry, rendered the conditions of the Americans still more wretched . . . and far from obtaining independence increased the obstacles that opposed it."[18] As a consequence of that belief, Iturbide explained: "I sallied out then to be useful to the Mexicans, to the King of Spain, and to the Spaniards." For him, preserving order was being useful to Mexico, even if it also served the king of Spain. One of the problems with the historiography is that it rarely takes Iturbide's own words seriously; yet in his explanation that to preserve order he fought for Spain, and that in so doing he was also preserving Mexicans and their fortunes, we have the fundamental explanation why such a vast portion of the Mexican population—creole, native, and caste—also fought for Spain. Why then did he convert to the side of independence in 1821? By his own testimony, if we believe him, it was again to save the country, not from the radical decrees of the restored Cortes, but from the factionalism and risk of explosion that political events in Spain unleashed in Mexico. The Plan of Iguala was his instrument, and "without bloodshed, without incendiaries, without murders, without robberies, in short, without tears and without lamentations, my country became free."[19]

Obviously, the rebels, who according to Iturbide aspired to either the annihilation or expulsion of the Spaniards, who favored decisive abrupt revolution over gradual evolution, and who, most of all, failed to achieve

[18]*Memoria de Livorno.*
[19]Ibid.

the status after Córdoba that they hoped to achieve, could not forgive Iturbide. Rocafuerte insisted that if Iturbide were a true patriot he would have abandoned the guarantees of Iguala in his talks with O'Donojú and would have broken all links with Spain. To confirmed revolutionaries, Iguala was a sign of Iturbide's servilism to Spain and refusal to upset the powerful Spaniards in the country.[20]

If, as Hamnett has recently demonstrated, the movement for independence was a regionally based insurgency pitting the "provincial bourgeoisie" and popular classes against the entrepreneurial elite, merchant-investors, and big landlords, in short, an expression of regional social tensions,[21] then Iturbide fundamentally misunderstood the foundations of his power and the new state he was attempting to create. Turning his back on the regional leaders, as represented by the local caciques and rising caudillos such as Guerrero, Juan Alvarez, and Antonio López de Santa Anna, in favor of the creation of a unified monarchy, he failed to build on the new power centers, both military and civilian, that had started to emerge. The status of national autonomy achieved under Iguala and Córdoba could have no effect but to unleash the demand for regional autonomy. The defection of the regions was incipient from the very beginning, and after the Plan of Casa Mata it was triumphant.[22] Although the monarchy in Spain had actually been based on an ancient tradition of regional autonomy, Bourbon absolutism and the passage of centuries had served to mute that tradition. In Mexico, although the original autonomists in 1810 had called for the creation of a separate Mexican provisional junta as but one of many regional juntas of the monarchy, ten years of brutal warfare had served to mute that memory. Thus, in 1821 few if any voices were raised in support of a monarchy based on regionalism, and devolution to the provinces became the object of the incipient republicanist movement. Indeed, one suspects that, with the exception of a few thinkers based in Mexico City such as José María Luis Mora, Carlos María de Bustamante, or Mier (who had a nationalist perspective and were well versed in the philosophy of Europe and North America), when advocates of republicanism used that term they meant it as a surrogate for regional autonomy. Furthermore, Iturbide's insistence on creating a unified centralist empire would certainly serve to drive the advocates of regionalism away from him and from the whole idea of monarchy.

A seriously complicating factor to impede Iturbide's task of creating a unified nation was the fact that at the very moment of the Treaty of

[20]Rocafuerte, *Bosquejo*, 58, 67.

[21]Hamnett, *Roots of Insurgency*, 24, 45.

[22]Nettie Lee Benson, "The Plan of Casa Mata," *Hispanic American Historical Review* 25:1 (February 1945), 45–56.

Córdoba the territorial division of the country was in a state of confusion, resulting from the fact that the constitutional guarantee of provincial deputations had only been partially applied in Mexico. Even as O'Donojú prepared to sail for Mexico the Mexican deputies in the Cortes, led by José Miguel Ramos Arizpe, were arguing that the Constitution of 1812 granted a provincial deputation to each Mexican intendancy, but that only six had thus far been created. When O'Donojú arrived at Veracruz he carried a recent Cortes decree calling for the creation of provincial deputations in all the intendancies that did not yet have them. When Iturbide gained control of some provinces, such as Puebla, for example, he authorized the creation of provincial deputations there. When independence was declared, eight provincial deputations were functioning and another six were authorized but not yet established. In the elections for the Constituent Congress yet other regions claimed the status of province, until by November 1822 there were eighteen, and a nineteenth, Nuevo México, functioned without legal recognition. By the end of 1823, after the overthrow of Iturbide, there were twenty-three provinces.[23] Though the movement for regional devolution was irresistible, Iturbide does not seem to have been equipped to deal with it. The Plan of Casa Mata had only to tap this wellspring of regional interest to overwhelm Iturbide.

Yet a further complicating factor was, of course, the status of Central America. When Guatemala City proclaimed its adhesion to the Plan of Iguala it manifestly did not represent the entire region. El Salvador, most notably, had to be subdued by force of arms.[24] When the first Congress met in Mexico City, Central America was represented by substitute deputies chosen in the capital (as were Yucatán, Tabasco, the Californias, and the Eastern and Western Internal Provinces). At no time during the Iturbide period was it entirely clear what the membership of Congress was or, for that matter, exactly what constituted the jurisdiction of the empire. One may surmise that at no time did Iturbide have the sort of absolute control over the empire that his critics implied he had, or that historians sometimes assume. He never did control Yucatán, for example, or the region of the south where caciques like Juan Alvarez and Gordiano Guzmán ruled. Only the personal adherence of Vicente Guerrero, the major caudillo of the south, kept that region in apparent loyalty, however briefly.[25] He obviously never had control over Central America or of most of the northern provinces either.

[23]Nettie Lee Benson, *La diputación provincial y el federalismo mexicano* (Mexico, 1955), 47, 57, 59, 61, 62, 68–69, 82–83.

[24]Gastón García Cantu, "Bustamante y el principio de la autodeterminación de los pueblos," *Cuadernos Americanos*, 179 (November–December 1971), 139–154.

[25]Hamnett, *Roots of Insurgency*, 194–197.

The fundamental political problem Iturbide faced stemmed from the inherent weakness of the Plan of Iguala itself. As a few authors later pointed out, the Plan of Iguala was a simple political project, not a fundamental code for a nation.[26] From this flowed a host of associated legal problems. Rocafuerte argued that Iturbide should have created the junta called for in the Plan, or even a Congress, before the arrival of O'Donojú, and that Guadalupe Victoria had so advised him. If this had occurred the ensuing legal document, the Treaty of Córdoba, would have had the status of an agreement between a junta or Congress and the Spanish Superior Political Chief.[27] Instead, Iturbide waited until after Córdoba to handpick the members of the Sovereign Provisional Governing Junta, which according to Alamán was more a *tertulia* of friends than a deliberating body.[28] According to Iguala, the Junta's only job was to organize the Mexican Cortes, or Constituent Congress. Many critics then accused the Junta of overstepping its mandate as a mere transitional body by making too many decisions on important matters.[29] Even so, a modern historian, Javier Ocampo, has pointed out that the Junta actually failed to come to grips with the needs and opportunities presented in the task of creating a new government. After analyzing all of the meetings and enactments of the Junta during its period of existence (22 September 1821–25 February 1822), Ocampo concluded that 54 percent of its 125 orders and 39 decrees related to subjects that were not critical or even necessary to the organization of a newly independent nation, while only 46 percent of its actions related to substantial political and economic matters.[30]

The most important decision of the Junta, however, was its convocation of the Constituent Congress, which can only be described as a complicated muddle. According to the Plan of Iguala, the Congress was supposed to be chosen along the same lines as the Spanish Cortes, but the absence of valid census figures for Mexico and the fluctuating recognition of provinces made that impossible. Iturbide then proposed a Congress of two houses, the upper house representing the clergy, military, cities, and audiencias, and the lower house elected by proportional representation.[31] Rocafuerte insisted Iturbide was motivated by the desire to have at least one house under his control.[32] Two days later it appears that Iturbide proposed a Congress based on social class or estates (*estamentos*), consisting

[26]Ortiz de Ayala, *México considerado como nación*, 10.

[27]Rocafuerte, *Bosquejo*, 61.

[28]Lucas Alamán, *Historia de Méjico desde los primeros movimientos que prepararon su independencia en el año de 1808 hasta la época presente*, 5 vols. (reprint, Mexico, 1942), V, 297.

[29]José María Bocanegra, *Memorias para la historia de México independiente, 1822–1846*, 2 vols. (Mexico, 1892–1897), I, 14; Alamán, *Historia de Méjico*, V, 310–311.

[30]Ocampo, *Las ideas*, 284–303.

[31]*Semanario político y literario de Méjico*, tomo IV, no. 2; Rocafuerte, *Bosquejo*, 76–77.

[32]Rocafuerte, *Bosquejo*, 80.

of public officials, clergy and thinkers, merchants, manufacturers, and miners, the military, titled nobles, and the rest of the population.[33] Iturbide himself appeared before the Junta to urge it not to be bound by the dictates of the Spanish Constitution in convoking the Mexican Congress,[34] a clear violation of the spirit of Iguala.

The upshot was that the Junta on 17 November 1821 decreed that Congress would be composed of deputies from each intendancy or province equal to two-thirds the number of partidos. Thus the intendancy of Mexico, with 43 partidos, had 28 deputies; Guadalajara, with 28 partidos, had 17 deputies, and so on. The problem was that the distribution of partidos had developed in the Spanish colonial era as a reflection of territorial extent and defense needs rather than population distribution, so that, incredibly, the Internal Provinces of the East (Nuevo León, Nuevo Santander, Coahuila, Texas) had one deputy each, but among the Internal Provinces of the West, Durango had 34 partidos (hence 23 deputies), Arizpe had 12 partidos (thus 8 deputies), and Nuevo México had one deputy for its one partido. Durango, with 200,000 inhabitants, thus had 23 deputies, while Guanajuato, with more than 400,000 inhabitants, had only 7 deputies.[35] Twelve provinces or intendancies thus had several deputies each; eight had only one. Each province with more than one deputy was to have among its representatives an ecclesiastic, a member of the army, and a magistrate or lawyer. Furthermore, certain provinces were to have representatives from certain professions or estates.[36] Thus, Mexico ended up with a Congress based neither on population nor on estates, but on a rather clumsy combination of both. In addition, the proposal for an upper house was changed into an agreement that Congress, once it started meeting, would divide itself into two chambers of equal size, but when Congress did in fact start to meet this matter was dropped as it clearly served no identifiable purpose.[37]

Neither side was happy with the convocation of Congress. Iturbide later blamed it for creating what he called "monstrous inequality" among the provinces. Zavala said the Congress was based on "the most monstrous amalgam of heterogenous elements" that sowed the "seed for the destruction of the congress and of civil war."[38] Rocafuerte said discontent with the

[33] *Semanario político y literario de Méjico*, tomo IV, no. 2; William Spence Robertson, *Iturbide of Mexico* (Durham, 1952), 138.

[34] *Diario de las sesiones de la Soberana Junta Gubernativa del Imperio Mexicano* (Mexico, 1821), 83–85.

[35] "Estado que manifiesta los Diputados proprietarios y suplentes que se han de nombrar para el Congreso constituyente del Imperio Mexicano" (Mexico, 1821), BLAC, W. B. Stephens collection.

[36] Decree of Sovereign Junta, Mexico, 17 November 1821, Biblioteca del Instituto Nacional de Antropología e Historia, Mexico, T-3, 35, Antigua Colección.

[37] Alamán, *Historia de Méjico*, V, 259, 315, 317, 320; *El Sol*, 23 February 1822.

[38] Zavala, *Ensayo crítico*, I, 102–103.

convocation of Congress is what provoked the first anti-Iturbide plot in Mexico City, which led to the arrests on 26 November 1821 of several leading old-time revolutionaries such as Nicolás Bravo and Guadalupe Victoria.

With a Congress that was neither fish nor fowl, things were bound to deteriorate rapidly. When the Congress first met on 24 February 1822—the first anniversary of Iguala—its members took an oath to uphold the four fundamental principles of Iguala—religious intolerance, ethnic union, independence, and a moderated constitutional monarchy. Thus, as Rocafuerte asserted, Congress, which Iguala said was supposed to be constituent and therefore free to determine what form the future government would take, was bound from the beginning, by force of the same Plan, to create only a monarchy. Republicans, such as Poinsett and Rocafuerte, firmly insisted that Congress did have the power to make decrees that altered the Spanish Constitution of 1812, yet Rocafuerte denied the Sovereign Junta had the right to alter the Spanish constitutional method of electing Congress.[39] Zavala believed that Congress was hopelessly discredited, and consequently he led the struggle to reform Congress along lines that also happened to be more acceptable to Iturbide.[40]

An even more fundamental problem, unsolvable without conflict, was that at its first meeting the Congress voted that sovereignty resided in itself. Yet Iturbide claimed that his authority, based as it was on the fundamental acts of Iguala and Córdoba, was the only voice for expressing the national will. There was thus presented, as Luis Villoro has pointed out, a crisis of "dual sovereignty."[41] Zavala had the clearest understanding of what this meant. In his famous "Plan for the Reform of Congress," which his enemies thought stamped him as an Iturbidist, he pointed out that Congress on its first day, before all its proprietary members were even present and before discussing the most pressing problems of the day, had declared that sovereignty resided in itself and had delegated the executive power to the Regency. After Iturbide's election as emperor, Congress had then forced him to take an oath to support the Spanish Constitution (which also vested sovereignty in the Cortes). It had then proceeded even to limit his powers by refusing the emperor the right of veto.[42] Thus Mexico had a Congress that had no choice but to create a monarchy, and a monarch who had no choice but to recognize the sovereignty of Congress. The two main contenders for power were thus severely weakened. On the one hand was a

[39]Joel R. Poinsett, *Notes on Mexico Made in the Autumn of 1822* (New York, reprint, 1969), 274; Rocafuerte, *Bosquejo*, 80.

[40]Raymond Estep, *Lorenzo de Zavala, profeta del liberalismo mexicano* (Mexico, 1952), 75.

[41]Villoro, "Ideological Currents," 217.

[42]Estep, *Lorenzo de Zavala*, 75; Lorenzo de Zavala, "Proyecto de reforma del Congreso Mexicano" (Mexico, 1822), BLAC, W. B. Stephens collection.

Congress defective in its makeup and defensive, even pugnacious, in insisting on its superiority; on the other hand was an emperor intemperate in his actions, poorly advised, and putative in his refusal to take second place.

Iturbide was convinced that Congress's main object was to despoil him of the power that he believed the people had given him. He argued that the powers of Congress only extended to those he had chosen to grant since, as he put it, "When I entered Mexico my own will was the Law; I commanded the public force. . . . And who compelled me to divide the powers? Myself, and myself alone, because I thought it was right. If I did not choose to be absolute then, why should I have wished to be so afterwards?"[43] When he dissolved Congress he believed that he had the general support of the army and leading notables since he had large numbers of representations from provincial deputations, army commanders, civilian officials, and private citizens urging him to do so.[44] When the Junta Instituyente was installed, Iturbide, at the opening ceremony, reasserted his primacy with the same blatancy with which he had attempted to uphold it, declaring: "My voice . . . constituted the single organ of the general will of the inhabitants of this empire."[45]

The continuing presence of a large contingent of Spanish military forces awaiting transfer back to Europe, the Spanish control over San Juan de Ulúa commanding the entry of the port of Veracruz, and concerns over whether Spain would recognize the Treaty of Córdoba all constituted a further source of weakness. Contemporary commentators disagreed over its impact. Rocafuerte and the opponents of Iturbide felt that the continued presence of Spanish troops in Mexico was a ploy on Iturbide's part to convince the people there was danger of reconquest and that he purposely delayed their departure.[46] Other commentators, like Bulnes, insist that the presence of 6,000 Spanish troops in Mexico meant that a genuine threat existed and that it was necessary to rally around the one man who could command the support of an army.[47] Still others insist that Iturbide broke the provisions of the Plan of Iguala from the very start. Navarro y Rodrigo argues that Iturbide had annulled all the guarantees of Iguala by the time of his overthrow; Poinsett insisted Iturbide's seizure of money sent by Spanish merchants to Veracruz was a violation of the third guarantee.[48]

[43] *Memoria de Livorno.*

[44] Ibid.; Zavala, *Ensayo crítico*, I, 141-143.

[45] "Acta de la instalación de la Junta Nacional Instituyente" (Mexico, 1822), BLAC, Hernández y Dávalos collection.

[46] Jaime E. Rodríguez O., *The Emergence of Spanish America: Vicente Rocafuerte and Spanish Americanism, 1808-1832* (Berkeley, 1975), 53-55.

[47] Bulnes, *La guerra de independencia*, 258.

[48] Navarro y Rodrigo, *Vida de Iturbide, 196*; Joel Roberts Poinsett, *The Present Political State of Mexico*, ed. by L. Smith Lee (Salisbury, N.C., 1976), 43.

One pressure that all sources agree existed was the demand of *empleomanía*, of raised expectations for advancement and reward from the army, the professionals, and from those Spaniards who had gone over to Iturbide. One of Iturbide's supporters insisted that everyone aspired to be a general.[49] Zavala wrote: "It is not easy to conceive of how many ambitions, both great and small, it was necessary to satisfy in order not to make for discontent."[50] Several original supporters—notably Santa Anna and Nicolás Bravo—broke with Iturbide in part because of failure to receive the ranks and appointments they had been led to expect.[51] Navarro y Rodrigo says that by December 1821 among the troops stationed at Mexico City there was already one officer of the rank of corporal or higher for every two soldiers.[52]

A closely related problem, which all commentators also agree on, is that Iturbide lacked the one thing necessary to consolidate his power—an economic base.[53] Government revenues were never adequate to meet the demand, and Iturbide was literally forced to beg, borrow, and steal. Poinsett concluded that the principal subject of dispute between Iturbide and the Congress was the frequent demand for money. It is true, as Tenenbaum says, that Congress under Iturbide did not enact a single new tax law but engaged in a fiscal battle with the emperor.[54] The disruption of the mining sector and the merchant-investors, and the flight of Spanish capital during the war, along with the deterioration of the treasury revenues that had occurred since well before the outbreak of the struggle for independence, would have made financing the new state difficult enough. The fact that so many interest groups needed to be rewarded for their part in bringing about the consensus of Iguala added an extra burden. Iturbide attempted various measures to meet the financial exigencies—discounts on salaries, forced loans, paper money, property taxes, and direct taxes (the latter three decreed by the Junta Nacional Instituyente after the closing of Congress). These merely served, however, to create a formidable alliance against him of civil servants, army members, merchants, and property owners which no power could resist. When Iturbide left in 1823 fewer than half of the bills were being paid.[55] The ultimate paradox, of course, is that the Itur-

[49]"Callen unos y hablen otros" (Mexico, 1821), BLAC, W. B. Stephens collection.

[50]Zavala, *Ensayo histórico*, 133.

[51]Leonard D. Parrish, "The Life of Nicolás Bravo, Mexican patriot (1786–1854)," (Ph.D. dissertation, University of Texas, Austin, 1951), 104; Antonio López de Santa Anna, *The Eagle: The Autobiography of Santa Anna*, ed. by Ann Fears Crawford (Austin, 1967), p. 16.

[52]Navarro y Rodrigo, *Vida de Iturbide*, 134.

[53]Bulnes, *La guerra de independencia*, 386. See Barbara A. Tenenbaum, *The Politics of Penury: Debts and Taxes in Mexico, 1821-1856* (Albuquerque, 1986), 14–20.

[54]Poinsett, *Notes on Mexico*, 270; Barbara A. Tenenbaum, "Taxation and Tyranny: Public Finance during the Iturbide Regime, 1821-1823," in this volume.

[55]Anna, "The Rule of Iturbide," 79–110; Stanley C. Green, *The Mexican Republic: The First Decade, 1823-1832* (Pittsburgh, 1987), 150.

bide victory had been achieved almost without cost; it had been a cheap success compared to the destruction and deprivation that had accompanied the eleven years of insurgency and insurrection before 1821. Yet, once separation from Spain was achieved, the elites consistently refused to pay for the new government from which they expected to receive so much and opposed all new taxes as they were proposed.

A final point worthy of brief comment was the personality of Iturbide himself. Whether he was the power-mad demagogue of unstable personality with a childhood history of torturing small animals as Rocafuerte portrayed him, or whether he was the "Honor and Glory of America," as his adulators painted him, it is clear that he could not retain the loyalty of even his closest companions like Pedro Celestino Negrete or José Antonio Echávarri, much less those of men like Guerrero, Bravo, or Santa Anna who had joined his side because the Plan of Iguala had seemed like the best way to achieve separation from Spain. The only thing that he cannot be accused of is personal cowardice. For all else he was a mere mortal. While Rondero insists Iturbide refused to be a dictator when he had the chance, and Bulnes says Iturbide wanted to be a dictator,[56] the evidence is clear that he refused to submit the nation to a civil war merely to hold onto his throne. In addition, as even such a hostile source as Valle admits, Iturbide descended the throne a poor man with no support but the pension granted him by Congress.[57] Bulnes points out, referring to Iturbide's ill-fated return to Mexico, that if the ex-emperor had been as designing as everyone feared, he would not have returned directly to Mexico, and to his death at Padilla, but would have gone first to Havana or New Orleans to build up a base of support for his restoration. One of the few really objective contemporary foreign observers, Captain Basil Hall, wrote concerning Iturbide's return to Mexico: "The result will show how far Iturbide's decision is a wise one: that it is a patriotic and disinterested decision, I have not the smallest doubt; and there does not appear the least reason for apprehending that his views have any other direction than the service of Mexico."[58]

It is clear that Iturbide faced many insuperable obstacles to the establishment of orderly government. Conscious of at least some of the troubles that would face him, his own testimony that in May 1822 he accepted the

[56]Rondero, "Diseño crítico de la consumación de la independencia," 141; Bulnes, *La guerra de independencia*, 400.

[57]Rafael Heliodoro Valle, *Como era Iturbide* (Mexico, 1922), 17.

[58]Bulnes, *La guerra de independencia*, 412; Captain Basil Hall, *Extracts from a Journal Written on the Coasts of Chili, Peru, and Mexico in the Years 1820, 1821, 1822*, 2 vols., 3d ed. (Upper Saddle River, N.J., reprint, 1968), II, 263.

throne feeling that "I was obliged to yield and to bear this misfortune, which was the greatest for me,"[59] may not be as self-serving as always assumed. It is also clear that his overthrow left a power vacuum that would not soon be filled. None of the leaders who immediately followed Iturbide possessed anything like the degree of initial public support and enthusiasm that he enjoyed in 1821 and 1822. If his task was difficult, theirs would be even more so.

[59]*Memoria de Livorno.*

Taxation and Tyranny: Public Finance during the Iturbide Regime, 1821–1823

Barbara A. Tenenbaum

On the morning of September 28, 1821, Agustín de Iturbide selected the 38 members of Mexico's new governing junta; in the afternoon they declared the nation free and independent from Spain. On May 18, 1822, Congress proclaimed Iturbide Emperor Agustín I. Less than one year later, on March 19, 1823, the Emperor abdicated, ending the first Mexican Empire and making way for the first federal republic. This essay explores the fiscal legacy which Iturbide inherited, his efforts to grapple with it, and the precedents which that struggle bequeathed to his successors.

The Fiscal Context

The Bourbon reforms in the late eighteenth century significantly altered the colonial tax structure. In 1760, the crown collected $4,675,178 pesos in revenue, and in 1790 a total of $11,493,748 – a 246 percent increase over a thirty-year period. Most gains appeared in tariffs, miscellaneous collections, and taxes on salaries. The new tobacco monopoly, established in 1766, whose proceeds went directly to Spain, provided 9 percent of total revenues for 1790.[1]

The increase in tax collections combined with payments for imported goods contributed to a widespread shortage of cash throughout New Spain. As a result, business was often transacted on credit. In a society where

[1]Fabián Fonseca and Carlos de Urrutia, *Historia general de Real Hacienda*, Volume 1 (Mexico: Imprenta de Vicente García Torres, 1845), introduction, pp. i-xxxviii and Chart 3; John TePaske with the collaboration of José and Mari Luz Hernández Palomo, *La Real Hacienda de Nueva España: La real caja de México (1576–1816)* (Mexico: Departamento de Investigaciones Históricas, Seminario de Historia Económica. Colección Científica, Fuentes [Historia Económica de México] 41, 1976), no page number, and a photocopy of "Sumario General de Cartas Cuentas de Veracruz," supplied by John TePaske, Duke Univerisity.

landholdings were the only acceptable collateral for loans, merchants, with their marketing operations and access to cash, formed alliances with hacendados, and both, particularly in the Bajío, were often involved in mining operations. As a result, an elite family enterprise formed and became the basis for colonial society, buttressed by the wealth of the church.[2]

By the end of the eighteenth century, the crown's need for money threatened the traditional role of that venerable institution as well. In 1798 Spain ordered the church to sell all property belonging to welfare institutions, brotherhoods, pious works, and church officials, and forced it to lend the proceeds to the royal treasury at 3 percent annual interest. Then on December 26, 1804, Viceroy José Iturrigaray promulgated the Consolidation Law, the culmination of the Bourbon attack on clerical power and wealth which began with the expulsion of the Jesuits in 1767. The Consolidation decreed that loans owed to the clergy be paid up and the funds loaned to Spain. By 1809 the church had sent over ten million pesos to Spain, 25 percent of which had come from the archdiocese of Mexico alone.[3]

The situation worsened with the outbreak of the Hidalgo revolt in September 1810. As a result, officials in Mexico City raised rates on sales taxes (*alcabala*) and trade taxes (*almojarifazgo*), taxed pulque and tobacco, called for new donations, and discounted the salaries of all public officials.[4]

The Hidalgo revolt shocked both Spaniards and creole nationalists into a new loyalty to Spain. From 1808 to 1810 landowners supplied the crown with eight million pesos and, until 1812, voluntarily loaned additional sums to the colonial government.[5] But by 1812, loans were no longer voluntary and Viceroy Venegas was forced to impose higher rates on all commodities consumed in urban areas. In Mexico City officials put a 10 percent tax on all urban real estate, and a 3 to 12 percent tax on income. They also levied a special convoy tax and were particularly assiduous in collecting the alcabala.[6]

[2]John E. Kicza, *Colonial Entrepreneurs: Families and Business in Bourbon Mexico City* (Albuquerque: University of New Mexico Press, 1983), 13–42; Richard B. Lindley, *Haciendas and Economic Development: Guadalajara, Mexico at Independence* (Austin: University of Texas, 1983), Chapter 2.

[3]Doris M. Ladd, *The Mexican Nobility at Independence 1780–1826* (Austin: Institute of Latin American Studies, University of Texas, 1976), p. 99; table 20, pp. 100–101; pp. 102–103.

[4]John J. TePaske, "The Financial Disintegration of the Royal Government of Mexico during the Epoch of Independence," in this volume. The author thanks Professor TePaske for sending her an advance copy and permitting her to cite this work.

[5]Lindley, *Haciendas*, 89–122; Brian R. Hamnett, "Royalist Counterinsurgency and the Continuity of Rebellion: Guanajuato and Michoacán, 1813–1820," *Hispanic American Historical Review* 62 (1982), 19–48; Timothy E. Anna, *The Fall of the Royal Government in Mexico City* (Lincoln: University of Nebraska Press, 1978), 151-158.

[6]TePaske, "Financial Disintegration."

When it became apparent that the crown could not repay previous loans, merchants and other creditors became highly reluctant to lend it more money. After 1812, merchants began to refuse solicitations for funds unless they received assurances of satisfactory collateral such as mortgages on future tax collections. Viceroy Félix Calleja complained as early as 1813 that the government had fallen completely into the hands of its creditors and by April he calculated a monthly deficit of $260,000. But, when he approached the elites for a loan, they demanded a mortgage on alcabala receipts from Mexico City and surrounding areas, on the pulque revenues, the two mill tax on road usage, and the war tax on food. Calleja had to pledge one half of the tax collections from Mexico City to obtain enough money to keep the tobacco monopoly, the gunpowder factory, and the mint in operation.[7]

On September 13, 1813, the Spanish Cortes issued a Nuevo Plan de Contribuciones Públicas which suggested the replacement of alcabalas and monopolies with port taxes and head taxes together with a 10 percent tax on urban property, 1 percent on coined silver, and a 50 percent price increase on tobacco. Calleja wrote to his superiors at court noting that if such a plan were implemented, "my government will inevitably be detested."[8]

On July 21, 1814, Calleja established new principles for augmenting tax revenues with committees throughout the kingdom assessing rates and drawing up lists for monthly regional collections. After the fall of the Cortes in 1814, Calleja renamed the new taxes "temporary war levies" (*subvención temporal de guerra*) and experienced such difficulty in getting residents to contribute to a forced loan that he had to resort to threats. At the close of 1815, the situation had grown so serious that Calleja tried to establish a forced lottery—an idea he soon abandoned.[9]

As TePaske has noted, by the end of 1815 the rate of debt increase had slowed considerably because the colony had been bled dry. Even church and household silver had been given to finance the war effort. By the end of 1816, one estimate indicated that the treasury of Mexico owed 81 million pesos.[10]

To make matters worse, many wealthy Spaniards preferred to leave Mexico after the Hidalgo revolt or simply ship their wealth out of the country and wait for better times. Regrettably it is still impossible to estimate the amount of capital flight, but José María Quirós set it at 786 million pesos.[11]

[7]Brian R. Hamnett, *Revolución y contrarrevolución en México y el Perú* (*Liberalismo, realeza, y separatismo 1800–1824*) (Mexico: Fondo de Cultura Económica, 1978), 87–88.

[8]Ibid., 93–94.

[9]Anna, *The Fall of the Royal Government*, 155–158.

[10]TePaske, "Financial Disintegration."

[11]Ladd, *The Mexican Nobility*, 148–153. For in interesting view of the problem of capital flight, see Romeo Flores Caballero, *Counterrevolution, the Role of the Spaniards in the*

Agustín de Iturbide and the Plan de Iguala with its three guarantees promised to solve two nagging questions about the future of New Spain. He pledged that the Catholic church would be secure in the new political environment and that Spaniards too would find a protected home there. Thus the Iturbide movement tried to assure its partisans that credit would be reestablished much as before, and that wealthy *peninsulares* need not send their capital abroad. These reassurances and fears of what might happen to a New Spain ruled by a liberal Spanish Cortes helped pave the way to independence.

Powerful interest groups—the church, merchants, mineowners, landowners, the army—expected that they would soon be restored to their former glory and that the prosperity predicted by von Humboldt would soon be theirs with the coming of independence. Yet, in addition to the different viewpoints of insurgent and royalist and the legacy of flooded mines, enormous debts, and widespread property damage, the Mexican nation faced three unacknowledged challenges to its becoming a viable country.

First, it would have to reestablish political and fiscal control over its territory. As TePaske has shown, the regional treasuries had virtually cut off their payment of yearly tax revenues to the central *caja* in Mexico City; the new nation would need those funds to establish a viable regime.[12]

Second, Iturbide had to reclaim the loyalty of a population disaffected by frequent exactions and constant insecurity. He would have to do this quickly and convincingly in order to reverse a long-standing trend toward alienation and atomization. That done, the new state could look forward to easy access to loans and public confidence.

Third, the new regime would have to create a new and workable tax base from the ruins of the colonial structure so that it could pay the army. The national government had to design a system which could satisfy its needs without sacrificing too much of its popularity.

Iturbide undoubtedly believed that his personal popularity as the Liberator of Mexico would give him enough support to construct a viable government for the new nation. He was unaware that the creole elites believed that Mexican independence meant a liberation from the burdens of Spanish colonial taxation and its incessant demands for unsecured loans. They had no intention of giving any Mexican leader the funds required to run a stable government. They expected Iturbide (and his successors) to find those sums elsewhere. Unhappily for Emperor Agustín I, they arrived too late.

Independence of Mexico, 1804–1838, trans. Jaime E. Rodríguez O. (Lincoln: University of Nebraska Press, 1974), 72.

[12]TePaske, "Financial Disintegration."

Iturbide and the Onset of Deficit

From the fiscal perspective, the Iturbide regime can be divided into three distinct periods: (1) the government before the installation of a Congress on February 24, 1822, and the issue of the first Memoria de Hacienda, (2) the administration during the Congressional period from February 24 to October 31, 1822, and the appearance of the second Memoria de Hacienda, and (3) the Empire under the Junta Instituyente from October 31, 1822, to Iturbide's abdication on March 19, 1823.[13]

During its first four months in power, the Iturbide administration slowly began to discover the nature of the fiscal system it had inherited. Initially, it wanted simply to establish an interim fiscal structure.

In October it abolished the taxes on *aguardiente* and *mescal*, the temporary war levies, the direct war tax, the convoy tax, the 10 percent tax on the value and rent of houses and exports, the taxes on henequen, and all extraordinary payments. In addition, it reduced the alcabala on domestic goods from 16 to 6 percent and on imported ones from 16 to 8 percent.[14]

Iturbide ordered that positions once held by employees who had emigrated during the independence wars were to be considered vacant and that openings for positions worth over $1,000 were to be published. More importantly, he established the Junta de Crédito Público to investigate the state of the public debt, thereby seeming to assure creole creditors that their debt paper would be redeemed. He also reestablished the tobacco monopoly.[15]

During the same month, the government fixed Iturbide's salary at $120,000 annually. It set payment for the three regents at $10,000 each, secretaries at $8,000, and the widow of Juan O'Donojú, the last viceroy of New Spain, was allotted a pension of $12,000.[16]

During November the regency established regulations for the organization of the four ministries (Foreign Relations, War, Justice, and Treasury) at an annual cost of $21,720 each. In order to help mine owners, the goverment combined eleven separate taxes into one 3 percent ad valorem duty, and to calm the fears of the elites about the possibility of additional taxation, it ended the Administración de Arbitrios, which had determined new taxes during the independence wars. The government followed a similar

[13]This essay does not treat the establishment of an empire as a significant fiscal event.

[14]Rafael Pérez Maldonado, *Memoria que el ministro de Hacienda presenta al soberano Congreso sobre el estado del erario* (Mexico, 1822), 9.

[15]Ibid., 18–19.

[16]Manuel Dublán and José María Lozano, *Legislación mexicana o colección completa de las disposiciones legislativas espedidas desde la independencia de la República* (Mexico: Imprenta del Comercio, 1876–1912), I, 552–553.

pattern in December with the publication of a new 25 percent ad valorem tariff (down from 36.5 percent) and the restoration of property confiscated during wartime.[17]

But by the end of 1821, the Treasury contained a mere $6,647.[18] Early in January the government authorized Iturbide to borrow $1,500,000. On January 4 Iturbide urged the Junta to heed his pleas and pay the army. Five days later, he asked the bishoprics of Guadalajara, Durango, and Oaxaca for $750,000 to be paid within six months.[19]

As early as January 1822 the elites showed themselves unwilling to place their confidence in Iturbide. In an obvious attempt to halt continuing capital flight, the government ordered a 15 percent surcharge on the exportation of coins. It also demanded that each of the regional treasuries supply the Treasury Ministry with monthly accounts including income, expenses, and funds on hand. Further, Iturbide named a committee to design a treasury structure for Mexico including Francisco Sánchez de Tagle, Máximo Parada (the intendent for Sonora), Fernando Navarro (secretary of the Junta de Crédito Público), Antonio Batres (treasurer of the Junta), and Vicente Carbajal.[20]

On February 1, the Regency reported to the Junta that it urgently needed funds to support the army and that the treasury could only pay expenses by transferring monies from the consulado of Mexico City, from the mint, and from donations for *obras pías*.[21] Therefore, it reopened the mint in Zacatecas, forbade the making of gunpowder, and improved port facilities in Guaymas and Mazatlán so that they could be opened to receive foreign vessels. Two weeks later, it combined eleven separate taxes on coins and silver into a straight 3 percent duty on their specie value and reduced duties on assay and other coinage taxes. On February 16, the Regency specifically forbade the export of specie except that needed for trade without specific permission from the government in an obvious attempt to halt capital flight. Several days later, it also raised taxes on foreign aguardiente to 20 percent (up from 6 percent), and set those on domestic liquors at 12 percent (February 20).[22]

[17]Pérez Maldonado, *Memoria de Hacienda 1822*, 9 and 19; Dublán and Lozano, *Legislación mexicana*, I, 554, 563–564, 567–587.

[18]*Memoria de Hacienda 1870*, 67–68.

[19]William Spence Robertson, *Iturbide of Mexico* (New York: Greenwood Press, 1968), 152–153.

[20]Pérez Maldonado, *Memoria de Hacienda 1822*, 20; Dublán and Lozano, *Legislación mexicana*, I, 590.

[21]Robertson, *Iturbide*, 153.

[22]Pérez Maldonado, *Memoria de Hacienda 1822*, 10 and 21; Dublán and Lozano, *Legislación mexicana*, I, 594–596.

The first Congress of the Mexican nation was officially installed on February 24, 1822. Three days later, Treasury Minister Rafael Pérez Maldonado presented his Memoria de Hacienda. Although he offered a budget for the ten months from September 1821 to June 30, 1822, in which expenses ($11,311,063) would outstrip income ($10,212,373) by $1,921,973, the report has a confident and optimistic tone. Pérez Maldonado believed that the colonial tax system would soon begin to function smoothly, and would produce substantial increases in income. For example, he noted that the tobacco, card, and gunpowder monopolies yielded an average of 2.5 million pesos during the period from 1803 to 1812.[23]

The Treasury Minister argued that the restoration of peace following the independence wars would soon stimulate commerce and agriculture and that the elites, now freed from arbitrary taxation, would return to business as usual and reinvest their wealth. He urged Iturbide to encourage mining and improve the administration of the tobacco monopoly so that revenues would return to their previously high levels. He also suggested streamlining the civilian government, reducing the army by developing national militias, and establishing a moderate direct contribution, since the Treasury had found itself forced to borrow $900,000 in less than six months.[24]

Pérez Maldonado was much too optimistic, but he had little understanding of the situation which the Mexican nation had inherited from New Spain. He assumed incorrectly that the new regime could call upon a fully operational Spanish colonial tax structure which would soon produce substantial revenues given time and proper management. But as TePaske has pointed out, the colonial fiscal system had been deteriorating since the late 1780s.[25] In addition, the Treasury Minister conveniently forgot to include the huge debts which the new nation had agreed to honor in order to win creole and peninsular support.

Pérez Maldonado also failed to allow for the elites' unspoken assumption that they could avoid contributing to the support of the new government. The strength of their commitment to that position led to a serious confrontation between Congress and the Liberator of Mexico.

Iturbide and Congress

During its first month Congress acted quickly to preserve the elites' wealth at the expense of the national treasury. The fiscal battle between

[23]It would be interesting to discover the Treasury Minister's sources. According to TePaske and Hernández Palomo, the card monopoly averaged $145,968.4 in those years, and the gunpowder *estanco* yielded an average of $84,078.2 for 1804–1809 (exclusive of 1807 for which there are no figures). No collections are given for tobacco in those years. Pérez Maldonado, *Memoria de Hacienda 1822*, 14.

[24]Ibid., 15–17, 21.

[25]TePaske, "Financial Disintegration."

Iturbide and the elites represented by Congress began on March 16, 1822, when the delegates ordered that officials stop collecting the $1,500,000 forced loan and made it voluntary. On March 22, Congress repealed the law against the export of specie and permitted people to leave the country on a month's notice with whatever sums they wished.[26]

Congress did not enact a single new tax law, although it did permit a $600,000 loan to be levied principally on merchants in Mexico City and salary reductions of up to 20 percent for officeholders. It handled the revenue shortage by looking to foreigners for the necessary funds. Therefore, it authorized a twenty-five to thirty million peso foreign loan with the entire national treasury to serve as collateral. It mandated the inventory of all property belonging to Philippine missionaries and the "holy places of Jerusalem," extended the 2 percent tax on coined gold and silver to copper, and altered the duties on liquors.[27]

In the meantime the fiscal crisis worsened because many in the army believed themselves deserving of special favors, promotions, or bonuses, much as in the rest of newly liberated Spanish America. As Lorenzo Zavala exaggerated it, "one half of the nation asked for this or that recompense."[28] Their response was hardly unusual for when Iturbide did not receive what he considered to be just recognition for his loyalty to the crown, he suddenly became an insurgent.[29] As Joel Poinsett noted, "so long as (Iturbide) possessed the means of paying and rewarding (officers and soldiers), so long will he maintain himself on the throne; when these fail he will be precipitated from it."[30] The situation had crystallized by April 1822. Iturbide faced an army hungry for reward and a Congress unwilling to enact the new taxes necessary to provide it.

As usual, the figures, undoubtedly fraudulent, tell the story. According to the accounting for March 1822 printed in *Gaceta Imperial de México*, the government collected $819,184 and spent $813,612, leaving a surplus of only $5,672. Most of the income ($304,854 or 37 percent) either came from the forced loan on the consulados, or from customs receipts ($163,000 or 20 percent). But by May with the forced loan rescinded, income had declined to $302,892 of which $143,502 or 47 percent came from a Treasury

[26]*Colección de órdenes y decretos de la soberana junta provisional gubernativa y soberanos congresos generales de la nación mexicana*, (Mexico, 1839), II, 13, 17, 34.

[27]Ibid., 7, 49, 52–53, 56–57, 72–73; Dublán and Lozano, *Legislación mexicana*, I, 617–619.

[28]Lorenzo Zavala, *Ensayo histórico de las revoluciones de México*, (Mexico, 1918), I, 126 as cited in Robertson, *Iturbide*, 203.

[29]Timothy Anna, "The Independence of Mexico and Central America," in Leslie Bethell, ed., *The Cambridge History of Latin America*, (Cambridge: Cambridge University Press, 1985), III, 87.

[30]Joel Poinsett, *Notes on Mexico* (Philadelphia, 1824), 68 as cited in Robertson, *Iturbide*, 192.

surplus in the preceding month. Since the Treasury had only $969 on hand on June 1, income for the next 28 days declined to $245,419, most of which ($79,886 or 32.5 percent) came from tariff revenues.[31]

Iturbide clearly recognized the problem and wisely shifted his Minister of War, Antonio Medina, to the Treasury on July 1. No doubt he believed that Medina would be able to find solutions to his two most pressing problems—army discontent and an empty treasury. But by October 1822, the fiscal situation had grown so desperate that Iturbide was forced to seize a *conducta* carrying silver worth $1,200,000 belonging to merchants in Perote. He justified his "expropriation" by correctly noting "there were no funds to pay the army or government employees, the treasury was empty, money couldn't be borrowed in the country and the foreign loans needed more time."[32]

Medina presented his very straightforward and realistic *Memoria de Hacienda* on October 28, 1822. After reporting that the Treasury would have a deficit of $2,826,630 by the end of 1822, he forthrightly advised Iturbide: "No doubt your excellency will prefer to take the most convenient steps to balance income and expenses . . . but in the future, new sources of revenue will be necessary."[33]

Medina attribued the obvious imbalance between income and expenses to reductions in tax collections and the additional needs of the army, which included the costs of maintaining Spanish soldiers who had capitulated to the insurgent army and were awaiting repatriation to Spain.[34] He devoted most his *Memoria de Hacienda*, however, to an extremely detailed examination of each and every tax category still extant from colonial times. He noted that collection costs, particularly for salaries, remained fixed and that receipts were down for every tax, except the alcabala, which should have produced more because of greater trade. Even the lottery registered a 75 percent decline due to general poverty![35]

[31]*Gaceta Imperial de Méjico*, chart opposite issues for April 1, June 5, and July 1, 1822.

[32]Lorenzo Zavala, *Umbral de la independencia* (Mexico: Empresas Editoriales, 1949), 196 as cited in Jan Bazant, *Historia de la deuda exterior de México (1823–1946)* (Mexico: El Colegio de México, 1968), 15.

[33]Antonio de Medina, *Memoria de Hacienda* (Mexico, 1822), Iturbide Papers, Library of Congress, Washington, D.C., Microfilm, roll 9, pp. 1–2. The author wishes to thank Wanda Turnley, Benson Latin American Collection, University of Texas at Austin, for her help in reconciling the manuscript edition of this report with the printed version.

[34]Ibid., 2–3, 7. According to Medina, they cost approximately $35,000 per month.

[35]Medina, *Memoria de Hacienda 1822*. Although his careful analysis pales in comparison with that of Manuel Payno y Bustamante in 1844, it was far superior to that classic discussion of the colonial revenue system which Matías Romero lifted from Fonseca and Urrutia, *Historia general*, to use in his *Memoria de Hacienda 1870*.

The Treasury Minister suggested that Mexico could either ask for voluntary loans or institute new taxes. Since the new nation could not endow a fund to pay interest and amortization charges for a voluntary loan, it would soon become a forced exaction. Although Medina also mentioned the possibility of emiting paper money, he noted that it too, like a voluntary loan, required confidence in the Treasury, which "was in a critical state" because troops had to be paid their arrears and current wages.

He concluded that Iturbide should push for the establishment of a provisional tax to be divided among wealthy residents to cover the deficit and allow Congress time in which to take more permanent action. These new revenues would help restore the tobacco monopoly and aid mining. Direct and indirect taxes could then be added in the future. Otherwise, he warned, grievances would accumulate and the Treasury (and the entire government) would be discredited.[36]

Many Mexican politicians were already working to produce such an outcome. On August 26, 1822, Iturbide was informed of a plot against the empire and arrested fifteen prominent Congressmen and thirty-five others. In retaliation, the Commander of the Interior Provinces of the East, Felipe de la Garza, led an uprising to effect their release. And as Jaime Rodríguez has noted, Vicente Rocafuerte worked tirelessly to ensure that Iturbide did not receive significant assistance from the United States.[37]

The day after Medina presented his report, Congress passed a new law ending the tobacco monopoly in 1825, thus depriving the government of one of its major sources of revenue. But Congress would not approve plans for a new loan, even though Iturbide pledged its repayment.[38]

These activities clearly indicated Congressional irresponsibility in view of the financial crisis and its determination not to contribute to the maintenance of the government. As Anna has noted, "during its nine months in existence, Congress had failed to address the basic issues of the consolidation of the empire."[39] In light of such Congressional opposition, Iturbide concluded that he would not be able to implement Medina's recommendations for raising revenue. Indeed, Congress would have been likely to obstruct any and all of his efforts to enact appropriate measures to solve the crisis.

[36]Medina, *Memoria de Hacienda 1822*, 2–7.

[37]Timothy Anna, "The Rule of Agustín de Iturbide: A Reappraisal," *Journal of Latin American Studies* (May, 1985), 17:1, 100; Jaime E. Rodríguez O. *The Emergence of Spanish America: Vicente Rocafuerte and Spanish Americanism, 1808–1832* (Berkeley: University of California Press, 1975), 60–64.

[38]*Colección de decretos*, II, 87–89.

[39]Anna, "Iturbide," 100–101.

On October 31, 1822, Iturbide forced the adjournment of Congress, complaining that among its other sins, it had not devised a tax structure for an independent nation.[40] Historians, unaware of the desperate confrontation between the Emperor and Congress over fiscal measures, have generally condemned Iturbide for what they perceived to be an arbitrary measure. Yet Iturbide could hardly have permitted Congress to deny him new taxes if he expected his government to survive. For example, shortly after Congress was dissolved, Joaquín Obregón, head of its Finance and Commerce Commissions, urged that the government order a study to determine the full extent of the treasury situation, just days after Medina had submitted his quite thorough *Memoria de Hacienda.*[41] Obregón already knew the disastrous state of the Mexican treasury and the reasons for it. He and other members of the elites simply did not want to contribute their fortunes to revitalizing the tax structure of the nation.

Taxes and Tyranny

Once he had disbanded Congress on October 31, 1822, Iturbide quickly established a smaller Junta Instituyente of former Congressmen, which declared its intention to design new taxes to reduce the deficit. Mostly, it simply followed Medina's advice. On November 5, the Junta decreed a forced loan of 2.8 million pesos, followed on December 20 by the emission of 4 million pesos in paper money. The following day, Treasury Minister Medina presented his budget for 1823 which listed expenses as $20,328,740 and predicted a deficit of $6,000,000. Following the budget announcement, Iturbide declared that each province would be assessed to pay direct taxes of four reales per year per person (with Mexico and Querétaro supplying $1,884,906 of the sum). All secular property owners would have to contribute 40 percent of the assessed value of their land; the Church would pay just 5 percent.[42]

On December 2, 1822, General Antonio López de Santa Anna revolted against the Empire after Iturbide removed him from his command in Jalapa. Royalist troops still loyal to Spain holding the castles of San Juan de Ulúa at the mouth of Veracruz harbor had already jeopardized revenues from the nation's chief port, but Santa Anna's revolt simply deprived the government of those revenues altogether.[43] The effect on the Treasury appears

[40] Ibid.

[41] Flores Caballero, *Counterrevolution*, 65–66.

[42] "Presupuesto por el año de 1823," Antonio de Medina, Mexico, December 21, 1822, INAH, T-3, 35, Colección Antigua. *Decreto del Emperador y de la Junta Nacional Instituyente*, December 21, 1822. Merchants were required to accept up to one-third of payments for merchandise in the new paper money. The author wishes to thank Timothy Anna, University of Manitoba, for supplying her with the information for this citation.

[43] Robertson, *Iturbide*, 221–225.

in the shocking income figures for January to March 1823, a mere $49,303, $49,143, and $43,259 respectively.[44]

Iturbide abdicated on March 19, 1823. Demands for money coupled with gradually more viable alternatives as finally articulated in the Plan of Casa Mata on February 1 doomed Mexico's first empire. As one complainant against the emission of paper money wrote so perceptively, "Perhaps the government of today is the tyrant of yesterday."[45]

Pernicious Precedents

The fall of Iturbide set three unforunate fiscal precedents which would determine much of the history of nineteenth-century Mexico. The first and most significant was the elites' steadfast refusal to pay additional taxes from 1821 to 1834. In fact, the entire revenue structure of the first federal republic was based on the premise that taxes on foreign trade would yield more than adequate revenue to fill the treasury. During the years from 1824 to 1827, the administration of Guadalupe Victoria was freed from the problem because of the windfall provided by two loans from British banking houses. When the treasury was empty again, governments routinely borrowed internally from moneylenders (*agiotistas*) for short periods at high rates, which were often directly repayable at the customs, the sole reliable source of revenue.

In 1829 Treasury Minister Lorenzo Zavala had the audacity to decree new taxes. They were quickly repealed and Zavala fired.[46] The next administration of Anastasio Bustamante and Lucas Alamán promulgated the incorrect notion that it could pay for government by reducing expenditures, but it too had to resort to borrowing. Its successors, liberals like Gómez Farías and Zavala, devised a strategy of filling the treasury by forcing the Church to sell its property, an idea which eventually led to the collapse of the first federal republic. Thus, during the years from 1821 to 1834, not one single new tax was added to the revenue system. Finally in 1836 the centralist regime of Antonio López de Santa Anna under the leadership of Treasury Minister Manuel Gorostiza decreed the first series of taxes on

[44]*Gaceta Imperial de Méjico*, January 9, 1823, 16; February 8, 1823, 70; March 6, 1823, 120; *Gaceta de México*, April 10, 1823, 182.

[45]"Quejas del pueblo contra el papel moneda" (Mexico, 1823), Hernández y Dávalos Collection, Benson Latin American Collection as cited in Anna, "Iturbide," 99.

[46]*Memoria de Hacienda 1870*, 97–98, 100–103. Historians have generally failed to acknowledge that only Santa Anna was able to convince the elites to pay more taxes. For more on this and other aspects of fiscal precedents, see Barbara A. Tenenbaum, *The Politics of Penury: Debts and Taxes in Mexico, 1821–1856* (Albuquerque: University of New Mexico Press, 1986).

urban property (2 pesos per mill), rural property (3 pesos per mill), and income taxes on urban businesses.[47]

Military expenses remained a sizable drain on inadequate revenues throughout the period. Except for the costs of repaying agiotista loans in the 1840s, military salaries was the biggest item of the Mexican budget during much of the nineteenth century. When the treasury was empty, armies went unpaid, and soldiers revolted, which accounts for the large number of separate governments that ruled Mexico from 1821 to 1856. The instability which resulted hardly convinced the elites to be more cooperative in supplying funds to the treasury and hurt Mexican efforts to borrow more or lure European capital investment.

The wrongheadedness and self-serving character of Mexican debate over fiscal problems remained consistent from the Iturbide period to the Reform. Mexican political leaders persisted in viewing expenses as the fundamental problem rather than the lack of income, despite the fact, as Antonio de Medina correctly noted in 1822, that administrative costs were largely fixed. Naturally, this interpretation arose from elites' reluctance to pay taxes.

The insistence on focusing on expenses as the problem rather than inadequate income is amply demonstrated by contemporary and historical attacks on Iturbide's regime which emphasized his lavish royal household and extravagant salary, rather than the disintegration of the colonial tax structure, the destruction of the mining economy, and eleven years of political uncertainty, not to mention the elites' unwillingness to pay more taxes or lend additional sums at nominal interest.[48] The persistent fixation on expenses fueled factional struggle as each side accused the other of waste and playing favorites, an interpretation which still continues in modern times.

The problems that Iturbide faced were hardly unique to Mexico. Every leader of a newly liberated Latin American nation confronted hostile elites, overly large and clamorous armies, and empty treasuries, and hardly any succeeded where Iturbide failed.[49] But fate and history have been kinder to most of them than to the Liberator of Mexico.

[47]Ibid, 152–154, 162–163.

[48]See Anna, "Iturbide," 96–99.

[49]For an analysis of comparable problems see Linda A. Rodríguez, *The Search for Public Policy: Regional Politics and Government Finances in Ecuador, 1830–1940* (Berkeley and Los Angeles: University of California Press, 1985), 53–87.

Mexico's First Foreign Loans

Jaime E. Rodríguez O.

New Spain, as I have argued elsewhere, stood in stark contrast to republican Mexico. During the late eighteenth century the viceroyalty not only generated sufficient revenue to cover its own expenses, but it also subsidized Spain's possessions in Central and North America, the Caribbean and the Philippines and even remitted funds to the royal treasury in Madrid.[1] This favorable situation ceased, however, with the onset of the French Revolution which unleashed twenty years of war in Europe. Throughout the crisis, from 1789 forward, the crown demanded that New Spain subordinate its economic needs to those of an imperiled metropolis—something it had never before required in the three hundred years of colonial history.

When Father Miguel Hidalgo initiated the struggle for independence in 1810, he precipitated an eleven-year civil war. Following twenty years of European conflict, the wars for independence shattered what remained of the viceroyalty's economy and institutions. Mining, commerce, and agriculture declined significantly. But the greatest blow to Mexican interests was the systematic draining of the country's credit and financial system. Beginning with the crown's exorbitant demands to finance its struggle in Europe and later by the viceregal government, to quell the rebellion at home, Spain devastated the credit and financial system of the viceroyalty. Huge forced loans and crushing taxes siphoned specie from New Spain. More significantly, these actions alienated the elite. Traditionally, wealthy New Spaniards had aided the crown in times of crisis. But the demands of the

Author's Note: An earlier Spanish version of this work was presented at the colloquium "Pasado y presente de la deuda externa de México" held at the Instituto de Investigaciones Dr. José María Luis Mora in Mexico City on July 21–22, 1986. Research for this study was made possible by a grant from the University of California, Irvine Academic Senate Committee on Research.

[1] Jaime E. Rodríguez O., *Down from Colonialism: Mexico's Nineteenth-Century Crisis* (Los Angeles, 1983), 15.

royal government after 1789 were so exorbitant and so detrimental to elite interests that they gradually lost confidence in the political system and eventually refused to assist their government. Their alientation would plague Mexico during subsequent decades.[2]

In 1821, Agustín Iturbide faced vast responsibilities without adequate resources. The old fiscal system no longer functioned: political expedience forced the abolition of many taxes; the government ignored others because it lacked the power to collect them. Most of the wartime levies, which had been imposed to finance the struggle against the insurgents, were abolished after independence to gain a modicum of political support for the new government.

Desperate for funds to sustain his administration, Iturbide issued unbacked paper money, imposed forced loans, and confiscated shipments of bullion. These, and other, arbitrary actions completed the process of elite alientation begun in 1789. Unable to establish an effective fiscal system, the new imperial government sought foreign loans to supplement its meager income until it could restore public confidence and prosperity. That tactic failed to accomplish its purpose.

The Supreme Executive Power, the triumvirate which succeeded the first Mexican empire in 1823, found the treasury empty. The establishment of the federal system, which divided tax revenues between the national government and the states, exacerbated the government's financial difficulties. Lacking adequate revenues, the republic, like the Iturbide regime before it, also turned to foreign bankers for assistance.[3]

Mexican leaders accepted foreign loans, regardless of their cost, in order to obtain the economic relief needed to restore national prosperity. They expected that the deficits accumulated during the first years of independent life would disappear rapidly once the economy recovered and tax revenues increased. Both Mexicans and foreigners believed that the new nation possessed immense unexploited wealth; post-independence economic difficulties constituted only minor impediments which would be overcome once the new government restored internal order. Foreign investors, particularly the British, were also convinced that, freed of Spain, Mexico would rapidly achieve wealth and power. Consequently they were eager to help the new nation through its initial period of difficulty. Foreigners, of course, expected to profit by aiding Mexico.

[2]Romeo Flores Caballero, *La contrarrevolución en la independencia: los españoles en la vida política, social y económica de México, 1804–1838* (Mexico, 1969), 15–103; Doris M. Ladd, *The Mexican Nobility at Independence, 1780–1826* (Austin, 1976), 89–161; Richard B. Lindley, *Haciendas and Economic Development: Guadalajara, Mexico at Independence* (Austin, 1983), 89–111.

[3]Flores Caballero, *La contrarrevolución*, 83–103; Barbara A. Tenenbaum, *México en la época de los agiotistas, 1821–1857* (Mexico, 1985), 35–42.

Unfortunately, the contemporary financial system encouraged speculation. In the early nineteenth century, governments floated loans by selling bonds in the European markets. After the Napoleonic wars, London emerged as the leading financial center. In the early 1820s, English financiers possessed surplus capital which they were eager to invest in the new nations of Latin America, particularly Mexico. Typically, a commercial import-export house, such as Baring Brothers or Barclay, Herring, Richardson & Company, agreed to handle the loan. The firm assumed the responsibility for all aspects of the transaction, from printing the bonds to selling them in the financial markets. Bonds were not sold at par, but at some percentage of their face value, generally in proportion to the investors' confidence in the government selling the bonds. Usually bonds were sold in two stages: during the first phase, large financiers, often commercial houses, bid on the issue. The winners subsequently resold the bonds on the bourse to numerous smaller investors. The commercial house charged a commission for the sale as well as administrative costs for handling the sale. The firm also retained an amortization fund to pay the quarterly dividends to the bondholders, and, in some cases, acted as financial agent, purchasing equipment, disbursing funds, and generally acting as a banker for the government which had floated the loan. All of these services brought commissions to the commercial houses. But in addition, governments often negotiated with intermediaries who arranged with foreign investment bankers to float loans. These individuals also received a commission for their services. Consequently, floating a government loan could be a very profitable undertaking for all those involved. It was only natural that countless speculators eagerly sought to assist a potentially wealthy country like Mexico to obtain foreign loans. The zeal of such speculators reaffirmed the government's view that Mexico was rich and that it could eventually liquidate any loan.

The political turmoil that accompanied independence complicated the process of negotiating foreign loans. Although most Mexicans accepted independence in 1821, they often acted from different motivations. Some merely wanted home rule; others sought to escape the liberal regime in Spain; a few favored a republic. The Plan of Iguala managed to reconcile temporarily these groups. Iturbide's short-lived empire gave way to a triumvirate, the Supreme Executive Power, and then a struggle ensued between the supporters of centralism and federalism. The latter triumphed, establishing a federal republic in 1824. Thereafter, former monarchists, Iturbidists, centralists, and federalists entered into shifting coalitions with one another creating further political turmoil. During that period of rapid political change, the various regimes authorized certain individuals to negotiate foreign loans for Mexico. Because these financial agents often had conflicting political allegiances, and because domestic political struggles intensified after 1824, serious rivalries emerged among them which negatively affected the credit of the new nation.[4]

The discord among Mexico's financial agents began with the first loan authorization. Francisco Borja Migoni, a Mexican merchant who had lived in London many years, wrote Iturbide in 1822 offering to negotiate a loan in England. As a monarchist, who had associated himself with Iturbide, Borja Migoni expected to be named minister plenipotentiary in London. Although he did not obtain the appointment, the Supreme Executive Power nonetheless authorized him to negotiate a new loan in 1823. President Guadalupe Victoria subsequently named him consul general in London. The Supreme Executive Power included among its members José Mariano Michelena, a strong foe of Iturbide, who was accused of authoritarian tendencies and driven from office during the Lobato revolt in January 1824. Although many distrusted him, among them Minister of Finance José Ignacio Esteva, Michelena was named minister plenipotentiary to England. Borja Migoni, who opposed the federal republic and resented Michelena's diplomatic appointment, became the minister plenipotentiary's bitter enemy and refused to cooperate with him. In the ensuing dispute, first over the use and then over the safety of the loan funds, Minister of Finance Esteva believed Borja Migoni rather than Michelena or his colleague and later Mexico's chargé d'affaires in London, Vicente Rocafuerte. These animosities deepened as differences between moderates and radical factions arose in Mexico. The moderates favored Michelena and Rocafuerte. Esteva, allied with the radicals, sided with Consul General Borja Migoni, who despised the moderates because they had overthrown Iturbide and later denied him the top diplomatic post in London. Thus, personal rivalries and partisan politics in Mexico divided the nation's officials as they grappled with the complex problem of securing foreign loans.[5]

Although various insurgent groups had attempted to obtain loans in the United States and in Europe during the struggle for independence, the first official effort occurred under Iturbide. In May 1822, Borja Migoni offered to negotiate a loan in England, claiming that his nine years of residence in London would allow him to obtain the best possible terms

[4]On the politics of the period see: Timothy E. Anna, *The Fall of the Royal Government in Mexico City* (Lincoln, 1978), 191–226; Javier Ocampo, *Las ideas de un dia: el pueblo mexicano ante la consumación de su independencia* (Mexico, 1969); William S. Robertson, *Iturbide of Mexico* (Durham 1952), 163–314; Nettie Lee Benson, *La diputación provincial y el federalismo mexicano* (Mexico, 1955); José Barragán Barragán, *Introducción al federalismo: la formación de los poderes, 1824* (Mexico, 1978); Jaime E. Rodríguez O., *The Emergence of Spanish America: Vicente Rocafuerte and Spanish Americanism, 1808–1832* (Berkeley, 1975), 47–88.

[5]These issues are treated in Rodríguez, *The Emergence of Spanish America*, 86–128.

for Mexico. An English loan, he argued, would not only solve the new nation's financial crisis, but it would also ensure that England had a stake in the independence and well-being of Mexico. Gran Colombia had already obtained a two million pound loan and as a result, Borja Migoni declared, England was committed to aiding that new nation and would not allow Spain to reconquer it. Finally, to demonstrate the accessibility of the English market, he mentioned that the governments of France, Spain, Prussia, Austria, Denmark, and Persia had also floated loans in London.[6]

Borja Migoni's offer arrived at an opportune time. A foreign loan would not only fill the imperial treasury's virtually empty coffers, but it would also permit the new country to buy armaments to drive the remaining Spanish forces from the fortress of San Juan de Ulúa. Capturing the fort was critical because it controlled the entrance to Veracruz, the main port of entry and the source of most customs revenues. Until the port were freed, Mexican commerce, and therefore government finances, could not recover. In addition, Spain would be less likely to attempt to recover its former colony as long as the fortress remained under Mexican control.

In June 1822 congress authorized the negotiation of a foreign loan of between 25 and 30 million pesos. It instructed the government to obtain the best possible terms and authorized it to mortgage present and future revenues to guarantee the loan.[7] Armed with that authority, Iturbide named Borja Migoni Mexico's financial agent in London. But before any agreement could be reached, the emperor fell from power. In 1823, the Constituent Congress authorized a foreign loan of eight million pesos, and the Supreme Executive Power sent Borja Migoni new credentials.[8]

Before Borja Migoni could obtain a loan in London, several English agents arrived in Mexico offering to secure loans for the hard pressed government. Although some of these offers were extremely onerous, the Mexican government seriously considered accepting the terms because it desperately needed the money and because it was convinced that the nation's wealth was so great that the government could afford to pay usurious rates to obtain funds quickly. Robert P. Staples, a representative of the London house of Thomas Kinder, Jr., for example, offered to negotiate a million pound loan at 5 percent which would provide Mexico 57.24 percent of face value. The better offer by Bartholomew Vigors Richards, a representative of the London commercial house of Barclay, Herring, Richardson & Com-

[6]Francisco de Borja Migoni to Agustín de Iturbide, London, May 26, 1822, in Mexico, Secretaría de Relaciones Exteriores, *La diplomacia mexicana*, 3 vols. (Mexico, 1910–1913), II, 137–140. (Hereafter, *La diplomacia mexicana.*)

[7]Manuel Dublán y José María Lozano, *Legislación mexicana . . .* , 34 vols. (Mexico, 1876–1904), I, 617. (Hereafter, *Legislación mexicana.*)

[8]Lucas Alamán to Borja Migoni, Mexico, April 24, 1823; March 4, 1823, Mexico, Archivo General de la Secretaría de Relaciones Exteriores H/121.32"823–24"/1. 40–11–12. (Hereafter, AGSREM.)

pany, ended negotiations with Staples. On December 5, 1823, José Ignacio Esteva, the new minister of treasury, signed a contract with Richards for a loan of twenty million pesos at 6 percent annual interest. Mexico agreed to issue bonds for that amount and Barclay promised to buy them at 70 percent of face value. (Since the pound sterling was worth five pesos, Mexico negotiated a loan of 4 million pounds, but would receive only £2,800,000.) The agreement stipulated that the contract was canceled if the London office of Barclay did not ratify and return the contract to Mexico by June 24, 1824. The Mexican government inserted the clause to ensure that Barclay acted expeditiously.[9]

During this period, Borja Migoni was negotiating Mexico's first foreign loan in London. Unfortunately, because he was a monarchist and former partisan of Iturbide, he was quite willing to exploit the new republican government. Instead of contracting with the leading merchant bankers, such as Rothschild, Barring Brothers, or Barclay, who were eager to make the loan, he entered into a secret agreement with B. A. Goldschmidt and Company. The firm agreed to act as agent for a group of London merchants headed by Borja Migoni. These men planned to purchase Mexico's bonds at a price considerably lower than face value. Once the merchants acquired the bonds, they would resell them at a large profit. To accomplish their goal, they needed time to raise the capital. Accordingly, Borja Migoni delayed by informing Mexico that none of the great banking houses would deal with the infant nation. He reassured the government, however, that the smaller but important firm of Goldschmidt was interested. The negotiations, he said, had been delayed by news of the French invasion of Spain and the resulting fear that the Holy Alliance would reconquer Mexico. Despite these problems Borja Migoni promised to continue working to obtain the loan on favorable terms.[10]

While Borja Migoni's associates accumulated their funds, a new complication ensued. Dr. Patrick Mackie, England's agent to Mexico, returned to London on November 15, 1823. Knowing that the American nation fervently sought a loan, he contacted Borja Migoni, pledging to intercede with the British government. Mackie, of course, expected to benefit from helping to secure a loan. Borja Migoni found himself in a quandary: he could not deal with Mackie without compromising his own enterprise. Faced with such a difficult situation, the Mexican agent temporized. Borja Migoni

[9]Rodríguez, *The Emergence of Spanish America*, 108.

[10]Francisco de Borja Migoni, "Exposición del consul general de México en Londres sobre el empréstito que fue encargado," *El amigo del pueblo*, September 12, 1827, pp. 3–7. The official correspondence Borja Migoni exchanged with the government on this matter is found in *La diplomacia mexicana*, II, 137–206; José Mariano Michelena to Alamán, London, July 24, 1824, in *La diplomacia mexicana*, III, 218–221; Vicente Rocafuerte to Juan de Dios Cañedo, London, January 28, 1828, and November 19, 1828, AGSREM, H/300(72:861) "823.30"/1.LE 1700 and H/131"823"/14. LE 1621(6).

allowed Mackie to introduce him to several associates who agreed to finance the loan for Mexico. Fortunately for the merchant, Mackie's group did not have direct access to funds. During the following weeks they acted so recklessly that Borja Migoni, denouncing the group as adventurers, severed relations with them. He charged that Mackie had abused his diplomatic post to take advantage of Mexico.[11] But Mackie and his friends refused to be dismissed so easily, demanding several hundred thousand pounds in compensation. Borja Migoni initially refused the demand, but eventually settled their claim with bonds worth £39,000, which he hid under administrative expenses in the Goldschmidt contract. Subsequently, Borja Migoni explained that he had authorized the gift to ensure the goodwill of these influential men.[12] Mackie and his associates, however, were hardly capable of deciding the future of Mexico. The bribe was designed to protect the exorbitant profits that Borja Migoni and his friends intended to realize from the loan to Mexico.

Freed from Mackie, and anxious to prevent any further threat to his enterprise, Borja Migoni entered into a verbal contract with Goldschmidt on January 2, 1824. Although the negotiations were secret, rumors that Mexico was going to float a loan had been circulating for some time. By January 20 the London *Times* speculated that the details of the loan would be made available soon because potential subscribers were eager for information. When no announcement appeared either from Goldschmidt or from Borja Migoni, the *Times* started an investigation. It reported on January 27 that bonds would soon be sold and that some buyers—Mackie and his associates—had received preferential scrip. The newspaper, however, could not provide the identities of these subscribers or the reason for their preferential treatment. The bonds were sold privately to the few men who had been invited to participate, rather than at a public auction which might have driven up the price. Borja Migoni's tactic succeeded; when the bonds were later resold in the bourse, the original buyers realized a substantial profit.[13]

On February 9, Borja Migoni wrote the minister of the treasury to announce the successful completion of the loan. He did not, of course, include information on the circumstances surrounding its negotiation and sale. Under the terms of the contract signed on February 7, 1824, Goldschmidt undertook to provide Mexico with £1,600,000 within fifteen

[11]Borja Migoni, "Exposición sobre el empréstito," 9–18. Michelena subsequently denounced Borja Migoni's activities. After reading the legation papers, he referred to Borja Migoni's official correspondence as "lies and contradictions" with which he and his associates entertained the government while they made their preparations. Michelena to Alamán, London, July 24, 1824, in *La diplomacia mexicana*, III, 218–221.

[12]Borja Migoni, "Exposición sobre el empréstito," 10–20.

[13]*Times* (London), no. 12,088 (January 20, 1824), p. 2; no. 12,094 (January 27, 1824), p. 2; 12,097 (February 11, 1824), p. 2; Borja Migoni, "Exposición sobre el empréstito," 18–20.

months. The Mexican government agreed to issue bonds for $3,200,000 to mature in thirty years at 5 percent interest. The bonds were to be sold at a guaranteed price of 58 percent of face value. Mexico would receive 50 percent of face value and the commercial house the remaining 8 percent as its commission for the sale of the bonds. Goldschmidt would also receive a 1-1/2 percent commission for any funds it administered. To guarantee payment of the loan, the Mexican government agreed to mortgage one-third of its customs receipts beginning in April 1, 1825. The sum of £400,000 would be retained by Goldschmidt to pay interest and to establish an amortization fund. The commission for the loan, the cost of printing the bonds, and other administrative costs, which came to £62,768.6 would be deducted from Mexico's share. Finally, clause twelve of the contract prohibited Mexico from making another foreign loan for one year and required that one quarter of any subsequent loan be used to amortize the Goldschmidt transaction.

Borja Migoni assured the minister of the treasury that he had obtained the best possible terms – given the fact that the specter of the Holy Alliance had frightened investors who would otherwise have been interested in Mexican bonds. The agent acknowledged that Gran Colombia had received better terms, but maintained that the South American nation had obtained its loan when the market was more favorable to Spanish America. Indeed, Borja Migoni boasted that the loan he negotiated carried the lowest interest rate that any nation had received in the London market. He maintained that a 42 percent discount was justified because other countries had been forced to accept even less favorable terms. Finally, to demonstrate his selfless dedication, Borja Migoni indicated that he would forego the commission customarily granted the person who negotiated a government loan.[14]

Borja Migoni's assertions were false. He sold Mexican bonds to his coterie of speculators at 58 percent of face value. They, in turn, resold the bonds at 84 percent, thus making a 45 percent profit. The speculators had known from the very beginning that they would profit handsomely from their involvement because there was an intense demand for Spanish American bonds in the London money market. Indeed, at the time of the original sale, the securities of Peru, Chile, Argentina, and Gran Colombia were selling in the London bourse at 80, 82, 85 and 88 percent respectively.

Borja Migoni also lied when he declared that the threat of the Holy Alliance had depressed the bond market. Although there had been a decline in the value of Spanish American securities in April 1823, when French troops entered Spain, prices returned to normal as soon as it became evident that England would not permit European intervention in American

[14]Borja Migoni to José Ignacio Esteva, London, February 9, 1824, in *La diplomacia mexicana*, II, 185–194. The Goldschmidt contract is reproduced in José María Luis Mora, *Obras sueltas*, 2a. ed. (Mexico, 1963), 437–444.

affairs. Furthermore, since Borja Migoni kept the first sale of the Mexican issue at an artificially low price, he was forced to borrow sixteen million pesos—twice the sum authorized by Congress—in order to produce the requisite sum of eight million pesos.

The Mexican merchant, who had lived in London many years and who had secretly become a British citizen, was supremely confident of his ability to deceive his former countrymen. His audacity is underscored by the fact that, during the same period, Gran Colombia obtained a loan from Goldschmidt at 86 percent. The South American country had not negotiated, as Borja Migoni maintained, at a time when the market was more favorable. Rather the difference in the terms of the two loans can be explained only if one assumes that the Gran Colombia agent had his country's interest in mind while Borja Migoni did not. Indeed, as Table 1 demonstrates, the Mexican contracted the most onerous loan negotiated by any Latin American nation during the years before the great economic dislocation of 1826.[15]

TABLE 1. British Loans to Latin America

Country	Amount in Pounds	Sale Price (%)	Price in Bourse (%)	Year
Chile	1,000,000	68.00	70.00	1822
Gran Colombia	2,000,000	82.00	84.00	1822
Peru	450,000	86.00	88.00	1822
Brazil	1,686,000	73.00	75.00	1824
Argentina	1,000,000	83.00	85.00	1824
Gran Colombia	4,750,000	86.50	88.50	1824
Mexico	**3,200,000**	**58.00**	**84.00**	**1824**
Peru	750,000	80.00	82.00	1824
Brazil	4,000,000	83.00	85.00	1825
Guatemala	167,000	70.00	73.00	1825
Mexico	**3,200,000**	**86.75**	**89.75**	**1825**
Peru	616,000	76.00	78.00	1825

SOURCE: Andreas Andreades, *History of the Bank of England* (New York, 1966), 249–250; Corporation of Foreign Bondholders, *Sixty-Fourth Annual Report* (London, 1937).

Furthermore, Borja Migoni profited twice from the loan. In October 1824 the value of Mexican bonds declined temporarily to 48 percent because it was feared that Iturbide would overthrow the government. The new Mexican minister to England, José Mariano Michelena, tried to use the six million

[15]For criticisms of the loan see: Michelena to Alamán, London, 26, 1824, and July 24, 1824, AGSREM, H/311.1(42:72)"824"/1, and *La diplomacia mexicana*, III, 218–221; Rocafuerte to Cañedo, London, January 22, 1828, and November 19, 1828, AGSREM, H/300(72:861)"823–30"/1. LE 1700 y H/131"823"/14. LE 1621(6); Murphy to Michelena, Paris, October 1, 1824, Hernández y Dávalos Papers, University of Texas, Austin, 17-5-4122. (Hereafter HD.)

pesos in the hands of Goldschmidt to buy Mexican bonds at that low price, planning to resell them when the scare had subsided and the bonds returned to a high price, which would have earned nearly 50 percent for Mexico. Borja Migoni, who retained sole authority to disburse the funds, refused. Instead, he and his friends bought the bonds as individuals and resold them later at a great profit.[16]

The clause in the Goldschmidt contract which prohibited new foreign loans until February 1825 prevented the Mexican government from concluding the Barclay negotiations. Mexico had initiated discussions with Barclay on the understanding that the money would be used to purchase ships and arms. But following its verbal agreement with Borja Migoni, Goldschmidt took steps to prevent the Barclay loan. Three weeks before the signing of the official agreement, and acting without authority, Goldschmidt informed Barclay that Mexico could not negotiate a new loan until February 7, 1825. The admonition arrived after Barclay had advanced funds to Mexico and had begun to purchase the war materiel urgently requested by the Mexican minister of war. Barclay suspended all acquisitions until the situation was clarified. David Barclay and Charles Herring demanded that Borja Migoni either modify the restrictive clause of the Goldschmidt contract or reimburse their firm for sums advanced to Mexico and employed to purchase equipment. The Mexican agent refused, claiming that he could not act without instructions from his government.[17]

In an effort to resolve the impasse, Barclay dispatched two agents, William Marshall and Robert Manning, to Mexico with instructions to obtain an extension for the ratification of the contract negotiated by Richards. An extension, the firm believed, would provide the time necessary to modify the Goldschmidt clause. In April, while the British agents were still en route to Mexico, Barclay received a new order from the minister of war to purchase arms. Although the company informed the Mexican government that as long as the Goldschmidt clause remained in effect, all previous agreements were null and void, Barclay arranged to purchase two forty-four gun frigates. When the Barclay Company learned that Mexico was sending a minister plenipotentiary to Great Britain, it hastened to express its "infinite satisfaction" and hope that the new envoy would be authorized to resolve the firm's dilemma.[18]

[16]Michelena to Carlos Alvear, London, November 10, 1824, HD 17-4.4203.

[17]Manuel de Mier y Terán to Michelena, Mexico, April 14, 1824; B. A. Goldschmidt to Barclay, Herring, Richardson & Co., London, January 12, 1824; David Barclay and Charles Herring to Borja Migoni, London, March 26, 1824, and March 31, 1824; Borja Migoni to Barclay, Herring, Richardson & Co., London, March 30, 1824, and April 3, 1824; Borja Migoni to Alamán, London, March 30, 1824; AGSREM, H/121.32"823-24"/1. 40-11-21.

[18]Barclay, Herring, Richardson & Co., to Esteva, London, April 1, 1824, and May 7, 1824, AGSREM, H/131.32"823-24"/1. 40-11-21.

One of the purposes of the Michelena mission was to procure large quantities of arms and ships to capture the fortress of San Juan Ulúa. Immediately after the plenipotentiary left Mexico, the minister of war began sending Michelena specifications for vessels. Since time was a crucial factor, the minister authorized the envoy to purchase the best available ships; even converted merchantmen would be acceptable.[19] Upon his arrival in London on June 24, 1824, Michelena dispatched his staff to search for weapons in the Low Countries, France, and England. The Mexican minister assumed that he could purchase the armament with the six million pesos on hand from the Goldschmidt loan. Yet despite threats and exhortations, Borja Migoni, first as financial agent and later as consul general, refused to appropriate any money without specific instructions from the minister of the treasury.[20]

Mexico's minister plenipotentiary to Britain found himself in an anomalous situation. Although Borja Migoni's diplomatic superior, he lacked authority to disburse Mexico's funds from the Goldschmidt loan. Only Borja Migoni could do that. In addition, Michelena lacked the authority to secure any changes in the clause which prevented a new loan until 1825. The Mexican diplomat, spurred by the fear of a Spanish invasion of Mexico, made repeated efforts to obtain arms on credit. The minister found himself in a humilitating position. Everyone knew he could not touch the six million pesos available to cover Mexican expenses because Borja Migoni, his subordinate, would not permit it. This impasse proved disastrous for Mexico. In August and September, Michelena located acceptable ships but lost the opportunity to buy them because he could not make the down payment.[21]

Although Barclay remained distressed that the Mexican plenipotentiary could not modify the Goldschmidt contract, the company continued to be interested in handling Mexico's business. The firm provided Michelena credit for weapons purchases believing that it would obtain a new contract from Mexico. By September the firm had advanced the new nation more

[19]Mier y Terán to Michelena, Mexico, April 4, 1824, AGSREM, H/121"823-24"/1. 40-11-21. Mier y Terán to Michelena, Mexico, September 4, 1824, HD 17-4.4073.

[20]Michelena to Alamán, London, August 21, 1824, AGSREM, H/131.1(42:72)l"824"/1. When Michelena told Borja Migoni that the Barclay company expected to be paid for its efforts, Borja Migoni replied sarcastically: "I have deduced that the government expected the generous patriotism of those gentlemen to provide an advance to cover the cost of military purchases. . . . The extraordinary outpouring of gratitude which the government and the Minister bestow upon them does not permit me to believe that these gentlemen expect money to make the purchase. If I am in error, I do not have the power to correct that error." Borja Migoni to Michelena, London, July 31, 1824; Michelena to Alamán, August 1, 1824, HD 17-4.4090, 4093.

[21]Michelena to Alamán, London, September 23, 1824 (letters 1 and 2), HD 17-4.4108; Michelena to Alamán, November 4, 1826; November 23, 1824, University of Texas, Austin, Lucas Alamán Papers, legajo II, nos. 116-117.

than 750,000 pesos. But without a contract to protect its outlay, the commercial house was reluctant to continue to grant funds.[22] Nevertheless, when, in late September, Michelena found an outstanding merchantship for sale at a low price, the firm lent the Mexican minister the funds to meet the down payment and agreed to outfit the vessel for war. In December news arrived that the Mexican government had authorized a new contract with Barclay.[23]

The Mexican decision to renegotiate the contract with Barclay did not signify that it had become disenchanted with Borja Migoni. The government upheld the consul's right to disburse funds from the Goldschmidt loan. Although it authorized Michelena to arrange a second loan, the terms of the agreement had to comply with the stipulations of the Goldschmidt contract. One-fourth of the amount derived from the new transaction would be used to amortize the earlier loan. The Barclay contract, moreover, could not go into effect until February 7, 1825. While Michelena would have the authority to disburse the funds from the second loan, he still would not have access to the Goldschmidt funds.[24]

The Mexican minister immediately negotiated a new contract with Barclay. Mexico agreed to issue thirty-year bonds for £3,200,000 at 6 percent interest; Barclay would receive 6 percent commission for the sale; and Mexico would guarantee the loan by mortgaging one-third of its maritime customs receipts. Michelena further stipulated that bonds could not be sold below 85 percent of face value. During these negotiations Barclay indicated that the firm wanted to become Mexico's sole financial agent. Although the Mexican minister was reluctant to agree since that would give the house excessive power and influence, he referred the matter to his government at the firm's insistence. Michelena advised against granting such authority, but Minister of Finance Esteva approved Barclay's request as a reward for the assistance rendered the nation and because the firm's agents in Mexico lobbied strongly for it.[25]

On Monday, February 7, 1825, Barclay sold Mexico's bonds. The company announced that the Mexican minister had established a minimum sale price, but it did not divulge the amount. Within a short time the entire issue was purchased by B. A. Goldschmidt who offered the highest bid of

[22]Barclay, Herring, Richards & Co., to Michelena, London, September 8, 1824, HD 17-4.4075.

[23]The correspondence on the purchase of the ships is located in HD 17-5.4142 to 18-2.4367.

[24](Decree authorizing the contract with Barclay and Company for the sale of Mexican bonds in London.) Mexico, August 25, 1824, AGSREM, H/121.32"823-24"/1. 40-11-21; Esteva to Michelena, Mexico, October 27, 1824, HD 17-5.4170.

[25]The Barclay contract is reproduced in Mora, *Obras sueltas*, 445-449. Michelena to Esteva, London, December 25, 1824; Michelena to Alamán, London, January 4, 1825, HD 17-7.731, 18-1.4266.

86.75 percent. The sale yielded £2,999,900; the Barclay Company received £166,560 as commission and £336,000 to establish an amortization fund. The cost of printing the bonds and other administrative costs amounted to £6,780 10s. Three days later Goldschmidt resold the bonds on the bourse at 89.75 percent of face value. The *Times* declared that there had been enough subscribers to float a £40,000,000 loan, indicating "how rapidly [the credit of] this fine country is rising in public estimation."[26] Indeed, as Table 1 indicates, the bonds from Mexico's second loan sold at the highest price of any Latin American securities on the London bourse. This was in stark contrast to the loan negotiated by Borja Migoni, which was sold to a few cronies at an artificially low price and later resold at much higher prices on the bourse. Table 2 compares the Goldschmidt and Barclay loans.

TABLE 2. Goldschmidt and Barclay Loans Compared
(In Mexican Pesos)

	Goldschmidt	Barclay
Amount	16,000,000	16,000,000
Interest (%)	5	6
Commission (%)	8	6
Sale Value (%)	58	86.75
Net amount after commission	8,000,000	13,048,000
Administrative cost	313,843	33,902
Amount received by Mexico after all deductions	5,686,157	11,333,298

As soon as arrangements for the Barclay loan were completed, Michelena again turned his attention to securing armaments for Mexico. Once he obtained the needed ships and weapons, he decided to return home. Consequently, after arranging to have Vicente Rocafuerte named chargé d'affaires, he departed in July 1825. Michelena took the new Mexican squadron to Mexico where it encountered and dispersed a smaller Spanish fleet. The Mexican ships subsequently besieged the fortress of San Juan de Ulúa forcing it to capitulate, thus assuring Mexican independence.[27]

Although as chargé d'affaires Rocafuerte was empowered to negotiate with all European nations, he lacked the authority to administer Mexico's funds. This situation worried the Mexican diplomat because he feared the growing instability of the English money market. Liberal policies were allowing credit to expand rapidly and British investors, enthusiastic about the

[26]*Times* (London), February 8, 1825, p. 2; February 11, 1825, p. 4. It is often asserted that Bolívar's victory in Peru contributed to the high price of American bonds in London. This is not the case. Accounts of Gran Colombian victories did not appear in the London press until March, a month after the loan was made. *Times* (London), March 3, 1825, p. 2.

[27]Rodríguez, *The Emergence of Spanish America*, 118–119.

future of Spanish America, seemed willing to finance any enterprise, from silver mining in Mexico to pearl hunting in Venezuela.[28] Since speculative fever also gripped the continental money markets, Rocafuerte feared that the entire financial structure of Europe might collapse. Barclay added to the chargé's concerns by convincing Minister of the Treasury Esteva to communicate directly with the firm or with its agents in Mexico, Manning and Marshall, but not with Mexico's diplomatic envoy in London. Because of domestic politics, the minister of the treasury believed Consul General Borja Migoni's reassuring reports and failed to heed Rocafuerte's warnings.[29]

Powerless, Rocafuerte watched as Barclay and Company speculated with Mexico's money. The chargé believed that the only way to protect his country's capital was to remove it from Barclay's hands. Thus, on August 2, 1825, after he received instructions from Esteva directing the Barclay Company to pay interest on the funds deposited with it, Rocafuerte instead suggested that the firm either deposit the money in the Bank of England or invest it in Bills of Exchequer. The chargé d'affaires hoped to protect his government's funds by placing them in institutions guaranteed by the British government and simultaneously to earn the interest desired by the minister of finance. Barclay rejected Rocafuerte's recommendations, since they would have reduced the firm's working capital and diminished its activity in the market. The chargé warned his government repeatedly that he was unable to restrain Barclay and insisted that Mexico's funds be deposited in the Bank of England. Despite his warnings, Esteva failed to act.[30]

Unfortunately, Rocafuerte's dire predictions materialized—the English financial situation worsened in the succeeding months. Goldschmidt was the first major commercial house to fail. Rocafuerte informed his government on February 15, 1826, that the firm was in serious financial difficulties and had suspended dividend payments. He noted that despite the critical circumstances the directors of Goldschmidt had acted with "great delicacy" and had not demanded that £50,000 from the Barclay loan destined to amortize part of Mexico's 1824 loan.[31]

[28]John Clampham, *The Bank of England*, 2 vols. (Cambridge, 1958), II, 89-100.

[29]Vicente Rocafuerte, *Exposición de las razones que determinaron a Vicente Rocafuerte a prestar a la República de Colombia la suma de £63,000* (London, 1829), 4-9; Manuel Gómez Pedraza to Rocafuerte, Mexico, October 31, 1825, AGSREM, H/310 (72:00)"835"/1. 4-2-36; *El sol*, no. 69 (August 22,1823), p. 276; Rocafuerte to Juan José Espinosa de los Monteros, London, n.d.; Rocafuerte to Cañedo, London, March 19, 1828, AGSREM, H/300 (72:861)"823-24"/1. LE 1700.

[30]Rocafuerte, *Exposición de las razones*, 6-9, 18-19. The Rocafuerte and Barclay correspondence appears on pages 9-17. Esteva to Michelena, Mexico, May 16, 1825, HD 18-4.4409. Rocafuerte to Camacho, London, May 4, 1826; Alamán to Rocafuerte, Mexico, August 19, 1825, AGSREM, III/352 (72:42)/2. 7-16-61. H/122.32 (72:42)"825"/1.

[31]Rocafuerte to Camacho, London, February 15, 1826, partially reproduced in Joaquín D. Casasus, *La deuda contraída en Londres* (Mexico, 1885), 103. The number of bankruptcies

The Goldschmidt disaster did not substantially affect Mexico finances, since only £4,000 of the proceeds of the first loan remained in the firm's hands. However, some of the bondholders of the 1824 loan had not collected their January dividends and since Goldschmidt had failed, they would not be paid. In order to retain the public's confidence in Mexico and halt the decline of the bonds from the Goldschmidt loan, Rocafuerte arranged with Barclay to indemnify the bondholders with funds from the 1825 loan.

The Goldschmidt bankruptcy provided Mexico an opportunity to redeem some of its bonds at bargain rates. Rocafuerte used the £50,000 from Barclay, which had originally been earmarked to amortize the 1824 loan to buy the depressed Goldschmidt bonds. Since repayment at maturity or through Goldschmidt would have been at face value, Mexico not only retrieved part of the first bond issue but also saved 35 to 40 percent. The large purchase also triggered a rally, increasing the price of Mexican bonds to 70 percent. Considering the depressed state of the market, the rise was spectacular, renewing confidence in Mexico.[32]

Gran Colombia and Peru did not enjoy such good fortune. Both lost large sums when Goldschmidt failed. Creditors demanded payment for millions of pounds outstanding in Peruvian and Gran Colombian drafts on Goldschmidt accounts. If Gran Colombia or Peru did not meet their dividend payments, confidence would decline. Action by Gran Colombia was particularly crucial because it and Mexico were considered the most important Spanish American nations.[33]

In desperation, Gran Colombia's minister, Manuel José Hurtado, implored Rocafuerte to help the South American country pay its April dividends. Hurtado assured him that Gran Colombia would remit funds to cover its obligations, but they could not possibly arrive in time. The Mexican diplomat agreed with Hurtado that the American nations had to work together to maintain their credit. He also believed that Mexico's funds would be safer in the hands of Gran Colombia rather than in Barclay's

---

grew to immense proportions at the turn of the year. The *Index to the Times Newspaper* shows this clearly. The January–March, 1825, *Index* has ten pages of bankruptcies; the one for April–June has eight pages and, thereafter, the number declines drastically. *Palmer's Index to the Times Newspaper* (London, 1898), Janauary-March, pp. 5-14; April-June, pp. 4-11. On the economic situation in England see *Times*, May 2, 1826, p. 4; May 4, 1826, p. 2. The Peruvian envoys reported to their government: "The great and extraordinary shock which the English economy has suffered appears to have no equal in its history. More than 500 bankruptcies have occurred and some of them were of great and wealthy [commercial] houses." José G. Paredes and José Joaquín Olmedo to the Peruvian Minister of Foreign Affairs, London, February 3, 1826, in José Joaquín Olmedo, *Epistolario* (Puebla, 1960), 522–523.

[32]Rocafuerte to Camacho, London, March 2, 1826, in Joaquín Ramírez Cabañas, ed., *El empréstito de México a Colombia* (Mexico, 1930), 5–7.

[33]Rocafuerte to Cañedo, London, March 19, 1828, AGSREM H/300(72:861)"823-30"/1. LE 1700.

coffers. Thus, he requested that Barclay advance the funds to Hurtado. The firm concurred. On April 6, 1826, Rocafuerte and Hurtado signed an agreement that advanced Gran Colombia an interest-free loan of £63,000, payable in eighteen months.[34]

While the loan permitted Gran Colombia to meet its April dividends, other means had to be found to make the remaining quarterly payments. In addition, Peru and Chile also requested assistance from Mexico. Rocafuerte rejected their requests because he did not believe those countries capable of servicing their loans punctually and because he had already overstepped his authority in making the loan to Gran Colombia. Chile managed to cover its dividends, but Peru did not.[35]

When the public learned that Lima would not meet its obligations, the price of Spanish American securities declined; even Mexican bonds fell to 60 percent. Realizing the gravity of the situation, Rocafuerte, Hurtado, and the minister from Argentina, Manuel de Sarratea, suggested that Peru float a loan with the Paris branch of the House of Rothschild. The minister of Peru, José Joaquín de Olmedo, refused, believing that this stopgap measure would substantially increase his nation's indebtedness while only providing his government a temporary respite from its financial difficulties. When it became known that Peru would not service its debts, English public opinion turned violently against all the Spanish American states. Prime Minister George Canning was savagely criticized by the opposition and the press for recognizing the new countries and for signing commercial treaties with Gran Colombia and Argentina. The public outcry threatened the pending commercial treaty with Mexico.[36]

The Spanish American nations were the victims of a European economic dislocation. Unemployment was increasing in Europe and, along with it,

[34]Although Gran Colombia attempted to repay the loan, it was unable to do so for many years. This caused contemporaries and later writers to criticize Rocafuerte unduly. The details of the loan are treated in greater length in Jaime E. Rodríguez O., "Rocafuerte y el empréstito a Colombia," *Historia Mexicana* 18 (April-June 1969), 485-515.

[35]José María del Castillo to Goldschmidt & Co., Bogotá, April 8, 1826, *El sol*, no. 1176 (September 2, 1826), p. 1780; Olmedo to José de la Mar, London, June 10, 1826, Olmedo, *Epistolario*, 535-543.

[36]Rocafuerte to Camacho, London, May 4, 1826, AGSREM, III/352(72:42)2. 7-16-61. Olmedo described the situation in the following terms: "The principal cause of our worry is that April 15 has passed, the day on which the dividends should have been paid and Mr. Kinder has not paid them. . . . The government which does not pay, be it because of its own bad will or that of its agents, be it because of poverty, or because its funds have been accidentally delayed, always, always, loses its credit. . . . The creditors do not let us live in peace one instant; they come to see us in droves; they complain; they lament; they ask us for explanations; they ask us for hope; in short they don't leave us alone. Because as I have said, not to be paid is bad in any circumstances, in the present it is horrible and deadly since many families live from these interests. Everything is paralyzed today; more than 600 bankruptcies have occurred. Money does not circulate and no one has the means to live." Olmedo to Simón Bolívar, London, April 22, 1826, in Olmedo, *Epistolario*, 532-533.

discontent. The British government, for example, had to use the army to quell riots in industrial centers.[37] The economic crisis frightened investors who sold their Spanish American holdings. Consequently, as capital evaporated, many foreign, and particularly British, enterprises in America failed. When the new nations had difficulties servicing their foreign debts, the price of their securities declined drastically. Gran Colombia's bonds fell to 34 percent in June when it became evident that the South American country could not meet its future dividends.[38]

Mexico's situation seemed better than those of its sister republics. The government dispatched a half-million pesos to cover its debt. The arrival of these funds temporarily restored English confidence. As the *Times* laconically noted, "Mexican bonds were rather in more demand."[39] However many bondholders knew that the market remained shaky and that the Barclay Company itself might fail. Thus, in spite of Mexico's positive action, the decline of securities continued.

English creditors had ample reason for fear because the Mexican government, despite Rocafuerte's repeated warnings, was doing nothing to protect its funds. Quite the contrary, Minister of the Treasury Esteva attempted to allay the chargé's concerns by extolling the "moral security" provided by Barclay.[40] Sadly, this assurance proved unfounded. Barclay, Herring, Richards & Company failed in August. The bankruptcy cost Mexico £303,928 which remained in the mortgage fund. While Mexico had attempted to save Spanish American credit by assisting Gran Colombia, no one could help Mexico. British investors reacted in a predictable fashion. The *Times* reported on August 10 that rumors concerning the declining credit of Mexico and Gran Colombia had produced panic in the bond market.[41]

Even before the bankruptcy, Rocafuerte had contacted the influential Alexander Baring requesting that he become Mexico's financial agent in England. The failure of Barclay only strengthened Rocafuerte's resolve to transfer his government's agency to Baring Brothers. He convinced Baring that Mexico could meet its obligations but required time. He proposed that in return for paying the September dividends, Baring Brothers could become Mexico's sole agent. Since the country was wealthy, with a bright economic future, Baring, he argued, would profit from the association. Furthermore, Rocafuerte assured the firm that Mexico was determined to protect its credit

[37]Rocafuerte to Camacho, London, May 4, 1826, AGSREM, III/352(72:42)2. 7-1661.

[38]Olmedo to De la Mar, London, June 10, 1826, Olmedo, *Epistolario*, 535–543; *Times* (London), June 21, 1826, p. 3.

[39]Rocafuerte to Camacho, London, June 9, 1826, AGSREM, H/300 (72:861)"823-30"/1. LE 1700; *Times* (London), June 18, 1826, p. 2.

[40]Rocafuerte to Espinosa de los Monteros, London, July 1, 1826, AGSREM, H/300(72:861)"823-30"/1. LE 1700.

[41]*Times* (London), August 10, 1826, p. 2.

and as proof supplied copies of minister of the treasury directives instructing customs officials to dedicate one-half of all receipts to service the foreign debt. When Baring agreed to consider the matter, Rocafuerte convinced Barclay to relinquish its contract as Mexico's financial agent. Then, on September 13, Baring Brothers agreed to handle Mexico's affairs in Europe. The firm would pay the dividents as well as the salaries and expenses of the country's diplomats. The advances would earn 5 percent interest and were to be repaid as soon as possible. Baring also dispatched an agent to Mexico to ratify the provisional agreement and to negotiate a formal contract.[42]

Rumors of the pending agreement stabilized the market in Mexican securities. Rocafuerte announced on the fifteenth that Baring Brothers would pay Mexico's dividend for September. The press reacted favorably, believing that Baring would not have agreed to represent Mexico without making certain that the federal republic would meet future dividends. Mexican bonds climbed to 66 percent at a time when "the English market was [otherwise] totally deserted."[43] The following month, Minister Plenipotentiary Sebastián Camacho arrived with funds to cover the January dividends and to repay part of Baring's advances. As a result, Mexican securities advanced still higher, to 69 percent, while the bonds of other Spanish American nations remained below 30 percent.[44]

Mexico managed to maintain dividend payments through April 1827. The October dividends, however, could not be met. The other American nations had not paid their dividends for nearly a year; now Mexico, the largest, wealthiest, and most stable of the Spanish American states, seemed to be in the verge of default. Although Gran Colombia's new minister, José Fernández de Madrid, reported to his government that Mexico's failure to meet its October payments harmed all the new nations, initially public reaction was mild.[45] When Rocafuerte announced that money was en

[42]On August 30, *Times* could find no grounds for believing that Mexico could pay its dividends. *Times* (London), August 30, 1826, p. 2. Barclay & Co. to Rocafuerte, London, September 10, 1826; Rocafuerte to Alexander Baring, London, September 11, 1826; Baring to Rocafuerte, London, September 13, 1826, AGSREM, 2-5-25-4. Esteva to maritime customs officials, Mexico, December 28, 1825; agreement calling for D. Vicente Rocafuerte, financial agent for Mexico, to transfer the agency, previously in the hands of Barclay, Herring, Richardson and Co., to Baring Brothers, London, September 20, 1826, AGSREM, H/121.332"823-24"/1. 40-11-21.

[43]*Times* (London), September 13, 1826, p. 2; September 14, 1826, p. 2; September 15, 1826, p. 2; September 16, 1826, p. 2; Rocafuerte to holders of Mexican bonds, London, September 15, 1826, *Times*, September 15, 1826, p. 2.

[44]Rocafuerte to Espinosa de los Monteros, London, November 9, 1826, AGSREM, III/352 (72:42)/2. 7-16-61; *El sol*, no. 1276 (December 14, 1826), 2190; no. 1280 (December 17, 1826), 1206 [sic] (in error for 2206); no. 1275 (December 12, 1826), 2186.

[45]José Fernández de Madrid to Bolívar, London, September 21, 1827, Simón O'Leary, *Memorias del General O'Leary*, 29 vols. (Caracas, 1880), IX, 299-300.

route, many bondholders hoped that payment was merely being delayed. When they finally realized that Mexico could not meet its obligations, the creditors reacted with fury, accusing the federal republic of fraud, deception, and treachery.[46]

As a consequence of the public outcry, parliament named a commission to investigate the Spanish American debt. Sir Robert Wilson, a member of parliament and a friend of the new nations, informed Rocafuerte that if the dividends could be paid, the entire question would lapse. If, on the other hand, payment were not forthcoming, relations between Great Britain and the new countries would deteriorate.[47] Rocafuerte informed his government of the gravity of the situation and exhorted the president to act. Newspapers in Mexico also expressed concern. *El Amigo del Pueblo* warned that action had to be taken because "a nation's credit, like virginity, can only be lost once."[48]

When it became apparent that Mexico could not pay its dividends in 1828, President Guadalupe Victoria authorized the recapitalization of the nation's foreign debt. Baring Brothers, however, argued that it was futile to exchange new bonds for old, unless the government could give assurance that it would service the debt; the promised allocation of customs revenues, all too often diverted to other uses in cases of emergency, would not suffice to restore credit. Mexico had already broken too many promises; it should make no new ones. Until substantial changes could be implemented in the tax structure, Alexander Baring suggested that things be allowed to remain as they were.[49]

The foreign loans which Mexico obtained in England were critical to the country's well-being. Because the new nation's tax structure was inadequate, as Barbara Tenenbaum has shown,[50] the government needed foreign loans to remain in power. Indeed, as a result of those loans, Guadalupe Victoria became the only chief executive to complete his term between independence and 1848.[51]

[46]Joel Warrington, an English bondholder, was among the many who demanded their dividends. He voiced a commonly held opinion when he said: "Now your nation is *without honor, without credit*, derided and despised by every honest man in Europe." Joel Warrington to Rocafuerte, London, February 16, 1828: Rocafuerte to Camacho, London, February 20, 1826, AGSREM, H/122.32(72:42)"827"/79.

[47]Rocafuerte to Cañedo, London, April 20, 1828; Esteva to Cañedo, Mexico, April 22, 1828, AGSREM, H/122.32 (72:420"827"/79. Rocafuerte to Lord Dudley, London, April 19, 1828, Great Britain, Public Record Office, Foreign Office Papers, FO 50/51, ff. 9–13.

[48]*El amigo del pueblo* 4 (April 2, 1828), 2, 4–5.

[49]Alexander Baring to Rocafuerte, London, December 25, 1828; Rocafuerte to Cañedo, London, January 22, 1829; José Ignacio Pavón to Baring Brothers, Mexico, March 30, 1829, AGSREM H/300 (72:861)"832-30"/1. LE 1700.

[50]Tenenbaum, *México en la época de los agiotistas*, 35–65.

[51]Rodríguez, *Down from Colonialism*, 9.

Because of conflicting reports and inadequate statistics, it is difficult to determine exactly either how much Mexico received or when it received it. My calculations indicate that after deducting commissions and other costs, Mexico obtained 17,019,455 pesos from the two British loans. Of that amount, approximately 1,854,640 pesos was lost in the London crisis, including the £4,000 from the Goldschmidt loan, the £63,000 loan to Gran Colombia, and the £303,928 from the Barclay bankruptcy. Thus, Mexico actually received a little more than 15,000,000 pesos from the two loans. That amount equaled the ordinary government revenue in 1826–1827, one of the best years for government income during the 1820s. The Mexican government used most of the 15,000,000 pesos, about 70 percent to cover general operating expenses, primarily for army salaries. The rest it spent on armaments and for debt repayment. The money from the loans was critical because it covered large deficits from 1824 to 1827.

Mexican needs and British interests coincided during the 1820s. Initially English investors looked to Mexico as a safe place to invest their capital. But they were rapidly disappointed by the relative poverty and instability of the government. After the financial crisis of 1826, British investors turned to other regions offering better opportunities. Mexico would not obtain a new loan in England until the 1860s. Thus the early 1820s were an anomalous period during which Mexico could obtain credit on excellent terms. The 1824 and 1825 loans, for example, sold at the bourse at 84 percent and 89-3/4 percent of face value respectively; these were among the best terms obtained by any government at the time.

Unfortunately, the leaders of Mexico had little experience negotiating foreign loans. They were so certain of their country's potential wealth and they were so desperate for money that they were willing to accept onerous terms so long as they obtained funds rapidly. A number of speculators, among them Borja Migoni, betrayed the government's confidence. Clearly the greatest loss occurred when Borja Migoni manipulated the market against Mexico. Given the state of the market at the time, it is likely that an open loan would have sold for at least 80 percent of face value rather than the 58 percent which Borja Migoni arranged. An 80 percent loan would have raised 12,800,000 pesos instead of the 9,280,000 pesos the Goldschmidt loan obtained. Borja Migoni's duplicity cost Mexico more than 3,500,000 pesos.

Mexico's domestic political strife also affected the management of the loan funds. Minister of Finance Esteva's hostility toward Minister Plenipotentiary Michelena and Chargé d'affaires Rocafuerte blinded him both to Consul General Borja Migoni's machinations and to the danger posed by the speculative fever of the London financial markets in 1825/1826. As a result, Mexico lost nearly two million pesos in the bankruptcies of its London agents. Because of poor decisions on the part of Mexico's government, the nation actually received about 50 percent of the loans it contracted instead of the 85 percent it could have obtained.

Only by keeping in mind the virulent political struggles in Mexico can we understand why officials were willing to accept adverse terms to secure funds rapidly. They, no doubt, believed that the nation's potential would eventually allow them to overcome the waste and mismanagement associated with these loans. Clearly foreigners were willing to lend large sums because they too believed in Mexico's legendary wealth. Both Mexicans and foreigners erred. The new republic failed to establish internal order and prosperity for nearly fifty years. After the initial flurry of interest in Mexico, foreign investors turned to other more stable areas of the world. Although the early foreign loans contributed to consolidating Mexico's independence, they also became a serious burden which the country overcame only with great difficulty.

Modernidad, mito y religiosidad en el nacimiento de México

Jaime del Arenal Fenochio

EL 28 DE SEPTIEMBRE DE 1821, al firmar el Acta de Independencia del Imperio Mexicano sus autores reconocieron los esfuerzos realizados por los hijos de la nación mexicana por liberarla del yugo español. Pero la fase inicial de esos esfuerzos la encontraron en el momento en que "un genio superior a toda admiración y elogio" proclamó en Iguala las Tres Garantías.[1] Ninguna referencia se hizo entonces a la lucha entablada por casi un década por los viejos insurgentes, negándoseles, así, su participación en la gesta que daría libertad a la oprimida Nueva España.

Casi dos años después el nuevamente establecido Soberano Congreso Constituyente decretó la nulidad de la coronación de don Agustín de Iturbide como Emperador de México, y la insubsistencia del Plan de Iguala y de los Tratados de Córdoba, únicamente en lo relativo a la forma de gobierno en ellos contemplada.[2] Como dicha coronación había sido obra de la violencia y de la fuerza, según el Constituyente, y como "jamás hubo derecho para sujetar a la nación mexicana a ninguna ley ni tratado", no hubo lugar, aquel día, ni siquiera a discutir sobre la abdicación de un emperador que, así se consideró en base a una absurda ficción legal, nunca pudo existir.

De esta formas, inaugurándose el uso de extrañas ficciones —a las que tanto recurriremos posteriormente los mexicanos—, los dos proyectos

NOTA DEL AUTOR: Una primera versión del presente ensayo fue el comentario que acompañó a la ponencia de Ernesto Lemoine en el Coloquio celebrado en el Instituto de Investigaciones Jurídicas de la Universidad Nacional Autónoma de México (UNAM) a principios de 1984 y que fue publicado en el libro *La formación del estado mexicano*, María del Refugio González, ed. (México: Porrúa, 1984), 43–48. La presente versión modifica y complementa ese comentario.

[1] *Colección de órdenes y decretos de la Soberana Junta Provisional Gubernativa y Soberanos Congresos Generales de la Nación Mexicana*, 2a. ed. (México: Imprenta de Galván, a cargo de Mariano Arévalo, 1829), I, 9.

[2] Ibid., II, 91 y 92, decretos del 8 de abril de 1823.

políticos que a lo largo de la segunda década de la pasada centuria se fueron perfilando con el objeto de consumar la independencia del Virreinato se negaron recíprocamente, para revindicar, cada uno para sí, la exclusiva paternidad del nuevo Estado. No es, pues, fortuito, que éste cuente con dos actas de nacimiento, la del 6 de noviembre de 1813, obra del Congreso del Anáhuac, y la del 28 de septiembre de 1821, creación de la Junta Provisional Gubernativa.

¿Pero esos proyectos, esas dos "posibilidades históricas" de las que nos habla O'Gorman en su ensayo sobre el monarquismo mexicano, se sustentaban hacia 1821 sobre principios del todo incompatibles? Hasta ahora ha sido usual analizar por parte de historiadores, politólogos y juristas las diferencias existentes entre ambos proyectos y preocuparse por oponer, sin posibilidad alguna de conciliación, la gesta libertadora de Hidalgo a la hazaña independentista de Iturbide. Poco, por el contrario, se ha hecho para encontrar los posibles puntos de conexión entre aquéllos. En este ensayo, quiero reflexionar sobre este último punto, que, quizás, pasiones e intereses políticos en pro de una historia de bronce no han pemitido estudiar con detenimiento.

Aclaro de antemano que no niego las diferencias; muchas se han encontrado para ser negadas gratuitamente. Ellas se hacen tan evidentes a medida que la insurgencia avanza hacia los planteamientos de Apatzingán y Puruarán que resultaría absurdo negarlas. Es más, creo que a éllas se les debe atribuir el fracaso inicial del programa insurgente y la victoria aun transitoria, del iturbidista. Pero al márgen de estas discrepancias, considero que la Historia del Derecho, dirigida a estudiar las ideas que o se mueven detrás de las formas y de las instituciones, o luchan por materializarse en éstas, sirve para encontrar —aplicando a los textos jurídico-políticos que produjo la independencia mexicana su particular óptica— notables coincidencias entre ambos proyectos, hijos al fin y al cabo de una misma realidad: la sociedad novohispana que los engendró. Para tal efecto, también ayuda acercarnos a las creencias populares de entonces, compartidas por la élite criolla que acaudilló ambos proyectos independentistas, creencias que, igualmente, quedaron plasmadas en esos documentos.

Tres son, a mi entender, los puntos de coincidencia más claros e inmediatos existentes en ambos programas.

Un elemento coincidente, permante a lo largo de los once años de lucha por la independencia, respetado por tirios y troyanos, fue la religión católica, apostólica y romana. Tanto los Elementos Constitucionales de Rayón, en su artículo primero, los Sentimientos de la Nación de Morelos, el Decreto Constitucional, conocido con el nombre de Constitución de Apatzingán, como el Plan de Iguala, las Bases Constitucionales y el Reglamento Provisional del Imperio, reconocen que la religión católica sea la única del nuevo

Estado, sin tolerancia de alguna otra.[3] Y aunque Hidalgo y su grupo no hayan promulgado un documento similar a los anteriores nadie puede pensar que no compartiesen la misma idea.

Otro factor que asemeja a los dos programas fue la monarquía, pero ahora concebida como limitada o constitucional, que si bien en el campo de las ideas insurgentes se abandonaría en cierto momento, ello no fue sin oposición y sin discusiones, de tal suerte que, viva aun la idea monárquica, Iturbide debió tomarla en cuenta tal vez porque en 1821 era considerada por la élite política novhispana —insurgente y no insurgente— como necesaria para facilitar el tránsito hacia la absoluta independencia del reino. Cabe precisar que, ciertamente, el proyecto insurgente lanzado por Hidalgo y elevado a su cúspide por Morelos y los hombres de Chilpancingo evolucionó hacia la adopción de las ideas republicanas, pero también es necesario no olvidar que todavía hacia 1813, en el proyecto de Discurso elaborado por Carlos María de Bustamante para ser leído por Morelos al abrirse las sesiones del Constituyente de Chilpancingo, se manejó la idea de restaurar en el trono a Fernando VII. La idea republicana fue abriéndose paso lentamente entre los insurgentes, pero todavía pasarían algunos años para que fuera opuesta radicalmente a la monárquica. Apenas importa recordar el éxito obtenido por el Plan de Iguala y los Tratados de Córdoba al respecto. La monarquía, pues, no desune inicialmente a los, por otros lados, antagónicos programas, aunque una vez consumada la independencia se convierta en el primero y principal punto de controversia entre las élites mexicanas.[4]

Un factor más de identidad fue, precisamente, la idea de independencia absoluta respecto de España,[5] que une en cuanto al objetivo final y divide en cuanto al modo de llevarla a cabo.

Todos estos principios o ideas que encontramos, tanto en el programa Hidalgo-Morelos-Chilpancingo-Apatzingán como en el programa Iturbide-Iguala-Córdoba, constituyen además elementos de cohesión, entre la insurgencia rural que dirige Morelos y las clases medias urbanas que forman e informan ideológicamente al Cura de Carácuaro, y que apoyaron

[3]Elementos Constitucionales (EC), a. 1; *Sentimientos de la Nación* (SN) a. 2; *Decreto Constitucional* (DC), a. 1; *Plan de Iguala* (PI), a. 1; *Bases Constitucionales* (BC), segunda declaración; *Reglamento Provisional del Imperio* (RPI), a. 3; Véase Felipe Tena Ramírez, *Leyes fundamentales de México* (1808–1983) México: Porrúa, 1983), passim,

[4]EC, a. 5; Ernesto Lemoine, "México independiente: de Iguala a las vísperas de Ayutla", *El territorio mexicano: la nación* (México: IMSS, 1982), I, 178, 180, 182 y 183. PI, a. 3; Tratados de Córdoba (TC), 116; BC, tercera base; RPI, a.5.

[5]EC, a. 4; SN, a. 1; Acta Solemne de la Declaración de la Independencia de América Septentrional de 6 de noviembre de 1813; Acta de la Independencia del Imperio Mexicano, de 28 de septiembre de 1821; PI, a. 2; TC, a. 1; RPI, a. 5.

decididamente las tres garantías. Puntos de unión que coexisten junto con los no menos evidentes elementos de antagonismo, como pudieran ser el odio al gachupín —antiguo, latente, popular y explosivo— la idea republicana de gobierno que se va ir paulatinamente imponiendo —igualmente explosiva— y, sobre todo, la revolución que Lemoine ha calificado de "populista y rural".[6]

Pero más allá de las obvias e inmediatamente perceptibles diferencias o coincidencias que separan o unen a ambos proyectos, es posible encontrar en el trasfondo de la lucha librada por lograr el nacimiento y determinar las características de un nuevo Estado, la común intención de constituirlo sobre los principios derivados del pensamiento *ius* naturalista racionalista europeo, y la preocupación compartida igualmente, por reafirmar su identidad sobre símbolos nativos, pertenecientes a la tradición o a la cultura *mexicana*, es decir, la que paulatinamente se fue formando durante el virreinato. Examinemos brevemente estos dos presupuestos.

Los principios jurídico-racionalistas que dominaron tanto la ideología de los autores del Decreto Constitucional de Apatzingán como la de los hombres del Primer Imperio fueron: (1) el reconocimiento de los derechos del hombre consagrados, por ejemplo, en los artículos 4, 6, 17 19, 22, 23 y 24 a 40 de la Constitución de Apatzingán y en los artículos 7 y 19 del Reglamento Provisonal del Imperio, entre otros documentos. Ahí quedaron de una vez fijados los derechos de sufragio, de igualdad, de libertad (en sus diversas manifestaciones), de propiedad y de privacidad;[7] (2) la consagración de la soberanía, nacional o popular; "La soberanía reside originalmente en el pueblo" afirmará la Constitución de Apatzingán; Los Tratados de Córdoba proclamarán que el Imperio Mexicano sea una nación soberana; y el Reglamento del Imperio que la nación mexicana sea soberana;[8] (3) la aceptación de un gobierno representativo basado en elecciones populares que se plasma en los artículos 5 y 7 de los Elementos Constitucionales de Rayón, en el quinto sentimiento de Morelos, en los 5 a 8 y 48 del Decreto Constitucional, en el 14 de los Tratados de Córdoba, en la primera Base Constitucional de febrero de 1822, en los artículos 23 y 24 del Reglamento imperial, así como en el decreto de 17 de noviembre de 1821;[9] (4) la división de poderes dispuesta entre ejecutivo, legislativo y judicial, con claro predominio del segundo sobre el primero, y evidente menosprecio al judicial; afirmará el artículo 23 del Reglamento Provisional del Imperio que "el sistema de gobierno político del imperio mexicano se compone de los poderes legislativo, ejecutivo y judicial, que son incom-

[6]Véase Lemoine, "Morelos y la generación de la independencia" en *La Formación*, 33–41.

[7]Véase, además, EC, aa. 24, 29, 31 y 32; SN, aa. 15, 17 y 18; PI, aa. 12 y 13; TC, a. 15; BC, sexta base.

[8]Véase EC, a. 5; SN, a. 5; DC, aa. 5–11; TC, a. 1; BC, primera declaración; RPI, a. 5.

[9]*Colección*, I, 31–36; sobre convocatoria a Cortes.

patibles en una misma persona o corporación", ratificando lo que documentos insurgentes anteriores habían consagrado;[10] (5) el monopolio en la creación del Derecho por parte del Estado intentado por éste desde siglos anteriores y que ahora el nuevo Estado hará realidad, en detrimento del viejo y anquilosado *ius comune* obra de juristas doctos y de los usos y costumbres de las comunidades indígenas;[11] (6) la fe absoluta en la ley como factor casi único de la felicidad popular y la supremacía de ésa, con el consecuente desplazamiento de cualquier otra fuente del Derecho;[12] (7) la codificación del derecho positivio sobre los principios de la codificación racionalista;[13] y (8) la delimitación previa de facultades, obligaciones y organización impersonal del gobierno.[14] Todo esto consagrado y reconocido dentro del marco de un documento concebido como superior a cualquier persona o institución, súbdito o gobernante: la Constitución, síntesis del propio Estado que nacía.[15]

La recepción de estos principios fue prácticamente absoluta y unánime por parte de la minoría ilustrada y dirigente de la sociedad novohispana (clérigos, militares, comerciantes, burócratas, universitarios, colegiales, seudo aristócratas, mineros, y sobre todo abogados; es decir, la burguesía de entonces) y dio lugar a la primera gran revolución intelectual habida en el seno de esa sociedad, sin la cual no se entienden cabalmente las revoluciones que habrían de venir. Su aceptación —consciente o inconsciente, casi imperceptible pero no menos avasalladora— únicamente contó con la oposición de quienes, como en el caso de los conjurados de la Profesa, se aferraron en mantener instituciones e ideas típicas del antiguo régimen, como la Monarquía absoluta, la Inquisición o el predominio absoluto político y social de los peninsulares en las esferas administrativas, comerciales o judiciales. Esta postura se resquebrajó en Apatzingán y quedó definitivamente hecha trizas al declararse, el 13 de diciembre de 1821, como "Bases Fundamentales" del Imperio Mexicano la independencia absoluta del Imperio, la monarquía hereditaria constitucional moderada, el gobierno representativo y la división de poderes,[16] y al jurar el Congreso Constituyente, el 24 de febrero siguiente, las Bases Constitucionales del

[10]EC, aa. 5 y 21; SN, a. 6; dC, aa. 11, 12 y 44; TC, aa. 3, 11 y 14; BC, cuarta base.

[11]Véase María del Refugio González, "Historia del derecho mexicano" en *Introducción al derecho mexicano* (México: UNAM, 1981), I, 46 y ss.

[12]SN, aa. 12, 13 y 14; DC, aa. 2, 11, 18 a 23; BC, cuarta base; RPI, aa. 2, 55 y 56.

[13]María del Refugio González, *Estudios sobre la historia del derecho civil en México durante el siglo XIX* (México: UNAM, 1981), 87. Decreto de la Soberana Junta Provisional Gubernativa, en *Colección*, I, 95 y 96.

[14]EC, passim; SN, aa. 5, 6, 7 y 11; DC, passim; PI, passim; TC, passim; BC, passim; RPI, passim.

[15]EC; DC; PI, aa. 3 y 11; TC, aa. 2 y 12; BC, tercera base; RPI, a. 5 y Bases organicas de la Junta Nacional Instituyente de 5 de noviembre de 1822, la. 2a. y 3a. base.

[16]Reglamento de Libertad de Imprenta a. 1, en *Colección*, I, 45.

mismo.[17] La influencia de los principios jurídico racionalistas sobrepasó, incluso, a cualquier posible proyecto político de tipo personal y por lo mismo los encontramos nítidamente expresados aún en el muy iturbidista Reglamento Provisional Político del Imperio.[18] Son estos principios, en fin, los que reafirmaron la participación de nuestro país —en el momento en que nacía como nación libre y soberana— en la cultura jurídica occidental, a la cual ya pertenecía bajo el nombre de Nueva España, desde tres siglos atrás, gracias al esfuerzo cultural desplegado por la vieja España.

Claro está que su recepción teórica no fue todo lo fácil y feliz que los fundadores del Estado mexicano imaginaron y menos aún la conformación de la sociedad mexicana y de sus instituciones sobre las bases propuestas por éllos: la codificación tardaría cincuenta años en triunfar del todo; la ley, y más concretamente la constitución, por sí mismas no conseguirían la felicidad del pueblo como creyeron, entre otros muchos, los diputados locales que promulgaron las primeras constituciones estatales; de los tres poderes, dos lucharían encarnizadamente para conseguir la hegemonía; las deseadas elecciones poco y mal se llevarían a cabo, y las constituciones, federales o centralistas, o las particulares de cada entidad federativa, se elaborarían atendiendo más al mundo de los ideales que a la compleja y contradictoria sociedad mexicana. Un sólo ejemplo nos ilustra a este respecto.

La supremacía del legislativo sobre los otros dos poderes, lejos de constituir la llave de la felicidad nacional, se convirtió en uno de los principales obstáculos para gobernar al nuevo Estado. Tanto Morelos como Iturbide, uno por creer ciegamente en esa supremacía, otro por atreverse a ponerla en entredicho, pagaron no sólo con sus respectivas carreras políticas sino con sus vidas el reconocimiento que en su momento hicieron a este nuevo mito. Y es que su aceptación, lógica consecuencia de la aversión al omnímodo poder personal, central, despótico e impopular, era indispensable para definir al nuevo ente político como Estado moderno, si bien lo convirtiera en algo ingobernable. Mucha sangre habría de correr en su suelo antes de que se encontrara una salida a la tensa relación que se fue estableciendo entre el poder legislativo —al fin y al cabo el poder popular— y el ejecutivo, previsto como siervo incondicional de la voluntad del pueblo.

El segundo presupuesto que encontramos en el transfondo ideológico de los dos proyectos políticos propuestos ente 1810 y 1821 lo constituye la intención de afirmar la identidad del nuevo Estado sobre símbolos locales, no importados, es decir *mexicanos*. Estos se encontraron en la tradición prehispánica que ahora se renueva con afanes nacionalistas y en el catolicismo popular.

[17]Tena Ramírez, *Leyes fundamentales*, 124.
[18]Ibid., 125–144.

La primera se nos evidencia en los nombres elegidos para designar a la nueva nación: el Anáhuac, América Mexicana, México o Imperio Mexicano;[19] o en el uso reiterado de una nueva ficción: aquella que se reflejaría en la reunión de un Congreso *del Anáhuac*[20] o en la declaración formulada por los firmantes de nuestra segunda Acta de Independencia en el sentido de considerar que la Nación mexicana, a la que entonces proclamaban como independiente, existía desde trescientos años atrás, lo que presupone la intención de estar liberando a un imperio azteca hasta entonces dormido, encubierto o latente en la estructura misma del virreinato, idea igualmente compartida por Morelos.[21] La tradición prehispánica también se refleja en la unánime adopción de la figura del águila sobre el nopal como escudo nacional,[22] sancionada en forma definitiva por los decretos de 2 de noviembre de 1821 y 7 de enero de 1822 promulgados por el Imperio de Iturbide.

El catolicismo popular aportaría el elemento más significativo y trascendente para definir y comprender cabalmente al México independiente en términos de unidad cultural y de identidad nacional. Me refiero, claro está, al culto a la Virgen de Guadalupe, no "expropiada" —como quiere Lemoine— sino, por el contrario, propiedad ancestral y exclusiva de criollos, indios y castas,[23] culto fomentado por Hidalgo y Morelos. El primero, al tomar la imagen de la Guadalupana en Atotonilco para usarla como pendón de los insurgentes; el segundo, el declarar, entre otras disposiciones guadalupanistas, en sus Sentimientos de la Nación que la

[19]DC para la libertad de la *América Mexicana*; Acta de Independencia de 1813; TC, a. 1; RPI, a. 5.

[20]Lemoine, "México", 187.

[21]Discurso de Morelos de 14 de septiembre de 1813: "Vamos a restablecer el Imperio Mexicano". En Ernesto Lemoine *Morelos. su vida revolucionaria a través de sus escritos y otros testimonios de la época* (México: UNAM, 1965), 369. El Acta principiará con estas palabras: "La Nación mexicana que, por trescientos años, ni ha tenido voluntad propia, ni libre el uso de la voz, sale hoy de la opresión en que ha vivido". Véase. Tena Ramírez, *Leyes fundamentales*, 122.

[22]Lemoine, *Morelos*, 560 y 561 y en *Colección*, I, 26 y 86.

[23]Lemoine, "Morelos", 35. Recientemente, Enrique Florescano en un artículo publicado bajo el surgerente título de "Guadalupe de todas" reconoce que la Virgen de Guadalupe se convirtió en "un símbolo nacional que identificó a indios, criollos y mestizos en una misma y celebrada creencia", no obstante lo cual, más adelante, parece inclinarse a considerar a la Virgen como objeto de una disputa patrimonialista entablada entre criollos e indígenas, reivindicando, en consecuencia, la paternidad original indígena del culto (Véase *Nexos* 10:109 (enero 1987), 29-37, interpretación, esta última, con la cual no estoy de acuerdo. No puede dejarse de mencionar, al respecto, el libro de J. Lafaye, *Quetzalcóalt y Guadalupe*: *la formación de la conciencia nacional en México* (México: Fondo de Cultura Económica, 1977), y la estupenda reseña al mismo de Edmundo O'Gorman publicada en *Historia Variae*, Vol. 1 (México: Universidad Iberoamericana). De este autor lamento no haber tenido todavía en mis manos su último libro, apenas salido de las prensas, *Destierro de sombras*: *Luz en el origen de la imagen y culto de Nuestra Señora de Guadalupe del Tepeyac*. Fidel de Jesús Chauvet,

Constitución del nuevo Estado estableciera "la celebración del 12 de diciembre en todos los pueblos, dedicado a la patrona de nuestra libertad, María Santísima de Guadalupe, encargando a todos los pueblos, la devoción mensual".[24] Este catolicismo popular fue reconocido por Iturbide al redactar los Estatutos de la Orden Imperial de Guadalupe,[25] y por el primer Congreso Constituyente al reconocer a la Virgen del Tepeyac como Patrona de la Nación y señalar al día 12 de diciembre como "el más grande para esta América, por la maravillosa aparición de María Santísima de Guadalupe".[26]

Considero que en estas dos grandes y trascendentes raíces ideológicas —racionalista la primera y mítico-religiosa la segunda, extraída una de allende el océano y la otra del propio suelo— encontró la generación de la independencia los elementos propicios para echar a caminar al Estado mexicano y para definir la nueva nacionalidad que iba forjándose. Cuando la Monarquía da paso a la República, ésta, al margen del sistema adoptado, se proclamará "moderna" al hacer suyos, también, los principios jurídico-políticos propios del Estado de Derecho que emergía en la historia política occidental, y afirmará su mexicanidad, al insistir en recuperar —aun cuando fuera únicamente en el discurso político— raíces prehispánicas en contra de las hispánicas[27] y al defender una religiosidad muy personal lograda dentro del catolicismo.

Quizás el hecho de que esta religiosidad, fundamentalmente guadalupana, se haya forjado poco a poco durante casi trescientos años y la misma haya sido adoptada paulatinamente por todas las capas de la masa social novohispana, explique el que se haya convertido en el factor de cohesión social y cultural más importante (y casi único) de una sociedad mexicana envuelta en infinidad de conflictos y divisiones desde antes de la independencia. Por el contrario, su poca vocación por los principios racionalistas; su tradicional desprecio y ambigua posición frente a la ley del Estado; la violencia provocada en las viejas instituciones e ideas por la imposición de ideas e instituciones fraguadas en otras latitudes; la terquedad por adoptar principios ajenos a una realidad que también tercamente se oponía a cambiar; su incapacidad para generar o revitalizar ideas políticas propias que le permitiesen crear su propia y particular modernidad, por un lado, y, por otro, el aventurado e incongruente —si bien explicable—

"Historia del culto guadalupano", y Luis Medina Ascencio, "Fuentes esenciales de la historia guadalupana: Su valor histórico". Ambos en *Album del 450 aniversario de las apariciones de Nuestra Señora de Guadalupe* (México: Ediciones Buena Nueva, 1981).

[24]Véase también de Rayón, EC, aa. 33 y 34.

[25]Decreto de 20 de febrero de 1822. *Colección*, I, 122.

[26]Decreto de 16 de agosto de 1822. *Colección*, II, 75 y Chauvet, "Historia del culto", 69.

[27]Recuérdese, por ejemplo, el cambio de nombre que sufrieron algunas provincias novohispanas al erigirse en estados soberanos.

deseo de revivir y mantener un pasado indígena totalmente acabado ayudaron, en buena medida, a que esa sociedad se escindiera aun más de lo que podía estar y se viera envuelta en aquellos conflictos.

Inadecuadamente modernos, decididamente religiosos y míticamente indigenistas los dos proyectos elaborados por la élite novohispana para independizar a México colaboraron a construir esa Nación premoderna, mítica y profundamente religiosa que fue la mexicana del pasado siglo, y a la cual hoy, en mucho, no hemos renunciado todavía.

Sin embargo, habría que precisar que los fenómenos anteriores no se dieron exclusivamente en y para el ámbito mexicano, sino que, por el contrario, fueron compartidos por casi todos los países hispanoamericanos, y por la propia España en sus luchas contra el francés y en favor de su propia modernidad. En todos ellos se acudió lo mismo a elementos culturales tradicionales como a las ideas modernas, bien para fundar sobre estas bases un Estado nuevo o para darle al antiguo bases y formas novedosas. La recuperación de un pasado propio, por más mítico que fuera, les permitió a todos legitimar la independencia y llevar a cabo las transformaciones políticas, económicas y sociales que pugnaron por realizar. No a otra cosa obedecen el renacimiento de las Cortes españolas y, en general, de la idea de "Cortes" en el mundo hispano (Martínez Marina); de los concejos americanos (México, Buenos Aires) y peninsulares ante la invasión napoleónica, e inclusive, la presencia de las ideas políticas provenientes de la escolástica castellana (Suárez), como lo ha demostrado Stoetzer.[28]

Ese pasado, junto con la religiosidad popular y la renovación de mitos —indígenas para el caso de América o medioevales para el caso de España— jugaron, tal vez, para todos aquellos países el mismo papel aunque con distinta intensidad. Lo propio de cada uno estaría dado, entonces, no tanto por la ausencia o presencia de esos elementos (para el caso de Argentina y Uruguay quizá, sólo por lo que se refiere al "indigenismo" criollo) sino por el *contenido* de los mismos y por el peso que para los habitantes de cada región tuvo cada uno de ellos. Así se explicarían, por ejemplo, las diferencias (dentro de las grandes similitudes) del constitucionalismo americano, en una época tan reciente como los primeros años de vida de las nuevas naciones independizadas de España, como lo notó Vicente Rocafuerte,[29] o que sólo en México se diera el "guadalupanismo", aún cuando en otras partes de América a la Virgen Morena se le brindara un determinado e importante culto, o brotasen similares fenómenos de religiosidad popular. También encontrarían explicación, desde esta perspec-

[28]O. Carlos Stoetzer, *Las raíces escolásticas de la emancipación de la América Española* (Madrid: Centro de Estudios Constitucionales, 1982).

[29]Vicente Rocafuerte, "Examen analítico de las constituciones formadas en Hispano-América", *Revista de Historia de América*, 72 (julio—dic. 1971), 419–484, precedido por Jaime E. Rodríguez O., "An Analysis of the First Constitutions of Spanish-America", 413–419.

tiva, la visión popular acerca de la Ley o del gobernante y, en general, la poca vigencia *real* de las ideas *ius* racionalistas en cada país. De estas diferencias en el grado de intensidad y alcances de la recepción de las nuevas ideas, y en la reflexión sobre sus símbolos, mitos y pasado propios, nacerá la propia personalidad política de los habitantes de las distintas regiones de América hispana, mismas que los distinguirá de sus vecinos. Pero no por esto, se perderán los vínculos raciales, ideomáticos y religiosos que los identifican en nuestros días como iberoamericanos; dueños de una cultura compleja, rica e igualmente, como las naciones que ellos forman, premoderna, mítica y religiosa.

Ilustrados, regalistas y liberales

María del Refugio González

Este ensayo tiene por objeto introducir algunos elementos de la investigación jurídica institucional en el análisis de los fenómenos históricos de la primera mitad del siglo XIX. El trabajo de los historiadores del derecho y de las instituciones es útil para ayudar a comprender mejor los fenómenos históricos en el mediano y el largo plazos. Este tipo de especialista está obligado a transitar a lo largo de varias decenas e incluso centenas de años para averiguar la génesis y el desarrollo de las instituciones. El análisis de largo plazo le permite ver la secuencia y la evolución de los fenómenos en relación a los modelos que les dan origen. Al hacerlo puede evaluar muchos de estos fenómenos históricos con una perspectiva diferente a la que tiene el historiador general.

El historiador del derecho y de las instituciones tiene en su contra el hecho de que su conocimiento sobre los períodos que estudia es más superficial que el de los historiadores en general, por eso tiene que recurrir a los trabajos historiográficos más diversos a fin de completar su información.

La advertencia anterior tiene por objeto explicar la perspectiva del trabajo que se presenta, el cual se inscribe en la historia de las instituciones. Desde esa perspectiva se busca introducir algunas propuestas para el análisis de las primeras décadas de la vida independiente de la nación mexicana, sobre todo en el aspecto relativo a las relaciones de la Iglesia y el Estado. La idea central es aportar elementos para explicar la manera en que el pensamiento ilustrado de la segunda mitad del siglo XVIII se fue transformando ya sea en liberal o en conservador. Para lograrlo conviene definir o mejor dicho, proponer, algunas hipótesis para la identificación del grupo más fácil de diferenciar: el conservador.

Hace algún tiempo empecé a trabajar en torno al pensamiento de los conservadores, con el fin de averiguar si existieron elementos que los identificaran. El análisis de muy diversos textos de carácter jurídicio y de algunas de las obras clásicas de nuestra historia me ha llevado a observar que los conservadores parecen hallarse identificados en torno a dos enunciados: la asunción de la doctrina cristiana que postula el pecado original con todas sus consecuencias; y la existencia de un programa político de acción,[1] mediante el cual buscaban conservar lo que había sido la "última Nueva España".[2]

Dado que la mayor parte de la población del virreinato era católica podría pensarse que toda era conservadora, y sabemos a ciencia cierta que no fue así. No todos los católicos fueron conservadores porque no todos estuvieron dispuestos a asumir por completo los postulados de la doctrina cristiana, y menos aún, todas las consecuencias de admitir los dogmas de la misma.

Hay que señalar que si bien los dogmas de la religión cristiana han sido y son inmutables y en consecuencia los católicos no pueden cuestionarlos, al lado de estos dogmas ha existido siempre un corpus doctrinario en el que es posible la interpretación por parte de los Papas o los Concilios. Como ejemplo se puede citar la condena expresa al racionalismo en el texto del *Sylabus* de 1864 frente a la tolerancia e incluso la práctica de actividades racionalistas por parte de la propia Iglesia de tiempos anteriores.

Así pues, en ocasiones sólo la condena de alguna práctica o filosofía ha llevado a los católicos a renunciar a ellas a pesar de haber participado en su ejercicio o en su elaboración antes de haber sido prohibidas o condenadas. Tal es el caso de los ilustrados, los regalistas y los liberales de la Nueva España y el México independiente. Todos ellos fueron católicos y participaron en la elaboración de ideas, doctrinas o actos que fueron expresamente prohibidos o condenados en 1864. Estos hechos hacen que el análisis de su pensamiento deba hacerse teniendo en cuenta lo que sucede en el seno de la Iglesia universal. Muchos de los católicos novohispanos, y luego mexicanos, fueron primero ilustrados y regalistas y después liberales. Otros se afiliaron al pensamiento y la acción conservadores. Creo que los que así procedieron no eran tan numerosos, descontada la Iglesia, por supuesto, y que al final fueron más los católicos que de ilustrados o regalistas pasaron a ser liberales tibios o moderados. Algunos ejemplos de conservadores propiamente dichos podrían ser Lucas Alamán, Clemente de Jesús Munguía, Juan N. Rodríguez de San Miguel, Bernardo Couto y J. J. Pesado. De ellos Couto[3] fue profundamente regalista en su juventud. Entre los liberales que fueron regalistas en alguna época de su vida, se puede señalar a José María Luis Mora, Fray Servando Teresa de Mier, Valentín Gómez Farías y Luis de la Rosa.[4]

[1]María del Refugio González, "El pensamiento de los conservadores mexicanos: hipótesis para su estudio", *Christus* (México), 587 (agosto 1985), 47-53.

[2]Roberto Moreno, "La última Nueva España", en *La formación del estado mexicano*, Coordinación María del Refugio González (México: Porrúa, 1984), 15-22.

[3]Bernardo Couto, *Disertación sobre la naturaleza y límites de la autoridad eclesiástica* (México, 1825).

[4][José María Luis Mora], *Disertación sobre la naturaleza y aplicación de las ventas y bienes eclesiásticos, y sobre la autoridad a que se hallan sujetos en cuánto a su creación,*

Liberales, regalistas, ilustrados y conservadores conviven hasta el fin del II Imperio. A partir de la Restauración de la República en 1867 los conservadores se convirtieron simplemente en reaccionarios por haber sido derrotado su programa de acción.[5] Los regalistas y los ilustrados ya no sobrevivieron a la constitución de un Estado laico y los liberales se diferenciaron por su grado de radicalización frente a las distintas doctrinas del ideario liberal. La coexistencia de tan variadas corrientes de opinión y la presencia en el mismo personaje de ideas de uno y otro bando fueron posibles porque no hay impedimento doctrinal para que un conservador sea liberal en materia económica; por eso, hay que buscar otros elementos para distinguir a unos y a otros. Sólo resta agregar que el conservadurismo a que se ha hecho referencia es el que se inspira en los pensadores que fueron contrarios a la obra de la Revolución francesa, como Edmund Burke.[6] De esta manera, en principio, los conservadores mexicanos habrían comenzado a manifestarse como tales, poco después de la Revolución. Pero la radicalización de su pensamiento sólo se presenta después de la insurrección y la guerra de independencia. Antes de ella no parecía posible una "horrorosa revolución" que fuera capaz de subvertir el orden de las cosas.

Ilustrados, regalistas y liberales

Dejemos pues de lado a los conservadores y pasemos a analizar qué tienen en común y cuáles son las diferencias entre el resto de nuestros personajes. El marco para el análisis será, como se dijo, el de las relaciones Iglesia y Estado por una razón muy simple: originalmente comparten postulados y doctrinas sobre la naturaleza de las relaciones entre ambas potestades y luego es este el asunto que los separa entre sí y los distingue de los conservadores.

Planteamiento General

La Ilustración, el regalismo y el liberalismo son fenómenos históricos de gran complejidad y no es el objetivo de estas páginas explicarlos sino solamente dar la idea general del sentido en el que son utilizados en el texto.[7]

---

aumento, subsistencia, o supresión. Su autor, un ciudadano de Zacatecas. Impresa de orden y a costa del H. Congreso de Zacatecas (México: Imprenta de Galván, a cargo de Mariano Arévalo, 1833).

[5]Jorge Adame Goddard, *El pensamiento político y social de los católicos mexicanos, 1867-1914* (México: UNAM, 1981).

[6]Edmund Burke, *Reflections on the Revolution in France and the Proceedings in Certain Societies in London Relative to That Event* (London, 1969).

[7]José María Luis Mora, *Revista política de las diversas administraciones que ha tenido la República hasta 1837*, prólogo po María del Refugio González (México: Coordinación

La Ilustración

El conjunto de ideas, prácticas y proyectos que conocemos como "Ilustración" no es igual en todos los países europeos. En cada lugar asume o se presenta con las características que le imprime a este fenómeno el pasado histórico local. Sin embargo, podría afirmarse que hay Ilustración en aquellos lugares en que se postula que la sociedad puede y debe organizarse conforme a lo que los hombres han deducido de su razón, y no de los designios divinos. La razón, y no Dios, debía pues presidir e inspirar los actos humanos. Esta afirmación no conducía necesariamente a negar a Dios, ni a la religión, ni a la Iglesia. La Ilustración no lleva aparejada la negación del dogma religioso y puede ser inclusive de signo católico, como lo fueron la española o la alemana.

Presididos por la razón, los hombres debían planear sus sociedades, señalando en constituciones o códigos el papel que cada quien habría de desempeñar en ellas. La razón permitiría distinguir las instituciones más ventajosas para el "bien común". Los reyes y sus vasallos, entre los cuales se hallaban los letrados que conformaban la naciente burocracia, debían ir dotando de nuevos contenidos a la acción estatal. El rey poco a poco se fue convirtiendo en absoluto y los vasallos, también poco a poco, hubieron de pensar en el modo de garantizar sus derechos como individuos frente al Estado. En el camino, fue redefiniéndose la acción estatal y, de simple testigo, el Estado comenzó a inmiscuirse cada vez más en los asuntos relacionados con los gremios, el comercio, la enseñanza, la moneda, etc. La Iglesia misma no era ajena a la intervención del Estado, aunque ésta sólo se redujera a los aspectos administrativos.

Esta política fue apoyada por aquellos que no formaban parte de la nobleza y que buscaban acomodarse en la sociedad por lo que sabían y no por lo que habían sido sus antepasados. También los que se dedicaban al comercio buscaban conseguir más mercados para colocar sus productos, al amparo de las nuevas ideas. Unos y otros fueron constituyendo la burguesía de la Europa continental, cuyos orígenes últimos habría que buscarlos allá por el siglo XI y que ya para el siglo XVII se hallaba plenamente desarrollada, aunque con características que la diferencian de la inglesa.

El regalismo

Dentro de las corrientes ilustradas puede señalarse por separado aquella que postula que el rey tiene el derecho de inmiscuirse en los asuntos de la Iglesia. El Origen de esta corriente de pensamiento se encuentra en la

---

de Humanidades-Miguel Angel Porrúa, 1986), xx-xxiv; transcribo textualmente el planteamiento que ahí realicé.

tradición medieval de la concesión del patronato a los particulares que hubieran ayudado a la edificación de una iglesia. En las Partidas quedó claramente establecido que el "vicario" de Dios en el reino era precisamente el rey (II, 1 y 5). Sin embargo, vicariato y patronato fueron en la práctica distintos, aunque con el tiempo llegaron a identificarse. Esto no debe extrañarnos, ya que en las Partidas está el sustento jurídico de la monarquía absoluta.

En el siglo XV, el papa Alejandro VI concedió a los reyes de Castilla y Aragón y a sus sucesores en la corona de Castilla, el patronato de la Iglesia indiana. El patronato se fue convirtiendo en vicariato, a medida que se acrecentaba el poder de los reyes de la dinastía austriaca y con el cambio de siglo y de dinastía se convirtió en regalía. Carlos III y Carlos IV veían como un derecho inherente a sus reales personas la intervención, cada día más grande, que tenían en los asuntos de la Iglesia. El fenómeno no es exclusivo de España, pero puede afirmarse que el patronato indiano fue el más amplio concedido a rey alguno. El regalismo se toca, y a veces se confunde, con la Ilustración y el liberalismo, cuando se trata de planear qué se hace con los bienes de la Iglesia. El regalismo puede, incluso, ser el origen de una política desamortizadora que se considere primero ilustrada y luego liberal. El liberalismo en la Europa continental parece la consecuencia natural de la Ilustración. La "razón" abrió el sendero de la "libertad". El nuevo grupo encontró su acomodo en la organización burocrática, en las asambleas parlamentarias, las magistraturas e incluso, si era el caso, a la cabeza de la República; sólo le hacía falta ejercer libremente los derechos que desde tiempo atrás comenzaron a postularse como inherentes al ser humano individualmente considerado. Poco o poco se fue consolidando el poder de este grupo que se apoyaba en el postulado de la libertad natural del hombre para pensar, escribir, elegir su credo religioso, contratar, producir y decidir la forma en que debía tener el Estado del cual formaba parte.

El liberalismo

El origen del liberalismo como doctrina y como programa político podría situarse en la Inglaterra revolucionaria del siglo XVII. La inglesa es la primera revolución burguesa de los tiempos modernos. Sus aspiraciones pueden condensarse en unas cuantas propuestas: exigencia de libertades para el hombre individualmente considerado, tolerancia religiosa, constitucionalismo y garantía de derechos políticos. Poco a poco se irían incorporando a estas propuestas la teoría y la práctica de la libertad económica. El liberalismo sería, pues, un conjunto de ideas, métodos y prácticas cuyo objetivo común era lograr una libertad mayor para los individuos. Esta libertad individual había de reivindicarse frente a los gobernantes o corporaciones, que eran quienes la limitaban. En el continente, el liberalismo fue asumiendo peculiaridades propias en cada uno de los lugares en que fue adoptado como credo político o económico.

Al tiempo que se producía en Inglaterra la primera de las revoluciones burguesas, en el continente europeo se difundía, cada vez más, una serie de ideas que a la larga conducirían también a la adopción del ideario liberal. Las estructuras políticas y económicas de la Europa continental se transformaron más lentamente que las inglesas, y antes de entrar de lleno a las corrientes liberales, transitaron por los burocráticos vericuetos del despotismo ilustrado. Los gobernantes del continente buscaron gobernar con "la razón" las monarquías que se fueron constituyendo entre los siglos XVII y XVIII en varios lugares del continente europeo.

Muchos de los postulados ilustrados desembocaron en el ideario liberal en el cual fueron llevados hasta sus últimas consecuencias sobre todo en la propia Inglaterra y Francia. En forma muy esquemática podría afirmarse que en estas naciones se encontraban los prototipos del liberalismo hasta que el liderazgo fue adquirido por los Estados Unidos de América. Para caracterizar en unas cuantas palabras a estos liberalismos podría decirse que el inglés fue sobre todo económico, en tanto que el francés fue más social y político. Inglaterra y Francia fueron los ejemplos a seguir para consequir la "modernización" de las estructuras. A su vez, la Revolución francesa fue el origen de la reacción conservadora de los reyes y los grupos de la sociedad que veían amenazado su poder por la mera difusión de las ideas y los logros revolucionarios.

En el terreno de las relaciones entre la Iglesia y el Estado tanto los ilustrados como los regalistas piensan en una Iglesia conducida por un Estado, normalmente de cuño católico. En ese contexto la adopción de una política desamortizadora no necesariamente es un acto anticlerical ya que incluso puede contarse con la anuencia de la Iglesia. En tanto que en el seno del liberalismo, la idea de la libertad de cultos y el interés por la secularización, puede llevar a la constitución de un clero de Estado, e incluso se contempla la posibilidad de constituir un Estado laico. En este contexto, la desamortización de bienes de la Iglesia no necesariamente contaba con su anuencia, es más, podía ser incluso contraria a dicha institución.

En forma breve, ha quedado perfilado el contexto en el que se movían unos y otros.

La Nueva España y el México Independiente

De este lado del Atlántico las ideas y las instituciones que tenían su cuna en algún lugar de Europa adquirían su propio perfil, el cual estaba dado por las condiciones en las que tenían que operar. Esta advertencia es útil y permite dejar de lado las periodizaciones que se han establecido para explicar el desarrollo del pensamiento y las instituciones europeas.

Hay coincidencias, por supuesto, pero es mejor conformar los distintos períodos en relación directa a los acontecimientos locales.

La Ilustración novohispana estaría dividida, según ha explicado Roberto Moreno, en cuatro etapas: Antecedentes, 1745-1767; Etapa criolla, 1768-1788; Etapa oficial o española, 1788-1803; y Etapa de síntesis. Para este autor el corolario está en la Independencia, la cual, a su juicio, no termina con el pensamiento ilustrado, ya que "las generaciones formadas en las etapas anteriores actúan dentro de los marcos de esa corriente, cuyas manifestaciones se prolongan con fuerza hasta mediados del siglo XIX".[8]

El modelo que elaboró Roberto Moreno se basa en el desarrollo del pensamiento científico de manera que las etapas podrían variar un poco si estudiamos otras áreas del conocimiento. Pero, para la explicación del asunto que nos ocupa lo que interesa destacar es la supervivencia del pensamiento ilustrado en las primeras décadas de la nación mexicana. El interés por constatar su presencia radica sobre todo en la necesidad de explicarnos la actuación "regalista" de buena parte de los líderes mexicanos. Si la Ilustración sobrevive en otros terrenos, la hipótesis que aquí se maneja se fortalece, pero para los fines de este ensayo es suficiente constatar la presencia del "regalismo", aunque ya no haya monarca.

Al lado del pensamiento ilustrado comenzó a desarrollarse el liberal. Para México se han señalado por Jesús Reyes Heroles, dos etapas: La de los orígenes, 1808-1824; y la de las realizaciones, 1824-1857. De esta última etapa el autor ha dicho que se podría extender hasta 1873, año en que se otorga nivel constitucional a las Leyes de Reforma.[9]

Para Reyes Heroles el liberalismo no se da en una sola línea, ni abarca una sola materia. Distingue el liberalismo económico y social del político jurídico. En el primero el autor ubica a la propiedad y a la disyuntiva: libre cambio-proteccionismo; y en el segundo encuadra las libertades, la secularización de la sociedad, la vinculación con la democracia y la identidad liberalismo-federalismo.[10]

Vista así la cuestión queda claro que en México coexistieron la Ilustración y el liberalismo, por lo menos, dos décadas. La primera se hallaba en su ocaso y el segundo en sus orígenes cuando sobrevino la independencia.

[8]Roberto Moreno, *Joaquín Velázquez de León y sus trabajos científicos en el Valle de México, 1773-1775* (México: UNAM, 1977), 13-17.

[9]Jesús Reyes Heroles, *El liberalismo mexicano*, 3 vols. (México: Fondo de Cultura Económica, 1974).

[10]Ibid., passim.

Liberales e ilustrados

Tanto en España como en América entre la Ilustración y el liberalismo hubo siempre una diferencia de método. A los ilustrados les interesaba mejorar sin revolucionar; no eran afectos a la rebelión y censuraban toda postura que la implicara. El hombre de la Ilustración quedó espantado con la Revolución francesa, sobre todo tras la muerte de la familia real.[11] El liberalismo, por el contrario, es revolucionario y en su versión francesa, anticatólico. Su fuente de inspiración está en los movimientos revolucionarios de los burgueses europeos y uno de sus objetivos fue la delimitación de las facultades de la Iglesia y las del Estado.

En España el liberalismo pudo abrirse camino gracias a la invasión napoleónica, la cual resultó la coyuntura ideal para buscar la modificación de las estructuras. Incluso los partidarios del absolutismo tuvieron que aceptar algunos cambios ya que si la soberanía se reflejaba completa en el rey, y éste la cedía al francés, los súbditos habrían tenido que obedecer.[12] Sin embargo, sólo los liberales se adhirieron al concepto de la soberanía nacional, no así los ilustrados y los afrancesados.[13] De todas maneras el primer liberalismo español no fue muy lejos en la mayoría de sus planteamientos[14] y menos aún en los que aquí nos interesan, los de las relaciones entre la Iglesia y el Estado. Sobre este particular Emilio La Parra López afirma que

> El primer liberalismo expañol tuvo que acomodar a la realidad del país sus principios ideológicos. Esto le obligó a ciertas incongruencias en algunas ocasiones, en especial en el terreno religioso. Hubo que renunciar a la libertad de creencias porque el pueblo no asimilaría de buen grado esta innovación, porque las fuerzas conservadoras pesaban mucho y porque de adoptar este principio las disputas teológicas subsiguientes podrían obstaculizar todo intento renovador. Tampoco pretendió nuestro primer liberalismo diferenciar a la Iglesia del Estado y de la sociedad. En parte su excesiva dependencia del regalismo ilustrado impedía atisbar una vía diferenciadora. . . .[15]

[11]María Esther Martínez Quinteiro, *Los grupos liberales antes de las Cortes de Cádiz* (Madrid: Narcea, S.A. de Editores, 1977), 98.

[12]Ibid., 187–189.

[13]Ibid., 99–100.

[14]*Colección de decretos y órdenes de las Cortes de Cádiz*, 2 vols. (Madrid: Publicaciones de las Cortes Generales, 1987); María Cruz Seoane, *El primer lenguaje constitucional español* (*Las Cortes de Cádiz*), prólogo de Rafael Lapesa (Madrid: Editorial Moneda y Crédito, 1968).

[15]Emilio La Parra López, *El primer liberalismo español y la Iglesia: las Cortes de Cádiz*, prólogo de Antonio Mestre Sandchis (Alicante, España: Instituto de Estudios Juan Gil Albert, 1985), 64–65.

Algo semejante, pero más agudo, se presentó en la Nueva España y en el México Independiente. Las ideas ilustradas habían penetrado ampliamente en ciertos grupos de la sociedad colonial. Algunas de ellas se llevaron a sus últimas consecuencias durante la insurrección y en la elaboración de los cuerpos jurídicos de los insurgentes, sobre todo en los que elaborarían José María Morelos y los hombres que lo seguían.[16] Ellos plasmaron en textos que estaban destinados a ser de observancia general el concepto de la soberanía del pueblo, que es el de Rousseau y no el de Cádiz; el de la igualdad de las clases sociales, el cual no se aceptó en Cádiz; y el sufragio universal directo y secreto, que no formó parte de ningún texto constitucional del siglo XIX incluyendo a la Constitucíon de Cádiz. Asimismo garantizaron la propiedad y la seguridad.[17] Estas ideas tan radicales sólo volvieron a plasmarse juntas en la Constitución de 1857.

Una vez sofocada la insurgencia el país fue entrando por una vía más conforme y consecuente con lo que había sido su pasado. La insurrección fue quedando atrás, y sus consecuencias no siempre parecían tan favorables. En una posición un poco extremosa Lucas Alamán afirmaba que

> Esta horrenda revolución es sin embargo, la que se ha querido que la república mejicana reconozca por su cuna. Los individuos que la promovieron no sólo no hicieron la independencia, sino que la retardaron e impidieron y con los principios que propagaron fueron causa de que cuando llegó a verificarse, no ha producido ninguno de los frutos que debía, y no ha sido para la nación mejicana más que un fuente continua de desgracias. . . . [18]

Si seguimos a Martínez Quinteiro en lo que afirma de los ilustrados, podríamos decir que después de la independencia se buscó "mejorar" sin "revolucionar" y que los actores de esta búsqueda fueron, sobre todo, los mexicanos que habían nacido en la "última Nueva España". Entre ellos se encuentran Alamán, Couto, Gómez Farías, Mora, Zavala y muchos más. Todos ellos un poco liberales, sobre todo en materia económica, y un poco ilustrados e incluso conservadores en lo que se refiere a educación, representación, propiedad y otros temas. Ven en la educación el remedio a los males de su patria, al igual que los ilustrados. Buscan modernizar las estructuras políticas de la nación pero sin marcar una clara preferencia por una forma de gobierno determinada ya que todos aceptaron la monarquía constitucional moderada de Agustín de Iturbide y en sus escritos no desdeñan la monarquía como opción posible y viable para el gobierno

[16]Decreto Constitucional para la libertad de la América Mexicana", en Felipe Tena Ramírez, *Leyes fundamentales de México, 1808-1975*, 6a. ed. (México: Porrúa, 1975).

[17]La mera revisión de los artículos correspondientes a estos temas en los diversos textos constitucionales y proyectos de constitución permite confirmar este aserto; ver Tena Ramírez, *Leyes fundamentales*, passim.

[18]Lucas Alamán, *Historia de Méjico*, 5 vols. (México: Editorial Jus, 1942), II, 212.

de su patria. Estos hombres no admitían cabalmente la igualdad entre los mexicanos porque lo que veían los había convencido de que era impracticable; al no admitirla, no podían conceder que el sufragio fuera universal, secreto y directo. Por último, cabe señalar que respecto de las relaciones entre la Iglesia y el Estado, aunque estuvieran en pro de la separación de ambas potestades quedaba claro que tal cosa se haría en el seno de un Estado católico en el que la intolerancia religiosa fuera la regla. En general pensaban que la Iglesia debía reducir su participación en la sociedad en forma voluntaria.

Todas estas ideas están plasmadas tanto en los escritos de los autores mencionados y otros más, como en los textos constitucionales, planes y pronunciamientos políticos anteriores a la invasión norteamericana. Parecería que este último hecho llevó a la radicalización de las posiciones. Quizá un factor importante fue el ingreso a la lucha política de nuevos protagonistas y la muerte de otros. Otro factor importante debió ser la oposición radical y violenta de la Iglesia para colaborar en la constitución de un Estado basado en ideas y prácticas contrarias al derecho natural. No debe olvidarse que para la doctrina cristiana la base de la sociedad está constituida por la familia y no por el individuo.

Ilustrados y regalistas

En la Nueva España siempre había existido una identidad de miras entre el Estado y la Iglesia. Las Bulas por las que se otorgó el Patronato insistieron una y otra vez en la necesidad de convertir a los naturales y de extender las fronteras del cristianismo. Asimismo se hacía énfasis en que a los reyes de Castilla y de León se les otorgaba el mandato apostólico para conseguir dichos fines.[19] Las Indias deberían quedar al margen de las cruentas luchas religiosas europeas y conservarse como bastión del catolicismo, al igual que lo era en la península, la naciente monarquía hispánica. A las Indias, pues, no debían pasar moros, ni judíos, ni conversos, ni ningún sospechoso de heterodoxia religiosa. Pero, esta política se volvió impracticable al tiempo que comenzaron a llegar los barcos con los libros, folletos y pasquines que contenían las ideas ilustradas y liberales y las tesis condenadas como heréticas por una Iglesia que para comienzos del siglo XIX se hallaba en franca defensa de su poder político frente a los cada vez más poderosos monarcas europeos.[20]

[19]Alberto de la Hera, *El regalismo borbónico en su proyección indiana* (Madrid: Ediciones Rialp, 1963), "La legislación del S. XVIII sobre el patronato Indiano, en *Anuario de Historia del Derecho Español* 40 (1970); Rafael Gómez Hoyos, *La Iglesia de América en las Leyes de Indiás*, (Madrid: Instituto Gonzalo Fernández de Oviedo, Instituto de Cultura Hispánica de Bogotá, 1961).

[20]Roberto Moreno, "Un caso de censura de libros en el siglo XVIII novohispano: Jorge Mas Theóphoro", *Suplementos al Boletín del Instituto de Investigaciones Bibliográficas* (México: UNAM, 1978); Monelisa Pérez Marchand, *Dos etapas ideológicas del siglo XVIII en México a través de los papeles de la Inquisición* (México: El Colegio de México, 1945).

A lo largo de la época colonial el Patronato de la Iglesia en Indias había correspondido al Rey, y era ejercido en América por varios vicepatronos. Las Leyes de Indias recogen la real cédula de Felipe II de 1 de junio de 1574 en la que se afirmaba:

> Por cuanto el derecho de Patronato Eclesiástico nos pertenece en todo el Estado de las Indias, así por haberse descubierto y adquirido aquel Nuevo Mundo, edificado y dotado en él las Iglesias y monasterios a nuestra costa y de los señores Reyes Católicos nuestros antecesores, como por habérsenos concedido por Bulas de los Sumos Pontífices de su propio motu, para su conservación y de la justicia que a él tenemos. Ordenamos y mandamos, que este derecho de Patronazgo de las Indias único e isolidum siempre sea reservado a Nos y a nuestra Real Corona, y no pueda salir de ella en todo ni en parte, y por gracia, merced, privilegio o cualquier otra disposición que Nos o los Reyes nuestros sucesores hiciéremos o concediéremos, no sea visto que concedemos derecho de Patronazgo a persona alguna, Iglesia ni Monasterio, ni perjudicarnos en el dicho derecho de Patronazgo (ley 1, títulos V, libro I, *Recopilación de Indias*).

El derecho de Patronato de los Reyes no se cuestionó nunca, y a su amparo, los soberanos pudieron intervenir en una forma muy amplia en todas aquellas cuestiones de la vida de la Iglesia indiana que no tuvieran que ver con el dogma religioso. Al monarca le tocaba decidir qué órdenes religiosas pasaban a las Indias, cuántos conventos se levantaban, cuántos curatos podía haber, cuáles eran los candidatos a las sedes vacantes, etc.

Estos hechos se corresponden cronológicamente con la lucha dentro del seno de la propia Iglesia por decretar la infalibilidad del Papa, lo cual se consigue hasta el primer Concilio Vaticano, en 1870, con el Papa Pío IX. A este pontífice le correspondió también la promulgación del *Sylabus* de 1864, texto en el que finalmente se condenan todos los errores que había perseguido la Iglesia desde la aparición de las corrientes reformistas y de las principales ideas ilustradas. Ahí se condena todo aquello que habían venido sosteniendo los jansenistas, los regalistas, los panteístas, los racionalistas, los socialistas y los comunistas y los miembros de las sociedades secretas, bíblicas y clérico liberales.[21] Muchas de estas tesis no habían sido condenadas anteriormente, sobre todo las que se referían a la intervención del Soberano temporal en asuntos de la Iglesia. Estas tesis se habían mantenido siempre dentro de la más pura ortodoxia religiosa[22] aunque a

[21]Enrique Denzinger, *El magisterio de la Iglesia* (Barcelona: Editorial Herdes, 1963), 404–413.

[22]Conde de Campomanes, *Tratado de la regalía de amortización* (edición facsimil), estudio preliminar de Francisco Tomás y Valiente (Madrid: Ediciones de la Revista de Trabajo, 1975). De sumo interés resulta consultar los dictámenes tanto civiles como eclesiásticos, los cuales son muestra de la ortodoxia del texto, pp. 287–296.

medida que el patronato se fue convirtiendo en vicariato, los textos de los autores regalistas se fueron incorporando al Indice de libros prohibidos por la Iglesia.[23] De cualquier manera, no se excolmugó a ningún rey por el ejercicio del Patronato por amplio que fuera.

A medida que crecía el poder real se fue perfilando un conjunto de doctrinas que reivindicaba para el soberano facultades que habían correspondido a la Iglesia en educación, salubridad pública, atención de las clases menos favorecidas de la sociedad y muchas otras. En materia de las relaciones Iglesia y Estado a las tesis que preconizaban la superioridad del último sobre la primera se les llamó regalistas. Regalías eran las atribuciones que en determinado asunto correspondían en forma *exclusiva* al soberano. Regalía fue, pues, su intervención en los asuntos de la Iglesia antes de que se admitiera en forma amplia que el monarca era el vicario de Dios en el reino. Esta idea ya estaba presente en el texto de las Partidas pero tocó a los reyes borbones hacerla efectiva en el terreno de la praxis política.

Al amparo de todas estas ideas comenzo la "modernización" del Estado español con muy buenos augurios. Este proceso encontró en la península graves obstáculos en las "clases" tradicionalmente privilegiadas, la nobleza y la Iglesia, y en las corporaciones del más diverso signo.[24]

De acuerdo a los postulados ilustrados la modernización implicaba no sólo reivindicar para el Estado facultades que habían correspondido a diversas corporaciones y estamentos de la sociedad sino también modificar las bases de sustentación del propio Estado. Los vasallos tenían que ser iguales frente al aparato estatal a fin de que éste les fijara a todos las reglas para comerciar, tributar, elegir representantes, etc. A cambio de haber cedido una buena parte de sus privilegios los vasallos participarían en la formulación de las leyes y la administración pública y de justicia por derecho propio y no por delegación de facultades. La Iglesia misma tendría que dejar de lado buena parte de sus privilegios y estar sometida a un estatuto semejante al del resto de los vasallos. Este planteamiento implicaba que los bienes de la Iglesia debían ser tratados como los demás bienes; su falta de circulación era un obstáculo para la prosperidad del Estado. La

[23]Juan de Solórzano Pereira, *Política indiana sacada en lengua castellana de los dos tomos del Derecho y gobierno municipal de las Indias occidentales* . . . (Madrid, 1647). Hay varias reimpresiones antiguas de este texto que figuró en el Indice de libros prohibidos, 1736 y 1803, y varias contemporáneas, 1930, 1972. Las antiguas muestran que tuvo amplia circulación a pesar de la prohibición que existía en su contra.

[24]Para una panorámica de las doctrinas pactistas puede verse Luis Legaz y Lacambra et al., *Et pactismo en la historia de España (Simposio)* (Madrid: Artes Gráficas Soler, 1980), y para la doctrina del contrato social lo mejor es consultar al propio Juan Jacobo Rousseau, *El contrato social*, traducción del francés por Consuelo Berges, prólogo de Antonio Rodríguez Huescar, 7a. edición, Biblioteca de Iniciación Filosófica (Buenos Aires: Aguilar, 1965).

desamortización debía comprender los bienes de todas las corporaciones tanto las civiles como los religiosas. En España, el proceso desamortizador se inició con las primeras. No sucedió lo mismo en la Nueva España.

Desamortización de bienes de corporaciones civiles y religiosas

Hasta aquí se han explicado las características fundamentales del pensamiento ilustrado, regalista y liberal tomando como punto de partida las relaciones de la Iglesia y el Estado. La razón para proceder así es que en este tema se presentaron las posiciones más radicalizadas en los casos que se atacaron normas que desde tiempos muy remotos formaban parte del bagaje jurídico de la Iglesia.

Un anómino católico mexicano lo explicaba de la siguiente manera en 1858, año en que las posiciones sobre este particular se encontraban especialmente radicalizadas.

> [En el concilio segundo de Aquisgrán, Aix de la Chapelle, 836 d.C. se hizo la deducción siguiente] . . . . Porque en verdad sabemos perfectamente que Cristo y su Iglesia son una misma persona y por consiguiente, *las cosas que son de la Iglesia, son de Cristo; lo que se quita a la Iglesia, se quita sin duda alguna al mismo Cristo.* La Iglesia había de poseer dinero; y por lo mismo predios, derecho de propiedad e innumerables ornamentos de toda especie. . . .[25]

Poco antes de que el texto anterior se escribiera habían sido promulgadas las llamadas Leyes de Reforma entre las que se hallaba la de desamortización de fincas urbanas y rústicas de corporaciones civiles y religiosas, y la de nacionalización de bienes de la Iglesia. Estas leyes encontraban su origen último en la política que bajo el signo de la Ilustración y las doctrinas regalistas iniciaron los reyes de la dinastía borbónica con el fin de mejorar el estado general del reino.

Tomás y Valiente ha estudiado el marco político de la desamortización en España y en su análisis ve con claridad cómo se fue radicalizando esa política a medida que crecía la deuda pública. La desamortización se había visto como provechosa, pero los teóricos del asunto recomendaron comenzarla por los bienes concejiles y esperar a convencer a la Iglesia de que colaborara con la monarquía en el proceso desamortizador, en el entendido de que se defendía a un gobierno católico a carta cabal.[26]

[25]"Un católico mexicano," *La Cruz* 7:6 (25 de marzo 1858), 172.

[26]Francisco Tomás y Valiente, *El marco político de la desamortización en España*, 2a. ed. (Barcelona: Ediciones Ariel, 1972), 12–37.

El déficit de la Hacienda Pública llevó a Carlos IV, apoyado por la Santa Sede, a legislar para conseguir que algunos de los bienes de manos muertas, incluidos los de la Iglesia, se subastaran en beneficio del erario público. Pío VII expidió un Breve en 1806 por el cual concedió al rey la facultad de enajenar "la séptima parte de los predios pertenecientes a las iglesias, monasterios, conventos, comunidades, fundaciones y a otras cualesquiera personas eclesiásticas, incluso los bienes patrimoniales de las cuatro Ordenes Militares y la de San Juan de Jeruzalén", todo aplicado a cambio de la venta del 3 por ciento "a la extinción de vales reales y al socorro de las urgentísimas necesidades de la monarquía".[27]

No es este el lugar para explicar el camino que siguió la desamortización española de los bienes eclesiásticas, la cual incluso en las Cortes de Cádiz fue planteada en forma muy tibia ya que sólo los bienes de la Inquisición pasaron al patrimonio del Estado. Interesa solamente hacer hincapié en el espíritu de colaboración que tenía la Iglesia frente a la desamortización de parte de sus bienes en beneficio de la monarquía hispánica, la cual para principios del siglo XIX era uno de los pocos baluartes del catolicismo en Europa.

La Nueva España y el Mexico Independiente

En la Nueva España la cuestión se planteó sobre las mismas bases que tenía en el resto de la monarquía y este fue el espíritu que embargó a los hombres que se ocuparon del asunto durante las primeras décadas de vida independiente.

Una vez conseguida la emancipación política se tenía que empezar a constituir un *Nuevo Estado* en lo que había sido el virreinato de la Nueva España. Los mexicanos eran católicos todos y pensaron que la Iglesia colaboraría en la construcción del nuevo ente y así habría sucedido si no se hubieran planteado algunas propuestas de origen ilustrado que se fueron convirtiendo en liberales y que dejaban fuera a la Iglesia. Por otra parte, la Santa Sede no reconoció la independencia hasta que el propio monarca español la sancionó. Este hecho tuvo consecuencias incalculables ya que los mexicanos que habían vivido en la "última Nueva España" estaban familiarizados con la práctica del regalismo y comenzaron a actuar conforme a ella ejerciendo, de facto, el Patronato. Esto es, proponer candidatos a las sedes vacantes, presentar personas aptas para todos los beneficios mayores y menores, religiosos y seculares, dar el *placet* para la aplicación de la legislación pontificia, celebrar concordatos, etc.

[27]Ibid., 38–42.

La Santa Sede tenía otra idea sobre el particular y en consecuencia obstaculizó la tarea de los primeros gobiernos mexicanos[28] y fue radicalizando su posición a medida que del regalismo se transitó al liberalismo.

De 1825 es el texto de Bernardo Couto, *Disertación sobre la naturaleza y límites de la autoridad eclesiástica*,[29] en el que se ocupa de esta cuestión dentro de la más pura teoría regalista. Este texto fue criticado por Florentino Mercado por contener opiniones "demasiado libres y hasta hostiles a la Santa Sede" y sostener la tesis de la "independencia de la autoridad de los obispos relativamente al santo padre de Roma".[30] Hay que recordar para extender este párrafo que Mercado era liberal, y para esos años Couto era conservador.

Años después el propio Couto escribió un texto muy distinto del que escribiera en su juventud. En este nuevo texto titulado *Discurso sobre la Constitución de la Iglesia*[31] ya se incorporan las tesis preconizadas en esos tiempos por la Santa Sede y la Iglesia universal sobre intolerancia, desamortización, supremacía del Papa sobre los obispos, etc. De su obra de juventud Couto decía que los excesos en que cayó sólo podían entenderse en función de la época que se vivía.

> Lo único que puede explicar el hecho es el vértigo general que entonces se había apoderado de las cabezas, y cuyos amargos resultados demasiado ha sentido la República. De ese vértigo queda una prueba visible en el dictamen de los tres censores que calificaron la disertación y le aplicaron el premio. Todas eran personas caracterizadas y de no vulgar ciencia; dos eran eclesiásticos en edad provecta, y uno constituido en dignidad. En el público nadie alzó

[28]Jaime E. Rodríguez O., "The Conflict between the Church and the State in Early Republican Mexico," *New World* 2 (1987), 93–112; Anne Staples, *La Iglesia en la primera república federal mexicana (1824–1835)*, traducción de Andrés Lira (México: SEP, 1976 [Sep Setentas No. 237]); y Anne Staples, "Secularización: Estado e Inglesia en tiempo de Gómez Farías", *Estudios de Historia Moderna y Contemporánea de México* 10, 109–123.

[29]Couto, *Disertación.*

[30]Florentino Mercado, *Libro de los Códigos o prenociones sintéticas de codificación romana, canónica, española y mexicana, por . . . , ministro del Superior Tribunal del Distrito. Obra necesaria para emprender el estudio de Leyes, de Cánones y de Teología: util aún a los que no profesan ninguna de las tres ciencias designadas, siempre que quieran tener idea histórica y exacta de los Cuerpos del Dcrecho, de las partes de que se compone, de su prelación y del modo antiguo y moderno conque se citan o alegan. Todo lo cual se facilita con el auxilio de numerosas listas de Abreviaturas, de un Glosario de voces anticuadas, y de las Tablas de Correspondencia de la Nueva y Novísma Recopilación del Derecho Romano, Canónico y Español* (México: Imprenta de Vicente G. Torres, Calle de San Juan de Letrán núm. 3, 1857), 853 y ss.

[31]Bernardo Couto, *Discurso sobre la constitución de la Iglesia* (México: Imprenta de Andrade y Escalante, 1857).

la voz contra ella. Tal era el imperio del error, que para decir verdad venía ya de años atrás, y no tenía por cuna a México.[32]

Por esos mismos años José María Luis Mora, eclesiástico, habiá escrito la famosa *Disertación sobre la naturaleza y aplicación de las ventas y bienes eclesiásticos*[33] en la que sostenía que la Iglesia es cuerpo místico y como tal no tiene necesidad, ni puede tener bienes temporales. La propiedad de los bienes la adquiría como comunidad política y como tal, debía sujetarse a las reglas del lugar en que se asienta, las cuales son dictadas por los reyes y emperadores.[34]

Años después, cuando algunos de los regalistas se hicieron conservadores, como Bernardo Couto, y otros se hicieron liberales como el propio Mora o Luis de la Rosa, el asunto de la propiedad de la Iglesia ya no era materia de interpretación y, o se admitía que no era posible desamortizarlos, en cuyo caso se estaba con la tesis conservadora, o se propugnaba por lo contrario, y se estaba con los liberales. El famoso obispo de Michoacán Clemente de Jesús Munguía planteaba el asunto en los términos siguientes:

> Varias son las formas y distintos los aspectos bajo los cuales se pueden considerar los bienes del clero y las propiedades; pero de cualquier modo que se miren, siempre será cierto que la universal propiedad de ellos es sagrada y respetable para los que creen y siguen el Evangelio de Jesús, y que sus derechos son inajenables e imprescriptibles como los de otro cualquiera.[35]

El obispo insiste una y otra vez en que estos bienes no pueden ser de la nación ya que "pertenecen al cuerpo de toda la Iglesia; de forma que faltando uno u otro cuerpo particular, sus bienes y propiedades deben quedar sujetos a las leyes de la propiedad del clero, como propiedad que son de todo él".[36]

Por esos mismos años en el periódico "exclusivemente religioso" *La Cruz* se denunciaban las tesis "regalistas" como contrarias al pensamiento católico[37] y J. J. Pesado, conservador de pura cepa, enlistaba las tesis en

[32]José Bernardo Couto, *Obras del doctor D. . . .* , tomo I, Opúsculos Varios (México: Imp. de V. Agüeros, Editor, 1898), xviii y xix.

[33]Mora, *Disertación.*

[34]María del Refugio González, prólogo a *Revista Política*, de José María Luis Mora, xii y xiii.

[35]Clemente Munguía, *Del Derecho Natural en sus principios comunes y en sus diversas ramificaciones, o sea, curso elemental de derecho natural y de gentes, público, político, constitucional, principios de legislación por el Lic. . . .* , 4 vols. (México: Imprenta de la Voz de la Religión, Calle de San José el Real, No. 13, 1849). Cita procede de tomo IV, pp. 327–238.

[36]Ibid., 328.

[37]Algunos artículos muy interesantes son los de J. J. Pesado aparecidos en *La Cruz* entre 1857 y 1858: "Controversia pacífica sobre la nueva constitución política"

que se contenía la doctrina recta, y con las que se daba por tierra a las exóticas y absurdas paradojas del regalismo:

1. La Iglesia tiene un gobierno propio, independiente en todo el poder civil
2. El gobierno de la Iglesia, por su propia condución, es santo, es perfecto, es inalterable y es perpetuo
3. Los gobiernos temporales son, por su naturaleza, profanos, imperfectos, mudables y perecederos
4. La Iglesia influye en el bien intrínseco del Estado: ningún Estado, por poderoso que sea, influye en el bien intrínseco de la Iglesia
5. La protección que el Estado dispense a la Iglesia es rigurosamente obligatoria: las remuneraciones honoríficas con que la Iglesia recompense a los gobernantes son meramente graciosas
6. La protección referida no da, ni puede dar en ningún caso, derecho de intervenir en la disciplina (ya se le de el nombre de interna, ya de externa) ni en el culto[38]

Antes de una década estas tesis serían simplemente reaccionarias y la Iglesia y el Estado se verían obligados a dar nuevas bases a su relación. Del regalismo quedaría la tesis, convertida en norma jurídica constitucional en 1917, de que los bienes de la Iglesia son del dominio directo de la nación.

(tomo V. no. 4, junio de 1857, 97–103); "Controversia. Reflexiones sobre la Iglesia y el Estado" (tomo V, no. 8, 2 julio de 1857, 233–241); "Controversia. Cuestiones sociales y religiosas" (tomo VI, no. 1, 1 de octubre de 1857, 1–7); "Controversia. Observaciones sobre la verdadera ciencia política, V. La Soberanía" (tomo VII, no. 3, 4 de marzo de 1858, 65–71); "Controversia. Observaciones sobre la verdadera ciencia política, VIII. Las Leyes humanas" (tomo VII, no. 5, 18 de marzo de 1858, 129–135). Por supuesto que no son los únicos, pero sí son representativos del pensamiento conservador propiamente dicho.

[38]J. J. Pesado, "Controversia. Reflexiones sobre la Iglesia," 240–241.

El pensamiento económico moderno en el México independiente

Beatriz Urías Horcasitas

Como muchos de sus contemporáneos, Lorenzo de Zavala llegó a considerar la ruptura con España como un cambio brusco para el que la sociedad novohispana no estaba todavía preparada. En su opinión, "una variación gradual y progresiva hubiera sido más natural y sin los sacudimientos que han experimentado todas las naciones al hacer estas violentas transiciones". Y añadió que "México se colocó en una falsa posición al pasar repentinamente del régimen colonial al de un sistema democrático cuyas bases esenciales son la instrucción popular, las costumbres, y la cómoda subsistencia y fácil modo de vivir de las masas".[1]

Para los liberales mexicanos, la consolidación del Estado moderno no dependía únicamente de las transformaciones políticas y jurídicas que habían sido iniciadas a partir de la independencia, sino también de la modernización de una sociedad con costumbres y formas de vida tradicionales. El proceso de modernización de la sociedad colonial estuvo vinculado a dos elementos —la educación utilitaria[2] y el enriquecimiento de las mayorías— que habían sido planteados en el contexto del proyecto reformista que los Borbones aplicaron en España y las colonias americanas en el último tercio del siglo XVIII.[3]

La transformación de la condición moral y económica del hombre colonial enfrentó, sin embargo, repetidos obstáculos durante los primeros años de vida independiente. Las fuerzas que representaban el antiguo orden

[1]Lorenzo de Zavala, *Memoria de la gestión del gobierno del Estado de México, 30 de marzo de 1833, Fondo Reservado, Colección Lafragua*, v. 473.

[2]B. Urías, "Educación para la democracia: el Ateneo Mexicano (1840-1852)", *Estudios*, (Instituto Tecnológico Autónomo de México), No. 12 (primavera de 1988).

[3]José Luis Aranguren ha señalado que las ideas acerca de la "*felicidad* secularizada como *bienestar* y de la *educación en función del desarrollo*" que animaron la política del despotismo ilustrado fueron reformuladas por los liberales a lo largo del siglo XIX y continúan estando en el centro de las preocupaciones del hombre contemporáneo. J. L. Aranguren, *Moral y sociedad: la moral española en el siglo XIX* (Taurus, Madrid, 1981), 168.

—fundamentalmente el clero y la milicia— oponían una resistencia feroz a un cambio que suponía la desaparición de fueros, privilegios y viejas jerarquías. Por otra parte, el rompimiento del modelo económico implantado por los Borbones en las postrimerías de la colonia y el empobrecimiento producido por diez años de guerra, habían sumido al país en una profunda crisis económica. La instauración del centralismo en 1836 puso además en peligro la experiencia política que había sido iniciada. Confrontados a esta situación, los liberales temieron que el Estado en formación no pudiera consolidarse, y que la sociedad mexicana —pobre, tradicional e ignorante— no pudiera vivir bajo un régimen democrático.

Algunos escritores, que probablemente estuvieron en contacto con las Sociedades Económicas de Amigos del País, abordaron estos problemas desde una perspectiva singular.[4] Utilizaron las ideas económicas que circulaban en México desde las postrimerías de la época colonial, para ofrecer una solución a la crisis por la que atravesaba el país después de la independencia.[5] Publicaron una folletería que tuvo un tiraje limitado y que aparentemente no presentó un punto de vista original en relación con el pensamiento económico europeo, cuyo interés radica en que a través del análisis de problemas coyunturales hizo aparecer una concepción del hombre en sociedad que paulatinamente revolucionó la vida del México independiente. Esta concepción planteaba que el trabajo individual —y por consiguiente, el ocio y la falta de ocupación productiva— era un asunto de interés público que excedía los límites de la esfera privada.[6]

[4]Las Sociedades Económicas de Amigos del País difundieron las ideas económicas europeas entre los miembros de la élite criolla hispanoamericana desde fines del siglo XVIII. En México, existió una sola Sociedad Económica después de la independencia, bajo el Imperio de Iturbide (1822). Sin embargo, el pensamiento económico también fue asimilado por los liberales moderados y algunos conservadores patriotas, a través de las logias masónicas y las asociaciones científicas y literarias. R. J. Shafer, *The Economic Societies in the Spanish World, 1763-1821* (Syracuse: Syracuse University Press, 1958).

[5]Eduardo Arcila Farías afirmó que los pensadores económicos hispanoamericanos del último tercio del siglo XVIII entrelazaron las doctrinas fisiocrática y mercantilista, con viejas tradiciones españolas y con instituciones típicamente indianas. Esto dio lugar a un pensamiento económico "híbrido" que no encajaba rigurosamente dentro de ninguna corriente. En términos generales, el pensamiento económico hispanoamericano fue más conservador que el español. Carlos III y sus colaboradores fueron vistos por muchos escritores indianos como innovadores irresponsables que inspiraban desconfianza. Por otra parte, existió un atraso en relación con la moda europea. En efecto, antes de la década de 1810 a 1820 es difícil encontrar elementos de la doctrina librecambista, ya que los criollos no podían concebir que el Estado dejara de intervenir en los asuntos económicos. E. Arcila Farías, *Reformas económicas del siglo XVIII en Nueva España*, Colección Sep Setentas, vols. 117 y 118 (México: Secretaría de Educación Pública, 1974); y *El pensamiento económico hispanoamericano en Baquijano y Carrillo* (Caracas: Consejo Nacional de la Cultura, Centro de Estudios Latinoamericanos Rómulo Gallegos, 1976).

[6]En otro contexto, Hannah Arendt ha señalado que esta concepción estuvo ligada a las transformaciones profundas que antecedieron la Revolución Industrial en Europea; en par-

La recepción del pensamiento económico europeo fue entusiasta, sin embargo su adaptación a las condiciones que prevalecían en México después de la independencia dio lugar a una serie de contradicciones. Este ensayo aborda algunas de ellas a través del análisis de cuatro problemas centrales: el trabajo productivo, el ocio, el interés individual y el papel del Estado en la vida económica.

"La nación jamás podrá ser feliz si su felicidad no la procuran todos y cada uno de sus individuos"[7]

Pensar el trabajo individual como un asunto público implicó concebir la prosperidad de la nación en relación con el esfuerzo de todos los ciudadanos, en vez de la acumulación de metales preciosos por parte del Estado. El imperativo de que la sociedad en su conjunto realizara un trabajo productivo se inscribía dentro de una nueva noción de la riqueza planteada por la economía política clásica en Europa.[8] En oposición a los mercantilistas, los clásicos asentaron que la riqueza estaba contenida en los bienes que resultaban del trabajo libre y productivo de la sociedad. Smith concibió el mercado como un complejo y gigantesco mecanismo social que hacía posible el intercambio del trabajo de los individuos, y además permitía que los intereses egoístas de todos y cada uno de los individuos fueran armonizados y hechos compatibles. Tomando en consideración que el mecanismo del mercado operaba independientemente de la voluntad de los agentes que en él intervenían, Smith atribuyó la armonización natural de intereses a la acción de una "mano invisible", que conducía a cada uno de los individuos "a promover un fin que no entraba en sus intenciones" y que, "al perseguir su propio interés, promueve el de la sociedad de una manera más efectiva que si esto entrara en sus designios".[9] El Estado veía

---

ticular, la división creciente del trabajo y la mecanización de la producción. H. Arendt, *On Human Condition* (Chicago: The University of Chicago Press, 1958).

[7]"Economia política", *El Farol*, periódico semanario de la Puebla de los Angeles en el Imperio Mexicano, domingo 2 de diciembre de 1821, p. 47.

[8]El surgimiento de la economia política clásica representa la culminación del proyecto de la filosofía política de los siglos XVII y XVIII; es decir, demostrar que la vida social descansa sobre principios inmanentes. El primero en formalizar los supuestos de la nueva corriente de pensamiento fue Adám Smith en *La riqueza de las naciones* (1776). Antes de esta obra, autores como Cantillon, Petty, Stewart y Quesnay contribuyeron a fijar las bases de esta nueva concepción de la sociedad. Entre 1815 y 1821, David Ricardo consolidó el prestigio de la economía política, elevándola a la categoría de disciplina científica. Autores como Mill, Say, Malthus y Torrens se inscriben dentro de la tradición iniciada por Smith y continuada por Ricardo.

[9]A. Smith, *Investigación sobre la naturaleza y causas de la riqueza de las naciones* (México: Fondo de Cultura Económica, 1981), 17.

limitada su esfera de acción al no poder intervenir en el terreno donde imperaban las leyes del interés individual, a riesgo de obstaculizar la acción conciliadora de la mano invisible. En efecto, la armonía social no provenía ya del control ejercido por el poder político sino del enriquecimiento que todos lograrían al vender e intercambiar.

La condición para que estos supuestos pudieran operar era que las llamadas "clases ociosas" —aquellas que no creaban riqueza— hubieran desaparecido. La folletería económica que se escribió en México durante los primeros años de vida independiente articuló dos interpretaciones acerca de la ociosidad de las clases menesterosas, cuya consecuencia más alarmante era un cuadro de pobreza generalizada.

Ociosidad y pobreza

Una Comisión Especial de Minería (1822) examinó el estado de la economía nacional después de la independencia. El informe atribuyó el "lánguido y moribundo estado" en que se encontraban "todos los ramos, todas las fuentes" de la riqueza pública a la fuga o a la destrucción de los capitales que circulaban en los últimos años de la época colonial.

> Inmensos capitales han sido presa de la más escandalosa rapiña, y los que se salvaron del naufragio general, buscaron los unos su seguridad refugiándose a países extraños, y los que permanecieron, condenados a la ociosidad más absoluta por falta de empleo, se extinguieron sucesivamente, como debió suceder.[10]

Este fenómeno se tradujo en una disminución de las inversiones, lo que provocó la falta de "ocupación a gran número de brazos, y con ella, los medios de conseguir su subsistencia y la de sus familias: de aquí la miseria y el empobrecimiento universal".[11]

La situación ya no parecía poder ser solucionada a través de un viejo paliativo —la beneficencia— que no hacía más que enmascarar la ociosidad y sus nefastas consecuencias. Se requería, por el contrario, atacar la raíz del problema y estimular el trabajo productivo de todos los ciudadanos. La Comisión recomendaba en este sentido

[10]"Exposición hecha por la Comisión Especial de Minería a la Soberana Junta Gubernativa, sobre la necesidad de fomentar este ramo principal de industria con la baja de derechos que propuso en su dictamen de 24 de octubre próximo pasado", Imprenta de don Mariano Zúñiga y Ontiveros (México 1822), 4, *Fondo Reservado, Colección Lafragua*, v. 745.

[11]Ibid., 5.

> abrir las fuentes de la riqueza pública, proporcionando a los cortos capitales que nos han quedado, negocios lucrativos que no sólo reemplacen la subsistencia que anticipan a los brazos que emplean, sino que además dejen ganancias con las cuales se habiliten para ocupar y dar subsistencia al mayor número de brazos, así es únicamente como puede animarse la ocupación general y volver a la vida al imperio casi exánime.[12]

La ociosidad de las clases populares fue por lo general atribuida a la falta de fuentes de trabajo, más que a la holgazanería. En este sentido, Diego Solís (1822) estableció una clara diferenciación entre los ricos ociosos "que sólo están comiendo lo que tienen", y los menesterosos que proliferaban entre las "innumerables familias de mis honrados paisanos que perecen, y no por vicios, sino porque los destinos que antes tenían, se han variado"[13] Dicho esto, la ociosidad de las clases menesterosas fue considerada una carga que pesaba injustamente sobre aquellos que tenían un medio de subsistencia.

> Un gran número de estos involuntarios ociosos, inutiliza así a todo el resto de habitantes quitándoles el bocado de la boca con la mendicidad, con el chasco, con el juego, con la estafa, con el robo y aun con el homicidio. Aun hay otro mal: que estos mismos hombres de bien deseando trabajar como es justo, se tiran a cualquier giro en que ven que otros comen y si éste (por ejemplo) era suficiente para sustentar a mil hombres, no siéndolo para tres mil, todos perecen; y esto mismo sucede en todo ejercicio.[14]

Solís señalaba que el ocio tenía además profundas repercusiones sobre la vida política, ya que "la pobreza sólo hace súbditos rebeldes y venales",[15] y concluía que el Estado se vería beneficiado con la creación de nuevas fuentes de trabajo.

A diferencia de Diego Solís, otros escritores plantearon que el ocio de las clases populares era deliberado y que el trabajo debía hacerse obligatorio. José María Quirós (1822) —líder de la corporación mercantil veracruzana— recomendaba aplicar a los ociosos fuertes sanciones que les hicieran cambiar de "conducta" y les inculcaran el sentido del interés individual, elemento central en la producción de riquezas.

[12] Ibid., 5.

[13] D. Solís, "Específico y único remedio de la pobreza del Imperio Mexicano", Oficina de don Urbano Sanromán, Guadalajara 1822, 3, *Fondo Reservado, Colección Lafragua*, v. 439.

[14] Ibid., 3–4.

[15] Ibid., 4.

> Despiértese en estos infelices el apego al interés propio y el amor al trabajo: oblígueseles a ser útiles en lugar de gravosos a la sociedad, destinándose a los presidios y al servicio de la marina nacional a los incorregibles, y privándoseles del carácter de ciudadanos a los ociosos, y que no usen siquiera camisa, pantalón o calzones como lo exige la honestidad pública, y poco a poco sacudirán su desidia y variarán de conducta; máxime si se les quitan los hijos para darles educación, ponerlos a oficio o en algún otro destino en que no tengan a la vista los malos ejemplos de los que les dieron el ser.[16]

Estas ideas entraban en contradicción con los supuestos elementales del pensamiento económico de los clásicos europeos. En primer lugar, porque la conducta humana —susceptible de ser modificada por medio de sanciones (jurídicas, morales)— no puede ser equiparada a la conducta económica que sólo responde a los estímulos que se derivan del interés individual. Por otra parte, porque este último sólo puede desarrollarse cuando el individuo se encuentra en absoluta libertad para elegir el trabajo que desea desempeñar. El sentido que se le dio a la noción del interés individual es más claro a la luz de la noción de propiedad.

El interés individual

Un trabajo presentado por Manuel Ortiz de la Torre (1825) en San Ildefonso analizó extensamente el tema del interés individual. De acuerdo con las premisas del pensamiento europeo, Ortiz de la Torre afirmó que la búsqueda irrestricta del beneficio personal era la clave de la prosperidad material de la sociedad. La intervención del Estado era innecesaria, al no tener éste un interés directo en acrecentar el capital.

> La autoridad pública sólo se ha establecido en las sociedades, para que se haga por su medio aquello que o no es posible, o no es conveniente, atendido el bien común, que los individuos en particular practiquen por sí mismos, entre lo que ciertamente no se comprende la industria productora. Todo lo contrario. Cuanto su misma naturaleza exige, que se dirija y ejecute por los individuos particulares, otro tanto resiste que se ejecute y dirija por la autoridad pública.[17]

El papel del poder político quedaba limitado a dar apoyo a la actividad económica de los agentes individuales. Esto se lograba, en primer lugar, garantizando la libertad del "hombre industrioso".

[16]J. M. Quirós, "Ideas políticas económicas de gobierno", Memoria de Instituto formada por el secretario de la Junta Gubernativa del Consulado de Veracruz, con cuya lectura han de abrirse sus sesiones en el año venidero de 1822 (Veracruz: Imprenta del Gobierno Imperial Mexicano de Priani y Socios, 1822), 34, *Fondo Reservado, Colección Lafragua*, v. 1487.

[17]Ibid., 5–6.

> Parece, pues, cierto que con tal que el hombre industrioso se encuentre libre para producir riquezas y entienda los modos de poderlo hacer, su interés individual, que es el resorte más seguro de las acciones humanas, lo impelerá con eficacia a solicitar brazos y capitales, a dedicarlos a las labores más ventajosas, y a tomar los arbitrios que sean conducentes al mayor lucro posible.[18]

En segundo lugar, removiendo los viejos obstáculos que entorpecían la libre producción de mercancías. En particular, "los reglamentos, aprendizajes y maestrías de las artes industriales que impiden ejercitarlas a todos los que en el caso de no existir tales trabas, lo verificarían, y quizá con mayor destreza y perfección".[19]

Al insistir en la importancia de que el "hombre industrioso" viera incentivado su interés personal por parte del Estado, Ortiz de la Torre subrayó la necesidad de "asegurar a los *empresarios* el goce pacífico de los productos de su trabajo, evitando mediante una buena legislación, una policía exacta y una recta administración de justicia, toda clase de ataques contra la *propiedad*".[20] Desde esta perspectiva, la noción de interés individual quedaba limitada a la problemática del "hombre industrioso", es decir el propietario.

La argumentación presentada por Ortiz de la Torre no es un caso aislado. En términos generales, los escritores económicos de la primera mitad del siglo XIX no hicieron extensivas las leyes económicas a todos los agentes de la producción; es decir, dejaron sin examinar la naturaleza del interés de los "individuos productores". Prueba de ello es la ausencia de una reflexión en torno al salario en la folletería económica de la época.[21]

El desconocimiento del interés de los trabajadores tuvo consecuencias importantes. En primer lugar, excluyó la posibilidad de realizar la armonización "natural" de intereses a través del mercado, en el sentido que para los clásicos europeos la participación de los "individuos productores" aseguraba que las leyes del mercado pudieran operar. En segundo lugar, justificó que el Estado interviniera para garantizar la armonización

[18]M. Ortiz de la Torre, "Discurso sobre los medios de fomentar la población, riqueza e ilustración de los Estados Unidos Mexicanos, presentado en el certamen literario, con que el Colegio de San Ildefonso de México recibió a su alumno el Ciudadano Guadalupe Victoria, Primer Presidente de la República" (México: Imprenta de la Federación Mexicana, 1825), 5, *Fondo Reservado, Colección Lafragua*, v. 708.

[19]Ibid., 10.

[20]Ibid., 18.

[21]A través de la noción de salario los clásicos europeos analizaron el beneficio que los no-propietarios obtenían de su trabajo. En este contexto, Smith demostró que el interés de los trabajadores contribuía a la armonización de la vida social en la misma medida que el interés de los propietarios.

"artificial" a través de la instancia política, a pesar de que con ello la libertad de la naciente clase empresarial se veía coartada. No deja de ser paradójico que inicialmente esta clase reclamó al Estado libertad y estímulos para dar rienda suelta a su interés. Los planteamientos de Esteban de Antuñano pueden ayudarnos a comprender la manera en que esta cuestión fue abordada por los empresarios mismos.

El papel del Estado

De acuerdo con Antuñano, el poder político debía imponer límites al interés personal. Esta aseveración, contraria a las ideas de los clásicos, cuyas obras leyó con interés durante su estancia en España e Inglaterra, se apoyó en el supuesto de que

> Las sociedades democráticas necesitan más que ninguna otra, leyes protectoras de los derechos, y celadoras de los deberes; porque estando más libre la voluntad individual, pueden las acciones personales de los hombres, hacer más perjuicios a sus conciudadanos y a su patria.[22]

Por otra parte, en el marco de su defensa al proteccionismo, Antuñano sostenía que sólo en países "ilustrados" —como Inglaterra y Francia— los individuos particulares podían juzgar mejor que el hombre de Estado lo que convenía para acrecentar la riqueza de la nación. Así, por ejemplo, en México

> [si] el Banco de Avío representando al gobierno no hubiera dirigido, movido, ilustrado y auxiliado con fondos el interés particular, tal vez hubiera pasado un siglo, sin que hubiéramos tenido una máquina de algodón.[23]

No obstante, Antuñao luchó por consolidar la autonomía de la esfera económica frente al poder político, y desaprobó que los gobiernos quisieran "dirigir el interés individual", sin antes "consultar y recibir la opinión de los individuos",[24] sobre todo cuando el Estado aplicaba medidas que afectaran a los propietarios.

[22]E. de Antuñano, *Economía política en México* (Puebla: Imprenta Antigua en el Portal de Flores, 14 de febrero de 1839), 3, *Fondo Reservado, Colección Lafragua*, v. 1487.

[23]E. de Antuñano, "Memoria breve de la industria manufacturera de México, desde el año de 1821 hasta el presente; señalando los motivos de su aniquilamiento, los efectos que éste ha producido sobre la moral y la riqueza, y el remedio análogo para poner nuestra industria en un estado animado." Oficina del Hospital de San Pedro, Puebla, julio de 1835, p. 11.

[24]Ibid., 12.

La obra de Antuñano no plantea que exista oposición sino convergencia de intereses entre gobernantes y gobernados:

> porque siendo el amor propio [el interés propio] la madre de todas las pasiones, la más poderosa, vigorosa y exactamente instintiva por la naturaleza animal y racional, y como que el gozar comodidades físicas y morales, es el anhelo del interés personal, y como que la riqueza es el instrumento más eficaz para conseguir aquéllos; parece que no es temeridad el persuadirse, que el amor patrio que se funda principalmente sobre los intereses personales, es el más racional y seguro.[25]

El corolario a este razonamiento es que el enriquecimiento de la nación permitiría lograr la estabilidad política, pues la ambición de poder sería contrarrestada por la obtención de riquezas, y el logro del bienestar alejaría el peligro de la tiranía.[26]

> El *espíritu público* enlaza los intereses individuales, y éstos bien combinados conservan el orden y la dignidad nacional; pero el *espíritu público* [el amor patrio] es *moneda falsa, es la máscara de la ambición, de la tiranía y otras pasiones infames*, cuando no está radicado sobre, y sugerido por, un noble y físico interés personal, y como que éste sólo se adquiere, generalmente, por medio de una ocupación material ilustrada y lucrativa, de aquí se sigue, *que la ilustración industrial, la ocupación útil y honesta, la práctica de las clases productoras, agricultura y artes fabriles*, forman el único sólido pedestal sobre que se funda, progresa y conserva toda sociedad humana civilizada.[27]

Antuñano vivió confrontado a los peligros que acarrearía el crecimiento ilimitado de un Estado susceptible de asumir las riendas de una nación en crisis, y luchó por desarrollar una sociedad civil sólidamente fincada en los principios democráticos. Este propósito chocó, sin embargo, con la

[25]E. de Antuñano, *Economía política en México*, "De las clases productoras: su influencia sobre la riqueza, población, ilustración y espíritu público" (Puebla: Imprenta de San Pedro, julio de 1838), 8, *Fondo Reservado, Colección Lafragua*, v. 923.

[26]Esta idea se inscribe dentro de una vieja corriente del pensamiento político occidental que, según la interpretación de Albert O. Hirschman, antecedió el triunfo del capitalismo en Europa. De acuerdo con este autor, durante el siglo XVII la filosofía política desarrolló un argumento a favor de que se diese rienda suelta a las actividades adquisitivas privadas para contrarrestar las pasiones políticas de los poderosos. A lo largo del siglo XVIII, autores como Montesquieu, Sir James Stewart y John Millar propusieron diferentes versiones de esta premisa original. Los Fisiócratas y Adam Smith pusieron fin a una larga polémica política, al llegar a la conclusión de que las actividades económicas por sí solas no podían neutralizar la ambición de poder. En efecto, Smith llegó a desarrollar una justificación estrictamente económica de la legitimidad del interés individual. A. O. Hirschman, *The Passions and the Interests: Political Arguments for Capitalism before Its Triumph* (Princeton, N.J.: Princeton University Press, 1977).

[27]Ibid., 10–11. (El subrayado aparece en el texto original.)

realidad histórica. En efecto, las condiciones que prevalecían en México después de la independencia no dieron lugar a un proceso de industrialización que integrara a las mayorías dentro de una economía de mercado, a pesar de que algunos empresarios aislados promovieron la mecanización de la producción. De hecho, hasta antes del Porfiriato sería difícil identificar la existencia de una sociedad civil —integrada por una burguesía y una clase trabajadora libre de ataduras corporativas—, cuyos objetivos estarían claramente diferenciados de aquellos del Estado.

Ante la ausencia de condiciones que dieran lugar a la transformación económica de la nación independiente, la incipiente clase empresarial se vio obligada a recurrir constantemente al poder político en busca de protección y ayuda. En efecto, la biografía de Antuñano muestra que los defensores de la autonomía de la sociedad civil frente al Estado establecieron alianzas con regímenes, en su caso el santanista, que ejercieron el poder en forma arbitraria y personalista.

Las contradicciones en que incurrieron los pensadores económicos mexicanos al tratar de resolver el problema de la ociosidad en una sociedad donde no se había constituido una economía de mercado, y donde la naciente clase empresarial mantenía una actitud discutible frente al Estado y las clases productoras, se derivan en buena medida de las dificultades que planteó el rompimiento del sistema colonial. La primera República Federal fue un período de transición y como tal, un momento de ambigüedad. Dicho en palabras de José María Luis Mora (1836), "En México no hay ningún orden establecido; no el antiguo porque sus principios están ya desvirtuados y medio destruidos los intereses que lo apoyaban; no el nuevo aunque las doctrinas en que se funda y los deseos que ellas exitan son ya comunísimos en el país, todavía no se ha acertado con los medios de combinarlas con los restos que existen aún del antiguo sistema, o de hacerlos desaparecer; en suma, no se puede volver atrás ni caminar hacia adelante sino con grande dificultad".[28]

[28] J. M. L. Mora, *México y sus revoluciones* (México: Editorial Porrúa, 1965), 472.

Territorial Integrity in Mexican Politics, 1821–1833

Nettie Lee Benson

PRIOR TO INDEPENDENCE IN 1821, the Viceroyalty of New Spain had at one time encompassed modern-day Mexico, Central America (except Panama), and most of the southwestern part of the United States. The only area in which Spain had relinquished its claim to territory in New Spain west of the Mississippi River was in the north, where the 1819 Adams-Onís Treaty between Spain and the United States had granted to the United States the area north "of the mouth of the Sabine River on the Gulf of Mexico, continuing North, along the western bank of that river, to the 32 degree of Latitude, where it strikes the Rio Roxo, or Red River, then following the course of the Rio Roxo Westward to the degree of Longitude, 100 West from London and 23 from Washington, then crossing the said Red River, and running thence by a line due North to the River Arkansas, thence, following the Course of the Southern Bank of the Arkansas to its source in Latitude 42 degrees North, and thence by that parallel of Latitude to the South-Sea [Pacific Ocean] . . . ."[1] When King Ferdinand VII presented this treaty to the Spanish Cortes in 1820, it was confirmed, but over the protest of all New Spain's deputies in that Cortes. Furthermore, the provisions set forth for surveying the actual boundary line had not yet been carried out when on February 24, 1821, the Plan de Iguala established the independence of New Spain and erected the Mexican Empire.

[1]Article 2 of the Adams-Onís Treaty ceded the two Floridas to the United States and Article 3 spelled out the boundary of the United States territory west of the Mississippi River and how the treaty should be implemented. For an English translation, see Philip Coolidge Brooks, *Diplomacy and the Borderlands: The Adams-Onís Treaty of 1819*, University of California Publications in History, no. 24 (Berkeley: University of California Press, 1939), 205–214; C. Alan Hutchinson, *Frontier Settlement in Mexican California* (New Haven: Yale University Press, 1969), 101–102; Tadeo Ortiz de Ayala, *Resumen de la estadística del imperio mexicano* (Mexico: Imprenta de doña Herculena del Villar y Socios, 1822), 9–11.

With the declaration of independence on September 28, 1821, by Iturbide and the Mexican Sovereign Governing Junta, one of the many issues that body faced was that of the extent of the national territory. Prior to independence the creation of the audiencia of Guatemala and the captaincy-generalships of Yucatán and Guatemala had removed those southern provinces from the jurisdiction of the Viceroyalty of New Spain.[2] The independence of Mexico also inspired those provinces to declare their independence; shortly thereafter those provinces, encouraged largely by the forceful prompting of Iturbide, soon joined the Mexican Empire.[3] Hence during the period January 1822–June 1823, Mexican territory extended from the southern limits of the province of Costa Rica in the south to the Sabine River on the northeast and to 42 degrees on the northwest coast of North America.

Twelve days after the Sovereign Governing Junta began its sessions, Tadeo de Ortiz de Ayala presented to Iturbide a statistical resume of the Mexican Empire—its geography, population, wealth, and internal and external problems. He concluded with the warning that Mexico need not fear foreign invasion through Veracruz (doubtless referring to the continued threat from Spain with its control of San Juan de Ulúa); instead, the danger lay in New Mexico, Texas, and the Isthmus of Tehuantepec. He emphasized that the English descendants on Mexico's northern boundaries of Texas, New Mexico, and California had already taken advantage of the weak Spanish government to disposses it of its former territories and that they continued to covet more of those regions, that the Russians were but thirty leagues (seventy-eight miles) from San Francisco and that their presence there might be due to some secret agreement with Spain, and that all the great maritime nations were interested in the southern extremities of the Mexican territory from Tehuantepec south. He pointed out the vagueness still existing in the boundary between the United States and Mexico under the treaty of 1819 and the need for Mexico to settle that matter as soon as relations with the government in Washington were established. To maintain the territorial integrity of the empire he recommended the colonization of those vast areas on its north and south, the establishment of strong local government within the provinces bordering those areas, and the fortification of the northern and southern boundaries of the empire.[4]

Previous to Iturbide's reception of this résumé the Sovereign Governing Junta, on September 30, had appointed Francisco Azcárate, Manuel de

[2]Edmundo O'Gorman, *Breve historia de las divisiones territoriales* (Mexico: Editorial Polis, 1937), xxii–xxiii.

[3]Ibid., 15–18; see also Rafael Heliodoro Valle, *La anexión de Centro América a México (documentos y escritos de 1821–1822, tomo III)*, Archivo Histórico Diplomático Mexicano, Serie II, no. 40 (Mexico: Publicaciones de la Secretaría de Relaciones Exteriores, 1936).

[4]Ortiz de Ayala, *Resumen de la estadística del imperio mexicano*, 7–101.

Heras Soto, and José Sánchez Enciso to its Committee on Foreign Affairs.[5] The committee read its first report to the Junta on December 24, but discussion was postponed because other matters requiring immediate attention were declared more urgent.[6] Although the report was brought up again and declared urgent, it was never discussed by the Junta. The committee's final draft was presented to the Junta on February 23, 1822; however, action on its various proposals was left to the constituent congress to be installed on the following day.[7]

The committee report read on December 24 dealt only with the dangers threatening the nation on the north: first from the barbarous Indian nations and second from the Anglo-Americans. With regard to the Indians the committee recommended that they be won not by war, but through trade, adhering faithfully to the treaties made with their leaders, converting them to the Catholic religion, and making them useful citizens of the empire. With regard to the Anglo-Americans, the committee, after giving an exact description of the territory acquired by the United States under the Adams-Onís Treaty of 1819, stated that the northern republic now wanted to expand its territory by taking the province of Texas, thus obtaining control of the Bay of Espíritu Santo, San Bernardo, Orcoquisac, and other ports of the Mexican gulf in order to conduct clandestine trade with adjoining Mexican provinces. The committee pointed out that according to Spanish law the king did not have the right to sell or alienate any territory as he had done in the Adams-Onís Treaty of 1819 and in the cession of the Floridas. The committee recommended that if the United States should ask for ratification of the Adams-Onís Treaty of 1819, Mexico should treat the matter very, very slowly, exercising the greatest delay possible. Under existing circumstances, however, the Empire should avoid any break in relations since it was still organizing itself; therefore it needed time as well as dedication and money. When delay became impossible, however, it would be necessary to ratify the Adams-Onís Treaty of limits.[8] Last, after describing Texas as a veritable paradise, the committee recommended that the government proceed at once to populate that province, so coveted by the United States, with settlers from New Orleans, from the Mexican Empire itself, and from Europe. It recommended that, momentarily at least, the

[5] *Diario de las sesiones de la soberana junta provisional gubernativa mexicana . . . 1821–1822* (Mexico: Imprenta Imperial de don Alejandro Valdés, 1821), 70.

[6] Ibid., 173.

[7] Ibid., 345; *Actas constitucionales mexicanas (1821–1824)*, 7 vols. (Mexico: Universidad Autónoma Nacional de México, 1980), I, 345.

[8] "Dictamen presentado a la soberana junta provisional gubernativa del imperio mexicano por la Comisión de Relaciones Exteriores, 29 de diciembre del año 1821, primero de la Independencia," in Juan Francisco Azcárate y Lezama, *Un programa de política internacional*, Archivo Histórico Diplomático Mexicano, Serie II, No. 37 (Mexico: Publicaciones de la Secretaría de Relaciones Exteriores, 1932), 3–9.

provisions of the colonization law enacted by the Spanish Cortes in June 1821[9] be used except that the measurement of the land offered be in acres rather than in the terms provided in the law, because in Europe and America that terminology was better known and understood and would attract more settlers.[10]

Whereas in its first report the committee had limited itself entirely to the territorial dangers Mexico faced on its northern frontier, in its final report, in the form of appendixes, it made recommendations for the maintenance of the empire's territorial integrity as then envisioned, even including the possibility, though remote, that the Philippine and Mariana islands would also form a part of the empire. In its first appendix, after describing the threat from the Russians in the Californias and southward on the Pacific, the committee recommended that Chinese merchants and traders be given inducement to establish themselves in the Californias and to settle there permanently. It also pointed out that Mexico should at once press Russia for a treaty whereby it would abandon its settlements in Upper California. The committee argued that because of the great distances to California both from internal Mexico and from China, the only viable solution was to populate the Californias by Chinese; this would be possible only if the Philippines and/or the Marianas formed a part of the Mexican Empire. Chinese immigrants should also be given land in the same manner as had been recommended for immigrants to Texas. The committee also suggested that criminals sentenced to die in the prison dungeons of Veracruz or to two years of presidial service might be given the choice of settling in California.[11]

Next the committee took up the matter of the independence of the provinces of the Audiencia of Guatemala and their becoming a part of the territory of the Mexican Empire. This led to the committee's consideration of the British operations in Honduras and along the Mosquito coast of the province of Nicaragua. The committee reported that the empire should be continuously alert to that situation. It argued that under the Treaty of Versailles, of September 3, 1783, Spain had retained sovereignty over those areas and that with independence and their union with Mexico sovereignty passed to the Empire. Hence the Mexican Empire should seek

[9]See ibid., 65–71, for the provisions of that law and Nettie Lee Benson, "Texas as Viewed from Mexico, 1820–1834," *Southwestern Historical Quarterly* 90:3 (January 1987), 220–223, for an account of the role played by the Mexican deputies to the Spanish Cortes in the passage of this law.

[10]Azcárate y Lezama, *Un programa de política internacional*, 12–20.

[11]Ibid., 20–27. On pages 36–41 of its report the committee returned again to the subject of China and what Chinese immigration and trade could mean for California as well as for the enrichment of the Mexican Empire.

a treaty to that effect as soon as relations with Great Britain had been established.[12]

The committee ended the report by focusing again on the need to proceed at once with getting the frontier regions in accordance with the provisions of the Spanish colonization law of June 1821, until the empire could enact its own legislation. The committee declared that military force could not possibly be expected to protect the vast unpopulated open frontier. Only a large loyal population in Texas, Coahuila, New Mexico, New Santander, and Upper and Lower California could prevent their loss to the empire.[13]

Although the newly installed constituent congress named a Committee on Colonization early in its session, presumably to draw up a colonization law, no report from it was soon forthcoming. José Antonio Gutiérrez de Lara, deputy from New Santander, on April 15, 1822, proposed that the safeguarding of the frontier of the Eastern Interior Provinces be the responsibility of 500 well-equipped, well-paid natives of those provinces commanded by Miguel Eça y Múzquiz; that after these troops had carried out their assignment for five years, they each would receive a square league of land in Texas, and that they found a town in the memory of Miguel Hidalgo; that all the native Indians be conceded an equal right to found towns under a name of their own choosing as soon as they accepted the Catholic religion and a civilized life; and that foreign Catholics having some craft or skill be given land. This proposal was read for the second time on May 5, 1822, and sent to the Committee on Colonization.[14]

José Refugio de la Garza, deputy for Texas, Gutiérrez de Lara, Lt. Col. Antonio Elozua, deputy for Coahuila, Juan Bautista Arizpe, deputy for Nuevo León, all representing the Eastern Interior Provinces, and Francisco Rivas, deputy for Upper California, dissatisfied with the response to their earlier appeals for attention to their proposals regarding those provinces, asked Congress for permission to go directly to Emperor Iturbide to explain to him the necessity of fortifying various points in the province of Texas.[15]

By June 1822, more than half a dozen petitions for contracts to settle land in Texas had been presented to the Mexican government, among them the request by Stephen F. Austin to assume his deceased father's contract of 1820 and a proposal offered by Diego Barry, Tadeo Ortiz de Ayala, and Felipe O'Reilly to settle 10,000 Irish and Canary Islanders in Texas.[16] When

[12]Ibid., 29–34.

[13]Ibid., 62–65.

[14]*Actas del congreso constitucional mexicano*, 5 vols. (Mexico: En la Oficina de Alejandro Valdés, 1822), I, 26, 27, 67, 89, and 2da foliatura, 36–37.

[15]Ibid., 341.

[16]Not all of these petitions had been presented to Congress; for those that had, see ibid., I, foliatura 2a., 253, 275; II, 7–8, 21–25; Herbert E. Bolton, *Guide to the Materials*

the Colonization Committee's approval of the Barry-Ortiz-O'Reilly proposal was read, on June 3, 1822, a heated argument began. It continued on June 5, with Congress finally voting to refer the matter back to the Colonization Committee, along with a proposal for a colonization law (which Gutiérrez de Lara stated he already had in draft form), until the committee could present a project for a general colonization law for congressional consideration.[17]

Garza of Texas, on August 5, 1822, again reminded Congress of the miserable conditions in Texas, the lack of population in that province, and of the great danger the Empire faced by not safeguarding the port of Matagorda. He concluded that measures should be taken immediately to prevent Texas and perhaps all the Eastern Interior Provinces from becoming part of the United States. He received immediate support in speeches delivered by Servando Teresa de Mier of Nuevo León, Pablo de la Llave of Puebla, and Manuel Mier y Terán of Chiapas.[18]

The Colonization Committee's project for a general law was finally read on August 20, 1822, along with the project that Gutiérrez de Lara had offered earlier and one drawn up by Valentín Gómez Farías.[19] The committee's project received considerable attention before Congress voted to return the material to the committee for further revision. The projects offered by Gutiérrez de Lara and Gómez Farías were not discussed at the time. On September 26, 1822, the committee presented for approval a revised version of the Gómez Farías project, in the place of its earlier proposal. Debate ensued and the committee moved rapidly toward approval, but proceedings were abruptly cut off when Iturbide dissolved the Congress and installed a handpicked Junta Nacional Instituyente.[20]

Shortly thereafter, on November 7, 1822, Iturbide's Minister of Foreign and Internal Affairs, José Manuel Herrera, asked the Junta Nacional Instituyente to expedite a colonization law, because of the number of impresarios in Mexico City still seeking grants for settlements in Texas. By January 3, 1823, the slightly expanded 28-article project first offered by the

---

for the History of the United States in the Principal Archives of Mexico (Washington, D.C., 1913), 350–353; Eugene C. Barker, *The Life of Stephen F. Austin* (Austin: University of Texas Press, 1980), 44–46.

[17]*Actas del congreso constituyente de México*, II, foliatura 2a., 21–24. For an account of the Barry-Ortiz-O'Reilly plan and the Report of the Colonization Committee to Congress, see Edith Louise Kelly and Mattie Austin Hatcher, eds. and trans., "Tadeo Ortiz de Ayala and the Colonization of Texas, 1822–1833," *Southwestern Historical Quarterly* 32 (July 1928–January 1929), 78–83.

[18]Ibid., II, 393.

[19]Ibid., II, 15–88; Juan A. Mateos, *Historia parlamentaria de los congresos mexicanos*, 25 vols. (Mexico: V. S. Reyes, impresor, 1877–1912), I, 808–850.

[20]Ibid., 991–1010.

Colonization Committee of the recently dissolved Congress was approved with scarcely any debate and signed on January 4 by Iturbide.[21]

It appeared that finally action would proceed on the much heralded measure, a colonization law that would provide for maintenance of the territorial integrity of the empire through populating the frontier provinces, especially Texas. One of the first grants or contracts considered was that of Stephen F. Austin, who expected prompt action. But such was not to be. Before all the details could be worked out, Iturbide called for the restoration of the dissolved Congress and abdicated as Emperor of Mexico on March 19, 1823. Immediately after obtaining a quorum, the restored Congress abrogated all the laws and decrees of the Junta Instituyente Mexicana and declared all actions taken by Iturbide null and void; Mexico was again without a colonization law and the empresarios, including Austin, without approved contracts to make settlements.[22]

During his brief rule as Mexican Emperor, Iturbide also took action with regard to the boundary between the United States and Mexico. He sent José Manuel Zozaya as his minister to Washington with secret instructions to learn the views of the United States government on the limits of Louisiana and to discover if any settlements had been effected or were being planned under the treaty of February 22, 1819, between the United States and Spain which would prejudice the rights of the Mexican Empire.[23] On December 26, 1822, Zozaya reported from Washington that he believed the question of the boundary between Texas and the United States should be left undecided. (It should be noted that this opinion coincided with the attitude expressed in the colonization project presented by the Committee on Foreign Relations to the Sovereign Governing Junta on February 23, 1822.) Zozaya also reported that both in Congress and in the state legislatures the talk was about nothing other than "in the arranging of the army and militia, which doubtless had no other object than that of fulfilling their ambitious designs on the Province of Texas."[24]

The first item relating to Texas taken up by the restored Constituent Congress in early 1823 was the matter of concessions made by Iturbide to colonizers in Texas. Prompted by this action, Stephen F. Austin asked the new government to confirm the grant made to him by the Iturbide

[21]*Diario de la junta nacional instituyente del imperio mexicano* (Mexico: En la Oficina de D. Alejandro Valdés, Impresor de Cámara de México, 1822), 25, 47–55; Mateos, *Historia parlamentaria*, II, 18–19, 21, 25, 28–29, 57–58.

[22]Barker, *Life of Stephen F. Austin*, 64–68; Hubert Howe Bancroft, *History of Mexico*, 6 vols. (San Francisco, 1883–1888), IV, 790–855.

[23]"Instrucciones reservadas para José Manuel Zozaya, 31 de octubre de 1822," in *La diplomacia mexicana* 3 vols. (Mexico: Tipografía Artística, 1910), I, 85; William R. Manning, "Texas and the Boundary Issue, 1822–1829," *Southwestern Historical Quarterly* 17:3 (January 1914), 217.

[24]Zozaya, Washington, D.C., December 26, 1822, in *La diplomacia mexicana*, I, 101–103.

government. Congress instructed the Supreme Executive Power to confirm those grants already made, if it thought that best. An executive order confirming Austin's grant followed;[25] if others were issued, they were apparently not confirmed.

Mexico was again without a much needed colonization law and at least eleven empresarios were still awaiting permits to bring settlers to colonize Texas. Among them were Haden Edwards, Daniel Stuart, and Arthur Wavell, who had first submitted their petitions in 1822. Lucas Alamán, the new Minister of Foreign and Internal Affairs, asked Francisco Fagoaga, who had served on the Colonization Committee in Spain, to draw up a project for a colonization law for the Supreme Executive Power to present to Congress for its consideration. Fagoaga's project of 28 articles appeared without other comment in the newspaper *El Sol*.[26] The Supreme Executive Power presented it to Congress on May 31, 1823, along with a lengthy evaluation, obviously written by Alamán.

The evaluation stated that it was unnecessary to demonstrate the need for an increase in the population in the interior provinces "bordering on the United States to impede a quiet occupation invited by their present abandonment and the invasions by Indian tribes that threaten the existing population there." The distribution of the vacant land in "provinces as distant as Texas, Sonora, etc., however, needed general direction and administration." It would not be easy according to the evaluation, for "the provincial deputations and municipal councils to be able to carry out the distribution of that land in those provinces with prudence," as provided in this project and as had been provided in the Spanish colonization law. Regardless of the form of government, the executive power should exercise the distribution of its land as in the United States, where the distribution and sale of land was exercised only by the president without intervention by the national government or the states. (This argument is of particular interest in relation to Mexico's later colonization law of April 6, 1830.) The Supreme Executive Power recommended that some of the vacant lands be sold; for that reason, the land should be classified and the best sold at moderate prices. Surprisingly, Article 28 received no criticism; it proposed that foreigners not only be permitted to settle along the coasts but also be allowed to bring their slaves. It concluded that the increase in population and progress in those areas could only result from foreign immigration and that

[25]*Diario de las sesiones del congreso constituyente de México*, 5 vols. (Mexico: En la Oficina de Valdés, 1823), IV, 119, 122; *Colección de los decretos y órdenes del soberano congreso mexicano desde su instalación en 24 de febrero de 1822 hasta 30 de octubre de 1823 en que cesó* (Mexico: Imprenta del Supremo Goberno, 1825), 100; *Colección de órdenes y decretos de la soberana junta provisional gubernativa y congresos generales*, 2d ed., 7 vols. (Mexico, 1829), II, 94.

[26]*El Sol* (Mexico City), I, No. 3 (June 1, 17, 1823), 9–10.

present in the capital was a multitude of contractors for establishing colonies, whose proposals had already suffered long delays.[27]

From May 1823 until the end of its session in October 1823, the national Congress was too busy with other more serious internal problems[28] to give attention to the law for colonization. The Supreme Executive Power, on August 6, 1823, reminded Congress of the recommendation made on May 31 and again appealed for the passage of a general colonization law, in view of the increasing number of families establishing themselves in Texas without order or rules.[29]

José Anastasio Torrens, the Mexican chargé d'affaires in Philadelphia, on August 21, 1823, notified his government that the newspapers there frequently reproached the United States government for not having obtained Texas from the Spanish government and accused John Quincy Adams of having ceded Texas to the Spanish in the Adams-Onís Treaty. Torrens then advised his government not to permit the Anglo-American population to become preponderant in Texas.[30] After receiving this report, Alamán instructed Torrens to proceed as diligently and actively as possible to secure United States confirmation of the Adams-Onís Treaty and to obtain from the United States the naming of its commissioners to lay out the exact boundary line between Texas and the United States.[31]

To this Torrens replied that the United States was posing difficulties even to recognizing the treaty. Not only had the time for marking the boundary expired, but also Ferdinand VII of Spain had declared void all actions of the Spanish constitutional government, thereby nullifying the treaty. Torrens was certain that the United States would attempt to take advantage of this new pretext and explained that he would not be surprised if the troops on the frontier were ordered to advance into Texas territory. So unlimited was American ambition for Texas that General Jackson had declared in his presence that "the United States should never have lost the opportunity to obtain it" and that "the way to obtain a territory was to

[27]"Indicación del supremo poder executivo al soberano congreso sobre colonización," *El Sol*, I, No. 6 (June 20, 1823), 22–24.

[28]For a discussion of many of these problems, see Nettie Lee Benson, *La diputación provincial y el federalismo mexicano* (Mexico: El Colegio de México, 1955, 2d ed., Mexico, LI Legislatura, Cámara de Diputados, 1980), 122 ff; Nettie Lee Benson, "The Plan of Casa Mata," *Hispanic American Historical Review* 25:1 (February 1945), 49–56.

[29]"Esposición hecha al supremo poder ejecutivo por unos ciudadanos sobre la colonización," signed by Lucas Alamán, to which he attached the above cited comments on a proposal for a settlement in southern Mexico, only part of which was published in *El Sol*, I, No. 66 (August 19, 1823), 365.

[30]José A. Torrens to Lucas Alamán, Philadelphia, August 21, 1823, in *La diplomacia mexicana*, II, 22–24; Manning, "Texas and the Boundary Issue," 218.

[31]Ibid., 219; Alamán to Torrens, Mexico, October 1, 1823, in *La diplomacia mexicana*, II, 33–34.

occupy it, and after having possession, treat for it, as was done in Florida."[32]

Torrens reported to Alamán in June 1823 that according to rumors in the United States the Russians were planning to take all of the northwest coast in order to dominate the Pacific. Then in November 1823 he reported that it was being said that Spain had ceded California to Russia before Mexican independence and before the Spanish-United States treaty of 1819. He seemed to think, however, that actions taken by the U.S. president in regard to Russian activities in that area would remove the Russian threat there.[33]

Previously the Mexican government under Iturbide, realizing the great need for more information about California, had sent Canon Agustín Fernández de San Vicente to California to gather information on the situation there. After some time, he reported that "we shall lose the precious and fertile province of California, the western key to our continent";[34] returning to Mexico in 1823, he brought with him three Russian deserters to confirm Russian designs on California.[35]

Since Russia had yet to recognize Mexico, the new nation could not protect that territory diplomatically. Colonization with Chinese immigrants and development of trade with China were recommended as the best solutions for maintaining Mexican territorial integrity in the Pacific by the committees on colonization and by Alamán, the secretary of state, in 1823.[36]

In the spring and summer of 1823, after the abdication of Iturbide, the union of the Central American provinces was irrevocably broken except for that of Chiapas. When deputies representing those provinces asked Congress for permission to return home, a special committee was appointed to consider the matter. Not until the Congress of the Central American Confederation notified the Mexican Congress that it had declared its independence from Mexico, however, did the Mexican Congress vote that all Central American deputies might leave, except those from Chiapas, which had decided to remain united with Mexico.[37] The withdrawal of the

[32]Torrens to Alamán, Washington, January 26, 1824, in ibid., 73-74; Manning, "Texas and the Boundary Issue," 220-221.

[33]Hutchinson, *Frontier Settlement in Mexican California*, 100-104; Torrens to Alamán, in *La diplomacia mexicana*, II, 26-27, 48-50.

[34]Agustín Fernández de San Vicente to José Ygnacio García Illueca, April 12, 1823, Mexico, Archivo General de la Nación, Provincias Internas, vol. XXIII, 142; Hutchinson, *Frontier Settlement in Mexican California*, 99-100.

[35]Ibid., 100.

[36]Ibid., 111-112; Azcarate y Lezama, *Un programa de política internacional*, 22-27; *Memoria que el secretario de estado presenta* (Mexico, 1823), 33.

[37]Nettie Lee Benson and Charles Berry, "The Central American Delegation in the First Constituent Congress of Mexico, 1822-1823," *Hispanic American Historical Review* 49:4 (November 1969), 699-700; Mateos, *Historia parlamentaria*, II, 429, 497-498, 500, 502, 552.

Central American provinces not only brought about the loss of much territory in the south but also created an additional threat to the remaining territory, the Central American Federation to Chiapas, Soconuso, and other areas bordering on Guatemala.[38]

Although colonization of the frontier was universally considered the best means of maintaining the territorial integrity of the nation, not until August 18, 1824, was a colonization law for the Mexican Republic finally promulgated. It was a very general law, because a previously adopted article of the constitution of the Mexican federal republic provided that each individual state, not the national administration, should have complete jurisdiction over the vacant land within its boundaries and that each state should establish laws or regulations for the distribution of its vacant lands and should promote colonization.[39] Alamán who believed that vacant lands belonged to the nation, not to the states, had argued against this provision in the constitution. José Miguel Ramos Arizpe maintained that the vacant lands belonged to the individual states whose ancestors had conquered and settled them; the states knew the quality of their lands and the need to allocate more or less depending on the quality.[40] This provision was also contained in the earlier Spanish colonization law, which gave similar jurisdiction to the provincial deputation of each province.

The provision pertaining to jurisdiction over vacant lands was a factor in the debate over which provinces should be recognized as states and which should become territories under the jurisdiction of the national government, especially those located on the frontier. All provinces and territories were represented in the national congresses. Most of the frontier provinces, including Texas, asked for territorial status, for they recognized their lack of resources and need for assistance from the national government. The Texas deputy Erasmo Seguín stated on September 10, 1824, that Texas preferred to be a territory of the national government, not a part of the state of Coahuila and Texas, because poverty and underpopulation prevented it from developing its resources and wealth. Texas, therefore, needed the aid of the national government to defend itself against the barbarous Indians, aid that Coahuila could not give because it too was not a rich province. No action was taken, but when Congress returned to Seguín's proposal again on October 2, 1824, Servando Teresa de Mier y Noriega of

[38]Andrés Clemente Vázquez, *Bosquejo histórico de la agregación a México de Chiapas y Soconusco* (Mexico: Publicaciones de la Secretaría de Relacions Exteriores, 1932).

[39]*Colección de órdenes y decretos de la soberana junta provisional*, III, 64–65; for an English translation, see H.P.N. Gammel, *The Laws of Texas 1822–1897* (Austin, Texas: Gammel Book Co., 1898), I, 38–40.

[40]*Constitución federal de 1824. Crónicas*, 2 vols. (Mexico: Comisión Nacional para la Conmemoración del Sesquicentenario de la República Federal y del Centenario de la Restauración del Senado, 1974), II, 602–603, 606–607, 618, 622, 624–626, 626–629, 639, 652, 658–662; *Aguila Mexicana*, August 1–19, 1824; *El Sol*, August 1–19, 1824.

of Nuevo León, José Cirilo Gómez Anaya of Mexico, and Carlos María Bustamante of Oaxaca supported it. Bustamante argued for the importance of having Texas directly under the vigilance and custody of the national government in order "to impede the introduction of foreign adventurers and an invasion on the part of those prejudicial to the interest of the Mexican republic." Deputies Carlos Espinosa de los Monteros of Sonora and Sinaloa, Crescencio Rejón of Yucatán, and Ramos Arizpe of Coahuila argued that Coahuila and Texas should be combined as one state. When the vote was taken, Congress approved the creation of the state of Coahuila y Texas by a vote of forty to thirty-six.[41]

Thus under the Constitution of 1824 the areas of the Californias and New Mexico became a territory under the sole jurisdiction of the national government, charged with providing regulations for colonization, internal government, and development within the territorial boundaries. Although the administration continued to emphasize the need for population growth, as the best way to maintain territorial integrity, not until November 21, 1828, did it finally produce the regulation for the colonization of the territories, especially of California and New Mexico.[42] Needless to say the national government did little in regard to colonization in those areas prior to that date.

Fortunately, however, for those empresarios who had been waiting so long for action on their petitions, the state of Coahuila y Texas took action on the matter even before completing its constitution. The state passed a colonization law on March 24, 1825,[43] which incorporated much of the thinking underlying the earlier proposals of Gutiérrez de Lara and Gómez Farías in regard to religion, the Indians and other Mexican settlers, limitations on foreigners settling within a given distance of the coast or the border with the United States, the amount and quality of land to be dispensed to each empresario and individual, and the way land was to be sold. Many articles in the law related to foreign immigrants, not because they were preferred over natives but because there was a need for greater control of who they were and where they settled. Articles 10 and 19 of the colonization law specifically stated that Christianized Indians were preferred over foreigners. Other articles provided for natives to become empresarios and various Mexicans were given empresario grants, among them Zavala, Ortiz de Ayala, José Antonio Mejía, Juan Domínguez, and Ramos Arizpe. Mexico, however, recognized that it had a vast amount of territory and lacked

[41]Ibid., *Constitución federal de 1824. Crónicas*, 671, 732–735, 812–822.

[42]*Colección de órdenes y decretos de la soberana junta provisional*, III, 75–80; Hutchinson, *Frontier Settlement in Mexican California*, 169; see pp. 133–168 for discussion of the problems faced in California in applying the general law of colonization of 1824.

[43]*Colección de órdenes y decretos de la soberana junta provisional*, III, 92–99; and English translation on the law in Gammel, *The Laws of Texas*, I, 40–46.

the population to develop it adequately. Therefore, it needed foreign immigrants.

While the colonization of Texas had moved from the control of the national government to that of the state of Coahuila y Texas, the problem of the state boundary with the United States remained under the jurisdiction of the national government, but was of great concern also to those in Texas. On April 15, 1824, José Antonio Sauceda, the political chief of Texas, advised Minister Alamán that he was certain that the United States was "trying to annul or has the idea of annulling the treaty of 1819" and that he believed the United States government would then assert its claim to the banks of the Rio Grande.[44] Hence, in August 1824 Alamán instructed Pablo Obregón, Mexico's minister to the United States, to do everything possible to secure United States acknowledgment of the Adams-Onís Treaty of 1819.[45]

The maintenance of territorial integrity was also a factor in the Congressional debates over the opening of Texas ports at Galveston and Atascosito. Senator José Manuel Santibáñez y Ceballos, on March 22, 1825, pointed out that opening those ports was the only means of enriching the state of Coahuila y Texas and "increasing the population within Texas, whose native sons united with those new colonies between the navigable Colorado and Brazos rivers," would bring prosperity to the state and to the nation, which had not been realized until then "because of the lack of beasts of burden . . . ." He declared that President Guadalupe Victoria, in the interest of the well-being of coastal Texas, had urged him to deliver his discourse.[46] When the Senate took up the request for a port at Galveston, both Ceballos and Senator Agustín Viezca of Coahuila y Texas argued for the port's immediate opening. Ceballos stated that there could be no more appropriate point than Galveston where a small military force could be in position to defend the Texas boundary. He asked that action be taken to prevent the return of pirates and invasions that could result in the loss of all Coahuila y Texas and to facilitate trade of cotton, flour, beans, tobacco, and lumber along the navigable Colorado, Brazos, and Trinity rivers.[47]

When Joel Roberts Poinsett was appointed United States minister to Mexico in March 1825, Secretary of State Henry Clay instructed him that the Adams-Onís Treaty of 1819 was obligatory between the United States and Mexico, even though it had not yet been fully executed. Clay quoted

[44]José Antonio Sauceda to Lucas Alamán, Bejar, April 15, 1824, in Bexar Archives, University of Texas at Austin; Lester G. Bugbee, "The Texas Frontier 1820–1825," *Publications of the Southern Historical Association* 4 (March 1900), 115; Manning, "Texas and the Boundary Issue, 221.

[45]Ibid., 222–223; "Instrucciones mui reservadas, August 30, 1824," MS., Archivo de la Secretaría de Relaciones Exteriores, Mexico.

[46]*Aguila Mexicana*, II, No. 342 (March 22, 1825).

[47]Ibid., III, No. 26 (May 26, 1825).

Article 3 of the treaty, which described the boundary line, and Article 4, which provided for a binational commission for its demarcation. He then recommended that Poinsett discuss with the Mexican government the advisability of establishing a new and more satisfactory boundary, perhaps "that of the Río Brasos de Dios, or the Río Colorado, or the Snow Mountain, or the Río del Norte in lieu of it."[48]

Two days after Poinsett's formal reception by President Guadalupe Victoria and before Poinsett had the opportunity to open negotiations, on June 3, 1825, Azcárate wrote a letter to Victoria informing him that when Poinsett arrived on the coast of Mexico in 1822 he had sought an interview with Azcárate to discuss an interesting matter. In that meeting Azcárate indicated that Poinsett had produced a map of Mexico on which he had traced a line, which showed that he wanted the United States to absorb all of Texas, New Mexico, and Upper California, and parts of Lower California, Sonora, Coahuila, and Nuevo León. Azcárate stated that he angrily replied that by virtue of the Treaty of Iguala [and Cordoba?] the Mexican government would always respect the Adams-Onís Treaty and would never cede a handbreadth of territory. In a second interview, on the next day, Poinsett declared that he was in Mexico as a traveler and was only expressing his personal view.[49]

When Poinsett met with Foreign Minister Alamán on July 12, 1825, he suggested that although the United States was bound to the Adams-Onís Treaty, it would appear more becoming to an independent country to lay aside the treaty altogether and to establish a more easily defined boundary and one mutually more advantageous. Alamán agreed and proposed that the two governments appoint commissioners to carry out a reconnaissance of the area adjacent to the boundary formerly set by the Adams-Onís Treaty in order to obtain information in regard to "that portion of our respective territories to enable us to act understandingly on the subject." Poinsett objected to Alamán's proposal because of the inherent delay in carrying it out. Alamán, however, insisted that his government would be unwilling to set limits based on the very meager information it then possessed. The governments came to no agreement on the subject at that time. Mexico continued to argue for a binational boundary commission to survey the entire area under dispute. Poinsett believed that the delay would favor the United States, for in the meantime Texas would continue to be settled by squatters or grantees, a population difficult to govern, and perhaps after a short time Mexico might not oppose parting with that

[48]Manning, "Texas and the Boundary Issue, 223–224; Clay to Poinsett, March 26, 1825, MS., Department of State, Instructions X, 225.

[49]Juan Francisco Azcárate to Guadalupe Victoria, June 3, 1825, MS., Archivo de la Secretaría de Relaciones Exteriores, Mexico; Manning, "Texas and the Boundary Issue, 224–226.

portion of its territory.[50] Nothing appeared in print about the meeting between Alamán and Poinsett; however, the Adams-Onís Treaty was published in its entirety in the government-subsidized newspaper *El Aguila Mexicana* on September 22, 1825.

A law controlling the activities of foreigners in Mexico was signed by President Victoria on June 5, 1825, and published in *El Sol* on June 12, 1825. According to the editors, the law was required because of the danger of political invasion if foreigners were allowed to acquire large landholdings in the country.[51] It covered all foreigners, including empresarios who had received grants of land for colonizing. It recognized the grants made by previous governments but specified that all foreigners had to abide by the provisions of the law. It stated that the purchase of land for colonization was solely under the jurisdiction of the national government. State legislatures could distribute uninhabited land within their territory to empresarios of colonies under the conditions that: (1) a fourth of the colonists be Mexicans; (2) the grant be divided into holdings not exceeding a square league of 5,000 Castilian rods within five years; (3) the foreign empresario not reserve for himself a piece of land exceeding sixteen square leagues, which should be transferred in twelve years after the grant was divided into holdings; (4) the fees placed on the colonists not be for longer than twenty years from the time they received their holdings.[52]

In his address to Congress on January 1, 1826, President Victoria stated that a definitive settlement of the boundary dispute between Mexico and the United States was most urgent. In referring to the defense of the nation, he noted that military supplies for troops had been sent to San Antonio de Bejar in Texas, to New Mexico, and to Chiapas.[53] He said, however, that Mexico continued to insist on a binational boundary commission survey of the area in dispute, especially that in Texas, before approving a treaty with the United States.[54] In the meantime Mexico was planning to send its boundary commission to Texas to acquire precise information on that boundary.[55]

Beginning in 1823 two political groups had formed in Mexico. The Centralists favored a strong national government based in Mexico City. Many centralists were members of the Scottish Rite (*escocés*) lodge, some

[50]Ibid., 226–228.

[51]"Revista política del año de 1825," *El Sol*, III, No. 932 (January 1, 1826), 801–802.

[52]"Dictamen de la Comisión de Gobernación del Senado," *Aguila Mexicana*, III, No. 185 (October 17–18, 1825).

[53]"Discurso del presidente Guadalupe Victoria al congreso general, 1 de enero de 1826," in ibid., III, No. 934 (January 3, 1826), 809–812.

[54]Manning, "Texas and the Boundary Issue," 225–231.

[55]A binational commission would give each nation the right to view both sides of the boundary; whereas a unilateral commission would be handicapped in moving across the stated boundary; for that reason Mexico insisted on the binational boundary commission.

were monarchists, who continued to hope that monarchy could be restored, and some were Spaniards residing in Mexico. H. G. Ward, the British foreign minister and a Scottish Rite Mason, was an influential member of this group since his arrival. The federalists were more representative of the states and their rights. Many belonged to the more recently organized York Rite (*yorkino*) lodge, which had expanded tremendously throughout the states, especially after the establishment of its Grand Lodge in Mexico City in 1825, with help from the United States minister Poinsett.

By 1826 the rivalry between the two groups had escalated. Neither attacked the other as centralist or federalist but rather indirectly through the secret masonic lodges, as escoceses or yorkinos. The Coahuila y Texas Senator Ceballos proposed, on April 21, 1826, a law prohibiting secret societies as being contrary to Catholic Church. Three days later, after the Senate had refused to admit it, Ceballos made the proposal again and the Senate again refused to accept it for discussion, doubtless because a fair number of Senate members belonged to a masonic lodge.[56] Nonetheless, Ceballos presented his proposal again on December 5, 1826.[57] In the same month, Minister of Internal and External Affairs Juan José Espinosa, in an address to the Senate, reported that according to the governor of Coahuila y Texas a masonic lodge in that state had influenced the election of deputies to the national congress and wanted to do the same in regard to other elections. The governor apparently did not state whether the lodge was Scottish or York Rite.[58] Most likely it was York Rite, for in the 1826 elections, the yorkinos won in most of the state elections, especially those for seats in the Chamber of Deputies.[59] Unquestionably the government was becoming concerned about the existence of the lodges and began an investigation of their activities.

The York Rite lodge in 1826 began the publication of its own daily newspaper, *Correo de la Federación Mexicana*, edited and directed by Lorenzo de Zavala, among others. *El Sol* generally represented the Scottish Rite and centralist group, and was largely edited by Lucas Alamán. The *Aguila Mexicana*, initiated and subsidized by the Mexican government to speak for the goverenment, edited at times by Ramos Arizpe and Zavala among others, was accused by *El Sol* of also being a York Rite organ. The

[56]*El Sol*, III, Nos. 1056 and 1058 (May 5, 7, 1826), 1302, 1310. Ceballos's proposal and the speeches of Lorenzo de Zavala and Juan de Dios Cañedo against its admission were reproduced in full in *El Sol*, III, No. 1053 (May 2, 1826), 1290.

[57]*El Sol*, IV, No. 1272 (December 9, 1826), 2171, which again reproduced Ceballos's proposal in full, this time bearing the date December 1, 1826.

[58]Romeo Flores Caballero, *Counterrevolution: The Role of the Spaniards in the Independence of Mexico, 1804–1838*, translated by Jaime E. Rodríguez O. (Lincoln: University of Nebraska Press, 1974), 90–93.

[59]*El Sol,* IV, No. 1285 (December 22, 1826), 2223–2226.

government, the lodges, and the newspapers kept the secret society issue sizzling, contributing greatly to Mexico's internal turmoil.

Fear of foreign aggression had been prevalent among Mexicans even prior to independence. The north and west were vulnerable to the United States and Russia, and the south before 1823 to Great Britain and after 1823 to both the British and Guatemala or the Central American Confederation. After 1826 there developed the additional fear of a Spanish reconquest. The question of Mexican territorial integrity became intertwined with the activities of the secret societies and the internal maneuvering of the federalists and centralists for domination of the government during the period 1826–1833.

The northern frontier, especially Texas, was the area most threatened during these years. Fear of territorial loss had been part of the debate over a strong law to guard against undesirable foreigners, especially Anglo-Americans and Spaniards, obtaining citizenship and large landholdings in Mexico. The fear of losing territory would become a factor in the expulsion of the Spaniards in 1827 and in the coup d'etat of Anastasio Bustamante in 1829, after the aborted attempt by Spain to reconquer Mexico. The same concern strengthened the argument of the centralist-escoses for a strong national government and more control over colonization, and was among the reasons for opposition to the Bustamante government and the execution of Vicente Guerrero in 1831.

Although the fear of a Spanish reconquest as well as widespread animosity toward the Spaniards remaining in Mexico had been constant after independence, the discovery of the Joaquín Arenas conspiracy to restore Spanish dominion over Mexico, in January 1827, inflamed passions, damaging both Spaniard and Mexican, especially the centralist-escoses. The federalist-yorkinos seized on the conspiracy theme to launch a vigorous attack against the Spaniards remaining in Mexico, some of whom were members of the centralist-escoses group, which at first tried to discount the validity of the conspiracy and accused the federalist-yorkinos of fabricating the conspiracy theory.

Congress, the newspapers, and the pamphleteers were so taken up with the Arenas conspiracy and the secret societies that they paid only slight attention to the short-lived Fredonian Rebellion in Texas in December 1826 and January 1827.[60] On the same day that Father Arenas was arrested, the minister of war gave a very garbled account of the rebellion to the Senate.

[60]Benjamin Edwards, brother of empresario Haden Edward, on December 16, 1826, with some thirty followers, rode into Nacogdoches under a flag inscribed "Independence, Liberty, and Justice" and proclaimed the Republic of Fredonia. Their attempt to attract support from the Indians, from the United States, and from settlers in Texas was unsuccessful. By January 31, they had fled across the Sabine. Barker, *Life of Stephen F. Austin*, 148–177; *Texas Handbook*, 3 vols. (Austin: Texas Historical Society, n.d.), I, 643.

In that session, Senator Ceballos declared that according to his reports the uprising did not constitute an invasion from the United States.[61] No other action was taken until February 17, when the minister of war informed Congress of what had happened at Nacogdoches.[62] The following day, Senator Llano of Nuevo León stated that his state had instructed him to propose a national law whereby *the supreme government of the Mexican Union received a 50 league strip of land on the border from Texas to Upper California to be colonized on its own account.* Llano also recommended that the Senate give preferential attention to the immediate preparation of a budget for the expenses of a commission to survey the Mexico–United States boundary.[63]

Congress approved a decree on February 23, 1827, that the government employ up to 4,000 militiamen from Coahuila y Texas, Nuevo León, Tamaulipas, and the territory of New Mexico and that 50,000 pesos be made available for extraordinary expenses to preserve the integrity of the republic on the northern frontier and for gifts for the Indians living there. Food and flour for the maintenance of the troops in that area were to be made available through the ports of Galveston, Bahía del Espíritu Santo and Lavaca.[64] Actually, none of these measures were carried out because the welcome news that the revolt had been brought to an end in late January reached Mexico City before the end of March.[65] In his closing address to Congress, President Victoria said that to avoid a repetition of similar attacks on the frontier a respectable defense force would be installed there.[66]

At the same time the Mexican government was dealing with the Fredonian revolt, actions by President John Q. Adams and Henry Clay attracted Mexico's attention to the boundary issue. Believing that the numerous and extensive land grants being made in Texas by the state of Coahuila y Texas showed a lack of value of the possession of that frontier area, Adams and Clay instructed Poinsett, on March 15, 1827, to negotiate a change of the boundary line through purchase of some territory in Texas. Poinsett was authorized to offer between $500,000 and $1,000,000, depending on where the new boundary was set. In May, Poinsett cautiously approached the

[61]*El Sol*, IV, No. 1315 (January 21, 1827), 2343. On the same day the newspaper carried the notice of Father Arenas's arrest.

[62]Editorial, *El Sol*, IV, No. 1343 (February 18, 1827), 2458.

[63]Italics his, *El Sol*, No. 1346 (February 23, 1827), 2476.

[64]*Colección de órdenes y decretos de la soberano junta provisional*, IV, 70; editorial, *El Sol*, IV, No. 1348 (February 23, 1827), 4278, which exaggerated greatly the amount of men and troops allocated and also in *El Sol*, IV, Nos. 1355–1356 (March 2–3, 1827), 2503, 2507.

[65]Benson, "Texas as Viewed from Mexico," 253–255; *El Sol*, "Aventureros," IV, No. 1342 (February 17, 1827), 4252–4253; "Natchitoches, 6 de febrero," *El Sol*, No. 1344 (February 19, 1827), 2461; *El Sol*, No. 1360 (March 7, 1827); editorial, including a letter from Antonio Padillo of Saltillo and the excerpt of February 6 from Natchitoches, *El Sol*, No. 1370 (March 17, 1827), 2556; and *El Sol*, No. 1390 (March 1827), 2670; No. 1395 (April 2, 1827), 2690–2691.

[66]"Discurso del Presidente," *El Sol*, No. 1440 (May 28, 1827), 3029.

Mexican foreign minister suggesting the importance of settling as early as possible and in a permanent manner the issue of the boundary between the two countries, and informed him that he, Poinsett, was empowered to treat on the subject.

On January 8, 1828, Poinsett reported that when he had "hinted at a remuneration to the Mexican government as an inducement to extend our boundary to the Río del Norte" in a private conversation with a Mexican authority, he was assured that neither the Mexican government nor the congress would consent to such a measure, because it would be considered a dismemberment of Mexican territory, prohibited by the constitution and by the fact that the territory was a part of Coahuila y Texas and thus did not belong to the central government. Poinsett stated further that any attempt to alter the boundary line by purchase would fail and would only incite unfriendly feelings in Mexico.[67]

When the secretary of the treasury in May presented to the Chamber of Deputies his report on the funds needed to cover the boundry commission's expenses, it appeared that action would be taken on sending the commission to survey the northern frontier. The proposed budget received immediate approval from the Chamber of Deputies, which sent it to the Senate.[68] The Senate apparently did not consider the matter urgent, however, for it took no action before the end of the regular session. Furthermore, when the Senate Committee on Internal Affairs, in a special session of the congress in late August, gave its opinion on the budget, immediately the question arose as to whether the commission should survey the entire northern frontier or only the area of the state of Coahuila y Texas. No agreement being reached, the bill was returned to the committee with instructions to obtain further opinion from the secretary of foreign and internal affairs before additional discussion in the Senate. The secretary reported and the Senate again returned the bill to the committee for revision.[69]

The boundary commission, headed by General Manuel Mier y Terán, left Mexico City for the Texas frontier on November 10, 1827. Its departure was not mentioned in any Mexico City newspapers nor cited in the minutes of either branch of congress. Ohland Morton suggests this meant the government wanted to keep its departure secret.[70] Secret from whom and why?

[67]Manning, "Texas and the Boundary Issue," 234–239.

[68]"Sesión de la Cámara de Diputados," *El Sol*, IV, No. 1472 (June 17, 1827), 3029; Mateos, *Historia parlamentaria*, IV, 206.

[69]"Sesiones de la Cámara de Senadores, *El Sol*, V, Nos. 1552–1553 (September 6–7, 1827), 3353, 3357.

[70]Ohland Morton, *Terán and Texas: A Chapter in Texas-Mexican Relations* (Austin: The Texas State Historical Society, 1948), 47–55. For comments on its secrecy see footnote 22, p. 56. Morton indicates that the Commission was escorted only by several cavalrymen and that the local presidios usually furnished sixteen men to accompany it through their districts.

The commission's composition, financing, and purpose had been openly discussed in both chambers of congress and reported in the newspapers since independence. Furthermore, Obregón, in Washington, informed Secretary Clay of its departure and Poinsett, in Mexico City kept Clay thoroughly informed on all subjects related to the commission.[71] I believe that the lack of attention paid to the departure of the commission indicated that the government in Mexico City, its opposition, and the newspapers were heavily involved with other events, like the Arenas conspiracy, the expulsion of the Spaniards, and the Plan of Montano, in preparation at the time.

Owing to the increase in anti-Spanish sentiment stimulated by the Arenas conspiracy, the government introduced a bill into the Chamber of Deputies in April 1827 calling for the removal of any individual born in Spain and living in the Federal District or the national territories from government, civil, and military employment until Spain recognized Mexico's independence. The measure was approved on May 10, but instead of moderating the tension, its passage seemed to cause the situation to deteriorate further. Many of the state legislatures had also passed laws controlling Spaniards within their boundaries. Seven of them went so far as to expel some or all Spaniards from their jurisdiction. Heated debate in Congress over state laws on the issue and numerous revolts for or against the national and state laws eventually led the anti-Spanish federalist-yorkino Congress, on December 20, 1827, to pass the first national law of expulsion.[72]

Not surprisingly, the pro-Spanish centralist-escoceses proclaimed their Plan de Montano at Otumba, Veracruz, only three days later. The plan called for the abolition of all secret societies, a complete change in the president's cabinet, the immediate expulsion of Poinsett from the country, and strict compliance with the constitution and existing laws. Poinsett was well known not only for his involvement with the York Rite lodge and the desire of the United States to acquire Texas and Mexican northern territory as far south as the Rio Grande River but also for his involvement in the internal anti-Spanish movement led by Vicente Guerrero in 1827.[73]

Immediately after the Plan of Montano was proclaimed, Vice-President Nicolás Bravo, Grand Master of the Scottish Rite masons, who had been

[71]Manning, "Texas and the Boundary Issue," 238–239, which thoroughly documents the correspondence between Poinsett and Clay concerning the Boundary Commission.

[72]Flores Caballero, *Counterrevolution*, 81–112; Harold D. Sims, *Descolonización en México: el conflicto entre mexicanos y españoles, 1821–1831* (Mexico, 1982), 18–21, 26–37, 243–248.

[73]Juan Suárez y Navarro, *Historia de México y del general López de Santa Anna* (Mexico: Imprenta de Ignacio Cumplido, 1850), 90; Leonard Duvin Parish, "The Life of Nicolás Bravo, Mexican Patriot" (Ph.D. dissertation, The University of Texas at Austin, June 1951), 183–184; Sims, *Descolonización en México*, 30–33; Flores Caballero, *Counterrevolution*, 116–118.

elected to the vice-presidency by the centralist-escoses, took over the rebelling forces. The government sent General Guerrero, a staunchly active federalist-yorkino, to quell the revolt. He quickly did so at Tulancingo, where Bravo and his staff were captured, putting a swift end to the Montano affair. Bravo lost his position as vice-president and he and sixteen of his supporters were exiled from Mexico for a period of six years, in June 1828.[74]

Bravo's exile was a serious blow to the centralist-escoses, for 1828 was an important election year and Bravo, their leading candidate for the presidency, was in exile. Population growth declined in 1827 both because of the expulsion of the Spaniards and the departure of others who feared the unstable conditions and because the political climate was not conducive to colonists. Also, the introduction by the Coahuila y Texas state legislature of a bill to expel some Spaniards and severely restrict their movement and activities as early as March 24, 1827,[75] raised the possibility that it might do the same against incoming foreign colonizers from any country. In California, in 1827, political chief José María Echandia, however, did not apply the laws against the Spanish missionaries, even though they refused to take the oath of allegiance to the Mexican constitution. He argued that Mexican substitutes had to be present to take their places before they could be expelled.[76] Hence only five Spaniards were expelled from California out of a total of sixty-eight. None were expelled from New Mexico.[77]

Although Mexico had always insisted on the binational survey of the northern boundary prior to approval of the Adams-Onís Treaty, negotiations between Poinsett and the Mexican authorities began upon approval of the treaty on January 8, 1828, before the Mexican boundary commission arrived in Texas. The negotiating parties signed the ratification of the Treaty of 1819, on January 12, 1828. But although it was approved by both the United States congress and the Mexican congress, the treaty did not go into effect, because the Mexican minister of foreign affairs delayed its final execution.[78]

During the remainder of 1828, Mexico was so involved in state and national elections, especially the presidential election, that the issue of territorial integrity received little attention. Not until November 21, 1828, was the government finally able to issue regulations governing the colonization of its territories. Its proclamation, however, did not help colonization in the territories, especially in California, because it stated that mission lands could not be colonized until it was determined whether they belonged to

[74]Ibid., 117; Súarez y Navarro, *Historia de México*, 91–97; Sims, *Descolonización en México*, 38–40; Parish, "The Life of Nicolás Bravo," 182–208.

[75]*El Sol*, V, No. 1659 (December 13, 1827), 3750; Benson, "Texas as Viewed from Mexico, 264–267.

[76]Hutchinson, *Frontier Settlement in Mexican California*, 135–136.

[77]Sims, *Descolonización en México*, 59.

[78]Manning, "Texas and the Boundary Issue," 241–244.

mission Indians and Mexican settlers or not.[79] The few settlers in the region were convicts shipped there by the government despite protests by the Californians.

Only in the state of Coahuila y Texas did colonization, the recommended protector of Mexican territorial integrity, continue to proceed fairly rapidly. Mier y Terán, along with the boundary commission, had reached Nacogdoches by 1829 and continued to survey the area and to report his findings. In his report of June 30, 1828, Mier y Terán described the population there as a strange mixture unparalleled in Mexico—numerous tribes of peaceful but armed Indians ready at any moment for war, whose steps toward civilization required the close supervision of a strong and intelligent government; foreign colonists, more aggressive and better informed than the Mexican inhabitants, but also more shrewd and unruly (among them fugitives from justice, vagabonds, and criminals); and slaves. He declared that both Mexicans and colonists complained about the union of Texas with Coahuila and favored the organization of Texas as a federal territory.[80]

Evidence that the threat to territorial integrity in the northern area in early 1829 was not of great concern to the Mexican government is the fact that President Victoria ordered Mier y Terán, on January 11, 1829, to return immediately to Mexico City. By early March, he and the other members of the commission had reached Matamoros, Tamaulipas, where he received orders to remain.[81]

Anti-Spanish feeling continued to grow during 1828, despite the first law of expulsion. By January 9, 1829, the Committee for Public Safety presented to the Chamber of Deputies a new and much more stringent bill to expel the remaining Spaniards. After heated debate in both the Chamber of Deputies and the Senate this second expulsion law was approved on March 30, 1829.[82]

Even before the passage of this law, the Spanish government with the aid of some of the exiles expelled earlier had begun plans to regain New Spain. Both England and the United States seemed to be aware of Spain's plans to invade its former colony. Although it had feared such an invasion and had used this fear to justify the expulsion laws, the Mexican government was unprepared for the arrival of General Isidro Barradas's expedition of 4,000 men at Cabo Rojo, near Tampico, on July 27, 1829—a threat not only to Mexico's territorial integrity but also its very independence

[79]Hutchinson, *Frontier Settlement in Mexican California*, 137.

[80]Barker, *Life of Stephen F. Austin*, 261–262; Morton, *Terán and Texas*, 58–60; Alleine Howren, "Causes and Origin of the Decree of April 6, 1836," *Southwestern Historical Quarterly* 16 (1912), 395–398.

[81]Morton, *Terán and Texas*, 77–79.

[82]Flores Caballero, *Counterrevolution*, 116–131; Sims, *Descolonización en México*, 61–122.

as a nation. General Mier y Terán, headquartered at Matamoros, was able to restrain the progress of the invaders until the Mexican government could send reinforcements. The weather, the unhealthy coastal conditions, and the Mexican army forced Barradas to surrender to Mier y Terán on September 11, 1829.[83]

This Spanish threat to Mexican independence united briefly all Mexicans inside and outside Mexico. Two weeks prior to the arrival of the Barradas expedition, generals Nicolás Bravo (the former vice-president), Miguel Barragán, José Antonio Echavarri, and Lt. Tiburcio Canas, all political exiles from either the Montano revolt or the Arenas conspiracy and all centralist-escoses, wrote the Mexican minister of war, Francisco Moctezuma, from New York City, offering to fight for Mexico against the anticipated Spanish invaders, if permitted to return to Mexico.[84]

Unity, however, quickly dissolved with the Mexican victory. Shortly before the news of Barradas's surrender reached Mexico City, President Guerrero pardoned the leaders of the Montano revolt and Arenas conspiracy and granted them permission to return to Mexico. During the last half of 1829 *El Sol* had begun a bitter attack against the United States and Poinsett by reprinting in its entirety the pamphlet *Conozca México Entero al Comisionado Regio*, which accused Poinsett of being not only an agent of the United States but also of Spain, who had informed Ferdinand VII that the time was right for the invasion of Mexico. The pamphlet concluded by asking for the dismissal of Poinsett from Mexico and suggested that "he carry in his suitcase with him Lorenzo de Zavala."[85]

Before the news of victory over the Spanish invaders had reached Mexico City, *El Sol*, in August and September, continued to emphasize the desire of the United States to invade Texas and Coahuila as well as other border areas.[86] The U.S. threat to Mexican territorial integrity was heightened in November when *El Sol* published a letter, dated New York, September 22, 1829, from Nicolás Bravo to Minister of War Moctezuma. Bravo urged the national government to "open its eyes and provide remedies for the evil threatening Texas by the Anglo-Americans, who were trying to usurp it." He was not referring to those who had settled Texas legally but to those who entered illegally, and especially to the threat of invasion by the United States so constantly evident in newspapers in New Orleans, Nashville, New York, and elsewhere.

[83]Flores Caballero, *Counterrevolution*, 137–140.

[84]The letter dated July 13, 1829, was sent to Carlos María Bustamante for transmittal to the Mexican minister; however, it was not transmitted to the Mexican minister until October 8, 1829. It appeared in *El Sol*, I, No. 150 (November 7, 1829), 517–518.

[85]*Conozca México entero al comisionado regio*, No. 2 (Mexico: Impreso en la Oficina a cargo de C. José Uribe Y Alcalde, 1829); *El Sol*, I, No. 13 (July 29, 1829), 113–114.

[86]Ibid., Nos. 48, 53, 54, 78 (August 17, 22, 23, and September 16, 1829), 192, 209, 214, 312.

Bravo had sent his letter to Carlos María Bustamante for transmittal to the minister of war along with a lengthy manifesto addressed to the Mexican people and signed "A Mexican" and some United States newspaper clippings to support his argument.[87] In the manifesto he called upon his fellow citizens to maintain the integrity of the Mexican Republic in the face of the aggrandizing appetite of the Anglo-Americans, who had forgotten the wise counsel of the immortal founder of American liberty, George Washington. Bravo mentioned the veiled attempt to purchase Texas and stated that even he had been approached in New York on the subject. After quoting Washington at length on the dangers of allowing foreigners to intervene in the internal politics of the United States, he asked why Mexico did not follow Washington's wise advice.[88] After the publication of Bravo's manifesto in *El Sol*, the editors denounced the yorkinos and Poinsett and alleged that the latter had probably influenced the naming of the new minister of foreign affairs, Agustín Viezca, a Coahuiltecan yorkino, who had assumed office on the previous day. They maintained that if the United States had loaned the Mexican government five million dollars with its payment secured by a portion of Texas, the purchase and sale would have been completed and Poinsett would have achieved his principal objective.[89]

The yorkino newspaper *El Correo de la Federación* responded to the manifesto, stating that the Guerrero government had not considered selling any part of the country and that the boundary treaty between the United States and Mexico soon to be ratified would show clearly that Texas remained a part of Mexico.[90] The centralist-escoceses, who never accepted the Guerrero government, continued their campaign against him, which began when he took office on April 1, 1829.

Guerrero named Mier y Terán commandant general of the Eastern Internal Provinces in September 1829 and ordered him in October 1829 to prepare for a military expedition into Texas to defend it against the United States. In response to this order, Mier y Terán, on November 14, repeated almost verbatim part of the denunciation of the United States designs on Texas that Bravo had made in his earlier letter to Carlos María Bustamante. Mier y Terán, a member of the Scottish Rite lodge, certainly believed in a strong

[87]Ibid., No. 126 (November 3, 1829), 502–503. For more detail in English about this episode, see also Benson, "Texas As Viewed from Mexico," 264–267.

[88]Bravo's manifesto was published in full in *El Sol*, I, No. 127 (November 4, 1829), 505–507, followed by a report (pp. 507–508) of the reasons for the offer of a purchase of Texas taken from the *Nashville Republican*. The manifesto appeared in full also in the *Gaceta Constitucional de Nuevo León*, Nos. 175–178 (November 20, December 3, 10, and 17, 1829), 4, 1-2, 3–4, and 2. It possibly appeared in other Mexican newspapers not available to the author.

[89]*El Sol*, No. 127 (November 4, 1829), 508.

[90]*Correo de la federación mexicana*, IX, No. 565 (November 8, 1829), 4.

national government.[91] He wrote to Bustamante, also on November 14, enclosing a secret annotated report upon which he, Bustamante, during the coming year would base his story of "The Catastrophe of Texas," which would "irresistibly occur on the Mexican yorkino scene during the year 1830." After explaining what Poinsett and his cohorts were already doing in Texas, Mier concluded by asking Bustamante to give Bravo a warm embrace.[92] On December 29, 1829, Mier wrote letters to both Minister of War Moctezuma and to Bustamante, repeating again that the entire coast and frontier were already in possession of the Anglo-Americans; that all means of communication within Texas were in their hands; and that they were continuing to settle in the most important places in the interior. He said it was his duty to recommend to the Mexican government that "if the colonization contracts in Texas by North Americans were not suspended and if conditions of their establishment were not watched" that "precious portion of our territory will be lost."[93]

Vice-President Anastasio Bustamante, who had headed the Army of the Reserve in Veracruz during the attempted Spanish reconquest, continued in that command and had not returned to Mexico by December. The conspiracy against the Guerrero government which had been brewing under the centralist-escoses since April culminated on December 4, 1829, with the proclamation of the Plan of Jalapa by the Army of the Reserve. The proclamation called upon Anastasio Bustamante to accept the Plan and become its leader, which he promptly did. Guerrero took the field briefly against his rebellious vice-president, but heavily outnumbered, he soon resigned the presidency and returned to his home near Acapulco. Vice-President

[91]Manuel Mier y Terán, Pueblo Viejo de Tampico, November 14, 1829, MS. No. 20-2-4713 of the Hernández y Dávalos Collection in the Benson Latin American Collection, University of Texas at Austin; for an English translation, see Morton, *Terán and Texas*, 99-101.

[92]Mier y Terán to Carlos María Bustamante, Pueblo Viejo de Tampico, October 14, 1829, MS. No. 20-2-4748 of the Hernández y Dávalos Collection in the Benson Latin American Collection, University of Texas at Austin.

[93]Mier y Terán to Secretary of War Francisco Moctezuma, Pueblo Viejo de Tampico, December 29, 1829, MS. No. 20-2-4724 of the Hernández y Dávalos Collection in the Benson Latin American Collection, University of Texas at Austin; Carlos María Bustamante published almost verbatim excerpts both from the October 14, 1829, report and the letter accompanying it, and the December 29 report in supplement No. 2 of his *Voz de la patria*, II (February 5, 1830). He did not indicate the author of the reports, to whom they had been directed, or their dates. Compare Morton, *Terán and Texas*, 104-105, who took his information from an excerpted account of José Antonio Facio, minister of war, made to Alamán on January 23, 1830. It should be noted that Moctezuma served as minister of war from April 1, 1829, until January 13, 1830, and all Mier's correspondence during that period was addressed to him and not to Facio, who became minister on January 14, 1830; for more detail on these communications, see Benson, "Texas as Viewed from Mexico," 268-269.

Bustamante with congressional approval became acting president of Mexico on January 1, 1830.[94]

During January, *El Sol* and the new government newspaper *Registro Oficial* continued to keep the United States attempt to purchase Texas before the public,[95] doubtless to gain support from the public and Congress for a new and much more stringent colonization law. On February 8, Alamán, the new minister for internal and foreign affairs, presented such an initiative to Congress in a secret session, which was immediately referred to a joint committee of the two houses.[96]

While the committee was preparing a bill based on Alamán's initiative, the government kept the Texas issue before the public through articles in its *Registro Oficial.* A lengthy review of William Walton Morris's *Considerations on the Propriety and Necessity of Annexing the Province of Texas by the United States* appeared on February 17. On the following day a three-column editorial on Texas appeared which stated that Texas had been won originally by the Mexicans and should remain a part of Mexico and that the Mexican Republic under any circumstances would be able to preserve the integrity of its territory. On February 23, after printing another passage on the United States attempt to negotiate with Mexico on the acquisition of Texas, the editors hastened to say that the current government had not been approached on the subject by the United States, nor would it listen to such a proposal, because it could not dispense with a hand's length of its national territory. The article concluded with the statement: "We have not inherited at this point the errors of the Spanish cabinet that sold its rich possessions to become poor and burdened with debts."[97]

Exactly one month after receipt of Alamán's initiative, the Chamber of Deputies began discussion on the joint committee's nineteen-article bill titled "Proposal for a Law to Preserve the Integrity of the Territory of the Republic." During the following three days, all articles passed quickly without discussion and all but three passed unanimously.[98]

[94]Flores Caballero, *Counterrevolution*, 140–141; Lorenzo de Zavala, *Ensayo histórico de las revoluciones de México desde 1808 hasta 1830*, 2 vols. (Paris: D. Dupont et G. Laguione, 1831–1832), II, 462–467, 492–495.

[95]*El Sol*, II, No. 193 (January 9, 1830), 772, and No. 207 (January 23, 1830), 825; *Registro Oficial*, No. 4 (January 24, 1830), 12; and No. 7 (January 24, 1830), 25.

[96]"Iniciativa de la ley de 6 de abril 1830," signed February 8, 1830, first published in Vicente Filisola, *Memoria para la historia de la guerra de Tejas*, as a *folletín* in the newspaper *El Universal*, 2 vols. (Mexico, 1848–1849), II, 589–615; published also in *Diccionario universal de historia y geografía*, 10 vols. (Mexico, 1853–1855), I, 48–56.

[97]*Registro Oficial*, No. 28 (February 17, 1830), 108–109; No. 29 (February 18, 1830), 113–114; No. 34 (February 23, 1830), 138, 140.

[98]Mateos, *Historia parlamentaria*, VI, 86–96; "Session of Chamber of Deputies," *El Sol*, II, Nos. 281–283 (April 7–9, 20, 1830), 1121, 1125, 1129, 1173.

The Senate took up the approved bill on March 27 and the twenty senators present immediately approved Articles 1 through 11 and 13 through 19, most of them unanimously and with little discussion. After extremely heated debate in the Senate, Article 12 was withdrawn by the joint committee and its withdrawl was approved by the Chamber of Deputies. Article 12 read: "With the permission of the national government foreigners shall be permitted to purchase rural and urban real estate on the northern frontier and in both Californias." Those who argued against it claimed that it would allow foreign countries to promote the purchase of large tracts of territory and would thereby pose an even greater threat to the maintenance of territorial integrity than the law of Colonization of 1824.[99]

The law passed by Congress and promulgated on April 6, 1830, was a much weaker and more diplomatic law than the one recommended in Alamán's initiative. Alamán strongly attacked the United States for not having yet confirmed the boundary treaty and for its effort to take Texas, asked that Stephen F. Austin's contract be greatly modified, called for much stricter control of the United States settlers there, and urged the transfer of the authority to colonize the department of Texas from the state of Coahuila y Texas to the national government.

Minister of War José Antonio Facio had notified Mier y Terán on January 30, 1830, that he was sending at once supplies and recruits and six days later informed him that he had been named commanding general of Texas. Soon thereafter Facio ordered various state governors to send militiamen to Texas to serve under Mier. Even though the law did not make Texas a territory as Mier y Terán had suggested, he must have been pleased with it and felt that the "Catastrophe of Texas in 1830" which he had predicted had been aborted.

Laws and orders were more easily issued than carried out, however, as Mier y Terán was soon to learn. By February 1830, President Bustamante and his supporters appeared to have control of the Mexican government; but the opposition was not to be so easily put aside. On March 11, 1830, at Santiago Barrabas in Michoacán, Colonel José Codallos issued a proclamation charging the Bustamante government with not only failing to uphold the constitution of 1824 but also of not taking sufficiently energetic measures to preserve the integrity of the federation under attack in the Californias, in the fertile lands of Texas, and in the peninsula of Yucatán. He said that the Bustamante government evidently had had a hand in the

[99]"Sessions of the Senate," *El Sol*, II, Nos. 314, 317, 320–321 (May 10, 13, 16–17, 1830), 1281-1282; see also Alleine Howren, "Causes and Origin of the Decree of April 6, 1836," *Southwestern Historical Quarterly* 16 (1912-1913), 378–421; note that she states that she was unable to locate the congressional debates of this law; Barker and Morton also admit their failure to locate these debates.

events taking place in those areas or that its fear of losing power weighed more heavily on it than the issues of national independence or territorial integrity. According to Article 6 of the Codallos proclamation, as soon as the nation accepted his plan "part of the permanent army would be sent to Yucatán, Texas, and other frontiers of the republic to maintain its integrity."[100] Soon former president Guerrero and others in the states of México, Michoacán, and Oaxaca joined Codallos. The government sent generals Bravo and Gabriel de Armijo to oppose these rebels. With this serious rebellion in the south of Mexico threatening the very existence of the Bustamante government less than three months after its inception, attention was diverted from the northern frontier during most of 1830 and into 1831.

During 1830–1832, therefore, Mier y Terán was left to his own devices to raise troops and carry out his orders to organize an expedition to Texas. He did not receive the militiamen from the various states as the government had directed because the states claimed the order was unconstitutional and refused to comply.

Deputy José María Alpuche e Infante wrote Mier y Terán on January 23, 1830, that the plan of the Bustamante goverment was to provoke a civil war, and then to send him (Mier y Terán) to Texas, where he would find no success because of his lack of resources there. Alpuche continued that this action by the government would be the first step in making Texas "independent of the Mexican nation, which is what they want and the reason why they do not attend to its needs." He said that "among their other plans is to shoot us when the first disturbances occur." Alpuche began the letter by calling on Mier y Terán to lead the opposition against the Bustamante forces supporting the Plan of Jalapa.[101] Apparently Alpuche was not aware that Mier y Terán was a Scottish Rite mason and a friend of Anastasio Bustamente and of Bravo and had already accepted the Plan of Jalapa. Mier y Terán quickly sent Alpuche's letter to the Bustamante government.[102]

The events of 1830 to 1832 certainly seemed to prove Alpuche's prediction on every point. Although he enjoyed immunity from arrest and prosecution as a deputy to Congress and president of the Chamber of Deputies when Alpuche wrote the letter, he was arrested, on March 7, 1830, and sentenced to six years in exile. Other congressional members were executed for opposing the government, as was former president Guerrero. Prior to his arrest, Alpuche wrote Guerrero warning him that "the government was prosecuting all those opposed to it, even when they maintained silence,"

[100]Zavala, *Ensayo crítico de las revoluciones*, II, 514–515.

[101]*El Sol*, II, No. 255 (March 12, 1830), 1018.

[102]The editors of *El Sol*, No. 260 (March 17, 1830), 1040, asked why Alpuche had not been arrested immediately on receipt of this letter from Mier y Terán.

and that "six assassins have been released from prison in Mexico City and paid large sums to murder you." This letter influenced Guerrero's decision to support Codallo's Plan.[103]

During 1830 various states charged that the Bustamante goverment was using all of its regular forces in the south in pursuit of Guerrero and his supporters. The government continued this action until early 1831 as well as its propaganda campaign accusing Guerrero of offering Texas to the United States in return for money to finance his government and resist his enemies. The government newspaper carried such propaganda in its issues nine and ten days after Guerrero's capture by his betrayer Captain Francisco Picaluga in Acapulco and twenty days before Guerrero's execution before a government firing squad on February 14, 1831.[104]

One of the charges brought against Guerrero at his trial was that he had offered Texas to the United States as security for a loan to finance his government. To this charge Guerrero gave an unqualified rebuttal.[105] José María Tornel, named minister to the United States by Guerrero, was accused of having been sent to the United States to obtain money, with Texas as security. Tornel denied the accusation. Tornel did not reach New York until January 13, 1830, and had been in no position to offer such a deal. Furthermore, he continued as minister in the Bustamante government until mid-1831. Tornel reported to Alamán, Bustamante's minister of foreign affairs, on March 6, 1830, that Anthony Butler's replacement of Poinsett, as United States minister to Mexico, had been made with a view toward buying the province of Texas and that these steps indicated that perhaps Poinsett had given his government hopes of such an acquisition, but that he, Tornel, since his arrival in the United States, had tried constantly to dispel that idea through his newspaper articles.[106]

[103]William Forrest Sprague, *Vicente Guerrero, Mexican Liberator* (Chicago: Printed by R. R. Donnelly & Sons, 1931), 114–118; Suárez y Navarro, *Historia de México*, 226–236.

[104]Ibid. and *Registro Oficial*, IV, No. 21 (January 23, 1831), 91; No. 22 (January 24, 1831), 96; Sprague, *Vicente Guerrero*, 114–118. Eduardo del Castillo Nagrete, *México en el siglo XIX, o sea su historia desde 1808 hasta la época presente*, 25 vols. (Mexico, 1875–1892), XIX, 326–327.

[105]Suárez y Navarro, *Historia de México*, 230, 232.

[106]José María Tornel, *Manifestación del ciudadano José María Tornel al público* (Mexico: Imprenta del ciudadano Alejandro Valdés, 1833), 53–59, 70–73; Carlos Bosch García, *Material para la historia diplomática de México y los Estados Unidos, 1820–1848* (Mexico: Escuela Nacional de Ciencias Sociales, Universidad Nacional Autónoma de México, 1957), 120–121, 131–138, 178; Tornel to Alamán, Baltimore, March 6, 1830, in Archivo de la Secretaría de Relaciones Esteriores, MS. No. 6-19-6, leaf 2. Guerrero, on July 1, 1829, wrote a confidential letter to President Andrew Jackson, asking for the recall of Poinsett but inexplicably that letter did not reach Secretary Martin Van Buren's hands until October 1829, and no publicity was given to this action until years later. Hence the continued belief in Mexico that Guerrero was supporting the continuance of Poinsett in that country. See Dorothy Parton, *The Diplomatic Career of Joel Roberts Poinsett* (Washington, D.C.: The Catholic University of America, 1934), 137–145.

The Bustamante government, after the passage of the Law of April 6, 1830, prohibiting the continued settlement of Anglo-Americans on the northern frontier, was unable to entice Europeans or Spanish and Mexican families living in Louisiana or the Floridas to return to settle in Texas or on the northern frontier. Hence Alamán proposed an addition to Article 14 of that law, which suggested that some of the $500,000 provided in the law be used to pay transportation expenses of destitute Mexican women and children living in New Orleans (as a result of the laws of expulsion of 1827 and 1829) to come to Texas to settle. Consul Ortiz de Ayala had been writing Alamán repeatedly from Bordeaux, France, between June 26 and November 30, 1830, warning of the almost certain loss of Texas if the government did not act promptly to separate Texas from Coahuila and make it a national territory under strict government control. Ortiz de Ayala in a letter addressed to Vice-President Bustamante, dated November 30, 1830, included an extensive colonization and military plan and a budget for realizing it.[107] In his report to Congress in January of the following year, Alamán again asked that body to recognize the many flaws in the colonization system, which he had pointed out earlier, and to make the necessary reforms. He also indicated that the Coahuiltecan government was attempting to confront the difficulties on its frontier as best it could by issuing colonization contracts and organizing the national militia, measures which were supported by the national government as much as possible.[108]

The Bustamante government was so embroiled in the struggle to maintain itself against the opposition now struggling to restore Gómez Pedraza to the presidency that it paid no further attention to the issue of territorial integrity. The long delayed boundary treaty, encompassing the acceptance by both the United States and Mexico of the Adams-Onís Treaty of 1819, however, was finally signed by Bustamante and Alamán on January 14, 1832, and by President Jackson on April 5, 1832. Not until March 5, 1833, did it finally appear in print without comment in Mexico City. Melchor Múzquiz, acting interim president after Bustamante was forced to take the field against his opponents, ordered it published and circulated in December 1832; however, its publication failed to materialize until two months into the brief administration of President Gómez Pedraza.[109]

[107] Annual report of the Minister of Internal and External Affairs, *El Sol*, No. 627 (March 19, 1831), 2506. See Kelly and Hatcher, "Tadeo Ortiz de Ayala," 33–86, 152–164, 222–245, for translations of this correspondence and the responses of Alamán and Mier y Terán.

[108] Mexico, Secretaría de Relaciones Exteriores, *Memoria de la . . . leida el 10 de enero 1832 al congreso* (Mexico, 1832), 13–14, and its "Observaciones al estado relativo al censo de la república mexicana," 5–6.

[109] *El Telégrafo; periódico oficial del gobierno e los estados unidos mexicanos*, I, No. 54 (March 5, 1833), 1–2.

After Gómez Pedraza had assumed the presidency in late December 1832, Anastasio Bustamante and many of his former supporters were punished by exile or were dubbed deserters and forced to serve in the army. Gómez Pedraza ordered the Minister of War, on February 11, 1833, to send these so-called deserters to Texas to augment the 11th and 7th batallions defending the frontier there.[110]

Senator José Antonio Mejía wrote Austin on March 27, 1833, asking for his opinion on the derogation of Article 11 of the Law of April 6, 1830, the article that prohibited emigrants from nations bordering on Mexico to settle in the states or territories adjacent to their own nation. Mejía doubted the time was right to obtain such a change. What prompted Mejía to address Austin on this subject is presently not known; possibly it was the result of a letter from Ortiz de Ayala, dated Matamoros, February 2, 1833, addressed to President Gómez Pedraza, reporting on Ortiz's official trip to Texas between February 1832 and February 1833.[111]

An initiative from the Coahuila y Texas legislature asking that the law of April 6, 1830, be declared unconstitutional was received in the Chamber of Deputies in May 1833.[112] Carlos García, the new minister of internal and external affairs, informed Congress on May 20, 1833, that the colonization of Texas and the frontier was continuing, and that to achieve its objective and to improve relations with the inhabitants of the rest of Mexico all obstacles should be removed through inducements for the well-being of those colonists. He stated that the government would present initiatives to Congress to realize that important goal.[113] Finally the government, directed by Vice-President Gómez Farías, through an editorial in its newspaper on October 9, 1833, reminded the Chamber of Deputies of the pending "solicitude of Austin's colonists"—a solicitude on which depended the fate of many thousands of Mexicans, whose political situation was insupportable. The editorial continued that if this important matter did not receive the individual attention it deserved, Mexico would be in danger of losing a very large, rich part of its territory.[114]

On October 22, 1833, the Chamber of Deputies took action on a bill based on the initiative sent by Coahuila y Texas for reform of the colonization law of April 6, 1830. The first article, which derogated Article 11 of the 1830 law, passed unanimously without debate. All four articles were

[110]Ibid., I, No. 34 (February 3, 1833), 1; on deserters, see ibid., No. 113 (May 3, 1833), 1.

[111]José Antonio Mejía to Austin, Mexico, March 27, 1833, in *Austin Papers*, 3 vols. (Washington, D.C. and Austin: American Historical Association, 1924–1928), I, 933; Kelly and Hatcher, "Tadeo Ortiz de Ayala," 311–343.

[112]Session of the Chamber of Deputies, *El Telégrafo*, II, No. 30 (June 9, 1833), 1.

[113]Report of the Minister of Internal and External Affairs, *El Telégrafo*, II, No. 96 (August 14, 1833), 2.

[114]Ibid., III, No. 26 (October 3, 1833), 4.

quickly passed and transmitted to the Senate on the same day.[115] When the bill was considered by the Senate on the following day, all articles passed, although not unanimously.[116]

Vice-President Gómez Farías had supported the reform measures of the colonization bill and other matters relating to Texas and the frontier. Why the bill was not passed to him for his signature immediately after its passage is not presently known. It was not sent to the president for his signature until October 27, 1833, after the sudden return of Santa Anna to occupy the presidential chair for fifty days. After nine days, Santa Anna returned the bill to the Senate with the recommendation for an addition to Article 4 stating that the derogation of Article 11 in its Article 1 would not take effect until six months after publication of the law. Both houses agreed to the addition and the law was signed on November 21, 1833.[117]

Vice-President Gómez Farías and his cabinet members were well aware that in California, where the Spanish missionaries continued to control much of the land as well as the Indians, colonization would continue to be almost impossible. Hence it was not surprising that Minister of Eclesiastical Affairs Ramos Arizpe presented to the Chamber of Deputies, as early as April 13, a bill to secularize the missions of Upper and Lower California. That bill became law on August 17, 1833, with little opposition. But when a bill to allocate the vast mission lands was introduced, on April 16, 1833, it suffered a different fate. After some debate and revision, the Chamber of Deputies approved it by May 9 and sent it to the Senate, where it was sent to its committee on colonization, which never reported it out for consideration.[118]

Nevertheless, Gómez Farías, using the extraordinary powers voted him by Congress, continued his campaign to encourage colonization in California. He began appointing to positions in California those who believed that the population had to be increased to ward off the expanding threat from not only the Russians but also from the increasing number of Anglo-American hunters and traders. Recently arrived Deputy Juan Bandini of California joined Gómez Farías in this struggle for a strong colonization program for California. Bandini presented a bill, on November 7, 1833, "to authorize the government to use every means possible to assure the colonization, and make effective the secularization of the missions of

[115]Ibid., III, No. 72 (November 20, 1833), 1–2; Mateos, *Historia parlamentaria*, VIII, 442–450.

[116]Session of Senate, *El Telégrafo*, III, No. 80 (November 20, 1833), 1.

[117]Mateos, *Historia parlamentaria*, VIII, 477; *Colección de leyes y decretos del congreso general de la nación mexicana de los años 1833 a 1835*, . . . , 17 vols. (Mexico: Imprenta del Galvan, 1840), VII, 74; Barker, *Life of Stephen F. Austin*, 314; Austin to Samuel M. Williams, Mexico, November 26, 1833, in *Austin Papers*, I, 1015.

[118]Hutchinson, *Frontier Settlement in Mexican California*, 160–174, gives a thoroughly documented account of these bills.

Upper and Lower California." Under this bill money was to be made available from the estates belonging to the pious funds of these territories to provide resources for the families going there from Mexico City and the commission directing them. The bill, approved by both chambers by November 11, was signed into law by President Santa Anna on November 26, 1833.[119] By the end of 1833, Vice-President Gómez Faríaz again occupied the presidency and had the tools to proceed with his colonizing plans in Texas and California. His opportunity to use them, however, was short-lived, for in 1834 he and many of his supporters were removed from office and forced to flee the country for their own safety. "The Castrophe of 1830" predicted by Mier y Terán occurred not in 1830 but in early 1836. By that date Gómez Farías and many others were living in New Orleans, eking out a meager existence, and Mier y Terán had committed suicide in mid-1832, probably because he realized his inability to prevent that catastrophe.

As a nation, Mexico had reached the tender age of twelve in September 1833. Like all young nations, it was still trying to decide what it wanted to be: a constitutional monarchy, a federal republic, with most power vested in the states, or a central republic divided into departments, similar to the French Republic, with little power vested in the departments. Each form of government had its adherents, who from time to time during these years switched from one dominant group to another—the centralists and federalists. Unfortunately, although all the actors supported the notion of territorial integrity some were not averse to using the issue to achieve their own political goals. Their adherence to the maintenance of territorial integrity became more chauvinistic and malicious than genuine. To them, acquisition of political power and maintenance of the power was far more important than territorial integrity. Nevertheless, the use of the principle of "territorial integrity" proved to be a good justification for grasping power by any means, even overthrowing governments, as well as an excuse for revenge against political opponents. Sadly, the practice continued for many years to come.

[119]Ibid., 175–193.

III
Comparisons

Comparing Mexican Independence with the Revolution: Causes, Concepts, and Pitfalls

Paul J. Vanderwood

SCHOLARS OF MEXICAN HISTORY have for some time now flirted with the idea of comparing the nation's Independence movement of 1810 with its great Revolution which erupted a century later. In the main, their efforts have been hit, miss and run for cover. The investigators have been uncertain of the purpose of such comparisons, and they seem to wonder why do it at all. Maybe they're right. Where would a point-by-point comparison of the two events lead us? Probably not very far. Yet other historians treating different countries have shown that historical comparisons can be meaningful. The problem for the Mexicanists has been one of approach, of conceptualization. While similarities and dissimilarities between the two major social upheavals have been relatively easy to identify, there has been a general failure to fit the rebellions where they belong in the overall flow of Mexican history. That is, the analysts have tended to treat the revolts as special events rather than as integral parts of the nation's historical development over time. As George Steiner might say, they have observed the froth on the waves rather than the main currents of Mexican history.

Let me state at the start that I do not really think that a truly meaningful comparison of the Independence movement and the Revolution can yet be made. We can ponder the topic and can speculate on possibilities here and there, but we Mexicanists have yet to produce the kinds of quality studies which allowed a Barrington Moore to write so intelligently and in a comparative way about the social origins of dictatorship and democracy or Charles, Louise, and Richard Tilly to examine in a comparative sense the changing nature of popular collective violence in three European countries during the rebellious century which they stretched between 1830 and 1930.[1] We Mexicanists may congratulate ourselves on progress, as

[1]Barrington Moore, Jr., *Social Origins of Dictatorship and Democracy* (Boston: Beacon Press, 1966), and Charles Tilly, Louise A. Tilly, and Richard Tilly, *The Rebellious Century, 1830–1930* (Cambridge, Mass.: Harvard University Press, 1975).

evidenced by the fine essays presented in this volume, but despite their individual excellence, when taken as a whole they represent for me how very far we have to travel—both in an empirical and theoretical sense—before learned comparisons can be drawn.

Comparisons should begin with a question. Moore observed that national regimes ran the spectrum from democractic to authoritarian, and asked how each country's history determined where it settled on that range. In his search for a response he could have settled upon any number of variables, but he finally selected the relationships between patrons (lords) and peasants in the countryside. The Tillys looked at the ways in which popular protest (they termed it collective violence) fluctuated and changed as a function of two givens—state making and the development of capitalism—in Italy, France, and Germany during the rebellious century. But in the case at hand we are not comparing the Mexican experience with that of other countries, which, by the way, could be a valuable exercise. Instead, we are comparing two events, Independence and Revolution, and doing it as a tool to illuminate the flow of Mexican history over what the French Annalists would call the *longue durée*. At least, in my opinion this is what we ought to be doing. So what I am urging is a certain conceptual approach: to think of Independence and the Revolution not as singular events which occurred a century apart and somehow deserve comparison, but more simply as two important conjunctures—two rather large bleeps—along the continuum of Mexican history. We may ask the question, as is normally done, what were the peculiar circumstances that caused these two specific events to occur and to proceed as they did—but this approach tends to lift the events out of the ongoing context of Mexican history. Or we can ask how it was that two large popular rebellions, among many other seemingly smaller ones, incited by elites and middle groups were then controlled and halted, which leads us into an examination of the variable of collective protest and its linkages to social groups (notice my adversion to the word class) within the *given* context of colonialism, nation building, and capitalist development, which characterized Mexico (and a good part of the world) at the time.

At first glance one seems to see broad similarities between the causes of the Independence movement and the Revolution. The generally accepted argument goes something like this. Rather long periods of substantial economic growth (in the eighteenth century under the Bourbons and in the nineteenth century under Porfirio Díaz) mainly profited elites, invigorated an expanded and aspiring middle sector, while steadily worsening the lot of common people. The relatively good times ended abruptly; for the colonialists with the advent of the Napoleonic Wars and for the Porfiristas in the convulsions of international capitalism in the early twentieth century. In both epochs, the clump caused a credit crisis and overall declining conditions were compounded by drought and dearth. Finally a sharp political shock—in the case of the colonists the crisis with their king, and with the nationalists the question of the presidential succession—sparked the respective rebellions.

If all this seems dreary and familiar, it's because it is. The thesis rests upon the famous "J" curve of James Davies, which allows that revolution is most likely to occur when a long period of rising expectations and fulfillment is suddently interrupted. Expectations continue to rise, but satisfactions decline. The result is individual dissatisfaction which leads to economic and social upheaval and a coalition of groups interested in revolution as a remedy for their ills.[2] Now it may be difficult to disprove the J-curve model, but it's not hard to see what Davids did not do, and that is to compare his findings with similar circumstances in which revolutions did not occur—and goodness knows, Mexican history is full of them. Furthermore, Davies is not explicit enough about the social status of those people he is investigating. What might be true of the bourgeoisie may not be so for more common people. The curve may fit the middle class, but how about the masses?

A basic problem with the Davies curve also concerns its reliance on deprivation theory, or that of relative deprivation, of which so many Mexicanists, indeed Latin Americanists, seem to be especially fond. For them, the amount of discontent in a population is the primary cause of rebellions. Hence, the oft-used phrase "growing discontent." It's plausible the revolution may occur when discontent reaches a certain threshold, but whether or not deprivation drives it up—at least to the point of open rebellion—is another question. In fact, a number of historians of revolution have now decided that deprivation is not a principal cause of rebellion, even though it may have occurred. Indeed, I remember chatting informally with colleagues at the Mexicanist conference in Oaxtecpec in 1971 about deprivation as a cause of the Revolution, and we decided that the rebellion probably would not have occurred when it did had it not been for the crisis created by the presidential issue. No one at the time denied that deprivation, or relative deprivation, had taken place, although even that thesis has been more recently challenged, and I believe with reason. However, all agreed that deprivation was not a primary cause of the rebellion. The Tillys have now found that the chronological distribution of collective violence was far from random, and they concluded that the timing of these various rebellions did not depend upon the rate of urbanization, industrialization, or other structural changes that were normally thought to generate "increasing discontent." Instead, they located popular protest at times of national

[2]James C. Davies, "The J-Curve of Rising and Declining Satisfactions as a Cause of Revolution and Rebellion," in Hugh D. Graham and Ted R. Gurr, *Violence in America: Historical and Comparative Perspectives* (Beverly Hills: Sage, 1979), 690–730.

power struggles, which could be a powerful conceptual tool for us Mexicanists to employ, even if at the same time difficult questions concerning the nature of Mexican nationhood must be addressed.[3]

The shortcomings of deprivation theory have led some scholars to look in other directions. For instance, Theda Skocpol concentrates upon the structure of the state and its ability to employ force to defend itself against threats, both foreign and domestic. She also grants considerable importance to village power structures in accounting for agrarian rebellions.[4] All this has not been lost on Mexicanists. John Hart's recent book stresses U.S. economic dominance in Mexico as a primary cause of the Revolution. He equates foreign investment with an invasion, and in a sense sees the Revolution as a war of decolonization.[5] In some of his latest work Frederich Katz stresses the structure of government, while not eschewing factors of deprivation.[6] Two anthropologists, María Teresa Korek and Anna María Alonzo, who are completing dissertations at the University of Chicago, note that widening fissures in village hierarchy mobilized revolutionary discontent.[7] My own work in the Valley of Papigochic in the state of Chihuahua confirms the same point: that there may have been a variety of reasons for rebellion in Chihuahua, but that deprivation—relative or not—doesn't seem to have been one of them.

While conflicts within the political structure of villages is becoming a new, and I believe fruitful, way to examine oncoming revolution in 1910, there is no comparable work that I know of being done for the Independence period. Brian Hamnett's *Roots of Insurgency* moves in that direction, but as provocative as it is, it does not provide the specifics needed for comparative analysis. He intelligently treats the relationships between villages, private proprietors, district administrators, merchants, shopkeepers, even priests, but he does not penetrate the political structure of the village itself.[8] Christon Archer is also investigating regions during Independence, and

[3]Tilly, Tilly, and Tilly, *Rebellious Century*, Chapters 5 and 6.

[4]Theda Skocpol, *States and Social Revolutions: A Comparative Analysis of France, Russia, and China* (Cambridge: Cambridge University Press, 1979).

[5]John M. Hart, *Revolutionary Mexico: The Coming and Process of the Mexican Revolution* (Berkeley: University of California Press, 1987).

[6]Frederich Katz, "Mexico: Restored Republic and Porfiriato, 1867–1910," in Leslie Bethell, ed., *Cambridge History of Latin America* (Cambridge: Cambridge University Press, 1986), V.5, 28–78.

[7]María Teresa Korek, "Social Organization and Land Tenure in a Mestizo Community in Northern Mexico: Cuchillo Parado, Chihuahua, 1865–1900," presented at VII Reunión de Historiadores Mexicanos y Norteamericanos, Oaxaca, Mexico, October 22–26, 1985. Anna María Alonzo, "U.S. Military Intervention, the Villista Movement and Defensas Sociales: Popular Revolutionary Mobilization and Ideology in the Chihuahuan Sierra, 1916–1917," presented at the symposium, "Rural Revolt, the Mexican State and the U.S.," University of California, San Diego, February 18–19, 1987.

[8]Brian R. Hamnett, *Roots of Insurgency: Mexican Regions, 1750–1824* (Cambridge: Cambridge University Press, 1986).

has uncovered some village rivalries as a source of conflict subsumed by the Independence movement.[9] Meanwhile, Eric Van Young is looking at tension and conflict in Indian villages around Guadalajara in the late colonial period.[10] All of this work is highly suggestive of kindred events before and during the Revoltuion, but the timing and data needed to make valid comparisons are not yet there.

This is the way it is throughout the field of Mexican history, Enrique Florescano with corn prices before Independence, but no comparable study for Revoltuion.[11] Van Young's stimulating foray into messianism as ideology during Independence, but no one has yet seriously considered this possibility for the Revolution.[12] Even if there was no such widespread messianism in the Revolution (although one or two people have suggested that Madero was a messianic figure for common Mexicans), it would be important to know why the strains of messianism evident in the popular protest of 1810 had disappeared or had not resurfaced during the Revolution. Such research might well lead to an examination of the Reform and its aftermath from a religious point of view, something which is badly needed and has yet to be done.

I recently reviewed two books dealing with two states – Chihuahua and Yucatán – on the eve of the Revolution; that is, Mark Wasserman on Chihuahua and Allen Wells on Yucatán.[13] Both are decent scholarly accounts and one would think they could be compared: Chihuahua, where revolution broke out and persisted, versus Yucatán, which remained relatively calm throughout. But because their analyses come from different directions, they do not ask the same questions of their material. Hence we have apples and oranges and not much to compare. Wasserman tries it, but in a rather cavalier way which in my opinion yields distorted results. Had Wasserman had the benefit of Wells' work, which was published after his own, he might have altered his conclusions.

Geographic districting is one logical way to begin disciplined thinking about Independence and the Revolution in a comparative sense. We would

[9]Christon Archer, "Banditry and Revolution in New Spain, 1790–1821," *Biblioteca Americana* 1 (November 1982), 59–89.

[10]Eric Van Young, "Conflict and Solidarity in Indian Village Life: The Guadalajara Region in the Late Colonial Period," *Hispanic American Historical Review* 64 (February 1984), 55–79.

[11]Enrique Florescano, *Precios de maíz y crisis agrícolas en México, 1708–1810: ensayo sobre el movimiento de los precios y sus consecuencias económicas y sociales* (Mexico: El Colegio de México, 1969).

[12]See Van Young's essay in this volume.

[13]Mark Wasserman, *Capitalists, Caciques and Revolution: The Native Elite and Foreign Enterprise in Chihuahua, Mexico, 1854–1911* (Chapel Hill: University of North Carolina Press, 1984) and Allen Wells, *Yucatan's Guilded Age: Haciendas, Henequen and International Harvester, 1860–1915* (Albuquerque: University of New Mexico Press, 1985).

be talking about the Bajío and the far north with some emphasis on Chihuahua. Katz has noted that each region experienced pronounced economic growth on the eve of their respective revolts.[14] There was, in each case, heavy investment in mining, but probably the most important investment came in the form of mercantile capital which both stimulated commerce and created a panorama of debts, especially during the bad economic times which periodically occurred. In terms of land tenure, both regions were characterized by their prevalence of agricultural small holdings worked by people whom historians have, according to their personal bent, alternately labeled campesinos, peasants, rancheros, *labradores*, or agriculturalists. Mexicanists have long been at pain to find a term that adequately fits the ordinary rural Mexicans they are describing. Of course, this dilemma is complicated by the fact that the Mexicans themselves—and this is clear in the contemporary documentation—had no overall term which they consistently used to describe themselves. Perhaps they were telling us something: stop trying to categorize us. Nevertheless, conceptually speaking such categories make no sense, because groupings do not necessarily depend only on factors such as land and labor, but also on *mentalidad*—how the individuals thought of themselves and perceived of their world of which land and labor are only one part. Hence small landowners in the north (peasants or otherwise) were in all epochs different from smallholders in the center, because they thought differently about their land and their society, and their daily lives, among many other things.

The relationship between the Bajío in 1810 and Morelos and the far north in 1910 might also bear consideration. Like the Bajío in late colonial times, Morelos experienced rapid economic development before 1910, but it was concentrated in sugar and did not seem to stimulate the regional economy in the diversity of ways in which development did in Chihuahua, for example, at the same time. Also, most of the capital invested in Morelos came from domestic sources, as opposed to foreign in Chihuahua, which could have affected mentalidad in the respective places. Also, the campesinos of Morelos seem to have been much more solidified than were the common rural people of the north, again as a consequence of their mentalidad, which was naturally formed by a long historical process entirely different from that in the north. In essence, the campesinos of Morelos seem to have been looking backward—toward their past—for a solution of their problems. To the contrary, the Villistas and Carrancistas looked forward—ahead to participation in a changed political atmosphere, which certainly did not preclude it from being republican and capitalist.

[14]Frederich Katz, "Rural Rebellions after 1810," in Frederich Katz, ed., *Riot, Rebellions and Revolution: Rural Social Conflict in Mexico* (Princeton, N.J.: Princeton University Press, 1988), 521–560.

Partially because so much historical analysis presently relies on broad Marxist formulations, which is not to say it is wrong, the fate of popular movements has normally been linked to the relationship of the rebelling masses to other social groups. It is presumed that common people cannot go it on their own, at least in so far as revolution is concerned. And this consideration leads us to another point of possible comparison. The popular uprisings of Independence and the Revolution did not suddenly spring from below; the masses were called into action by groups, or segments of social groups, generally conceded a higher social status than *los de abajo*. These segments saw rebellion as a way to settle their ills and to advance their ambitions; other segments of the very same groups did not agree, even though they may have had the same grievances and ambitions. Van Young finds this relationship especially muddled outside the Bajío during Independence.[15]

In whatever way they were divided, historians have normally assembled these groups, loosely at best and sloppily at worst, as "the bourgeoisie." Now scholars have begun to focus upon the so-called provincial bourgeoisie, though they have yet to confront the wrinkles in their arguments—for instance, that northern hacendados led and abetted the Revolution as no other hacendados did in the country. And in Morelos, Katz finds that the Zapatistas were not allied to any other social groups, although their spokesmen and intellectual leadership came from Mexico City.[16]

For Independence, Hamnett has attempted to resolve the contradictory attitudes of elites and middle groups toward the rebellion by clumping them into categories, bound to be controversial, which go far beyond the shredded but still revered tapestry of creoles versus peninsulares, traditional elites versus an aspiring middle sector, and so on. He emphasizes that independence was only one option considered by the Mexican upper groups in their search for self-government.

Most preferred some form of autonomy within the Spanish Imperial system. In an original way he then slices up the bourgeoisie into various components: a Mexican or resident elite, which was a hybrid of noble and bourgeois individuals, both peninsulares and Mexican-born; a bureaucratic elite of individuals who expected to return to Spain; and a provincial elite wracked by social tensions. These groups were not monolithic and the Independence movement split them apart, and Hamnett concludes that ultimately linkages between the professional bourgeois and the popular

[15]Van Young, comments on this essay delivered as a paper at the symposium "The Independence of Mexico and the Creation of the New Republic," University of California, Irvine, February 20–21, 1987.

[16]Katz, "Rural Rebellions."

classes were unable to defeat the alliance between an entrepreneurial elite and the colonial power.[17]

Whether or not one agrees with the groupings designed by Hamnett, it is the overall thrust of his approach that intrigues me. Rather than viewing the Independence movement in its essence as a break from Spain, he edges toward a concept of civil war—different Mexican groups struggling for power inside of Mexico itself—regardless of the Spanish connection. And when elaborated, this kind of conceptualization will help us to compare it in a much more meaningful way to the Revolution.

Factors which frustrated the popular movement for Independence seem easier to come by than those which eventually controlled popular aspirations in the Revolution. For Independence, options other than rebellion were open to upper groups who wanted significant change but who feared a race war. Furthermore, popular participation seems to have been more limited during the Independence upheaval and, for reasons yet to be clarified, lacked the large-scale stick-to-itiveness of the revolutionaries of 1910, factors that must have aided the successful counterinsurgency of Calleja. Then again Van Young senses that perseverance may be overrated for the Revolution and understated for Independence.[18]

Much of the work on the Revolution has also identified bourgeois liberal participation in the struggle, although this important subject has been approached with more passion than method. Some have written of a national bourgeoisie, an important concept because of the word "national," which is presumably different than "regional." No doubt the entire question of social nationalization which assuredly took place in the period from Independence to the Revolution needs to be examined as to form, content, degree, and limits. Such research would also focus our attention on mentalidad, which in turn may help us to understand the mechanisms that allowed middle groups to control popular passion and to direct the rebellion toward their ends.

Judging by Hamnett's work and the outpouring of fair to middling to quite good regional studies published in recent years, approaching both Independence and the Revolution from a regional perspective can be enticing, even enlightening, although fraught with difficulties which begin with the problem of what one means by "region." Regardless of its uncertain accomplishments, even the best of this type of history inclines toward the type of investigation that Barrington Moore rather than Theda Skocpol would applaud. And what seems to be increasingly clear is that both the

[17]Hamnett, *Roots of Insurgency*, especially Chapter 1.

[18]Van Young, comments on this essay delivered as a paper at the symposium "The Independence of Mexico and the Creation of the New Republic," University of California, Irvine, February 20–21, 1987.

Independence movement and the Revolution were rooted in local grievances of very long standing which remained unresolved and probably were complicated by the rebellions. Certainly the local conflicts unearthed, mediated, and created by the Independence wars continued right on into the nineteenth century, to the Revolution, and through it. I believe that conceptually speaking this is the way to approach the two events—and this relates to my earlier comments concerning the necessity to view Mexican history over the longue durée and to see Independence and the Revolution as two conjunctures, not as turning points, along the route.

This means that Independence and the Revolution should be studied in the context of issues that have always characterized Mexican history—questions of land, water, ethnicity, local autonomy, regionalism, village structure, religious feeling and practice, climate, resources, dependency, power relationships, and violence (both official and otherwise). And it should be centered upon those social structures which have been and still are capable of withstanding political upheaval. And this is why François-Xavier Guerra's history of the Revolution, which emphasizes the long-term, ongoing conflict between traditionalism and modernization, is so interesting, even though it is bound to be roundly criticized for many of its broad generalizations and unconvincing conclusions.[19]

John Tutino also studies Mexican agrarian life over a long period, from before Independence through the Revolution, and develops a model to explain why peasants rebel at certain times in specific regions. But his thesis rests upon deprivation theory, and his case studies lack documentation. Tutino invites debate on his book; he will get it.[20]

To tug at the continuing threads of Mexican history rather than exaggerating singular events certainly does not imply that the long course of Mexican history has not been marked by changes in both attitude and practice. Katz has noted (citing William B. Taylor's work) that protest in the colonial period was mostly spontaneous and concerned local matters such as abuses by colonial officials which were quickly redressed by superior administrative order. Noticeably absent were conflicts concerning land, because, according to Katz, capitalist expansion of rural estates had yet to impinge upon small farmer and village holdings.[21] I am not sure that all colonialists would concur with that opinion, and I would not be surprised if we discover land at issue when disciplined research begins to unravel

[19]François-Xavier Guerra, *Le Mexique de l'ancien régime a la révolution*, 2 vols. (Paris: Editions L'Harmattan, 1985).

[20]John Tutino, *From Insurrection to Revolution in Mexico: Social Bases of Agrarian Violence, 1750–1940* (Princeton, N.J.: Princeton University Press, 1986).

[21]Katz, "Rural Rebellions in Colonial and Pre-Conquest Mexico," in Katz, ed., *Riot, Rebellions and Revolution*, Chapter 3; William B. Taylor, *Drinking, Homicide and Rebellion in Colonial Mexican Villages* (Stanford: Stanford University Press, 1979).

what really happened at the local level during the turbulence of the Independence wars. In fact, Christon Archer's essay in this book inclines in that direction; local and regional land questions seem to have characterized much of the Independence struggle. Tutino would certainly concur.

Land certainly seemed at some issue during the Mexican Revolution, although possibly much less so than official rhetoric before and after the fighting would have us believe. For instance, Robert H. Holden concludes that the labor and results of the *dislindadores*—those bêtes noires of historiography concerning the Revolution—who surveyed and divided up so much territory in the 1880s, did *not* contribute in any important way to the development of revolutionary pressures.[22] My own work in the Valley of Papigochic, which was the *cuna* of the Revolution, does not find land as a primary cause of discontent, but others disagree. Anna María Alonzo, who is studying Namiquipa, one of the villages in the Valley of Papigochic, tells me that encroachment by a neighboring hacienda was a major cause of rebel mobilization in the town. I would put more emphasis on the split in that village's power structure which occurred before the Revolution, but the revolutionaries certainly complained of land usurpation, even if their losses judged by today's perceptions may appear to have been minimal.

The role of land in the Independence movement and the Revolution, and before, between, and after these events, again is only another way to make comparisons. On another tack, we might take a lead from the Tillys and examine the changing nature of collective violence in Mexico. They note how singular food riots, tax protests, and resistence to military conscription became much larger and better organized movements during the period of state building and intense capitalist development which characterized the aforementioned rebellious century in Europe. The transition from disparate mobs to organized units did not follow a smooth track; it had its exceptions and contradictions. But when one looks at mobilization patterns, their texture, extent, and strength, for Independence and Revolution, the change becomes apparent. The Tillys would weigh them against their models of competitive, proactive, and reactive movements,[23] but the way to understand them returns us to mentalidad. The collective consciousness of Mexicans had changed between the two events because of what had been and was happening along the longue durée.

Collective consciousness is a heady concept which defies proof; most historians avoid it, although the Annalists have made it a basic tenet of their approach. In constructing a hypothesis for comparing Independence and the Revolution, one could posit that while long-standing local grievances

[22]Robert H. Holden, "The Mexican State Manages Modernization: The Survey of the Public Lands in Six States, 1876–1911" (Ph.D. dissertation, University of Chicago, 1986).

[23]Tilly, Tilly, and Tilly, *Rebellious Century*, 248–254.

form the bedrock of both popular movements (setting aside the linkages to other social groups), it was the way in which common Mexicans perceived of their grievances and sought to redress them that had changed. What this rejects is the exasperation of futility of a Mariano Azuela[24] and gives ordinary Mexicans—both rebels and *pacíficos*—their due: an ideology, as dense, and even as contradictory, as it probably was.

Scholars know public consciousness exists but have found it nearly impossible to decipher it. Marxists have had the best of it, because of their concerns for class consciousness; most other historians, excluding the Annalists, avoid it. We are back again talking about mentalidad, and some intriguing possibilities have been set forth. We have forward- and backward-looking peasants in the same village which helps to explain social rifts. James C. Scott situates village people in a moral economy, where their differences are resolved through cooperative mechanisms and realities.[25] Not so, says Samuel L. Popkin; rural commoners are agressive and acquisitive and the competition among them does not cease.[26] Tutino probes the peasant's sense of security, but more as a novelist than a historian.[27] E. P. Thompson is properly acclaimed for his intuitions about the mentalidad of ordinary people, although his insistence on their innate sense of justice—just price, just wage and all that—has been challenged.[28] And George F. E. Rudé is exciting with his models, specifically the thesis that mentalidad is a combination of inherent and derived notions and beliefs—*inherent* insofar as they stem from the direct experience, oral tradition, or folk memory of the ordinary people, and *derived* in the sense of ideas and beliefs borrowed from the "outside," meaning from others. As time proceeds, an amalgam takes place, although to an uncertain degree and at different levels of sophistication. Circumstances and experience determine the blend, which explains why in revolution people with similar inherited and derived beliefs sometimes take an opposite tack.[29]

These are not rules, but thoughts, and despite my admiration for the ideas of Rudé and others, they have not made me more confident about my own work on the messianic rebellion at Tomochic. In fact, I have only recently decided that it was messianic at all. Eric Hobsbawm and most others

[24]Mariano Azuela, *The Underdogs* (New York: New American Library, 1962).

[25]James C. Scott, *The Moral Economy of the Peasant: Rebellion and Subsistence in Southeast Asia* (New Haven: Yale University Press, 1976).

[26]Samuel L. Popkin, *The Rational Peasant: The Political Economy of Rural Society in Vietnam* (Berkeley: University of California Press, 1979).

[27]Tutino, *Insurrection to Revolution.*

[28]E. P. Thompson, "The Moral Economy of the English Crowd in the Eighteenth Century," *Past and Present* (February 1971), 76–136.

[29]George F. E. Rudé, *Ideology and Popular Protest* (New York: Pantheon Books, 1980), especially Chapter 2.

insist that millennial movements are backward looking,[30] a position confirmed by today's liberation theologists. But the rebels at Tomochic were not looking back, at least not in the sense of the Sioux Indians who were ghost dancing at the same time in South Dakota. The insurgents at Tomochic were looking forward to a world of equality, they said, devoid of clerics, doctors, and even money. At least they saw money as one of mankind's major evils, and they were willing to die for their beliefs. Maybe they even thought they *had* to die in order to bring about their new world.

So to them money was quite evil—or was it? I recently encountered a document which indicated that while they were in rebellion before being crushed by the army that they were quite interested in money. They insisted that money owed them from business transactions before the revolt be paid up. And their leader averred that each rebel soldier was being paid four pesos a day, which for the times would have been an extraordinary wage for most ordinary Mexicans. So I have a contradiction to work out—but damn the contradictions—and remember that at the time of Garibaldi's wars in the 1860s, an Italian brigand issued a proclamation to the effect:

> Out with traitors, out with beggars, long live the fair kingdom of Naples with his most religious sovereign, long live the vicar of Christ, Pius IX, and long live our ardent republican brothers.[31]

Or, as the Cuban bandit-patriot, Manuel García, asserted in a leaflet, issued in 1891, when he considered himself at war with Spain:

> We are so oppressed in every way that we have determined to proclaim the Independence of our island and constitute the Republic of Cuba, *annexed* to the United States. . .
>
> We now respectfully ask the Foreign Governments to maintain neutrality on this civil war, and if the reasons we have to declare war in Spain draw your sympathy, *come and help us.*[32]

So there you have it: damn the contradictions and on with our study of Independence and the Revolution in a comparative sense but imbedded in the mainstream of Mexican history and with our attention riveted on mentalidad.

[30]Eric J. Hobsbawm, *Primitive Rebels: Studies in Archaic Forms of Social Movement in the 19th and 20th Centuries*, 2d ed. (New York: Praeger, 1963), especially Chapters 4 and 5.

[31]Rudé, *Ideology and Popular Protest*, 31.

[32]Rosalie Schwartz, "Lawless Liberators: Patriots, Brigands and Cuban Independence," MS. (San Diego, Calif., 1987), 84.

Independence and Revolution: Continuities and Discontinuities

Linda B. Hall

THERE ARE MANY SIMILARITIES between the movement begun by Father Miguel Hidalgo for the independence of the Mexican state from Spain, 1810–1821, and the revolution against the dictatorship of Porfirio Díaz, 1910–1920, although the outcomes were quite different. There is still a great deal of disagreement about the causes and processes of these widespread armed uprisings, but recent scholarship has indicated that many of the same sorts of grievances continued throughout the intervening century. Moreover, the opportunity for these grievances to culminate in a major national movement, much longer and more successful in the case of the latter, depended greatly on the vacuum of power at the center, that is, the weakness of the state.[1] The processes involved seem to have been much the same as well—a groundswell of local disturbances along with the emergence and increasing power of local leaders, harnessed for a time to a central cause but always difficult to control. Indeed, the integration of these powerful leaders into a unified, institutionalized state proved virtually impossible for the first part of the nineteenth century, and only the consensus-building talents of a remarkable leader made centralization possible (though incomplete) in the decade after the Mexican Revolution.

Brian Hamnett's work on the development of insurgency in the various regions of Mexico in the period after 1750 has shown that local grievances were widespread and led to sporadic outbreaks of protest and violence. As with the Mexican Revolution, many of those conflicts were focused on the land, although the sources of the problems seem to have been somewhat different. Indian population recovery in the eighteenth century seems to have

[1]In this discussion, I draw extensively from Brian Hamnett's work on independence, *Roots of Insurgency: Mexican Regions, 1750–1824* (Cambridge: Cambridge University Press, 1986), and Alan Knight, *The Mexican Revolution*, 2 vols. (Cambridge: Cambridge University Press, 1986).

been an important factor in causing pressure on the land, and fencing by the landlords of areas traditionally used by Indian and peasant communities led increasingly to disturbances. Although the normal action for the Indian community was to seek redress through the courts, asking not only for the land that they currently held but also additional land to provide for the increase in their numbers, conflict was accelerating as the independence struggle approached. In actions similar to those taken by peasant communities at the outbreak of the Mexican Revolution in 1910, villagers sometimes actually invaded the lands in question and began to use them.[2] In addition, landlords, eager to secure a ready supply of labor, tried to tie laborers to their own service in various ways. Although the Crown tried to prevent the spread of debt-peonage, which would have reduced the laborers of the hacienda to an immobile servitude, and additionally inveighed against corporal punishment, royal officials were nevertheless enjoined to prevent laziness and sloth. Thus Spanish officials did conspire with local notables to provide forced labor for the haciendas. Still, protest by the villagers in general was confined to those individuals actually near at hand as opposed to the King, who continued to be seen as a sort of protector.[3] The importance of land questions, both related to the possession of land and the labor arrangements that pertained to it, is quite clear in the case of the Mexican Revolution as well, and I agree with Alan Knight and Frank Tannenbaum that it was in its essence a "popular, agrarian movement."[4]

It is important to keep in mind, of course, that the pressure on the land at the time of the latter conflict was closely tied to questions of the integration of Mexico into the world market and the growth of commercial agriculture. Knight argues that the agrarian motivation during the Revolution was relatively stronger in areas such as Morelos than it was in the north, where it was combined with a resistance to central control, but in this respect as well, the 1910–1920 period was similar to Independence. Hamnett argues that in the latter part of the eighteenth century, as the Crown sought to extend a more sound administrative control over New Spain, "The actions of over-zealous Visitors-General after 1765 initiated a process of breakdown of consent, which threatened to endanger the balance which previous metropolitan governments had managed to hold intact." Although Hamnett indicates that protest was more widespread and effective in New Granada and Peru during this period than it was in New Spain, nevertheless it was a factor to be contended with. Examples in New Spain were protests engendered by the attempts by Spanish officials to enforce the tobacco monopoly and to tax the production of pulque for local village use. Changes in traditional practices and what were seen as administrative abuses also

[2]Hamnett, *Roots of Insurgency*, 88–89, 92.

[3]Ibid., 84–87, and Eric Van Young's essay in this volume.

[4]Knight, *The Mexican Revolution*, I, xi.

became flashpoints for protest. One such abuse, actually prohibited by the law, was the *repartimiento*, the provision of trade monopolies by administrators in local areas to merchants who repaid the favor through payoffs to the same underpaid officials.[5]

These legal and illegal intrusions of officialdom into the countryside are similar to what Knight sees as the root causes of "serrano" rebellion in 1910–1920. He indicates that the problems were greatest in those remote areas, many of them in mountainous regions of northern Mexico, "wherever the authority of state and landlord was tenuous," which had been able to maintain a relative independence from both state and landlord until the time of Porfirio Díaz. Protest was not unknown in these relatively undisturbed areas, as "The local urge to independence, conflicting with the state's unremitting, if sometimes ineffectual, quest for obedience, produced numerous serrano rebellions, from the colonial through the independence periods and down to the Porfiriato." But as the state's ability to extend its control more effectively grew during the latter decades of the nineteenth century, the potential for revolt grew as well. Although some areas were protected by "old-style" Indian or mestizo caciques, individuals, and families whose power in local areas served to slow down the advance of the power of the center into their neighborhood, their ability to perform this function was eroding toward the end of the Porfiriato. Indeed, in many areas local leaders were replaced officially by persons from outside of the community, and the quest to recover "municipal autonomy" would become a major goal in the northern revolutionary movement. Another point about serrano rebellion is that it had the power to mobilize virtually the entire community, top to bottom, and thus exhibited less class division than was apparent in the more strictly agrarian regions to the south.[6] In this way, these movements bear considerable resemblance to some portions of the Independence forces, such as those of the Bravo family in Chilpancingo or of Hermenegildo Galeana of Morelos, affectionately known as "Tata Gildo" to his people, who brought with him to the struggle "a wide series of relatives, dependents, neighbors and compadres, as well as a great number of their negro and mulatto workers."[7]

A further similarity between the outbreak of the Independence movement and the Revolution was the question of economic dearth just preceding the beginning of violence. In New Spain, the loss of two harvests in a row would lead to disaster, as a drop in agricultural production would affect all sectors of the economy, given the importance of animals in both transportation and production in commerce and industry. Price rises in one agriculture product were quickly shifted to other items as attempts were

[5]Hamnett, *Roots of Insurgency*, 77–82.
[6]Knight, *The Mexican Revolution*, I, 115–127.
[7]Hamnett, *Roots of Insurgency*, 146.

made to substitute one for another. In addition, late colonial shortages were made more immediately acute for the population, as the period after 1760 was marked by a general inflationary trend. At the time of the Hidalgo rebellion, Mexico had suffered a period of two years of bad harvests. Crown officials had the responsibility of providing relief in these situations, and, as Hamnett correctly points out, any failure of the authorities to do everything possible to deal with these problems was likely to produce protest. "As a result, instances of inefficient administration, notorious corruption, and evident partiality, tended to have both social and political consequences." Resentments may well have been expected to be directed at the visible symbols of the Crown's lack of effectiveness in these matters, which may explain the viciousness of the attack on the *alhóndiga* in Guanajuato.[8] Similarly, Mexico at the time of the Revolution was experiencing difficulties and scarcity in some key areas. Such a case was the Laguna region, which was to become a center of radical peasant action and was one of the areas most receptive to the activities of Francisco I. Madero in the period just preceding the Revolution. Economic crisis in the United States in 1907, combined with drought in the Laguna itself, had caused serious want among the workers of the area. Food was in short supply and the alternative employment that they were accustomed to seeking across the border was unavailable. Thus the workers were pushed to action. Violence in the area increased markedly, with protests by hacienda workers, increased activity by bandit groups, and a corresponding growth in police actions aimed at repression. These incidents assumed an increasingly political air. In June 1908 a group of armed men attacked Viesca, shouting "long live the Mexican Liberal Party" as they robbed the bank, attacked police, and released prisoners from jail. The raid was blamed on "hunger and crop failures" and "hunger and poverty stemming from the present financial crisis," as opposed to political motives, but the Partido Liberal Mexicano took credit for the raid. Its relative success indicated to the workers that they could actually take effective action against the upper classes and constituted authority.[9]

An additional similarity between the two periods was the weakness of the state at the time that the two violent movements spread from merely local conflicts into a broader, more national context. I argue that the very possibility that they would so spread was dependent on significant weakness at the center of the nation. Theda Skocpol has suggested that an important similarity between successful revolutions is precisely the failure or generalized

[8]Ibid., 102–130.

[9]See William K. Meyers's excellent article "La Comarca Lagunera: Work, Protest, and Popular Mobilization in North Central Mexico," in Thomas Benjamin and William McNellie, eds., *Other Mexicos: Essays on Mexican Regional History, 1876–1911* (Albuquerque: University of New Mexico Press, 1984), 259–264.

weakness of state power at the center.[10] This weakness provides an opportunity for successful anti-state action, and this success itself builds as other areas observe it and come to take part in the conflict. In the case of the Independence movement, New Spain was faced with considerable economic difficulties as well as political confusion. As John TePaske has pointed out in his contribution to this volume, the financial system of the royal government of Mexico was collapsing in the two decades before the outbreak of the Hidalgo revolt. Although income from the viceroyalty had reached its highest point ever by 1810, inflation seriously affected the value of Crown revenues, and expenditures for war and defense were increasing precipitously. The Crown went far beyond its usual revenue measures to require religious and lay institutions to provide forced loans or to purchase government bonds from their capital funds. It seems possible that this sucking of capital funds from the colony may well have contributed negatively to Mexico's possibilities for economic recovery after the decade of Independence. In any case, New Spain was suffering a financial crisis that contributed significantly to the weakness of the central state. This economic crisis was mirrored in Mexico at the time of the Revolution by the negative effects on the economy caused by the international recession of 1907–1908 and the widespread local agrarian protests and industrial unrest that accompanied it.[11]

More important still was the disarray in political power at the center. At the time of Independence, as Hamnett points out, it seems probable that even given the long-maturing "social dislocation" in the countryside, with its accompanying growth of a sense of grievance and despair, widespread violence would not have been possible without "(1) the availability of leadership to articulate and direct grievances, that in their origins may be local, and (2) a crisis at the center and the existence of political uncertainty in provincial capital cities."[12] In New Spain, confusion in the viceregal political situation arising out of the kidnapping of the Spanish king by the French led to division between local elites and the emergence of available creole leadership which could mobilize mass support, just as confusion and opportunity at the center as Porfirio Díaz aged caused political jockeying among elites and the initial alliance of the elite leadership of Francisco Madero with the masses who would furnish the muscle of the Revolution. Further, initial successes encouraged more to join Hidalgo's

[10]Theda Skocpol, *States and Social Revolutions: A Comparative Analysis of France, Russia, and China* (Cambridge: Cambridge University Press, 1979), 47–51.

[11]For local examples, see Mark Wasserman, "Chihuahua: Family Power, Foreign Enterprise, and National Control," in Thomas Benjamin and William McNellie, eds., *Other Mexicos: Essays on Mexican Regional History, 1876–1911* (Albuquerque: University of New Mexico Press, 1984); and Meyers, "La Comarca Lagunera."

[12]Hamnett, *Roots of Insurgency*, 204.

struggle. Although finally engulfed by the counterrevolution of newly unified creole and Spanish elites, the fact that the Hidalgo movement could spread so far so fast is testimony both to the extent of grievances and the temporary weakness at the center. Indeed, despite the political accommodation of the Iturbide period, the unrest unleashed in 1810 continued to have effects in local areas for many decades to come.[13] Although elites in New Spain at the time of Independence, caught between "Royalist militarism and marauding insurgency," had opted for a return to unified elite government, pockets of insurgency led by local leaders or "caudillos" continued.[14] Much as Francisco Madero tried futilely to control his troops at Ciudad Júarez in 1911 and later attempted to replace revolutionary armies with the Federal Army that he had just defeated, elites in Mexico, frightened by the Hidalgo movement, quickly closed ranks. As Timothy Anna points out, Iturbide later staffed his government principally with members of the old elite—holders of high office from the viceroyalty, the Spanish, the high clergy, aristocrats, and the upper ranks of the military. Francisco Madero's later use of Mexico's pre-1910 political and economic elite to staff his own government seems quite similar—an attempt not just to accommodate potential opposition but actually a return to that group of people with experience in governing, people whom he felt were qualified and, quite mistakenly, people he felt he could trust.

A further consideration in the continuities and discontinuities of the Independence period and the Mexican Revolution is the growth and continued importance of regional and local leadership, "caudillismo" and "caciquismo." Although the post-Independence period has not been carefully studied in this regard, it is clear that such leaders continued to be extremely important during the first half of the nineteenth century. Indeed, the regional disintegration of Mexico after Independence and the continual loss of territory may be seen at least partly as a result of the attempt to bring local leadership under centralized control. Anna refers to the difficulties that Iturbide had in controlling the south, where caciques like Juan Alvarez and Gordiano Guzmán exerted their power. At the national level, of course, the struggle between central and regional power became one of the major issues of post-Independence politics. In the case of the Revolution, the question of subordinating local and regional leaders to central power, undertaken quite carefully at first, became the major task in the 1920–1940 period. Only with the fall of Saturnino Cedillo in San Luis Potosí toward the end of this period was the government of Lázaro Cárdenas able to bring the major areas of Mexico under centralized, institutional control.

[13]Ibid., 210–211.
[14]Ibid., 207.

Thus, many similarities between the struggle for Independence and the Revolution a century later can be cited. Agrarian questions and resistance to central authority were important motivating factors in both. The emergence of local leadership able to gain the support of many levels within local society was apparent in 1810 with the Bravos and in serrano movements during the Revolution. Both movements were preceded by periods of scarcity—economic difficulties, droughts, and bad harvests. And both were able to fuse local conflicts into a broader national struggle largely because of financial and political weaknesses at the level of the central state. However, the Independence movement, with its return to control of pre-revolutionary elites, was unable to centralize the nation successfully and to bring local and regional caciques and caudillos to heel. Attempts to do so during the Porfiriato were successful in some instances, but the extension of central control in some areas was actually important in bringing on the violence of 1910–1920. However, the Revolution in the post-1920 period was ultimately successful in forging an alliance between mass groups and old elites and in bringing under its control those who had emerged as powerful in regional areas and putting in place a political system which has remained stable for more than sixty years.

Mexican Independence in Comparative Perspective

Steven Topik

Mexico's independence was one of those rare epoch-making movements. Sitting at the nexus of the prosperous, stable colonial period and the turbulent, impoverished first decades of nationhood, the independence period has an immense legacy. The long shadow cast by the events of these few years between 1810 and 1821 has led to an emphasis on their unique aspects. As a result, little research has been done on comparative independence movements, though much exists on comparative revolutions. On the infrequent occasion that the comparative perspective is adopted for Mexico, the comparison is made with other Spanish American nations. The Spanish colonial system and culture are key variables. This is logical and appropriate. But some other examples might be introduced to stimulate new questions or question old answers. This essay briefly considers the Mexican independence experience in the light of some other movements.

First I compare Mexico's violent upheaval with another event, or rather a non-event—Brazil's independence. Brazil gave an independence movement and no one came. Rather than a Grito de Dolores, we have a Grito de Ypiranga. On September 7, 1822, Prince Dom Pedro I, heir to the throne of Portugal, suffering from a bout of diarrhea, returned from relieving himself to face a letter calling him back to Portugal. A priest in attendance recalled that "Dom Pedro, trembling with rage, grabbed the letters from my hands, crumpling them up, threw them on the ground and stomped on them." After a moment of thought, he turned to the priest and said: "they asked for it and they will get it. The Cortes is persecuting me and calling me an adolescent and a Brazilian. Well, now let them see their adolescent in action. From today on our relations with them are finished. I want nothing more from the Portuguese government, and I proclaim Brazil forevermore separated from Portugal." The Prince then turned to his adjutant and said: "Tell my guard that I have just declared the complete independence of Brazil. We are free from Portugal."[1] And that pretty much was that. With relatively little combat, Brazil was independent. No decade of warfare, no bloodbath, burning of fields, inflaming of passions.[2] There were a number of regional revolts in the 1830s and 1840s, but none seriously threatened the state. Indeed, so successful were Brazilians in compromising that they became known as an especially passive, accommodating people, unlike their supposedly hotheaded Spanish American neighbors. The Spanish Americans with their caudillo tradition were viewed as fighters while Brazilians, because of their tradition of the "homen cordial," were seen more as lovers.[3]

Why did Brazil enjoy the peace that Mexico sought? A number of structural reasons can be cited. (1) Brazil's seaboard settlement, export orientation,slave plantation system, and the marginalization of the less complex indigenous population led to a more uniform linking of political society to the international economy. Brazil's elite consequently had more common interests than did Mexico's; (2) the Pombalian reforms placed Brazilians in important newly created offices rather than replacing the native-born with Spaniards as the Bourbon reforms did. Thus the Portuguese system seemed less an external imposition; (3) many mercantilist monopolies and privileges, which were points of contention in Mexico, were already abolished by the time of independence in Brazil; (4) the Brazilian Catholic church had far less economic and political power than did the Mexican church, and it exercised no important control over laborers. Thus the Brazilian elite had no economic grounds for attacking the Church. Consequently, Church-State issues did not divided the elite;[4] (5) the Brazilian elite was trained in the Portuguese university of Coimbra to represent Portuguese interests rather than narrow regional ones;[5] (6) fear that inter-elite struggles would incite massive slave rebellions united Brazil's oligarchy.

[1]Included in E. Bradford Burns, *A Documentary History of Brazil* (New York: Alfred Knopf, 1966), 198–199.

[2]José Honório Rodrigues, *Independencia: Revolução e Contra-Revolução, as Forças Armadas* (Rio de Janeiro: Livraria Francisco Alves Editora, 1975), argues that the Brazilian independence movement succeeded so easily because the nation rose up, defended by its militias. Even though little actual fighting broke out, thousands of troops faced each other and it took over a year for the Portuguese troops to completely succumb.

[3]See Gilberto Freyre on the "homen cordial" in *The Masters and the Slaves* (New York: Alfred Knopf, 1946).

[4]The Jesuits had been important intermediaries in the labor market in the Amazon where they oversaw "aldeias" of Tupis. This contributed to their expulsion in 1759. See John Hemming, *Red Gold* (Cambridge: Harvard University Press, 1978).

[5]José Murillo de Carvalho, "Political Elites and State Building: The Case of Nineteenth-Century Brazil," *Comparative Studies in Society and History* 24:3 (July 1982), 378–400, finds elite education the most compelling reason for Brazilian unity after independence.

These are compelling reasons for Brazil's rather peaceful transition from colony to nation. But they do not completely convince. After all, the Mexican elite also maintained a high degree of cohesiveness and a united front at least initially. They set aside many of their differences once confronted by Hidalgo's enormous horde.[6] It is not self-evident that the Church in Mexico would be divisive; it did offer the elite loans and a tranquil peasantry and the clergy's leaders supported independence.[7] The specter of indigenous rebellions bound the elite together in Mexico just as the threat of slave uprisings did in Brazil since the Mexican peasantry had a history of violence.[8]

I suggest that perhaps the key difference between the processes of independence in Brazil and Mexico were not structural but conjunctural. Historical contingency, not historical necessity, led Mexico to destruction. Napoleon's armies invaded the Iberian peninsula in 1808, not realizing that they would be confirming Theda Skocpol's thesis on the importance of international wars and state structures in the promotion of revolution.[9] The responses of the two Iberian monarchs serve as a healthy reminder of the importance of free choice.

Charles IV and his son Ferdinand VII foolishly allowed themselves to be captured in Bayonne by the French. The Spanish people revolted, establishing local juntas to contest French rule. Spanish administrators in the colonies found their legitimacy undercut; rival creole groups began to vie for power. As John TePaske shows, Mexico's capital was drained in the effort to defend Spain. Thus Napoleon's actions on the other side of the Atlantic eroded state power in the Spanish New World.

Portugal's King Dom João VI found discretion the better part of valor and fled to Brazil with his entire court, treasury, library, and much of the navy and merchant marine. After more than three centuries of colonial rule, an Iberian monarch laid eyes on his possessions for the first time. Indeed Dom João did much more than look; he transferred intact the machinery of government of the Portuguese empire. Brazil ceased being a colony; it became a co-kingdom. Mercantilist restrictions were lifted, and

[6]D. A. Brading discusses the close economic and familial ties between creoles and peninsulares in *Miners and Merchants in Bourbon Mexico, 1763–1810* (Cambridge: The University Press, 1971). John Tutino emphasizes the unity of the elite in the face of mass unrest in *From Insurrection to Revolution in Mexico: Social Bases of Agrarian Violence, 1750–1940* (Princeton, N.J.: Princeton University Press, 1986).

[7]Enrique Dussell, *A History of the Church in Latin America*, translated by Alan Nelly (Grand Rapids, Mich., 1981), 90–91; Michael P. Costeloe, *Church Wealth in Mexico: A Study of the Juzgado de Capellanías in the Archbishopric of Mexico, 1800–1856* (Cambridge: The University Press, 1967).

[8]William B. Taylor, *Drinking, Homicide, and Rebellion in Colonial Mexican Villages* (Stanford: Stanford University Press, 1979).

[9]Theda Skocpol, *States and Social Revolutions: A Comparative Analysis of France, Russia, and China* (Cambridge: Cambridge University Press, 1979).

the ports opened. Taxes which had flowed to Lisbon now remained to build up Rio de Janeiro and enlarge the imperial bureaucracy. Profits which had been repatriated to Portugal now were invested by nobles in their new home, helping to finance Brazil's coffee boom. Thus to a considerable degree it was the French in Portugal who gave Brazil a national state. When Dom João reluctantly returned to Lisbon after more than a decade, he left his son and heir in charge. Brazil already had a developed state apparatus and a recognized legitimate ruler before it officially broke the bonds of dependence. Brazil's independence, then, was not a break but simply a royal succession, an inheritance.

Am I suggesting that Mexico's first ruler, Agustín de Iturbide, was right: monarchy was the cure for Mexico's ills? Not exactly. Timothy Anna and Barbara Tenenbaum have persuasively demonstrated that Iturbide's failure stemmed not from personality flaws; he took appropriate actions. Rather Mexico's first monarchy collapsed because of the predatory manner in which the elite viewed the new state and the weakened, impoverished state apparatus that the independence struggles had bequeathed. After a decade of guerrilla movements and ideological ferment, even the "correct" form of government could no longer remedy the serious erosion of the state's legitimacy. But is is intriguing to consider what might have been had Ferdinand VII fled to Mexico in 1808 or had he been able to deliver an adequate heir. There are many structural reasons we can marshal to demonstrate that independence was inevitable: the influence of the Enlightenment; the contradictory economic and political effects of the Bourbon reforms; growing creole nationalism; demographic pressures and the impoverishment of the indigenous population; the demands of the Industrial Revolution; the demonstration effect of the "Age of Revolution." But for all of their persuasiveness, were not conjunctural events of tremendous importance? Had Mexico received a ruler whom the elite could jointly accept might not independence have come later and been less cataclysmic? The direction of history was not apparent to most people at the time. Certainly it was not obvious to Brazilians in 1799 that their colony would not be convulsed by a Haitian-like upheaval. Nor was it obvious in 1820 that their country would be independent within two years. I suspect that the same was true for Mexico. The jealousy of creole for peninsular was counterbalanced by their joint fear of eruption of the popular classes. The indigenous population's resentment of Spanish tribute and caste restrictions were offset by their distrust of the rapacious creoles and, as Eric Van Young points out, their veneration of the king. Mexico, after all, of all Latin America, had the richest, most self-sufficient, developed economy.[10] John TePaske demonstrates that

[10]See Jaime E. Rodríguez O., *Down from Colonialism: Mexico's Nineteenth-Century Crisis* (Los Angeles: Chicano Studies Research Center, University of California, Los Angeles, 1983).

it also had, at least until the Napoleonic Wars made greater demands, a healthy treasury that centralized revenue in Mexico City. In addition, the colonial regime was staffed by a fairly professional civil service, who enjoyed widespread judicial authority, and, as Christon Archer shows, commanded a strong army and militia that exercised before the revolt a monopoly of the forces of repression.[11]

The essays in this volume suggest that not only were the structures for an easy transition to nationhood in place in Mexico, but also that there was no organized, committed opposition to the colonial regime in 1810. Virginia Guedea shows that the Masons, who would be so important in the Republic, only rose to prominence a decade after Hidalgo's Grito. They were an effect of independence more than a cause. Nor was the elite split into conservative and liberal factions in 1810. María de Refugio González points out that the main division occurred between Ilustrados and Regalistas, who shared many assumptions. And while Hugh Hamill cautions us that caudillos existed in form and even name in the colonial period, they did not yet hold political power. The indigenous population, while often erupting in localized revolts, apparently had no wider organization or program. To the extent that messianism appealed to them, argues Van Young, it was more likely to induce loyalty than rebellion.

Eleven years later, after the death of perhaps a tenth of Mexico's population, state authority was splintered and discredited, the treasury was bare, the financial links between Mexico City and the rest of New Spain were destroyed, bandits freely plundered passengers and cargo on the highways, and the age of the caudillo had arrived. Mines filled with water, North Americans poured into Texas, and Iturbide faced an impossible situation. None of this was inevitable or even foreseeable in 1810. Clearly Mexico's independence was not merely an event, a political moment on the path from colony to nation. Rather, it was a tortuous and tortured process that delivered to independent Mexico a new and frightful world, not simply somewhat altered colonial institutions and traditions. Independent Mexico was forged in the fire of insurgency. Thus one should not fault too strongly either "the colonial heritage" of Mexico or nineteenth-century liberals for the dismal nineteenth-century performance of the economy and the society.[12] The independence struggle itself apparently reshaped and retarded the country.

[11]For the extent of the colonial state's reach see Woodrow W. Borah, *Justice by Insurance: The General Indian Court of Colonial Mexico and the Legal Aids of the Half-Real* (Berkeley: University of California Press, 1983).

[12]Stanley J. Stein and Barbara H. Stein, *The Colonial Heritage of Latin America* (New York: Oxford University Press, 1970), blame the colonial period while E. Bradford Burns, *The Poverty of Progress* (Berkeley: University of California Press, 1980), holds nineteenth-century neocolonialism at fault. John Coatsworth, "Obstacles to Economic Growth in

If this is so it raises an interesting theoretical point: the political becomes privileged over the economic. While social and economic conditions prepared Mexico for rebellion, the political moment was the catalyst. Moreover, the political struggles, caused as much by contingency as by underlying economic grievances or changing relations of production, restructured the economy. Not only was capital lost and wasted and wealth redistributed, but also the national market was constricted. Brigandage led to recalculations of transport costs and turned many producers inward.[13] The state became the most lucrative client for the new money lenders.[14]

The fine essays in this volume, then, remind us of the central importance of the independence struggles. They do not tell us, unfortunately, enough about what those struggles were about. Much work remains to be done on the regional manifestations of rebellion. In the interstices between the arguments one can get a glimpse of the movements. It is clear that we are not dealing with a coherent national war of liberation. In fact there was little national about this struggle for nationhood. Rather, there were a series of local conflicts. The independence movement was much like the elephant that was described by three blind men: it was a complex amalgam of failed social revolutions, diverse jacquaries, coups, mercenary raids, and messianistic movements. It could serve as a laboratory for all of the categories of revolutionary movements in Chalmers Johnson's typology.[15] Everyone seems to have fought for his own reason or perhaps no reason. Creoles fought peninsulares; they both fought the *populares* who also fought each other; the cities fought the *campo*; and the regions fought the center. Motivations are refracted in a prismatic countrywide crisis of identity. More local research will probably reveal a complex pattern similar to that which erupted one hundred years later in the Mexican Revolution.

Comparison with the Revolution raises an interesting question. Both struggles were nearly a decade long, bloody, chaotic, regionally diverse, initially lacking central leadership. Both left destruction and armed bands. Both succeeded in overthrowing the previous regime. In both instances victory was initially won by a leader with close ties to that previous regime.[16]

Nineteenth-Century Mexico," *American Historical Review* 83:1 (February 1978), 80–100, points out how badly Mexico's nineteenth-century economic performance retarded development.

[13]See Paul Vanderwood's excellent study, *Disorder and Progress: Bandits, Police, and Mexican Development* (Lincoln: University of Nebraska Press, 1981).

[14]Barbara Tenenbaum, *The Politics of Penury: Debts and Taxes in Mexico, 1821–1856* (Albuquerque: University of New Mexico Press, 1986).

[15]Chalmers Johnson, *Revolutionary Change* (Boston: Little, Brown, 1966). Also see Harry Eckstein, *Internal War* (New York: Free Press, 1964).

[16]Iturbide and Madero were able to win over most of the ruling class to the side of rebellion because they promised to restrict change to the political level, leaving most of the ancient regime intact.

Yet in the case of independence, on the one hand, the age of caudillos and civil war followed. State power virtually collapsed as regional warlords staked out private domains. The Revolution, on the other hand, quickly led to a consolidation of central state authority and the subsumption of local caciques. Scholars usually are not surprised that the centralized colonial state was shattered. Simply listing the internal civil wars, foreign invasions and threats, and economic decline seem sufficient reason. And perhaps they are. But civil wars continued after 1917 with the Cristero rebellion, the United States threatened to invade Mexico and undercut state authority, and the economy was seriously disrupted in many sectors. Yet these challenges strengthened the state.

If we move our gaze to the experiences of other lands, we find that armed struggle more often creates centralized states than weak federations. It is true that Mexico's independence experience does not stand out when compared to the independence movements of the rest of Spanish America. Only Paraguay, and to a lesser extent Chile, avoided the splintering of the state. Elsewhere caudillismo emerged and prevailed for fifty years or so. But if we look to other national wars of liberation in Asia or Africa we find that long struggles usually led to a national perspective and a national organization on the part of the combatants. Once victorious they have formed highly centralized interventionist states.[17] The major revolutions in China, France, Russia, and the United States have also led to increased centralization. Why was the Mexican independence movement different?

There is only space in this essay to posit some possibilities. Perhaps the level of development of the world economy in the nineteenth century which relegated Mexico to export agriculture and mining and ignored the relatively small internal economy did not encourage a stronger state. In the twentieth century planning and financing the industrialization drive require much greater state participation which is readily recognized by influential members of civil society.

Ideology influenced the ultimate victors in Mexico, the liberals, to dismantle the colonial state. They attributed Spain's relative backwardness to its mercantilism and Britain's progress to its laissez-faire regime. In the more recent past the strong entrepreneurial state roles in such successful cases as Germany, Russia, and Japan have made a larger state more attractive. So has the political success of socialism.

Advances in technology have facilitated centralization. Revolutions in transportation, communications, and weapons have made it easier for the few to dominate the many and have homogenized peoples, reducing regional differences.

[17]For a discussion of recent new states see Hamza Alavi, "The State in Post-Colonial Societies, Pakistan and Bangla Desh," *New Left Review* 76 (1972), 59–82.

While these generic explanations are attractive and probably played a role, the nature of the independence movement itself was perhaps key. The movement began with no coordination or planning. It attracted followers in diverse areas for a variety of reasons, who disagreed about what they opposed and about what they wanted. In many cases they quite literally did not speak the same language. And they did not agree on an ideology or a leader. Fighting took place in compartmentalized regional theatres. A century later, socioeconomic developments had led to greater homogenization. While the Revolution was still split by regional differences, vertical networks of caciques, caudillos, and national leaders could be formed. Regional armies moved over much greater areas, sweeping diverse peoples into their movements and bringing them together under a few national leaders. National leaders had an interest in appealing to the masses now even if they did not find the mass's interests appealing. Probably other reasons can be adduced for the disastrous legacy of Mexico's independence. While much remains to be done, one thing is clear: the struggle to make Mexico independent delayed its birth as a true nation.

Random Thoughts Comparing the Role of the Army in the Independence Movement and the Fall of the Porfiriato

William F. Sater

GIVEN THE DIVERSE NATURE of the various essays in this volume, it is quite difficult to formulate a statement both global as well as sage. Clearly the contributors have broadened our understanding of Mexico. What has emerged is a series of conclusions. We have learned that the once highly centralized imperial regime imploded; that a series of regional power centers, economically self-sufficient and under the control of autonomous men, replaced the baroque edifice of colonial government. Ideology, we discovered—at least if it is crudely defined as merely a struggle between liberal and conservative tenets—had less of an impact than earlier believed. The Royalist army, invigorated by new blood and reinforced by seasoned veterans, managed to prolong the war for Independence. Even these recently acquired skills, however, could not restrain those who so fervently sought independence. Secret societies formed and proliferated, influencing the course of the Independence movement. Lower down on the social scale, Indians also rebelled. The world they aspired to build, however, seemed less sophisticated than that sought by their more educated fellow countrymen.

Predictably, the revolutionary turmoil adversely affected Mexico's economy. The mines, the nation's fiscal lifeblood, suffered so many disruptions that many ceased producing ore. Just as predictably Madrid never received the metals produced by Mexico's few remaining mines; these were either squandered in New Spain or were seized by regional warlords, caciques, or caudillos, who materialized even before the empire sounded its final death rattle.

Typical perhaps of the intellectual process, these essays, while resolving certain issues, raise more questions. Why did Indians rebel? After years of apparent passivity, what eventually drove them to adopt such a violent solution? Did Mexico's Indians share the same goals as other messianic movements, like those of Brazil or the followers of Tupac Amaru? Why did secret societies suddenly appear and, more significantly, why did they disappear or become the nucleus for subsequent political organizations? Were they merely a more elegant version of the Indian movements, futilely seeking some secular utopia? What is a caudillo and when does he burst onto the scene? Clearly the strongman seems to have materialized before the completion of the independence movement. He also seems more vulnerable than previously believed. Apparently even caudillos must accept limitations. If so, did Chile's Diego Portales succeed because he could forge a consensus with the oligarchy while Iturbide failed because he could not?

I, of course, can fearlessly raise these questions because I, happily, do not have to answer them. To show that I am not completely irresponsible, I should like to follow the example of my fellow commentators and compare some aspects of the collapse of the colonial empire and that of the Porfirian government.

There is a certain similarity between the colonial period and the Porfiriato. Both were, comparatively speaking, periods of political stability. Yet, whereas the struggle for Mexican Independence lasted for a decade, the Díaz administration, despite its impressive Belle Epoque facade, collapsed in almost indecent haste. It is interesting, and perhaps even profitable, to speculate on some of the reasons for this debacle, particularly by focusing on the role of the military.

The Spanish army, which sought unsuccessfully to keep Mexico tethered to Madrid's imperial leash, was larger than the armed forces which defended the Porfiriato. The colonial army had an additional advantage: it could draw upon the militia for reinforcements. Indeed, as Christon Archer has noted, the Spanish army was singularly well suited to deal with Morelos and Hidalgo: Royalist officers applied in Mexico the experience they gained during the Napoleonic Wars. Was the Spanish Empire, therefore, more capable of defending itself than the Porfirian military?

Porfirio Díaz instituted some important military reforms. His administration revived the Colegio Militar in order to train junior officers; it also created a General Staff to coordinate the efforts of the various technical branches and the combat arms. In addition, the armed forces developed a number of auxiliary schools, not only to train technical officers but also enlisted personnel. The army, moreover, also obtained new armaments both heavy and light; it revised the table of organization in order to incorporate the latest technology.[1]

These reforms reflected part of a general process to improve the level of the armed forces. In 1888, for example, the *Revista Militar Mexicana* appeared. A particularly truculent journal (its first editorial insisted that "war is the most important factor in progress", it sought to "put Mexico

[1]U.S. Archives, Military Intelligence Division, 1640–3; 1640–12. (Hereafter cited as MID.)

on the new path of technical advances."[2] The need for such reform was obvious: war was not only an essential part of the human condition, but Mexico specifically was "the advance guard of the Latin race, on whose shoulders weighs the immense responsibility, upon whose valor is resting a powerful and iron will, in order to stave off the Anglo-Saxon race."[3] For almost a decade, this journal fulfilled its share of this mission by informing its readers of the latest military innovations: German cavalry maneuvers, Austrian rifles, French artillery, and Italian explosives.[4]

The results of the various reform efforts appear mixed. The Colegio Militar annually turned out such skilled officers that civilian employers eagerly sought their services. Even the American military attachés, one of whom believed that the Colegio's discipline lacked a certain rigor, nonetheless pronounced its graduates as "intelligent and well educated." Many of the changes did not touch the enlisted ranks. American observers described them as "poor in quality, badly clothed and equipped, with poor quarters and food and a very poor pittance in pay."[5] Since the state press-ganged its recruits, perhaps it did not feel that it had to provide such reluctant patriots creature comforts. Others argued that the state simply lacked the financial resources to provide more to its soldiers.[6] Regardless of the reasons, recruitment and retention problems plagued the army where approximately a third of the men deserted.[7] To rectify this problem, in 1898 the government passed a law requiring compulsory military service. The impact of this measure, however, did not seem to fall unduly upon the *gente decente*.

Despite these limitations, the army still inspired respect, if not fear. One American military attaché noted that if U.S troops invaded Mexico they would encounter "formidable resistance" which, while not up to European standards, would nonetheless pose problems. General Winfield Scott, commented one American officer, might have easily vanquished the Mexican army of the 1840s because it was then a "poorly armed, undisciplined mob of Indians, poorly officered and poorly led." This situation was no longer the case. Mexican troops were hardy, capable of marching long distances, and of absorbing enormous punishment while demonstrating an almost reckless bravery in the face of fire.[8]

But, if the troops possessed such military virtues and the quality of the officers and equipment had improved so much, why then did the Porfirian army fail? In part this became a matter of numbers. Díaz had

[2]"Nuestro Programa," *Revista Militar Mexicana* 1 (1888), 3–4. (Hereafter cited as RMM.)
[3]"El Ejército," RMM 1 (1889), 68.
[4]See RMM 1 (1889), 163–164, 198–207, 367–373, 442–443.
[5]MID, 1640–4; 1640–12.
[6]P. Velasco, "Reclutamiento," RMM 2:6 (1890), 179–181.
[7]Ramón Arturo, "El Ejército," RMM 1:11 (1889), 312–313.
[8]MID, 1640–2; 1640–12.

so systemically reduced the size of the army that by 1910 it could field only 14,000 men. Thus, in proportion to the nation's population, the new Federal army was smaller than the one that defended Spain's empire a hundred years earlier. Some claim that Díaz, who knew better than most about the evils of predatory militarism, deliberately emasculated the military. Others, besides Díaz, favored reducing the size of the armed forces. Mexico, they argued, did not require a large standing army. Better to have a smaller, more quality military. Certainly economic pressures contributed. The fall of the price of silver, in 1893, for example, reduced government income. Consequently, the state cut the number of enlisted personnel by 30 to 40 percent.[9]

Lack of command experience may also have proved crucial. Many of the Royalist commanders had served in the Napoleonic Wars before arriving in Mexico. They applied this newly gained knowledge when fighting the rebels during the struggle for independence. Conversely, only a few of the Porfirian officers had seen active service. And, moreover, those who had combat experience had participated in the Mayan or Yaqui wars which did not necessarily prepare them for more conventional forms of combat. Finally, and perhaps more significantly, most officers had never commanded large units. Thus, the officer corps, despite its advances, lacked critical practical experience of soldiering in war.

Technology constituted another problem. The Porfirian army was not badly equipped. It possessed new French field and mountain artillery batteries; it had created machine gun companies as well as assigned automatic weapons to company level units. Once in combat, moreover, the army used this equipment well. At Cerro Prieto and Casas Grandes, for example, the regular army's artillery proved invaluable in repelling the rebels. Indeed, except for Ciudad Júarez—which capitulated at the end of the Porfiriato—the Federal forces did not lose a city and were not defeated on the field of battle.

Unlike the Royalists, however, the Porfirian army did not possess a monopoly on military technology. The rebel forces easily obtained automatic weapons as well as small arms in the United States. Indeed, this is why control of the frontier was so important; access to the United States allowed Madero's men to arm themselves. Althought the insurgents did not have artillery, they did have dynamite which, while not as elegant a tool, nonetheless allowed them to blast their way into various cities. Mastering automatic and semiautomatic weapons, moreover, proved relatively easy. Indeed, it was far simpler for a peon to learn how to shoot a machine gun than to complete the complex techniques needed to load and fire more primitive weapons of the early nineteenth century. The rebels of 1810 were

[9]Spencer St. John, Earl of Roseberry, 30 June 1893, Public Record Office: Foreign Office Papers FO 50/488.

not so lucky and hence had to struggle longer before vanquishing their opposition.

In part, Díaz must share a large portion of the blame for his army's problems. Don Porfirio, knowing full well the evils of a restive armed forces, apparently deliberately kept the army dispersed. In order to protect the seat of power, the president stationed more than a third of the regular army in Mexico City. The remainder he divided into small units, none larger than a regiment, which he assigned to various military districts. This policy not only fragmented the command structure, but also made it difficult to concentrate sufficient troops to crush resistance. Furthermore, the aging leader compounded the problem by arrogating to himself all command decisions. Consequently, troop commanders often had to wait upon the army's primitive communications system and don Porfirio's pleasure before they could react to any developing military situation.[10]

The government did try to develop a method to compensate for dispersing its military units. In case of a tactical emergency, it planned to use the nation's extensive rail system to collect and deliver military units to any trouble spot. This strategy had worked earlier when the Díaz administration, for example, successfully quashed the Yaqui and the Mayans.

Yet, paradoxically, by depending upon the rail system, the government increased its vulnerability. Anyone with enough wit and dynamite could easily destroy bridges, tunnels, or sections of rails, thus either isolating troops in the garrisons or stranding them once they left their barracks. Early in the war, for example, federal troops could not reinforce Pedernales because the rebels so terrified the train engineers that they refused to drive the locomotives. Even when the military corrected this problem, attacks on rail bridges slowed and sometimes stopped completely train traffic.[11] The rebels of 1910, however, proved less considerate than those of 1810. Rebellions erupted in Sonora, Chihuahua, and Durango, only to spread throughout the nation. Simply put, the army did not have sufficient resources to meet the needs of a spreading crisis.

The insurgents seemed to have developed this successful strategy more by accident than design. Incapable of routing the federal forces, the rebels continued to resist, as had the Yaquis, from the countryside. The regular army, however, could not eradicate the enemy. Outnumbered and fighting on various fronts, the Porfirian army did not have the manpower or resources to take the offensive. Simply pacifying Chihuahua would have consumed virtually the entire army. Consequently, the army had to retreat to the cities, giving the rebels both control of the countryside and the time to build an army.

[10]Secretaría de Guerra y Marina, *Campaña de 1910 a 1911* (Mexico, 1913), 14–16.
[11]Ibid., 26, 175–179.

The military was not fighting a guerrilla war as much as a conventional struggle which overtaxed their reserves. When the rebel forces moved on the cities in late 1910 and early 1911, they discovered that the various federal garrisons still resisted, holding off vastly larger forces. The federal discipline, moreover, remained intact. As Paul Vanderwood noted, don Porfirio's troops showed more mettle than their commander.[12]

It may be argued that the collapse of 1911—like France's decision to quit Algeria—was a political, not a military, decision. The federal army resisted until don Porfirio quit. Most of the troops remained loyal and the officers did not turn their coats. This situation stands in sharp contrast with the events of 1810–1821.

Colonial officers like Calleja and de la Cruz managed to protect the state during the critical months of 1810. Having repelled the first rebel advance, the war stalemated: the Royalists created flying detachments which employed terror to cow, if not pacify, their opposition; the insurgents occasionally would descend from their mountain redoubts to scorch the earth and occupy, albeit temporarily, various towns. The struggle degenerated into a tedious contest. In the end, however, it was politics, not military skill, which decided the struggle. After so many years stationed in Mexico, various Royalist officers and troops had "gone native." The combination of their increasing identification with Mexico and the restoration of the Spanish Constitution, in 1820, proved irresistible. So many of the military withdrew their support from the monarchy, pledging it instead to the cause of independence, that, as Christon Archer noted, "Lacking an army committed to Spain, New Spain simply collapsed."[13] In 1821 the army's decision to side with the insurgents brought down the government. Ninety years later the Mexican army had remained at its post while the Porfiriato's political leaders bartered away their legitimacy.

[12]Paul Vanderwood, "Response to Revolt: The Counter-Guerrilla Strategy of Porfirio Díaz," *Hispanic American Historical Review* 56:4 (1976), 571–572.

[13]Christon Archer, "The Army of New Spain and the Wars of Independence," *Hispanic American Historical Review* 61:4 (1981), 714.

Bibliography

Adame Goddard, Jorge. *El pensamiento político y social de los católicos mexicanos*, 1867–1914. Mexico, 1981.

Adas, Michael. *Prophets of Rebellion: Millenarian Protest Movements Against the European Colonial Order.* Chapel Hill, 1979.

Aguila Mexicana, 1824–1825.

Alamán, Lucas. *Historia de Méjico.* 5 vols. Mexico, 1849–1852.

———. *Historia de Méjico desde los primeros movimientos que prepararon su independencia en el año de 1808 hasta la época presente.* 5 vols. Mexico, 1942.

Alamán, Lucas, et al. *Dictamen de la comisión especial nombrada para informar sobre el importante ramo de minería.* Impreso de orden de las Cortes. Mexico, 1821.

Alavi, Hamza. "The State in Post-Colonial Societies, Pakistan and Bangla Desh." *New Left Review* 76 (1972), 59–82.

Aldama, Juan. "Declaración rendida por . . . en la causa que se le instruyó por haber sido caudillo insurgente." In *Documentos históricos*, vol. 6, by Genaro García. 2d ed. Mexico, 1985.

Alden, John R. *The American Revolution.* New York, 1954.

Alperovich, M. S. *Historia de la independencia de México, 1810–1824.* Mexico, 1976.

El amigo del pueblo, 1828.

Ancona, Eligio. *Historia de Yucatán desde la época más remota hasta nuestros días. Parte tercera, época moderna.* 2d ed. Barcelona, 1889.

Anderson, W. Woodrow. "Reform as a Means to Quell Revolution." In *Mexico and the Spanish Cortes*, edited by Nettie Lee Benson, 185–196. Austin, 1966.

Anna, Timothy E. *The Fall of the Royal Government in Mexico City.* Lincoln, 1978.

———. "The Independence of Mexico and Central America." In *The Cambridge History of Latin America*, vol. 3, edited by Leslie Bethell, 51–156, Cambridge, 1985.

———. "The Last Viceroys of New Spain and Peru: An Appraisal." *American Historical Review* 81:1 (February 1976), 39–40.

———. "The Role of Agustín Iturbide: A Reappraisal." *Journal of Latin American Studies* 17 (1985), 79–110.

Antuñano, E. de. *Economía política en México.* "De las clases productoras: su influencia sobre la riqueza, población, ilustración y espíritu publico." Imprenta de San Pedro. Puebla, julio de 1838.

______. *Economía política en México.* Imprenta Antigua en el Portal de Flores. Puebla, 14 de febrero de 1839.

______. "Memoria breve de la industria manufacturera de México, desde el año de 1821 hasta el presente; señalando los motivos de su aniquilamiento, los efectos que éste ha producido sobre la moral y la riqueza, y el remedio análogo para poner nuestra industria en un estado animado." Oficina del Hospital de San Pedro, a cargo del C. Manuel Buen-Abad. Puebla, julio de 1835.

Aranguren, J. L. *Moral y sociedad: la moral española en el siglo XIX.* Taurus, Madrid, 1981.

Archer, Christon I. *The Army in Bourbon Mexico, 1760–1810.* Albuquerque, 1977.

______. "The Army of New Spain and the Wars of Independence." *Hispanic American Historical Review* 61:4 (1981), 705–720.

______. "Banditry and Revolution in New Spain, 1790–1821." *Biblioteca Americana* 1 (November 1982), 59–89.

______. Los dineros de la insurgencia." In *Repaso de la independencia,* edited by Carlos Herrejón Peredo, 39–70. Zamora, Michoacán, 1985.

______. *El ejército en el México borbónico, 1760–1810.* Mexico, 1983.

______. "The Officer Corps in New Spain: The Martial Career, 1759–1821." *Jahrbuch Für Geschichte von Staat, Wirtschaft und Gesellschaft Lateinamerikas* (1980), 137–158.

______. "The Royalist Army in New Spain: Civil Military Relationships, 1810–1821," Journal of Latin American Studies 13:1 (May 1981), 57–83.

______. "Surviving the Chaos of Insurgency: Urban-Rural Relationships in Mexico, 1810–1821." In *Proceedings of the VII Conference of Mexican and North American Historians,* edited by Roberto Moreno de los Arcos and Eric Van Young, Mexico, forthcoming.

______. "Where Did All the Royalists Go? New Light on the Military Collapse of New Spain, 1810–1821." In *The Mexican and the Mexican American Experience in the Nineteenth Century,* edited by Jaime E. Rodríguez O, 24–43. Tempe, 1989.

Arcila Farías, E. *El pensamiento económico hispanoamericano en Baquijano y Carrillo.* Caracas, 1976.

______. *El siglo ilustrado en América: reformas económicas del siglo XVIII en Nueva España.* Caracas, 1955.

______. *Reformas económicas del siglo XVIII en Nueva España.* Mexico, 1974.

Arendt, H. *On Human Condition.* Chicago, 1958.

Arrom, Silvia M. *The Women of Mexico City, 1790–1857.* Stanford, 1985.

Arturo, Ramón. "El Ejército." *Revista Militar Mexicana* 1:11 (1889), 312–313.

Ascencio, Luis Medina. "Fuentes esenciales de la historia Guadalupana: su valor histórico." In *Album del 450 aniversario de las apariciones de Nuestra Señora de Guadalupe.* Mexico, 1981.

"Aventureros." *El Sol* 4, no. 1342 (February 17, 1827), 4252–4253.

Azcarate y Lezama, Juan Francisco. *Un programa de política internacional.* Archivo Histórico Diplomático Mexicano, Serie II, No. 37. Mexico, 1932.

Azuela, Mariano. *The Underdogs.* New York, 1962.

Bak, Janos, and Gerhard Benecke, eds. *Religion and Rural Revolt.* Manchester, 1984.

Bancroft, Hubert Howe. *History of Mexico,* 6 vols. San Francisco, 1883–1888.

Barker, Eugene C. *The Life of Stephen F. Austin.* Austin, 1980.

Barragán Barragán, José. *Introducción al federalismo: la formación de los poderes, 1824.* Mexico, 1978.

Bastide, Roger. *Les Religions africaines de Brésil.* Paris, 1960.

Bataillon, Claude. *Las regiones geográficas en México.* Mexico, 1969.

Bazant, Jan. *Cinco haciendas mexicanas.* Mexico, 1975.

______. *Historia de la deuda exterior de México (1823–1946).* Mexico, 1968.

Benson, Nettie Lee, "Comparison of the American Independence Movements." *Dos Revoluciones: México y los Estados Unidos,* Mexico, 1976, 117–127.

______. *La diputación provincial y el federalismo mexicano.* Mexico, 1955.

______. "The Plan of Casa Mata." *Hispanic American Historical Review* 25:1 (February 1945), 45–56.

______. "Texas as Viewed from Mexico, 1820–1834." *Southwestern Historical Quarterly* 90:3 (January 1987), 219–291.

______. ed. *Mexico and the Spanish Cortes.* Austin, 1966.

Benson, Nettie Lee, and Charles Berry. "The Central American Delegation in the First Constituent Congress of Mexico, 1822–1823." *Hispanic American Historical Review* 49:4 (November 1969), 699–700.

Berry, Charles R. "The Election of Mexican Deputies to the Spanish Cortes." In *Mexico and the Spanish Cortes,* edited by Nettie Lee Beson, 12–13. Austin, 1966.

Bocanegra, José María. *Memorias para la historia de México independiente,* 1822–1846. 2 vols. Mexico, 1892–1897.

Bolton, Herbert E. *Guide to the Materials for the History of the United States in the Principal Archives of Mexico.* Washington, D.C., 1913.

Borah, Woodrow W. *Justice by Insurance: The General Indian Court of Colonial Mexico and the Legal Aides of the Half-Real.* Berkeley, 1983.

Borja Migoni, Francisco de. "Exposición del consul general de México en Londres sobre el empréstito que fue encargado." *El amigo del pueblo* (12 de septiembre de 1827), 3–7.

Bosch García, Carlos. *Material para la historia diplomática de México y los Estados Unidos, 1820–1848.* Mexico, 1957.

______. *Problemas diplomáticos de México independiente.* 2d ed. Mexico, 1986.

Brading, David A. "El Bajío." In *Mineros y comerciantes en el México borbónico (1763–1810).* Mexico, 1975.

______. *Miners and Merchants in Bourbon Mexico, 1763–1810.* Cambridge, 1971.

______. "Tridentine Catholicism and Enlightened Despotism in Bourbon Mexico." *Journal of Latin America Studies* 15 (1983), 1–22.

Bricker, Victoria Reifler. *The Indian Christ, the Indian King: The Historical Substrate of Maya Myth and Ritual.* Austin, 1981.

Brinton, Crane. *The Anatomy of a Revolution.* Rev. ed. New York, 1957.

Briseño Senosian, Lillian, et al. *La independencia de México: textos de su historia.* Mexico, 1985.

Brooks, Philip Coolidge. *Diplomacy and the Borderlands: The Adams-Onís Treaty of 1819.* University of California Publications in History, no. 24. Berkeley, 1939.

Bruchey, Stuart. *The Roots of American Economic Growth, 1607–1861.* New York, 1965.

Brundage, Burr Cartwright. *The Fifth Sun: Aztec Gods, Aztec World.* Austin, 1979.

Bugbee, Lester G. "The Texas Frontier 1820–1825." *Publications of the Southern Historical Association* 4 (March 1900), 115.

Bulnes, Francisco. *La guerra de independencia: Hidalgo-Iturbide.* Mexico, 1910.

Burke, Edmund. *Reflections on the Revolution in France and the Proceedings in Certain Societies in London Relative to That Event*, edited by Conor Cruise O'Brien. London, 1969.

Burns, E. Bradford. *A Documentary History of Brazil.* New York, 1966.

______. *The Poverty of Progress.* Berkeley, 1980.

Bustamente, Carlos María. *Campañas del General D. Félix María Calleja.* Mexico, 1828.

______. *Continuación del cuadro histórico de la revolución mexicana.* 4 vols. Mexico, 1953–1963.

______. *Cuadro histórico de la revolución mexicana.* 3 vols. 3d ed. Mexico, 1961.

Callcott, Wilfred Hardy. *Santa Anna: The Story of an Enigma Who Once Was Mexico.* Norman, 1936.

Cárdenas, Barrios, René. "Plan de Independencia de la América Septentrional." In *1810–1821: Documentos básicos para la independencia.* Mexico, 1979.

Cardinales de dos independencias. Mexico, 1978.

Casasus, Joaquín D. *La deuda contraída en Londres.* Mexico, 1885.

Castañeda Delgado , Paulino. "La condición miserable del indio y sus privilegios." *Anuario de Estudios Americanos* 28 (1971), 245–335.

Castillo Negrete, Eduardo del. *México en el siglo XIX, o sea su historia desde 1808 hasta la época presente.* 25 volts. Mexico, 1875–1892.

Chauvet, Fidel de Jesús. "Historia del culto Guadalupano." In *Album del 450 aniversario de las apariciones de Nuestra Señora de Guadalupe.* Mexico, 1981.

Chávez Orozco, Luis, ed. *La guerra de independencia y el crédito agrícola. Mexico, 1953.*

Clapman, John. *The Bank of England.* 2 vols. Cambridge, 1958.

Coatsworth, John. "The Limits of Colonial Absolutism: The State in Eighteenth-Century Mexico." In *Essays in the Political, Economic and Social History of Colonial Latin America*, edited by K. Spaulding, 25–52. Newark, Del., 1982.

______. "Obstacles to Economic Growth in Nineteenth-Century Mexico." *American Historical Review* 83:1 (February 1978), 80–100.

Cohn, Norman. "Medieval Millenarism: Its Bearing on the Comparative Study of Millenarian Movements." In *Millennial Dreams in Action: Studies in Revolutionary Religious Movements*, edited by Sylvia L. Thrupp, 31–43. New York, 1970.

______. *The Pursuit of the Millenium: Revolutionary Messianism in Medieval and Reformation Europe and Its Bearing on Modern Totalitarian Movements.* 2d ed. New York, 1961.

Conozca México entero al comisionado regio, no. 2. Mexico, 1829.

Correo de la federación mexicana, 1829.

Costeloe, Michael P. *Church Wealth in Mexico: A Study of the Juzgado de Capellanías in the Archbishopric of Mexico, 1800–1856.* Cambridge, 1967.

______. *La primera república federal de México, 1824–*1835. Mexico, 1975.

Couto, Bernardo. *Discurso sobre la constitución de la Iglesia.* Mexico, 1857.

______. *Disertación sobre la naturaleza y limites de la autoridad eclesiástica.* Mexico, 1825.

______. *Obras del doctor D. . . .* Mexico, 1898.

Cunniff, Roger L. "Mexican Municipal Reform, 1810-1822." In *Mexico and the Spanish Cortes*, edited by Nettie Lee Benson, 59-86. Austin, 1966.

Davies, James C. "The J-Curve of Rising and Declining Satisfactions as a Cause of Revolution and Rebellion." In *Violence in America: Historical and Comparative Perspectives* by Hugh D. Graham and Ted R. Gurr. Beverly Hills, 1979.

Dealy, Glen C. "Prolegomena on the Spanish American Political Tradition." *Hispanic American Historical Review* 48:1 (February 1968), 37-58.

———. *The Public Man: An Interpretation of Latin American and Other Catholic Countries*. Amherst, 1977.

Decreto Constitucional para la libertad de la América mexicana." In *Leyes fundamentales de México, 1808-1975*, by Felipe Tena Ramírez. 6th ed. Mexico, 1975.

Denzinger, Enrique. *El magisterio de la Iglesia*. Barcelona, 1963.

El Despertador Americano, 1810.

Díaz Díaz, Fernando. *Caudillos y caciques: Antonio López de Santa Anna y Juan Alvarez*. Mexico, 1972.

"Discurso del Presidente." El Sol, no. 1440 (May 28, 1827), 3029.

Dos revoluciones: México y los Estados Unidos. Mexico, 1976.

Dublán, Manuel, and José María Lozano. *Legislación mexicana o colección completa de las disposiciones legislativas espedidas desde la independencia de la República*. 34 vols. Mexico, 1876-1912.

Dussell, Enrique. *A History of the Church of Latin America*, translated by Alan Nelly. Grand Rapids, 1981.

Eckstein, Harry. *Internal War*. New York, 1964.

"El Ejército." *Revista Militar Mexicana* 1 (1889), 68.

Elliot, John H. *The Revolt of the Catalans*. Cambridge, 1963.

Estep, Raymond. *Lorenzo de Zavala, profeta del liberalismo mexicano*. Mexico City, 1952.

Estrada, Francisco. *El centinela de Santiago: diálogo entre la ronda de la Tecpan y un clérigo*. Mexico, 1810.

Fagoaga, José María, et al. *Exposición hecha por la comisión especial a la soberana junta gubernativa, sobre la necesidad de fomentar este ramo principal de industria con la baja de derechos que propuso su dictamen de 24 de octubre próximo padado*. Mexico, 1822.

El Farol, 1821.

Farriss, Nancy M. *Crown and Clergy in Colonial Mexico: 1759-1821*. London, 1968.

———. *Maya Society Under Spanish Colonial Rule: The Collective Enterprise of Survival*. Princeton, 1984.

Fernández de San Salvador, Agustín Pomposo. *Silva Libre*. (Mexico, July 30, 1808), 3.

Ferrer Benimeli, José A. *Masonería española contemporánea, Vol. I, 1800-1868*. Madrid, 1980.

———. *La masonería española en el siglo XVIII*. Madrid, 1974.

Flores Caballero, Romeo. *La contrarrevolución en la independencia: los españoles en la vida política, social y económica de México, 1804-1838*. Mexico, 1969.

———. *Counterrevolution, the Role of the Spaniards in the Independence of Mexico, 1804-1838*. Translated by Jaime E. Rodríguez, O. Lincoln, 1974.

Florescano, Enrique, ed. *Fuentes para la historia de la crisis agrícola, 1785-1786*. 2 vols. Mexico, 1981.

______. "Guadalupe de todos." *Nexos* 10:109 (January 1987).

______. *Precios de maíz y crisis agrícolas en México, 1708–1810*. Mexico, 1969.

Florescano, Enrique, and Isabel Gil, eds. *Descripciones económicas generales de la Nueva España, 1784–1817*. Mexico, 1973.

Fonseca, Fabián, and Carlos de Urrutia. *Historia general de Real Hacienda*. Vol 1. Mexico, 1845.

Freyre, Gilberto. *The Masters and Slaves*. New York, 1946.

Gaceta constitucional de Nuevo León, 1829.

Gaceta Imperial de México: semanario político y literario de Méjico, 1821–1822.

Gammel, H.P.N. *The Laws of Texas 1822–1897*. Austin, 1898.

García Cantu, Gastón. "Bustamente y el principio de la autodeterminación de los pueblos." *Cuadernos Americanos* 179 (November–December 1971), 139–154.

García, Genaro. *Documentos históricos mexicanos*. 7 vols. 2d ed. Mexico, 1985.

Gibaja y Patrón, Antonio. *Comentario crítico, histórico, autentico a las revoluciones sociales de México*. 2 vols. Mexico, 1926.

Glassborow, Gilly, and Gillian Freeman, eds. *The Atlas of the United States*. New York, 1986.

Gómez Hoyos, Rafael. *La Iglesia de América en las Leyes de Indias*. Madrid, 1961.

Gómez Pedraza, Manuel. *Manifiesto que . . . , ciudadano de la República de Méjico dedica a sus compatriotas, o sea una reseña de su vida pública*. 2d ed. Guadalajara, 1831.

González, María del Refugio. *Estudios sobre la historia del derecho civil en México durante el siglo XIX*. Mexico, 1981.

______. "Historia del derecho mexicano." In *Introducción al derecho mexicano*. Mexico, 1981.

______. "El pensamiento de los conservadores mexicanos: hipotesis para su estudio." *Christus* 587 (Mexico, August 1985), 47–53.

González Navarro, Moisés. *Anatomía del poder en México*. Mexico, 1977.

González Obregón, Luis and Juan Pablo Baz. *Fray Melchor de Talamantes: biografía y escritos póstumos*. Mexico, 1909.

Green, Stanley C. *The Mexican Republic: The First Decade, 1823–1832*. Pittsburgh, 1987.

Greene, Jack P. "The Social Origins of the American Revolution: An Evaluation and an Interpretation." *Political Science Quarterly* 88 (1973), 1–22.

Greenleaf, Richard E. "The Mexican Inquisition and the Masonic Movement: 1751–1820." *New Mexico Historical Review* 44:2 (April 1969), 92–117.

Gruzinski, Serge. *Les Hommes-dieux du Mexique. Pouvoir indien et société, XVIe-XVIIe siecles*. Paris, 1985.

Guedea, Virginia. "The Beginning of Relations between Mexico and the United States." Paper presented at the University of Calgary's "Mexico Week," March 21–26, 1988.

______. "Comentario a las ponencias de María del Refugio González, Jaime E. Rodríguez O. y Christon Archer." Paper read in the session "The Emergence of Independent Mexico" at the annual meeting of the American Historical Association, Washington, D.C. December 30, 1987.

______. "Los Guadalupes de México." *Relaciones. Estudios de Historia y Sociedad*, no. 23 (1985), 71–91.

______. "Criollos y peninsulares en 1808: dos puntos de vista sobre lo español." Licenciatura thesis, Universidad Iberoamericana, 1964.

———. "The Historiography of Independence." Paper presented at the University of Calgary's "Mexico Week," March 21-26, 1988.

———. "Los indios voluntarios de Fernando VII." *Estudios de Historia Moderna y Contemporánea* 10 (1986), 11-83.

———. *José María Morelos y Pavón: coronología*. Mexico, 1981.

———. "José Nemesio Vázquez, un correo insurgente." In *De la historia: homenaje a Jorge Gurría Lacroix*, edited by Antonio Pompa y Pompa et al., 287-295. Mexico, 1985.

———. "México en 1812: control político y bebidas prohibidas." *Estudios de Historia Moderna y Contemporánea* 8 (1980), 23-66.

———. "La organización militar." In *El gobierno provincial en la Nueva España, 1570-1787*, edited by Woodrow Borah, 125-148. Mexico, 1985.

Guerra, François-Xavier. *Le Mexique de l'ancien régime a la révolution*. 2 vols. Paris, 1985.

Hall, Captain Basil. *Extracts from a Journal Written on the Coasts of Chile, Peru, and Mexico in the Years 1820, 1821, 1822*. 2 vols. 3d ed. Reprint. Upper Saddle River, N.J., 1968.

Hall, Linda B. *Alvaro Obregón: Power and Revolution in Mexico, 1911-1920*. College Station, 1981.

Hamill, Hugh M., Jr. "Un discurso formado con angustia: Francisco Primo de Verdad el 9 de agosto de 1808." *Historia Mexicana* 28:3 (January-March 1979), 439-474.

———. *The Hidalgo Revolt: Prelude to Mexican Independence*. Gainesville, 1966.

———. "Royalist Counterinsurgency in the Mexican War for Independence: The Lessons of 1811." *Hispanic American Historical Review* 53:3 (August 1973), 470-489.

———. "Was the Mexican Independence A Movement a Revolution?" In *Dos revoluciones: México y los Estados Unidos*, 43-61. Mexico, 1976.

Hamnett, Brian R. "Anastasio Bustamente y la guerra de independencia, 1810-1821." *Historia Mexicana* 28:12 (April-June 1979), 518.

———. "The Appropriation of Mexican Church Wealth by the Spanish Bourbon Government." *Journal of Latin American Studies* 1 (1969), 85-113.

———. "The Economic and Social Dimension of the Revolution of Independence in Mexico, 1800-1824." *Ibero-Amerikanisches Archives* 6:1 (1980), 1-27.

———. *La política española en la época revolucionaria*. Mexico, 1985.

———. *Revolución y contrarrevolución en México y el Perú (Liberalismo, realeza y separatismo 1800-1824)*. Mexico, 1978.

———. *Roots of Insurgency: Mexican Regions, 1750-1824*. Cambridge, 1986.

———. "Royalist Counterinsurgency and the Continuity of Rebellion: Guanajuato and Michoacán, 1813-1820." *Hispanic American Historical Review* 62:1 (February 1982), 19-48.

Harrison, J.F.C. *The Second Coming: Popular Millenarianism, 1780-1850*. London, 1979.

Hart, John M. *Revolutionary Mexico: The Coming and Process of the Mexican Revolution*. Berkeley, 1987.

Hartz, Louis. *The Founding of New Societies*. New York, 1964.

Hemming, John. *Red Gold*. Cambridge, 1978.

Hera, Alberto de la *El regalismo borbónico en su proyección indiana*. Madrid, 1963.

Hernández y Dávalos, Juan E. *Colección de documentos para la historia de la guerra de independencia de México de 1808 a 1821*. 6 vols. 2d ed. Mexico, 1985.

Herr, Richard. *The Eighteenth-Century Revolution in Spain*. Princeton, 1958.

Herrejón Peredo, Carlos. *Morelos: antología documental*. México, 1985.

Higgenbotham, Don. *The War of American Independence*. New York, 1971.

Hirschman, A. O. *The Passions and the Interests: Political Arguments for Capitalism before Its Triumph*. Princeton, 1977.

Hobsbawm, Eric J. *Industria e imperio: una historia económica de Gran Bretaña desde 1750*. Barcelona, 1977.

______. *Primitive Rebels: Studies in Archaic Forms of Social Movement in the 19th and 20th Centuries*. 2d ed. New York, 1963.

Horne, Alister. *A Savage War of Peace: Algeria, 1954–1962*. London, 1977.

Howe, Walter. *The Mining Guild of New Spain and Its Tribunal General, 1770–1821*. Cambridge, 1949.

Howren, Alleine. "Causes and Origin of the Decree of April 6, 1836." *Southwestern Historical Quarterly* 16 (1912), 378–421.

Humboldt, Alexander von. *Personal Narrative of Travels to the Equinoctial Regions of the New Continent During the Years 1799–1804*. 4 vols. 3d ed. London, 1822.

Hutchinson, C. Alan. *Frontier Settlement in Mexican California*. New Haven, 1969.

Ilustrador americano, 1812.

"Indicación del supremo poder executivo al soberano congreso sobre colonización." *El Sol* 1, no. 6 (June 20, 1823), 22–24.

"Instrucciones reservadas para José Manuel Zozaya, 31 de octubre de 1822." In *La diplomacia mexicana*. 3 vols. Mexico, 1910.

Israel, John, I. *Race, Class and Politics in Colonial Mexico*. Oxford, 1975.

Jameson, James Franklin. *The American Revolution Considered as a Social Movement*. Princeton, 1926.

Jensen, Merrill. *The American Revolution within America*. New York 1974.

______. *The Articles of Confederation*. 2d ed. Madison, 1959.

______. *The New Nation*. New York, 1950.

Johnson, Chalmers. *Revolutionary Change*. Boston, 1966.

Jones, Ricardo Rees. *El despotismo ilustrado y los intendentes de la Nueva España*. Mexico, 1979.

Katz, Frederich. "Mexico: Restored Republic and Porfiriato, 1867–1910." In *Cambridge History of Latin America*, edited by Leslie Bethell. Cambridge, 1986.

______. "Rural Rebellions after 1810." In *Riot, Rebellions and Revolution: Rural Social Conflict in Mexico*, edited by Frederick Katz. Princeton, 1988.

Kelly, Edith Louis, and Mattie Austin Hatcher, eds. and trans. "Tadeo Ortiz de Ayala and the Colonization of Texas, 1822–1833." *Southwestern Historical Quarterly* 32 (July 1928–January 1929), 78–86, 152–164, 222–245, 311–343.

Kenwood, A. G., and A. L. Lougheed. *Historia del desarrollo económico internacional desde 1820 hasta la primera guerra mundial*. Madrid, 1973.

Kicza, John E. *Colonial Entrepreneurs: Families and Business In Bourbon Mexico City*. Albuquerque, 1983.

Knight, Alan. *The Mexican Revolution*. 2 vols. Cambridge, 1986.

Labastida Martín del Campo, Julio, comp. *Dictaduras y dictadores*. Mexico: Siglo Veintiuno, 1986.

Ladd, Doris M. *The Mexican Nobility at Independence, 1780–1826*. Austin, 1976.

Lafaye, Jacques. *Mesías, cruzadas, utopías: el judeo-cristianismo en las sociedades ibericas*. Mexico, 1984.

———. *Quetzalcóatl and Guadalupe: The Formation of the Mexican National Consciousness, 1531–1813*, translated by Benjamin Keen. Chicago, 1976.

———. *Quetzalcóatl y Guadalupe: la formación de la conciencia nacional en México*. Mexico, 1977.

Lafuente Ferrari, Enrique. *El Virrey Iturrigaray y los orígenes de la independencia de México*. Madrid, 1941.

Lavrín, Asunción. "The Execution of the Law of Consolidation in New Spain." *Hispanic American Historical Review* 52 (February 1973), 27–49.

Legaz y Lacambra, Luis, et al. *El pactismo en la historia de España (simposio)*. Madrid, 1980.

"La legislación del S. XVIII sobre el Patronato Indiano." In *Anuario de historia del derecho español*. 40 (1970).

Lemoine Villicaña, Ernesto. *La revolución de independencia, 1808–1821* Vol. 3 of *La república federal mexicana*. Mexico, n.d.

———. "Mexico independiente: de Iguala a las vísperas de Ayutla." *El territorio mexicano: la nación*. Mexico, 1982.

———. *Morelos: su vida revolucionaria a través de sus escritos y otros testimonios de la época*. Mexico, 1965.

———. "Morelos y la generación de la independencia." In *La formación del estado mexicano*. Mexico, 1984.

León-Portilla, Miguel. *Aztec Thought and Culture: A Study of the Ancient Nahuatl Mind*. Norman, 1963.

Lindley, Richard B. *Haciendas and Economic Development: Guadalajara, Mexico, at Independence*. Austin, 1983.

Llorens, Vicente, *Liberales y románticos: una emigración española en Inglaterra*. 2d ed. Madrid, 1968.

López, Juan, ed. *La rebelión del Indio Mariano—un movimiento insurgente en la Nueva Galicia, en 1801; y documentos procesales*. 3 vols. Guadalajara, 1985.

López de Santa Anna, Antonio. *The Eagle: The Autobiography of Santa Anna*, edited by Ann Fears Crawford. Austin, 1967.

Lovett, Gabriel. *Napoleon and the Birth of Modern Spain*. 2 vols. New York, 1965.

MacLachlan, Colin M., and Jaime E. Rodríguez O. *The Forging of the Cosmic Race: A Reinterpretation of Colonial Mexico*. Berkeley, 1980.

Macune, Charles. *El Estado de México y la federación mexicana*. Mexico, 1978.

Manning, William R. "Texas and the Boundary Issue, 1822–1829." *Southwestern Historical Quarterly* 17:3 (January 1914), 217–218.

Martínez Quinteiro, María Esther. *Los grupos liberales antes de las Cortes de Cádiz*. Madrid, 1977.

Mateos, José María. *Historia de la masonería en México desde 1806 hasta 1884*. Mexico, 1884.

Mateos, Juan A. *Historia parlamentaria de los congresos mexicanos*. 25 vols. Mexico, 1877–1912.

Mayer, Brantz. *México lo que fue y lo que es*. Mexico, 1953.

Medina, Antonio de. *Memoria de hacienda*. Mexico, 1822.

Melchor de Talamantes, Fray. "Congreso Nacional del Reyno de Nueva España." In *Fray Melchor de Talamantes: biografía y escritos póstumos*, by Louis Gonzáles Obregón and Juan Pablo Baz. Mexico, 1909.

Memoria acerca de los medios que se estiman justos para el fomento y pronto restablecimiento de la minería, presentada por el Tribunal del mismo cuerpo al Supreme Poder Ejecutivo. Precede el discurso con que el tribunal dio cuenta a la junta general del cuerpo de las pretensiones y negocios que tenía pendientes, en el que se recapitula cuando se expuso al gobierno supremo en la Memoria. Mexico, 1824.

Memoria presentada a las dos cámaras del Congreso General de la Federación, por el Secretario de estado y del despacho de Relaciones Exteriorres e Interiores al abrirse las sesiones del año de 1825. Sobre el estado de los negocios de su ramo. Mexico, 1825.

Memoria que el Secretario de estado y del Despacho de relaciones exteriores e interiores presenta al soberano congreso constituyente, sobre los negocios de la Secretaría a su cargo. Leida en la sesión del 8 de noviembre de 1823. Impresa de orden del soberano Congreso. Mexico, 1823.

Memoria sobre la utilidad e influyo de la minería en el reino: necesidad de su fomento, y arbitrios de verificarlo. Mexico, 1819.

Menéndez y Pelayo, Marcelino, *Historia de los heterodoxos españoles*, edited by Félix F. Corso. Buenos Aires, 1945.

Mexico. *Actas constitucionales mexicanas (1821–1824)*. 9 vols. Mexico, 1980.

_______. *Colección de los decretos y órdenes del soberano congreso mexicano desde su instalación el 24 de febrero de 1822 hasta 30 de octubre de 1823 en que cesó.* Mexico, 1825.

_______. *Colección de leyes y decretos del congreso general de la nación mexicana de los años 1833 a 1835.* . . . 17 vols. Mexico, 1840.

_______. *Colección de órdenes y decretos de la soberana junta provisional gubernativa y soberanos congresos generales de la nación mexicana.* 7 vols. 2d ed. Mexico, 1829.

Mexico. Congress. *Actas del Congreso Constituyente Mexicano.* 2 vols. Mexico, 1822–1823.

Mexico. *Constitución federal de 1824. Crónicas.* Vol. 2. Mexico, 1974.

_______. *Diario de la junta nacional instituyente del imperio mexicano.* Mexico, 1822.

_______. *Diario de las sesiones del congreso constituyente de México.* 5 vols. Mexico, 1823.

_______. *Diario de las sesiones de la Soberana Junta Provisional Gubernativa del Imperio Mexicano.* Mexico, 1821.

_______. "Dictamen de la Comisión de Gobernación del Senado." *Aguila Mexicana* 3, no. 185 (October 17–18, 1825).

_______. "Dictamen presentado a la soberana junta provisional gubernativa del imperio mexicano por la Comisión de Relaciones Exteriores, 29 de diciembre del año 1821, primero de la Independencia." In *Un programa de política internacional*, by Juan Francisco Azcarate y Lezama. Archivo Histórico Diplomático Mexicano, Serie II, no. 37. Mexico, 1932.

Mexico. Secretaría de Relaciones Exteriores. *La diplomacia mexicana.* 3 vols. Mexico, 1910–1913.

Mexico. "Sesión de la Cámara de Diputados." *El Sol* 4, no. 1472 (June 17, 1827), 3029.

_______. "Sesiones de la Cámara de Senadores." *El Sol* 5, nos. 1552–1553 (September 6–7, 1827), 3353, 3357.

_______. Session of the Chamber of Deputies. *El Telegrafo* 2, no. 30 (June 9, 1833), 1.

_______. Session of the Senate. *El Telegrafo* 3, no. 80 (November 20, 1833), 1.

______. "Sessions in the Senate." *El Sol* Serie 3, Año 2, nos. 314, 317, 320–321 (May 10, 13, 16–17, 1830), 1281–1282.

Meyers, William K. "La Comarca Lagunera: Work, Protest, and Popular Mobilization in North Central Mexico." In *Other Mexicos: Essays on Mexican Regional History, 1876–1911*, edited by Thomas Benjamin and William McNellie. Albuquerque, 1984.

Michelena, José Mariano. "Verdadero origen de la revolución de 1809 en el Departamento de Michoacán." In *Documentos históricos*, vol. 1, by Genaro García. 2d ed. Mexico, 1985.

Miller, John C. *The Federalist Era, 1789–1800*. New York, 1960.

Miranda, José. *Las ideas y las instituciones políticas mexicanas*. 2d ed. Mexico, 1978.

Moore, Jr., Barrington, Jr. *Social Origins of Dictatorship and Democracy*. Boston, 1966.

Mora, José María Luis. *Disertación sobre la naturaleza y aplicación de las ventas y bienes eclesiásticos, y sobre la autoridad a que se hallan sujetos en cuánto a su creación, aumento, subsistencia, o supresión. Su autor, un ciudadano de Zacatecas. Impresa de orden y a costa del H. Congreso de Zacatecas*. Mexico, 1833.

______. *México y sus revoluciones*. 4 vols. Paris, 1836.

______. "Revista política de las diversas administraciones que la república mexicana ha tenido hasta 1837." En *Obras sueltas de . . . ciudadano mexicano*. 2d ed. Mexico, 1963.

Morelos, José María. "Nombramiento de comisionados para el reconocimiento de las existencias de las rentas reales y administración de estas. 18 de abril de 1811." In *Legislación mexicana o colección completa de las disposiciones legislativas expedidas desde la independencia de la república ordenada por los licenciados* . . . , by Manuel Dublán and José María Lozano. Mexico, 1876.

Moreno Bonett, Margarita. *Nacionalismo novohispano*. Mexico, 1983.

Moreno, Roberto. "Actitudes españolas ante la independencia de los Estados Unidos." In *Cardinales de dos independencias*. Mexico, 1978.

______. "Un caso de censura de libros en el siglo XVIII novohispano: Jorge Mas Theóphoro." *Suplementos al Boletín del Instituto de Investigaciones Bibliográficas*. Mexico, 1978.

______. *Joaquín Velázquez de León y sus trabajos científicos en el Valle de México*. Mexico, 1977.

______. "La última Nueva España." In *La formación del estado mexicano*, edited by María del Refugio González. Mexico, 1984.

Morris, Richard B. "The American Revolution and the Mexican War for Independence: Parallels and Divergences." In *Dos revoluciones: México y los Estados Unidos*. Mexico, 1976.

Morse, Richard M. "Toward a Theory of Spanish American Government." *Journal of the History of Ideas* 15 (1954), 71–93.

Morton, Ohland. *Terán and Texas: A Chapter in Texas-Mexican Relations*. Austin, 1948.

Munguía, Clemente. *Del Derecho Natural en sus principios comunes y en sus diversas ramificaciones, o sea, curso elemental de derecho natural y de gentes, público, político, constitucional, principios de legislación por el Lic.* . . . , 4 vols. Mexico, 1849.

Murillo de Carvalho, José. "Political Elites and State Building: The Case of Nineteenth-Century Brazil." *Comparative Studies in Society and History* 24:3 (July 1982), 378–400.

Navarro, Bernabé. *Cultura mexicana moderna en el siglo XVIII*. Mexico, 1964.

______. *La introducción de la filosofía moderna en México*. Mexico, 1948.

Navarro Y Rodrígo, Carlos. *Vida de Agustín de Iturbide*. Madrid, 1919.

"Nuestro Programa." *Revista Militar Mexicana* 1 (1888), 3–4.

Nuñez y Domínguez, José de J. *La Virreina mexicana: doña María Francisca de la Gándara de Calleja.* Mexico, 1950.

Ocampo, Javier. *Las ideas de un dia: el pueblo mexicano ante la consumación de su independencia.* Mexico, 1969.

Ochoa, Alvaro. *Los insurgentes de Mezcala.* Morelia, 1985.

O'Donojú, Juan. *Manifiesto que por conducto del señor gobernador intendente y jefe político de esta provincia hace a sus moradores el Excmo. Señor Capitán General y Jefe Superior político D.* . . . Veracruz and Puebla, 1821.

O'Gorman, Edmundo. *Breve historia de las divisiones territoriales.* Mexico, 1937.

O'Leary, Simón. *Memorias del General O'Leary.* 29 vols. Caracas, 1880.

Olmedo, José Joaquín. *Epistolario.* Puebla, 1960.

Olveda, Jaime. *Gordiano Guzmán: un cacique del siglo XIX.* Mexico, 1980.

Ordenanzas de minería y colección de los órdenes de esta materia posteriores a su publicación a las que van agregadas las reformas de que son susceptibles algunos de los artículos vigentes de las mismas ordenanzas y dos láminas para explicar los métodos más económicos de despuntar las vetas. . . . Paris, 1851.

Ortiz de Ayala, Tadeo. *México considerado como nación independiente y libre.* 2 vols. 1832. Reprint. Guadalajara, 1952.

______. *Resumen de la estadística del imperio mexicano.* Mexico, 1822.

Ortiz de la Torre, M. "Discurso sobre los medios de fomentar la población, riqueza e ilustración de los Estados Unidos Mexicanos, presentado en el certamen literario, con que el Colegio de San Ildefonso de México recibió a su alumno el Ciudadano Guadalupe Victoria, Primer Presidente de la República." Imprenta de la Federación Mexicana. Mexico, 1825.

Ots Capdequi, J. M. *España en América: el régimen de tierras en la época colonial.* Mexico, 1959.

Parra López, Emilio La. *El primer liberalismo español y la Iglesia: las Cortes de Cádiz.* Alicante, España, 1985.

Parton, Dorothy. *The Diplomatic Career of Joel Roberts Poinsett.* Washington, D.C., 1934.

Pérez Maldonado, Rafael. *Memoria que el ministro de Hacienda presenta al soberano Congreso sobre el estado del erario.* Mexico, 1822.

Pérez Marchand, Monelisa. *Dos etapas ideológicas del siglo XVIII, en México a través de los papeles de la Inquisición.* Mexico, 1945.

Phelan, John L. *The Millennial Kingdom of the Franciscans in the New World.* 2d rev. ed. Berkeley, 1970.

______. *The People and the King: The Comunero Revolution in Colombia, 1781.* Madison, 1978.

Pietschmann, Horst. *Die Einfuhrung des Intendantensystem in Neu-Spanien.* Cologne, 1972.

Poinsett, Joel. *Notes on Mexico.* Philadelphia, 1824.

______. *The Present Political State of Mexico,* edited by L. Smith Lee. Salisbury, N.C., 1976.

Popkin, Samuel L. *The Rational Peasant: The Political Economy of Rural Society in Vietnam.* Berkeley, 1979.

Quirós, José María. "Ideas políticas económicas de gobierno." Imprenta del Gobierno Imperial Mexicano de Priani y Socios. Veracruz, 1822.

______. "Memoria de estatuto. Idea de la riqueza que daban a la masa circulante de Nueva España sus naturales producciones en los años de tranquilidad, y su abatimiento en las presentes conmociones, 1817." In *Descripciones económicas generales de la Nueva España, 1784–1817*, compiled by E. Enrique Florescano and Isabel Gil. Mexico, 1973.

Ramírez Cabañas, Joaquín, ed. *El empréstito de México a Colombia*. Mexico, 1930.

Randall, R. W. *Real del Monte: una empresa minera británica en México*. Mexico, 1977.

Rangel, Nicolás. *Los precursores ideológicos de la guerra de Independencia: la masonería en México, siglo XVIII*. 2 vols. Mexico, 1932.

Registro oficial, 1830–1831.

"Report of the Minister of Internal and External Affairs." *El Telégrafo* 2:96 (August 14, 1833), 2.

"Revista política del año de 1825." *El Sol* 3, no. 932 (January 1, 1826), 801–802.

Reyes Heroles, Jesus. *El liberalismo mexicano*. 3 vols. Mexico, 1974.

Ribeiro, René. "Brazilian Messianic Movements." In *Millennial Dreams in Action: Studies in Revolutionary Movements*, edited by Sylvia L. Thrupp, 59. New York, 1970.

Ricard, Robert. *The Spiritual Conquest of Mexico: An Essay on the Apostolate and the Evangelizing Methods of the Mendicant Orders in New Spain: 1523–1572*, translated by Lesley B. Simpson. Berkeley, 1966.

Robertson, William S. *Iturbide of Mexico*. Durham, N.C., 1952.

[Rocafuerte, Vicente.] *Bosquejo ligerísimo de la revolución de Méjico*. Philadelphia, 1822.

______. "Examen analítico de las constituciones formadas en Hispano-América." *Revista de Historia de América* 72 (July–December 1971), 419–484.

______. *Exposición de las razones que determinaron a Vicente Rocafuerte a prestar a la República de Colombia la suma de £63 000*. Londres, 1829.

Rodrigues, José Honorio. *Independencia: Revolução e Contra-Revolução, as Forças Armadas*. Rio de Janeíro, 1975.

Rodríguez O., Jaime E. "An Analysis of the First Constitutions of Spanish America." *Revista de Historia de América* 72 (July–December 1971), 413–419.

______. "The Conflict between the Church and the State in Early Republican Mexico." *New World* 2 (1987), 93–112.

______. *Down from Colonialism: Mexico's Nineteenth-Century Crisis*. Los Angeles, 1983.

______. *The Emergence of Spanish America: Vicente Rocafuerte and Spanish Americanism, 1808–1832*. Berkeley, 1975.

______. "Intellectuals and the Mexican Constitution of 1824." In *The State and Intellectual Life in Mexico*, edited by Roderic A. Camp, Charles A. Hale, and Josefina Zoraida Vásquez. Mexico and Los Angeles, forthcoming.

______. "Rocafuerte y el empréstito a Colombia." *Historia Mexicana* 18 (April–June 1969), 485–515.

______. ed. *La formación de un republicano* Vol. 4 of *Obras completas de Servando Teresa de Mier*. Mexico, 1988.

______. ed. *The Mexican and the Mexican American Experience in the Nineteenth-Century*. Tempe, 1989.

Rodríguez, Linda A. *The Search for Public Policy: Regional Politics and Government Finances in Ecuador, 1830–1940*. Berkeley, 1985.

Rondero, Javier. "Diseño crítico de la consumación de la independencia." *Cuadernos Americanos* 180 (January-February 1972), 128-142.

Rouquié, Alain. "Dictadores, militares y legitimidad en América Latina." In *Dictaduras y dictadores*, compiled by Julio Labastida Martín del Campo, 10-26. Mexico, 1986.

Rousseau, Juan Jacobo. *El contrato social*. 7th ed., translated by Consuelo Berges. Buenos Aires, 1965.

Rubio Mañé, J. Ignacio. "Los sanjuanistas de Yucatán y Manuel Jiménez Solís, el padre Justis." *Boletín del Archivo General de la Nación*, 2a. serie, 8, no. 3-4 (1967), 1211-1234; 9, no. 1-2 (1968), 193-243; no. 3-4 (1968), 401-508; 10, no. 1-2 (1969), 127-252.

Rudé, George F. E. *Ideology and Popular Protest*. New York, 1980.

Safford, Frank. "Politics, Ideology and Society in Post-Independence Spanish America." In *The Cambridge History of Latin America, Vol. 3: From Independence to c. 1870*, edited by Leslie Bethell. Cambridge, 1985.

Sarraihl, Jean. *La España ilustrada de la segunda mitad del siglo XVII*. Mexico, 1957.

Scott, James C. *The Moral Economy of the Peasant: Rebellion and Subsistence in Southeast Asia*. New Haven, 1976.

Sejourné, Laurette. *Burning Water: Thought and Religion in Ancient Mexico*. London, 1957.

Seoane, María Cruz. *El primer lenguaje constitucional español* (*las Cortes de Cádiz*). Madrid, 1968.

Shafer, R. J. *The Economic Societies in the Spanish World* (*1763-1821*). Syracuse, 1958.

Shepperson, George. "The Comparative Study of Millenarian Movements." In *Millennial Dreams in Action: Studies in Revolutionary Religious Movements*, edited by Sylvia L. Thrupp, 44-52. New York, 1970.

Sims, Harold D. *Descolonización en México: el conflicto entre mexicanos y españoles, 1821-1831*. Mexico, 1982.

———. *La expulsión de los españoles de México, 1821-1828*. Mexico, 1974.

———. *La reconquista de México: la historia de los atentados españoles, 1821-1830*. Mexico, 1984.

Skocpol, Theda. *States and Social Revolutions: A Comparative Analysis of France, Russia, and China*. Cambridge, 1979.

Smelser, Marshall. *The Winning of Independence*. Chicago, 1972.

Smith, Adám. *Investigación sobre la naturaleza y causas de la riqueza de las naciones*. Mexico, 1981.

Smith, Peter H. "Political Legitimacy in Spanish America." In *New Approaches to Latin American History*, edited by Richard Graham and Peter H. Smith, 225-255. Austin, 1974.

El Sol, 1823-1830.

Solís, D. "Específico y único remedio de la pobreza del Imperio Mexicano." Oficina de don Urbano Sanromán, Guadalajara, 1822.

Solórzano Pereira, Juan de. *Política indiana sacada en lengua castellana de los dos tomos del Derecho y gobierno municipal de las Indias occidentales. . . .* Madrid, 1647.

Soustelle, Jacques. *La Pensée cosmologique des anciens mexicains*. Paris, 1940.

Spain. Cortes. *Colección de decretos y órdenes de las Cortes de Cádiz*. 2 vols. Madrid, 1987.

Sprague, William Forrest. *Vicente Guerrero, Mexican Liberator*. Chicago, 1931.

Staples, Anne. *La Iglesia en la primera república federal mexicana* (*1824-1835*), translated by Andrés Lira. Mexico, 1976.

———. "Secularización: Estado e Iglesia en tiempo de Gómez Farías." *Estudios de Historia Moderna y Contemporánea de México* 10, 109–123.

Stein, Stanley J., and Barbara H. Stein. *The Colonial Heritage of Latin America*. New York, 1970.

Stoetzer, O. Carlos. *Las raíces escolasticas de la emancipación de la América Española*. Madrid, 1982.

Suárez y Navarro, Juan. *Historia de México y del general López de Santa Anna*. Mexico, 1850.

Tamayo, Jorge L. *Geografía general de México*. 4 vols. 2d ed. Mexico, 1962.

Tavera Alfaro, Xavier. *Dos etapas de la independencia: documentos*. Morelia, 1966.

Taylor, William B. *Drinking, Homicide and Rebellion in Colonial Mexican Villages*. Stanford, 1979.

El Telégrafo; periódico oficial del gobierno de los Estados Unidos Mexicanos, 1833.

Tena Ramírez, Felipe. *Leyes fundamentales de México (1808–1983)*. Mexico: Porrúa, 1983.

Tenenbaum, Barbara A. *México en la época de los agiotistas, 1821–1857*. Mexico, 1985.

———. *The Politics of Penury: Debts and Taxes in Mexico, 1821–1856*. Albuquerque, 1986.

TePaske, John J. "Economic Cycles in New Spain in the Eighteenth Century: The View from the Public Sector." In *Iberian Colonies, New World Societies: Essays in Memory of Charles Gibson*, edited by R. L. Garner and W. B. Taylor. University, Pa., 1985.

———. "La política española en el caribe durante los siglos XVII y XVIII." In *La influencia de España en el caribe, la Florida y la Luisiana, 1500–1800*, edited by Antonio Acosta and Juan Marchena, 76–82. Madrid, 1983.

———. *La Real Hacienda de Nueva España: la real caja de México, 1576–1816*. Mexico, 1976.

TePaske, John J., and Herbert S. Klein. *Ingresos y egresos de la Real Hacienda de Nueva España*. Mexico, , 1986.

Thompson, E. P. "The Moral Economy of the English Crowd in the Eighteenth Century." *Past and Present* (February 1971), 76–136.

Thrupp, Sylvia L., ed. *Millennial Dreams in Action: Studies in Revolutionary Religious Movements*. New York, 1970.

Tilly, Charles, Louise A. Tilly, and Richard Tilly. *The Rebellious Century, 1830–1930*. Cambridge, 1975.

Timmons, Wilbert H. "Los Guadalupes: A Secret Society in the Mexican Revolution for Independence." *Hispanic American Historical Review* 30:4 (November 1950), 453–479.

Tomás y Valiente, Francisco. *El marco político de la desamortización en España*. 2d ed. Barcelona, 1972.

Tornel y Mendívil, José María. *Breve reseña histórica de los acontecimientos más notables de la nación mexicana, desde el año de 1821 hasta nuestros días*. Mexico, 1852.

———. *Manifestación del ciudadano José María Tornel al público*. Mexico, 1833.

Torre Villar, Ernesto de la, ed. *Los "Guadalupes" y la independencia*. ed. Mexico, 1985.

Turner, Victor. *Dramas, Fields, and Metaphors: Symbolic Action in Human Society*. New York, 1974.

Tutino, John. *From Insurrection to Revolution in Mexico: Social Bases of Agrarian Violence, 1750–1940*. Princeton, 1986.

Urías, B. "Educación para la democracia: El Ateneo Mexicano (1840–1852)." *Estudios* (Instituto Tecnológico Autónomo de México), no. 12 (Spring 1988).

Valle, Rafael Heliodoro. *La anexión de Centro América a México (documentos y escritos de 1821–1822, tomo III)*. Archivo Histórico Diplomático Mexicano, Serie II, no. 40. Mexico, 1936.

______. *Como era Iturbide*. Mexico, 1922.

Vanderwood, Paul J. *Disorder and Progress: Bandits, Police, and Mexican Development*. Lincoln, 1981.

______. "Response to Revolt: The Counter-Guerrilla Strategy of Porfirio Díaz." *Hispanic American Historical Review* 56:4 (1976), 571–572.

Van Young, Eric. "Conflict and Solidarity in Indian Village Life: The Guadalajara Region in the Late Colonial Period." *Hispanic American Historical Review* 64 (February 1984), 55–79.

______. *Hacienda and Market in Eighteenth-Century Mexico: The Rural Economy of the Guadalajara Region, 1675–1820*. Berkeley, 1981.

______. "Millennium on the Northern Marches: The Mad Messiah of Durango and Popular Rebellion in Mexico, 1800–1815." *Comparative Studies in Society and History* 21 (1986), 385–413.

______. "Who Was That Masked Man, Anyway?: Popular Symbols and Ideology in the Mexican Wars of Independence." In *Proceedings*. Annual meeting of the Rocky Mountain Council on Latin American Studies, I, 18–35. Las Cruces, New Mexico, 1984.

Vázquez, Andrés Clemente. *Bosquejo histórico de la agregación a México de Chiapas y Soconusco*. Mexico, 1932.

Vázquez Mantecón, Carmen. *Santa Anna y la encrucijrda del Estado: la dictadura (1853–1855)*. Mexico, 1986.

Velasco, P. "Reclutamiento." *Revista Militar Mexicana* 2:6 (1890), 179–181.

Villoro, Luis. "The Ideological Currents of the Epoch of Independence." In *Major Trends in Mexican Philosophy*, edited by Mario de la Cueva et al., 215, 217–218. Notre Dame, 1966.

______. *El proceso ideológico de la revolución de la independencia*. 3d ed. Mexico, 1981.

Voz de la patria, 1830.

Wallace, Willard M. *Appeal to Arms: A Military History of the American Revolution*. Chicago, 1964.

Ward, Henry George. *México en 1827*. Mexico, 1981.

Warren, Harris G. *The Sword Was Their Passport*. Baton Rouge, 1943.

Wasserman, Mark. *Capitalists, Caciques and Revolution: The Native Elite and Foreign Enterprise in Chihuahua, Mexico, 1854–1911*. Chapel Hill, 1984.

______. "Chihuahua: Family Power, Foreign Enterprise, and National Control." In *Other Mexicos: Essays on Mexican Regional History, 1876–1911*, edited by Thomas Benjamin and William McNellie. Albuquerque, 1984.

Wasserstrom, Robert. *Class and Society in Central Chiapas*. Berkeley, 1983.

Wells, Allen. *Yucatán's Guilded Age: Haciendas, Henequen and International Harvester, 1860–1915*. Albuquerque, 1985.

Zavala, Iris M. *Masones, comuneros y carbonarios*. Madrid, 1971.

Zavala, Lorenzo de. *Ensayo histórico de las revoluciones de México desde 1808 hasta 1830*. Vol. 1 of *Obras*. Mexico, 1969.

______. *Ensayo histórico de las revoluciones de México desde 1808 hasta 1830*. 2 vols. Paris, 1831–1832.

———. *Memoria de la gestión del gobierno del Estado de México, 30 de marzo de 1833.*
———. *Umbral de la independencia.* Mexico, 1949.

Index

Abad y Queipo, Manuel, 85–87, 96
Absolutistas, 45
Acapulco, 64, 141, 303
Acta de Independencia, 243
Aculco, 86, 90
Acuña, Vicente, 53–56
Adams, John Quincy, 3, 283, 292
Adams-Onís Treaty, 275, 277, 283, 287–289, 295, 304
Administración de Arbitrios, 205
Aduana, 71, 81
Africa, 337
Age of Caudillismo, 174
Age of Revolution, 334
Agiotistas, 212, 213
Agriculture, 2, 11, 87, 130, 133, 135–137, 140, 149, 151, 166, 207, 215, 293, 316
Aguardiente, 71, 205, 206
Aguascalientes, 105
El Águila, 50
Aguirre, Guillermo, 28
Aguirre, Matias de, 101
Agustín I, Emperor. *See* Iturbide, Agustín de
Alamán, Lucas, ix, 39, 43, 59, 102, 131, 132, 138, 140, 149, 156, 157, 159, 161, 187, 212, 248, 255, 282, 284, 285, 287–290, 300, 301, 303, 304
Alcabala, 68, 70, 202, 203, 209
Alcalá, José María, 51
Alcaldía, 149
Aldama, Juan, 30, 31
Alejandro VI, 251
Alférez, Real, 172
Algeria, 344
Alhóndiga, 326
Allende, Ignacio, 11, 30–32, 48, 110, 121, 124, 125, 127
Almojarifazgos, 70, 202
Alonzo, Anna María, 314, 320
Alperovich, M. S., 19
Alpuche e Infante, José María, 302
Álvarez, Juan, 191, 192, 328
Alvear, Carlos, 52
Amaru, Tupac, 339
America, 33, 34, 40, 53, 106, 124, 231, 245, 254, 257
American Constitution, 22, 23
American Revolution, 63
Americans, 86, 190
American Spaniards, 3, 4, 24, 26, 28, 31, 32, 36
Anahuac, 156, 243
Anaya family, 94
Ancona, Eligio, 60
Anglo-Americans, 277, 283, 291, 297, 299, 304
Anna, Timothy, xi, 12, 102, 185, 210, 328, 334
Antecedentes, 253
Antonio de Andrade, José, 95
Antuñano, Esteban de, 272–274
Apam, 140
Apatzingán, 238, 239, 241
Apezochea, Fermín de, 132
Apodaca, Juan Ruiz de, 59, 61, 101–104, 106
Apolbón, Manuel, 55
Aquisgrán, Aix de la Chapelle, 259
Aragón, 22, 251
Aranjuez, 46
Arbitrios de milicias, 106
Archduke John of Austria, 124
Archer, Christon I., ix, x, xi, 6, 11, 38, 85, 172, 314, 320, 335, 340, 344
Arenal Fenochio, Jaime del, xi, 12, 13, 237, 246
Arenas, Joaquín, 291
Arenas Conspiracy, 291, 294, 297
Argentina, 222, 230, 245

Arkansas River, 275
Armijo, Gabriel de, 302
Army of the Center, 86, 88, 90, 91, 101, 173
Army of the Reserve, 299
Army of the Right, 94
Army of the South, 98, 101
Army of Three Guarantees, 69, 73
Articles of Confederation, 3
Asia, 150, 337
Atascosito, 287
Atlautla, 119
Atotonilco, 243
Audiencia of Guatemala, 278
Audiencias, 29, 34, 38, 72
Austin, Stephen F., 279, 281, 301, 305
Austria, 219
Autonomists, 10, 21, 28, 32, 33, 36, 39, 40, 191
Autonomy, 10, 11, 21, 26, 27, 29-31, 35, 38, 42, 185, 188, 191
Ayuntamiento of Mexico City, 25, 277
Ayuntamientos, 48, 107
Ayuntamientos of New Spain, 27
Azcárate, Juan Francisco, 27, 29, 276, 288
Aztec, 113
Azuela, Mariano, 321

Bahía del Espíritu Santo, 277, 292
Bahía de Lavaca, 292
Bajío, 4, 30, 91, 124, 130, 131, 135, 137, 140, 141, 167, 170, 202, 316
Banco de Avío, 272
Bandini, Juan, 306
Bank of England, 228
Barclay, David, 224
Barclay, Herring, Richardson & Company, 217, 219, 220, 224-229, 230-232, 234
Baring, Alexander, 231, 233
Baring Brothers, 220, 232, 233
Barradas, Isidro, 296, 297
Barradas, José, 95
Barragán, Miguel, 173, 297
Barreiro, José Miguel, 97
Barry, Diego, 279
Base Constitucional, 240
Bases Constitucionales, 239, 241
Bases Fundamentales, 241
Batres, Antonio, 206
Bautista Arizpe, Juan, 279
Bayonne, 333
Benson, Nettie Lee, xi, 13, 275
Beristáin de Sousa, José Mariano, 29
Bernardez, hacienda de, 133
Beye Cisneros, Francisco, 29
Beye Cisneros, José, 35
Bledos, 172
Bonds, 217, 220-224, 226, 227, 229-232, 327
Bordeaux, France, 304
Borja Migoni, Francisco, 218-234
Boundaries, 281-301
Bourbon Reforms, 201, 243
Bourbons, 6, 63, 65, 189, 265, 266, 312, 332
Bravo, Nicolás, 189, 195, 197, 198, 266, 294, 295, 297-299, 302, 325, 329
Brazil, 14, 331-334, 339
Brazilian Catholic Church, 332
Brazilians, 331
Brazos River, 287
Brinton, Crane, 63
Buenos Aires, 39, 53, 245
Bulas, 256, 257
Bulas de santa cruzada, 73
Bulnes, Francisco, 187, 196, 198
Burke, Edmund, 249
Bustamante, Anastasio, 173, 212, 291, 299, 301-304
Bustamante, Carlos María de, 36, 191, 239, 286, 298, 299
Bustamante, M. M., 154
Butler, Anthony, 303

Caballero, 171
Caballeros Racionales, 53, 58
Cabildo, 25, 37, 72
Cabo Rojo, 296
Caciques, 166, 171, 191, 325, 328, 337-339
Caciquismo, 166, 328
Cadena, Conde de la, *See* Flon, Manuel de
Cádiz, 27, 28, 34, 47, 52, 53, 56, 103, 137, 254, 255
Caja Real de Madrid, 215
Cajas, 64, 67, 68, 71, 204
Calderón, 86, 90, 91
California, 276, 278, 284, 286, 295, 306, 307
Californias, 192, 278, 286, 301
Callcott, W. H., 163
Calleja, María Francisca, 172, 173
Calleja del Rey, Félix María, 11, 12, 32, 36-39, 52, 86-108, 123, 138, 139, 144, 168-174, 203, 318, 344
Camacho, Sebastián, 232
Campeche, 60, 61
Campesinos, 11, 32, 95, 316
Canada, 21, 40
Canary Islanders, 279
Canas, Tiburcio, 297
Cano y Moctezuma, Dionisio, 51
Capellanías, 21
Carbajal, Vicente, 206

Cardeña, Joaquín, 55
Cardeña, Ramón, 52, 56
Cárdenas, Lázaro, 328
Caribbean, 65, 69, 70, 71, 73, 215
Carlos I, 26, 33
Carlos III, 251
Carlos IV, 24, 251, 260
Carmen, Monastery of, 28
Carrancistas, 316
Carrasa, 88
Cartas cuentas, 64
Casa de moneda, 69
Casas Grandes, 342
Castile. *See* Castilla
Castilian centralism, 26
Castilla, 22, 65, 251, 256
Castro Terreno, Conde de, 98
Catalans, 26
Catholic Church, 46, 204
Catholics, 279
Catastrophe of 1830, 301, 307
Caudillaje, 11, 167, 169
Caudillismo, 163-174, 337
Caudillo de la gente Española, 169
Caudillo de Israel, 169
Caudillos, 11, 163-174, 191, 328, 329, 335, 336, 338-340
Causa Buena, La, 85-108, 172
Cedillo, Saturnino, 328
Celaya, 89, 122, 135
Central America, 192, 215, 275
Central American Confederation, 285, 291
Centralist-escoceses, 9, 217, 242, 289-291, 295, 297-299, 307
Cerro Prieto, 342
Chalco, 124
Chamber of Deputies, 290, 293, 294, 296, 300, 302, 305, 307
Chapultepec, 104
Charles IV, 333
Chiapas, 284, 285, 289
Chihuahua, 125, 314-316, 343
Chile, 39, 222, 230, 337
Chilpancingo, 239, 325
China, 278, 284, 337
Chinese, 278
Chism, Richard, 48
Christ, 117
Church, 13, 34, 118, 202, 211, 212, 247-263, 333
Cia, Francisco, 56
Clay, Henry, 287, 292, 294
Coahuila, 194, 279, 286-305
Coatsworth, John, 164-168
Codallos, José, 301, 302
Coimbra, University of, 332
Colegio Militar, 341
Colonialists, 312, 319
Colonization, 279-305
Colonization, Law of, 305, 306
Colorado River, 287
Columna, Antonio, 100
Comisión Especial de Minería, 268
Commerce, 11, 22, 87, 139, 141-144, 151, 207, 215, 219, 250, 316, 325
Commission to Reconnoiter the Boundary of Mexico with the United States, 292-294, 296
Committee on Colonization, 279-281
Committee on Foreign Affairs, 277, 281
Committee on Public Safety, 296
Comunistas, 257
Concilio Vaticano, 257
Concilios, 248
Conducta, 209
Confederación Patriótica, 61
Congreso, 154, 155, 157, 159, 223
Congreso del Anáhuac, 238, 243
Congress of the Central American Confederation, 284
Congreso Constituyente Mexicano, 219, 241, 244
Consejo de Guerra, 106
Consejo de Regencia, 47
Conservatives, 9, 13, 27, 35, 186, 247-249, 255, 262, 339
Consolidation, Law of, 21, 202
Constitucionalistas, 45
Constitución de Apatzingán, 238-240
Constitución de Cádiz, 58, 59, 255
Constitución de 1857, 255
Constituent Congress, 192, 193
Constitutional cabildos, 34, 39
Constitution of 1812, 34, 35, 37-40, 51, 60, 106, 107, 192-194
Constitution of 1814, 58, 60
Constitution of 1824, 285, 286, 301
Constituyente de Chilpancingo, 239
Constituyente de 1821, 237
Consulado, 66, 72, 208
Consulado de Veracruz, 103
Contribuciones militares, 106
Corona, 153
Cortes, 7, 22, 23, 25, 33, 34, 37-41, 149-151, 160, 190, 192, 195, 203, 204, 245, 331
Cortes de Cádiz, 27, 34, 51, 260
Cortes españolas, 58, 245
Costa Rica, 276
Counterinsurgency, 20, 39, 85-108, 167, 318
Counterrevolutionaries, 190
Coup d'etat, 24, 29
Couto, Bernardo, 248, 255, 261, 262
Couto, José Maria, 34
Covarrubias, José María, 154
Creole elites, 204, 238, 327
Creole nationalists, 202

Creoles, 186, 190, 207, 334, 336
Criollos, 29, 30, 36, 38, 53, 56, 85, 168, 172, 243, 245
Cristero rebellion, 337
Cristo, 259
Cristo y Conde, José del, 29
Crown, 26, 201, 202, 208, 324-327
Cruz, José de la, 94-96, 102, 104, 123, 344
Cruz, Manuel, 55
Cuautla Amilpas, 86, 92
Cuauhtitlán, 110, 122
Cuautla, 123
Cuba, 66, 71, 322
Cuernavaca, 122, 124
Cuerpo Urbano, 90
Cuerpos volantes, 95, 95
Cuevas, 187
Cura de Carácuaro, 239
Cura de Dolores, 170

Davies, James, 313
Debt, 10, 12, 63-84, 165, 203, 204, 205-207, 316
Decentralization, 86
Declaration of Independence, 276
Decreto Constitucional, 238, 240, 241
Deficits, 10, 72, 216, 234
Democracy, 187
Denmark, 219
Depósitos, 67, 73
Deprivation theory, 313, 314, 319
Deseado, El, 122, 124
Deseado del Sosiego, El, 100
Destacamento volante, 93-96, 105
Díaz, Manuel, 50
Díaz, Porfirio, 14, 15, 168, 312, 323, 325, 327, 340, 341, 343, 344
Dislindadores, 320
Dolores, 31, 89
Domínguez, Juan, 30, 48
Domínguez, Miguel, 286
Dom João VI, 333
Dom Pedro I, 331
Donations, 66, 69, 70, 94, 202, 206
Durango, 64, 68, 109, 126, 160, 194, 343

Early Republic, 163, 164, 168
Eastern Interior (Internal) Provinces, 37, 42, 192, 279, 280, 298
Eça y Múzquiz, Miguel, 279
Ecclesiastical fueros, 27
Echandia, José María, 295
Echavárri, José Antonio, 198, 297
Edwards, Haden, 282
Eguia, José Joaquín de, 146
El Salvador, 192
Elementos Constitucionales de Rayón, 239, 240
Elhuyar, Fausto de, 59
Elites, 198, 205, 207, 208, 213, 215, 239, 312, 317, 318, 327-329, 332-335
Elozua, Antonio, 279
Empire of Mexico, 188
Empleomanía, 197
Empresarios, 286, 289
England (Great Britain), 5, 9, 99, 218-220, 224, 231-234, 251, 252, 272, 279, 291, 296, 337
English, 171
Enlightenment, 21, 63, 334
Epazoyuca, 120
Equilibristas, 36
Escoceses, 58, 289, 290, 294, 298
Espinosa, Juan José, 290
Espinosa de las Monteros, Carlos, 286
Estado de Derecho, 244
Estatutos de la Orden Imperial de Guadalupe, 244
Esteva, José Ignacio, 218, 220, 228, 231, 234
Etapa criolla, 253
Etapa oficial o española, 253
Etapa de síntesis, 253
Europe, 2, 3, 5, 7, 34, 72, 150, 156, 191, 196, 215, 217, 218, 228, 230, 232, 251, 252, 267
Europeans, 120, 304
European Spaniards, 3, 4, 6, 21, 24, 27-32, 35, 39, 40, 110
Evangelio de Jesús, 262
Expenditures, 76, 83

Facio, José Antonio, 301
Fagoaga, Francisco, 282
Fagoaga, José María, 58, 150
Farriss, Nancy, 167
Federal Army, 328, 342, 343
Federal District, 294
Federalism, 42, 43
Federalist-yorkinos, 9, 217, 242, 290, 291, 294
Felipe II, 257
Fernández de Lizardi, José Joaquín, 36
Fernández de Madrid, José, 232
Fernández de San Salvador, Agustín Pomposo, 169
Fernández de San Vicente, Agustín, 284
Fernández de Villamil, Bernardo, 173
La Fernandita, 170
Fernando VI, 46, 47
Fernando VII, 24, 30, 31, 38, 39, 110, 119-121, 124, 170, 188, 239, 275, 283, 297, 333, 334

Fiallo, Evarista, 53, 55, 56
Finance and Commerce Commission, 211
First Constituent Congress, 41, 42
Flon, Antonio de, 97
Flon, Manuel de, 90
Florescano, Enrique, 315
Florida, 66, 71, 284
Floridas, 277, 304
Franc Massones. *See* Freemasonry
France, 5, 19, 23, 38, 219, 225, 252, 312, 337
Fredonian Rebellion, 291, 292
Freemasonry, 32, 46, 58
Free trade, 27
French, 33, 86, 93, 171, 327, 333
French Annalists, 312, 320
French Republic, 307
French Revolution of 1789, 3, 23, 63, 215, 249, 252, 254

Gachupines, 28, 30, 36, 120, 122, 124, 170, 189, 240
Galicia, Francisco Antonio, 38, 51
Galeana, Hermenegildo, 132, 325
Galveston, 287, 292
Gándara, Manuel de la, 172
Gándara, María Josefa de la, 173
García, Albino, 91, 132, 142
García, Carlos, 305
García, Gabino, 133
García, Manuel, 322
García Conde, Diego, 96
Garibay, Pedro, 29
Garza, Felipe de la, 210
Garza, José Refugio de la, 279
Geographic districting, 315
Germany, 312, 337
Gibaja y Patrón, Antonio, 48
God, 124, 251, 258
Godoy, Manuel, 24, 28
Goldschmidt and Company, 220–234
Gómez Anaya, Cirilo, 286
Gómez Farías Valentín, 154, 187, 212, 248, 255, 280, 286, 305–307
Gómez Pedraza, Manuel, 39, 173, 304
González, María del Refugio, xi, 13, 247, 335
González Carvajal, Ciriaco, 27
Gordoa, José Miguel, 35
Gorostiza, Manuel, 212
Gortari Rabiela, Hira de, xi, 11, 129
Gran Colombia, 219, 222, 223, 229, 230, 231, 234
Grand Lodge, 47, 48, 290
Grants or contracts, 280
Grito de Dolores, 11, 63, 169, 174
Guadalajara, 30, 41, 64, 65, 68, 72, 95, 101, 104, 144, 160, 194, 315
Guadalupana, 243
Guadalupe, Monastry of, 28
Guadalupe, Virgin of, 110, 120, 122, 124, 125, 170, 171, 243
Guadalupes, 32, 35, 36 49–52, 57, 58, 61
Guanajuato, 30, 32, 37, 64, 65, 68, 69, 86, 89–91, 93, 104, 131, 132, 134, 141, 142, 160, 194
Guatemala, 37, 39, 276, 291
Guatemala City, 192
Guaymas, 206
Guedea Rincón Gallardo, Virginia, ix, x, xi, 6, 10, 36, 45, 335
Guerra, Francisco-Xavier, 319
Guerrero, Vicente, 189, 192, 198, 291, 294, 297, 298, 299, 302, 303
Guevara, Ernesto "Che", 123
Gulf of Mexico, 275, 277
Guridi y Alcocer, José Miguel, 34
Gutiérrez de Lara, José Antonio, 279, 280, 286
Guzmán, Gordiano, 192, 328

Hacienda de los Morales, 105
Hacienda Pública, 260
Hall, Basil, 198
Hall, Linda, xii, 14, 323
Hart, John, 314
Havana, 56, 103, 198
Heras Soto, Manuel de, 276
Herrera, José Manuel, 280
Herrera-Sobek, María, x
Herring, Graham y Powels, 283
Heterodoxy, 115–117
Hidalgo y Costilla, Miguel, ix, 4, 6, 12, 30–32, 48, 86, 109, 110, 121–126, 132, 145, 168–171, 185, 190, 215, 238, 239, 243, 279, 323, 340
Hidalgo Revolt, 31, 65, 67, 69, 73, 173, 202, 203, 326–328, 335
Hilario, Pablo, 120
Hamill, Hugh M., Jr., xii, 11, 12, 31, 163, 335
Hamnett, Brian, 102, 135, 141, 147, 167, 185, 188, 191, 314, 317, 318, 323, 324, 326, 327
Historia del Derecho, 238
Hobsbawm, Eric, 321, 322
Holden, Robert H., 320
Holy Alliance, 5, 220, 222
Hombres de bien, 21, 43
Honduras, 278
Huasteca, 167
Huichapan, 94
Humboldt, Alexander von, 22, 204
Hurtado, Manuel José, 229, 230

Iberian Peninsula, 28, 333

Ilustración, 250, 251, 253, 254, 259
Ilustrados, 247-262, 272, 335
Imperio Mexicano, 240, 241, 243
Independence, 14, 19, 86, 164, 168, 252-259, 274, 294, 311-344
Indians, 28, 30, 66, 70, 85, 87, 97, 110, 113-120, 124-127, 243, 256, 277, 279, 286, 292, 296, 323, 339
Indies, 67
Indulgences, 66, 72
Industrial Revolution, 334
Industry, 27, 87, 130, 136, 166, 325
Infantry Regiments of Ordenes Militares and Voluntarios de Navarra, 103
Infantry Regiment of Zaragoza, 105
Inflation, 65, 72, 106
Insurgency, 20, 33, 37-39, 45, 49-51, 57, 58, 61, 85-91, 93, 96-102, 107, 126, 135, 139, 144, 167, 185, 191, 238, 239, 255, 323, 328, 335
Insurgent army, 209
Insurgents, 23, 36-38, 51, 56, 86, 87, 89-108, 110, 124, 133-145, 167, 170, 189, 204, 208, 216, 218, 237, 239, 243, 255, 322, 342-344
Intendancy of Mexico, 95
Internal Provinces of the East, 194
Internal Provinces of the West, 194
Inquisition, 27, 47, 58, 59, 241, 260
Irapuato, 89, 135
Irish, 279
Italy, 32, 124, 312
Iturbide, Agustín de, 5, 8, 11, 12, 14, 40-42, 60, 107, 108, 142, 143, 152, 167, 185-199, 201, 204-213, 216-220, 223, 237-239, 242, 276, 279-281, 284, 328, 334, 335, 340
Iturrigaray, José, 25, 27-29, 35, 202

Jackson, Andrew, 283, 304
Jacobins, 187
Jala, hacienda de, 135
Jalapa, 39, 52-57, 61, 99, 103, 211
Jalisco, 4, 41, 42, 102
Jansenistas, 257
Japan, 337
Jaral de Berrio, Marqés de, 88, 172, 174
Jefferson, Thomas, 3
Jerusalem, 208
Jesuits, 202
Jesus, 125
Johnson, Chalmers, 336
Juárez, Benito, 168
Juárez, Ciudad, 328, 342
Juchipila, 120
Junta de crédito público, 206
Junta Gubernativa de Naolingo, 55, 56
Junta Nacional Instituyente, 196, 197, 205, 206, 211, 280, 281
Junta Provisional Gubernativa, 40, 151, 152, 189, 193, 195, 238, 276, 277
Junta de Puebla, 42
Junta de San Juan, 61
Junta Supreme Central, 29, 33
Juzgado de intestados, 72

Katz, Frederich, 314, 316, 319
Kinder, Thomas, Jr., 219
King of Spain, 110, 114, 121, 190, 324
Knight, Alan, 324, 325
Korek, María Teresa, 314

Ladd, Doris, 26
Lafaye, Jacques, 123
Laguna, 326
Laguna de Chapala, 95, 116
Latin America, 167
Latin Americanists, 313
Law of April 6, 1830, 304
Laws of the Reform, 187
Lemoine, Ernesto, 253, 259
León, hacienda de, 243
León, 256
Leyes de Indias, 50
Liberalism, 5, 9, 13, 35, 37, 60, 257, 337, 339
Liberals, 38, 47, 165, 186, 247-263, 265, 266
Liñan, Pascual de, 103, 104, 107
Lisbon, 334
Lizana y Beaumont, Francisco Javier, 29, 30
Llano, Ciriaco de, 92, 107
Llano, Manuel María, 292
Llanos de Apan, 95
Llave, Pablo de la, 280
Loans, 7, 8, 12, 66, 69, 70, 156-161, 201-213, 215-235, 327
Lobato, José María, 218
Lobera, Company of, 95
London, 53, 159, 217-220, 222, 225, 228, 234
López-Irianni, Geneva, x
López Rayón, Ignacio, 51
López de Santa Anna, Antonio. *See* Santa Anna, Antonio López de
Louisiana, 281, 304
Lowe, Karen, x
Lower California, 279, 288, 306, 307
Luaces, Domingo, 105
Lucas de Olabarrieta, Juan, 56
Lucido José Mariano, 55

Machismo, 168, 170, 172
Mackie, Patrick, 220, 221
Madero, Francisco I., 168, 315, 326-328
Madison, James, 3
Madrid, 24, 64, 339

Madrid, Mariano la, 143
Mal gobierno, 21
Manning, Robert, 224, 228
Mariana Islands, 278
Mariano, el indio, 117, 122, 126
Márquez y Donallo, José Joaquín, 95
Marshall, William, 224, 228
Martínez, Juan, 36
Martínez de Aragón, Felipe, 59
Martínez Marina, Francisco, 22, 245
Martínez Quintero, María Esthér, 255
Marxists, 321
Masonería, 46–49, 53, 57–62, 335
Matagorda, 280
Matamoros, 169, 296, 305
Mateos, José María, 48
Matrix treasury, 64, 67, 71
Maximilian, 168
Mayans, 343
Mayan Wars, 342
Mazatlan, 206
Medellín, 92
Medina, Antonio, 209–211
Medina, Conde de, 27
Medina, Teresa, 55
Medina del Campo, 171
Mejía, José Antonio, 286, 305
Memoria de Hacienda, 205, 207, 209, 211
Mentalidad, 14, 316, 318, 320–322
Mercado, Florentino, 261
Mérida, 60, 61
Mescal, 205
Mesoamerican Classic Era, 113
Messianism, 11, 109–127, 335
Metztitlán, 119, 225
Mexican Army, 341
Mexican Congress, 194–197, 201, 207–211, 279–305
Mexican Empire, 201, 205, 212, 275–281
Mexican Liberal Party, 326
Mexican Republic, 261, 285, 286, 298, 300
Mexican Revolution, 14, 311–322, 323–329
Mexico: intendancy, 194; province, 37, 56, 57, 135; state, 302; topography, 2
Mexico City, 7, 20, 25, 26, 28, 32, 36, 42, 48, 50, 51, 55, 58, 59, 61, 64, 65, 67, 68, 71–73, 85, 90, 94, 95, 99, 100, 103, 107, 120, 122, 131, 141, 165, 172, 174, 191, 192, 197, 202–204, 206, 208, 280, 289, 292, 296, 297, 303, 304, 307, 317, 335, 343
Mezcala, 95, 116
Michelena, José Mariano, 30, 39, 218, 223, 225–227, 234
Michoacán, 37, 42, 102, 167, 170, 302
Mier y Noriega, Servando Teresa de, 23, 52, 58, 86, 187, 191, 248, 280, 285
Mier y Terán, Manuel, 280, 293, 296, 297, 299, 301, 302, 307
Military caudillos, 43
Militia, 42, 71
Millenarianism, 11, 109–127
Mina, Francisco Javier, 52, 58, 61, 113
Mining, 11, 27, 129–161, 202, 207, 210, 213, 215, 316, 335, 337, 339
Mint, 69, 79, 203
Mississippi River, 275
Mixteca, 135
Miyares Mancebo, Fernando, 101
Moctezuma, Francisco, 297, 299
Molango, 119
Monarchists, 290
Monarquía, 244
Monduí, Ramón, 92
Monroe Doctrine, 5
Monroy Guerrero y Luyando, Manuel, 48
Montano Revolt, 297
Montezuma II, 168
Moore, Barrington, 311, 312, 318
Mora, José María Luis, 58, 191, 248, 255, 262, 274
Morales, Alejandro, x
Morelos, 316, 317, 324, 325
Morelos, José María, ix, 4, 49, 51, 58, 68, 73, 86, 91, 123, 125, 132, 133–135, 140, 144, 239–243, 255, 340
Moreno, Roberto, 253
Morillo, Pablo, 103
Mornay, Arístides Franklin, 158, 159
Morris, William Walton, 300
Morton, Ohland, 293
Mosquito Coast, 278
Mungía, Clemente de Jesús, 169, 248, 262
Muñí, Enrique, 48
Murphy, Tomás, 58
Múzquiz, Melchor, 304

Nacogdoches, 292, 296
Namiquipa, 320
Napoleon I, 3, 23, 47, 53, 120, 169, 333
Napoleonic Wars, 312, 335, 342
Nashville, 297
Nationalism, 19, 22, 190
Navarro, Fernando, 206
Navarro y Rodrigo, Carlos, 185, 197
Negrete, Pedro Celestino, 198
Negroes, 85
New Granada, 39, 324
New Jerusalem, 126
New León. *See* Nuevo León
New Mexico, 33, 192, 194, 276, 279, 286, 288, 289, 292, 295
New Orleans, 98, 198, 277, 297, 304, 307
New Santander, 194, 279

New Spain, 37, 39, 324-328, 335, 335, 339, 344
New Spaniards, 22, 23, 25, 37-40
New World, 33, 35, 126, 257
New York City, 297
Nicaragua, 278
Nieto, 88
Nononalco, 104
Nopala, 94
North America, 191, 215, 299
Novenos, 73
Nueva Galicia, 37, 104, 170
Nuevo León, 194, 279, 288, 292
Nuevo Plan de Contribuciones Públicas, 203
Nuevo Santander, 279

Oaxaca, 37, 42, 72, 135, 143, 286, 302
Obeso, José María, 30
Obras pías, 21, 206
Obregón, Joaquín, 211
Obregón, Pablo, 287
Ocampo, Javier, 193
O'Donojú, Juan, 61, 186, 191-193, 205
O'Gorman, Edmundo, 238
Olmedo, José Joaquín de, 230
Ometusco, 135
Orcoquisac, 277
Ordenanzas de minería, 157
Ordenes Militares, 260
O'Reilly, Felipe, 279
Oriente, 144
Ortiz de Ayala, Tadeo, 187, 276, 279, 286, 304, 305
Ortiz, Francisco, 133
Ortiz, Juan Bautista, 53, 55
Ortiz de la Torre, Manuel, 270, 271
Ortiz Monasterio, Leonor, x
Osorno, José Francisco, 132, 135, 140
Otumba, Veracruz, 95, 135, 294

Pachuca, 95, 132
Pacific Ocean, 275, 278, 284
Pacíficos, 321
Padilla, 198
Padre de la Patria, 170
Países Bajos, 225
Panama, 275
Panteístas, 257
Papa Pío IX, 257
Los Papas, 248
Paraguay, 337
Parra López, Emilio La, 254
Partidas, 258
Patronato, 256-258
Paz, 154
Pedernales, 343
Pedro el Negro, 104
Peimbert y Hernández, Juan Nazario, 50
Premartin, 56,
Peña, Antonia, 50
Peninsula, 24, 64, 145
Peninsulars, 22, 27, 29, 32, 186, 204, 207, 241, 245, 334, 336
Peninsular War, 68
Pérez, Antonio Joaquín, 35, 117
Pérez Maldonado, Rafael, 206, 207
Perote, 53, 55, 105, 209
Persia, 219
Peru, 39, 103, 222, 229, 230, 324
Pesado, J. J., 248, 262
Pesos fuertes, 69
Philadelphia, 186, 283
Philippines, 65, 66, 71-73, 215, 278
Picaluga, Francisco, 303
Pío VII, 260
Plan of Casa Mata, 191, 192, 212
Plan of Iguala, 8, 40, 107, 185-199, 204, 217, 237, 239
Plan of Jalapa, 299, 302
Plan of Montano, 294
Plan for the Reform of Congress, 195
Poinsett, Joel Roberts, 187, 195, 197, 208, 287-303
Pombalian reforms, 332
Poncitlán, 116
Poniente, 144
Popkin, Samuel I., 321
Porfirian army, 14, 341-343
Porfiriato, 14, 274, 325, 329, 340
Portales, Diego, 340
Portugal, 331-334
Post-Independence period, 328
Poverty, 13, 268-270
Prado, Bernardo del, 27
Presidio del Carmen, 71
Presidios, 65, 69, 73
Primer Imperio, 240
Primo de Verdad y Ramos, Francisco, 27-30, 48
Products, 5
Production, 271
Propios y arbitrios, 70
Proposal for a Law to Preserve the Integrity of the Territory of the Republic, 300
Provincial deputation, 34, 37, 39, 41, 196
Provincial Dragoon Regiments, 87
Provincial Regiment of Celaya, 90
Prusia, 219
Puebla, 26, 37, 39, 42, 87, 88, 90, 91, 99, 107, 135, 141-143, 174
Puente del Rey, 98
Puerto Rico, 66, 71
Puruarán, 238

Quebradillo, 132
Querétaro, 30, 37, 42, 88, 90, 94, 97, 99, 105, 110, 135, 170, 211
Quetzalcóatl, 11, 109, 113
Quevedo, José, 98
Quiros, José María, 137, 146, 203, 269, 270

Racionalistas, 257
Radicales, 218
Ramos agenos (ramos particulares), 66, 67, 70, 72, 73
Ramos Arizpe, José Miguel, 34, 35, 38, 39, 192, 285, 286, 290, 306
Rancho de Tejar, 92
Rayas, Marqués de San Juan de, 27, 31
Raz y Guzmán, Juan Bautista, 50, 51
Real Acuerdo, 27
Real Casa de México, 146
Real de Catorce, 154
Real Contaduría, 64
Real Corona, 257
Reales Cajas, 146
Real hacienda, 6, 67, 71–73
Rebels, 86–108, 185, 189, 190, 321
Recopilación de Castilla, 157
Reforma, 9, 13, 164, 213, 315
Regalism, 13
Regalistas, 247–263, 335
Regency, 206
Regiment of Dragones Fieles de Potosí, 101
Regiment of Dragoons of San Luis, 95
Regiment of Lobera, 53, 95
Regiment of Mexico, 95
Regiment of Ordenes Militares, 100
Regiment of Querétaro, 95
Regiment of San Carlos, 174
Regionalism, 7, 8, 12, 37, 86, 191
Regionalists, 41
Regional treasuries, 65, 67
Regla, Conde de, 27
Reglamento Provisional del Imperio, 238, 240–242
Rejón, Crescencio, 286
Religión Católica, 238
Republic, 164, 173, 187–189, 201, 217, 244, 251, 335
Republicanism, 186, 191, 239
Republicans, 187
Restauración de la República, 249
Revenues, 64, 67–69, 71, 74, 75, 77, 82
Revillagigedo, Juan Vicente de Güemes Pacheco, Conde de, 171
Revolution for Independence, 14, 188, 249, 311–322, 323–329, 338
Revolution of 1910, 164
Revolutionaries, 190, 191, 195
Reyes Heroles, Jesús, 253
Riaño, Juan Antonio, 89
Richards, Bartholomew Vigors, 219, 220, 224
Riego, Rafael, 60, 106
Rincón, Mariano, 55
Rincón Gallardo, Manuel José, Marqués de Guadalupe Gallardo, 173
Río Grande River, 287, 294
Río de Janeiro, 334
Río del Norte, 288, 293
Río Roxo, 275
Río Verde, 173
Rivas, Francisco, 279
Rivero, Agustín del, 28
Roa Bárcena, José María, 59
Rocafuerte, Vicente, 186, 189, 191, 193–198, 210, 218, 227–234, 245
Rodríguez, Eloy, x
Rodríguez, Linda Alexander, x
Rodríguez O., Jaime E., x, xii, 10, 12, 19, 164–168, 210, 215
Rodríguez de San Miguel, Juan N., 248
Rondero, Javier, 198
Rosa, Luis de la, 248, 268
Rothschild, House of, 220, 230
Rousseau, Jean Jacques, 255
Royalists, 6, 11, 14, 37, 86–108, 110, 123, 142, 143, 167, 170, 172, 185, 204, 342, 344
Royal Order of Carlos III, 66
Rudé, George F. E., 321
Rugama, Francisco, 56
Ruíz de Apodaca, Juan. *See* Apodaca, Juan Ruiz de
Russia, 278, 284, 291, 337
Russians, 86, 278, 284
Rutineros, 60

Sabine River, 275, 276
Saints, 125
Salamanca, 89, 91, 135, 142
Salvatierra, 133
Samaniego, Comandante, 143
San Andrés, 140
San Antonio de Béjar, 289
San Bernardo, 277
San Carlos, 52, 88
Sánchez Enciso, José, 277
Sánchez de Tagle, Francisco, 206
San Francisco, 276
San Ildefonso, 270
San Juan, 51, 60
Sanjuanistas, 60
San Juan Teotihuacán, 95
Sa Juan de Ulúa, 60, 196, 211, 219, 225, 227
San Lorenzo Huichichilapan, 117

San Luis, 88, 95
San Luis de la Paz, 97
San Luis Potosí, 37, 42, 64, 88-90, 97, 144, 149, 170, 171, 173, 174, 328
San Miguel, 89, 96, 97
San Miguel El Grande, 30, 124
Santa Anna, Antonio López de, 163, 172, 191, 197, 198, 211, 212, 306, 307
Santanismo, 167
Santa Sede, 260, 261
Santiago Barrabas, 301
Santibáñez y Ceballos, José Manuel, 287, 290, 291
Santo Domingo, Monastery of, 28
Santo Domingo, 66, 85
Sarratea, Manuel de, 230
Sater, William F., x, xii, 14, 15, 339
Sauceda, José Antonio, 133, 287
Scott, James C., 321
Scott, Winfield, 341
Scottish (Rite). *See* Escoceses
Second Constituent Congress, 42
Seguín, Erasmo, 285
Senate Committee on Internal Affairs, 293
Senate, 290, 293, 296, 301, 306
Sentimientos de la Nación, 238, 243, 244
Serviles, 35
Shamanism, 113, 117
Sichú, 97
Silao, 89
Sinaloa, 286
Singuilucan, 135
Sioux Indians, 322
Situados, 65, 66, 69, 70-72
Skocpol, Theda, 314, 318, 327, 333
Smith, Adam, 267
Snow Mountain, 288
Soberanía, 170
Soberano, V., 154
Soberano Congreso Constituyente, 237
Socialistas, 257
Sociedad Económica de Amigos del País, 266
Sociedades secretas, 45-61, 257, 290, 291, 294, 339
Solís, Diego, 269
Sombrerete, 64, 65
Sonora, 123, 282, 286, 288, 343
South Dakota, 322
Spain, 5, 6, 9, 13, 22, 24, 26, 33, 34, 38-41, 46, 47, 53, 60, 63, 66, 67, 69, 70, 73, 91, 93, 94, 112, 120, 185, 186, 188, 190, 191, 196, 198, 202, 209, 211, 215-217, 219, 220, 222, 239, 242, 245, 251, 254, 259, 265, 272, 275-278, 281, 282, 284, 291, 294, 296, 297, 317, 318, 322, 333, 337
Spaniards, 7, 91, 116, 120, 121, 190, 201, 202, 204, 283, 290, 291, 294, 295, 304, 324, 332
Spanish America, 63, 190, 222
Spanish Americans, 332
Spanish Army, 11, 340
Spanish Constitution, 188, 194, 344
Spanish Cortes, 33-41, 193, 275, 278
Spanish Empire, 340
Spanish Imperial system, 317
Spanish Indies, 63
Spanish King, 127, 170, 327
Spanish liberalism, 20
Spanish New World, 333
Spanish Superior Political Chief, 193
Spanish-United States Treaty of 1819, 284
Staples, Robert R., 219
Stein, Stanley, 164
Steiner, George, 311
Stoetzer, O. Carlos, 245
Stuart, Daniel, 282
Suárez, Francisco, 245
Subsidiary treasuries, 68
Sultepec, 132
Suprema Junta Nacional Americana, 50, 51
Supremo Poder Ejecutivo, 216, 217, 219, 282
Sylabus de 1864, 248, 257

Tabasco, 192
Tacones, 53
Tacuba, 104
Talamantes, Fray Melchor de, 26, 27, 29, 30
Tamariz, José María, 55
Tamaulipas, 292, 296
Tampico, 296
Tannenbaum, Frank, 324
Tariffs, 201, 209
Taxco, 148
Taxes, 10, 12, 21, 41, 63-73, 74, 77, 78, 81, 82, 87, 96, 97, 103, 105-107, 114, 127, 165, 197, 201-213, 215, 216, 324, 334
Taylor, William B., 319
Tehuantepec, 276
Téllez, Manuel, 55
Temascaltepec, 132
Temporalidades, 67, 73
Tenenbaum, Barbara, xii, 7, 12, 41, 197, 201, 233, 334
Tenientes de policía, 99
Tenth Brigade, 87, 171
TePaske, John, xii, 7, 10, 11, 63, 203, 204, 207, 327, 333, 334
Tepetates, 135
Tepic, 109

Terán, 140
Teresas, Sisters, 59
Tesorería, 145
Texas, 9, 194, 276–307, 335
Texcoco, 95, 124
Thompson, E. P., 321
Thrupp, Sylvia, 112
Tierra Firme, 39
Tilly, Charles, 311, 313, 320
Tilly, Louis, 311, 313, 320
Tilly, Richard, 311, 313, 320
Timmons, Wilbert H., 49
Tithes, 67
Tlacotepec, 49
Tlaxcala, 37, 90, 122
Tobacco, 201, 203–207, 210, 324
Toluca, 90, 134
Tomás y Valiente, Francisco, 259
Tomochic, 322
Topik, Steven, xii, 14, 331
Tornel, José María, 157, 187, 303
Torre, Ernesto de la, 49
Torrens, José Anastasio, 283
Torres, P., 140
Trade, 64, 287
Treasury, 206, 207, 209, 210
Treaty of Córdoba, 186, 187, 190–193, 195, 196, 237, 239, 240
Treaty of Iguala, 288
Treaty of Versailles, 2, 278
Tres Garantías, 237
Tribunal de la Acordada, 100
Tribunal de Cuentas, 64
Tribunal de Minería, 160
Trinity River, 287
Tula, 94
Tulancingo, 95, 295
Tutino, John, 319, 321

Uluapa, Marqués de, 27
Unemployment, 13, 265–274
Unión, La, 159, 161
Union of Arms, 26
United States: aid, 210; arms, 342; army, 341; colony, 1, 4, 5, 6; congress, 295; Constitution of 1787, 3; economics, 326; founding fathers, 21; invasion by, 9, 337; loans, 218; territory, 275–307, 322; topography, 2; war for independence, 3, 337
Upper California, 278, 279, 288, 292, 306, 307
Urías Horcasitas, Beatriz, xii, 13, 265
Uruapan, 104
Uruguay, 245

Valenciana, 133
Valladolid, 30, 42, 72, 85, 101, 104, 134
Valle, Rafael Heliodoro, 198
Valle de Santiago, 133
Valley of Papigochic, 314, 320
Vanderwood, Paul, xii, 14, 311–322, 334
Van Young, Eric, xii, 11, 109, 315, 317, 318, 334, 335
Velázquez, 55
Venadito, Conde del. *See* Apodaca
Venegas, Francisco Xavier, 35–37, 51, 70, 87, 88, 90–94, 174, 202
Venezuela, 103, 228
Veracruz, 37, 39, 56, 57, 64, 71, 87, 90, 92, 93, 98, 101–104, 108, 141, 142, 144, 146, 192, 196, 211, 219, 276, 278, 299
Viceroyalty of New Spain, 37, 165, 275, 276
Victoria, Guadalupe, 8, 12, 189, 193, 212, 218, 233, 287–289, 292, 296
Viesca, 326
Viezca, Agustín, 287, 298
Villa, Pancho, 123
Villagrán family, 167
Villaurrutia, Jacobo, 27, 36, 51
Vilistas, 316
Villoro, Luis, 19, 188, 195
Viña, Agustín, 91
Virgen Morena, 245
Virgen del Tepeyac, 244
Virgin of Guadalupe. *See* Guadalupe, Virgin of
Virreinato, 145, 238
Visigoths, 22
Visitors-General, 324
Vite, Luis, 119

Ward, Henry G., 153, 290
War of 1812, 99
Washington, D.C., 275, 281
Washington, George, 3, 298
Wasserman, Mark, 315
Wavell, Arthur, 282
Wells, Allen, 315
Western Interior (Internal) Provinces, 37, 192
Wilbert, Johannes, ii
Wilson, Robert, 233

Yaquis, 343
Yaqui Wars, 342
Yautepec, 117
Yermo, Gabriel, 27, 29, 33
Yorkinos, 48, 289, 290, 294, 298
York Rite Lodge. *See* Yorkinos
Yucatán, 9, 33, 37, 42, 60, 61, 276, 286, 302, 315

Zacatecas, 42, 43, 64, 68, 69, 131, 132, 148, 160, 206

Zacualpan, 153
Zapata, Emiliano, 123
Zapatistas, 317
Zavala, Lorenzo de, 60, 154, 186, 187, 194–197, 208, 212, 255, 265, 286, 290, 297
Zempoala, 95, 120, 135
Zimapan, 153
Zitácuaro, 50, 86, 92, 134, 174
Zozaya, José Manuel, 281